TWENTIETH-CENTURY AMERICAN FOREIGN POLICY, ed. by John Braeman and others. Ohio State, 1971. 567p (Modern America, 3) 78-141495. 10.00. ISBN 0-8142-0151-2

CHOICE *NOV. '71*

History, Geography &
Travel

North America

There has been in recent years a great interest in 20th-century U.S. foreign policy. This anthology, edited by three distinguished historians, is part of a series which focuses upon the problems of change and continuity in 20th-century U.S. history. The present effort contains 11 essays, two of which are historiographical. David Trask's historiographical contribution, "Writings on American foreign relations: 1957 to the present," is especially valuable because it reviews thoroughly the recent works written on 20th-century U.S. diplomacy. Other essays include Waldo Heinrichs, Jr., "Bureaucracy and professionalism in the development of American career diplomacy," a hitherto neglected area; Paul Verg, "The United States a world power, 1900–1917: myth or reality?"; Manfred Jonas, "The United States and the failure of collective security in the 1930's"; Lawrence Kaplan, "The United States and the Atlantic Alliance: the first generation"; Allan Millett, "The United States and Cuba: the uncomfortable 'Abrazo,' 1898–1968"; and Warren Cohen, "From contempt to con-

tainment: cycles in American attitudes toward China." All essays are perceptively written and might serve as supplemental readings in college diplomatic history courses.

Travel

North America

Twentieth-Century

American

Foreign Policy

Twentieth-Century

American

Foreign Policy

Edited by
John Braeman
Robert H. Bremner
David Brody

OHIO STATE UNIVERSITY PRESS

CONTENTS

INTRODUCTION

The present volume is the third in the series "Modern America," dealing with the problems of change and continuity in twentieth-century United States history. The first, *Change and Continuity in Twentieth-Century America,* was published by the Ohio State University Press in 1964; the second, *Change and Continuity in Twentieth-Century America: The 1920's,* in 1968. The eleven essays comprising this volume explore aspects of, and issues in, American foreign policy in the storm-tossed years since the beginning of this century.

Two of the essays are historiographical. Charles E. Neu of Brown University analyzes the changing assumptions and presuppositions underlying the writing of American diplomatic history from its coming of age in the 1920s to the present in his paper "The Changing Interpretive Structure of American Foreign Policy." In his "Writings on American Foreign Relations: 1957 to the Present," David F. Trask of the State University of New York—Stony Brook surveys the major scholarly works on American foreign policy and diplomacy of the last decade—a decade exceptionally rich in important new contributions.

Waldo H. Heinrichs, Jr., of the University of Illinois (Urbana-Champaign), in his paper "Bureaucracy and Professionalism in the Development of American Career Diplomacy," traces the development in the twentieth century of an American career foreign service—and in so doing, illuminates an aspect of diplomatic history hitherto too largely ignored.

Three of the essays are concerned with the changing relationship between the United States and the rest of the world. Paul A. Varg of Michigan State University reexamines the question "The United States a World Power, 1900–1917: Myth or Reality?", and finds that the answer depends upon which part of the world you are talking about. Manfred Jonas of Union College documents the continuing American resistance during the 1930s to any form of collective security in his paper "The United States and the Failure of Collective Security in the 1930s." Lawrence S. Kaplan of Kent State University, in his essay "The United States and the Atlantic Alliance: The First Generation," shows how the United States in the aftermath of World War II abandoned its traditional isolationism by taking the lead in the formation and maintenance of NATO.

The remaining essays appraise United States relations with a specific foreign country. Robert Craig Brown of the University of Toronto, in his paper "Canada in North America," reviews twentieth-century United States–Canadian relations from the Canadian viewpoint. Lyle C. Brown of Baylor University and James W. Wilkie of the University of California —Los Angeles detail and explain the dramatic improvement in United States–Mexican relations since World War II in their paper "Recent United States–Mexican Relations: Problems Old and New." Allan R. Millett of Ohio State University provides in "The United States and Cuba: The Uncomfortable *Abrazo*, 1898–1968" an account of the historical background indispensable for understanding Castro and his hostility toward the United States. A. E. Campbell of Keble College, Oxford University, questions the meaning of "The United States and Great Britain—Uneasy Allies." And Warren I. Cohen of Michigan State University reassesses American policy toward China in his paper "From Contempt to Containment: Cycles in American Attitudes toward China."

The editors would like to take this opportunity to express their appreciation to Weldon A. Kefauver and Robert S. Demorest, director and editor respectively, of the Ohio State University Press, without whose kind assistance and patience this volume—and series—would not be possible.

The fourth volume, devoted to the New Deal, is in preparation.

JOHN BRAEMAN
ROBERT H. BREMNER
DAVID BRODY

The Changing Interpretive Structure
of American Foreign Policy

CHARLES E. NEU

THE STUDY of American foreign policy matured in an era that was, in many ways, unfavorable to its growth. American diplomatic history came to life in the 1920s, when the conservative, evolutionist school of historical writing, from which it drew so much of its inspiration, was in a state of decline, and when the rising tide of progressive history offered little encouragement to students of American foreign policy. Conservative evolutionists emphasized the homogeneity and continuity of the American past, set within a framework of evolving institutions. They minimized conflict, focused upon the development of institutions and principles, and confidently identified with the growth of American unity and power. In contrast, progressive historians were preoccupied with the process of change, determined to widen the area of historical inquiry, and convinced that history must serve the purposes of current political reform. They viewed the past in terms of persistent and clear-cut conflicts between easily identifiable groups and sought to discover the fundamental social forces in American society. For progressive historians the meaning of American history resided in the unending struggle for liberal reform, not in the gradual strengthening of the American Union.[1]

There was, to be sure, a considerable overlap between the two approaches to history. Both were grounded upon a belief in progress and the cumulative nature of historical knowledge, and both ignored the intangible aspects of human experience. But the conservative, evolutionist approach was more conducive to the study of diplomatic history. It encouraged historians to concentrate upon the European background of American civilization and the interaction between European and American institutions. Progressive historians were absorbed in the nature of the American experience; to them American foreign policy seemed subordinate and peripheral. As John Higham observes, "progressive thought . . . was critical of tradition, insensitive to institutional continuities, and preoccupied with domestic conflict."[2]

Though major trends of American historiography were adverse in the years after World War I, both events and a significant prewar tradition nourished diplomatic history.[3] The strong interest in the war-guilt question and the origins of World War I, as well as the availability of recent diplo-

1. John Higham's brilliant essay in John Higham with Leonard Krieger and Felix Gilbert, *History* (Englewood Cliffs, N.J., 1965) greatly enlarged my understanding of the historiography of American history, as did Richard Hofstadter's *The Progressive Historians: Turner, Beard, Parrington* (New York, 1968). I am grateful to Ernest R. May and Louis Galambos for their critical readings of the manuscript, and to Waldo H. Heinrichs, Jr., for his comments on a far shorter version read at the December, 1969, meeting of the American Historical Association.

2. Higham, *History,* p. 189.

3. Apparently, the consciousness of being a specialist in American diplomatic history developed slowly and imperceptibly in the twenties. Samuel Flagg Bemis, for example, does not remember when he first began to think of himself in this way. It is interesting, however, that Thomas A. Bailey, who entered academic life about a decade later than Bemis, recalls 1932 as the date of his transformation from a political to diplomatic historian. By the early thirties, diplomatic history was a clearly recognized specialty. Interview with Samuel Flagg Bemis, September 17, 1968; letter from Thomas A. Bailey to author, March 10, 1969.

matic documents, gave a stimulus to European diplomatic history; this in turn affected those studying America's relation to the world. Events themselves seemed to endow the history of American foreign policy with an obvious relevance, and an extensive monographic literature written mostly in the decade and a half before the war provided a solid structure upon which diplomatic historians in the twenties could build.[4] Nearly all of these monographs were dry, precise, and narrowly defined—the very epitome of scientific history. They were accompanied, however, by a number of more broadly conceived books written by prominent scholars such as Archibald Cary Coolidge, Carl Russell Fish, Albert Bushnell Hart, John H. Latané, and John Bassett Moore.[5] None of their studies were based upon extensive archival research, but they did embody certain themes and characteristics that would be developed in the twenties and thirties.

All of these authors wrote of a distinctive American diplomatic tradition, one based upon a clear concept of neutrality, freedom of the seas, the Monroe Doctrine, and the Open

4. Some of the more prominent prewar monographs were: Ephriam Douglass Adams, *British Interests and Activities in Texas, 1838–1846* (Baltimore, 1910); James Morton Callahan, *The Diplomatic History of the Southern Confederacy* (Baltimore, 1901); Edward S. Corwin, *French Policy and the American Alliance of 1778* (Princeton, N.J., 1916); John H. Latané, *The Diplomatic Relations of the United States and Spanish America* (Baltimore, 1900); Jesse S. Reeves, *American Diplomacy under Tyler and Polk* (Baltimore, 1907); Frank A. Updyke, *The Diplomacy of the War of 1812* (Baltimore, 1915); Mary Wilhelmine Williams, *Anglo-American Isthmian Diplomacy, 1815–1915* (Washington, D.C., 1916).

5. Archibald Cary Coolidge, *The United States as a World Power* (New York, 1908); Carl Russell Fish, *American Diplomacy* (New York, 1915), *The Path of Empire: A Chronicle of the United States as a World Power* (New Haven, Conn., 1919); Albert Bushnell Hart, *The Foundations of American Foreign Policy* (New York, 1901), *National Ideals Historically Traced, 1607–1907* (New York, 1907), *The Monroe Doctrine: An Interpretation* (Boston, 1916); John H. Latané, *America as a World Power, 1897–1907* (New York, 1907), *From Isolation to Leadership: A Review of American Foreign Policy* (New York, 1918); John Bassett Moore, *American Diplomacy: Its Spirit and Achievements* (New York, 1905), *Four Phases of American Development: Federalism—Democracy—Imperialism—Expansion* (Baltimore, 1912), *The Principles of American Diplomacy* (New York, 1918).

Door policy. The United States, they argued, had pioneered in the development of international law and the application of arbitral procedures to international disputes. Their writing had a legalistic cast as they described boundary disputes, the growth of neutrality law, and various quarrels submitted to arbitration. In general, American diplomacy seemed to them exceptionally pure, and they praised the uninterrupted advance of the United States in world affairs. Carl Russell Fish entitled the last chapter of his *American Diplomacy* "Success and its Causes"; Albert Bushnell Hart wrote that "with few reservations, I feel pride in the purposes and results of American diplomacy." [6] All approved, sometimes enthusiastically, the consequences of the Spanish-American War. Coolidge believed, for example, that the American people were prepared to meet their unprecedented burdens with "joyous self-reliance." [7] But most were uncertain about the nature of these responsibilities, and there was sharp disagreement over whether a new phase had begun in American foreign policy. Coolidge, who defined world power as the extent to which the United States figured in the calculations of the great European nations, saw a definite break with the past in 1898; Moore contended the United States had always been a world power in terms of ideological leadership; and Hart went even further, claiming that the United States had consistently asserted its influence throughout the globe to defend its vital interests. [8]

Despite such differences, these writers believed the established principles of American diplomacy still applied after 1898. [9] All would have accepted Fish's judgment that Ameri-

6. Fish, *American Diplomacy*, p. 497; Hart, *Foundations of American Foreign Policy*, p. v.

7. *United States as a World Power*, p. 133.

8. *Ibid.*, pp. 121, 131; Moore, *American Diplomacy*, p. 2; Hart, *Foundations of American Foreign Policy*, p. 4.

9. With the exception of Hart, who thought that the Monroe Doctrine, in its original sense, was no longer relevant. *Monroe Doctrine*, pp. 299–300.

can diplomatic success had "rested upon a continuity, both of detail and of general policy, which is remarkable." [10] In retrospect, one is struck by the extent to which these authors agreed upon the substance of the American diplomatic tradition and shared a common approach to its study. But their books were only sketches, offering an optimistic, affirmative synthesis that had yet to be rooted in systematic research.

In the twenties historians examined in much greater depth both the continuities of principle and policy and the international setting of American diplomacy. [11] Prominent texts by John H. Latané and Louis Martin Sears typified this development, [12] as did the decade's two most impressive books, those by Tyler Dennett and Dexter Perkins. Dennett, in his monumental *Americans in Eastern Asia*, explored the essence of the Open Door policy, which, he claimed, was "as old as our relations with Asia." The precedents upon which that policy was grounded retained a "remarkable consistency"; the real questions centered around methods, not ends. [13] The first volume of Dexter Perkins's history of the Monroe Doctrine was an even more outstanding work. Based upon multiarchival research, this book set a new standard of excellence and not only placed American foreign policy in its European setting but also examined with care the growth of those ideas expressed in the Monroe Doctrine. Perkins devoted consid-

10. *American Diplomacy*, p. 498.

11. Important titles were: Ephriam Douglass Adams, *Great Britain and the American Civil War*, 2 vols. (New York, 1925); Samuel Flagg Bemis, *Jay's Treaty: A Study in Commerce and Diplomacy* (New York, 1923), and *Pinckney's Treaty: A Study of America's Advantage from Europe's Distress, 1783–1800* (Baltimore, 1926), ed., *The American Secretaries of State and Their Diplomacy*, 10 vols. (New York, 1927–29); Howard C. Hill, *Roosevelt and the Caribbean* (Chicago, 1927); Payson J. Treat, *Japan and the United States, 1853–1928* (Stanford, Calif., 1928); Alice Felt Tyler, *The Foreign Policy of James G. Blaine* (Minneapolis, 1927).

12. John H. Latané, *A History of American Foreign Policy* (New York, 1927); Louis Martin Sears, *A History of American Foreign Relations* (New York, 1927).

13. Tyler Dennett, *Americans in Eastern Asia* (New York, 1922), pp. v, 4.

erable attention to the impact of domestic politics and public opinion upon the formulation of American policy. He gloried in his work, believing that the principles of Monroe were still relevant. "No task," he wrote in the preface to the second volume of his trilogy, "can be more attractive than that of tracing the evolution and consolidation of fundamental principles." [14]

While studies of American foreign policy gained in solidity and sophistication, they lost neither their optimism nor their belief in the need for American participation in world affairs. Latané and Sears were untroubled by the repeated involvement of the United States in wars that, in their judgment, generally could have been avoided. One of Dennett's purposes was to prove the necessity for a cooperative policy in Eastern Asia among the United States, Great Britain, and Japan. The choice, Dennett believed, was that nations "must either fight each other or cooperate." Three years later, in 1925, Dennett praised Theodore Roosevelt for his realization that America must help preserve the balance of power in Europe and East Asia. [15]

During the thirties Samuel Flagg Bemis emerged as the foremost writer in the conservative, evolutionist school of American diplomatic history. Bemis had written two monographs in the twenties, but it was in the following decade that he created a powerful codification and elaboration of the traditional synthesis, one which remains influential to our own day. [16] Bemis's approach was multiarchival, his focus

14. Dexter Perkins, *The Monroe Doctrine, 1823–1826* (Cambridge, Mass., 1927), and *The Monroe Doctrine, 1826–1867* (Baltimore, 1933), p. vii.

15. *Americans in Eastern Asia*, p. viii, and *Roosevelt and the Russo-Japanese War* (New York, 1925).

16. His major publication was, of course, *A Diplomatic History of the United States* (New York, 1936); but during the decade he also produced, aside from a variety of articles, *The Diplomacy of the American Revolution* (New York, 1935), and, in collaboration with Grace Gardner Griffin, *Guide*

upon both the European context of American diplomacy and on its continuities. His work was marked by an exuberant patriotism and a frequent use of superlatives to describe the triumphs and errors of American statesmen. "The heroic period of American nationality" occurred in the late eighteenth century, and Bemis looked wistfully back at great figures such as Franklin, Washington, Hamilton, and Adams, who had so wisely guided the nation through perilous times. Not only had the nation prospered under their tutelage but by 1796 they had laid the foundations of American foreign policy, which only needed to be capped in 1823 by the Monroe Doctrine. In the first edition of his text (1936) Bemis listed eight of these fundamentals, including freedom of the seas, nonentanglement in European politics, continental expansion, and the various tenets of the Monroe Doctrine. His belief in the relevance of most of these basic principles never altered; they were the unchanging continuities of American foreign policy. Washington's Farewell Address, which "embodied the experience and wisdom of the Fathers . . . became so firmly established an American policy as to stand, even in our days in a vastly altered world." [17]

Unlike his predecessors, Bemis did not view American diplomacy as a continual triumph extending to the thirties. He saw a sharp break in American foreign policy at the end of the nineteenth century. Until then, guided by the aphorisms of the Founding Fathers, American diplomatists had made no serious mistakes. After 1898 one catastrophic error followed another. American imperialism was a "Great Aberration," entangling the nation in the politics of Europe and

to the *Diplomatic History of the United States, 1775–1921* (Washington, D.C., 1935). The most recent assessment of Bemis is H. C. Allen's "Samuel Flagg Bemis," in Marcus Cunliffe and Robin W. Winks, eds., *Pastmasters: Some Essays on American Historians* (New York, 1969).

17. *John Quincy Adams and the Foundations of American Foreign Policy* (New York, 1949), p. 3; *Diplomatic History*, p. 110.

Asia, where it possessed no vital interests. The acquisition of the Philippines, in Bemis's judgment, was the "greatest blunder" of American diplomacy; the Open Door Notes a "grandiose and sentimental floriation," a "protean error." Bemis deplored the departure of the United States from a policy of isolation and its involvement in affairs outside the Western Hemisphere. He doubted, in retrospect, the wisdom of entering World War I and felt that the Senate's rejection of the League had worked to the nation's advantage. America could wait, secure in its own hemisphere, for the world to grow better. And so, in the mid-thirties, he urged Americans to avoid a confrontation with Japan and to withdraw from China, which was "not in any sense vital." Shifts in American foreign policy in the thirties such as neutrality legislation and the liquidation of imperialism seemed to Bemis a "clarification," a grasping of enduring principles lost sight of in previous twentieth-century diplomacy. The United States, he argued, should remain aloof from turmoil in Europe and East Asia and develop, in the inter-American system, a noncompulsory concept of collective security as a model for the world.[18]

Bemis's views were partly a reflection of the profoundly isolationist mood of the middle years of the decade, but they also expressed a firmly held set of convictions that transcended the period in which he wrote. Though he later came to accept the need for American involvement in World War II and for the postwar confrontation with the Soviet Union, he could never comfortably adjust to the new position of the United States. For him there was always the belief that American principles set the nation apart from the rest of the world, always a nostalgia for the late eighteenth and early nineteenth centuries.

18. *Diplomatic History*, pp. 463, 482, 501, 806; Bemis, "A Clarifying Foreign Policy," *Yale Review* XXV (1935), 221–40.

Other scholars continued to write in the tradition of diplomatic history that Bemis most successfully embodied. Despite the dominance of progressive history and the unfavorable climate it produced, the decade saw a great burst of scholarship in foreign policy.[19] Charles Callan Tansill published several detailed diplomatic histories; Dexter Perkins extended his study of the Monroe Doctrine; and A. Whitney Griswold, building upon the work of Dennett, produced a seminal book on the history of American Far Eastern policy.[20] Griswold shared Bemis's belief that in 1898 "American diplomacy departed from the traditions of one century and assumed the obligations of another," and he was also critical of the involvement produced by twentieth-century American diplomacy. Emphasizing the European context of American policy, he saw a consistent, cyclical pattern of advance and retreat in the pursuit of illusory objectives in East Asia.[21] His interpretation was to remain an influential one because of its breadth of conception and high level of analysis. Like so much of the work done in American foreign policy in the thirties, it has yet to be replaced.

19. Philip Coolidge Brooks, *Diplomacy and Borderlands: The Adams-Onís Treaty of 1819* (Berkeley, Calif., 1939); John H. Ferguson, *American Diplomacy and the Boer War* (Philadelphia, 1939); Alice M. Morrissey, *The American Defense of Neutral Rights, 1914–17* (Cambridge, Mass., 1939); Payson J. Treat, *Diplomatic Relations between the United States and Japan, 1853–1905*, 3 vols. (Stanford, Calif., 1932–38); and Richard Heathcote Heindel, *The American Impact on Great Britain, 1898–1914* (Philadelphia, 1940), though it moved beyond the conservative, evolutionist tradition in its emphasis on the interaction of the two civilizations. Bemis expressed this sense of momentum among diplomatic historians in "Fields for Research in the Diplomatic History of the United States to 1900," *American Historical Review* XXXVI (1930), 68–75.

20. Charles Callan Tansill, *The Purchase of the Danish West Indies* (Baltimore, 1932), *The United States and Santo Domingo, 1798–1873* (Baltimore, 1938); Dexter Perkins, *The Monroe Doctrine, 1826–1867*, and *The Monroe Doctrine, 1867–1907* (Baltimore, 1937); A. Whitney Griswold, *The Far Eastern Policy of the United States* (New York, 1938).

21. *Far Eastern Policy*, p. 3; Robert H. Ferrell and Waldo H. Heinrichs, Jr., comment upon Griswold's thesis and its influence in Dorothy Borg, ed., *Historians and American Far Eastern Policy* (New York, 1966), pp. 14–21, 38–41.

While Bemis and others wrote in the conservative, evolutionist tradition, another school of diplomatic historians emerged that was in the mainstream of American historiography and that drew its inspiration directly from progressive history. These historians, neglecting the evolution of principles and the international setting of diplomacy, sought out the domestic sources of foreign policy—the economic, intellectual, and political forces that dominated the formulation of policy. Some were inspired by Frederick Jackson Turner and his followers, others by different strands of progressive historiography. The result was a different kind of diplomatic history that emphasized change far more than continuity.[22]

During the twenties Julius W. Pratt and Arthur P. Whitaker published monographs emphasizing the importance of the West and of sectional forces in American foreign policy.[23] In the next decade Whitaker became a specialist in Latin American history, and Pratt produced one of the most original books of the decade, *Expansionists of 1898*. In one sense, this book was path-breaking because it moved behind the facade of public opinion to an analysis of the views on expansion and war of specific groups, such as business and organized religion. Pratt displayed a vigorous interest in the ideas that affected foreign policy and offered an extensive analysis of what he termed the "new Manifest Destiny." Though an impressionistic book, *Expansionists of 1898* sug-

22. Aside from those mentioned below in the text, some of the best monographs in this genre were: John D. P. Fuller, *The Movement for the Acquisition of all Mexico, 1846–48* (Baltimore, 1936); Frank L. Owsley, *King Cotton Diplomacy: Foreign Relations of the Confederate States of America* (Chicago, 1931); Louis Martin Sears, *Jefferson and the Embargo* (Durham, N.C., 1927); Joe Patterson Smith, *The Republican Expansionists of the Early Reconstruction Era* (Chicago, 1933).

23. Julius W. Pratt, *Expansionists of 1812* (New York, 1925); Arthur P. Whitaker, *The Spanish-American Frontier, 1783–1795* (Boston, 1927).

gested approaches to the 1890s that would not be fully exploited for many years.[24]

Pratt was not alone in his use of intellectual history to enrich the study of American foreign policy. Harley Notter's semibiographical appraisal of Woodrow Wilson recreated the intellectual precedents for Wilson's foreign policy decisions, and Albert K. Weinberg's *Manifest Destiny* analyzed American expansionist thought over the whole of the nation's history. *Manifest Destiny* suffered from serious organizational flaws: it tended to isolate ideas from their historical milieu and, by seeking to unwind the various strands of Manifest Destiny, it failed to capture the wholeness of the ideology at any one time. But in its choice of subject, this book offered an important example for future diplomatic historians.[25]

Thomas A. Bailey served approximately the same function for this progressive approach to diplomatic history as Bemis did for the more conservative one. Most of Bailey's scholarship appeared during and after World War II, but in 1940 he published an influential and popular text that summed up the new attitude. Bailey, along with Pratt and Whitaker, viewed foreign policy from a domestic perspective, though he did not share their responsiveness to intellectual history. His text, like his first monograph on the Japanese-American crisis of 1906–9, focused on the influence of public opinion and domestic politics and on the alternatives confronting statesmen during foreign policy crises.[26] It also gave a more

24. Julius W. Pratt, *Expansionists of 1898: The Acquisition of Hawaii and the Spanish Islands* (Baltimore, 1936).

25. Harley Notter, *The Origins of the Foreign Policy of Woodrow Wilson* (Baltimore, 1937); Albert K. Weinberg, *Manifest Destiny: A Study of National Expansionism in American History* (Baltimore, 1935).

26. Thomas A. Bailey, *Theodore Roosevelt and the Japanese-American Crises* (Stanford, Calif., 1934); *A Diplomatic History of the American People* (New York, 1940).

prominent position to decision-making and to personalities and the images that the United States and other nations held of each other. Impressed with the power of public opinion, Bailey sought to reach a larger audience in order to destroy popular myths and illusions. Bailey wrote in reaction against diplomatic history "merely presenting digests of official correspondence" and with the conviction that "diplomatic affairs cannot be conducted in a vacuum . . . since they cannot be isolated from political, economic, and social developments." He specifically rejected the continuities of principle and policy emphasized in previous texts. "If, at times," he observed, "it seems as though the narrative were concerned with a series of unrelated incidents, it must be borne in mind that for considerable periods that is precisely what American diplomatic history has been." [27]

Though Bailey, Pratt and others added a new dimension to the writing on American foreign policy, they were in many ways dependent on the conservative, evolutionist tradition. Bailey's text, for example, was episodic; it provided no compelling themes, no synthesis to bind periods together. It also failed to give a larger meaning to the record of American diplomacy. It remained for Bemis and those who shared his views to provide an overview of American diplomatic history based upon the triumph of uniquely American principles. When diplomatic historians fused together the two traditions after 1945, the conservative, evolutionist framework retained its dominance because of its powerful, synthetic qualities.

Even in the twenties and thirties, however, the two traditions were closely related to one another. Whatever the major characteristics of a scholar's work, there were always portions of it that linked him to the other school, as well as

27. *Diplomatic History*, p. xi.

occasional shifts in an individual's point of view.[28] Moreover, diplomatic historians did not seem particularly conscious of a difference of approach and easily assimilated the insights of one another. Bemis, for example, incorporated the conclusions of Pratt on the origins of the War of 1812 into his text, while Bailey drew on Bemis's scholarship in his analysis of American diplomacy in the late eighteenth century. The underdeveloped state of historiography encouraged this blurring of what were, in fact, distinctive genres of diplomatic history. These seem far more evident now because of the passage of time and because of our own generation's need to locate itself more precisely in the historical spectrum.

Scholars who were specialists in other areas such as Latin America, Europe, or the British Empire, also made during the twenties and thirties, as they do today, substantial contributions to the literature of American foreign policy.[29] Generally their studies fitted closely into one tradition, though at times they fell somewhere in between. Charles Seymour wrote the decade's best analysis of American intervention in World War I, while Arthur P. Whitaker published one of the outstanding books of this period.[30] *The United States and the Independence of Latin America* presented, in Whitaker's own estimate, "a broader view of the subject than has been given before, by adding to the conventional

28. Bemis's early work showed some progressive influence. This was evident in his first article on "The Settlement of the Yazoo Boundary Dispute: The First Step in Southern Expansion," *Magazine of History* XVII (1913), 129–40, and in his first monograph, *Jay's Treaty*.

29. A. L. Burt, *The United States, Great Britain, and British North America from the Revolution to the Establishment of Peace after the War of 1812* (New Haven, Conn., 1940); Alfred L. P. Dennis, *Adventures in American Diplomacy, 1896–1906* (New York, 1928); Lionel M. Gelber, *The Rise of Anglo-American Friendship, 1898–1906* (New York, 1938); Charles Carroll Griffin, *The United States and the Disruption of the Spanish Empire, 1810–1822* (New York, 1937).

30. Charles Seymour, *American Diplomacy during the World War* (Baltimore, 1934), *American Neutrality, 1914–1917* (New Haven, Conn., 1935); Arthur P. Whitaker, *The United States and the Independence of Latin America, 1800–1830* (Baltimore, 1941).

narrative of diplomacy an account of economic interests, political ideas, and cultural relations." Whitaker traced the growth of concepts, such as the belief in inter-American unity, and also revealed the intricate interplay of forces shaping foreign policy decisions. It was a book that fused together the distinctive features of the conservative and progressive approaches to foreign policy.[31] Another Latin Americanist, J. Fred Rippy, employed a variety of techniques, the most original of which examined the private economic structure linking the United States to other nations.[32]

Whatever their approach to the subject, few diplomatic historians completely escaped the isolationist assumptions so prevalent in the thirties or the influence of revisionist writings on American intervention in World War I. There were, of course, some variations. Bailey and Perkins seemed to accept American involvement in world politics in the twentieth century, and even the critique of those such as Bemis was muted by their belief that the nation's record in foreign affairs was largely a noble and inspiring one. Still, the bulk of the writing dealing with twentieth-century American diplomacy had a critical tone, and, compared with earlier periods, some notable shifts in interpretations occurred.[33] Previously historians had applauded the skill of McKinley and Roosevelt in guiding the nation's emergence as a world power; now they often made a harsh and negative appraisal of their diplomacy. Interpretations of American East Asian policy underwent a similar change. Before World War I historians

31. *The United States and the Independence of Latin America*, p. xiii.
32. J. Fred Rippy, *The United States and Mexico* (New York, 1926); *Rivalry of the United States and Great Britain over Latin America, 1808–1830* (Baltimore, 1929); *The Capitalists and Colombia* (New York, 1931); *The Caribbean Danger Zone* (New York, 1940).
33. Ernest R. May traces some of these changes in "Emergence to World Power," in John Higham, ed., *The Reconstruction of American History* (New York, 1962), pp. 180–96.

had characterized the Open Door Notes as a bold and effective diplomatic démarche; in the twenties they had become more skeptical of their effectiveness and wisdom; in the thirties many condemned the notes and the misunderstanding of the nation's interests in East Asia which they generated. In 1922 Tyler Dennett had praised the Open Door Notes as exemplifying a cooperative policy in East Asia, but in 1933 Dennett portrayed them as motivated by Hay's extreme Anglophilia and by domestic political needs. According to Dennett, American interests in China were small, and Hay had wisely abandoned adventurous policies there once he realized where they might lead.[34]

Though the writing of nearly all diplomatic historians during the thirties revealed strains of isolationism and revisionism, the writers of major revisionist tracts—Edwin Borchard and William Potter Lage, C. Hartley Grattan, and Walter Millis—were not specialists in American foreign policy. The only exception was Charles Callan Tansill. Today their interpretations of American involvement in World War I are discredited; at the time, however, their books had a great influence upon scholars. This was particularly true of Tansill's *America Goes to War,* the most substantial work on American intervention to appear in the twenties and thirties. Revisionists pioneered in the study of the role of propaganda and economics in diplomacy, and Millis displayed a sensitive if impressionistic understanding of national psychology. But their writings suffered from a variety of weaknesses. They were often excessively polemical, sometimes vague and contradictory in their analysis of events, and frequently unbalanced in their emphasis upon economic factors and in their

34. See the comments by John A. Garraty and Ernest R. May on the Open Door Notes and Tyler Dennett in Borg, *Historians and American Far Eastern Policy,* pp. 4–13, 32–37. Dennett applauded the Open Door Notes in *Americans in Eastern Asia* and criticized them in *John Hay: From Poetry to Politics* (New York, 1933).

hostility to Great Britain and to most of Wilson's advisers. Finally, they thrived on a parochialism of outlook which, while it facilitated a condemnation of Wilson's diplomacy, ensured that multinational studies would one day place events in a broader framework.[35]

Charles A. Beard was the only revisionist who transcended the immediate issue of American intervention to offer a convincing interpretation of the whole of American foreign policy. Beard wrote no studies in diplomatic history until after World War II, but in *America in Midpassage,* the third volume of his great text, and in other books written during the thirties, he sought the domestic roots of foreign policy and historical justification for his concept of "continentalism." [36] Out of the early years of the young republic, Beard contended, two conceptions of foreign policy emerged, one Federalist-Whig-Republican or "industrialist," the other Jeffersonian or "agrarian." The first featured high tariffs along with commercial and territorial expansion abroad; the second concentrated upon agricultural exports, free trade, and international cooperation. Both traditions were vague

35. Edwin Borchard and William P. Lage, *Neutrality for the United States* (New Haven, Conn., 1937); C. Hartley Grattan, *Why We Fought* (New York, 1929); Walter Millis, *Road to War: America, 1914–1917* (Boston, 1935); Charles Callan Tansill, *America Goes to War* (Boston, 1938). Two good discussions of revisionism are: Richard W. Leopold, "The Problem of American Intervention, 1917: A Historical Retrospect," *World Politics* II (1950), 405–25, and Warren I. Cohen, *The American Revisionists: The Lessons of Intervention in World War I* (Chicago, 1967).

36. Charles A. and Mary R. Beard, *America in Midpassage* (New York, 1939). Aside from this volume, Beard expressed his ideas about the evolution of American expansionism most clearly in: *The Idea of National Interest: An Analytical Study in American Foreign Policy* (New York, 1934); *The Open Door at Home: A Trial Philosophy of National Interest* (New York, 1935); *A Foreign Policy for America* (New York, 1940). Appraisals of Beard's foreign policy views are offered by Hofstadter, *The Progressive Historians,* pp. 318–46; George R. Leighton, "Beard and Foreign Policy," in Howard K. Beale, ed., *Charles A. Beard: An Appraisal* (Lexington, Ky., 1954), pp. 161–84; Gerald Stourzh, "Charles A. Beard's Interpretations of American Foreign Policy," *World Affairs Quarterly* XXVIII (1957), 111–48; and Cushing Strout, *The Pragmatic Revolt in American History: Carl Becker and Charles Beard* (New Haven, Conn., 1958), pp. 135–56.

and contradictory, and neither was powerful enough to prevent the United States from following, until the late nineteenth century, an essentially isolationist foreign policy dedicated to the expansion of foreign trade without involvement abroad. It was only then that the industrialist outlook became intensified and elaborated, leading many to believe that the nation faced a "question of commercial expansion or stagnation and decay." And so until 1929 the United States, led by a "restless elite," aggressively pursued foreign economic expansion both to maintain prosperity at home and to distract the people from the unresolved problems of domestic reform. Wilsonian internationalism, Beard argued, was only an offshoot of industrialism, for Wilson believed in the necessity both of commercial expansion and of American predominance in world affairs. The great depression was the critical event that shattered the illusion of endless advance abroad as a solution to domestic problems, and in the thirties Beard invited the American nation "to open doors at home, to substitute an intensive cultivation of its own garden for a wasteful, quixotic, and ineffectual extension of its interests beyond the reach of competent military and naval defenses." [37] Americans must, in short, now turn to the enormous, unfinished task of developing the potentialities of their own unique civilization.

Beard was, of course, the most eminent progressive historian, and his work on foreign policy indicates how the thrust of progressive history, when carried to extremes, could be a distorting influence. In Beard's hands the exploration of the domestic sources of foreign policy often became an economic reductionism; the attempt to relate the history of ideas to foreign policy floundered upon what Richard Hofstadter aptly describes as his ineptitude in dealing "with ideas, with

37. *The Open Door at Home*, p. 38; *A Foreign Policy for America*, p. 148; *The Open Door at Home*, p. vii.

moral impulses, with cultural forces that could not be closely
tied to economic origins." [38] Beard ignored the international
setting of diplomacy and wrote as if American leaders had
no legitimate concern for national security or the actions of
other powers. His writings on foreign policy, dominated by
suspicion of Franklin D. Roosevelt and fears for the future
of American civilization, worked against the natural inter-
penetration of the progressive and conservative traditions of
diplomatic history. But their obvious polemical nature, their
confusing twists and turns required by Beard's efforts to fit
the history of American foreign policy into ever-changing
needs, undoubtedly weakened his impact on diplomatic historians during the decade. Beard was too obviously a historian with a cause. Nonetheless, his influence did persist in
the years after World War II in the writings of William
Appleman Williams and other "New Left" diplomatic historians. Though rejecting Beard's dualism, they found meaning in his economic realism and in his emphasis on the domestic origins of foreign policy. More than anything else,
however, they found in Beard an inspirational figure, committed to making history serve his social passions and cou-
rageously advocating his reforming vision.

Beard's weaknesses, like his strengths, were of massive
proportions compared with those of most other historians of
the time. What now seem to be significant shortcomings of
American diplomatic history in the twenties and thirties oc-
cupy a less dramatic scale. Conservative evolutionists, in focusing on continuities, displayed little sense of the shifting
meaning of fundamental principles and traditional policies.
On the other hand, progressive historians, who de-empha-
sized continuities and approached foreign policy from its
domestic perspective, were often superficial in their analysis

38. *The Progressive Historians*, p. 245.

of various domestic forces, particularly public opinion. Even when exploring the ideology of foreign policy, they seldom linked ideas to the decision-making process or suggested the extent to which concepts of policy are time-bound—tied to the peculiar intellectual and cultural environment of a given period.

Nor did specialists in American foreign policy dwell upon the tragic dimension of history—the unpredictability of events, the overpowering of governments and statesmen by the massive sweep of historical forces, or the illusions and irrationalities of nations and their leaders. The faith of these historians in rational, orderly progress still ran deep. Bailey and Bemis were fond of listing the mistakes or blunders of American statesmen, suggesting by implication that clear options existed if only men had been wise enough to see them. The multiarchival approach of Bemis, Perkins, and others brought an awareness of the interaction of American policy with that of other nations; but it did not breed much historical fatalism, partly because it was multiarchival rather than multinational—grounded too much on government archives and too little on a broader understanding of the relationship between domestic politics and foreign policy. There was, to be sure, a strong sense of fatalism in the work of Millis and Seymour; but this was not generally the case, and most diplomatic historians were not oppressed with a sense of inevitability in dealing with the coming of war in 1812, 1846, or 1898. They agreed that in 1812 knowledge of Britain's repeal of the Orders-in-Council would have prevented a declaration of war; that in 1846 neither the United States nor Mexico really tried to keep the peace; and that in 1898 the McKinley administration might have averted war by displaying more firmness toward the American public and more patience with Spain. American intervention in World War I seemed more complex, and most prominent diplomatic historians, with the exception of Tansill, felt ambivalent over the possibility of avoiding it.

Moreover, the results of the War of 1812 and the Mexican War aroused considerable enthusiasm. Bemis believed that the War of 1812 "galvanized American nationality. . . . [and] swelled a new pride in the Union which was to triumph over the great threat of state rights in the middle of the century." Though he condemned the war as a "rash departure" from traditional policy, Bailey agreed that it brought forth a new nation.[39] In assessing the Mexican War, few challenged Bemis's conclusion that no one would care to undo the results of Polk's aggressive diplomacy. Whether diplomatic historians praised or condemned the consequences of the Spanish-American War and American intervention in World War I, they were surprisingly gentle in appraising the diplomacy of McKinley and Wilson. All of these judgments reflected a pride in the American past and the relative freedom of this generation from the many burdens of our own time.

To some extent, however, diplomatic historians shared in what John Higham describes as the "crisis in progressive history" in the thirties. The best of the progressive historians had begun in that decade, if not before, to have doubts about scientific history and the cumulative nature of historical knowledge; they had begun to understand the way in which the historian, immersed in the values and perspectives of his own era, was bound by its assumptions in examining the past. Historical knowledge seemed less secure, less solid, as a crisis of confidence spread imperceptibly through the profession. Now some questioned the idea of progress, probed beneath man's surface motivations, and displayed a new awareness of the less tangible aspects of national and individual be-

39. Bemis, *Diplomatic History*, p. 171; Bailey, *Diplomatic History*, pp. 139, 158.

mis urged a return to national discipline and sac-
at the same time, nostalgically evoked the nine-
ury, those "happy, golden, bygone years of safety,
nocence, apart from the world around us." Like
y Adams, his personal motto was "A stout heart
conscience, and never despair." But he could not
ears for the future of his nation.[47]

cholarship showed the imprint of changing his-
udes, as well as a sensitivity to broader domestic
tional currents. The viewpoint of another con-
olutionist, Dexter Perkins, changed less dramat-
41 Perkins summed up and extended his history
oe Doctrine, but never again did he undertake
llectual task. Instead, he published a series of
ks generally designed to explain the American
oreign relations and to bring home the lessons
the public.[48] One of these books, *The American
Foreign Policy*, did display a new concern with
public's mood and suggested a diminishing be-
ationality of decision-making. Neither these in-
rkins's loss of faith in collective security altered
view of the history of American foreign policy,
5 he was unperturbed, if not complacent, about
le in world politics. He took pride and satisfac-

havior. Ideas, traditional values, and the role of the individual, all achieved more recognition. In the process the
interpretive structure of progressive history was seriously
undermined.[40]

Diplomatic historians, who were somewhat insulated from
the prevalent historical attitude, responded slowly to these
changes. But even in the thirties certain signs of the new historical outlook appeared in their writings. As we have seen,
there was a critical mood that emphasized the mistakes of
the past and a tendency, on the part of Bailey and Millis, to
portray the power and irresponsibility of public opinion. A
significant interest in biography also developed.[41] The most
impressive of these biographies was Dennett's *John Hay*,
which explored with perception and grace the tensions of
Hay's life. A subtle portrait emerged of a disunified man,
filled with unresolved contradictions between a love of com-
fort and idleness and a gnawing need to achieve worldly success and recognition. Hay was torn between an amateurish
diffuseness and a recognition that his talents must be focused
if he was to make a lasting impression upon the world. As
Dennett wrote, his was "no hero's tale," and yet there was a
"vein of heroism" in Hay's life because "indolent by nature
. . . evading most of . . . [life's] rough spots . . . he over-
came himself" and became a great secretary of state.[42] What
distinguished Dennett's *Hay* was the way in which it conveyed the sadness of Hay's life, the extent to which he lived
on the edge of tragedy and was rescued from it by forces
largely beyond his own control. It was a somber book, illu-

incy Adams and the Foundations of American Foreign
670; and American Foreign Policy and the Blessings of
14. This pessimism began in the thirties, when Bemis was
w Deal and disturbed by the apparent decline of traditional
s. In recent years it has deepened. Interview with Samuel
ptember 17, 1968.

ff: A History of the Monroe Doctrine (Boston, 1941);
Wars (Boston, 1944); The Evolution of American Foreign
rk, 1948); The American Approach to Foreign Policy
1); America's Quest for Peace (Bloomington, Ind., 1962);
of a New Age: Major Issues in U.S. Policy since 1945
d., 1967). Many of his essays are collected in Glyndon G.
Richard C. Wade, eds., Foreign Policy and the American
Dexter Perkins (Ithaca, N.Y., 1957). Perkins reflects on
f the Years (Boston, 1969).

40. Higham, *History*, pp. 198–211.

41. Philip C. Jessup, *Elihu Root*, 2 vols. (New York, 1938); Allan Nevins, *Henry White: Thirty Years of American Diplomacy* (New York, 1930), *Hamilton Fish: The Inner History of the Grant Administration* (New York, 1936); J. Fred Rippy, *Joel R. Poinsett: Versatile American* (Durham, N.C., 1935); Louis Martin Sears, *John Slidell* (Durham, N.C., 1925), and *George Washington* (New York, 1932).

42. *John Hay*, p. 443.

minating the darker sides of human existence, from which one could easily infer parallels between the fate of nations and men.

After World War II these new directions in diplomatic history fell into bolder relief. Scholars continued, of course, to work in the conservative-evolutionist and progressive traditions of foreign policy, but now substantial changes of tone and interpretation appeared. In the early forties Bemis turned to a study of the Latin American policy of the United States, one that emphasized continuities, particularly the evolution of a legal framework for inter-American relations. He reached optimistic conclusions, seeing steady progress in the development of the principles of hemispheric unity and cooperation and predicting that the inter-American system would become the cornerstone of the world's future peace structure.[43] He then moved on to biography, and produced, in 1949, the first of two volumes on John Quincy Adams. Bemis chose Adams in part because his career as diplomat and secretary of state embodied the foundations of American foreign policy and served as a convenient way in which to trace their formulation. The first volume, as Bemis pointed out, was a "diplomatic biography," [44] but the second was quite different. Foreign policy could no longer serve as a major theme around which to group Adams's activities; now Bemis saw him as a fervent nationalist and as an upholder of the Union. More importantly, the final volume had a much broader scope, ranging across many aspects of Adams's personal life—the tensions within his marriage and with his son, his melancholy, and his compulsive need for political contention. Bemis touched upon these inner dimensions of Adams's personality, yet felt inadequately prepared

43. Samuel Flagg Bemis, *The Latin American Policy of the United States: An Historical Interpretation* (New York, 1943).

44. *John Quincy Adams and the Foundations of American Foreign Policy*, p. ix.

to deal with them. "This tas[ ] ture biographers." [45]

Bemis also changed his [ ] rest of the world. By 194[ ] Japan menaced America's [ ] World War II, he accepted [ ] the necessity of the Cold [ ] Union involved precious [ ] the nation had lived in a [ ] after 1922. Now he mod[ ] about the course of Ameri[ ] took the stance of a politi[ ] power should dominate [ ] United States must rely u[ ] nations of the world form[ ] and vindicated Wilson's [ ] aspects of America's new [ ] and in the years after 19[ ] of confidence and reache[ ] contemporary American [ ] ings about American for[ ] nation in the role of "gl[ ] foresee a long armed p[ ] and endurance of the A[ ] address to the America[ ] vealed doubts about th[ ] that the American peo[ ] and propagate the "bl[ ] they had lost sight of [ ] softening, its people a[ ]

45. Samuel Flagg Bemis, [ ] 1956), p. 544.
46. Samuel Flagg Bemis, [ ] *Liberty and Other Essays* (N[ ]

gence." Be[ ] rifice and, [ ] teenth cent[ ] in lucky in[ ] John Quinc[ ] and a clear [ ] repress his [ ]

Bemis's s[ ] torical attit[ ] and interna[ ] servative ev[ ] ically. In 19[ ] of the Mon[ ] a major int[ ] smaller boo[ ] heritage in [ ] of history to[ ] *Approach to*[ ] shifts in the [ ] lief in the r[ ] sights nor P[ ] his optimisti[ ] and after 19[ ] America's ro[ ]

47. *John Qu*[ ] *Policy,* pp. 566[ ] *Liberty,* pp. 6, [ ] hostile to the N[ ] American virtue[ ] Flagg Bemis, S[ ]
48. *Hands O*[ ] *America and Tu*[ ] *Policy* (New Y[ ] (Stockholm, 195[ ] *The Diplomacy*[ ] (Bloomington, I[ ] Van Deusen and[ ] *Spirit: Essays b*[ ] his life in *Yield*[ ]

tion in both the past and present and believed that, on the whole, American diplomacy had been "remarkably successful."[49] It was an idealistic diplomacy, concerned with general principles, dependent upon public opinion, and reluctant to recognize the role of force. Americans were pacific and moralistic but also flexible and pragmatic in their response to particular problems. Though the occasional naïveté of American foreign policy worried Perkins, he praised its major characteristics.

Between 1947, when he predicted a "brilliant future" for Cuba, and 1967, Perkins's optimism about world affairs wavered but remained strong.[50] He clung to his belief that the trend was toward stability and order and that war was "more and more unlikely." "It may be," he wrote in 1962, "that we shall see a great decrease in international tension in the years ahead. Surely we should not wring our hands in futility. Great winds of hope are sweeping through the world, the hope of peace, the hope of economic progress, of a richer life for all. This is no time for despair." [51]

Diplomatic historians working within the progressive tradition also continued to publish in the postwar period, but with the exception of Thomas A. Bailey, they seemed uninterested in building upon their earlier writings. Julius W. Pratt showed no inclination to explore the new approaches opened up in *Expansionists of 1898*,[52] and J. Fred Rippy, a

49. *The American Approach to Foreign Policy*, p. 174; *Yield of the Years*, pp. 139–40.

50. *The United States and the Caribbean* (Cambridge, Mass., 1947), p. 32. This comes out clearly if one compares the preface of the 1947 edition with that of the 1966 revised edition.

51. *American Historical Review* LXXIII (1967), 87; Perkins, *America's Quest for Peace*, p. 122.

52. Julius W. Pratt, *America's Colonial Experiment: How the United States Gained, Governed, and in Part Gave Away a Colonial Empire* (New York, 1950); *Cordell Hull, 1933–44*, 2 vols. (New York, 1964); *Challenge and Rejection: The United States and World Leadership, 1900–1921* (New York, 1967).

Latin Americanist strongly influenced by progressive history, did not really improve his technique of historical analysis.[53] Rippy did, however, become dissatisfied with American foreign policy and pessimistic over the future. He complained that the United States devoted too little attention to the Western Hemisphere, still its "inner fortress," and too much to the rest of the world. America's "compulsory benevolence" around the globe was badly straining its own society and preventing the development of self-reliance in other nations. Rippy felt he lived "at a time of terrible crises in the history of the human race," when the American epic was "on the point of becoming a Greek tragedy." The world was "increasingly complex and dangerous . . . on the verge of greater material prosperity but growing more immoral, inhumane, and desolate spiritually." [54] Rippy had no regrets that his life span was nearing its end; the future seemed unlikely to be so good as the past.

Of all those historians concerned with the domestic sources of foreign policy, Thomas A. Bailey remained the most productive during and after World War II. An intense present-mindedness marked his work, along with an interest in the nature and education of public opinion. Fearful that the United States might "again run through the same tragic circle of disillusionment and isolationism," Bailey described, in two volumes, the lessons to be learned from Woodrow Wilson's efforts to make a just peace and secure its acceptance by the American people. Admitting his admiration for Wilson and his sympathy with his ends, Bailey focused closely on Wilson's various decisions as if they would be directly relevant to peacemaking in 1945. He concluded that

53. J. Fred Rippy, *Latin America and the Industrial Age* (New York, 1944); *Globe and Hemisphere: Latin America's Place in the Postwar Foreign Relations of the United States* (Chicago, 1958); *British Investments in Latin America, 1822–1949* (Minneapolis, 1959).

54. *Globe and Hemisphere*, pp. 28, 95; and *Bygones I Cannot Help Recalling: The Memoirs of a Mobile Scholar* (Austin, Tex., 1966), pp. vi, 95, 191.

Wilson moved too fast and that he failed to realize that "mankind is shortsighted and perverse." The failure to win Senate approval of the Treaty of Versailles was in part due to Wilson's own flaws and was "one of the supreme tragedies of human history." [55]

Bailey's interest in public opinion climaxed in 1948 with the publication of *The Man in the Street.* Relying heavily on public opinion polls, Bailey essentially described popular attitudes and illusions toward foreign affairs. There was a certain muckraking quality to the book, as Bailey decried the public's "appalling ignorance of foreign affairs" and equated ignorance with a bellicose feeling toward other nations. He also emphasized the deficiencies of American democracy and the way in which the people had disappointed "the high hopes of our friends and . . . fallen so far short of our ideals." [56] Yet there was, beneath the superficial disillusionment, a basic core of faith that the American people, as they gained more understanding of others, would become more mature, tolerant, and sophisticated in their foreign policy.

The Man in the Street left unanswered many questions about public opinion. It was, to be sure, a powerful force, but the book did not dissect it or establish a connection between the public's beliefs and decision-making. Nor did Bailey ever attempt to move beyond his 1948 analysis. He soon turned to another timely subject, Russian-American relations, and after 1950 his work trailed off in a number of directions, leaving to others the pursuit of his many original insights. [57] At the same time, he sought to revive his faltering

55. Thomas A. Bailey, *Woodrow Wilson and the Lost Peace* (New York, 1944), pp. v, 325; *Woodrow Wilson and the Great Betrayal* (New York, 1945), p. v.

56. Thomas A. Bailey, *The Man in the Street: The Impact of American Public Opinion on Foreign Policy* (New York, 1948), pp. 130, 46.

57. Thomas A. Bailey, *America Faces Russia: Russian-American Relations from Early Times to Our Day* (Ithaca, N.Y., 1950); *Presidential Greatness: The Image and the Man from George Washington to the Present* (New York, 1966); *The Art of Diplomacy: The American Experience* (New York, 1968); *Democrats vs. Republicans: The Continuing Clash* (New York,

confidence in America and its mission. But Bailey's claims
that the United States "towers gigantic and unique," the
home of a "remarkable people," seemed forced, designed
more to reassure himself than to convince others.[58]

To one extent or another, then, all of the older diplomatic
historians writing in the postwar period shared the loss of
confidence so evident in Bemis and Rippy. Both foreign and
domestic events shook the certitudes of these men; the continuities of the past seemed less reassuring and less relevant
to a precarious future.

John Higham remarks that the late forties and early fifties
were the "Indian summer" of progressive history, a time of
ripeness of interpretation, when the ferment of new historical attitudes was about to break through the surface in a
massive way.[59] Developments in American diplomatic history
ran parallel to this, though perhaps the upheaval was less
dramatic. In the late forties and early fifties, Bailey, Bemis,
Perkins, and Pratt still dominated the field, but the two separate traditions of American foreign policy that they represented became less distinct. Assimilating the insights of a
previous generation, younger scholars tended to blend together the two strands into a common interpretive structure.
This process was particularly noticeable in textbooks, which
were no longer so distinctive as those of Bemis and Bailey.[60]

1968). For a selection of his articles, see Armin Rappaport and Alexander
DeConde, eds., *Essays Diplomatic and Undiplomatic of Thomas A. Bailey*
(New York, 1969).

58. *The American Pageant: A History of the Republic*, 3d ed. (Boston,
1966), pp. v, 990.

59. *History*, p. 212.

60. Of the new texts published by the older generation of diplomatic
historians after 1945, Pratt's *A History of United States Foreign Policy*
(Englewood Cliffs, N.J., 1955), and L. Ethan Ellis's *A Short History of
American Diplomacy* (New York, 1951), were balanced syntheses of the
two traditions. Richard W. Van Alstyne's *American Diplomacy in Action*
(Stanford, Calif., 1944), stood somewhat apart because of its case study
approach and its emphasis on a dynamic, aggressive concept of American

Instead, scholars emphasized both continuities and the international context as well as specific crises and domestic influences upon foreign policy decisions.

But many of the generalizations produced about the American diplomatic experience now seemed to be commonplace and inadequate explanations of events. The old continuities—the foundations of American foreign policy and the tradition of equality, liberty, and hope, so vivid in the work of Bemis—would perhaps inspire some citizens but would hardly satisfy historians.[61] They began during these years to feel a need to examine American foreign policy in a different way in an attempt to achieve a deeper level of understanding. This meant, of course, that in the fifties a wide-ranging reworking of periods and problems began that brought the whole field of American foreign policy, as one critic alarmingly notes, into a "condition of serious intellectual disarray." [62] This was, however, a sign of health, not of decay, and it produced a new literature that saw the past as more pluralistic and fragmented and less related to contemporary concerns.

This restlessness over accepted generalizations stemmed from two sources. Partly it was a reflection of the cumulative impact of events upon diplomatic historians, who could not

security. Texts by younger scholars that revealed a substantial consensus were: Robert H. Ferrell, *American Diplomacy: A History* (New York, 1959); Richard W. Leopold, *The Growth of American Foreign Policy: A History* (New York, 1962); Alexander DeConde, *A History of American Foreign Policy* (New York, 1963). Wayne S. Cole, *An Interpretive History of American Foreign Relations* (Homewood, Ill., 1968) gave more weight to the domestic sources of foreign policy. There is, of course, a great variation in the quality of these texts.

61. The continuities are spelled out in Frank Tannenbaum's *The American Tradition in Foreign Policy* (Norman, Okla., 1955).

62. Francis L. Loewenheim, "A Legacy of Hope and a Legacy of Doubt: Reflections on the Role of History and Historians in American Foreign Policy since the Eighteenth Century," in Loewenheim, ed., *The Historian and the Diplomat: The Role of History and Historians in American Foreign Policy* (New York, 1967), p. 70.

help but be affected by the tensions and perils of the international situation. So many developments since the late thirties had suggested the irrational and chaotic nature of world politics that diplomatic historians inevitably viewed the past from a more somber perspective. In addition, they were affected, though sometimes belatedly, by the disintegration of the progressive synthesis in American history and by the emergence of many new ways of interpreting the past. No longer did historians see American history as a dramatic struggle between reform and reaction, one that involved clearly defined groups acting for rational purposes and the gradual triumph of liberal reform. Now some were struck by the widespread agreement upon a largely unarticulated liberal tradition, and they used this consensus as a backdrop against which the American experience could be placed. Others, more preoccupied with instability and friction, saw it in a much different way than did progressive historians. They decreased the scope of conflict and transformed its nature, emphasizing the impact of status considerations, rapid mobility, and myths and images upon individuals and their society. Much of the conflict was internalized in the form of psychic tensions that most Americans shared. The result was a recognition of the unconscious aspects of human behavior and a concentration upon the tragic side of American history, upon defeat and decay rather than upon fulfillment and progress. Finally, an increasing number of historians analyzed the basic patterns of American political life and broadened our concept of the political process, accelerating the movement away from traditional, event-oriented history.[63]

63. By far the best descriptions of these changes are Higham, *History*, pp. 212–32, and Hofstadter, *The Progressive Historians*, pp. 437–66. Samuel H. Hays, "Social Analysis of American Political History, 1880–1920," *Political Science Quarterly* LXXX (1965), 373–94, is also excellent for a more limited area.

All of these various approaches made the past seem more complex and raised questions both about man's ability to master himself and his society. Now the impact of traditional reform measures often seemed superficial and change appeared as both good and bad, part of a continual process of disintegration and reintegration that destroys as well as creates. The past seemed so ambiguous, peopled by so few heroes or lessons for the present, that historians became acutely aware of the tension between their historical knowledge and their sense of our contemporary crisis. As Richard Hofstadter observes, they were "caught between their desire to count in the world, and their desire to understand it." [64] For the moment, at least, most seemed to reject the present-mindedness of the progressive generation of scholars and instead to concentrate on the imaginative leap, the creative fusion of past and present, that they saw as the essence of their craft.

After 1950 numerous authors reexamined America's involvement in past wars. Generally their books were multinational studies that concentrated upon the process of decision-making and, at the same time, placed that process in a much broader context than historians had previously done. Nearly all of these books emphasized the haphazard nature of decision-making and the extent to which policy was based upon illusions about other nations. Far more than in previous studies, these historians portrayed statesmen as trapped by the bureaucratic structures that provided information and advice or by public opinion, which they dared not defy. Their range of choice seemed narrow, their vision and understanding limited, and their responsiveness to the needs of other nations impeded by intellectual assumptions and preconceptions.

A drift toward fatalism appeared in significant reinterpre-

64. *The Progressive Historians,* p. 464.

tations of most of the major wars in which the United States participated. In the twenties and thirties diplomatic historians had customarily labeled the War of 1812, the Mexican War, and the Spanish-American War as unnecessary, and generally had seen a possibility of continuing American neutrality in World War I.[65] New multinational studies, however, greatly altered these conclusions. In the preface to a major work on the War of 1812, Bradford Perkins wrote that "scholars have overemphasized the tangible, rational reasons for action and . . . have given too little heed to such things as national pride, sensitivity, and frustration. . . . Emotion, chance, and half choices often mold the relations between states as much as or more than cool reason." Perkins stressed the cumulative psychological consequences of British assaults and brought out the fundamental miscalculations of the British and American governments. The British had been insensitive to the mood of Americans and had failed to comprehend the economic interdependence of the two nations; the Americans had overestimated the power of economic coercion and assumed that Great Britain would react rationally to various American initiatives. Perkins judged harshly the "diplomatic ineptness," the "fumbling and confused analysis" of Jefferson and Madison. Through action and inaction,

65. For discussions of some aspects of the historiography of these wars, see: Warren H. Goodman, "The Origins of the War of 1812: A Survey of Changing Interpretations," *Mississippi Valley Historical Review* XXVIII (1941), 171–86; Peter T. Harsted and Richard W. Rush, "The Causes of the Mexican War: A Note on Changing Interpretations," *Arizona and the West* VI (1964), 289–302; Ernest R. May, *American Intervention: 1917 and 1941* (Washington, D.C., 1960); Daniel M. Smith, "National Interest and American Intervention in 1917: An Historiographical Appraisal," *Journal of American History* LII (1965), 5–24. There was no important reinterpretation of the Mexican War. It still awaits a multinational study of its origins to replace Justin H. Smith's *The War with Mexico*, 2 vols. (New York, 1919). In the thirties Charles Seymour, who put the most emphasis on the international context of American intervention in World War I, was the most fatalistic. "Wilson," Seymour wrote, "did not dictate circumstances, but was governed by them. As we survey these four years there is something reminiscent of a Greek tragedy in the obvious omnipotence of Fate" (*American Diplomacy during the World War*, pp. 396–97).

they had led the nation to a point where it had to accept either war or profound national humiliation. Perkins believed the war was "tragically unnecessary" and could have been avoided if Jefferson and Madison had displayed the wisdom and caution of Federalist foreign policy in the 1790s.[66] But this would have required an alteration of each man's basic assumptions.

Another study of the War of 1812, by Roger H. Brown, analyzed more closely the motives of Republicans in opting for war. Drawing insights from the work of Cecilia M. Kenyon and Bernard Bailyn, Brown identified a strain of uncertainty over the fate of the Republic, a pattern of thought that continued to exist after 1787. He described how, in the years before 1812, a consensus had slowly developed among Republicans that, if the United States failed to show that it could defend its honor and endure, a less democratic form of government might have emerged. By going to war in 1812 the nation had thus overcome a crisis of confidence.[67] The thrust of both these books, with their focus on decision-making and national psychology, was to add many dimensions to our understanding of the decision for war and to narrow the possibility of avoiding conflict.

The same tendency was evident in studies of the coming war in 1898, 1914, and 1941. In *Imperial Democracy*, Ernest R. May examined the intersection of Spanish and American policy and concluded that neither government was willing to accept the domestic consequences involved in the maintenance of peace. Ultimately Spain had preferred losing Cuba through war with the United States rather than through concessions to the Cuban rebels; President McKinley had "led his country unwillingly toward a war that he did not want

66. Bradford Perkins, *Prologue to War: England and the United States, 1805–1812* (Berkeley and Los Angeles, 1963), pp. vii, 121, 426.
67. Roger H. Brown, *The Republic in Peril: 1812* (New York, 1964).

for a cause in which he did not believe" rather than risk the destruction of his leadership and of his party's dominance in American politics. For the first time May placed the origin of the war in its international context and explored the domestic pressures upon the Spanish government.[68] He also moved beyond Pratt's analysis of the structure of American public opinion. Tracing the beginnings of the Cuban agitation and its spread to the masses of the people, he showed how a popular upheaval had overwhelmed timid politicians and caused traditional leaders of public opinion to reverse their judgment and accept the necessity of war. The root of the public's frenzy was an irrational connection between concern for Cuba and the various anxieties of the 1890s. May felt that war came from a "terrible human predicament" beyond the ability of statesmen to solve.[69]

In both *Imperial Democracy* and his previous book, *The World War and American Isolation,* May provided an exceptionally thoughtful canvass of the options of statesmen as well as a compelling account of the drift into war.[70] Earlier, Charles Seymour had argued that no American concessions to Germany, short of a complete abdication of rights, would have prevented that nation's decision for unlimited submarine warfare. But it was only in the fifties and early sixties that books by May, Robert E. Osgood, and Arthur S. Link revealed the full complexity of Wilson's thought and of the

---

68. Ernest R. May, *Imperial Democracy: The Emergence of America as a Great Power* (New York, 1961); the quote is from p. 159. Orestes Ferrara's *The Last Spanish War: Revelations in "Diplomacy,"* trans. William E. Shea (New York, 1937), used some European archives but was a sketchy account that concentrated upon Spain's search for European diplomatic assistance.

69. Ernest R. May, "Overseas Expansion: The Coming of War with Spain, 1895–98," in Merrill D. Peterson and Leonard W. Levy, eds., *Major Crises in American History: Documentary Problems,* 2 vols. (New York, 1962), II, 144.

70. Ernest R. May, *The World War and American Isolation, 1914–1917* (Cambridge, Mass., 1959).

decision-making process in the American government.[71] Each emphasized the importance of intangible factors such as national honor and prestige and Wilson's sense of international morality; each found little fault with that diplomacy; and each felt the decision for war inevitable, given the values of Wilson and the American people. May's book, however, provided the most unified account of American intervention because of its exploration of the domestic sources of British and German policy, its penetrating analysis of the beliefs of Wilson and his advisers, and its taut description of the relentless domestic and international pressures that drove the nation toward war. "Despite the paradoxes," May concluded, "close analysis cannot find the point at which he [Wilson] might have turned back or taken another road. In Wilson's dilemmas, as in the contests in London and Berlin, there were elements of high tragedy." [72]

In contrast to American intervention in World War I, no historians, except extreme revisionists such as Beard and Tansill, ever questioned the wisdom of going to war with Germany in 1941.[73] Both at the time and in retrospect, Nazi Germany seemed a threat to the nation's vital interests. Moreover, the course of events after World War II never created the intellectual atmosphere in which revisionism could thrive, and it was further discouraged by the early

71. Charles Seymour, *American Neutrality*, p. 79; Robert E. Osgood, *Ideals and Self-Interest in America's Foreign Relations: The Great Transformation of the Twentieth Century* (Chicago, 1953); Arthur S. Link, *Woodrow Wilson and the Progressive Era, 1910–1917* (New York, 1954), *Wilson the Diplomatist: A Look at His Major Foreign Policies* (Baltimore, 1957), *Wilson: The Struggle for Neutrality, 1914–1915* (Princeton, N.J., 1960), *Wilson: Confusions and Crises, 1915–1916* (Princeton, N.J., 1964), and *Wilson: Campaigns for Progressivism and Peace, 1916–1917* (Princeton, N.J., 1965).

72. *The World War and American Isolation*, p. vii.

73. Assessments of the literature on American entry into World War II are: Ernest R. May, *American Intervention: 1917 and 1941;* Wayne S. Cole, "American Entry into World War II: A Historiographical Appraisal," *Mississippi Valley Historical Review* XLIII (1957), 595–617.

publication of William L. Langer's and S. Everett Gleason's
impressive defense of the American decision for war.[74] But
the coming of war with Japan raised different and more subtle issues, and historians have been preoccupied with the
might-have-beens of Japanese-American relations in the
thirties. Japan, after all, was less powerful than Germany, its
leaders less irrational, and its expansionist aims less dangerous to the interests of the United States. Until the very end
the two governments discussed the terms of a compromise
settlement, and historians have tried to understand why
these efforts failed. The first authoritative account, by Herbert Feis, assumed that failure was inevitable.[75] Feis's narrative, however, was narrow in scope, dealing primarily with
the American side. It left too many questions unresolved to
quiet historians' interest in the possibility of a last-minute
agreement. Eight years after Feis wrote, Paul W. Schroeder
published the most forceful statement of this position. Condemning the moralistic tone of American diplomacy,
Schroeder suggested that, since Japan was on the defensive
by late 1941, a *modus vivendi* could have grown into a permanent accord.[76] More recently Waldo H. Heinrichs, Jr.,
argues, in his excellent biography of Joseph Grew, that flexible and imaginative American diplomacy might have resulted in a settlement with Japan.[77] But Heinrichs's own

74. William L. Langer and S. Everett Gleason, *The Challenge to Isolation, 1937–1940* (New York, 1952), and *The Undeclared War, 1940–1941*
(New York, 1953). James V. Compton's analysis of Hitler's bizarre attitude
toward the United States in *The Swastika and the Eagle: Hitler, the United
States, and the Origins of World War II* (Boston, 1967) has only further
underlined the impossibility of peacefully coexisting with the Second Reich
and its leader.

75. Herbert Feis, *The Road to Pearl Harbor* (Princeton, N.J., 1950).

76. Paul W. Schroeder, *The Axis Alliance and Japanese-American Relations* (Ithaca, N.Y., 1958). F. C. Jones anticipated some of Schroeder's
arguments in *Japan's New Order in East Asia: Its Rise and Fall, 1937–45*
(New York, 1954).

77. Waldo H. Heinrichs, Jr., *American Ambassador: Joseph C. Grew and
the Development of the United States Diplomatic Tradition* (Boston, 1966).

analysis of Japanese expansionism and of the extraordinary
difficulty any Westerner faced in comprehending Japanese
policy tends to refute his own conclusions. In fact, those
scholars such as Robert J. C. Butow and Akira Iriye, who
have probed most deeply into Japanese politics, are pessimistic about the chances of altering the collision course on
which the two nations were set.[78] In other words, the more
historians know about the internal dynamics of Japanese
expansionism, the more fatalistic they become over the outbreak of war in the Pacific.

Thus as diplomatic historians have reached out to understand other nations and their foreign policies, the alternatives that past American statesmen faced seemed steadily to
decrease. Three outstanding books, two by George F.
Kennan and one by Roberta Wohlstetter, reinforced this
tendency. Both authors emphasized the faulty information
underlying foreign policy decisions and the enormous confusion inherent in the decision-making process. Both vividly
portrayed the difficulty of controlling bureaucratic structures
designed to serve statesmen; neither was optimistic about
the possibilities of correcting these deficiencies.[79] Much of
the recent literature on Vietnam, indicating an enormous gap
between reality and Washington's conception of it, confirms
the wisdom of Kennan and Wohlstetter in accepting this sort
of confusion as an important element in the shaping of foreign policy.[80]

Other developments in the writing of American foreign
policy have also underscored the unstable and uncertain

78. Robert J. C. Butow, *Tojo and the Coming of the War* (Princeton,
N.J., 1961); Iriye, *Across the Pacific: An Inner History of American-East
Asian Relations* (New York, 1967).

79. George F. Kennan, *Russia Leaves the War* (Princeton, N.J., 1956),
and *The Decision to Intervene* (Princeton, N.J., 1958); Roberta Wohlstetter,
Pearl Harbor: Warning and Decision (Stanford, Calif., 1962).

80. Perhaps the best example is John Mecklin's *Mission in Torment: An
Intimate Account of the United States Role in Vietnam* (New York, 1965).

foundations of decision-making. Although diplomatic historians generally have given considerable attention to public opinion, as derived from newspaper editorials or, for later periods, public opinion polls, they have not explored the process through which it is formed or the way in which politicians measure and interpret the public's response. Ernest R. May's survey of research by behavioral scientists suggests that there is no orderly transmission of views to governmental officials and that public opinion is far more complex and irrational than historians have assumed. Both the public and the statesmen who judge its opinions, May writes, "may . . . be arriving at judgments that are products of their own personalities and inner needs." [81]

Finally, a finer appreciation of the depths and nuances of human personality has increased the historian's emphasis upon the subjectivity of foreign policy decisions. Diplomatic historians largely ignored any analysis of individual personalities in the twenties and thirties, though a modest turn to biography began in the thirties.[82] Some wrote biographies of real distinction, but none pioneered in the study of group or individual psychology, as did Thomas Cochran in *America's Railway Leaders* or David Donald in *Charles Sumner and*

81. Ernest R. May, "An American Tradition in Foreign Policy: The Role of Public Opinion," in William H. Nelson, ed., *Theory and Practice in American Politics* (Chicago, 1964), p. 107. May's most recent book, *American Imperialism: A Speculative Essay* (New York, 1968), utilizes insights from behavorial scientists to explore the interplay between public opinion, the foreign policy elite, and government leaders in the 1890s. Robert H. Wiebe's *The Search for Order, 1877–1920* (New York, 1967), also contains illuminating comments on those groups dominating foreign policy in the late nineteenth and early twentieth centuries.

82. Postwar biographical or semibiographical studies written by diplomatic historians included: Bemis, *John Quincy Adams* (2 vols.); Wayne S. Cole, *Senator Gerald P. Nye and American Foreign Relations* (Minneapolis, 1962); Heinrichs, *Grew;* Richard W. Leopold, *Elihu Root and the Conservative Tradition* (Boston, 1954); Paul A. Varg, *Open Door Diplomat: The Life of W. W. Rockhill* (Urbana, Ill., 1952); and Robert Dallek, *Democrat and Diplomat: The Life of William E. Dodd* (New York, 1968).

the Coming of the Civil War.[83] There was, however, a spreading awareness of the many layers of personality as diplomatic historians drew upon the insights of outstanding biographers to penetrate into the conscious and subconscious motives of statesmen. Everywhere they turned, diplomatic historians were confronted with the dissolution of old certainties and of previously accepted generalizations.

In the fifties and sixties there was also a movement toward widening the context of decision-making, one that involved an assimilation of social and intellectual history. Before World War II some diplomatic historians had studied the intellectual concepts of statesmen and, in subsequent years, with the growing maturity of social and intellectual history, more became sensitive to the ideas behind foreign policy. One consequence was a major assault upon the conservative, evolutionist framework, which had assumed a continuity of principles meaning the same thing to different men at different times. Now these principles seemed relative to their time, part of a shifting complex of thought and values, and historians sought to understand how the assumptions of an age shaped men's outlook toward world affairs and influenced their particular decisions. Eventually, new generalizations about the history of American foreign policy will perhaps appear when a younger generation lays a comprehensive foundation of monographic literature. That process is, however, far from complete.

A number of books exemplify this new trend. Felix Gilbert has measured the impact of Enlightenment ideas upon the formulation of American diplomatic concepts in the late eighteenth century; Gerald Stourzh has traced the link be-

83. Thomas Cochran, *America's Railway Leaders, 1845–1890* (Cambridge, Mass., 1953); David Donald, *Charles Sumner and the Coming of the Civil War* (New York, 1960).

tween political action and thought in Benjamin Franklin's approach to foreign policy; and, for later periods, Howard K. Beale, John Morton Blum, Norman A. Graebner, Robert E. Osgood, and Arthur P. Whitaker have published important studies.[84] Blum and Beale, in different ways, have examined the intellectual underpinnings of Theodore Roosevelt's foreign policy and attempted to view it, in Blum's words, "against the background of the confidence he shared and fed." [85] Perhaps Osgood has succeeded better than anyone else in penetrating the whole intellectual atmosphere of early twentieth-century American diplomacy. He has put Roosevelt's generally realistic appraisal of international politics in perspective by exploring popular attitudes toward world affairs, particularly the significance of the peace movement. Finally, Whitaker has sketched the rise and decline of *The Western Hemisphere Idea,* which had inspired men since the early nineteenth century, and Graebner has analyzed the intense debate over foreign policy in the early fifties. More recently, the appearance of Graebner's *Ideas and Diplomacy* in 1964 symbolizes the assimilation of intellectual history into diplomatic history. Previous documentary collections consisted largely of official diplomatic correspondence and the texts of treaties; Graebner designed his readings to reveal the ideas behind American diplomacy and their relationship to the contemporary intellectual milieu.[86]

84. Felix Gilbert, *To the Farewell Address: Ideas of Early American Foreign Policy* (Princeton, N.J., 1961); Gerald Stourzh, *Benjamin Franklin and American Foreign Policy* (Chicago, 1954); John Morton Blum, *The Republican Roosevelt* (Cambridge, Mass., 1954); Howard K. Beale, *Theodore Roosevelt and the Rise of America to World Power* (Baltimore, 1956); Osgood, *Ideals and Self-Interest;* Arthur P. Whitaker, *The Western Hemisphere Idea: Its Rise and Decline* (Ithaca, N.Y., 1954); Norman A. Graebner, *The New Isolationism: A Study in Politics and Foreign Policy since 1950* (New York, 1956).

85. *The Republican Roosevelt,* p. 1.

86. Norman A. Graebner, *Ideas and Diplomacy: Readings in the Intellectual Tradition of American Foreign Policy* (New York, 1964).

Though this fusion of diplomatic, intellectual, and social history had widespread implications for the whole history of American foreign policy, the bulk of the new scholarship has crystallized around certain periods and issues. In the twenties and thirties diplomatic historians did not recognize the unique cluster of values and ideas embodied in the progressive era, partly because they were too close in point of time, partly because they did not attempt to isolate the intellectual characteristics of any period. Wilson's idealistic view of international affairs, for example, seemed an individual phenomenon with a continuing relevance. But once historians identified the distinctive aspects of the years before World War I,[87] the assumptions of Wilson's wartime diplomacy became far more comprehensible. Wilson's concept of a community of power appeared as the ultimate expression of an era that believed that nations could order their relations in a rational, legalistic, and humane way. As Robert E. Osgood has pointed out, "we live in a world he [Wilson] never envisioned. . . . [For his] conception of collective security was firmly rooted in nineteenth-century liberalism and twentieth-century progressivism."[88]

This development, combined with a comparative analysis of American and European politics, has also greatly enlarged our perspective on Wilson's role at the Paris Peace Conference. Diplomatic historians long realized that political conditions in Europe impeded the achievement of Wilson's goals, but they did not pursue this insight and exaggerated the gap between Wilson's aims and those of various European leaders. In 1961 Seth P. Tillman's study *Anglo-American Relations at the Paris Peace Conference of 1919*

87. Henry F. May's *The End of American Innocence: A Study of the First Years of Our Own Time, 1912–1917* (New York, 1959), was perhaps the most helpful analysis of our prewar culture.

88. Robert E. Osgood, "Woodrow Wilson, Collective Security, and the Lessons of History," *Confluence* V (1957), 349, 354.

pointed out the large area of agreement between the two governments, and two books by Arno J. Mayer explored with painstaking detail and intellectual subtlety the linkage between politics, ideology, and diplomacy in Europe and America. Mayer emphasized certain neglected aspects of Allied and American diplomacy—such as its counterrevolutionary impulse—and his conclusions reduced the importance of the questions American diplomatic historians traditionally asked about Wilson's efforts at peacemaking. The composition of the American delegation, Wilson's decision to go to Paris, and his appeal for a Democratic Congress now seemed peripheral as Mayer illustrated how different decisions would not have significantly altered events. Wilson could not have succeeded unless those political groups in Great Britain, France, and Italy that stood for moderate war aims and identified with his peace program—"the forces of movement"—greatly gained in strength during the war years. But their power actually lessened as the tensions generated by the war splintered those forces favoring liberal domestic and foreign reconstruction. By placing Wilson's diplomacy in a larger context, Mayer's works narrow the margin of Wilson's influence and further the absorption of his individual acts into broader historical currents.[89]

Recent scholarship has not only lessened the drama of Wilson's diplomacy but has also leveled out interpretations of American foreign policy in the thirties. Both developments were part of a major tendency in American historiography,

89. Seth P. Tillman, *Anglo-American Relations at the Paris Peace Conference of 1919* (Princeton, N.J., 1961); Arno J. Mayer, *Political Origins of the New Diplomacy, 1917–1918* (New Haven, Conn., 1959), and *Politics and Diplomacy of Peacemaking: Containment and Counterrevolution at Versailles, 1918–1919* (New York, 1967). Other important works were: Jere King, *Foch versus Clemenceau: France and German Dismemberment, 1918–1919* (Cambridge, Mass., 1960), and *Generals & Politicians: The Conflict between France's High Command, Parliament, and Government. 1914–1918* (Berkeley, Calif., 1951); John M. Thompson, *Russia, Bolshevism, and the Versailles Peace* (Princeton, N.J., 1966).

what John Higham has called "a massive grading operation
that smoothed and flattened the convulsive dialectic of progressive history." [90] In the past diplomatic historians had
neglected the study of foreign policy in the early and middle
thirties and had read back into this period the patterns and
beliefs of 1940 and 1941. They had assumed that throughout
the thirties Roosevelt remained a Wilsonian, committed to
the concept of collective security, and that, though he reconciled himself to the isolationist mood of the era, he never
accepted its assumptions. Over the last decade scholars have
deepened our understanding of isolationism in the thirties
and greatly altered Roosevelt's relationship to it. Though
they disagree on the origins of isolationism, Selig Adler,
Wayne S. Cole, and Manfred Jonas have done much to
advance our knowledge of its ideology and influence. [91]
Moreover, studies by Robert A. Divine and Dorothy Borg
indicate that Roosevelt's Wilsonianism eroded during the
decade and that he assimilated many isolationist attitudes.
Like most men of his time, he could not help but be affected
by the general loss of confidence in the nation's strength and
in its ability to carry out its historic mission in world affairs.
For this, and for many other reasons, the President pursued
a cautious and often passive foreign policy that only gradually changed as he realized, along with the American people,
the nation's stake in world affairs. Now Roosevelt appears as
more a man of his times, bound by the same limited vistas
as other men, to some extent sharing, along with his countrymen, the psychology of appeasement so prevalent in Great
Britain and France. [92]

90. Higham, *History,* p. 214.
91. Selig Adler, *The Isolationist Impulse: Its Twentieth Century Reaction* (New York, 1957); Cole, *Senator Gerald P. Nye;* Manfred Jonas,
Isolationism in America, 1935–1941 (Ithaca, N.Y., 1966).
92. Robert A. Divine, "Franklin D. Roosevelt and Collective Security,
1933," *Mississippi Valley Historical Review* XLVIII (1961), 42–59. *The*

Robert A. Divine's recent study of American internationalism during World War II also endows the president's wartime commitment to collective security with a more ambiguous, shadowy quality. When Roosevelt's ideas began to
emerge toward the end of the war, he seemed attracted to
the notion of the Four Policemen and eventually wove this
concept into the fabric of the United Nations. He occupied
a shifting, middle ground between realism and Wilsonian
internationalism that, in retrospect, is almost impossible to
pin down. It was a position typical of so much of Roosevelt's
diplomacy, with its endless shifts and clouded rhetoric.[93]
　　The rising importance of intellectual and social history has
left a large imprint on the writing of American diplomatic
history, as has the consensus history of Louis Hartz and
Daniel J. Boorstin. Their focus on the stability and continuity
of American history has many implications for foreign policy.
It helped to explain why American diplomatists were often
unsuccessful in projecting themselves outside of their own
ideological milieu to grasp the unique political traditions of
other nations, particularly non-Western ones. In his massive
study *America's Failure in China,* Tang Tsou demonstrated
how American diplomats, scholars, and politicians—unaware
of the unarticulated assumptions of their own liberal tradition—misunderstood the nature of Chinese culture and
underestimated the role of ideology in Chinese communism.[94]

Illusion of Neutrality (Chicago, 1962), *The Reluctant Belligerent: Ameri-
can Entry into World War II* (New York, 1965), and *Roosevelt and World
War II* (Baltimore, 1969); Dorothy Borg, "Notes on Roosevelt's 'Quarantine'
Speech," *Political Science Quarterly* LXXII (1957), 405–33, *The United
States and the Far Eastern Crisis of 1933–38: From the Manchurian Incident through the Initial Stage of the Undeclared Sino-Japanese War* (Cambridge, Mass., 1964). Willard Range's *Franklin D. Roosevelt's World Order*
(Athens, Ga., 1959) was only a partial modification of the traditional view.
　　93. Robert A. Divine, *Second Chance: The Triumph of Internationalism
in America during World War II* (New York, 1967).
　　94. Tang Tsou, "The American Political Tradition and the American
Image of Chinese Communism," *Political Science Quarterly* LXXVII (1962),
570–600; *America's Failure in China, 1941–50* (Chicago, 1963).

More recently, Hartz's schematic framework has been sys-
tematically applied to Wilson's view of world politics. The
sophisticated study by N. Gordon Levin, Jr., indicates how
fruitful this sort of intellectual analysis can be, but it also
suggests some of its pitfalls. Ignoring the play of events and
the chaos of decision-making, Levin overrationalizes Wilson's foreign policy and makes the sweeping, ahistorical
claim that Wilson's vision "of a peaceful liberal capitalist
world order under international law . . . continues to mo-
tivate America's foreign policy decision-makers." In short,
Wilson set the "main outlines of recent American foreign
policies." [95] There are, to be sure, aspects of Wilson's vision
that still live in the minds of American statesmen, but its
idealistic core, centered around a new community of power,
has largely faded away. It is possible, then, for those working within Hartz's framework to miss the way in which the
American liberal tradition was, at any given time, interwoven with the values and beliefs of a particular age, which
in themselves were subject to subtle and continuous changes.
Consensus history sets the limits of the American experience
but does not explain its essence.[96]

There was another dimension, too, in this shift toward the
intellectual aspects of foreign policy. Diplomatic historians,
influenced by works that explored symbol and myth in the
American past, have devoted more attention to the images
that the American people and their leaders held of other
nations (though they did not write some of the pivotal
books). Cushing Strout's *The American Image of the Old
World* concentrated upon literary images and their alteration
over time, and traced the rise and decline of the notion that

95. N. Gordon Levin, Jr., *Woodrow Wilson and World Politics: America's Response to War and Revolution* (New York, 1968), pp. vii, 1.

96. A superb discussion of the shortcomings of consensus history is in
Hofstadter, *The Progressive Historians*, pp. 444–63.

Europe is an alien world.[97] Tang Tsou and Akira Iriye have produced significant studies relating images much more directly to policy decisions. Both reach disturbing conclusions. Tang Tsou believes that illusions and miscalculations dominated America's China policy; Iriye finds a continual "gap between reality and perception" in the relations of China, Japan, and the United States and a surprising fluctuation in the images the three nations held of each other. He is struck by the fact that "policies have been made on the basis of considerations tangential to the Pacific, mutual images have been formed with little basis in fact, and wars have been fought even though policies and images have not postulated wars."[98] Though Iriye fears that the future may be no better than the past, he cautiously hopes, along with Strout and Tang Tsou, that America can achieve, in the words of Louis Hartz, "a new level of consciousness . . . in which an understanding of self and an understanding of others go hand in hand."[99]

In the early fifties some political scientists and historians took a didactic attitude toward leading the American public to this new level of awareness. Dissatisfied with the course of American foreign policy in the twentieth century, they touched off a major debate in scholarly circles. Their leading theoretician was Hans J. Morgenthau, whose brilliant abstractions concerning the struggle for power among nations served as a model against which American foreign policy could be measured.[100] Morgenthau and George F. Kennan in

97. Cushing Strout, *The American Image of the Old World* (New York, 1963). Within this genre, Phil Rahv's *The Discovery of Europe: The Story of American Experience in the Old World* (Boston, 1947), was a pioneering anthology.

98. *Across the Pacific*, pp. xvi, 82.

99. Louis Hartz, *The Liberal Tradition in America* (New York, 1955), p. 308.

100. Morgenthau's major theoretical work is *Politics among Nations: The Struggle for Power and Peace* (4th ed., New York, 1967), though he makes

1951 published stinging critiques of the moralism, legalism, and utopianism of twentieth-century American diplomacy.[101] Morgenthau decried the "intoxication with moral abstractions" and pleaded for the acceptance of the fact that "the struggle for power is . . . a continuum, with each solved problem giving rise to a new one in a never ending succession." He also called for an appreciation of the "contradictions and conflicts which are inherent in the nature of things and which human reason is powerless to solve." [102] Other scholars, such as Robert E. Osgood and Norman A. Graebner, have applied this approach with greatly varying results.[103] On the one hand, these efforts have brought a better understanding of the intellectual structure of American foreign policy and, as such, are a part of the larger fusion of diplomatic and intellectual history. On the other hand, some of this writing is marred by an excessive preoccupation with what went wrong, almost an obsession in pointing out

some interesting observations on the human condition in *Scientific Man vs. Power Politics* (Chicago, 1946). His views on the history of American foreign policy are expressed best in: *In Defense of the National Interest* (New York, 1951); "The Mainsprings of American Foreign Policy: The National Interest vs. Moral Abstractions," *American Political Science Review* XLIV (1950), 833–54; "Another 'Great Debate': The National Interest of the United States," *ibid.*, XLVI (1952), 961–88; *The Purpose of American Politics* (New York, 1960). Many of his essays are collected in *Politics in the Twentieth Century*, 3 vols. (Chicago, 1962).

101. Morgenthau, *In Defense of the National Interest;* George F. Kennan, *American Diplomacy, 1900–1950* (Chicago, 1951).

102. *In Defense of the National Interest*, pp. 4, 92, and *Scientific Man vs. Power Politics*, p. 206.

103. Osgood, *Ideals and Self-Interest.* Graebner stressed the gap between ends and means in a variety of works, particularly in his "The Year of Transition (1898)," in Norman A. Graebner, ed., *An Uncertain Tradition: American Secretaries of State in the Twentieth Century* (New York, 1961), *Cold War Diplomacy, 1945–1960* (Princeton, N.J., 1962), and *Ideas and Diplomacy.* Other books following Morgenthau's approach were: Stourzh, *Benjamin Franklin and American Foreign Policy;* Tang Tsou, *America's Failure in China;* Betty Glad, *Charles Evans Hughes and the Illusions of Innocence: A Study in American Diplomacy* (Urbana, Ill., 1966); and, to a lesser extent, Edward H. Buehrig, *Woodrow Wilson and the Balance of Power* (Bloomington, Ind., 1955). Osgood was most successful in achieving historical understanding, Glad and Buehrig least successful.

the alleged errors of American diplomacy. Though this may have served the cause of public education, it certainly does not serve the cause of history, because these scholars often fail to work inside the intellectual and social atmosphere of a given period and frequently obscure the reasons why men believed and acted as they did. The very questions they ask seem to blur their comprehension of the past.

They have also created their own historical myths. Morgenthau, *In Defense of the National Interest,* echoed Bemis in his veneration of the Founding Fathers. Hamilton in particular had formulated the realist position "with unsurpassed simplicity and penetration," and this legacy had basically endured until the end of the nineteenth century, when the moralistic period of American foreign policy ensued. Even then Morgenthau detected, beneath the idealistic rhetoric, a realist tradition that American statesmen instinctively had acted upon during major crises. Encouraged by the "great innovations of 1947," for a time Morgenthau saw "a slow, painful, and incomplete process of emancipation from deeply ingrained error, and a rediscovery of long-forgotten truths." [104] But his optimism soon passed as American foreign policy in the fifties and sixties seemed unable to respond with imagination to challenges far different from those of the late forties. Most recently, Morgenthau has softened many of his harsh strictures on American foreign policy in *The Purpose of American Politics.* There he paints the past in gentler shades, recognizing the "pragmatic genius" of American statesmen and displaying more sympathy than anger in dealing with the way in which Americans sought to apply their tradition of "equality in freedom" to foreign problems. [105]

Of all those who deplored the lack of realism in American

104. *In Defense of the National Interest,* pp. 14, 39, and *Politics in the Twentieth Century,* II, 2.
105. Pp. 22, 132.

diplomacy, the most eloquent was George F. Kennan. As a career diplomat, he viewed foreign policy from a unique perspective, one which valued orderly lines of communication, well-defined spheres of authority, and rational and unemotional exchanges among governments. As a devout Christian, the methods employed by statesmen concerned him as much as the results they achieved. Kennan was preoccupied with both the morality and the effectiveness of policies; he analyzed the past in order to understand how the West had reached its perilous contemporary position. More particularly, he scrutinized the history of American foreign policy in this century to pinpoint those alternatives that might, if pursued, have furthered the larger interests both of the United States and Western civilization. He saw, to be sure, that deeply embedded American traditions and ideals prevented the pursuit of some of these options, and in part his work was an effort to educate public opinion and policymakers. But he was originally concerned with the openness of history, with the re-creation of possibilities that were never followed. This was the outstanding characteristic of his first book, *American Diplomacy*, which made little attempt to penetrate the milieu in which statesmen operated. Kennan was impatient with American statecraft and contemptuously dismissed "the nonsensical timidities of technical neutrality" that so heavily influenced Wilson from 1914 to 1917.[106] With the passage of time and the maturation of his scholarship, however, certain shifts have occurred in Kennan's attitudes. In his two superb volumes on Soviet-American relations, he still sought to understand what went wrong during this initial encounter between the two opposing systems; and he argued that if only American military intervention had been avoided, "the entire subsequent course

106. P. 71.

of Soviet-American relations might have materially
changed." [107] But this thesis seems strained and artificial, for
the whole thrust of this study was to re-create the atmosphere of decision-making in Washington and Moscow and,
by doing so, to demonstrate how much statesmen are at the
mercy of chaotic conditions, dated and erroneous information, and national traditions and preoccupations that dim
their grasp of reality.

In effect, then, as Kennan became a better historian he became a less convincing critic of American foreign policy.
Confronted with the complexity of the historical process, he
perceived more clearly the limits upon effective action by
men and nations. There was always a brooding sadness in his
work, but this theme is more noticeable in his great autobiography, a somber, sensitive book, the tale of an intellectual's striving to find order and meaning in the modern
world. It is a book that still reflects many of the old criticisms
and often brilliantly discusses policies that, in retrospect,
seem superior to those adopted. But Kennan does not really
attempt to argue that these alternatives could have been
chosen, and a mood of pessimism and skepticism pervades
the book. Kennan is oppressed by the "vast, turgid, self-
centered, and highly emotional process" through which
decisions are made in Washington; by the plight of underdeveloped nations and the ineffectiveness of our aid to them;
and by the constant intrusion of domestic politics into the
foreign policy–making process. He wonders, increasingly, if
the American government can ever conduct "a mature,
consistent, and discriminating foreign policy." The United
States would be wiser to concern itself less with foreign problems and more with domestic ones, though he doubts our
ability to solve even these. In fact, Kennan hovers on the

107. *Russia Leaves the War*, and *The Decision to Intervene*, especially
p. 302.

edge of despair, convinced that man's ego is "demonic, anarchic, unbridleable," estranged even from himself. In a haunting metaphor Kennan writes that

> one moves through life like someone moving with a lantern in a dark woods. A bit of the path ahead is illuminated, and a bit of the path behind. But the darkness follows hard on one's footsteps, and envelops our trail as one proceeds. Were one to be able, as one never is, to retrace the steps by daylight, one would find that the terrain traversed bears, in reality, little relationship to what imagination and memory had pictured.[108]

Inevitably his *Memoirs* evokes comparison to *The Education of Henry Adams*. Both men identify more with the eighteenth century than with their own; both seek to overcome alienation from American society and to impose order on the relentless change of modern civilization; both fail and finally come to fear deeply for the future. And Kennan undoubtedly shares Adams's hope that some day, beyond his era, there will be a world "that sensitive and timid natures could regard without a shudder." [109]

If Kennan's *Memoirs* is symptomatic of a drift among diplomatic historians toward fatalism and despair, the "New Left" represents quite a different direction in scholarship.[110] This is, to be sure, a somewhat protean term, but it does refer to a certain intellectual mood and to a radical critique of American society. New Left history is infused with a feeling

108. George F. Kennan, *Memoirs, 1925–1950* (Boston, 1967). The quotations are from pp. 4, 295, 483. For a more recent statement of Kennan's pessimism about the future of American civilization, see his *Democracy and the Student Left* (Boston, 1968), p. 228.

109. *The Education of Henry Adams* (Modern Library Edition, New York, 1931), p. 505.

110. Irwin Unger's "The 'New Left' and American History: Some Recent Trends in United States Historiography," *American Historical Review* LXXII (1967), 1237–63, provides an excellent dissection of this historical phenomenon.

of acute dissatisfaction with the condition of American civilization and the course of American foreign policy; its goal is to create a "new past" that would substantiate its contemporary analysis. This is a formidable task, and the New Left reconstruction of domestic history is still in an early and contradictory stage. But in foreign policy the work of creating a new synthesis is much further along. As early as 1959 William Appleman Williams, in *The Tragedy of American Diplomacy*, outlined a comprehensive interpretation of American foreign policy that a younger group of American diplomatic historians has found extremely persuasive. Drawing upon the insights of Beard and Turner, Williams saw a conscious, highly-rationalized outward thrust as the main motif of the whole of American foreign policy.[111] With the closing of the internal frontier in the late nineteenth century, Americans had ended the continental phase of their expansion and had turned to the creation of an open-door empire abroad, meeting with remarkable success as "hard-headed and practical" statesmen gradually developed and implemented the vision of an American Century. They sought to evade domestic inequities and failures by attempting to sustain both democracy and prosperity through continued overseas expansion, a "twentieth-century Manifest Destiny." This was at the root of American involvement in every war

111. The fullest statement of Williams's foreign policy views is in *The Tragedy of American Diplomacy*, rev. ed. (New York, 1962). In *The Contours of American History* (Cleveland, 1961), he sets them within a broader context and deals with the entire span of American history, not just the twentieth century. *The United States, Cuba, and Castro: An Essay on the Dynamics of Revolution and the Dissolution of Empire* (New York, 1962), and *The Great Evasion: An Essay on the Contemporary Relevance of Karl Marx and on the Wisdom of Admitting the Heretic into the Dialogue about America's Future* (Chicago, 1964), cover limited, contemporary topics. Aside from Beard and Turner, Williams and those sharing his approach were apparently affected by Richard W. Van Alstyne's *The Rising American Empire* (New York, 1960), and by various ideas expressed by Fred Harvey Harrington. On the basis of his published writings, the reasons for Harrington's great influence are not clear.

since 1898, as well as the Cold War, and through its very success tied Americans to an oppressive status quo. According to Williams, the tragedy was that in the postwar period Americans failed to see the urgent need for a socialist commonwealth at home and instead continued to believe that their "freedom and prosperity depend upon the continued expansion of . . . [their] economic and ideological system through the policy of the open door." But Soviet and Chinese power now blocked this expansion, as did the worldwide revolutionary ferment; and if Americans persisted in pursuing their "vision of omnipotence," they might bring disaster upon themselves and the world.[112] Later, in 1964, Williams sees another alternative—that Americans might avoid confronting their domestic failure by creating a new frontier in space through which "the evasion will become literally projected to infinity." [113]

Despite the boldness of this analysis, Williams's elaboration of it is moderate. He recognizes the genuine idealism and humanitarianism of American statesmen and admits that their policies have often been beneficial. They were not evil men; nor did they understand the catastrophic consequences of the policies they pursued. In fact, Williams displays much admiration for Herbert Hoover, Charles Evans Hughes, and Henry L. Stimson, whom he credits with a lucid analysis of industrial society and a sophisticated concept of empire. Hoover in particular had the courage and insight to seek a partial withdrawal from open-door expansionism in order to avoid the imperialist wars it spawned. In the end Williams places his hope for the future upon the "enlightened conservatives" who might be able "to act upon

112. *The Tragedy of American Diplomacy*, pp. 50, 53, 203, 301–3. The Korean War is an exception to this, though Williams fits the decision to cross the thirty-eighth parallel into his interpretive pattern.
113. *The Great Evasion*, p. 12.

the validity of a radical analysis." [114] Nevertheless, this conclusion is overshadowed by Williams's tendency to strip
away the ethical pretenses of American diplomacy and to
show it for what he says it really was: expansionist, aggressive, and counterrevolutionary.

Many scholars have followed in Williams's footsteps,
sharing his assumptions and applying his framework to more
specific periods. In the process they have developed a substantial monographic literature that challenges prevailing
interpretations. [115] Like Williams, they admire many of the
creators of the American Empire and identify a broad consensus for open-door expansion, arguing that foreign policy
controversies revolved around means, not ends. In contrast
to Williams, however, these scholars emphasize the economic
rather than the ideological side of American expansion. Or
when, as in the case of Walter LaFeber's *The New Empire*,
they do venture into intellectual history, they stress the predominance of economic considerations in the thoughts of
major historical figures. They also oversimplify the link between economic forces and decision-making, and find a
coherence and consistency in the past that is in itself implau-
sible. In short, their approach to diplomatic history seems

114. *The Tragedy of American Diplomacy*, p. 309. As John Higham
shrewdly observes, Williams represents a "patriotic radicalism, which seeks
some positive basis in the American past for the hope of a collectivistic future" ("The Contours of William A. Williams," *Studies on the Left*, II
[1961], 75). Eugene D. Genovese makes the same observation in "William
Appleman Williams on Marx and America," ibid., VI (1966), 70–86.

115. Major titles are: Gar Alperovitz, *Atomic Diplomacy: Hiroshima and
Potsdam: The Use of the Atomic Bomb and the American Confrontation
with Soviet Power* (New York, 1965); D. F. Fleming, *The Cold War and
Its Origins, 1917–1960*, 2 vols. (London, 1961); Lloyd C. Gardner, *Eco-
nomic Aspects of New Deal Diplomacy* (Madison, Wisc., 1964); Gabriel
Kolko, *The Politics of War: The World and United States Foreign Policy,
1943–1945* (New York, 1968); Walter LaFeber, *The New Empire: An
Interpretation of American Expansion, 1860–1898* (Ithaca, N.Y., 1963),
America, Russia, and the Cold War, 1945–1966 (New York, 1967); Thomas
J. McCormick, *China Market: America's Quest for Informal Empire, 1893–
1901* (Chicago, 1967); Robert F. Smith, *The United States and Cuba:
Business and Diplomacy, 1917–1960* (New York, 1961).

somewhat traditional and dated. This obsolete methodology is most striking in Gar Alperovitz's impassioned assault on the widely accepted interpretation of the origins of the Cold War.[116] Attempting to demonstrate the aggressiveness of American policy, Alperovitz ignores the interplay of domestic politics and public opinion in the decision-making process and fails to measure the relative influence of Truman's advisers. Nor does he speculate upon the motives behind Soviet policy. Alperovitz's approach is, to be sure, narrower than that of most New Left diplomatic historians, but much of their writing on American foreign policy, like revisionism in the thirties, thrives on historical parochialism.[117]

In many ways it is unfortunate that the books of Williams and his followers are so infused with the emotions of current political controversy. They have, after all, isolated an important theme in the American past and are exploring some neglected aspects of American foreign policy. But their exaggerated presentism and their resistance to broader developments in American historiography blunts much of the effectiveness of their approach. Resentful of the liberal historical establishment and its consensus history,[118] they

116. New Left historians greeted this book with enthusiasm. Thomas C. Fiddick claimed that Alperovitz had provided "documentary proof of what Leftists have instinctively known for twenty years, namely, that the Cold War was begun by Anglo-American leaders even before World War II was ended"; Christopher Lasch argued that Alperovitz "proceeds with a thoroughness and caution which, in the case of a less controversial work, would command the unanimous respect of the scholarly profession" (*Studies on the Left,* VI [1966], 93–97; "The Cold War, Revisited and Re-Visioned," *New York Times Magazine,* Jan. 14, 1968, p. 51).

117. The parochialism of revisionism in the thirties is emphasized by Ernest R. May in "Emergence to World Power," in Higham, *The Reconstruction of American History,* pp. 195–96.

118. Christopher Lasch asserts, e.g., that "the defection of intellectuals from their true calling—critical thought—goes a long way toward explaining . . . the intellectual bankruptcy of so much recent historical scholarship. The infatuation with consensus; the vogue of a disembodied 'history of ideas' divorced from considerations of class or other determinants of social organization; the obsession with 'American Studies' which perpetuates a nationalistic myth of American uniqueness—these things reflect the degree

seem unable to assimilate methodological advances and instead, in their writings on foreign policy, emphasize rationality, the dominance of economic forces, and the continuity
of "a comprehensive world outlook."[119] Moreover, it is unlikely that the nature of the New Left approach to American
foreign policy will quickly change. To study, for example,
the structure of private, nongovernmental economic relationships and to accept a more varied and contradictory view of
the past would lessen the relevance of their scholarship to
current political controversy and weaken the contemporary
attack on American foreign policy.[120] In the short run, this
unwillingness to adopt a more neutral historical stance may
add to their influence and vitality if both domestic and foreign crises remain unsolved or deepen. But in the long run,
the New Left will probably be unable to create the new past
for which it longs, for it stands uncomfortably poised between the old tradition of progressive history and powerful
tides of historical reinterpretation. Eventually New Left
historians must either become more responsive to major
trends in American historiography and thus dilute much of
their purpose or be left farther and farther behind.

It is difficult, of course, for diplomatic historians to find a
balance between despair and anger, between Kennan's

---

to which historians have become apologists, in effect, for American national
power in the holy war against communism" ("The Cultural Cold War: A
Short History of the Congress for Cultural Freedom," in Barton J. Bernstein,
ed., *Towards a New Past: Dissenting Essays in American History* [New
York, 1968], p. 323). This is, of course, an extreme statement, and other
New Left historians show more appreciation of scholarship written from a
different point of view. Certainly Williams does so in *Contours*, as does
LaFeber in *America, Russia, and the Cold War*.

119. See, e.g., LaFeber, *America, Russia, and the Cold War*, p. 256, and
Gardner, *Economic Aspects*, p. 8.

120. It is interesting that New Left historians see no conflict between
asking what happened and what went wrong. In fact, several have vigorously
challenged this distinction. William Appleman Williams's review of May's
Imperial Democracy in *Studies on the Left*, III (1963), 94–99; Robert
Freeman Smith, "American Foreign Relations, 1920–1942," in Bernstein,
Towards a New Past, pp. 236–37.

pessimism and Williams's passion for change. Nor is it easy to find an enduring answer to the question of the historian's relationship to the world about him. New ways of looking at the past have opened exciting intellectual vistas and have aroused the hope that a new synthesis of the history of American foreign policy—more pluralistic and subtle than the old—is in the process of creation. But as diplomatic historians have absorbed these concepts of recent American historiography and have penetrated more deeply into the process through which foreign policy is made, they have come to sense that history is closing in, narrowing the possibilities of the future as well as those of the past. Those who acquiesce in this shedding of the old illusions about rationality and progress must struggle to avoid an all-encompassing fatalism and acknowledge that small but precious hold which men have over themselves and the fate of their nations. Those who employ their knowledge of the past to right the wrongs of the present must somehow remain reconciled to the dilemmas of nations and the ambiguities of man's condition. Perhaps all will remember that the certainties of our own time may become the historiographical curiosities of another era, and perhaps all will recognize the vastness and complexity of the historical drama of which they are a part.

Writings on American Foreign Relations: 1957 to the Present

DAVID F. TRASK

THE HISTORICAL STUDY of American foreign policy and diplomacy now enjoys remarkable popularity, but this development is of recent origin. A small but talented cadre of scholars established the field from the twenties to the middle fifties—in particular, Thomas A. Bailey, Samuel Flagg Bemis, Dexter Perkins, Julius Pratt, and Richard W. Van Alstyne—but these men were lonely exponents of a concern that often seemed peripheral to colleagues exploiting the domestic insights of historians like Turner, Parrington, and Beard. Nowadays all is altered. A great demand exists for historians of foreign relations; many of the most talented graduate students in the most prestigious graduate schools flock into the field. No issue of the *American Historical Review* or the *Journal of American History* fails to include reviews of several major works in foreign relations. Only recently, specialists in the field organized their own scholarly society.

What has caused this dramatic change? The principal reason is the vast international involvement of the republic since World War II. This reality has directed most younger scholars of diplomatic history to the study of twentieth-century phenomena. The perspective of the sixties imparts extraordinary cogency to the recent American experience of world politics, and historians have responded in scholarly terms to a pervasive national preoccupation. Another important influence was the continuing vigor of Bailey, Bemis, Perkins, Pratt, and Van Alstyne. All of them sustained their careers into the last decade. A third factor was the availability of new data as public records and private collections became available in bewildering volume. Finally, fellowships and grants for study abroad, notably the Fulbright and Ford programs, allowed many scholars to investigate materials in foreign archives.

The first fruits of a new generation of American diplomatic historians have appeared since 1957. What topics interest them? What interpretations have they advanced? What is the present shape of the field? What opportunities lie ahead?

I

The two "great traditions" in the writing of diplomatic history took modern form during the nineteenth century in the works of two German historians. One of these scholars was Leopold von Ranke; the other was Karl Marx.[1] Ranke concentrated on power relationships existing *between* nation-states at given points in time. His view placed exceptional emphasis on the international balance of power. The essence of diplomacy was to divine the nature of the balance and through that insight to safeguard the "national interest."

1. Recent scholars have contested certain customary assumptions about the views of Ranke and Marx concerning the nature of historical analysis, but these generalizations are legitimate in the broad sense discussed here.

Marx concentrated on the contest of various groups *within* given nations, specifically on the "class struggle." Foreign policy was a political consequence of social and economic conflict at home. It reflected the interest of the dominant class. In short, Ranke looked outward; Marx looked inward.

Of course, many historians avoid identification with either alternative, presenting analyses that give due consideration both to internal and external developments. Usually eclectic and syncretic in approach, such historians are much less susceptible of categorization; in the past they have perhaps been less influential than those who opted for some variant or extension of Rankean or Marxian interpretation.

Two historians writing since World War II produced profoundly influential interpretations of American foreign relations that represent contemporary extensions of the grand traditions. George Frost Kennan, who wrote *American Diplomacy, 1900–1950,* in 1951, was clearly within the conservative balance-of-power tradition, whereas William Appleman Williams, who published *The Tragedy of American Diplomacy* in 1959, reflected the continuing vitality of radical economic interpretation.[2]

Kennan began by observing "a lack of an adequately stated and widely accepted theoretical foundation to underpin the conduct of our external relations." Contemporary international problems "seemed in large measure to be products of the outcome of . . . two world wars." American deficiencies in world politics were "deeply rooted in the national consciousness, and any corrections would be difficult indeed." Obsessed with the decline in national security, Kennan traced it to "a significant gap between challenge and response in our conduct of foreign policy," a gap that had not

2. George F. Kennan, *American Diplomacy, 1900–1950* (Chicago, 1951); also available in paperback as a Mentor Book (citations are to the Mentor edition); William Appleman Williams, *The Tragedy of American Diplomacy* (Cleveland, 1959); also available in a revised and enlarged Delta Book edition (citations are to the Delta edition).

been closed and had put the republic in "grave peril." One difficulty involved machinery or means; the nation had not learned to cope with the "erratic and subjective nature of public reaction to foreign policy questions." Another problem was one of concept or ends. "I see the most serious fault in our past policy formulation to lie in something that I might call the legalistic-moralistic approach to international problems."

In magisterial prose, Kennan offered comments on critical events—particularly the Spanish-American War, World War I, and World War II—that graphically illustrated his general thesis. He questioned the Open Door policy, intervention in World War I, and the drive for "total victory" during World War II, sustaining at all points his critique of baneful public opinion and the legalistic-moralistic approach. Kennan called for a "realistic" approach to foreign relations, one that stressed the importance of power and attributed error to ideologically motivated leaders. An experienced diplomat, Kennan did not fail to offer general recommendations. To improve the machinery, he called for "much more effective use of the principle of professionalism in the conduct of foreign policy." To clarify concept, he advocated a restrained and reasoned concern for the national interest. Such an approach would mean

> that we have the modesty to admit that our own national interest is all that we are really capable of knowing and understanding—and the courage to recognize that if our purposes and undertakings here at home are decent ones, unsullied by arrogance or hostilities toward other people or delusions of superiority, then the pursuit of our national interest can never fail to be conducive to a better world. . . . Whatever is realistic in concept and founded in an endeavor to see both ourselves and others as we really are, cannot be illiberal.[3]

3. Kennan, *American Diplomacy*, pp. 5–6, 81–82, 88–89.

Kennan's sustained advocacy of the balance of power, his "realism," and his enlightened conservatism suggest an affinity for the Rankean tradition, to which he imparted qualities and modifications reflective of his own time and character.

Williams began his analysis by insisting upon the tragic nature of American diplomacy, tragic because it contained "several contradictory truths." Utilizing Cuban policy as an illustration, he noted three "truths"—the fact of American power; the absence of any reality in Cuba corresponding to American ideals; and a revolutionary movement in Cuba that eventually seized power because of the deployment and use of American strength. "The central and miserable truth is that there would have been neither revolution nor abortive invasion [in Cuba] if American policy had been successful within the framework of its own assumptions and logic." Although recognizing the humanitarian aspects of American policy, he held firmly: "Other societies come to feel that American policy causes them to lose their economic, political, and even psychological independence." Williams drew attention to the national conviction that "America's *domestic* well being depends upon . . . sustained, ever-increasing overseas economic expansion." Here was a "convergence of economic practice with intellectual analysis and emotional involvement that creates a very powerful and dangerous propensity to define the essentials of American welfare in terms of activities outside the United States." This propensity was dangerous because it caused neglect of internal developments and transferred blame for national problems on other peoples.

American leaders assumed that political and social objectives at home could be obtained only by economic methods, specifically by economic expansion overseas. In 1898, "American leaders went to war . . . as part of, and as the consequence of, a general outlook which externalized the opportunity and the responsibilities for America's domestic welfare; broadly in terms of vigorous economic expansion into Latin America and Asia." By 1900 the United States developed a general approach to world politics, the Open Door policy, which continued to shape American responses to international questions across the rest of the century. It was unlike previous strategies of aggrandizement in that it was a means of expanding without war. It assumed that American economic power could dictate pro-American policies in weaker countries. Much interested in the two World Wars, Williams argued that those conflicts deepened the notion that Americans were "defending an anti-colonial democracy charged with the duty to regenerate the world. They . . . also had come firmly to believe that their own prosperity and democracy depended upon the continued expansion of their economic system under the strategy of the open door." Contrary to Kennan, Williams did not attribute American decisions to legal or moral motivations; the Open Door policy "was extremely hard-headed and practical." Unless modified, it "was certain to produce foreign policy crises that would become increasingly severe." The key to Williams's historical analysis was the idea that the search for an "informal empire" explained growing national difficulties in world politics over the century.

What was to be done in order to avoid additional international difficulties? Williams proposed that the United States advocate an "open door for revolutions," working with rather than against the great social revolutions of the century. The United States faced "the traditional dilemma of empire. It could resort to war or it could disengage, safeguarding its strategic position by formulating a new outlook which accepted the reality of a world in revolution and devising new policies calculated to assist those revolutions to move immediately and visibly toward their goal of a better human life." His last words were prophetic in tone and content: "If the United States cannot accept the existence of . . . limits [upon its freedom of action] without giving up democracy and cannot proceed to enhance and extend democracy within such limits, then the traditional effort to sustain democracy by expansion will lead to the destruction of democracy."

Williams definitely embraced the tradition of economic interpretation. The reader of Lenin's analysis of imperialism finds a broadly comparable thesis for the United States in Williams's book, although *sans* the determinism and terminology of Marxist orthodoxy. It can be described as "neo-Beardian analysis." Williams explicitly claimed radical affiliation, offering "a fuller, more accurate picture of reality" and calling for fundamental changes in direction. His prose possessed a raw, insistent quality that exercised a compelling claim on its readers.[4]

Despite great differences in form and content, the two books have certain common characteristics. Both stress continuity rather than change in the American approach to foreign policy. Both discern a growing deterioration in national security. Both are intensely critical of the American record in world politics. Both offer solutions, however different in nature. Both have been remarkably influential, attracting the allegiance of many scholars writing on specialized subjects.

Of course, the work of many scholars cannot be easily classified in either category. One of the most notable of recent trends in the field has been a tendency to break away from the confining influences of traditional theories. Most of the works that reflect this tendency reveal a commitment to

4. Williams, *Tragedy of American Diplomacy,* pp. 6, 11, 37, 49–50, 200, 295, 309.

political liberalism as against the alternatives posed by
Kennan and Williams—conservatism or radicalism. The
reader finds in these works a general stress on description as
against judgment along with a rejection of theories of single
causation.

With these broad interpretive tendencies in mind, then,
let us discuss the literature of the past decade, utilizing one
of the generally accepted chronologies for the study of American foreign relations during this century: (1) the background and conduct of the Spanish-American War; (2) the
"imperial interlude" from 1898 to 1914; (3) World War I
from 1914 through the peacemaking concluding in 1921;
(4) the "long armistice" from 1919 to 1939; (5) World War
II from 1939 to 1945; and (6) the troubled postwar years
from 1945 to the present.

II

In recent years historians have eroded the view that the
years between the Civil War and the Spanish-American War
constituted the "nadir" of American involvement in world
affairs. In addition, they have considered anew the reasons
why the United States went to war in 1898 with Spain and
how President William McKinley conducted foreign policy
at the time.

In 1962 David Pletcher published his *The Awkward Years,*
a study of foreign relations from 1881 to 1885. The 1880s
bridged the "problems of the Civil War and Reconstruction
and those of the tempestuous *fin de siècle*." Through trial
and error Presidents James Garfield and Chester Arthur prepared the nation to some degree for Theodore Roosevelt's
imperialism and internationalism. Desires for prestige, markets, and security stimulated pressures for expansion during

the early 1880s. Various interest groups—isolationists, nationalists, and economizers—opposed this pressure, but they could not prevent expansion indefinitely. Secretaries of State Frederick Frelinghuysen and James G. Blaine opposed territorial acquisitions and warfare, but Pletcher holds that his evidence allows him to "trace the unfolding of expansionism under Garfield and Arthur, to relate it with political and economic developments inside the United States, and, as far as possible, to explain the reasons why their policies failed." He concludes that "foreshadowings and anticipations . . . suggest that the 'new imperialism' of the 1890's actually germinated before the first Cleveland administration, and that the outwardly stagnant years of Garfield and Arthur were actually a period of preparation and crude testing in response to impulses which, though strong, were still vaguely formed and not clearly understood." [5]

Walter LaFeber advances a comparable but more general thesis for the entire period 1860–98 in *The New Empire* (1963), analyzing "the crucial incubation period of the American overseas empire by relating the development of that empire to the effects of the industrial revolution on United States foreign policy." The empire of 1900 was a culmination rather than a break in American history. "Americans neither acquired the empire during a temporary absence of mind nor had the empire forced upon them." A series of internal disturbances caused by industrialization caused American leaders to resolve domestic dilemmas by overseas expansion. After exploring expansionist thought in the writings of Frederick Jackson Turner, Josiah Strong, Brooks Adams, and Alfred Thayer Mahan, and describing the strategic and economic goals of American diplomacy, LaFeber examines the Panic of 1893 as an instance of internal

5. David M. Pletcher, *The Awkward Years: American Foreign Relations under Garfield and Arthur* (Columbia, Mo., 1962), pp. x–xvi, 356.

disturbance leading to aggressive foreign policy—the Venezuelan boundary crisis. The Anglo-American crisis of 1895 was not a consequence of Manifest Destiny. "The two currents of economic overseas expansion and Olney's realization that the United States possessed the means to protect its interests converged into the Venezuelan controversy." Downgrading yellow journalism and congressional belligerence as causes of the Spanish-American War, LaFeber stresses "the transformation of the opinion of many spokesmen for the business community who had formerly opposed war." The war rescued the United States from a burgeoning "economic and political dilemma." [6]

The New Empire is a sophisticated example of economic interpretation, integrating diplomatic history and intellectual history in a way that lends credence to the "informal empire" thesis. LaFeber's debt to W. A. Williams is quite apparent. The writer's emphasis on ideas is everywhere evident and is one of the most striking developments in the historical analysis of foreign relations of late.

A collection of essays by John A. S. Grenville and George B. Young, published in 1966, centers mostly on personalities active in shaping American foreign relations between 1873 and 1900 and lends support to the views of George Kennan. The authors draw attention to the "baneful influence of [domestic] politics on American foreign policy." Internal political considerations rather than rational calculations based on realistic assessment of international conditions too often determined foreign policy. They maintain that "the harmonization of strategy and foreign policy was more often a matter of chance than of design," arguing that "an excessive regard for political advantage and a lack of attention to strategic considerations has in the past handicapped the

6. Walter LaFeber, *The New Empire: An Interpretation of American Expansion, 1860–1898* (Ithaca, N.Y., 1963), pp. vii, 403, 417.

conduct of American diplomacy." This criticism is frequently illustrated in the biographical essays themselves. Revisionist interpretations appear frequently, often critical of economic interpretations such as those of LaFeber and supportive of power-realist prescriptions for the conduct of foreign relations.[7]

Ernest R. May's *Imperial Democracy* (1961) is the most detailed study of the period 1895–1900 to appear in recent years. During these years the United States established itself as the "seventh power," and other nations attributed to the United States "a government not only commanding great resources but the will to use them." May considers this assumption a delusion. The United States "rarely displayed any purposefulness whatsoever." Unlike Pletcher and LaFeber, May holds that "in the 1890's the United States had not sought a new role in world affairs. Issues in Hawaii, China, Turkey, Venezuela, and Cuba had intruded almost of their own accord." Domestic affairs dominated Washington. American leaders "ran the risk of precipitating Europe into a coalition against America. Yet their actions had the paradoxical effect of convincing people abroad that the United States possessed not only the might but also the will to be a force among nations." May concludes mordantly: "Some nations achieve greatness; the United States had greatness thrust upon it."

What caused the war? May does not completely discount "moral revulsion" against Spanish policy in Cuba and imperial interest in Latin America and Asia, but he emphasizes the fact that McKinley, preoccupied by domestic problems, bowed ultimately to public hysteria. The president

7. John A. S. Grenville and George Berkeley Young, *Politics, Strategy, and American Foreign Policy: Studies in Foreign Policy, 1873–1917* (New Haven, Conn., 1966), p. xviii.

worked always in terrible consciousness of the division in
public opinion. . . . McKinley was not a brave man. In his
whole political career, there had been no act of boldness.
And the one resource he did not employ in 1898 was courage.
Rightly or wrongly, he conceived that he had some justification for demanding a final end to the violence in Cuba, that
his highest duty lay in keeping his own country united, and
that the alternative to war might be a domestic crisis tan-
tamount in his eyes to revolution. For these reasons he led
his country unwillingly toward a war that he did not want
for a cause in which he did not believe.[8]

Like many other historians, May has interested himself
in the role of ideas and public opinion in the making of foreign policy, a concern at the center of his *American Imperialism: A Reinterpretation* (1967). Why did imperialist ideas
gain currency in the 1890s? Why did they lose currency very
rapidly? May does not ignore the influence of "pressures
of the moment, a latent tradition of expansionism, Social
Darwinist ideas, naval technology, and economic forces,"
but he concentrates on "the impact in America of English
and European political debate." He seeks "an explanation
of the processes by which a variety of influences produced a
revolution in American attitudes." After postulating certain
assumptions about public opinion in the late nineteenth
century, May traces its evolution and emphasizes the importance of opinion leadership by elites. He discerns a notable
proliferation of British social-imperial thought in the United
States, attributing to this phenomenon a relatively important
role in shaping American behavior in 1898. The work reflects
the utility of a perspective and research design that is multinational. "Americans were members incorporate of an Atlan-

8. Ernest R. May, *Imperial Democracy: The Emergence of America as a
Great Power* (New York, 1961), pp. 159, 267, 269–70.

tic civilization." [9] Here is an arresting piece indeed, one that makes extensive use of modern theory and technique derived from ancillary social sciences.

H. Wayne Morgan strongly challenges May's assessment of McKinley in his biography *William McKinley and His America* (1963). The president's prewar intention was to force Spanish reforms. His failure was not to prepare alternatives to war if Spain failed to respond. McKinley opposed war, but "he would attain reform in Cuba by neutrality if possible, but by force if necessary." Morgan is as adamant in opposing the argument that McKinley had no spine as he is in refuting the view that Cleveland would have avoided war. "Blame for the intervention falls fairly among the Cubans, the Americans, McKinley's policies, and especially the Spanish." He admits that McKinley failed to lead public opinion. "Fearful of being misunderstood or adding impetus to the movement for Cuban relief, he remained silent in public, thus *seeming* to drift." But his final verdict is on the whole favorable:

> McKinley often lacked creative vigor, but he had great ability to synthesize views into policies acceptable to a majority of his people and his party. He did not move more rapidly in many fields simply because he detected no support for such motion. He was not a "great" president, but he fulfilled an exacting and critical role with success and ability displayed by no other contemporary.[10]

No consensus yet characterizes interpretations of these early events; a dichotomy is apparent between those like Pletcher and LaFeber who consider American policy a rational long-term design to resolve domestic class conflict

9. Ernest R. May, "American Imperialism: A Reinterpretation," *Perspectives in American History*, I (1967), 123, 279.

10. H. Wayne Morgan, *William McKinley and His America* (Syracuse, N.Y., 1963), pp. 375–77, 528.

by overseas expansion as against those like Grenville, Young, and May who discern drift, confusion, popular alarms, and absence of mind. The search for new evidence and new modes of analysis has greatly sophisticated but hardly resolved the problems of synthesis, interpretation, and criticism which remain open to additional investigation. On one point all agree; these were truly important formative years that deserve continuing investigation as dedicated as that of the past decade.

III

The expansion of 1898 signaled new departures in policy from that date until 1914 or so, in particular an experiment in colonial management and a novel set of relations with other great powers. Some important contributions to our understanding of American policy in the Caribbean and Pacific regions have appeared in recent years. Unfortunately, we still do not have sufficient studies on relations with European powers. The subject of relations with Britain, Germany, and other European powers is all too often treated simply as a by-product of the "imperial interlude," a tendency that obscures the role of the United States in the historical developments that led to the outbreak of World War I. Perhaps the approaching publication of research such as that of Samuel Wells, Jr., on Anglo-American relations for the period 1904–14 will begin to correct the balance.

The Spanish-American War was a landmark in the emergence of the modern Anglo-American relationship, the subject of Charles S. Campbell's *Anglo-American Understanding, 1898–1903* (1957). Nothing ordained the shift that materialized at the end of the century. The two nations "took advantage of favorable circumstance and some luck in order

to resolve serious controversies beclouding relations . . .
and even beclouding the peace." Campbell takes his readers
through many exchanges and negotiations that resulted in
the imposing settlements of 1902–3. What made these
achievements possible? British restraint during the war, the
British recognition of their need for American friendship
given continental difficulties, and the general Anglo-American agreement concerning the Far East all influenced the
relationship. "Never again, once the clash over canal policy
in Central America and once the perils lurking along the
Alaska boundary were removed, has an issue arisen that
appeared possibly incapable of peaceful settlement." [11] Extremely scrupulous in his research and judgment, Campbell
is flexible in outlook, difficult to classify definitively in any
particular school of analysis.

R. G. Neale has also examined the Anglo-American relationship during these years, writing *Great Britain and United
States Expansion: 1898–1900* (1966) largely from the British
perspective. Concerned primarily with diplomatic exchanges
stemming from American expansion, the author constantly
adverts to the "quality of friendship" between the two nations. Even before the Spanish-American War, Britain had
made it clear that it would avoid diplomatic initiatives unacceptable in Washington. Nevertheless, Britain made no
move to influence the behavior of other European powers
during the war, nor did it attempt to influence American
policy in East Asia after its conclusion. The extent of friendly
relations during the conflict has been exaggerated; the British
were interested but cautious, recognizing the virility of
Anglophobia across the sea. Alfred Hippisley and Lord
Beresford had no great impact on American policy; Britain
was moving toward cooperation with other Asian powers

11. Charles S. Campbell, Jr., *Anglo-American Understanding, 1898–1903*
(Baltimore, 1957), pp. 5, 347.

when the United States began to espouse the open door. Britain reached two broad conclusions concerning relations with the United States:

> Britain should wait upon the slow development of United States opinion and policy and then endeavour to accommodate to America's unilateral decisions British international commitments during this waiting period. . . . Britain should resign from any attempt to maintain in the American hemisphere those policies which the United States regarded as being in any way inimical to her national interests.[12]

Both Campbell and Neale demonstrate the utility of multiarchival research as well as scrupulously balanced evaluation of evidence. Both consider the general international context within which emerged the Anglo-American relationship. Hopefully, more studies of the American relationship with other European countries during these years will appear in the near future.

One such effort is that of Calvin D. Davis, who has published *The United States and the First Hague Conference* (1962). After tracing the origins of the meeting to 1899, Davis argues that "no nation went into the First Hague Conference with greater determination to defeat its original, primary objective [disarmament] than did the United States of America. Sincere in its desire to establish a permanent international tribunal, the Americans would countenance no agreement hindering improvement in their army and navy." The United States delegation supported the Permanent Court of Arbitration but fought hard for a resolution defending the Monroe doctrine and the principle of no entangling alliances. Nobody wanted to limit armaments in 1899. "The conference was essentially a failure. . . . It is doubtful if

12. R. G. Neale, *Great Britain and United States Expansion: 1898–1900* (East Lansing, Mich., 1966), p. 214.

any of its conventions other than those on the laws of war have ever benefited many people." [13] The reader senses that the imperial enterprise of the post-1898 years was a far more important influence on policy than the extensive movement for various restraints on warfare.

One of the more original contributions to the history of American policy in the Pacific–East Asian region is William R. Braisted's work on the role of the United States Navy in that area, *The United States Navy in the Pacific, 1897–1909* (1958). The author seeks to correct certain deficiencies in historical research:

> American diplomatic history has too often been written after an examination of strictly diplomatic correspondence without adequate consideration of the economic, military, intellectual, and other factors that motivate foreign policy, and second . . . American naval history has too often been confined to discourse on wars and campaigns without sufficient regard for the Navy's influence on American foreign and domestic affairs in times of peace.

Braisted analyzes the period 1897–1909 because during this time the United States greatly altered its Far Eastern policy and the Navy vastly expanded its operations in that region.

The central naval problem was the emergence of Japanese power; by 1909 the old European squadrons had been withdrawn to other stations. "There remained the United States and Japan to contend for, or to share, the mastery of the Pacific." Ironically, the United States was no more secure in 1909 than in 1897. The United States failed to achieve effective liaison between the State and Navy departments, although naval plans were developed in terms of the national diplomatic posture. The Japanese defeat of Russia in 1904–5,

13. Calvin D. Davis, *The United States and the First Hague Peace Conference* (Ithaca, N.Y., 1962), pp. 110, 112.

interfered with naval projects to develop an Asiatic battle fleet, a base at Subig Bay, and an advanced base in China. The cruise of the White Fleet was an effort to balance the power of Japan. Braisted believes that Subig Bay should have been developed. He does not fail to note the effect of European developments on the navy, in particular the evolution of planning concepts from a fleet equal to that of Germany to a fleet second to none. "In diplomacy European considerations weighed as heavily in determining American Far Eastern policies as Atlantic defense determined the Navy's outlook in the Pacific." [14]

Another recent work on the Far East is Raymond A. Esthus's *Theodore Roosevelt and Japan* (1966). The rise of Japanese power serves as Esthus's point of departure. President Roosevelt hoped to mediate the Russo-Japanese War because he believed "that a balance of power should be established in East Asia with a line of friction between Russia and Japan. In establishing that balance of power, he hoped to play a key role." T.R. supported the Japanese protectorate in Korea because it avoided outright annexation, an event delayed until 1910. Much of the book considers Japanese-American tensions rising from restrictive racial policies in the United States. Esthus discerns no world-shaking significance in either the Taft-Katsura agreed memorandum of 1905 or the Root-Takahira agreement of 1908. The first was merely "an honest exchange of views. . . . Nothing more than a community of interest with Japan and Britain in the Far East was implied." And further: "Throughout the [Root-Takahira] negotiations both governments had been motivated primarily by a desire to signalize the Japanese-American rapprochement with a publicity statement that would smooth over the friction of the preceding two years and

14. William R. Braisted, *The United States Navy in the Pacific, 1897–1909* (Austin, Tex., 1958), pp. vii–viii, 240, 244.

silence the war rumors." There was "no great confrontation
of China and Japan in the arena of American policy making."
T.R.'s compromise diplomacy is neatly summarized: "Roosevelt was willing to sacrifice the open door and the integrity
of China in favor of the strategic and economic interests of
Japan in Manchuria in order to compensate Japan for discrimination in the United States against Japanese and the
exclusion of Japanese laborers." [15]

Students of United States–Latin American relations during
the imperial interlude remain very active, and one, Dana G.
Munro, has offered a general study entitled *Intervention and
Dollar Diplomacy in the Caribbean, 1900–1921* (1964). He
attempts to show how and why the United States practiced
intervention in the Caribbean, believing that an understanding of this phenomenon will help the nation to avoid mistakes
like those of fifty years past. Munro stresses the strategic as
against the economic motivation for intervention, arguing
that the United States sought "to promote stable government
and economic progress as the best means of warding off
European influence." Dollar diplomacy was not "a design to
aid American bankers and other selfish interests in exploiting
the countries where it was applied." The Platt Amendment
and the Theodore Roosevelt Corollary were means of putting

> an end to conditions that threatened the independence of
> some of the Caribbean states and were consequently a po-
> tential danger to the security of the United States. Revolu-
> tions must be discouraged; the bad financial practices that
> weakened the governments and involved them in troubles
> with foreigners must be reformed; and general economic and
> social conditions, which were a basic cause of instability,
> must be removed.

Despite his critique of the argument for economic motivation, Munro decries American policy in many respects, es-

15. Raymond A. Esthus, *Theodore Roosevelt and Japan* (Seattle, 1966),
pp. 55, 107, 285, 308.

pecially the tendency to dispatch incompetent diplomatists to the region and the undue proclivity to utilize compulsion rather than persuasion.[16]

A useful study, *The United States in Cuba, 1898–1902* (1963), by David F. Healy, differs to some degree from Munro's views. After 1898 the United States had to decide how to govern its overseas dependencies. Cuba was one of the laboratories for this decision. There the United States worked out three elements of policy that were applied elsewhere as well—"the establishment of informal protectorates which left a large degree of internal self-government"; "the making, through trade treaties or financial arrangements, of strong economic ties with the United States"; and "economic penetration through United States investment and development." The anti-annexationist spirit that had generated the Teller Amendment, a self-denying ordinance passed by Congress at the beginning of the war with Spain, precluded the absorption of Cuba, but a prevalent racism presumed that nonwhite populations were incapable of full self-government. Direct intervention by "big business" is hard to find, but only because "the necessary decisions were made, not by businessmen, but by soldiers, politicians, and civil servants. If these decisionmakers sought to satisfy the desires of the business community—and obviously they did—they tried even harder to satisfy the voting public."

Healy recognizes that political as well as economic motives influenced American policy. "While American business interests soon got all they wanted in Cuba, they did so under a settlement shaped by many forces, prominent among which were the clash of domestic party politics and the demands of the oft-forgotten Cuban people." The Platt Amendment was "a middle course between altruism and annexationism. It was a realistic compromise designed to award each side its

16. Dana G. Munro, *Intervention and Dollar Diplomacy in the Caribbean, 1900–1921* (Princeton, N.J., 1964), pp. 161, 163, 531.

minimum demands." Elihu Root, who was the principal framer of the Platt Amendment, deplored the interventionist backsliding that came later on.[17]

Another much-praised study of United States activity in Latin America is Robert E. Quirk's work, *An Affair of Honor* (1962), about the intervention at Veracruz in 1914, during the early stages of the Mexican Revolution. The occupation of Veracruz accomplished little but left a permanent stain on Mexican-American relations. President Wilson "clothed American aggression with the sanctimonious raiment of idealism. Insisting upon the morality of his acts, he aroused both the hatred and the scorn of the Mexicans—hatred over the invasion but a deep scorn for what they saw as his hypocrisy." The United States must not revert to policy like that of Wilson. "We may offer encouragement, friendship, understanding, and (when asked) counsel. But never tutelage, never superiority, never condescension." Wilson's ends may have been noble, but his means were completely unacceptable.[18]

For the most part American historians have neglected non-Spanish regions of Latin America, but E. Bradford Burns's study of Brazilian-American relations between 1902 and 1912, *The Unwritten Alliance* (1966), begins to redress the balance. Writing from the Brazilian perspective, Burns's basic contention is that the tradition of Brazilian-American friendship, often dated from the nineteenth century, actually flowered when the Baron of Rio-Branco was foreign minister of Brazil (1902–12). Rio-Branco hoped to settle various boundary disputes with neighboring states and also to establish Brazilian diplomatic ascendancy in South America.

    17. David F. Healy, *The United States in Cuba, 1898–1902: Generals, Politicians, and the Search for Policy* (Madison, Wis., 1963), pp. xii, 211, 214.
    18. Robert E. Quirk, *An Affair of Honor: Woodrow Wilson and the Occupation of Veracruz* (Lexington, Ky., 1962), p. 6.

Good relations with the United States would further these objectives. At the same time, the United States saw in Brazil an ally in advancing its Latin American policies. The result was an unwritten alliance. During the Rio-Branco era, "Brazil shifted its diplomatic axis from London to Washington where it has since remained." Brazilian policy reflected a strong desire to find markets in the United States. No corresponding impulse to sell goods in Brazil motivated the Americans, but "dependence on the American importer . . . pulled Brazil closer to its giant neighbor in the north. Brazil's new diplomatic policies reflected that situation." [19]

Most of the historians writing about the years immediately after the Spanish-American War have dealt with the imperial consequences of that conflict; not enough has been written about American contributions during this time to the processes that led to World War I. The easy assumption that the United States was merely a bystander as Europe moved toward war may not withstand critical evaluation. There should be continuing study of United States relations with Latin America and East Asia, but a truly important field is the consequences of the imperial interlude for relations with Europe—relations that are an aspect of the origins and causation of World War I.

IV

The study of American foreign relations during World War I has recently been one of the most active interests of diplomatic historians. The years from 1914 to 1920 constituted the Pandora's box of the century; manifold problems materialized then that have endured to the present. The search

19. E. Bradford Burns, *The Unwritten Alliance: Rio-Branco and Brazilian-American Relations* (New York, 1966), pp. ix, 75.

for the origins of the contemporary international crisis has
led many investigators back to the Great War. Another influence has been the astounding richness of research materials becoming available since World War II. In addition,
the period permits a close examination of relations between
force and diplomacy.

Daniel M. Smith has produced a useful survey of the
entire period, significantly entitled *The Great Departure*
(1965), which concentrates for the most part on the traditional interests of American historians—explanation of the
intervention of 1917 and the peacemaking of 1919. His view-
points reflect the influence of power-realist analysis:

> Most Americans lacked an understanding of the basic reasons
> why the country entered the war and of the nation's specific
> stake in the peace settlement. The United States entered the
> war, in an involved controversy over neutral rights, because
> of national self-interests and an even greater concern in the
> creation of a stable and just postwar world society. American
> foreign policy, throughout the neutrality and war periods,
> was in general practical and based on these national interests.
> Even the Wilsonian concept of an idealistic peace and a
> global collective security system was related to practical
> national interests. But the majority of citizens was not made
> fully aware of that fact and was too easily wearied by the
> responsibilities of world leadership. There lay the tragedy of
> America in World War I.

Smith insists that the picture of Wilsonian moralism so general in former writings has been vastly overdrawn. He gives
special attention to the influential realism of Secretary of
State Robert Lansing and to the vain effort of Wilson to mediate the European conflict prior to the intervention.[20]

The towering character and personality of Woodrow Wil-

20. Daniel M. Smith, *The Great Departure: The United States and
World War I* (New York, 1965), p. x.

son dominates American writing about World War I. Arthur Link's magisterial biography has so far extended only to the intervention of 1917, but his views on *Wilson the Diplomatist* were summarized in 1957. In many ways this analysis extends the pro-Wilsonian interpretation offered by Ray Stannard Baker that flowered between the wars but encountered strong criticism from exponents of neutrality just before World War II and from realists as well as radicals after World War II. It rejects both trade expansion and unrestrained international moralism as single-cause interpretations of the war president's course. In analyzing neutrality, Link refutes the view either that Wilson was too neutral or not neutral enough. Responsive to public opinion, Wilson moved with the feelings of the American people. Intervention was in part a consequence of the absence of constructive alternatives and in part a desire to "achieve objectives to justify the misery of mankind." His discussion of the peace conference is a strong defense of Wilson; he argues for Wilsonian success at that time. The real failure of Versailles was lack of a will to achievement among the victors of Europe. Wilson's inability to obtain assent to the treaty at home is ascribed in part to his physical breakdown but mostly to his stubborn unwillingness to compromise principle beyond a certain point. Wilson ultimately chose the role of prophet rather than statesman.[21]

Works on neutrality have been relatively few in recent years, but one, Ernest R. May's *The World War and American Isolation, 1914–1917* (1959), has found broad acceptance. May stresses two interrelationships—that between European and American decisions and that between diplomacy and domestic politics in the United States, Great Britain, and Germany. "Scarcely any event in one of the three

21. Arthur S. Link, *Wilson the Diplomatist: A Look at His Major Foreign Policies* (Baltimore, 1957), p. 90.

states failed to affect the other two. . . . In Britain and
Germany questions of American policy became key issues in
domestic struggles for power." American policy was somewhat different:

> On the American side the drama was less a factional struggle
> than a contest within one man's conscience. A near-pacifist
> President found himself marching step by step toward war.
> . . . In the end he had to choose war because he dreamed
> of peace. Despite the paradoxes, close analysis cannot find
> the point at which he might have turned back or taken an-
> other road. In Wilson's dilemmas, as in the contests in Lon-
> don and Berlin, there were elements of high tragedy.

The submarine controversy led to American intervention.
May describes Sir Edward Grey's effort to preserve and extend the traditional Anglo-American understanding. The
development of German-American antagonism secured the
Anglo-American relation despite the strains of the war. Wilson hoped to achieve a general peace through the vehicle of
Anglo-American cooperation; unfortunately for Germany
there was no prior tradition of trust between that nation and
the United States. Chancellor Bethmann Hollweg's prudence
and Wilson's dedication to peace postponed the day of
reckoning but did not avoid it. May finds it difficult to label
the President's policy as "unrealistic." "He sought lasting
peace for its own sake. Since it offered the only sure escape
from the dilemmas of wartime relations with Britain and
Germany, it did have its practical side." By 1917 war was
unavoidable.[22]

May's work has a distinctive multinational perspective and
a multiarchival basis. It demonstrates the advantages of
avoiding an unduly restricted national perspective and evi-

---

22. Ernest R. May, *The World War and American Isolation, 1914–1917*
(Cambridge, Mass., 1959), pp. vii–viii, 437.

dential base. If the book lends new plausibility to older analyses like that of Charles Seymour, it is a model of scholarship and historical writing to which others might repair with profit. Though certainly within the Rankean tradition, it defies easy classification because of its complex analysis.

Victor S. Mamatey's influential *The United States and East Central Europe, 1914–1918* (1957), is appropriately subtitled *A Study in Wilsonian Diplomacy and Propaganda.* He seeks "to reconstruct . . . the story of the United States attitude toward the break-up of the old Habsburg Empire and the creation of Czechoslovakia and Yugoslavia, the reunification of Rumania, and the completion of the unification of Italy." Eclectic in outlook, Mamatey believes that "foreign policy is a set of reactions to impulses both at home and abroad." Wilson neither Balkanized East Central Europe nor represented bourgeois-nationalist opposition to social revolution. "British and Allied policy during the war was improvised in a pragmatic and empiric fashion almost from day to day; there was little or no planning for postwar days." Relying on little-known eastern European sources, Mamatey expounds a general thesis:

> The new nations of East Central Europe were not created by the Paris Peace Conference; they created themselves by their own efforts. Both American and Russian propaganda *stimulated* but did not *engender* their desire for independence. The Allies made their independence possible by crushing the main obstacle to it: the military might of the Central Powers. Victory over the Central Powers—*that* was the great Allied contribution to the freedom of the peoples of East Central Europe. Wilsonian America contributed to the Allied victory; Bolshevik Russia did not.[23]

23. Victor S. Mamatey, *The United States and East Central Europe, 1914–1918: A Study in Wilsonian Diplomacy and Propaganda* (Princeton, N.J., 1957), pp. viii, x, 152, 384.

This forceful but temperate work reflects the outlook of recent students, far removed from the passions of the period
and yet deeply involved in its significance for later events.

Lawrence E. Gelfand, in *The Inquiry* (1963), has contributed another striking study of Wilsonian activity by tracing
the work of Wilson's planners for the peace conference. Far
from being catch-as-catch-can, American preparations for
the sessions at Paris were quite extensive. The organization
and work of the Inquiry in regard to all parts of the world
becomes clear, the results of unusually thorough research.
Gelfand gives considerable space to the contributions of
Sidney Mezes, Isaiah Bowman, Walter Lippmann, James T.
Shotwell, and David Hunter Miller. Despite its effort, the
Inquiry had mixed results. Although it did not develop well-
conceived peace proposals, its work was of some use at the
peace conference; its global proportions at least indicated
that "the United States by 1917 had reached the status of a
great world power." Gelfand analyzes with particular care
the use of scholars for the first time as servants of the government. Like other recent students, he sees in Wilson "less of
the moralistic fiber than is customary." Trade expansion
does not appear as a dominating motive behind policy planning.[24]

Representative of the continuing preoccupation with the
relations between public opinion and foreign policy is a
recent collection of essays edited by Joseph P. O'Grady entitled *The Immigrants' Influence on Wilson's Peace Policies*
(1967). Various immigrant groups in America, ranging
from the Irish and Jews to the Carpatho-Ruthenians and the
British-Americans, attempted to guide policy by influencing
the general public, establishment leadership, local and national politicians, various departments and agencies, and

24. Lawrence E. Gelfand, *The Inquiry: American Preparations for
Peace, 1917–1919* (New Haven, Conn., 1963), pp. 314, 333.

finally the president and his staff. O'Grady summarizes the over-all conclusion: "only two of the immigrant groups studied really influenced Wilson and in neither case [Jewish and Polish] was the principal means the operation of public opinion." The essays frequently suggest that "realistic" calculations based on the relative strength of states were regular aspects of Wilsonian diplomacy. O'Grady minces no words in his final estimate:

> There are those who hold that diplomacy in the twentieth century is controlled by the people and not by the realities of power and geography, that it is free from the influence of the whims of individuals. Yet in the case of Wilson it would seem that geography did influence diplomacy, that power played its role, and that the whim of the individual had not been eliminated.[25]

This writer has examined the relations between American diplomacy and military decisions during 1917–18 in *The United States and the Supreme War Council* (1961). The Supreme War Council attempted to coordinate the political-military decisions of the Entente Powers and the United States, the first such enterprise in which the United States had taken part since the Revolution. Contrary to the views of the power realists, Wilson and his advisers appreciated the relations between military and political decisions. Five case studies of issues dealt with in the Supreme War Council led to the conclusion that "American relations with the Entente turned on two fundamental objectives, a clear-cut victory over the Central Powers and the maintenance of American diplomatic independence. President Wilson deemed both objectives necessary in order to insure the fulfillment of his plans for the postwar world." Wilsonian decisions dur-

25. Joseph P. O'Grady, ed., *The Immigrants' Influence on Wilson's Peace Policies* (Lexington, Ky., 1967), pp. 28–29.

ing the period of belligerency sought to insure American domination of the peace settlement—if necessary to dictate the outcome both to the victors and the vanquished of Europe.[26]

George Frost Kennan himself has investigated the war years in his study of *Soviet-American Relations, 1917–1920* (1956–). Throughout the two volumes that have appeared, he applies some of the general interpretive principles laid out in *American Diplomacy 1900–1950:*

> In the end it is only right principles, consistently applied—not the gift of prophecy or the pride of insight—that achieve the best [diplomatic] results. These results are never wholly predictable; nor are they even easy to distinguish when they appear. It is the tragedy of the diplomatic art that even the finest achievements are always mingled with ulterior causes and are seldom visible or intelligible to the broader public until many years have separated them from the decisions in which, in the main, they had their origin.

In *Russia Leaves the War* Kennan quickly establishes his distaste for Wilson, who did not use "diplomatic missions as a vital and intimate agency of policy." His general thesis is that American policy was misguided because no one really understood the situation in Russia and too many amateurs like Raymond Robins confused the issues. Discussing a curious effort to make John Reed the Soviet consul in New York, Kennan observes "the infinite possibilities for misunderstanding, confusion, intrigue, and malevolent exploitation that are always present when inexperienced people, whose status is unclarified, are permitted to dabble in the transactions between governments." This dabbling had enormous conse-

---

26. David F. Trask, *The United States in the Supreme War Council: American War Aims and Inter-Allied Strategy, 1917–1918* (Middletown, Conn., 1961), p. 172.

quences: "Out of the resulting confusion grew, in large part, the many myths and controversies by which their memory has been followed."

The second volume, *The Decision to Intervene*, elaborates this theme: "Confusion was the predominant element in the external relations of Russia in 1918." Kennan criticizes the inter-Allied intervention because it "sacrificed . . . the slender thread of communication with the new government in Russia which had existed in the form of official and semi-official staffs left after the Revolution in the territory held by the Bolsheviki." The writer's deep-seated conservatism and advocacy of diplomatic professionalism appear in his vale-dictory comment:

> The reasons for the failure of American statesmanship lay . . . in such things as the deficiencies of the American political system from the grievous distortion of vision brought to the democratic society by any self-abandonment —as in World War I—to the hysteria of militancy; the con-genital shallowness, philosophical and intellectual, of the approach to world problems that bubbled up from the fer-mentations of official Washington; and the pervasive dil-letantism in the execution of American policy. How pleasing it would be if one were able to record, in concluding this volume, that these deficiencies had been left behind.[27]

An entirely different analysis appears in Arno Mayer's *Wilson vs. Lenin: Political Origins of the New Diplomacy, 1917–1918* (1964). It is a lonely but distinguished study of the influence of domestic politics on foreign policy during World War I. Mayer analyzes the controversies within vari-ous European countries between "parties of order" and

27. George F. Kennan, *Soviet-American Relations, 1917–1920*, 2 vols. (Princeton, N.J., 1956—). Vol. I: *Russia Leaves the War*, pp. viii, 28, 410–11; Vol. II: *The Decision to Intervene*, pp. 14, 470, 471–72. A third volume is to appear.

"parties of movement" over war aims from March, 1917, to January, 1918. This chronology permits comparative study and encompasses certain critical events—the military stalemate in France, the American intervention, and the Bolshevik Revolution. Lenin's April Theses and Wilson's Fourteen Points symbolize the "new diplomacy." The old diplomacy stressed annexations, protectorates, and spheres of influence, appealing to self-defense, national honor, and freedom. The new diplomacy called for open diplomacy and nonannexationist objectives. Insisting on the primacy of "domestic political determinants," Mayer shows how the parties of movement espoused the new diplomacy:

> The triumph of the New Diplomacy during the last year of the war must be assessed not only in the light of Wilson's profound faith in the wisdom of open diplomacy and popular control of foreign policy, or of the Bolshevik practice of open diplomacy at Brest-Litovsk and their conversion to self-determination, but also in the light of the decided growth of the forces of movement in Austria-Hungary, Germany, France, and Great Britain.

During 1917, when World War I became "a worldwide revolutionary and ideological struggle," Wilson and Lenin pursued comparable principles for different ends. Wilson hoped to rekindle the fighting spirit of the Allies and strengthen the forces of movement in the enemy camp. Lenin hoped to advance the revolution of the proletariat by combining a compromise peace with domestic reform. Ultimately reform and revolution became antithetical to each other.[28]

In a sequel entitled *Politics and Diplomacy of Peacemak-*

28. Arno J. Mayer, *Wilson vs. Lenin: Political Origins of the New Diplomacy, 1917–1918* (Cleveland, Ohio, 1964), pp. 8, 33. Originally published under title of *Political Origins of the New Diplomacy, 1917–1918* (New Haven, Conn., 1959).

ing (1967) Mayer interests himself in the "political and diplomatic context and climate in which the principal peacemakers dealt with critical issues and problems involving fundamental policy considerations." The peace conference of 1919 revealed the ultimate recovery of the parties of order. Both Russia and America, although for different reasons, took leave of postwar European politics. "Russia was ostracized and quarantined because of her revolutionary transgression, and this transgression became both cause and excuse for treating Russia as if she were a decaying empire." On the other hand, "America's withdrawal, not unlike Russia's expulsion, was activated by political considerations in foreign policy and not by considerations of *raison d'état.*" Mayer summarizes his conclusion grimly:

> The end of the war emergency and the intensifying contest between revolution and counterrevolution pushed the primacy of foreign policy into the background. . . . The legacy of disorder, frustration, and exhaustion actually intensified political tensions beyond what they had been before the war; and disappointments with the outcome of the Peace Conference intensified these tensions still further. The signing of a diplomatic document could not lessen or liquidate the massive world crisis whose locus shifted from the international to the internal area. Hereafter foreign policy issues became caught up in partisan politics; foreign policy and diplomacy became pawns in the domestic struggle for power.[29]

Mayer's revisionism contrasts starkly with the measured tones of Seth Tillman's *Anglo-American Relations at the Paris Peace Conference of 1919* (1961). Tillman discerns considerable Anglo-American harmony at Paris but at no

29. Arno J. Mayer, *Politics and Diplomacy of Peacemaking: Containment and Counterrevolution at Versailles, 1918–1919* (New York, 1967), pp. vii, 876.

point "did the English-speaking powers identify their community of interests to the point of pursuing acknowledged common objectives by a coherent common strategy." If the United States maintained a general policy of diplomatic independence, indicating the continuing influence of the isolationist past, the author argues that "with certain exceptions, Britain and the United States were responsible for the most enlightened, most progressive, and most moral features of the treaties of peace." The Americans and the British clashed over colonies and mandates, sea power, and reparations and economic settlements, but they were in close accord on the European settlement and the covenant of the League. Tillman looks benignly on the settlement. "Whatever the defects of the particulars of the treaties, the settlement as a whole was a reasonable embodiment of the Fourteen Points, and, more broadly, of the democratic principles of Anglo-American society." Because the Americans repudiated the Versailles treaty legally, and the British morally, "the worst particulars of the treaties were enforced, while the best were stillborn." [30]

If the historical works on the diplomacy of World War I reveal the conventional division of view between power realism and economic interpretation, most scholars adopt either a neutral or favorable view of Wilsonian diplomacy, a definite reaction against the views extant just after World War II. No general consensus has as yet emerged, but the productivity of those interested in the period may provide the basis for a new general synthesis in the not too distant future. One universally accepted view is not likely to be abandoned—that the history of World War I has all the elements of high tragedy.

30. Seth P. Tillman, *Anglo-American Relations at the Paris Peace Conference of 1919* (Princeton, N.J., 1961), pp. vii, 401–2, 408.

V

In late years the interwar years have attracted more students of American foreign relations than any other field. Archival materials for the period 1919–39 have become available in great plenty. Some scholars have concentrated on the twenties, concerned with the aftermath of the war, but most have pioneered in the study of the years from 1929 to 1939, examining American behavior during the great international decline in security that culminated in World War II.

Perhaps the most influential general work on the over-all period is Selig Adler's *The Isolationist Impulse* (1957). The study is not diplomatic history. Like many other students of this era, Adler treats domestic attitudes toward involvement in world politics from the time of World War I. Ever since Sarajevo, "Americans have been torn between a desire to use their national power to stabilize the world, and a conflicting desire to remain aloof from overseas turmoil." No irreversible commitment was made from 1914 to the middle fifties. "Only in times of acute foreign or domestic crisis has one desire or another dominated public opinion." The author studies "mass opinion," analyzing the views of those in the middle as well as at the extremes. The result is insight into the way in which opinions penetrated into the consciousness of the American people.[31]

Waldo Heinrichs has written an unusually detailed biography of Ambassador Joseph C. Grew, *American Ambassador* (1966), which spans the interwar period, adding to an understanding of the broader course of national policy by tracing its impact on a leading member of the Foreign Serv-

31. Selig Adler, *The Isolationist Impulse: Its Twentieth Century Reaction,* paperback ed. (New York, 1957), p. 433.

ice. Grew had tours of duty in Washington, but he was principally a professional diplomat engaged in field operations,
notably in Ankara and Tokyo. Grew's ambassadorial role in
Japan from 1931 to 1941 is the highlight of the biography.
The emphasis in this biography is on the execution rather
than the formation of policy, an important dimension to
which other historians might give more attention.[32]

Historians writing about the twenties have emphasized
domestic influences on policy-making. They have dealt in
particular with the limiting effects of the great public reaction against Wilson's "crusade" and the shaping forces of the
"business civilization" that held sway during the presidential service of Harding, Coolidge, and Hoover. Recent scholars have been less bitter than those of earlier decades, but
they remain highly critical of American statecraft in the Republican era. Betty Glad's critical exploration of Charles E.
Hughes's service as secretary of state from 1921 to 1925, definitely exemplifies the views of the power realists as influenced by the political scientist Hans Morgenthau. The author argues that "American foreign policy between the
World Wars was not based on a solid intellectual foundation." Hughes had a somewhat jarring childhood, an experience that led him continually to seek personal calm. The
secretary was unduly concerned with the unsettling consequences of domestic political criticism. "In avoiding the politically objectionable, he may have left untouched the
really significant problems of his time." Above all, Hughes
failed to consider the relations between force and diplomacy.
"Holding to a nineteenth-century rationalist philosophy
which obscured the relationship of power to social order, he
had difficulty in formulating foreign policies adequately

32. Waldo Heinrichs, *American Ambassador: Joseph C. Grew and the
Development of the United States Diplomatic Tradition* (Boston, 1966).

geared to the new international situation of the United States." The final judgment is harsh: "because his philosophy and his personality would not permit him to face squarely the bases of political action, Hughes could not see the fundamental changes that had occurred in the international position of the United States and adjust his goals accordingly." [33]

Another useful study of an influential figure during the twenties is John C. Vinson's work on the chairman of the Senate Foreign Relations Committee, William E. Borah, Republican of Idaho. Neither a full-scale biography nor a study of policy, the book examines "Borah's actions and methods, and . . . his aims and motives in regard to the problem of America's proper responsibility in promoting world peace." The senator was "the archetype of absolute insistence on unfettered national will that has been loosely identified as isolationism." Vinson sees in his subject a "struggle to preserve in full the traditions of a small republic remote from strong neighbors against the inroads of recurring crises faced by a world power." Borah believed that complete independence in foreign affairs was compatible with cooperative endeavors to maintain the peace. Particularly fearful of unduly restrictive ties to Europe, Borah could favor the Kellogg-Briand pact despite his all-out opposition to the League because that treaty accorded with the positive aspects of his thought on international relations. Vinson concentrates on Borah's gradual acceptance of the principle of outlawing war. "The Pact of Paris met every test, for it did not entangle the United States in foreign politics, it was not an alliance, it did not obligate the United States, and it was not based on the use of force." Committed to the principles of nationalism, sovereignty, and independence, Borah could support the out-

33. Betty Glad, *Charles Evans Hughes and the Illusions of Innocence: A Study in American Diplomacy* (Urbana, Ill., 1966), pp. 152, 322, 326.

lawry of war wholeheartedly without abandoning his isolationist sentiments.[34]

Peter Filene's *Americans and the Soviet Experiment, 1917–1933* (1967), deals with domestic attitudes toward a particular issue of great significance. "Intensive analysis of this single intellectual theme will indirectly describe Americans' conceptions of democracy, of capitalism, and of themselves as a society and nation." Dealing with ideas advanced by specific interest groups, Filene traces the evolution of attitudes toward the Soviet Union through intervention, withdrawal, the new economic plan, the first five-year plan, and recognition. There was no dramatic shift from hostility to reconciliation, but feelings were "decidedly more benign" in 1933 than in 1918–19. Filene concludes that "American attitudes toward Soviet Russia always included the same set of values, but with the order of priorities revised in response to the varying situations of war, prosperity, and depression. The sequence varied from group to group and often differed within groups, of course, but the differences derived from disagreement on priority of values rather than the values themselves." Attitudes were both fickle and contradictory because American values were so pluralistic. The failure to make the world safe for democracy and for prosperity exerted great influence on attitudes; it forced America to realize that the Soviet Union would neither surrender nor accept defeat.[35]

Raymond O'Connor has written a useful study of the relations between sailors and statesmen in *Perilous Equilibrium* (1962), an investigation of the London Naval Conference of 1930. Conflicting attitudes troubled this relationship. "The

34. John Chalmers Vinson, *William E. Borah and the Outlawry of War* (Athens, Ga., 1957), pp. ix, 161.

35. Peter G. Filene, *Americans and the Soviet Experiment, 1917–1933* (Cambridge, Mass., 1967), pp. 3–4, 273, 274–75.

statesman strives for international conciliation and the professional reiterates that the fleet which exists is the fleet that wins." Great political differences separated the delegates of France and Italy from the representatives of the United States, Great Britain, and Japan at London. This situation led to a tripartite arrangement excluding the French and Italians. The three greatest naval powers agreed to some naval limitation, but the result was a perilous equilibrium because the negotiators did not decide clearly whether to base the treaty on the "moral force" principle of the Kellogg-Briand pact or the "military implications" of the League Covenant. The treaty insured that the United States would possess sufficient naval power to defend the Monroe Doctrine and probably its Pacific possessions but not enough to preserve the open door in East Asia.[36]

The thirties have attracted perhaps more interest than the twenties in recent years because of the coming of World War II. Among those scholars working on the thirties none has been more active than Robert H. Ferrell, whose study of the Hoover-Stimson foreign policy, *American Diplomacy in the Great Depression* (1957), generally "realist" in tone, has exercised broad influence. Ferrell bases his work on the premise that the Great Depression "underlay the deterioration of American foreign relations during the years1929–33." He considers the ways in which the national heritage, the characteristics of the diplomatists, and the events of the period combined to shape policy during the early depression years. Notably critical of Secretary of State Henry L. Stimson, Ferrell renders negative judgments on his policies during the Manchurian crisis of 1929 and the naval negotiations of 1930. He gives Hoover some credit in his handling of war

36. Raymond G. O'Connor, *Perilous Equilibrium: The United States and the London Naval Conference of 1930* (Lawrence, Kans., 1962); quotation is from the Preface, unpaginated.

debts and the moratorium but downgrades their importance. Most of the book treats the Manchurian crisis of 1931–32, and Stimson is roundly criticized once again. Good intentions were not enough. "Only a few individuals . . . were willing to try a diplomacy based on force rather than moral suasion and legal admonition." Stimson was entirely too legalistic; all too often events outran intelligence.[37]

Lloyd C. Gardner adopts an entirely different approach to foreign relations during the depression. His study of *Economic Aspects of New Deal Diplomacy* (1964) stresses the continuity of traditional American behavior. The passage of the Reciprocal Trade Agreements Act of 1934 committed the United States once again to its traditional foreign policy —trade expansion—and there has been no real change since. In 1933–34 the New Dealers organized for trade expansion in response to economic interests endangered by the domestic depression. During 1934–37 they made their initial efforts to penetrate Latin America, Asia, and Europe. From 1937 to 1941 these beginnings hardened as the Axis challenge to trade expansion became apparent. World War II enlarged the scope of America's trade expansion diplomacy to the entire world and led to the Cold War. Gardner's conclusion is firmly within the school of economic interpretation, and in particular the specific viewpoint of William Appleman Williams. "In Manchuria . . . , in the Middle East, in Latin America, in fact nearly everywhere, the United States wanted the Open Door Policy and an open world. Russia did not. And therein was the struggle which developed into Cold War."[38]

37. Robert H. Ferrell, *American Diplomacy in the Great Depression: Hoover-Stimson Foreign Policy, 1929–1933* (New Haven, Conn., 1957), pp.18, 280.

38. Lloyd C. Gardner, *Economic Aspects of New Deal Diplomacy* (Madison, Wis., 1964), p. 329.

Students of United States–Latin American relations during the thirties have continued their analysis of the Good Neighbor policy. The most comprehensive effort, *The Making of the Good Neighbor Policy* (1961), is by Bryce Wood. Like so many other recent scholars, Wood stresses ideas: "The development of ideas about compromise, collaboration, and leadership in unfamiliar political circumstances." During the period 1920–33 the United States realized that the use of force in the Caribbean was not only expensive and undemocratic but also injurious to the national interest. The Good Neighbor approach of Franklin D. Roosevelt developed not only the principles of nonintervention and noninterference but also the idea of "pacific protection." The national interest in security transcended business interests. Wood opts for the strategic emphasis of writers like Dana G. Munro as against the economic interpretations of Gardner and like scholars. His judgment of New Deal diplomacy in Latin America is positive, unlike that of the Williams group.[39]

E. David Cronon has dealt with a specific application of the Good Neighbor ideal in his *Josephus Daniels in Mexico* (1960). Cronon discerns a mixture of interest and idealism in Good Neighbor politics. "At times even President Roosevelt himself seemed unclear as to which aim was primary. Neither in motivation nor in application, then, was the Good Neighbor Policy a simple, consistent doctrine." Daniels was a true exemplar of the Good Neighbor. He realized that the United States would accomplish much more by "tact, discretion, patience, and understanding" than by bluster and force. The acid test was the crisis over the Mexican expropriation of foreign-owned oil properties in 1938. Daniels realized that the special interests of the oil companies must be sacri-

39. Bryce Wood, *The Making of the Good Neighbor Policy* (New York, 1961), p. vi.

ficed. "In the long run, a higher standard of living would bring a greatly expanded demand for American goods and capital in Mexico." Change was unavoidable; it was best to accept it gracefully, preserving whatever was possible. Cronon compares Daniels favorably with one of his predecessors. "Dwight Morrow was the able and effective representative of American capital in Mexico; Daniels represented the American people." Because the Good Neighbor policy was never really a well-articulated line, diplomats in the field greatly influenced its development. Cronon concludes that the reason for the happy outcome in Mexico was Daniels.[40]

Diplomatic historians of the last decade have not neglected relations with East Asia for the thirties. If students of relations with Latin America have been generally favorable to United States policy, those interested in East Asia have been generally uncomplimentary. As in other topics, a number of revisionist interpretations have been advanced. Armin Rappaport has restudied the Manchurian crisis in order to explain the failure of the United States and Great Britain to restrain Japan during the period 1931–33. *Henry L. Stimson and Japan, 1931–33* (1963) emphasizes the decision-makers and the public mood. Like Ferrell, Rappaport criticizes Stimson's inveterate legalism: "There was no "law" against which the conduct of nations could be assessed. In diplomacy he [Stimson] seemed to have forgotten, if he ever knew, that one cannot let emotion or morality be the only guide of conduct. One must neither hate nor love, only calculate and weigh." Stimson found no support abroad, but did earn the enmity of Japan. He brandished an unloaded pistol, "thereby transgressing the cardinal maxim of the statesman and placing his country in jeopardy." Although definitely in the

40. E. David Cronon, *Josephus Daniels in Mexico* (Madison, Wis., 1960), pp. ix, 286, 287.

"realist" camp, Rappaport nevertheless concedes that the
United States should have voiced shock at the Japanese aggression.[41]

Another important study of United States–Japanese relations is Dorothy Borg's *The United States and the Far Eastern Crisis of 1933–1938* (1964). Japan pursued two main policies during this obscure period. From 1933 to 1937 Tokyo
used peaceful methods of threatening China. Roosevelt neither appeased nor opposed Japan; he did nothing. Even
after the China Incident of 1937, the United States maintained a policy of inaction despite its interest in world peace.
Secretary of State Cordell Hull took a moral stand but
avoided use of sanctions. Given the rapid development of
the world crisis, Borg considers American passivity "aston-
ishing in retrospect." Lassitude rather than action was at the
core of the American failure to help keep the peace.[42]

A different approach to American-Japanese relations preceding Pearl Harbor is taken by Paul Schroeder in his important revisionist study, *The Axis Alliance and Japanese-
American Relations, 1941* (1958). Downgrading the role of
conspiracy and unreason stressed by many earlier scholars,
Schroeder argues that "the attack [on Pearl Harbor] was an
act of desperation, not madness. Japan fought only when she
had her back to the wall as a result of America's diplomatic
and economic offensive." The American demand that Japan
withdraw immediately from China was unwise, as was the
refusal to accept Premier Konoye's bid for a summit meeting
in 1941. Schroeder issues a severe indictment. "In the attempt to gain everything at once, the United States lost her
opportunity to secure immediately her essential require-

41. Armin Rappaport, *Henry L. Stimson and Japan, 1931–33* (Chicago, 1963), pp. 202, 203.
42. Dorothy Borg, *The United States and the Far Eastern Crisis of 1933–1938: From the Manchurian Incident through the Initial Stage of the Undeclared Sino-Japanese War* (Cambridge, Mass., 1964), p. 544.

ments in the Far East and to continue to work toward her long-range goals." Instead, the nation "succeeded . . . in making inevitable an unnecessary and avoidable war." The error was to abandon the policy of dividing Japan from the Axis. The quixotic endeavor to liberate China did not halt Japan; it brought on war. Like Joseph C. Grew, Schroeder believes that the United States should have sought a *modus vivendi,* delaying a showdown until victory in Europe permitted a desirable settlement in Asia. The American approach was inconsistent, unrealistic, and futile, "a policy designed to uphold principle and to punish the aggressor, but not to save the victor." A strong "realist," Schroeder holds that sound policy requires "fundamental attention to what is practical and expedient at a given time and to limited objectives within the scope of the national interest." [43]

Isolationist thought and practice has attracted numerous scholars. Robert A. Divine has studied the neutrality legislation enacted by Congress during the period 1935–37 in *The Illusion of Neutrality* (1962). Emphasizing the debate between isolationists and internationalists, Divine brings out the equivocal role of President Roosevelt. He failed to grasp the strength of isolationism, and later on could not moderate its influence. "Only when the reality of war finally began transforming public opinion did he move effectively to revise the neutrality legislation. And even then he had to compromise, accepting the cash-and-carry restrictions as the necessary price for the repeal of the arms embargo." Nevertheless, the principal responsibility rests with the neutrality bloc in Congress, especially Gerald P. Nye, Bennett Clark, and Hamilton Fish. Divine also attributes some of the blame to Key Pittman, chairman of the Senate Foreign Relations Committee. In the last analysis, however, the responsibility

43. Paul W. Schroeder, *The Axis Alliance and Japanese-American Relations* (Ithaca, N.Y., 1958), pp. 201, 203, 208, 214.

lay with the American people. They favored the democracies but feared involvement in the struggle. Only Pearl Harbor resolved their ambivalence.[44]

Wayne S. Cole has studied the career of one of the leading isolationists in *Senator Gerald P. Nye and American Foreign Relations* (1962). Cole believes that "important roots of isolationism may be traced to needs, desires, and value systems of major segments of the American agricultural society. Agrarian radicalism of the Great Plains and Middle West exerted fundamental influences on Nye's foreign policy views." Cole also traces the shift of isolationist thought from liberalism to conservatism. Isolationism was one means of waging war on urban society. After tracing Nye's career, Cole concludes that his failure was a logical outcome of urbanization—the emergence of a society based on commerce, industry, finance, and labor. Business initially attracted Nye's scorn, but as he became increasingly fearful of big government "he gradually began to move from liberalism to conservatism—without abandoning his isolationism." [45]

The most recent student of isolationism, Manfred Jonas, in *Isolationism in America* (1966) doubts that he is dealing with a full-fledged political philosophy, but as an intellectual historian he takes the phenomenon very seriously because it was "the considered response to foreign and domestic developments of a large, responsible, and respectable segment of the American people." Isolationist thought had positive as well as negative attributes. It tied together unilateralism and avoidance of war. It was unified not by geography, politics, class structure, or ethnic allegiance, but by the notion of going it alone out of fear. Isolationism gained strength in the

44. Robert A. Divine, *The Illusion of Neutrality* (Chicago, 1962), p. 334.

45. Wayne S. Cole, *Senator Gerald P. Nye and American Foreign Relations* (Minneapolis, 1962), pp. 4, 76.

thirties because of foreign troubles, the Great Depression, and revisionist history on the origins of World War I. The onset of the international crisis placed the isolationists in a dilemma. The nation could seek safety in strength or lead an anti-war movement. Unable to accept either alternative, the isolationists retreated into an impossible attempt to insulate the Republic from outside dangers. This strategy left ultimate political decisions to outside forces; the drift of events undermined the isolationist appeal. Jonas summarizes the isolationist outlook beautifully:

> Reduced to its least common denominator, the isolationism of the Thirties consisted of belief in the amorality of international affairs and the impregnability of the Western Hemisphere which, taken together, made American intervention in a foreign war both unavailing and unnecessary; of the idea that peace-loving nations such as the United States became involved in war largely through the machinations of selfish, greedy minorities; and of the conviction that, since all other countries were amoral, warlike, or vulnerable, it was essential for the United States to adhere to a policy of unilateralism in its foreign relations. Sustaining these attitudes in the face of world events that cast doubt on their validity was the dread of total war and its domestic consequences.
>
> As thus stated, isolationism is devoid of political, economic, or social content.[46]

Perhaps the most notable tendency among the historians of the interwar years is their great preoccupation with public opinion, attitudes, ideas, and domestic politics at home in their relations to foreign policy. Both power realism and economic interpretation have attracted adherents, as have the insights of intellectual history. There is need for many more

46. Manfred Jonas, *Isolationism in America, 1935–1941* (Ithaca, N.Y., 1966), pp. 273–74.

analyses of policy formation and execution, an emphasis that is now possible because extensive collections of government documents are becoming available. An early consensus on the history of the long armistice appears quite unlikely, but the contributions of the past decade have added greatly to historical understanding of the tragic years preceding World War II.

VI

The serious scholarship on foreign relations during World War II is limited, although there is an extraordinary collection of contemporary observation, journals, memoirs, and the like. The paucity of research reflects both the lack of official sources and the great complexity of the subject. At this point in time, however, the establishment of historical perspective and the growing availability of information make the period particularly attractive. Most historians to date have focused upon the question of how did coalition diplomacy work itself out during the period of belligerency. And most have approached this general problem by studying various more specific and often controversial policies and decisions in order to permit a more detailed and objective synthesis of the period.

Only a few general interpretations of the war period have appeared, of which the leading example is Gaddis Smith's *American Diplomacy during the Second World War, 1941–1945* (1965). Abandoning the search for culpability so characteristic of immediate postwar writings, Smith concentrates on a series of stereotypes to which President Roosevelt and his associates clung tenaciously. A lack of realism marred American statecraft during the war; "they [American statesmen] held too long to stereotypes about the United States

and other nations and acted too often on the basis of hopes
and illusion rather than ascertainable fact." False analogies
often substituted for actualities. Americans made unduly sim-
plistic assumptions about the motives of their enemies. Leaders distrusted public willingness to shoulder responsibilities
at war's end. They also overestimated the potential of the
United Nations, thus neglecting to consider many difficult
problems. "Reliance on these stereotypes simplified the task
of wartime leadership . . . but added immeasurably to the
tasks of . . . [their] successors." [47]

The most prolific and influential scholar of the war years
is Herbert Feis, formerly an official in the Department of
State. He has written *Churchill—Roosevelt—Stalin* (1957),
the most useful synthesis of the workings of the Grand Alliance. Considering fourteen stages in the evolution of the
wartime coalition, Feis makes a balanced but definite defense of Anglo-American diplomacy in relation to that of the
Soviet Union. Circumstances rather than error forced many
decisions criticized since, e.g., those made at Casablanca and
Yalta. Political decisions were necessarily delayed until victory was in sight. Feis attributes postwar difficulties largely
to the expansionist ambitions of the Soviet Union:

> Roosevelt and his colleagues were right; the nations needed
> moral law and freedom. Churchill was right; the nations
> needed magnanimity and balance of power. Stalin was sul-
> lying a right; the Russian people were entitled to the fullest
> equality and protection against another assault upon them.
> But under Stalin they were trying not only to extend their
> boundaries and their control over neighboring states but also
> beginning to revert to their revolutionary effort throughout
> the world. Within the next few years this was to break the
> coalition and, along with the spread of nationalist passion

47. Gaddis Smith, *American Diplomacy during the Second World War,
1941–1945* (New York, 1965), pp. 178, 179.

in hitherto passive parts of the world, create the turbulence in which we are now living.[48]

Anne Armstrong's *Unconditional Surrender* (1961) is a study of that decision. Roosevelt's support of the unconditional surrender principle "represented not only the American war aim in the Second World War but also a basic American attitude toward international politics, and toward war." Critics maintain that this demand prolonged the conflict, undermined anti-Nazi elements in Germany, and helped to create a power vacuum in central Europe. Defenders hold that it was not only morally sound but also dictated by the reality of total war. Armstrong shows that German military success, fears of Russian defalcation, and ideological commitment all influenced American policy. F.D.R. attributed sole blame for the war to Germany and believed that German defeat would insure a just and lasting peace. Any alternative to unconditional surrender would have required "a more flexible and a more realistic attitude toward both Germany and Russia, a view of war as the instrument of policy rather than of policy as the handmaiden of strategy." Generally within the realist school, the author does not suggest that F.D.R. could have acted much differently, but she questions unduly categorical and emotional decision-making.[49]

Stephen E. Ambrose has analyzed another prolific source of myths about World War II in *Eisenhower and Berlin, 1945* (1967). What circumstances led to the Russian occupation of Berlin? Ambrose interests himself in the relations between force and diplomacy, disposing of two specific myths —the idea that the United States could have avoided the

48. Herbert Feis, *Churchill—Roosevelt—Stalin: The War They Waged and the Peace They Sought* (Princeton, N.J., 1957), p. 655.

49. Anne Armstrong, *Unconditional Surrender: The Impact of the Casablanca Policy upon World War II* (New Brunswick, N.J., 1961), pp. ix, 261.

Berlin problem by occupying that city and the view that
President Roosevelt ordered General Dwight D. Eisenhower
to leave the place to the Russians. In any case the United
States would have withdrawn its forces westward to the
Elbe, established as the limit of the American advance. "The
best hope of the world in 1945 was American-Russian cooperation, and the achievement of this aim was worth almost
any effort. I do not believe that hope was doomed from the
start." Ambrose shows that the boundaries of the occupation
zones derived from an effort to divide Germany equally
among Russia, Britain, and the United States. The West
never contemplated violating the agreements on the zones
reached in late 1944. Eisenhower's aim was "quick defeat,
his purpose to overrun Germany, his method exploitation
under his best General [Omar Bradley]." Fully in agreement
with Eisenhower's estimates, Ambrose not only doubts that
the United States could have beaten the Russians to Berlin
but points out that over 100,000 Russians were lost in the
operation and that the United States received its zone of the
conquered city according to the agreement.[50]

Robert A. Divine has contributed a pioneering study
called *Second Chance* (1967), about the "transformation of
American attitudes toward international organization during
the Second World War." Hoping to avoid a third world conflict, the United States looked to the Wilsonian past for an
antidote to war. If Americans during World War II did not
succeed in abolishing warfare, they did manage to repudiate
the heritage of isolationism. Divine believes that the wartime debate was over what new departure to take, rather
than whether to chart a new course. Various individuals and
groups tried to influence public attitudes—pressure groups,
certain political leaders, and a number of publicists. Down-

50. Stephen E. Ambrose, *Eisenhower and Berlin, 1945: The Decision to
Halt at the Elbe* (New York, 1967), pp. 12, 41.

grading the roles of some men earlier deemed of prime importance in the movement toward collective security, including F.D.R. and Secretary of State Hull, the author gives considerable space to the activities of Republican Senator Joseph Ball of Minnesota, Wendell Willkie, Sumner Welles, and Clark Eichelberger of the League of Nations Association. The work ends on an ironic note: "Throughout the war the American people had looked forward to the creation of an international organization as the dominant feature of the postwar world. Their vision of the future centered in the fulfillment of Wilson's dream. Suddenly they discovered that scientists working secretly in laboratories in Chicago, Oak Ridge, Hanford and Los Alamos were the real architects of the brave new world." [51]

In recent years historians have reassessed the view that the wartime activities of the Soviet Union generated the Cold War. An example of this trend is Martin F. Herz's *Beginnings of the Cold War* (1966). After noting the striking difference between expectations at the time historical events take place and the outlook one later attributes to the time, Herz concentrates on the months between the Yalta and Potsdam conferences in 1945. The wrangle over Poland determined the future course of events—not the German question. Germany was partitioned because there was no other means of satisfying Russia's demand for capital goods for postwar reconstruction. "By the time of Potsdam (July 1945), it was clear that the Western Powers could not accept the *de facto* Russian sphere of influence in eastern Europe and that they had nothing to offer Russia to make it forego the establishment of such a sphere also in central Europe." Europe became divided on the basis of military power at the end of the war, "when the United States failed to throw into

51. Robert A. Divine, *Second Chance: The Triumph of Internationalism in America during World War II* (New York, 1967), pp. 4, 314.

the balance its economic power, which was later to play such an important role in the conduct of the Cold War." [52]

If Herz the realist places great emphasis on a sin of omission, the American failure to engage in economic diplomacy, Gar Alperovitz concentrates on positive acts in his *Atomic Diplomacy* (1965). One of the few works on World War II to assume the primacy of domestic considerations in the making of foreign policy, the writer points an accusing finger at President Harry S. Truman, who repudiated F.D.R.'s policy of accommodation and "launched a powerful foreign policy initiative aimed at reducing or eliminating Soviet influence from Europe." Alperovitz's basic contention is that "the atomic bomb played a role in the formulation of policy, particularly in connection with Truman's only meeting with Stalin, the Potsdam Conference." The bomb was dropped on Hiroshima and Nagasaki because "a combat demonstration was needed to convince the Russians to accept the American plan for a stable peace." Recognizing that his argument depends heavily on inference, the author finally concedes that "no final conclusion can be reached on this question," but he leaves little doubt as to his opinion. The Cold War was an American initiative based on the possession of a nuclear monopoly. [53]

Clearly, this brief survey of recent scholarship in foreign relations during World War II suggests that many fruitful topics remain to be studied and that historians are far from a general agreement on the conduct and outcome of that conflict. Recent works on the "myths" of the period depart radically from the initial consensus. Power-realist analysis is increasingly questioned by historians who stress domestic

52. Martin F. Herz, *Beginnings of the Cold War* (Bloomington, Ind., 1966), p. 188.
53. Gar Alperovitz, *Atomic Diplomacy: Hiroshima and Potsdam. The Use of the Atomic Bomb and the American Confrontation with Soviet Power* (New York, 1965), pp. 13, 240, 241.

influences on foreign policy and diplomacy. The study of
World War II provides many opportunities for those interested in the relation between force and diplomacy. As World
War II fades into the past, changing perspectives and new
evidence should result in broad reinterpretation comparable
to that which has reshaped the views of historians about
World War I.

VII

The conventional disadvantages of contemporary history
have inhibited study of events since World War II—lack of
perspective and evidence. Nevertheless, some scholars have
offered general syntheses, interpretations, and criticisms of
American foreign relations since 1945. Most of them are histories of the Cold War. In the earlier postwar years historians
concentrated on Russo-American conflict. In later years they
showed extensive interest in the rise of ex-colonial nations in
the Third World. Historians have shown great ingenuity in
analyzing recent events by utilizing advantages such as personal involvement, interviews, and contemporary reportage.
Representatives of both power realism and economic interpretation have discussed postwar developments, the former
school dominating the field in earlier years but giving some
place to dissenting views of late. Political scientists and even
practicing diplomats have been frequent contributors to the
historical debate.

In 1962 Norman A. Graebner produced one of the first interpretations of the United States in the Cold War, an intelligent application of analytical principles advanced by
George F. Kennan and Hans Morgenthau. Noting the modern proclivity to turn diplomatic controversies into crusades
for freedom, Graebner observes that "the tendency to pur-

sue abstractions rather than concrete interests continued to dominate American diplomacy in the postwar era." Stressing "the absence of any clearly-defined body of objectives that had some relation to American capability or even genuine intention," he considers the outcome tragic. "This neglect of the fundamental obligation of government to maintain some relationship between ends and means in national action accustomed the American people to expect too much of foreign policy." The United States refused to recognize the obvious reality of enhanced Russian power in Europe after World War II. This fact was hard to accept; the satiate quality of American life suggested an identity between international stability and democratic ideals, a correlation not easily accepted elsewhere in the world. "Only when the United States recognized officially that past changes, whatever their magnitude, were not synonymous with Communist aggression would it discard its feeling of universal obligation, eliminate the nagging character of its diplomacy, and cease to respond to every episode as if it were ushering in the Day of Judgment." Extremely critical of American responses during the period 1945–60, Graebner concludes with a general indictment:

> The nation, with its interests ill-defined in a general crusade for self-determination, entered a new period of drift after World War II not unlike that of the thirties. Thereafter through fifteen years of cold war experience American leadership could not prepare the country either to accept the necessity of coexistence with those forces which challenged its principles or the price required for dismantling the world which it could not accept.[54]

This general outlook appears in another detailed history of American foreign policy since World War II written by John W. Spanier. Highly critical of the national distaste for

54. Norman A. Graebner, *Cold War Diplomacy: American Foreign Policy, 1945–1960* (New York, 1962), pp. 9–10, 107, 132.

"power politics," which "hindered an adequate response to
the ideological, social, and strategic challenges of our age,"
Spanier is convinced that "the American penchant for separating war and peace into two mutually exclusive states of
affairs and divorcing force from diplomacy hampered a union of power and policy." Another important weakness of
the United States was its inability to understand "social
politics"; "economic progress [in the Third World] must be
attended by thorough transformation." Any alteration in the
American approach to foreign policy required domestic
change, because national attitudes were a "product both of
our experience and our predominantly middle-class culture."
Like Graebner, Spanier analyzes the American tendency to
view "international politics in terms of abstract moral principles instead of clashes of interest and power." In order to
avoid future error, the United States must recognize, first,
that power is not inherently evil and, second, that it must
make a great contribution to the social revolutionary process
in the Third World.[55]

   John Lukacs also adopts a realist approach in *A History of
the Cold War* (1961), but he places his major emphasis on
Europe. In his view the division of Germany rather than the
atomic bomb or communism was the principal source of
postwar instability. Impressed by the continuity of world
politics since World War I, Lukacs insists that Europe remains the center of world politics. His basic remedy for the
Cold War is "a truly united and truly independent Europe."
He is also much concerned with the moral dimension of the
crisis, believing that religious insight by the western world
might help to avoid future catastrophes. "Ultimately it is
the quality of America's stewardship and of Russia's adaptation of the Christian heritage that counts."[56]

   55. John W. Spanier, *American Foreign Policy Since World War II*, 2d.
ed. (New York, 1965), pp. v, vi, 22.
   56. John Lukacs, *A History of the Cold War*, paperback ed. (New York,
1962), p. 337. The original hard-cover edition was published in 1961.

The most recent realist analysis, *The Cold War as History* (1967), is that of Louis J. Halle, formerly on the Policy Planning Staff of the State Department. Taking Thucydides as his model, he treats the Cold War as "a phenomenon not without precedent in the long history of international conflict; as a phenomenon that, typically, goes through a certain cycle with a beginning, a middle, and an end." Mindful of the "absolute predicament" in which we find ourselves, his attitude is one of sympathy for both protagonists in the tragic struggle. Russia was, at least superficially, the initial aggressor in the Cold War, but "the historical circumstances, themselves, had an ineluctable quality that left the Russians little choice but to move as they did. Moving as they did, they compelled the United States and its allies to move in response." The struggle was between opposing constellations of power, not between good and evil, a fourth episode in the modern history of the balance of power, a "contest in which one expanding power has threatened to make itself predominant, and in which other powers have banded together in a defensive coalition to frustrate it." The Cold War precipitated the Asiatic involvements of the United States, but the opposed coalitions are now working toward an accommodation. Nuclear weaponry, paradoxically, had been a peace-keeping factor because the bomb was too dangerous to permit resolution of the conflict by force.[57]

Although analyses such as those of Graebner, Spanier, Lukacs, and Halle have found broad acceptance, a revisionist trend has developed in very recent years. Those who advance alternative views often stress the influence of domestic developments on foreign policy, particularly the pressures of capitalism. They usually maintain that the United States was at least as responsible for the Cold War as the

57. Louis J. Halle, *The Cold War as History* (New York, 1967), pp. xii, xiii, 9.

Soviet Union. Denna Frank Fleming's two-volume study *The Cold War and Its Origins, 1917–1960* (1961) was the first really influential contribution of this nature. Apocalyptic in outlook, Fleming believes that the outcome of the Cold War "will determine whether our civilization is to disappear in the nuclear flames of a final war of annihilation or find essential unity in one family of organized nations." At the root of the conflict was America's refusal to accept the position Russia had gained because of its contribution to the defeat of the Axis powers. President Roosevelt recognized the need for accommodation; President Truman reversed this course by opting for containment. Russia's response reflected a "dreadful fear of a fourth western attack, backed by the atomic bomb." Fleming ends with a chapter entitled "Why the West Lost the Cold War," in which he gives ten reasons for this outcome. The West refused to accept the consequences of World War II. The West relied too heavily on nuclear weapons while discounting Soviet science. We wrongly equated Stalin with Hitler. We wrongly equated communism with fascism. We disregarded the possibility of evolution in the Communist world. We adopted negative rather than positive policies toward other peoples. We copied the worst aspects of our opponents' system. We overcompensated for our isolationist past. We failed to realize that cold wars cannot be won. The policy of containment helped to foster the power we wished to restrict.[58]

Another revisionist, David Horowitz, argues in his *The Free World Colossus* (1965), that the United States consciously heads a global antirevolutionary movement. His leading thesis is that the outcome of World War II gave the United States "a near monopoly on the *strategic* decisions which would affect the basic structure of international rela-

58. Denna Frank Fleming, *The Cold War and Its Origins, 1917–1960*, 2 vols. (London, 1961), I, xi; II, 1045.

tions in the post-war world." As for Russia, its leaders, *"whatever their long-range intentions,* were bound by the same imbalance of power to make moves of primarily *tactical* significance." Containment theory was a self-fulfilling prophecy; it divided the world into the opposite camps it presumed at the outset. Horowitz makes lengthy analyses of crises in Greece, Turkey, Iran, Guatemala, Vietnam, South Korea, Lebanon, Laos, Cuba, and other places in an effort to show that the American motive was to preserve vested interests and the position of private capital. Our Russian policy attempted to deny the Soviet Union the fruits of victory in Europe and to seek the downfall of the Soviet system. The work concludes with a stinging indictment:

> When America set out on her post-war path to contain revolution throughout the world, and threw her immense power and influence into the balance against the rising movement for social justice among the poverty stricken two thirds of the world's population, the first victims of her deeds were the very ideals for a better world—liberty, equality, and self-determination—which she herself, in her infancy, had done so much to foster.

Horowitz's general outlook is inescapable; internal forces shape foreign policy, and the antirevolutionary scheme is both reasoned and mature. The author, of course, is deeply opposed to this kind of foreign policy.[59]

The most impressive analysis of Cold War history is Walter LaFeber's *America, Russia, and the Cold War, 1945–1966* (1967). Assuming that internal developments influence foreign policy, LaFeber makes four basic generalizations about American policy since the 1890s: first, that economic forces were most influential among domestic pressures in-

59. David Horowitz, *The Free World Colossus: A Critique of American Foreign Policy in the Cold War* (New York, 1965), pp. 19, 434.

fluencing international decisions; second, that American statesmen believed that restraints on the free flow of international trade had caused the crisis of the 1930s; third, that American leaders thought the United States could achieve its objectives by utilizing its economic, rather than its military, power; and finally, that American decision-makers were willing to use American economic power to gain their ends. Russian leaders were equally determined to protect their international interests. "Within a year after Hitler's demise, America's open-world diplomacy crashed against Stalin's iron curtain." Stalin's policies reflected the devastation that Russia had experienced during World War II. The United States reacted to Russian intransigence with military initiatives first in Europe and then in Asia. Concerned "to point out where and why American foreign policy began to pivot away from Europe and to focus on the newly emerging areas," LaFeber shows how the Cold War mentality was transferred to relations with the Third World, a trend he deplores. The requirement of the future was to use American power not to counteract revolutions abroad but to build "an equitable society at home. It would be a Promethean—or Sisyphean—effort." Here is an imposing challenge to the conventional wisdom of the realist school, clearly expressive of the Williams approach.[60]

Both realists and revisionists are intensely critical of American policy since World War II. Contemporary historians are a part of their times; the accounting of the recent past from Graebner to LaFeber reflects the commitment of the profession in the United States to peaceful and honorable resolution of international conflict in the interests of peoples everywhere. Historians have only begun to evaluate the Cold War. In all likelihood, the initial interpretations

60. Walter LaFeber, *America, Russia, and the Cold War, 1945–1966* (New York, 1967), pp. ix, 12, 259.

will not endure, but future reconstructions will rest securely on the distinguished labors of the first generation. It is also probable that the tendency to syncretize rather than to choose between the traditional Rankean and Marxian models, manifest in the work of scholars so different in outlook as Graebner and LaFeber, will gain strength during the coming years.

This survey considers only a few representative studies of American foreign policy in this century appearing in the years 1957–67, but it reveals the variety as well as the volume of that scholarship. Once diplomatic history was despised because of its undue preoccupation with chronicles based on official documents, but historians of American foreign relations now utilize multiple concepts and bodies of data that might yield fertile information and insight. Nothing has been more notable than the exploration of domestic intellectual and emotional influences on decision-making; students of foreign policy and diplomacy must continue to appropriate the insights of ancillary disciplines if they are to remain abreast of colleagues in other branches of historical investigation. Historians of foreign relations have also undertaken a truly extensive investigation of the critical relationship between force and diplomacy, an unavoidable and essential preoccupation. This concern must also sustain itself in the future.

Some scholars have experimented with new perspectives on American foreign relations, in particular multinational or international approaches. Multiarchival studies utilizing many foreign languages are beginning to make their appearance. This trend will continue; those who wish to enter this field must be willing to accept the burdens of travel and language study.

For a number of years historians of foreign relations have

devoted most of their energies to detailed monographic investigations. Some broad syntheses have appeared, but there is a growing need for over-all works that synthesize recent scholarship for the twentieth century as a whole and for major subdivisions of the period. Fortunately, those who presented monographs did so with larger interpretations in mind, and they have already helped generate outlooks and perspectives that bid fair to inform more comprehensive studies.

At times one detects undue revisionism in recent scholarship. Of course, bold analysis is essential. The dead hand of the past must not preclude imagination, but in the end wise restraint is the mother of lasting scholarship. Revision for the sake of revision might produce brilliant short-run success, but it can also force its exponents to lifelong defense of useful but overstated theses rather than to constructive progress toward fuller, more satisfactory views. New evidence, techniques, perspectives, and contexts naturally stimulate historical revision. Indeed, they must have this effect, but historians must always honor those sound canons of scholarship that ultimately foster humane historical thought.

No reader of the diplomatic history written in the recent past can fail to note its pervasive critique of the American past in world politics. Much that seemed entirely appropriate and reasonable at the time now appears generally unsound. The pace of change in the modern world forces a great discontinuity in historical thought. All too many of the initiatives and policies of the past now seem impossible to justify either on expediential or moral grounds. The common tie that binds diplomatic historians of all persuasions is a vast rejection of the established American theory and practice of foreign policy. Some historians might question this preoccupation with the "whether" as well as the "what" and the "why" of the past, but historians do have social and political as well as intellectual and academic responsibilities. We are American citizens as well as American scholars. Historians have a responsibility to help shape the future as well as to ransack the past. Those who have dedicated their professional activity to the history of American foreign relations in the past decade have not failed to accept this responsibility, and there is every reason to believe that they will continue on the same lines in the future.

Bureaucracy and Professionalism
in the Development of
American Career Diplomacy

WALDO H. HEINRICHS, JR.

Introduction

THE PRINCIPAL THEME in the history of American career diplomacy has been the triumph of careerism over amateurism. A number of accounts describe the succession of legislative and executive reforms that gradually established a special civil service system for American representation abroad.[1] What this study seeks to explain is why the system assumed the particular form it did. That objective requires a special method of inquiry.

Career diplomacy is a generic term embracing both diplomatic and consular work, though strictly speaking, these were two distinct kinds of foreign service activity. Diplomats conducted the official relations of the United States with for-

1. William Barnes and John Heath Morgan, *The Foreign Service of the United States* (Washington, 1961); Warren Frederick Ilchman, *Professional Diplomacy in the United States, 1779–1939: A Study in Administrative History* (Chicago, 1961); J. Rives Childs, *American Foreign Service* (New York, 1948); Tracy Hollingsworth Lay, *The Foreign Service of the United States* (New York, 1925); Graham H. Stuart, *The Department of State: A History of Its Organization, Procedure and Personnel* (New York, 1949).

eign nations. They resided in foreign capitals and dealt
directly with central governments. Their principal duties
were to represent the United States and its interests at the
highest level, to negotiate treaties and agreements, and to
report foreign developments of significance to their country.
Each chief of a diplomatic mission—ambassador or minister
—had the assistance of a staff, the size of which depended on
the importance of the mission. Staff members shared the
privileged status accorded by international practice to representatives of sovereign states and assumed the international
ranks of secretary of embassy or legation in various grades or
counselor of embassy or legation.[2] Consuls were also official
agents but lacked the favored status of diplomats and dealt
with local officials. They served in important foreign cities,
especially seaports, looking after American shipping and
Americans residing or traveling abroad and seeking out new
markets for American goods. Generally their tasks were
administrative, such as issuing visas and passports and certifying invoices. They ranked as consuls general, consuls, and
vice-consuls, depending on the size of the post and their
position in it.[3]

The history of American career diplomacy has been a
story of progress. In the nineteenth century patronage ruled
the separate diplomatic and consular services. The career
movement began under the pressure of enlarging world
interests at the end of the nineteenth century. Presidents
Theodore Roosevelt and William Howard Taft installed the
rudiments of merit systems in both services, and their successors gradually expanded them. In 1924 the Rogers Act combined the diplomatic and consular services into a single
career system, the Foreign Service. Subsequent acts of Con-

2. Harold Nicolson, *Diplomacy* (New York, 1939).
3. Lay, *Foreign Service,* chap. 5; Childs, *American Foreign Service,*
chap. 10.

gress and executive orders provide further benchmarks on the path of progress. Crises and backsliding were followed by reorganizations and new advances, and with each new advance the system became more elaborate, representative, adaptable, or efficient—in short, improved.

We see one system as it evolved through time, yet it is not difficult to conceive of constructing a career service in a number of ways. It could be semiautonomous or simply an extension of the home department. It could assume responsibility for all overseas activities or just traditional diplomatic functions. It could recruit at the bottom only or at all levels. The government might treat diplomacy as a single endeavor or as a host of separate skills. In preferment it might emphasize intellect or personality, seniority or achievement. Actually all these sets of values and more have been subjects of deliberation and vigorous contention in the history of career diplomacy. To define precisely what shape the system took and why, we must search out the alternatives, preferences, and principles of selection. To find out why the shopper chose the black coat, it is necessary to ask why he chose it instead of the green one. We must think in greens as well as blacks. The idea of an ever-improving career system stretching back to the wilderness of amateurism leads to a preoccupation with results as formally defined by law or executive order. It gives us blacks but not greens.

We achieve a more satisfactory result if we think of organizations and occupations instead of diplomats. In this light it is apparent that American career diplomacy had two patterns of organization, a professional one and a bureaucratic one. The origins of the Foreign Service coincided with the arrival of the bureaucratic orientation in American society. This mode of organization provided the techniques and management procedures for securing continuity, flexibility, predictability, expertness, and efficiency in a complex and fluid urban-industrial society. It provided these advantages also for the conduct of increasingly delicate and important foreign relations. In the same period the profession was gaining in numbers and importance as a form of occupation. As W. J. Goode says, "An industrializing society is a professionalizing society."[4] Diplomats found the profession the most satisfactory form of occupational identification and gave the Foreign Service in significant measure the attributes of a profession, including a pattern of organization that differed in some respects from the bureaucratic pattern.

American career diplomacy displays the distinctive characteristics of bureaucratic organization as conceived by Max Weber.[5] Administrators divided and subdivided tasks to achieve specialization and expertness. They factored diplomacy into political, economic, cultural, and other spheres, and compartmentalized work to the point where a political officer, for example, might watch over a single political party. Career diplomacy developed within a hierarchical authority structure, with each officer assigned a place in a pyramid extending up through the ambassador to the secretary of state and the president. Less pervasive was the characteristic of "a formally established system of rules and regulations [that] governs official decisions and actions." Classical diplomatic activities were not readily amenable to routine. However, the State Department regulated the form, timing, and scope of reporting, and international practice prescribed the manner of representation and negotiation. Most consular work involved nothing but the application of laws and regulations

4. Quoted in Bernard Barber, "Some Problems in the Sociology of the Professions," *Daedalus* XCII (1963), 671.

5. Max Weber, *The Theory of Social and Economic Organization*, trans. A. M. Henderson and Talcott Parsons; ed. with Introduction by Talcott Parsons (New York, 1947), pp. 329–41. The following discussion is based on the summary of Weber's distinctive characteristics of bureaucracy in Peter M. Blau and W. Richard Scott, *Formal Organizations: A Comparative Approach* (San Francisco, 1962), pp. 32–33.

to specific cases. Career diplomacy functioned in a bureaucratic way as a system of offices and ranks, designed for impersonality and emotional detachment and hence rationality and stability in foreign relations. It fully adopted protocol as a means of upholding an officer's quality as an official representative and inserted status distinctions to emphasize the difference between offices. Finally, the system ultimately provided a full-fledged career with security of tenure, entrance by examination, promotion by merit, remuneration in the form of salary, and provision for retirement.

To describe the system as bureaucratic would be only partially correct; the bureaucratic mode had limitations, especially in the case of diplomacy. The fact that the bureaucratic day did not occur at the same time everywhere was one limitation. A telegram dispatched in office hours at Washington might require action at midnight abroad. A diplomat could not shed his official role at 5 P.M.; he was always serving in a representative capacity. Working in small groups of their own nationality in an alien environment, diplomats were thrown upon one another and upon diplomats of other nations for companionship. Friendships and social groups arose that defied the hierarchical and status prescriptions of bureaucracy. The limitations went to the heart of the diplomatic function. The diplomat had to cross cultural frontiers and create his own universe outside bureaucratic guidelines to carry out the tasks assigned him. Furthermore, diplomacy was somewhat unpredictable, irrational, and inefficient. People and nations as corporate personalities acted from fear, pride, anger, and human liking, feelings that could not be pigeonholed in a bureaucratic profile. Aspects of diplomacy always lay beyond the reach of the bureaucratic pattern of organization.

Along the lines of Bernard Barber's useful definition, the

profession has four distinctive characteristics: a generalized and systematic field of knowledge; orientation to community service rather than self-interest; a system of rewards emphasizing prestige rather than monetary income; and self-regulation of behavior. Professionalism is a matter of degree: the extent to which these attributes are present in an occupation defines its place on a scale of professionalism.[6]

Diplomacy was relatively weak as a specialized field of knowledge. Diplomatic practice unlike law or medicine required no prolonged and sophisticated intellectual training. Nevertheless, the precisely appropriate method of communicating the views of one's government required special knowledge and remained a mystery to the layman. Though by no means exclusively an intellectual endeavor, diplomacy required constant acquisition of various kinds of knowledge even in highly sophisticated and specialized fields. American diplomats never agreed on a set of fields peculiar to diplomacy but took as their intellectual province the broad area of human behavior that pertained to international relations.

The second attribute, public service, was always present among American diplomats, though in varying degree. Some early careerists were primarily interested in the social advantages of diplomacy, but usually a career required considerable sacrifice and occasional hardship. As to the service they provided, American diplomats claimed a general responsibility for accommodating differences between foreign governments and their own and for protection and advancement of American interests. By having to understand, explain, and thereby in a sense represent foreign views to their own gov-

6. Barber, "Sociology of the Professions," pp. 672–73. See also: Everett C. Hughes, "Professions," *Daedalus* XCII (1963), 655–68; Morris L. Cogan, "The Problem of Defining a Profession," *Ethical Standards and Professional Conduct, Annals of the American Academy of Political and Social Science* CCXCVII (1955), 105–11; Roy Lewis and Angus Maude, *Professional People* (London, 1952), chap. 4.

ernment, diplomats acquired an international character and even on occasion an additional role as international conciliator.

Income has never been one of the rewards of diplomacy. The high social prestige attached to diplomatic status was an attraction but not a mark of professional achievement, since all diplomats enjoyed it. The rewards lay in becoming ambassador or minister. The chief of mission had a particular aura as representative of the sovereign person or state. Gaining a good share of the top posts for careerists was vitally important to professional development.

Self-regulation was far more prevalent than appears on the surface. Corporate consciousness developed early in American career diplomacy and persisted through construction of the Foreign Service and its subsequent reorganization. Elites and leaders emerged to secure key administrative positions enabling them to guard against encroachment and resist misguided reforms. They sought to win public support for professional diplomacy and even managed to secure legislation recognizing the autonomy of the Foreign Service and providing for a measure of self-regulation. Diplomats took a hand in establishing personnel policies, passing on candidates, and deciding promotions. They organized a nongovernmental association that on occasion served as a means of defining and representing their organized professional interests. In their attitudes toward their work and toward the Foreign Service, diplomats displayed a high sense of individual responsibility. To a significant extent they acted as a peer group.

Over time, career diplomacy shifted from a low point on the scale of professionalism to the middle range. At the beginning professionalism was an idea, a name, and a status symbol. As the system became less socially exclusive, the status factor declined in importance and professional ideology and behavior emerged in sufficient strength to affect the administration of the service. In other words, career diplomacy evolved according to a professional as well as a bureaucratic pattern.

This duality was not peculiar. The trend in business and government was for more professionals to work in bureaucratic settings. In government the two modes of organization had a number of common assumptions: universalistic criteria of judgment, emotional detachment, specialization, preferment by achievement, and public service motivation.[7] In addition, diplomats depended on bureaucracy for a career structure that provided them authority, position, and recognition. Occupying positions in an organizational hierarchy, they were bureaucrats as well as professionals.

At the same time there were grounds for incompatibility. The intellectual universe of the diplomat in the field and that of his superior in Washington were different, and the type of specialization deemed necessary was not always the same. The fact that the diplomat found all his professional associations within the Foreign Service and not partly elsewhere, as would the lawyer working for government, made for greater professional solidarity and capacity to resist bureaucracy. Above all, the authority structure of the two patterns was different, the bureaucratic based on disciplined obedience to orders of a superior and the professional characterized by implicit sanctions, individual responsibility, and peer group control.[8] These differences made for conflict.

Insofar as the bureaucratic and professional patterns were congruent, adaptation was easy; but when they conflicted, change was accompanied by tension and crisis. The result

7. Blau and Scott, *Formal Organizations,* pp. 60–63. On the relation between bureaucratic and professional forms of organization, see also: Robert C. Stone, "The Sociology of Bureaucracy and Professions," in Joseph S. Rouček, *Readings in Contemporary American Sociology* (Paterson, N.J., 1961), 491–506; Amitai Etzioni, *Modern Organizations* (Englewood Cliffs, N.J., 1964), chap. 8.

8. Blau and Scott, *Formal Organizations,* pp. 62–63.

might be ascendancy of one pattern or the other, or a compromise of the two, or a standoff. Over time, the inherent advantages and limitations of both patterns righted any imbalance. In other words, internal conflict might impede the functioning of the organization in the short run but assisted it in the long run. Thus the organization tended toward structural stability. This conceptual framework provides a more precise and comprehensive explanation of the development of American career diplomacy.

The Beginnings of Careerism, 1893–1917

The growing power of the United States at the end of the nineteenth century was not reflected in its representation abroad. As late as 1893, it had no ambassadors and fewer secretaries of legation than ministers. For consular work in important cities abroad the government employed full-time, salaried American officials, but in a larger number of small cities and ports it engaged Americans and foreign nationals on a part-time basis, permitting them to engage in outside business and compensating them with small salaries or the fees they collected in performing consular services. The top salary of a minister was $10,000, of a secretary $2,625, and of a consul $5,000, and the average was considerably less. The only allowance was five cents a mile for travel. Every appointment was to a particular post, and no appointment guaranteed tenure. The foreign services lacked permanency, adequate or uniform salary scales, provision for selection and promotion by merit, and retirement compensation—in short, any suggestion of a career system. It is true that many consuls and a few diplomats managed to retain their posts from one administration to the next or return to them when their party came back to power, but they were exceptions. Patronage was the rule. Every four years the shifting tides of

American politics deposited a new set of officials on foreign shores. Managing American foreign relations was a State Department of seventy-seven persons including messengers, with a budget of $131,500.[9]

Beginning in 1893 when Congress authorized the appointment of the first ambassadors, these quaint arrangements gradually gave way to modern systems. During the following quarter-century, war, empire, and trade expansion increased the volume and complexity of American activity abroad and public awareness of its significance. The need for improvement was widely acknowledged. Three principle themes are distinguishable in reform sentiment. Most widely held was the conviction that career services would protect and enlarge American markets abroad by attracting and retaining carefully selected and experienced officers. Second, civil service reformers contributed their support, viewing the foreign service as a desirable extension of the merit system. Finally, many argued that an improved foreign service establishment would enhance American dignity and prestige. Both the Diplomatic and Consular services felt the impact of these ideas. Reorganization proceeded steadily until by 1917 each had a distinct career system. However, reform sentiment played on the two services with varying emphasis, and each responded according to its character and mission. The Consular Service was the more in demand and reformed itself more quickly and thoroughly. It became the model foreign affairs system to which the sister service was expected to conform, and the pattern it set was thoroughly bureaucratic.

Consular work lent itself to bureaucratic solutions. Consuls moved in a world of specifics, issuing and certifying documents, assisting Americans in distress, or investigating poten-

9. Katherine Crane, *Mr. Carr of State: Forty-Seven Years in the Department of State* (New York, 1960), p. 21; Department of State, *Register of the Department of State, 1898* (Washington, 1898).

tial markets. Mostly they applied laws and regulations to particular cases. With such concrete, routine, and yet variegated functions, the more an officer specialized in one or several duties the more knowledgeable and proficient he and his clerks became, with resulting improvement in the quantity and quality of work. The larger offices could more effectively accomplish their business by subdividing into sections for commerce, visas, shipping, citizenship, and so forth, and the sections by subdividing to the point where a particular desk assumed a single function. Distinctions of rank between consul general, consul, and vice-consul facilitated a bureaucratic distribution of responsibility. The hierarchy of offices, from consulate general to consular agency, also provided a means of subdividing consular work in the host country into easily coordinated and supervised districts. With offices scattered all over the world, including colonial areas, consuls had little opportunity for familiarity with each other and relationships tended to be formal.[10]

The needs of the Consular Service coincided with the main currents of reform sentiment. Shabby consulates and instances of corrupt, dissolute, and uncouth consuls offended the progressive's sense of civic virtue and national pride.[11] But the most powerful impetus for reform was business con-

10. G. Howland Shaw, "The American Foreign Service," *Foreign Affairs* XIV (1936), 327.

11. U.S. Congress, House of Representatives, *Report of the Honorable Herbert H. D. Peirce on Inspection of United States Consulates in the Orient,* H. Doc. No. 665, 59th Cong., 1st Sess. (Washington, 1906); Editorial, *Independent* LII (1900), 561; E. L. Godkin, "Consular Reform," *Nation* LXI (1895), 218; Editorial, *ibid.*, LXXXI (1905), 67; "Our Consular Disgrace," *ibid.*, LXXXII (1906), 274; "Good Work for 'Good Americans,'" *ibid.* LVIII (1894), 247–48; William F. Wharton, "Reform in the Consular Service," *North American Review* CLVIII (1894), 412–22; Francis B. Loomis, "The Foreign Service of the United States," *ibid.* CLXIX (1899), 350–51; Francis B. Loomis, "Proposed Reorganization of the American Consular Service," *ibid.* CLXXXII (1906), 361; Julian Ralph, "A Monopoly to Our Rescue," *Harper's Weekly* XLIII (1899), 472; Editorial, *ibid.* XLIX (1905), 1922; "Consular Reform," *Outlook* LXV (1900), 203; "Consular Reform," *ibid.* LXX (1902), 167–68; "The Consular Service and the Spoils System," *Century* XLVIII (1896), 306–11.

cern for trade expansion. The consul as drummer for American trade was a persistent theme of reform literature. The constant turnover of political appointees, it was argued, and their general incompetence deprived business of accurate, up-to-date information about trade opportunities at a time when expanding foreign markets were crucial for prosperity and competition was keen. The United States required a permanent corps of specialists familiar with foreign conditions and practices.[12] Business became not only a client but a model. Patronage was wasteful. A merit system with careful selection, training, and supervision of recruits—in short, "businesslike" management—would ensure greater "efficiency."[13] In a broad sense, consular reform was one aspect of the fundamental restructuring of American society along bureaucratic lines. Especially in the Consular Service, because of the tangible services it rendered, expertness, continuity, and regularity would maximize return on investment.[14]

12. Gaillard Hunt, "To Reorganize the Foreign Service," *World's Work* III (1902), 1606–13; Louis E. Van Norman, "The Consular Service of the United States," *Chautauquan* XXXV (1902), 224–29; John Ball Osborne, "The American Consul and American Trade," *Atlantic* XCIX (1907), 161; J. Sloan Fassett, "Congress and the Consular Service," *American Review of Reviews* XXXIII (1906), 555–60; Harry A. Garfield, "The Business Man and the Consular Service," *Century* LX (1900), 268–71; Robert Adams, Jr., "Faults in Our Consular Service," *North American Review* CLVI (1893), 461–66; Henry White, "Consular Reforms," *ibid.* CLIX (1894), 711–21; Thomas R. Jernigan, "A Hindrance to Our Foreign Trade," *ibid.* CLXIII (1896), 443.
13. "Chance vs. Training in Appointments," Editorial, *Independent* LII (1900), 561–62; Harry A. Garfield, "The Remodeling of the Consular Service," *ibid.*, 658; E. L. Godkin, "The Tariff and the Consuls," *Nation* LVII (1893), 340; Edward J. Brundage, "Shall the Government Educate Its Commercial Agents?", *World Today* XVI (1909), 321–23; A. L. Bishop, "The Recent Reforms in the Consular Service of the United States," *Yale Review* XVI (1907), 41–43; Charles Dudley Warner, "Our Foreign Trade and Our Consular Service," *North American Review* CLXII (1896), 275–76; "Consular Reform," *Outlook* LXIV (1900), 247; "A More Businesslike Consular Service," *ibid.* CIX (1915), 250–51.
14. On the "efficiency craze" see Samuel Haber, *Efficiency and Uplift: Scientific Management in the Progressive Era, 1890–1920* (Chicago, 1964), pp. ix–xii, 99–116. Also Robert H. Wiebe, *The Search for Order, 1877–1920*

The State Department, which rarely finds a constituency of its own, responded eagerly to business interest in reform. The Department and its public looked at the problem somewhat differently, to be sure. Where businessmen would give the consul more work to do, administrative officers worried about his present burdens. From 1898 to 1913 foreign trade almost doubled and outgoing passengers more than quadrupled, burdening consuls with attendant invoices, registrations, protection cases, and other services.[15] As an index of the increasing volume of consular work, consular fees increased from $532,990 in 1898 to $1,613,835 in 1908.[16] But bureaucracy thrives on mission, as Willard Straight, fresh from service as consul general at Mukden, noted in a letter to the director of the Consular Service, Wilbur J. Carr. A more active role for the United States in China and South America, he wrote, should result in "considerable appropriations for, and added sympathy with, the creation of a sufficient and well organized foreign service." [17] Carr was well aware of the connection. He noted that consular Advance Sheets, daily trade bulletins that began appearing in 1898, created a favorable impression of what consuls could do and thereby "afforded a practical basis on which to demand a reorganization of the service." [18] Consequently, State Department officials actively encouraged business support and directed it into appropriate legislative channels. In articles, speeches,

---

(New York, 1967), chap. 6; Barry Dean Karl, *Executive Reorganization and Reform in the New Deal: The Genesis of Administrative Management, 1900–1939* (Cambridge, Mass., 1963), pp. 15–22; Frank Mann Stewart, *The National Civil Service Reform League: History, Activities, Problems* (Austin, 1929), pp. 84–90.

15. Table XVII, National Civil Service Reform League, *Report on the Foreign Service* (New York, 1919), p. 194.

16. Barnes and Morgan, *Foreign Service*, p. 155.

17. Willard Straight to Wilbur J. Carr, August 6, 1909, Carr Papers, Library of Congress.

18. Wilbur J. Carr, "The American Consular Service," *American Journal of International Law* I (1907), Part 2, 907–8.

and letters they stressed the need, as Carr put it, for "the development of this Governmental machinery to its highest state of efficiency in the battle for our proportionate share of the trade of the world." [19] In 1912 Assistant Secretary of State F. M. Huntington Wilson wrote over one thousand business organizations and another thousand newspapers soliciting support for a reform bill as a "matter of the greatest importance to our commerce and to the protection of the interests of our people abroad." [20]

No individual contributed more to the bureaucratic development of the foreign service than Wilbur J. Carr, in many ways the epitome of the bureaucrat. His career was a tribute to the merit system. An Ohio farm boy, he ventured forth to a commercial college to learn bookkeeping and shorthand and then after passing civil service exams entered the State Department as a clerk in 1892. By diligence and proficiency he rose through the hierarchy of clerks to become director of the Consular Service in 1909. Later he would be assistant secretary of state and finally minister to Czechoslovakia.[21] He worked in the same office of the old State Department building for thirty-four years.[22] Punctual, methodical, prudent, and disciplined, he was the typical bureaucrat. Consular work suited his mind well: it was "fascinating" to "take a collection of facts and apply to them principles of law." [23] He strove to introduce order and routine to the diverse and miscellaneous tasks of the Consular Service, starting a precedent file, writing an annotation of shipping acts, and revising the Consular Regulations. His was a world of

19. Draft of speech by Carr, n.d. [about 1910], Carr Papers.
20. File 120.1/21c, State Department Archives, National Archives. See also File 120.1/17,30, State Department Archives.
21. Crane, *Carr;* "The Little Father of the Consuls," *Saturday Evening Post* CXCV (January 27, 1923), 26.
22. "Interview with Herbert Hengstler in Commemoration of Wilbur J. Carr's Fortieth Year in the Department of State," *American Foreign Service Journal* IX (1932), 212.
23. Crane, *Carr,* p. 9.

figures, facts, cases. On one occasion, when serving on an oral examination board and noticing the candidate's jugular vein thumping under the tension, he took out his watch to count her pulse (120).[24] His own life was a search for maximum efficiency. He almost never lost his temper, but on one rare occasion when he did, he attributed it to the press of business, which

> caused my overstrained nerves of the brain to lose their power to coordinate, and created a condition quickly degenerating into passion. . . . This experience convinced me of two things. The loss occasioned by overstrain is most expensive and is economic waste.[25]

Carr was an exponent of scientific management. Government was a machine, and it was his function to make it run smoothly. His special responsibility was the Consular Service, and that organization, he would be proud to say in 1924, was "as near perfection as possible." [26]

To characterize Carr simply as a bureaucrat would be wrong. No faceless functionary could have transformed the foreign service as he did. A deeper understanding begins with the fact that he was an intensely ambitious person, eager for prominence in the political and diplomatic worlds of Washington. Ultimately his "great adventure," as he called it, might culminate in a significant policy-making role or an embassy. Yet at the same time he was acutely sensitive to the limitations of his little red schoolhouse background. He confided to his diary that he was "conscious always of an inferiority of preparation and of mind, lacking in information but by determination and endless hours of labor doing what better educated and more highly placed men had failed to

24. Carr Diary, January 20, 1925, Carr Papers.

25. *Ibid.*, October 19, 1919.

26. Joseph C. Grew to Hugh Gibson, June 5, 1924, Grew Papers, Houghton Library, Harvard University.

do." He took evening courses to secure a law degree and admission to the bar. Frequently he returned to the department at midnight to work several hours more. Exercises in self-improvement included Pliny, Aristophanes, Thucydides, Dante's *Inferno,* violin lessons, and the mandolin, altogether a Chautauquan conception of upper-class cultural attainments. However "comfortable" his clerkly niche seemed at times, Carr wanted something "greater." "Mere consular work" was dwarfing to the mind, he wrote in 1901. The pursuit of high office meant abandoning civil service security and exposing himself to political dismissal, however, and Carr was not prone to taking risks: "If only I did not have this curse of timidity . . . which apparently I have cultivated as a virtue until now it has come to deprive me of so much that I should give a great deal to have." [27] His problem was how to attain the high standing he cherished without risking the gains he had so painstakingly secured.

Carr's answer to his dilemma was to make himself indispensable. As chief of the Consular Bureau and director of the Consular Service, he secured absolute control over his specialty. All outgoing correspondence originated with him or passed across his desk. He retained final authority over promotions, transfers, and retirements. Needs and problems of consuls received his close and sympathetic attention. [28] He came to be a kind of father to the consular brood. One consul wrote him: "All of us have at times regarded you instead of the service as our employer." It was not a question of Carr's connection with the Consular Service, another consul recalled; he *was* the consular service. [29] At the same time Carr

27. Crane, *Carr,* pp. 6–7, 28, 146; Carr Diary, November 7, 1900, April 26, 1901, June 22, 1927, Carr Papers.

28. Crane, *Carr,* p. 131. On Carr's direction of the Consular Service and widening role in the department: *ibid.,* chaps. 7–17.

29. Stewart McMillan to Carr, August 21, 1924, Carr Papers; Crane, *Carr,* p. 122.

extended his influence laterally in the department by accepting fiscal and budgetary responsibilities. With grasp of the department's financial threads went knowledge of all its workings and assignment to appear before congressional appropriations committees. Patient, helpful, expert, economy-minded, he made an excellent impression on the Hill. With this strategic position inside the State Department and his relations with the business community on reform and with Congress on reform, appropriations, and constituents' problems of trade and travel, Carr amassed extraordinary power. In 1920 he was described to the new secretary of state, Bainbridge Colby, as the "backbone" of the department.[30] Secretaries of state could scarcely afford to carry on without him.

Carr's fiefdom in the department had an archaic personal quality about it, yet his role had great significance for bureaucratic development. He had to systematize the Consular Service to free himself from what he called "desk slavery." [31] As chief of the Consular Bureau, he trained an assistant to take over routine functions so he could concentrate on control and change. Bureaucratic solutions not only opened the way for him to broaden the scope of his responsibilities but also enabled him to mould the Consular Service to his image. Given a free hand by Secretaries Elihu Root and Philander C. Knox, he was in a position to effect radical change in procedure and organization. Furthermore, his position opened a new management echelon between the clerks, who would never escape their narrow spheres, and the assistant secretaries, who seldom remained long enough to understand, let alone change, the system. Thus Carr was a key figure in the transition to modern bureaucratic organization.

30. Carr Diary, March 23, 1920, Carr Papers.
31. *Ibid.*, January 31, 1925.

Acts of 1906 and 1915, an Executive Order of 1906, and Carr's innovations radically reorganized the Consular Service. Classification of consulates according to importance, assignment of specific territory to each, and increase in the numbers and supervisory functions of consulates general brought about a more rational division of labor and tighter control. Reduction in the number of hybrid offices, consular agencies and the like, more appropriate location of offices, provision of standard equipment and furniture, assignment of American clerks, replacement of fee compensation by salaries, and prohibition of outside business activity enhanced the official and American character of consulates. Introduction of the fee stamp system ensured honest accounting of funds. Most important in standardizing the service and raising its quality was the establishment of an inspection corps. Inspectors set forth on biennial rounds with thirty-page schedules devised by Carr that inquired exhaustively into the management and expenditures of offices. They rated officers on a scale of 100 for honesty, morality, sobriety, standing, force, and loyalty, as well as more tangible qualities. Appointment to class rather than post and provision for service in Washington allowed greater flexibility in assignment and broader experience. Entrance by written and oral examination at the two lowest grades and promotion on the basis of experience and efficiency records all but eliminated political jobbery. New officers received a month of orientation before going overseas. Tenure, the merit system, transportation allowances, and higher salaries offered young men substantial inducements to make a career.[32] All in all, the Consular Service developed according to a classical bureaucratic pattern.

32. Department of State, *Register, 1898, Register of the Department of State, 1915* (Washington, 1915); Lay, *Foreign Service*, pp. 287–88; Barnes and Morgan, *Foreign Service*, pp. 162–77; Crane, *Carr*, pp. 82–112, 121–26.

To a degree the Diplomatic Service grew according to the same pattern. Diplomatic secretaries tripled in number between 1898 and 1918, from thirty-one to ninety-seven; every mission received at least one and the larger embassies from three to seven.[33] As numbers increased, the pyramid of offices enlarged with the addition of counselors of embassy and second and third secretaries. During World War I busy embassies subdivided into sections, and senior secretaries emerged as administrative officers.[34] Like consuls, diplomats gained transportation and post allowances, a merit system of admission and promotion, and appointment to classes instead of posts. Congress permitted modest attempts to secure government-owned embassies and legations and, under Presidents Roosevelt and Taft, approved a significant number of promotions of secretaries to ministerships and even ambassadorships. No less than eighteen of Taft's chiefs of mission came from the lower service. The creation of geographical divisions in the State Department (the first being the Far Eastern Division in 1908), the introduction of a new filing system, instructions for more comprehensive reporting, the establishment of a student interpreter corps for Japan and China, and the beginnings of a training period for new officers suggest the systematization and specialization characteristic of bureaucratic development.[35]

There similarities end. The organization of American di-

33. Department of State, *Register, 1898,* and *1915.*

34. Waldo H. Heinrichs, Jr., *American Ambassador: Joseph C. Grew and the Development of the United States Diplomatic Tradition* (Boston, 1966), pp. 22–23. For a description of the division of labor in a typical embassy see the testimony of J. Butler Wright, U.S. Congress, House of Representatives, Committee on Foreign Affairs, *Foreign Service of the United States, Hearings on H.R. 17 and 6357,* 68th Cong., 1st Sess (Washington, 1924), p. 71.

35. Barnes and Morgan, *Foreign Service,* pp. 142–47, 155–57, 165–86, 195; "The Far Eastern Division," *American Foreign Service Journal* IX (1932), 385–90; Consul General James B. Stewart, "Foreign Service Officer Training School," *ibid.* X (1933), 224–27.

plomacy, such as it was, posed obstacles to bureaucratic change. The principle of appointing only career officers as heads of mission has never been accepted, and progress in that direction was wiped out by President Wilson's dismissal of nearly all of Taft's veterans.[36] The result was that career diplomats had no assurance that merit and experience would open a path out of the secretarial world. And a humble world it was. The highest diplomatic officer in the London embassy next to the ambassador received one-fourth the salary of the consul general.[37] Whereas in the Consular Service the differential between ranks was roughly the same, the gap in status and power between counselor or first secretary and ambassador or minister was enormous. Furthermore, since the head of mission was a creature of the president, not the secretary of state, he enjoyed considerable autonomy, making it difficult to manipulate offices and officers from Washington. Finally, no diplomatic figure emerged in the department with the power and permanence of Carr. A. A. Adee was a quaint reminder of the old days, more concerned with form than with system.[38] Huntington Wilson was an innovator comparable to Carr, but he was dismissed in the Democratic clean sweep of 1913, which Carr survived. William Phillips took an interest in diplomatic reform, but he was young and lacked forcefulness. As a result, the central control, inspection system, standardization of work, and rationalization of offices of the Consular Service did not carry over to the Diplomatic Service.

Diplomatic reform had to overcome deeply entrenched popular notions about diplomacy and diplomats that consular reform was largely spared. The America that was passing away clung to republican simplicity and was indifferent to,

36. Barnes and Morgan, *Foreign Service*, p. 184.
37. Department of State, *Register, 1915*.
38. Crane, *Carr*, chap. 5.

or unaware of, what happened abroad, if not profoundly suspicious of entanglement with Europe. The village mentality associated diplomacy with monarchy, aristocracy, intrigue, duplicity, and war. From this point of view those served best who served least, and political appointees by their very impermanence made the safest envoys. How much of this old view remained is difficult to determine, but reformers seemed painfully aware of it.[39] A modern version appeared in the notion that the advent of the cable made diplomacy obsolete. As Mr. Dooley said, "If me frind President Tiddy wants to know what's goin' on annywhere, all he has to do is subscribe to the pa-apers."[40] The reverse argument could be used against change as well. According to Edwin A. Grosvenor, the very importance of diplomacy made it necessary for the president to appoint men of his own mind, and no better preparation existed than "the practical school of American politics." In engaging foreign nations, "the American stroke is the stroke for us."[41] Out of their own limited view of American political interests abroad or perhaps in recognition of the strength of old prejudices, reform-

39. Perrin Galpin, ed., *Hugh Gibson, 1883–1954* (New York, 1956), p. 27; Edward G. Lowry, "Bryan's Diplomatic Appointments," *Colliers* LII (February 7, 1914), 9; An Anglo-American, "American Ambassadors Abroad," *North American Review* CXCVIII (1913), 310; An American Diplomat, "The Diplomatic Service: Its Organization and Demoralization," *Outlook* CVI (1914), 533; David Jayne Hill, "Why Do We Have a Diplomatic Service," *Harper's* CXXVIII (1914), 191; Hill, "Shall We Standardize Our Diplomatic Service?", *ibid.*, 690–98; Hill, "Can Our Diplomatic Service Be Made More Efficient?", *ibid.* CXXX (1915), 190–98; "Plush Pants," *Harper's Weekly* LIII (June 26, 1909), 6; "Our Legations Abroad," *Independent* LXIV (1908), 763; "Our Need For a Permanent Diplomatic Service," *Forum* XXV (1898), 702–11.

40. "A More Self-Respecting Diplomatic Service," *Outlook* XCVII (1911), 379; Henry Loomis Nelson, "The Need of Trained Diplomats and Consuls," *Harper's Weekly* XLV (1901), 599; "Literature and Diplomacy," *Nation* LXX (1900), 394; E. L. Godkin, "Ambassadors," *ibid.* LVI (1893), 247; Finley Peter Dunne, "Our Representatives Abroad," *Dissertations by Mr. Dooley* (New York, 1906), pp. 92–93.

41. Edwin A. Grosvenor, "American Diplomacy," *American Historical Association Annual Report* (New York, 1898), pp. 294, 299.

ers seldom alluded to the argument that expert representation abroad was more likely to preserve peace and protect
national security in a dangerous world.[42]

The same reform impulses that provided a favorable environment for change in the Consular Service helped overcome these prejudices and facilitate reform in the Diplomatic
Service as well. Both services received examination systems
simultaneously in 1905, and both gained a system of appointments to grades rather than to particular posts by the Stone-
Flood Act of 1915. Reformers emphasized the need in diplomacy no less than in consular work for expertness and
efficiency, acquired by training, specialization, and permanence. They stressed that diplomats no less than consuls
assisted in trade expansion.[43]

Pressure for reform of the Diplomatic Service, however,
was weaker. The merit system for diplomatic secretaries
lagged three years behind that for consuls, and it was only
at the insistence of the administration that the Diplomatic
Service was included in the reforms achieved in 1915.[44] Business remained primarily concerned with consular reform,
from which it expected more immediate and tangible re-

42. Those who did present this argument: Nelson, "The Need of Trained
Diplomats and Consuls," p. 599; An American Diplomat, "The Diplomatic
Service," p. 534; "Merit and Diplomacy," *Outlook* LXXXV (1907), 212;
Perry Belmont, "The First Line of National Defense," *North American Re-
view* CCI (1915), 886; Ilchman, *Professional Diplomacy*, pp. 52–53.

43. "Chance vs. Training in Appointments," *Independent* LII (1900),
561–62; "Our Diplomatic Service," *ibid.* LXXXI (1915), 446; Godkin,
"Ambassadors," 246–47; "Our Diplomatic Service," *Forum* LVI (1916),
611–18; Hill, "Can Our Diplomatic Service Be Made More Efficient?",
196–97; John Barrett, "An American School of Diplomacy," *Harper's Weekly*
XLIV (March 3, 1900), 193–94; "The First Year of the Wilson Administra-
tion," *Outlook* CVI (1914), 523–25; "For Efficiency, Not Wealth, in the
Diplomatic Service," *American Review of Reviews* XLVII (1913), 750–51;
James D. Whelpley, "Our Disorganized Diplomatic Service," *Century*
LXXXVII (1913), 123–27; "The Diplomatic Service," *Nation* LXXXIX
(1909), 398; An American Diplomat, "The Diplomatic Service," pp. 533–58;
Ilchman, *Professional Diplomacy*, p. 55.

44. Ilchman, *Professional Diplomacy*, pp. 106–7.

sults.[45] The National Civil Service Reform League also worried less about diplomatic than consular reform, and in 1913 limited itself to recommending establishment of a "merit tradition" in the appointment of envoys, while insisting on elimination of the spoils system elsewhere in the services.[46] In effect, the Diplomatic Service hitchhiked on the consular reform movement. It achieved its career system, yet remained somewhat shaded from the public values that encouraged bureaucratic solutions on the consular side.

The Diplomatic Service did not lack a distinctive reform theme. Again and again, the pages of magazines such as the *Nation, Independent, Outlook, Harper's,* and *North American Review* reflected concern over the impression made on foreigners by American envoys and their quarters. Writers warned that European governments viewed the ambassador as the "incarnation of national sovereignty" and laid much stress on outward appearances of rank and power. In this light the American representative cut a sorry figure. He lived in "conspicuous shabbiness" on a salary reflecting his government's "ostentatious parsimony." Often incompetent, ignorant of foreign ways and languages, even of "the ordinary usages of polite society," he became the laughing stock of the community. It was a "humiliating," "mortifying" condition. Ostentatious wealth seemed equally out of keeping with the character of the nation. The appointment of "dollar diplomats" smacked of plutocracy. America required salaries, allowances, residences, and offices adequate to maintain the dignity and self-respect of a great nation and allow its ablest citizens to serve. James Monroe was quoted in the *Arena* as advising:

45. Nelson, "The Need of Trained Diplomats and Consuls," p. 599; William Phillips, "Cleaning Our Diplomatic House," *Forum* LXIII (1920), 167; Ilchman, *Professional Diplomacy,* p. 70.

46. National Civil Service Reform League, *Report,* pp. 148–50.

A minister can be useful only by filling his place with credit in the diplomatic corps, and in the corresponding circle of society in the country where he resides, which is the best in every country. By taking the proper ground, if he possesses the proper qualifications, and is furnished with adequate means, he will become acquainted with all that passes. . . . Deprive him of the necessary means to sustain the ground, separate him from the circle to which he belongs, and he is reduced to a cypher.[47]

The period from 1893 to 1917 was the heyday of what might be called prestige diplomacy. In 1905 John Bassett Moore noted "a visible tendency toward conformity to customs elsewhere established . . . accelerated by the natural drift of a great and self-conscious people toward participation in world affairs."[48] Mark Twain reflected this new self-consciousness when he wrote from Vienna in 1899 that the idea of an ill-paid American ambassador was ludicrous, "a billionaire in a paper collar, a king in a breech clout, an archangel in a tin halo." America had come of age, he said, like a young girl reaching eighteen, who "adds six inches to her skirt . . . has a room to herself, and becomes in many

47. "Permanent Housing for Diplomats," *American Review of Reviews* XLIII (1911), 693; "Rich and Poor Ambassadors," *Literary Digest* XLVI (1913), 760; "American Diplomacy," *Nation* LVI (1893), 251; H. C. Chatfield-Taylor, "American Diplomats in Europe," *North American Review* CLXIII (1896), 125–28; Captain F. M. Barber, "The Government Ownership of Diplomatic and Consular Buildings," *ibid.* CXC (1909), 359; "Our Diplomatic Service," *Outlook* LXXXIII (1906), 309; "American Representatives Abroad," *ibid.* LXXXVIII (1908), 844–45; "The Kaiser, the Towers, and Mr. Hill," *ibid.* 806–7; Elizabeth Ballister Bates, "The Etiquette of American Diplomats," *Independent* LIV (1902), 2650; Editorial, "The Salaries of Our Diplomats," *ibid.* LXIII (1907), 580–82; Nicholas Longworth, "Bettering Our Diplomatic Service," *ibid.* LXI (1906), 19–23; "Our Ambassadors Abroad: The Embassy in France," *Harper's Weekly* XLIV (1900), 506; "Our Ambassadors Abroad: The Embassy at Rome," *ibid.* 754–55; Frances Benjamin Johnston, "The Eagle's Perch Abroad," *ibid.* LI (1907), 726–30; Sydney Brooks, "Our Embassy in London," *ibid.* LVII (1913), 11, and "Two Embassies," *ibid.* LVIII (1913), 7–8; Herbert H. D. Peirce, "Our Diplomatic and Consular Services," *Arena* XVII (1897), 916.

48. John Bassett Moore, "American Diplomacy: Its Influence and Tendencies," *Harper's* CXI (1905), 695.

ways a thundering expense. But she is in society now and papa has to stand it; there is no avoiding it." The *Nation* agreed: "If we are going into the game we must play it according to the rules." [49]

This concern for a proper American diplomatic establishment manifested itself most strongly in genteel magazines read by families of the old upper and upper middle classes. *Harper's Weekly* was only describing its readers when it said that the demand for diplomatic reform originated in the "politer" East. Similarly, *Outlook* found the origins among "more educated, and therefore more thoughtful people." [50] The readers were well-to-do, old-stock, Anglo-Saxon Americans in established businesses and professions, who regarded themselves as guardians of American traditions of public life. Among them were urban elites with the cosmopolitan outlook and additional wealth and status to mix in European court society, and who were accordingly most sensitive to America's image abroad. In this restricted environment of "seasoned wealth and seasoned conscience," to use Richard Hofstadter's happy phrase, the Diplomatic Service found its own constituency.[51]

E. L. Godkin's "respectable classes" looked on diplomacy as their special preserve. They believed in public servants of intellect and integrity, above selfish interest and party greed, in short, of the "better elements" of society themselves.[52] In a swiftly modernizing America one of the few

49. Mark Twain, "Diplomatic Pay and Clothes," 1899, reprinted in *Forum* XCV (1936), 137; "The Ambassadorship Muddle," *Nation* LXXXVI (1908), 298.

50. "Plush Pants," *Harper's Weekly* LIII (June 26, 1909), 6; "Uncle Sam's Tin Halo," *Outlook* CXXVII 1921), 253.

51. American residents in London increased in numbers by about thirty percent in the years 1899–1900 alone, according to Richard H. Heindel, *The American Impact on Great Britain* (Philadelphia, 1940), p. 47 n. 1. *The Age of Reform: From Bryan to F.D.R.* (New York, 1956), 139.

52. Haber, *Efficiency and Uplift*, pp. 99–102.

paths of public service not requiring a radical change of life style and values was diplomacy. The idea of diplomacy as a profession interested them. They noted that Europe considered it a profession, and they likened it to the army, the navy, law, medicine, and architecture. Diplomacy, if it provided a career, would be an honored calling suitable for sons of the best families. They were not sure about qualifications, but some spoke of diplomacy as a science, requiring special training. Others stressed experience, using the analogy of the sailor, whose seamanship came not only from a host of skills but also from weathering many gales. They stressed special aptitudes as well, such as intellect, character, personality, and social skills, which only the home and school provided.[53] When they visualized the career diplomat, they saw themselves or their sons. The connection was made explicitly by a career diplomat when he described the kind of recruits the Diplomatic Service should seek. They should come from "homes with tradition," said Hugh Gibson: "Some of them are simple homes—no butlers or footmen—but where the boys go to college—the bills are paid—Sunday observed, good books read, and where a standard obtains in respect to private life and public policies." Another diplomat put it this way: "We want men in our foreign service to represent the good will and good breeding of their country." [54] The origins and agents of prestige diplomacy had much in common.

In sum, two strains are evident in the movement for diplomatic reform. One was forward-looking, responding to the

53. G. L. Rives, "Our Need for a Permanent Diplomatic Service," *Forum* XXV (1898), 702–711; F. M. Huntington Wilson, "Improving the American Diplomat," *Harper's Weekly* LVI (August 24, 1912), 21; Wilson, "The American Foreign Service," *Outlook* LXXXII (1906), 499–501; Hill, "Shall We Standardize Our Diplomatic Service?", pp. 690–98; Belmont, "The First Line of National Defense," p. 886.

54. Galpin, ed., *Gibson*, p. 97; Francis B. Loomis, "The Foreign Service of the United States," p. 351.

dominant impulses of the progressive movement, emphasizing the rational organization and special skills of the modern bureaucratic society. The other looked backward, stressing individual qualities and elite rule, a last vestige of mugwumpery.[55] The progressive strain had the momentum and broad appeal to provide the formal definition of the new career, but the elite strain provided the wealth and motivation to staff it. Which strain would predominate only time would tell, but the diplomatic careerists possessed one crucial advantage, their indispensability. The continuity of Republican administrations from 1897 to 1913, the introduction of the merit system, the survival of the secretarial service under the Democrats, and the exigencies of World War I ensured that able recruits could remain and acquire skill. Since only the wealthy could afford to serve, no administration could afford to dispense with staff that knew the ropes. Consequently, the careerists were in a strategic position to define their role themselves.

Professionalism took hold among diplomatic secretaries who entered the service during the period 1893–1917. Theirs was a peculiar sort of professionalism, shadowy and incomplete in many respects, and somewhat spurious. Nonetheless, it had a distinct meaning and character that carried into the future. It derived from the background of the officers, their motivations in pursuing diplomacy, and their occupational and group experiences in the service.

It was an overwhelmingly upper-class group. Illustrating this fact are the following examples of secretaries who went on to become ministers and ambassadors. The wealth of Joseph C. Grew, later ambassador to Japan, derived from

55. For a definition of the mugwump outlook, see Geoffrey Blodgett, *The Gentle Reformers: Massachusetts Democrats in the Cleveland Era* (Cambridge, Mass., 1966), 33–47.

the wool business, the China trade, and western mining, and his wife, a Boston Perry and Cabot, had her own resources. As secretary at Berlin, he spent $15,000 a year on a salary of less than $3,000.[56] Ten thousand dollars a year in private income was considered the minimum necessary to support a bachelor secretary.[57] Peter Jay was a descendant of John Jay, and pre–Civil War railroad fortunes stood behind John W. Garrett and Leland Harrison.[58] Chicago meat-packing and soap manufacturing underwrote the careers of Norman Armour and Alexander Kirk.[59] Lloyd Griscom's family, descended from original Philadelphia Quakers, flourished anew in rails, oil, and shipping, and boasted liveried coachmen.[60] One grandfather of John Van Antwerp MacMurray, later minister to China, had founded an iron works in St. Louis, and the other, a descendant of original Dutch settlers, was a prosperous Albany banker.[61] One grandfather of Arthur Bliss Lane had built a $2,500,000 business, and the other was a successful cotton broker.[62] Corporation law and castor oil ("Castoria—Children Cry For It") set up Robert Woods Bliss in diplomacy, the Knickerbocker Club, and Dumbarton Oaks.[63] Irwin Laughlin was treasurer of Jones and Laughlin Steel Company at thirty-three when he entered diplomacy.

56. Heinrichs, *Grew*, pp. 3, 9, 16.

57. J. Pierrepont Moffat to Charles C. Curtis, December 14, 1927, Moffat Papers, Houghton Library, Harvard University.

58. On Harrison's grandfather see E. Digby Baltzell, *Philadelphia Gentlemen: The Making of a National Upper Class* (New York, 1958), 183–84.

59. On Kirk see George Kennan, *Memoirs, 1925–1950* (Boston, 1967), 112–15.

60. Lloyd C. Griscom, *Diplomatically Speaking* (New York, 1940), p. 8; Lloyd Griscom Transcript, Columbia Oral History Collection, Columbia University Library.

61. "Register of the Collection," p. 40, John Van Antwerp MacMurray Papers, Princeton University Library.

62. John A. Sylvester, "Arthur Bliss Lane, American Career Diplomat," (Ph.D. Dissertation, University of Wisconsin, 1967), p. 1.

63. Drew Pearson and Robert S. Allen, *Washington Merry-Go-Round* (New York, 1931), p. 144.

William Phillips, whose great uncle was Wendell Phillips, became financially independent at twenty-one.[64]

Most of these budding career diplomats had strikingly similar backgrounds. The typical recruit came from an upper-class stronghold such as New York, Boston, Philadelphia, Baltimore, or Chicago. He received a private early education with tutors, in a day school, or at a New England or European boarding school. Three New Yorkers, Sheldon Whitehouse, Peter Jay, and Leland Harrison, attended Eton. Usually the diplomatic secretary was a graduate of Harvard, Yale, or Princeton, one in three being a Harvard man. Several went on to the Ecole des Sciences Politiques. It was a small and probably self-conscious minority that did not receive some form of fashionable education.[65]

The boarding school performed a number of important functions. Generally the wealth of these young men had seasoned for at least a generation, but where acquisition was in the immediate background, the school was a means of upper-class ascription and acculturation. Hugh Wilson worked in his family's shirt manufacturing firm and knew where his money came from, but thanks to Hill School, Yale, and diplomacy felt comfortable about understanding "instinctively the social gradations . . . of any cosmopolitan group." Also, Groton and schools like it, by gathering in the

64. William Phillips Transcript, Columbia Oral History Collection.

65. Based on biographical statements on all diplomatic secretaries who served in Europe between 1898 and 1914 in Department of State, *Register, 1915.* Also *Who's Who in America* and *Dictionary of American Biography.* Of these ninety-five officers, information about colleges attended was available for sixty-three. Twenty-two attended Harvard and thirteen Yale or Princeton. Information about secondary schooling was available for only thirty of the sixty-three, of whom twenty-eight listed private schools, St. Paul's, St. Mark's, Groton, and Lawrenceville, in particular. Ilchman (*Professional Diplomacy,* pp. 170–71), working with secretaries recruited between 1914 and 1922, found that 72.3 percent attended boarding schools, that 84 percent received some form of private secondary education, and that 73.9 percent attended an Ivy League college. In my group of sixty-three, 85 percent received some form of fashionable education, including college as well as secondary school.

sons of city-bound elites, fostered a common upper-class identity, as did the college and its clubs.[66]

The boarding school way of life, modeled on the English public school, tended to encourage a professional rather than a bureaucratic orientation. The Grotonian—loyal, orderly, disciplined, imperturbable, formalistic—would seem well suited to bureaucratic life, and in these respects he was. In other respects he was not. Like his English counterpart bred to the idea of the gentleman amateur, he shied away from expertness and specialization. Viewing leadership in traditional or charismatic terms, he was essentially prebureaucratic. He learned to conform, but to an internalized gentlemanly code rather than to formal, explicit rules. The professional idea, with its implicit sanctions, avowedly ethical pursuit, sense of corporate identity, and mystique, would better fit private-school expectations. On the other hand, a reliance on taste, common sense, intuition, and instinct, and a disdain for theorizing and speculation, would not carry the Groton or Eton mind far into the intellectual realm of professional activity.[67]

As with any walk of life, it is difficult to generalize about why these men entered diplomacy. Most of them probably had no idea of devoting their lives to it because it offered no realistic prospect of success in terms of ministerships and ambassadorships.[68] Rather, diplomacy often represented a career rejection. Hugh Wilson claimed that a life in business held no appeal to young men of his background because

66. Baltzell, *Philadelphia Gentlemen*, pp. 293, 303; Hugh R. Wilson, *Diplomacy as a Career* (Cambridge, Mass., 1941), p. 33.

67. For a study of English public school values and their relation to government service, see Rupert Wilkinson, *Gentlemanly Power* (London, 1964), especially Parts I and II. Wilkinson does not make the distinction made here between professional and bureaucratic modes. Weber, *Theory of Social and Economic Organization*, pp. 328–41; Baltzell, *Philadelphia Gentlemen*, pp. 303, 316–17; Heinrichs, *Grew*, pp. 4–5.

68. Harold J. Coolidge and Robert H. Lord, *Archibald Cary Coolidge, Life and Letters* (Boston, 1932), p. 17.

ease and education made it difficult for them to understand the grimness with which their fathers pursued the amassing of fortunes. "If you ever hear of me starting in on State Street," Grew wrote a friend, "please send flowers as the end will not be far off." [69] Diplomacy more often than not was a second or third start. One in three attended law school first but undoubtedly found the law confining or simply boring, as Phillips did. [70] They also found their communities confining. Life at Albany, bound by a set of "provincial ideas," seemed "narrowing and numbing" to MacMurray. A Brahmin life in Boston looked pallid to Phillips. [71] According to Hofstadter, American provincial city elites suffered status loss at the end of the nineteenth century because "the arena for prestige, like the market for commodities, had been widened to embrace the entire nation." [72] Local social eminence counted for less with this generation. They went shopping for something interesting and more rewarding.

Diplomacy brought these young men into the national scene, and by a more genteel route than politics. At the least it would keep them decently occupied, as parents and society demanded, while they savored the life of European courts and satisfied their yen for travel. [73] There was an appeal to youthful idealism as well. The idea that the rich and well-born had an obligation to serve their nation, one constantly affirmed and exemplified by Theodore Roosevelt, was assiduously cultivated at schools like Groton. America's

69. Hugh Wilson, *Education of a Diplomat* (New York, 1938), pp. 2–4; Grew to Hugh Gibson, September 15, 1922, Grew Papers.

70. Department of State, *Register, 1915;* Phillips Transcript, Columbia Oral History Collection.

71. MacMurray to his mother, February 9, 1902, MacMurray Papers; Phillips, *Ventures in Diplomacy* (Boston, 1952), pp. 5–6.

72. Hofstadter, *Age of Reform,* p. 138.

73. MacMurray to his mother, May 6, 1902, MacMurray Papers; Wilson, *Diplomacy as a Career,* p. 2; Heinrichs, *Grew,* p. 8; Griscom, *Diplomatically Speaking,* chaps. 3–6; Coolidge and Lord, *Coolidge,* pp. 17–18.

emergence as an imperial power provided a natural focus
for such idealism in service abroad.[74] The ambitious sought
to satisfy a craving for national recognition but lacked a
Baedecker to point the way. A number of paths lay open,
including colonial administration and consular work as well
as diplomacy. A man might take one path and shift to another depending on opportunities. Indeed, Roosevelt felt it
would be debilitating for a young man to play at courtier
diplomacy too long.[75] Somewhere ahead lay a governor general's palace perhaps, or an embassy.[76] With no more precise
notion of what they were about than Kipling provided,
America's favored sons began working at diplomacy.

At his first posts the novice found more of a family than an
office. The embassy was a social unit, and the wife was no
less important than the officer in maintaining its standing in
the diplomatic community. Originally the secretary was part
of the ambassador's household if not actually his son, as was
the case with generations of Adamses. Some of the old feeling persisted and merged with the boarding school idea of
surrogate family, the ambassador and his wife carrying on
the father and mother roles of the Reverend and Mrs. Endi-
cott Peabody.[77] The rhythm of work defied scheduling. When
there was no work to be done, the diplomat was not supposed
to pretend to work.[78] Sport and other leisurely pursuits led to

74. Interview with G. Howland Shaw, January 6, 1959; Shaw, "American Foreign Service," p. 327; William Phillips Transcript, Columbia Oral
History Collection; Phillips, *Ventures in Diplomacy*; Heinrichs, *Grew*, pp.
8–9.

75. Ilchman, *Professional Diplomacy*, p. 88.

76. William Franklin Sands, "Basil Miles: An Appreciation," *American
Foreign Service Journal* VII (1930), 79–80.

77. Baltzell, *Philadelphia Gentlemen*, p. 303; Harold Nicholson, "The
British Foreign Service," *American Foreign Service Journal* XIII (1936),
430. On "family" feeling in the Diplomatic Service: Interview with William
Phillips, November 17, 1958; Frederick Dolbeare to Ellis L. Dresel, October
[?], 1920, Dresel Papers, Houghton Library, Harvard University; Diary of
Joseph C. Grew, July 3, 1915, Grew Papers.

78. Lord Strang, *The Foreign Office* (London, 1955), p. 99.

friendships with other secretaries that developed easily from common upper-class, boarding school, and Ivy League background. In a crisis everyone pitched in and worked twelve-, fifteen-, even twenty-hour days. In the case of the American embassy at Berlin, 1914–17, shared privations, constant tension, and an alien environment deepened group loyalty and internal cohesiveness.[79] Thus the embassy or legation, as a detached and isolated unit fusing social and occupational roles, developed primary group relations that supplied informal sanctions, loyalties, and procedures outside the formal organizational structure.[80]

As secretaries stayed on from one administration to the next, they shifted posts and enlarged acquaintance.[81] Occasionally they managed to move as a group and keep their "family" together, but in any case the service was becoming clannish.[82] With a good part of the world still colonial, nearly half of the secretaryships were in Europe, and it was convenient to visit neighboring embassies to renew acquaintance and exchange gossip. Assignment to Washington was also more frequent, and there, with other "sons of Empire" in Congress, the army, and colonial administration, they formed

79. Heinrichs, *Grew*, p. 23.

80. Charles Hunt Page, "Bureaucracy's Other Face," *Social Forces* XXV (1946–47), 89.

81. Whereas from 1867 to 1898 the secretary had only one chance in twelve of shifting posts, by 1914 four out of five had served in one or more mission. Nearly half of the prewar secretaryships were in Europe, so that by 1914 four-fifths of the secretaries on duty were serving in or had served in Europe. Diplomatic Service lists in the annual Department of State *Register* for the years 1867 to 1914 (Washington, 1867–1914).

82. One such "family" migrated as follows in the years 1915–21: Frederick Dolbeare: Vienna, Berne, Berlin; Allen Dulles: Vienna, Berne, Berlin; Ellis Dresel: Berlin, Berne, Berlin; Hugh Wilson: Berlin, Vienna, Berne, Berlin. Close ties are readily apparent in Grew's correspondence with Wilson, Gibson, J. Butler Wright, and Ulysses Grant-Smith in the Grew Papers, in the Dresel-Gibson and Dresel-Dolbeare correspondence in the Dresel Papers, in the correspondence of Gibson, Hugh S. Gibson Papers, Hoover Institution On War, Revolution and Peace, Stanford University, and in the Wilson correspondence, Hugh R. Wilson Papers, Herbert Hoover Presidential Library, West Branch, Iowa.

a bachelors' mess at 1718 H Street that became a sort of club for the social elite of the Diplomatic Service.[83] "The Service would have been far from a congenial career all those years," Grew recalled, "if it hadn't been for the little group of men who have known each other intimately, and when serving at different posts, have kept up their friendship." [84] Secretaries began keeping track of career progress in the group as a whole and taking pride in "this old Service of ours." They recognized a developing esprit de corps.[85] An amateur ambassador acknowledged the new corporate identity when he referred to them as a Secretaries' Union.[86] One of the most elitist of the secretaries described the service as a "club." [87] A club in fact is what it resembled in the sense of social exclusiveness, broad acquaintanceship and loyalty, knots of close friendships, and dislike of formal organization.

With corporate identity and esprit de corps there developed a sense of craftsmanship. Command of protocol, fluency in key languages, familiarity with elements of international law, polish in writing dispatches and diplomatic communications, facility in "certain finesses . . . certain little necessary discriminations," gave the secretaries a feeling of expertness.[88] MacMurray felt he had learned his letters during his first tour in Siam and looked forward to gaining finish at Petrograd by contact with the high politics of Eu-

---

83. On the 1817 H Street "club" see: Sands, "Basil Miles," p. 80; Leland Harrison Papers, Library of Congress; Carr Diary, March 25, 1935, Carr Papers; Grew to A. H. Frazier and E. L. Dresel, July 5, 1917, Grew Papers.

84. Grew to Frederick Dolbeare, February 29, 1928, Grew Papers. See also Hugh Wilson, *Diplomat Between Wars* (New York, 1941), p. 165.

85. Grew to John W. Garrett, October 18, 1919, Grew Papers.

86. Brand Whitlock, quoted in Ilchman, *Professional Diplomacy*, pp. 137–38.

87. Hugh Wilson used the term "pretty good club": Minutes of Foreign Service Personnel Board Meeting, March 30, 1927, Grew Papers. Shaw, "Foreign Service," p. 327.

88. Grew to his mother, December 7, 1914, Grew Papers; Heinrichs, *Grew*, pp. 17, 24–25.

rope.[89] Toward their amateur chiefs they felt the scorn of the professional naval officer for the landlubber who could not tell a binnacle from a pelican hook. They did the dirty work, rescued their chiefs from blunder, took charge in their absence, and thus felt qualified for top posts themselves.[90]

This sense of craftsmanship developed not in a vacuum but in the competitive environment of European diplomacy. There diplomats enjoyed a fully established career sanctified as a profession, a sort of Freemasonry with a corporate identity of its own apart from national identities. The Americans moved easily into this upper-class world. They and their foreign opposites learned the same ropes, worked up through the ranks the same way, sported together, and formed friendships. The Americans felt they measured up, and identified with the Europeans as colleagues in the same profession. Hugh Gibson, for example, particularly admired the British Diplomatic Service because of its long traditions.[91] The idea of diplomacy as a profession had a status value. An honored calling, a gentlemanly profession above "trade," would dignify their activities, especially for families who were footing the bill.[92] They recognized that American diplomacy was deficient in the crucial respect that it lacked a full career. Only when ambassadorships and ministerships, the real prizes, were within their grasp would American diplomacy qualify as a "permanent profession." [93]

89. MacMurray to his mother, October 14, 1908, MacMurray Papers.

90. MacMurray to his mother, February 19, 1914, MacMurray Papers; Page, "Bureaucracy's Other Face," p. 94; George Kennan, *Russia Leaves the War* (Princeton, N.J., 1956), p. 396.

91. MacMurray to his mother, October 14, 1908, MacMurray Papers; Harold Nicolson, *The Evolution of Diplomacy* (New York, 1962), p. 102; Joseph C. Grew, *Turbulent Era; A Diplomatic Record of Forty Years, 1904–1945,* ed. Walter Johnson, 2 vols. (Cambridge, Mass., 1952), I, 22–23; Perrin Galpin Transcript, Columbia Oral History Collection.

92. M. F. Egan, "Your Move, Mr. Harding," *Colliers* LXVII (February 5, 1921), 12.

93. Grew to Managing Editor, Harvard *Crimson,* November 12, 1913, in Grew, *Turbulent Era,* I, 114.

To sum up, the Diplomatic Service as of 1917 was an organization developing in two different ways. Formally it was becoming more bureaucratic. Informally it gained the group feeling, craftsmanship, and orientation of a profession.

The Establishment of the Foreign Service, 1917–1927

The following decade, from 1917 to 1927, witnessed a second wave of change in American representation abroad. The main impetus came from outside the Diplomatic Service in the form of legislation and executive reorganization that joined the Diplomatic and Consular services into one Foreign Service and tightened the administration of diplomatic personnel. This bureaucratic thrust evoked a professional response. The diplomats feared that proposed reforms would destroy their service and moved to its defense. By emphasizing professional aspects of diplomacy and by organizing to influence drafting of legislation and administration of the Foreign Service, they sought to restrict access and preserve their autonomy. For a time they succeeded, but their efforts provoked opposition that came to a head in 1927. In a showdown that year the diplomats lost, and their influence diminished.

Foreign service reform received strong support in the years following World War I. The argument in favor of amateur diplomats was the exception; generally, expressions of opinion favored opening top posts to career officers and providing them adequate compensation. Nevertheless, acceptance of the career principle did not mean approval of the kind of diplomacy represented by the Diplomatic Service. The war brought a shift in popular conceptions of diplomacy. The emergence of the United States as the most powerful nation in the world eased concern for its image

abroad. In periodicals the prestige consciousness of the turn
of the century, with its partiality for diplomatic reform according to elitist conceptions, diminished, and the upper
class itself lost influence. Meanwhile, Wilsonian ideals, the
Paris Peace Conference, and the fight over the Versailles
Treaty aroused old prejudices against diplomacy. It was associated with reactionary upper classes that arranged secret
treaties and incited territorial aggrandizement. Europe's
professional diplomats, said one commentator, had proved a
supreme failure in preventing the outbreak of the Great
War. Traditional diplomacy endangered rather than advanced American interests.[94]

The dominant themes of reform sentiment were those
that had earlier facilitated the more rapid and extensive reform of the Consular Service. Here the main function of diplomacy was the expansion of American trade. Arthur Sweetser in *World's Work* argued that the questions of the future
concerned solely "the struggle for markets and wealth, in
which an efficiently organized foreign service will greatly
benefit us." According to *Colliers*, an efficient State Department and competent ambassadors were needed "to keep the
wheels of American industry turning full time." Emphasis
on training, skill, economy—in short, efficiency—suggests
that as before the connection between reform and business
was not simply a matter of increasing wealth but also of
improving organization.[95] As Robert Wiebe says:

94. Will Irwin, "Business in Diplomacy," *Saturday Evening Post* CXCIII
(August 14, 1920), 66; William T. Ellis, "Frank Words On the Trained
Diplomat," *Outlook* CXXVII (1921), 383; Ilchman, *Professional Diplo-
macy*, pp. 138–39.

95. Egan, "Your Move, Mr. Harding"; Egan, "Our Extraordinary Envoys," *Collier's* LXVII (March 26, 1921), 7; Egan, "More Business in Diplomacy," *ibid.* LXIX (February 4, 1922), 9; Irwin, "Business in Diplomacy," pp. 29–30; Arthur Sweetser, "Why the State Department Should
Be Reorganized," *World's Work* XXXIX (1920), 514; Wilbur Carr, "To
Bring Our Foreign Service up to Date," *Independent* CV (1921), 207;
"Praise for Harding's Diplomats," *Literary Digest* LXXIV (September 2,

What emerged by the war was an important segment of the
population, a crucial one in terms of both public and private
leadership, acting from common assumptions and speaking
a common language. A bureaucratic orientation now defined
a basic part of the nation's discourse. The values of continuity
and regularity, functionality and rationality, administration
and management set the form of problems and outlined their
alternative solutions.[96]

Reformers made a sharp distinction between the two
services. The Diplomatic Service had a poor public image.
Rich career secretaries replaced rich amateur ambassadors
as the target for criticism. They seemed undemocratic, un-
American, and useless, mere social ornaments of an outdated
courtier diplomacy. Respecting class origins at least, the
image was accurate, and British dress and manner were
sufficiently common to make the diplomats a perpetual cin-
der in the public eye.[97] For example, Leland Harrison, Eton,
Harvard (Porcellian Club), Knickerbocker Club, served in
Washington as assistant secretary of state for several years,
where his accent, spats, Rolls Royce, and aloofness even
among social equals were not likely to appease democratic
instincts.[98] He was an extreme case, but extremes establish

1922), 16; National Civil Service Reform League, *Report*, p. 12; Remarks
by Representatives R. Walton Moore and Edward E. Browne, *Congressional Record*, 67th Cong., 4th Sess. (1923), 3163, 3165, and by Tom
Connally, *ibid.*, 68th Cong., 1st Sess. (1924), 7573.

96. Wiebe, *Search for Order*, 295.

97. "Representation Allowances For Our Ambassadors," *World's Work*
XLVIII (1924), 16; Egan, "Your Move, Mr. Harding," pp. 12, 27, 28;
Irwin, "Business in Diplomacy," pp. 30, 69; Sweetser, "Why the State De-
partment Should Be Reorganized," p. 515; Herbert Corey, "He Has Jobs for
Rising Young Men," *Collier's* LXXII (November 3, 1923), 14; Norval
Richardson, "My Diplomatic Education," *Saturday Evening Post* CXCV
(February 10, 1923), 8–9; "When Diplomats Write Ads," *New Republic*
XXXV (1923), 167–68; Heinrichs, *Grew*, pp. 48–50.

98. On Harrison: Grew to Major T. M. Langton, January 25, 1919,
Grew Papers; Diary of Gordon Auchincloss, August 4, 1918, Colonel Ed-
ward M. House Papers, Yale University Library; J. Pierrepont Moffat to
Gibson, June 29, 1921, Moffat Papers; Herbert O. Yardley, *The American*

popular stereotypes. Consuls, on the other hand, were mostly middle class. Fewer came from the Northeast; the rural West and South were better represented. Most had received some form of college education, often vocational, and the proportion of college graduates was increasing. But their education was typically middle class: three out of four consular recruits in 1924 attended public school and only one out of four an Ivy League college.[99] Theirs was a reorganized service, "keen, highly-trained, and efficient to the last degree," according to *Literary Digest*. They dealt with the general public more often and their work yielded practical, tangible benefits. They were the humble cousins of the diplomats, "working on quietly, unspectacularly, winning markets for American merchants." [100]

The obvious way to remedy the deficiencies of the Diplomatic Service was to make it resemble the Consular Service. This was the approach taken in legislation first introduced in 1919 by Representative John Jacob Rogers of Lowell, Massachusetts. A leading Republican on the Foreign Affairs Committee, Rogers was by far the outstanding congressional proponent of foreign service reform from 1919 until his death in 1925. In its final form the Rogers Bill encouraged promotion of the best officers to ministerships, though it failed to provide for a class of career ministers. It also drastically improved salaries, increasing the top class from $4,000 to $9,000, and authorized retirement benefits, paid home

---

Black Chamber (Indianapolis, 1931), p. 19. Grew believed Yardley's description of diplomats was a perfect portrait of Harrison (Grew Diary, July 13–27, 1931, Grew Papers).

99. Information on consuls derived from a sampling ("A" through "H" of the alphabet) of biographical statements in State Department, *Register, 1915*, and Ilchman, *Professional Diplomacy*, pp. 164, 170–71.

100. "The Yankee Consul, New Style, On the Job," *Literary Digest* LXVIII (January 29, 1921), 60–62; Irwin, "Business in Diplomacy," pp. 30, 66; Sweetser, "Why the State Department Should Be Reorganized," p. 515.

leave, and representation allowances. Such improvements would not necessarily alter the complexion of the Diplomatic Service, however, or alter it soon enough. Robert P. Skinner, consul general at London, had a quick solution. He proposed dissolving the Diplomatic Service and incorporating its members in the Consular Service. This would probably have caused a mass resignation of diplomats. The problem was to devise a combination of the two services that would take into account their separate functions and effect the necessary social change, yet not too radically. Wilbur Carr supplied the answer in the Foreign Service idea that was a central feature of the Rogers Act. This was a personnel system classifying secretaries and consuls together for salary and promotion purposes while keeping them functionally separate. Provision for interchange of officers at all levels would permit progressive integration of the two services to the point where assignment depended not on old service affiliation but on the interest of the government and the officer's abilities.[101]

Carr's was a classic bureaucratic solution. His scheme removed the artificial barrier between consular and diplomatic offices. The two services performed many similar and complementary functions anyway. A single source of personnel would improve coordination of political and economic work and permit the Department of State to meet the particular needs of an office from a broader range of skills. The plan

---

101. Excerpts from Carr Memo, May 2, 1920, enclosed in Carr to Grew, November 12, 1925, Carr Papers; Ilchman, *Professional Diplomacy*, pp. 148–50; Crane, *Carr*, pp. 248, 255–56. The text of the Rogers Act is in Lay, *Foreign Service*, Appendix E. As Ilchman concedes, Carr's authorship of the Foreign Service idea is based on inference (*Professional Diplomacy*, p. 150 n. 106), but this seems a reasonable inference. In addition to the circumstantial evidence Ilchman cites is the fact that Carr claimed all versions of the bill were drafted in his office (Crane, *Carr*, p. 284), and that Carr wrote Undersecretary Frank Polk as early as June 7, 1919, some months before any of Rogers's reform bills were introduced, that there was a need for a "much closer" relationship between the Diplomatic and Consular services, with secretaries subject to service as consuls and vice versa (File 120.1/57, State Department Archives).

offered the advantage of bringing consuls versed in commercial problems into embassies as well as that of assigning diplomats to politically sensitive consulates such as Calcutta, Ottawa, Capetown, and Melbourne, where no diplomatic mission existed. Furthermore, junior officers would be tested in a variety of situations and could then find the type of work best suited to them. The Foreign Service system would effect economies such as housing consulates in embassies and consolidating personnel offices. Carr was playing on popular themes but with the genuine enthusiasm of an exponent of scientific management.[102]

The Rogers Bill appealed to almost everyone. The themes of efficiency and trade echoed from committee hearing room to the floor of Congress to newspapers and periodicals and back again. A congressman expressed the consensus when he said: "Every rotary, every commercial organization wants this bill passed. Why? Because they want an efficient foreign service and know that it benefits business." [103] Congress also thumped lustily on the idea of making the Diplomatic Service more democratic and American. The irrepressible Tom Connally delighted a House hearing by mimicking, with appropriate gestures and accent, an American secretary

102. Memorandum by Carr, October, 19, 1922, and Secretary of State to Rogers, October 19, 1922, File 120/102a, State Department Archives; U.S. Congress, House of Representatives, Committee on Foreign Affairs, *Foreign Service of the United States, Hearings on H.R. 12543*, 67th Cong., 4th Sess. (Washington, 1922), pp. 5–6, 16, 46; U.S. House of Representatives, Committee on Appropriations, *Hearing Held before the Subcommittee in Charge of Departments of State and Justice Appropriation Bills*, 67th Cong., 2d Sess. (Washington, 1922), Part I, p. 19; *Hearings on H.R. 17 and 6357*, pp. 9, 11, 30, 130–31; Crane, *Carr*, p. 234.

103. Rep. Edward E. Browne in *Congressional Record*, 67th Cong., 4th Sess. (1923), 3165. Also Reps. Rogers and R. Walton Moore, *ibid.*, 3145, 3163; Rep. Tom Conally, *ibid.*, 68th Cong., 1st Sess. (1924), 7573; testimony of Carr and Skinner, *Hearings on H.R. 12543*, pp. 17, 39, 80; testimony of Carr, U.S. Congress, House of Representatives, Committee on Appropriations, *Hearings before the Subcommittee on Appropriations for the Department of State, 1925*, 68th Cong., 1st Sess. (Washington, 1925), p. 113. On the history of the Rogers Bill: Ilchman, *Professional Diplomacy*, chap. 4.

aping the Europeans, "trying to walk like one, holding his stick like one, wearing his handkerchief like one, and trying to talk like one [Laughter]." [104] Consular work would be good medicine for these young men and keep the new recruit's "American spirit fresh." [105] The State Department leadership, faced with a vast increase in postwar overseas responsibilities, saw the need for more and better recruits and the weeding-out of the incompetent and superannuated. Secretary of State Hughes testified himself and made the bill an administration measure. [106] Needless to say, consuls approved. [107] Carr tirelessly drafted all versions of the bill, worked to gain public support, and testified before Congress. [108] He undoubtedly saw a larger role for himself in the consequence. In 1921 he disengaged himself from direct supervision of consuls by setting up an office of consular personnel under his wing, which, he believed, would serve for diplomatic personnel as well in time. [109] The intent of Congress to make Carr chief of the Foreign Service was clear in an amendment to the Rogers Bill that abolished the office of director of the Consular Service and applied its salary to a

104. U.S. Congress, House of Representatives, Committee on Foreign Affairs, *Hearings on the Diplomatic and Consular Appropriation Bill,* 66th Cong., 2d Sess. (Washington, 1920), p. 75. Also *Congressional Record,* 67th Cong., 4th Sess. (1923), 3145, 3159, and 68th Cong., 1st Sess. (1924), 7565–7566.

105. Skinner testimony, *Hearings on H.R. 12543,* p. 77.

106. Correspondence between Charles Evans Hughes and President Warren G. Harding, and Memoranda by Carr, 1922 and 1923, File 120. Rogers Act/No. 1, State Department Archives; Hughes to Harding, August 22, 1922, File 120.1/70a, State Department Archives; Rogers, "Are Changes Provided by the Rogers Bill Necessary?", *Congressional Digest* III (1924), 124; Barnes and Morgan, *Foreign Service,* pp. 195–200; Crane, *Carr,* pp. 227–28.

107. See letters of congratulation from various consuls to Carr, 1924, Carr Papers.

108. On Carr's role see File 120.Rogers Act/No. 1; Carr, "To Bring Our Foreign Service up to Date," *Independent* CV (1921), 207, 220; Crane, *Carr,* chaps. 26, 27.

109. Crane, *Carr,* pp. 247–48.

new assistant secretaryship. The amendment circulated in the State Department beforehand and was approved.[110]

The diplomats found these proceedings painful, especially because the Rogers Bill went so far to satisfy their most urgent needs. In the postwar years pitifully few were attracted to diplomacy, and many within the service were tempted out by Wall Street.[111] The diplomats fully accepted the necessity of making the career attractive to less affluent men and regarded the bill's encouragement of service ministerships as a triumph for the career principle and their only hope of permanency.[112] What upset them was amalgamation, especially talk of free interchangeability, of officers "weaving back and forth" between consular and diplomatic work. Outnumbered four to one, they feared they would be swallowed up in the consular establishment. Lewis Einstein, the best mind among them, warned that extensive lateral entry, especially in the middle grades where "corporate consciousness" was formed, would destroy the esprit de corps of the Diplomatic Service.[113] Grew feared that the consular pattern of formal and hierarchical relationships, with Carr in control, would "bureaucratize" his own service.[114] The diplomats could not have been less enthusiastic about being shifted to

110. Reps. Otis Wingo and Rogers in *Congressional Record*, 68th Cong., 1st Sess. (1924), 8823–24; Diary of William R. Castle, Jr., May 19, 1924, examined when in Castle's possession, now in Castle Papers, Houghton Library, Harvard University; Grew Diary, May 13, 1924, Grew Papers.

111. Heinrichs, *Grew*, p. 98.

112. Grew to his mother, June 26, 1919, and to Thomas Sergeant Perry, January 19, 1924, Grew Papers; William Phillips, "Cleaning Our Diplomatic House," *Forum* LXIII (August 14, 1920), 164–72; Ilchman, *Professional Diplomacy*, p. 162.

113. Skinner testimony, *Hearings on H.R. 12543*, 77–78; Castle Diary, January 10, 1923; Pierre Boal to Rogers, August 2, 1923, Gibson Papers; circular letter of Lewis Einstein, June 20, 1923, enclosed in Fred M. Dearing to William Phillips, July 7, 1923, File 111/248, State Department Archives. On Einstein, see Lewis Einstein, *A Diplomat Looks Back*, ed. Lawrence E. Gelfand (New Haven, Conn., 1968). Memorandum, Phillips to Frank Polk, June 4, 1919, File 120.1/57, State Department Archives.

114. Grew, *Turbulent Era*, I, 619; Shaw, "Foreign Service," p. 327.

the world of visas, invoices, and stranded seamen.[115] Neither did they favor leaving the world of European chancelleries. Gibson supposed they would be sent to Singapore, Capetown, or Tegucigalpa "to learn us to chew tibacco [sic] and give up spats." The thought of transfer even to Tokyo made him feel as if his "spine had been removed by a turkey boning machine." [116] They feared a loss of corporate identity, bureaucratization, and shift to a different and less attractive type of work.

Woven into the amalgamation issue was a problem of social status. The case of Wilbur Carr is illustrative. In 1917 he had married a wealthy lady and moved into a mansion on Wyoming Avenue.[117] He had come far from his humble beginnings, and yet there always seemed much further to go. Most of the undersecretaries and assistant secretaries of the Harding administration were Harvard or Princeton diplomats, urbane, elegant men who seemed effortlessly to enjoy a position and maintain a style of life that he struggled so hard to attain. Carr made a point of noting down talk of "Harvard society type" diplomats in the department and evidence of their snobbishness.[118] American representatives, he contended, should come from "neither the most exclusive social circle nor from the circle in which no culture is found" —in other words, from middle-class people like himself.[119] If upper-class status was always somewhat beyond his reach, he might be able to make diplomacy more bourgeois.

115. Gibson testimony, *Hearings on H.R. 17 and 6357*, p. 21; Grew to Albert Ruddock, December 11, 1919, Grew Papers.

116. Gibson to William R. Castle, Jr., February 19, 1923, Gibson Papers; Gibson to E. L. Dresel, September 1, 1921, Dresel Papers.

117. Crane, *Carr*, pp. 201–2.

118. Carr Diary, January 26, March 17, 1923, July 27, 1925, Carr Papers; Hubert Herring, "The Department of State," *Harper's* CLXXIV (1937), 228.

119. Carr notes for speech in Diary, 1922–1923, n.d., Carr Papers.

Social tension was only to be expected in joining together a homogenous upper-class group and a predominantly middle-class organization. Though most consuls appear to have been more interested in the retirement benefits of the Rogers Bill than the opportunities for diplomatic work it provided, they resented the social precedence enjoyed by those with diplomatic status abroad and in Washington.[120] "The diplomatic privileges," wrote Nelson Johnson, "ah, there are the almost perfect insulations," making "the career secretariat immune to criticism by the uninitated." He supposed the diplomats would find it "infra dig" to be "jumbled in" with consuls.[121] Johnson the following year became chief of the Far Eastern Division, then assistant secretary of state and later minister and ambassador to China. Consul General Skinner, who testified before Congress about snobs in the Diplomatic Service, asked for a "proper" legation as soon as the Rogers Bill passed.[122] The status sensitivity of consuls in transition reflected the class barrier between the services.

Occasionally diplomats betrayed a snobbish attitude toward consuls. A diplomat's picture of a person in a "sweat" was a consul at an embassy dinner. Consular "standards of civilization" were lower, as shown in sentimentality, "a fondness for Y.M.C.A. standards and phraseology."[123] Generally the diplomats were on the defensive. Grew, who was minister to Switzerland at the time, wanted the "few rotters" in the Diplomatic Service eliminated and the "decent, red-blooded

120. Letters of Consuls to Carr, 1924, and Carr Diary, November 5, 1923, Carr Papers; Rep. Tom Connally, *Congressional Record,* 67th Cong., 4th Sess. (1923), 3147.
121. Nelson Johnson to N. B. Stewart, May 28, 1924, Johnson to M. L. Myers, July 15, 1923, Johnson Papers, Library of Congress.
122. Skinner testimony, *Hearings on H.R. 12543,* pp. 76–81; Skinner to Carr, June 26, 1924, Carr Papers.
123. Gibson to Grew, July 2, 1924, Leland Harrison Papers; Castle Diary, December 2, 1924, Castle Papers.

men" advanced. Minister to Poland Hugh Gibson, much to his chagrin, coined the term "cookie pusher." When the service tried to get rid of such incompetents, he contended, congressmen protected them.[124] Undersecretary of State William Phillips balanced an element of socially ambitious consuls against the element of snobbish diplomats.[125] This disarming frankness and even-handedness might suggest that the social factor in amalgamation was insignificant for the diplomats. On the contrary, status defense was a vital factor in their response, but expressed itself in a subtler manner.

The hard fact was that the forces marshaled behind the Foreign Service idea were too strong to be resisted. The Diplomatic Service would have to lose its formal identity to secure the career advantages its members regarded as essential. Nevertheless, their position was by no means hopeless. Charles Evans Hughes conducted a most active diplomacy, bilateral and multilateral, and skilled agents and staff were in urgent demand. He made it clear to Congress that he respected the qualities and motives of his diplomats and that, though he favored interchange of officers, it would be kept "within reasonable limits." [126] He chose diplomats for all high policy posts in the department and took every opportunity to appoint service ministers. No less than ten secretaries secured missions between the end of the war and the Rogers Act. Valued as they were, the diplomats believed that if they could not block the establishment of a single Foreign Service, they might at least influence the administration of it so as to keep their service substantially intact. In seeking this ob-

124. Grew to T. S. Perry, January 13, 1924, Grew Papers; Gibson testimony, *Hearings on H.R. 17 and 6357,* p. 40; Gibson to Castle, February 19, 1923, Gibson Papers.

125. Carr Diary, November 5, 1923, Carr Papers. Also, Pierre Boal to John J. Rogers, August 2, 1923, Gibson Papers.

126. Hughes testimony, *Hearings on H.R. 12543,* pp. 7–8; Pierre Boal to John J. Rogers, August 2, 1923, Gibson Papers; Ilchman, *Professional Diplomacy,* pp. 157–59.

ject they acted in ways that significantly departed from the bureaucratic structure and pattern.

The fortunes of the Diplomatic Service came to rest in the hands of an elite of six that included, besides Gibson, Grew, and Phillips, Hugh Wilson, a secretary serving in Berlin and then Tokyo, J. Butler Wright, assistant secretary of state and chief of the Diplomatic Bureau, and Ulysses Grant-Smith, minister to Albania. These six were assisted from time to time by another half-dozen senior careerists.[127] The group conformed to the social type of the Service and had extensive European experience, as well as in most cases departmental experience that acquainted them with the reform movement at home. They were characterized by strong esprit de corps, career idealism, and sensitivity to service opinion. In the cases of Phillips and Wright, activities assisting the service were a function of office, but the rest worked outside their bureaucratic roles. Gibson and Grew were *beaux ideals* of the service, the former a brilliant wit, mimic, and raconteur who charmed European society, as well as a shrewd, perceptive observer, the latter combining diligence and disarming sincerity with suavity, good looks, and a sporting instinct. Both had reputations as skilled diplomatists and both had panache.[128] The elite worked informally because it suited their style and because overt organizing was frowned on.[129] They made plans and achieved consensus by

127. Others identified included Robert Woods Bliss, Frederick Sterling, Lewis Einstein, Pierre Boal, Leland Harrison, and Ellis Dresel. Identification of the group from correspondence among members of the group in Grew, Dresel, Gibson, and Wilson papers.

128. On Gibson: Galpin Transcript, Columbia Oral History Collection; Galpin, ed., *Gibson;* Nancy H. Hooker, ed., *The Moffat Papers: Selections from the Diplomatic Journals of Jay Pierrepont Moffat, 1919–1943* (Cambridge, Mass., 1956), pp. 10–12. On Grew: Heinrichs, *Grew*.

129. In 1923 Lewis Einstein sent out a circular letter in the Diplomatic Service disapproving of Foreign Service amalgamation. Minister Fred M. Dearing strongly disapproved of such efforts to organize opposition to the Rogers Bill and forwarded Einstein's letter and his reply to Phillips. File 111/248, State Department Archives.

extensive personal correspondence and by seemingly casual get-togethers in Paris and Berlin.[130]

They moved to protect the service in a number of ways. Gibson felt that someone had to testify and show Congress that diplomats spoke American and could "find their way in and out of a drawing room without the use of a monocle." He tried Grew, who passed the assignment back, chuckling that "people who talk through their nose and spit on the floor will cut a lot more ice than those who try and talk like Englishmen." [131] Gibson went home and testified. In addition, the leadership developed its own ideas for the Foreign Service. In 1920 Hugh Wilson drew up a plan with separate Diplomatic and Consular divisions and no interchange of officers. Five diplomats meeting in Paris approved, but nothing came of it.[132] What the diplomats needed was stronger representation at the highest levels of the State Department. At Gibson's suggestion a Diplomatic Personnel Committee was formed in 1920. Composed of Assistant Secretary Van Santvoord Merle-Smith and four diplomats, its assignment was to formulate personnel policy, but it was abolished in the change of administration.[133] The chief of the Diplomatic Bureau was a key position, but Wright seemed too much under Carr's influence, and the undersecretaryship assumed all the more importance.[134] When Phillips left the latter post

130. On the meetings: Castle Diary, October 21, 1922, Castle Papers; Grew to Gibson, December 22, 1920, Grew to Grant-Smith, April 15, 1920, Grew to Robert Woods Bliss, September 30, 1921, and Wilson to Rep. Rogers, April 7, 1920, Grew Papers.

131. Grew to Gibson, March 23, 1923, Grew Papers; Gibson to Castle, February 19, 1923, Gibson Papers.

132. Wilson to John J. Rogers, April 7, 1920, Grew Papers; Grew to Grant-Smith, April 15, 1920, Grew Papers; excerpts from Carr Memorandum, May 2, 1920, enclosed in Carr to Grew, November 12, 1925, Carr Papers.

133. Grew to Castle, January 30, 1922, Grew Papers; Gibson to Moffat, January 23, 1920, Moffat Papers; Ilchman, *Professional Diplomacy*, pp. 155–56.

134. Grew to Gibson, October 15, November 3, 1923, Grew Papers; Castle Diary, November 2, 1923, Castle Papers.

in 1924, he strongly recommended Gibson and Grew, and Hughes was amenable. Gibson declined and urged it on Grew for the sake of the service. Grew, a man who would "stand hitched" when the Diplomatic Service needed protection, accepted.[135]

The widely held view that Carr would be appointed chief of the new Foreign Service was the major concern, and Grew, Gibson, and William R. Castle met in Berlin in 1922 to form a plan to counter the threat. Their idea was a powerful chief of personnel identified with neither branch. Their candidate was Castle, whom they recommended to Hughes.[136] In fact, Castle, chief of the Western European Affairs Division, was warmly sympathetic to the diplomats. "Joe Grew is wonderfully friendly about my being, in the opinion of the service men, really a part of the service," he wrote. A descendant of one of the original American grandee families in Hawaii, and a graduate of Harvard, he fitted easily into the club.[137]

The Rogers Bill became law on May 24, 1924. It was silent on the administration of the Foreign Service and the extent of amalgamation, and the opposing forces pressed forward with their separate plans. Carr's plan placed control of Foreign Service personnel in a board composed of the undersecretary and two assistant secretaries, as well as one consular and one diplomatic officer brought back from the field semiannually. Only the undersecretary and assistant secretaries would decide transfers between branches. They would constitute a quorum and could in any case outvote

135. Castle Diary, January 29, 30, 1924, Castle Papers; Grew to T. S. Perry, February 13, 1924, Grew Papers; Gibson to Wilson, April 16, 1924, Wilson Papers.
136. Grew to Hughes, February 18, 1923, Grew to Gibson, February 20, 1923, Grew Papers; Castle Diary, October 21, 1922, January 30, 1924, Castle Papers; Gibson to Hughes, January 17, 1923, Hughes Papers, Library of Congress.
137. Castle Diary, November 11, 1922, Castle Papers. On Castle, Robert Ferrell, *American Diplomacy in the Great Depression* (New Haven, Conn., 1957), p. 38.

the field representatives. With Carr now an assistant secretary and a permanent fixture in the department, the result was obvious to Castle: "Everything will lead gently but inevitably toward control by the one man who is permanent." [138] The plan of the diplomats, drawn up by Hugh Wilson, embodied the Gibson-Grew-Castle scheme of a high-ranking personnel chief from neither branch reporting directly to the secretary, bypassing the assistant secretaries. He was to be chairman of a Personnel Board composed of himself and one representative from each branch.[139] Carr bitterly rejected the idea, claiming the diplomats had no experience to justify their submitting a plan. He threatened to give up all consular work if someone from the outside took over his consular personnel. Further, he disapproved of a meeting the diplomats assigned to the department were calling to air their views. Undersecretary Grew met this problem by suggesting to the diplomats that they call on the chief of the Diplomatic Bureau on their own initiative, "singly or en masse." [140] They did so, held a two and one-half hour meeting, and voted fifteen to two to support the Wilson plan. With this sampling of diplomatic opinion, Grew felt in a position to recommend the Wilson plan to the secretary, and also, according to Castle, to advise him to keep the two branches distinct for the present.[141]

Hughes chose neither plan, or rather, chose both plans. The Executive Order for the administration of the Foreign

138. Memorandum, Carr to Phillips, January 14, 1924, Harrison Papers; Grew, *Turbulent Era,* I, 619–20; Memorandum, Castle to Grew, May 14, 1924, and Grew Diary, May 13, 1924, Grew Papers.

139. Gibson to Wilson, February 19, 1924, with attached Memorandum from Wilson, n.d., and Memorandum, Wilson to Grew, May 5, 1924, with attached draft memorandum by Wilson, n.d., and Memorandum from Wilson, June 2, 1924, Wilson Papers.

140. Grew Diary, May 13–27, 1924, Grew Papers.

141. Castle Diary, May 28, 1924, Castle Papers; Grew to Gibson, June 5, 1924, Grew Papers.

Service established a Personnel Board composed of two elements. One element was the undersecretary and two assistant secretaries with final authority over transfers, as in the Carr plan. The other element was an Executive Committee with a chairman and two Foreign Service officers, one from each branch, as in the Wilson plan, with full voting power except on transfers.[142] Carr resisted the compromise but finally accepted it and conceded that the two branches should remain distinct for the present. Grew believed it represented a substantial gain for the diplomats in that the service element would have a more prestigeful, powerful, and continuous role in administration. Castle disagreed and declined the position of chairman of the Executive Committee because of its reduced significance. He saw no future in a scheme that placed responsibility nowhere and left Carr in ultimate control through long-term influence in selecting the Executive Committee.[143] Whatever the future, the first Personnel Committee suited the diplomats well. Serving with Chairman Grew and Assistant Secretaries Wright and Carr was an Executive Committee consisting of two consuls and Hugh Wilson for the diplomats. Grew and Wright could block transfers, and on any other question the Board was evenly split between those identified with consuls and those with diplomats. The diplomats had by no means ensured their autonomy, yet their organized efforts had not been unavailing. They had gained permanent representation on the board and for the time being at least had halted the momentum for change in the composition of the American diplomatic establishment.

The Foreign Service concept forced the diplomats to or-

142. Text of Executive Order of June 7, 1924, in Lay, *Foreign Service,* Appendix F.

143. Grew Diary, June 5, 11, 1924, and Memorandums, Grew to Carr, June 5, 1924, and Grew to Gibson, June 5, 11, 1924, Grew Papers; Grew, *Turbulent Era,* I, 626; Castle Diary, June 5, 10, 1924, Castle Papers.

ganize in defense of their autonomy and give some thought to justifying it. Their professionalism had come by way of ascription, the reference group being European diplomats, and they had not bothered to validate their claim as long as it went unchallenged. To the extent that American diplomacy had been professionally incomplete by failure to provide permanency, the Rogers Act substantially remedied the deficiency. But this solution created a new problem. Now simply asserting the professional nature of diplomacy was not enough. The Foreign Service embraced consuls as well, and if the diplomats were to retain their identity, they would need to make some distinction between the two types of activity, would need, in other words, to establish professional criteria. Yet the more sharply they marked off their own field, the more they contradicted the combining theme that was so prominent in reform sentiment and the official State Department position. The problem is reflected in a speech Grew made to new Foreign Service Officers in 1926. He said: "I only wish I could give each of you, in addition to your commission, a roll of parchment tied up with a red ribbon conferring on you the honorable degree of Doctor of Foreign Affairs, for certainly the Foreign Service is just exactly as much a profession as law or medicine or the ministry." [144] What he undoubtedly meant and wanted to say in place of "Foreign Service" was "diplomacy" because he had referred only a few months earlier to "the consular and diplomatic professions," and because he derived his satisfaction from capping diplomacy as a profession in the old sense. [145] But of course these were Foreign Service Officers, most of whom would start in consulates and not all of whom

144. Speech by Grew at Foreign Service Officers Luncheon, May 3, 1926, Grew Papers.
145. Radio talk by Grew, February 24, 1926, Grew Papers.

would end in diplomacy, and so an adjustment was necessary.

Professional distinctions were hard to make for other reasons as well. It was difficult to apply a professional classification to the intellectual content of diplomacy. As a close student of the problem, himself a diplomat, admitted, "The technical knowledge peculiar to the Foreign Service is limited and may be acquired with relative ease and in a relatively short period of time. . . . "[146] At the same time, diplomacy was as much a matter of personality as intellect, embracing a variety of talents in dealing with people. Furthermore, so far as diplomacy served the ideal of accommodating differences between nations, the postwar years of nonentanglement were a discouraging time to advertise that service.

Operating under these paradoxes, constraints, and limitations, the diplomats presented a confusing and ambiguous professional image. Generally they preferred the business approach, contending that diplomacy no less than consular work procured dollar benefits. Indeed, according to Grew, it was eminently business-like. Like any profession it had undergone change and was no longer mysterious, but straightforward and practical, organized like a corporation to maximize efficiency. By thus striving to overcome prejudice and conform to the business mentality, Grew suggested a service his profession performed but not why it alone could perform it. Pierre Boal, a diplomatic secretary, used the business analogy but managed to insert a distinction by likening the diplomat to a corporation's general counsel in a foreign country and the consul to its local agent.[147] Gibson

146. Shaw, "American Foreign Service," p. 325.
147. Heinrichs, *Grew*, p. 103; Ilchman, *Professional Diplomacy*, p. 152; radio talk by Grew, February 26, 1926, Grew Papers; Boal to John J. Rogers, August 2, 1923, Gibson Papers.

alone rejected the notion of diplomacy as a business proposition. He told Congress it was a "specialized profession" requiring long experience, and one for which the businessman was rarely prepared. No one would allow an operation on himself by someone equipped only with common sense. When it came to specifying the precise function of the diplomat, however, he also took refuge in analogy. His diplomat was a weather forecaster who plotted a political barometric pressure chart from a variety of phenomena, while his consul reported varied but not necessarily related commercial phenomena.[148] Someone suggested that in a daily paper the diplomat's work would appear as a signed article on page one and the consul's in the market page or want ads.[149] Another comparison was between a carpenter and a plumber, with the diplomat identified with the craftsman, the carpenter.[150] These analogies implied a superior-inferior relation between diplomats and consuls. Together they were hardly likely to clarify the public's mind about the unique function of the diplomat.

The diplomats of this generation had a common conception of the qualifications necessary for their way of life. Intellect was less important than personality, and personality was related to social status. They looked for flexibility, adaptability, imagination, a broad liberal education, "personal cultivation," "taste for study," "worldliness." Rather than "mere knowledge," they wanted knowledge as a way of mingling, as a means of "social and intellectual intercourse with cultured people." When it came to personal qualities such as tact, bearing, and poise, they had in mind the gentlemanly ideal. Thus Grew spoke of the "inborn suavity, gracefulness of movement and lightness of touch" possessed

148. Gibson testimony, *Hearings on H.R. 17 and 6357*, pp. 41–42, 95–98.
149. Memorandum, n.a., n.d., Box 14–1A, Gibson Papers.
150. Grew to Albert Ruddock, December 11, 1919, Grew Papers.

by members of Boston's exclusive Somerset Club. When Wright, Gibson, and Castle mentioned "breeding" and Grew "background," they referred to their own upper-class upbringing and schooling.[151] The younger one learned languages the better, to the point where Grew worried that his youngsters were learning English before French. English should be written with the "old courtesy and grace of style and expression." [152] Let it be said that the diplomats emphasized hard work, loyalty, forcefulness, frankness, and initiative, too, that they were in many respects admirable men, and that the qualities they stressed had worked well for them and, broadly defined, would always be associated with diplomacy. Nonetheless, consuls by and large did not come from "homes with tradition" in Gibson's sense. Upper-class membership implicitly formed these definitions. Underlying the diplomats' professional criteria was a status-defense mechanism. After all, the Diplomatic Service would hardly be a club, to say nothing of Wilson's "pretty good club," if just anyone were let in.

During the first two and one-half years of the Foreign Service, the diplomats mostly succeeded in having their own way. The more attractive career with entrance only at the bottom eminently suited their needs. Candidates appeared for the written examination in numbers that exceeded expectations.[153] The diplomats regarded this as a preliminary

151. Grew address to Foreign Service Officers School, April 25, 1925, Grew to Senator Frank B. Willis, May 14, 1926, Grew to Dresel, January 28, 1920, Grew to Francis Peabody, December 30, 1925, Minutes of Foreign Service Personnel Board Meetings, June 13, November 24, 1925, November 4, 1926, January 11, 1927, Grew Papers; Wright to Milton Conover, May 2, 1925, File 120.1121/11, State Department Archives; Wilson, *Diplomacy As a Career*, p. 33; *Hearings on H.R. 17 and 6357*, p. 52; Gibson to Wilson, October 15, 1924, Wilson Papers; Castle Diary, October 9, 1922, Castle Papers.

152. Enclosure in Grew to Gibson, November 12, 1923, and Grew to his mother, October 18, 1919, and Grew speech at Foreign Service Officers Luncheon, May 3, 1926, Grew Papers.

153. Ilchman, *Professional Diplomacy*, p. 202.

screening, however, because it placed too great an emphasis on memorization of facts, and they sought to keep the passing score low. The crucial test for fitness was the oral examination where "mentality" and personality could be explored.[154] They strongly resisted the admission of women, and as for blacks, "we shall have to fail them . . . on the ground that they do not possess the necessary qualifications for the Service."[155] The diplomats opposed establishment of a special academy for the Foreign Service on the ground that diplomacy could not be taught but had to be learned by experience.[156] Nevertheless, Grew liked to think of the new Foreign Service School as a form of postgraduate professional training.[157] The training period was extended from one month to six or eight months, and in addition to bureaucratic orientation and technical instruction, recruits received lectures on the art of political reporting by Allen Dulles and on history, problems, and policy in sensitive areas such as China, Central America, and the Soviet Union. Other topics included economic problems, disarmament, and international organization. Wright gave a talk in which he urged them to build their vocabularies, pointing out that the "average cultivated" Englishman had one-third to one-half more words at his command than the American.[158] From the school the new officers went to consulates,

154. Milton Conover to Wright, May 2, 1925, and Wright to Conover, May 8, 1925, File 120.1121/11, State Department Archives; Memorandum from Grew, October 5, 1925, Grew Papers; Ilchman, *Professional Diplomacy*, p. 206.

155. Grew Diary, October 31, 1924. On the admission of women see also: Grew Diary, January 14, 1925, Memorandum, Grew to Wright, January 19, 1925, and Grew to Gibson, March 25, April 29, May 20, 1925, Grew Papers.

156. Memorandum by H. P. Fletcher, April 25, 1921, File 120.1/67, State Department Archives; Wilson, *Diplomacy As a Career*, p. 20.

157. Talk by Grew at Foreign Service School, October 27, 1926, File E-623, State Department Archives.

158. Talks by Wright, October 4, 1926, and others, File E-623, State Department Archives; James B. Stewart, "Foreign Service Officer Training School," *Foreign Service Journal* X (1933), 224–27.

where the most suitable were selected for diplomacy. In making assignments in the diplomatic branch, Grew preferred to hold open positions for these promising new men rather than fill them by transfer of established consular officers.[159]

Above the entering classes, the Personnel Board kept the two branches almost entirely distinct. Only a token number of interchanges occurred, four diplomats to consular work and six consuls to diplomatic. Personnel evaluation in the Diplomatic Service had been so haphazard that there was no basis of comparison with consuls for promotion purposes. Consequently, while uniform standards were being developed, the Board kept separate promotion lists.[160] Concern for morale in the diplomatic branch repeatedly cropped up in discussions of the Board regarding promotions and assignments. Hearing rumblings of discontent from the field, particularly from Gibson, Grew sent letters to all posts inviting statements of grievances.[161] The diplomatic side of the board could not prevent inclusion of consuls in lists recommending for minister, but Grew disapproved nonetheless. On one occasion he contended that consuls by their training and experience tended to rely too much on instructions and to use too little initiative, and were therefore generally less suitable to head a mission than diplomats who steadily trained for the post.[162]

In spite of their favorable position, the diplomats balked at any tightening of the reins. Gibson complained that the board was authoritarian and remote. He urged it to minimize formal administration and maximize the "human side." The board should give special and sympathetic consideration to

159. Grew to Grant-Smith, May 15, 1926, Grew Papers.

160. Heinrichs, *Grew*, pp. 106, 116.

161. Minutes of Foreign Service Personnel Board meetings, March 21, December 7, 1925, December 16, 1926, January 11, 1927, Grew Papers; Gibson to Grew, July 10, 1925, Wilson Papers; Heinrichs, *Grew*, pp. 116–17.

162. Heinrichs, *Grew*, pp. 118–19.

the problems of the individual. Men in the field should feel free to blow off steam and never doubt they were valued members of the "family," the "club." One of the first diplomatic inspectors objected to revealing adverse comments to the individuals involved. Lessons should be administered gently, he advised, preferably by example. He had no desire to play schoolmaster to men roughly his own age. These were sensitive people who could be led but not driven, he warned. Gibson rejected a new efficiency report form based on the consular system, with percentile ratings of enumerated qualities. He considered it absurd to attempt a mathematical estimation of tact, courage, loyalty, and so forth. Honesty, sobriety, and morality should be taken for granted unless evidence to the contrary existed. He suggested additional categories particularly relevant to diplomacy such as what sort of first impression a man makes, the appropriateness of his style of living, and his standing in the mission, the Diplomatic Corps, with residents, and with traveling Americans.[163] Additional criteria would of course make a common basis for evaluating performance in the Foreign Service all the more difficult to achieve. Gibson represented the reaction of a loosely organized, individualistic, informal, collegial group to extension of the bureaucratic pattern of organization.

The autonomy of the diplomatic branch lasted until "the famous State Department smash of 1927." [164] The trouble began with a side effect of separate promotion lists. Resignations and the weeding-out of incompetents resulted in a faster rate of promotion among diplomats than consuls. By

163. Gibson to Wilson, October 15, 1924, July 10, October 23, 1925, Frederick Dolbeare to Wilson, June 2, 1925, Wilson Papers. See also Grew Diary, October 11, 1924, Grew to Dolbeare, October 1, 1924, and Grew Memorandum, March 29, 1927, Grew Papers.

164. Pearson and Allen, *Washington Merry-Go-Round*, p. 142. For details see Heinrichs, *Grew*, pp. 119–25.

1927 the rate for diplomats was about twice that for consuls, and the disparity was particularly great in the upper classes.[165] Carr believed in substantial amalgamation but wanted to move toward it in an orderly way. Even so, he became increasingly distressed at the slowness of progress and the board's tenderness toward the diplomats. In May, 1926, the board agreed to work toward a single promotion list; but by 1927 it had still not been adopted, and complaints of consuls at the apparent favoritism shown diplomats were beginning to stir congressmen.[166] Then in February, 1927, the administration presented Congress a slate of nine high appointments to choice legations, an embassy, and assistant secretaryships. The list included Wright, Wilson, Gibson, Phillips, Bliss, Castle, and Harrison, as well as Frederick Sterling and Francis White. It was a group chosen by Secretary Frank Kellogg not on the basis of Personnel Board recommendations but largely from personal familiarity with the men. Whatever the basis of selection and however appropriate individually, appointment of that particular group at that time could not have been more ill-conceived. Not one consul was among them. All were wealthy, all except Gibson graduates of Harvard, Yale, or Princeton, all except Castle career diplomats, and all except White active in promoting the interests of the diplomatic branch. The

165. According to the State Department's estimate in June, 1927 (Kellogg to Congressman Charles Edwards, June 21, 1927, File 120.31/38, State Department Archives), of 109 diplomats in service at the end of 1926, 76 had received promotions since the Rogers Act came into force; and of 380 consuls, 136 had received promotions; or, respectively, 70 percent and 36 percent. Congress in reporting its investigation of the board's personnel policies, arrived at a slightly different result (63 percent and 37 percent), largely from using different figures for total strength. U.S. Senate, Committee on Foreign Relations, *Reorganization and Improvement of the Foreign Service,* Sen. Rep. No. 1069, 70th Cong., 1st Sess. (Washington, 1928), 3.

166. Carr Diary, April 6, May 7, 1926, February 2, 1927, Carr Papers; Congressman Edwards to Kellogg, June 16, 1926, and attached memoranda, File 120.1/114, State Department Archives.

diplomats had never presented so large and inviting a target.

The diplomats were in no position to resist now. The February list became notorious, with Grew and Wilson pictured as heads of an "inner circle of social diplomats which has set well-to-do diplomats over the hard-working consul." There was talk of repealing the Rogers Act and widespread public criticism of career diplomats in which the vice-president himself joined. Periodicals and newspapers that had solidly supported Foreign Service reform reflected the general disillusion. As the *Philadelphia Inquirer* said on October 15, 1928, "The word 'career' possessed an honorable meaning up to about two years ago." The president was reported deeply disturbed and began filling high posts from outside the service. The Senate delayed confirming the appointments (ultimately it confirmed them all) and launched an investigation. Meanwhile, the State Department moved to repair the damage. Its solicitor ruled that a single promotion list was mandatory under the Rogers Act, whereupon the Board adopted one and promoted forty-four consuls in reparation for inequities under the double list. The diplomats on the board moved to the field, Grew as ambassador to Turkey. Kellogg removed the undersecretary from the board and in assigning replacements ensured that those identified with the consuls outnumbered those identified with the diplomats four to two. Carr was named chairman.[167] The diplomats had decisively lost their fight for autonomy, and the development of the Foreign Service entered a new phase.

It was a fight the diplomats stood very little chance of winning. They could not long defy the manifest intent of

167. Grew, *Turbulent Era*, I, 698–99; Heinrichs, *Grew*, p. 124; Departmental Orders No. 407 and 437, April 23, 1927 and February 25, 1928, and Kellogg Circular Instruction, March 2, 1928, File 120.11/2,4,5, State Department Archives.

Congress to fuse the two services. Their professional defense, constrained and limited to begin with, contained a large element of social caste and was to that extent pseudoprofessional. Nevertheless, their efforts were not merely the last stand of a dying social order. In the idea of a powerful and independent chief of personnel they hit upon a device that the Foreign Service would come back to again and again to protect its autonomy. The diplomats entered the Foreign Service confidently and hopefully and stayed with it long enough for the esprit de corps and elite idea of the old Diplomatic Service to attach themselves to the Foreign Service. Finally, they bequeathed to the Foreign Service the idea of diplomacy as a profession. These civil servants would think of themselves as professionals not in the usual sense of individual specialists in a bureaucracy but as members of an integral profession within a bureaucracy. In important ways the Foreign Service reflected the Diplomatic Service, not its intended model the Consular Service.

The Development of the Foreign Service, 1927–1946

The "Diplomatic Scandal of 1927" opened a third phase in the development of American career diplomacy. It set the forces of bureaucratic reform in motion to remedy the deficiencies of the Rogers Act. New legislation provided better compensation to ensure that the man without private income would suffer no disadvantage and safeguards against favoritism in the administration of the Foreign Service. Carr moved into control and increased interchange of personnel to the point where the division between the branches was no longer significant. With reform carried as far as law and administration permitted, the bureaucratic drive slackened, and the initiative gradually passed back to the professionals, not the

old group but younger men who identified themselves with
the Foreign Service as a whole rather than with any segment of it. They grew increasingly restive under what
seemed a rigid and unimaginative direction of their service
and searched for a new professionalism devoid of social
bias and providing a more substantial intellectual foundation to justify a measure of self-administration. In 1937,
when Carr finally relinquished control and departed as minister to Czechoslovakia, the younger men moved into influential positions in the State Department hierarchy. At the
end of World War II they were in a position to draft legislation making the Foreign Service a largely distinct and self-
regulating agency. The Foreign Service Act of 1946, which
embodied the views of these Foreign Service officers,
marked the high point of professional autonomy in American diplomacy.

In view of the public outcry at the conduct of the diplomats on the Personnel Board, corrective action by Congress
was surprisingly mild. A number of circumstances contributed to a remedial rather than a root-and-branch solution.
No one favored a return to the spoils system, and Congress
was naturally loath to concede that its original formula, the
Rogers Act, was defective. Indeed, the evidence suggested
not that the idea was wrong but that it had been perverted
in practice. Action was delayed by a Senate investigation
and the variety of reform proposals this inspired.[168] In the
meantime, the State Department had an opportunity to set
its house in order and take some of the sting out of the attack. Kellogg and Carr explained the circumstances of the
February promotion list, exonerating the Personnel Board,
and Carr used his influence to soften some of the more re-

168. Ilchman, *Professional Diplomacy*, pp. 196–99. For one alternative,
the Porter Bill, see *New York Times*, Apr. 19, 1928.

strictive features of pending legislation.[169] The result, the Moses-Linthicum Act of 1931, was a restatement of the Rogers Act with amendments to remedy its deficiencies.[170] Its negative and prohibitive features were balanced by constructive provisions to make the career more attractive. For example, it authorized special allowances for posts where the cost of living was substantially higher than in the United States. With these features, and reflecting as it did administrative changes already effected in the department, the act came as a welcome relief to the Foreign Service.[171]

Those features that the diplomats found unattractive related to the administration of the Foreign Service. The Moses-Linthicum Act vested sole responsibility for its administration in a Personnel Board composed of not more than three assistant secretaries, with the assistant secretary in charge of administration (Carr, of course) as chairman. This arrangement was in effect a statutory enactment of the Carr plan. The act further provided for a Division of Foreign Service Personnel to handle housekeeping chores, to which no Foreign Service officer below Class I could be assigned. Assignment made an officer ineligible for recommendation for promotion to minister then and for three years thereafter. The chief of personnel might attend board meetings but could not vote, and had authority only of "a purely advisory character" over promotions and transfers. Every two years the chairman was to have a single promo-

169. Carr Diary, October 15, 1927, and Charles Bridgman Hosmer to Carr, February 19, 1931, Carr Papers; Grew, *Turbulent Era,* I, 704.

170. "An Act for the Grading and Classification of Clerks in the Foreign Service . . . (Moses-Linthicum Act), 71st Cong., 3d Sess. (1931), 46 U.S. Statues 1207 (February 23, 1931).

171. Carr Diary, February 18, 1931. Wilson, Castle, and Grew all reacted favorably to the Moses Bill, which was substantially incorporated in the final Act of 1931 (Wilson to Grew, June 5, 1928, and Castle to Grew, May 12, 1928, Wilson Papers; Grew to Wright, June 14, 1928, Grew Papers).

tion list prepared rating all officers in the service according to their relative efficiency. After approval by the board and the secretary of state, the list could not be changed except by the same process of approval for reasons of conspicuously meritorious conduct or serious misconduct recorded in the individual's efficiency record. Thus Congress disposed, in extraordinary and even humiliating detail, of the problem of favoritism in the Foreign Service. Administration by legislation was directed in this case toward more effective bureaucratic control, but, of course, it could be used for the opposite purpose, as a means of isolating the Foreign Service from control by the department and ensuring its self-regulation.

Carr ran the Foreign Service with a firm hand, determined finally to achieve consolidation. He had a position of unique authority, ranking above other assistant secretaries, with responsibility for virtually all the department's activities except foreign policy. He supervised the examination system and training school of the Foreign Service as well as managing its personnel.[172] He strove constantly for commonalty in the service: a single set of regulations, commissioning under both diplomatic and consular titles, and consolidation of diplomatic and consular work in capital cities. Under the new system, an ambassador could assign staff to either type of work as needed and through the head of his consular section supervise all the consuls in the country.[173] Service appointments to minister under President Hoover were generally to less-favored Latin American posts, and Carr was pleased to see Secretary Stimson deal severely with Leland Harrison for trying to beg off his assignment

172. Carr Diary, November 23, 1934, Carr Papers; Crane, *Carr*, pp. 304–5; Raymond Moley, "Shake-up," *Newsweek* X (July 17, 1937), 44.
173. Ilchman, *Professional Diplomacy*, p. 200; Childs, *American Foreign Service*, pp. 79–80; Barnes and Morgan, *Foreign Service*, pp. 229–30.

to Uruguay.[174] Franklin Roosevelt seemed no less inclined to discipline the diplomats. He instructed Carr to speed up interchange of officers, to extend it to the highest ranks, and to inform diplomats of pre-Rogers vintage that service in a consulate was considered a normal part of training for ministerial rank.[175] As a result, more and more diplomats found themselves in unaccustomed roles in faraway places, the counselor of embassy in Berlin as consul general in Calcutta and the counselor of embassy in Paris as consul general in Beirut. The momentum for consolidation became irreversible. By the end of the thirties the Foreign Service was a monolithic organization. Whatever distinctions remained between the two old services lay in the unreachable area of personal relations.

The period of Carr's greatest power proved to be his unhappiest. He was nearing retirement, and it seemed the "great adventure" might elude him. He wanted a policy role under Kellogg but was denied it. He hoped for the undersecretaryship in 1931, but Stimson appointed his enemy Castle, explaining he required a policy man.[176] Under Roosevelt the post went to diplomats Phillips and Sumner Welles. No one mentioned Carr for an embassy. High rank made his work less satisfying. He was no longer personally managing the careers of consuls, and it was "painful" to note how little real understanding they had of his part in the new service.[177] At the same time, broader responsibilities exposed him to more criticism. Particularly distasteful was the

174. Grew to Moffat, January 27, 1930, Grew Papers; Evan Young to Secretary of State, March 30, 1928, File 120/58, State Department Archives. On Harrison: Carr Diary, July 3, 1930, Carr Papers; Grew to Arthur Bliss Lane, May 24, 1932, Grew Papers.

175. Carr Diary, June 28, July 6, 1934, January 15, 1935, Carr Papers.

176. Memorandum, Robert Olds to Frank B. Kellogg, June 29, 1928, Kellogg Papers, Minnesota Historical Society; Carr Diary, March 28, 1931, Carr Papers.

177. Carr Diary, May 3, 1926, Carr Papers.

task of effecting radical economies during the depression. Demoralizing cuts in salaries and allowances together with the depreciation of the dollar meant income losses as high as fifty percent for some officers. Carr pleaded and warned, but loyally hacked away at the structure he had spent so many years building.[178] How bitter it was, then, to be described in a national magazine as an official who was popular on the Hill because he never begged very hard for appropriations![179]

For Carr the administration of the Foreign Service under Roosevelt was a nightmare. He detested his colleagues on the Personnel Board, Assistant Secretaries Welles and R. Walton Moore. They formed one of those unmatched teams Roosevelt placed in a department to see which man pulled hardest and to open up options. Welles was the personification of the social diplomat, Groton and Harvard like the president, one of the "old 1718 crowd," and owner of Oxon Hill Manor, which, Carr had heard, kept twenty gardeners busy. Welles would secure presidential intervention in behalf of certain diplomats while Moore, who shared Carr's antipathy for social diplomats, aroused him no less by seeking help outside the board against them, from the field, Congress, the secretary, and the president. Undersecretary Phillips had his own problems, and Secretary Hull seemed uninterested and diffident. In the circumstances it was impossible to administer the service methodically, and the board became "a constant humiliation."[180] Still, Carr hung on

178. *Ibid.*, January 7, 1935; File 120.31/182–213, State Department Archives; Ilchman, *Professional Diplomacy*, pp. 229–31; Crane, *Carr*, pp. 314–17.

179. Herring, "Department of State," p. 228.

180. Carr Diary, June 20, 1934, March 25, 1935, Carr Papers. On Carr's difficulties in the administration of the Foreign Service: Carr Diary, 1934–37, *passim*. On Moore see also: Robert Dallek, *Democrat and Diplomat: The Life of William E. Dodd* (New York, 1968), pp. 237–38.

grimly past retirement age until 1937, when the president asked him to go as minister to Czechoslovakia, figuring, Carr supposed, the Germans would get there first. After the appointment, Carr noticed how quickly people changed their greeting. And so, after forty-five years in the department, he left, nursing the thought that perhaps the machine would not run so smoothly when he was gone.

These demoralizing circumstances had their effect on Carr's leadership of the Foreign Service. He was most effective when his responsibilities were clearly defined and he had the support of strong secretaries of state with orderly administrative habits, like Root, Hughes, and Stimson. Now lonely eminence, crisscrossing lines of authority, and the whipsaw of powerful, aggressive personalities intensified Carr's insecurity. In 1936 Foreign Service Officer G. Howland Shaw wrote an essay in *Foreign Affairs* describing administration of the Service—by implication Carr's administration—as rigid, unimaginative, and unresponsive.[181] Such criticism only heightened Carr's anxieties. An article in *Harper's* of the type public officials must often suffer in silence, criticizing him for playing favorites and remaining insensitive to the glaring inadequacies of the Service, provoked Carr to consideration of action for libel.[182] The insecure and threatened bureaucrat frequently responds with exaggerated bureaucratic, or "bureaupathic," behavior, a form of ritualism characterized by undue emphasis on com-

181. Shaw, "American Foreign Service." Shaw, in an interview with the author, January 6, 1959, claimed that Carr sought to demote him for publication of the article. The allegation has not been verified, but Carr does note in his diary (November 14, 1935) that he placed before the Personnel Board a memorandum on the Shaw article and secured their approval of it. Shaw in the same conversation with the author claimed that Carr "grew very rigid."

182. Herring, "Department of State"; Memorandum, Keith Merrill to Carr, February 2, 1937, Carr Papers.

pliance with rules and stubborn resistance to change.[183] Carr may well have been such a case. He was caught in a circle: the more threatened he felt, the more rigid he became, and the more criticism he evoked. Thus the Foreign Service was being subjected not merely to an extension of the bureaucratic pattern of the old Consular Service, but to such a pattern in exaggerated form. The result was growing dissatisfaction around which formed a new professional movement.

In 1937 the Foreign Service consisted of seven hundred officers divided into eight classes and three probationary grades. It was more geographically representative than the Diplomatic Service had been, and the distortions—overrepresentation of the East and West coasts and urban states and underrepresentation of the South—were not a significant liability.[184] The defeat and consequent discouragement of the diplomats in 1927 as well as the temptations of business led to an "appalling" rate of resignations in the 1927–29 period.[185] Those who remained accepted the new discipline and orientation of the service. With the depression came financial hardship from budget slashing, but there were now few jobs outside the service. Consequently, the resignation rate for 1930–39 was a low 1.3 percent.[186] Foreign Service officers retained jobs, but prospects of promotion were discouraging. Due to the large intake of the postwar years and the rapid promotions of 1924–27, the top four classes were young, close to each other in median age, and thus far from retirement.[187] Movement upward slowed. The increase in service ministers

183. Victor A. Thompson, *Modern Organization: A General Theory* (New York, 1968), pp. 152–69.

184. "Statistical Survey of the Foreign Service," *American Foreign Service Journal* XVI (1939), 374.

185. Editorial by Dana Munro, *ibid.*, VI (1929), 410; Moffat Diary, April 2, 1929, Moffat Papers.

186. Ilchman, *Professional Diplomacy*, p. 223.

187. Selden Chapin, "The American Foreign Service," *American Foreign Service Journal* XIV (1937), 748–49.

and ambassadors under Hoover and Roosevelt was slight, from 41 to 48 percent, a numerical difference of nine.[188] Slow turnover at the top and statutory limitation on the numbers in each class, to say nothing of budgetary limitations, virtually halted career advancement. The Foreign Service of 1937 was different from the old Diplomatic Service in a number of ways. It was committed to the career by necessity if not by choice. It was more disciplined, more enured to hardship, less buoyant, and less illusioned.

The significant distinction in the Foreign Service after 1927 was not vertical, between consuls and diplomats, but horizontal, between pre-Rogers and post-Rogers officers. By 1937 the latter comprised more than a third of the Service, occupying that portion from Class VI down. This new group, having no stake in the quarrels of the older officers, indentified themselves exclusively with the Foreign Service. It had a distinct character that differentiated it from the older groups. The junior officer group was considerably better educated than the old Consular Service and somewhat better than the Diplomatic Service. The number holding college degrees in entering examination groups rose to 91.3 percent in 1939, and the number with no college experience dwindled to less than 1 percent. They were less fashionably educated than the Diplomatic Service officers. Approximately one-half had attended high school and one-third boarding school, contrasting with three-fourths from boarding schools in the older service. One-third had attended Harvard, Yale, or Princeton, compared with two-thirds in the Diplomatic Service. Possessing the means and motivation to go to college indicates a predominantly upper-middle-class group as contrasted with the stipulation of private income that marked the upper-class origins of the Diplomatic Service. The upper-

188. "Career vs. Non-Career Appointments, 1906–1940," *ibid.,* XVII (1940), 679.

middle class was the traditional recruiting ground of the professions.

This was a group with strong career motivation and professional orientation. They were likely to have taken social science courses and in some cases prepared themselves specifically by attending Foreign Service schools like Georgetown. Two-thirds, rising to three-fourths, had taken graduate work. Their entering age was younger: having a well-established career to pursue, they were less experimental in choosing the Foreign Service. To secure entrance they had survived keen competition. In contrast to the three or four dozen who generally took the Diplomatic Service examination, the numbers appearing for the Foreign Service examination ranged from 168 to 732 depending on the fortunes of the service and the economy. It became a more discriminating examination in 1931 when Stimson retained Joseph C. Green, a former Princeton professor, as secretary of the Board of Examiners. Green disposed of the Civil Service examination, which stressed factual knowledge, and asked a committee of experts in international law, diplomatic usage, educational theory, and testing to draw up a new one that placed greater emphasis on intellectual capacity. He also reduced the proportion passing the examination from an average of 19.4 percent to an average of 5.5 percent.[189] In terms of motivation, preparation, and mental capacity this was a superior group of officers, an intellectual elite in contrast to the social elite of the Diplomatic Service.

Upon entering the service, they had a number of opportunities for developing professional conceptions. A few were fortunate enough to secure area training. The department had long made provision for Chinese and Japanese language

189. U.S. Department of State, *Foreign Service List, January 1, 1940* (Washington, 1940); Ilchman, *Professional Diplomacy*, pp. 162, 170, 204–5, 218–22, 227, 236, 238–40; *Who's Who in America*.

training. Beginning in 1925 this was extended to Turkish, Arabic, Persian, and Slavic. In urging appropriation of funds, Kellogg pointed out that the break-up of empires made it necessary to prepare representatives to cope with exotic cultures. Under this program junior officers such as Raymond Hare and Charles Bohlen studied at the Ecole Nationale des Langues Vivantes Orientales in Paris, and George Kennan studied Russian language, literature, and history at the University of Berlin.[190] At Istanbul, Counselor of Embassy G. Howland Shaw encouraged junior secretaries to file dispatches that carried beyond the normal requirements of political reporting and amounted to scholarly studies of Turkish life and institutions.[191] Roosevelt economy measures apparently curtailed the programs, but the concept of special training for service in non-European areas had been established, adding a new dimension to American career diplomacy. The rigorous experience brought a distinct intellectual commitment and sense of competency within the broad field of diplomacy.

Junior officers would look in vain to the pre-Rogers diplomats for professional leadership. The older diplomats were much in demand, in spite of 1927. As heads of mission, counselors, and division chiefs, the old Diplomatic Service managed much of the regular business of diplomacy in the thirties. Grew was Ambassador to Japan, Phillips to Italy, and Wilson briefly to Germany. As ambassadors they had graduated from the Foreign Service and were unresponsive to its current needs. The satisfaction of achieving career diplomacy was soured by defeat, disillusion, and humiliation. They retained the conviction that the wrong approach

190. Kellogg to Rep. Charles Edwards, January 13, 1927, File 120.1/116, and File 120.377/1,6,7,52, State Department Archives; Kennan, *Memoirs*, pp. 23–24, 31–34; Ilchman, *Professional Diplomacy*, p. 240.

191. Heinrichs, *Grew*, p. 160.

had prevailed, with the effect of imprisoning good men in irrelevant work.[192] To battle for change was another thing. Republicans working for Democrats, Edwardians in a mass society, gentle civilizers in barbaric times, they could not accept, let alone comprehend or manipulate, their world.[193] They would do their duty, but for organizing and directing the Foreign Service they had no heart.

The older generation served as teachers rather than leaders. They were masters of technique and form. In the writing of diplomatic communications, they drummed into their secretaries the importance of precision, conciseness, clarity, an orderly structure of logic, and the avoidance of stylistic excrescences. It should be a matter of "professional pride" with any officer, Grew told his staff, to withhold his initials from a document until he was satisfied that its contents were as perfect as possible.[194] MacMurray dealt with the ethics of the profession in the *Foreign Service Journal*. He insisted that diplomacy had a code of conduct as rigorous as any profession. Far from being an affair of duplicity, as people imagined, diplomacy had strict rules of play that the practitioner disregarded at the peril of contempt from his colleagues of other nations. This concern for reputation might arise from "guild spirit," the natural desire of a man to

192. Grew Diary, March 20, 1928, and Grew to Arthur Bliss Lane, May 24, 1932, Grew Papers; Wilson to Grew, June 5, 1928, and to Hugh R. Wilson, Jr., September 17, 1936, Wilson Papers. Gibson, in "Diplomats Pay to Work," *Saturday Evening Post* CCIX (May 8, 1937), 25, worried about representation allowances and amateur ambassadors.

193. The Grew and Moffat diaries and the correspondence of Wilson offer many illustrations of this state of mind. See for example Moffat Diary, March 16–18, August 14, 1931, Moffat Papers, and Alexander Kirk to William Bullitt, October 16, 1939, Wilson Papers, as well as Heinrichs, *Grew*, and William W. Kaufmann, "Two American Ambassadors: Bullitt and Kennedy," in Gordon A. Craig and Felix Gilbert, eds., *The Diplomats, 1919–1939* (Princeton, N.J., 1953), p. 680.

194. Grew, "Efficiency Reports," *Foreign Service Journal* XIX (1942), 532–533; J. Theodore Marriner, "Use of English in Diplomatic Correspondence," *ibid.*, II (1925), 300; Grew, "Address to the Class of 1926," *ibid.*, III (1926), 181–83.

win the esteem of his particular group, but in any case no profession took more into account an individual's dependability, loyalty, and scrupulosity. People would be amazed to learn, MacMurray continued, that the tradition of diplomacy involved not only fair play but positive helpfulness. Diplomacy, he concluded, was very much a human institution.[195]

Young Foreign Service officers also learned their craft in subtler ways. Kennan writes of his debt to Alexander Kirk, under whom he served at Berlin in 1939–40. Kirk was old school, a junior to Grew in the same embassy during World War I. He was a wealthy and eccentric bachelor who insisted that he entered diplomacy to spare his dear mother the trouble of having her bags inspected by customs. "Unintellectual as he was," says Kennan, "his instincts were very sound; and when one learned enough to see through the poses and to look for the deeper meaning of the quips, he was a good teacher." [196] Kennan learned that how a diplomat went about his business was at least as important as what he sought to accomplish. Perhaps Kirk overstressed good form, and undoubtedly his conception of it was too exquisite for modern diplomacy. Nevertheless, ends and means were related in diplomacy, and Kirk, Grew, Gibson, and their generation helped mature the diplomatic personalities of the younger men by directing their attention to the impression made on others, to ambiance, tone, and style. They served as models additionally by having a clear sense of who they were and what they stood for. That identity may not have suited the younger generation, but they profited from the example of self-confidence and the easy assurance in action that flowed from it.

Joseph Grew further assisted by providing a definition of

195. MacMurray, "The Ethics of Diplomacy," *ibid.*, IX (1932), 3–8, 36.
196. Kennan, *Memoirs,* pp. 112–15.

the professional diplomat broader than that of mere agent of his government. The public service ideal and individual sense of responsibility that characterized the Diplomatic Service at its best were strongly represented in Grew, and his decades of service abroad gave him an objective view of the attitudes and policies of his own country. He went to Japan as ambassador in 1932 determined to establish a solid basis for Japanese-American understanding, like an architect building a house to last forever. When that hope dimmed, he used another professional analogy, the physician trying to save his patient, the patient being neither Japan nor America but their relationship. In the years before Pearl Harbor he repeatedly urged both governments to begin resolving their differences, on occasion taking unauthorized initiatives at Tokyo to "start the ball rolling toward peace." [197] The circumstances were not promising, and Grew played the role of middleman so circumspectly toward the end that he weakened his purpose. Nevertheless, by obviously trying to be a peacemaker, Grew offered a conception of professional service with the strongest possible emphasis on altruism.

One officer was willing—in fact, anxious—to lead the Foreign Service. He was Gardiner Howland Shaw, a Boston Brahmin, Harvard graduate, and member of the Somerset Club. Shaw entered the Diplomatic Service in 1918 and rose in twelve years to Class I in the Foreign Service. He was regarded as one of the most promising younger diplomats, sure to be minister and ambassador soon.[198] A close friend of Grew, he admired the qualities Grew represented and fitted that type easily. Yet he was also different. Entering the

197. Heinrichs, *Grew,* pp. 248, 253, 283, 291–99, 338–50.
198. Undersecretary Robert Olds to Kellogg, July 12, 1928, Kellogg Papers; *Who's Who in America;* Department of State, *Register, October 1, 1939* (Washington, 1939).

service during the war, he never experienced courtier diplomacy. Entirely atypical was his scholarly bent: election to Phi Beta Kappa, graduate work at Harvard, and lifelong study in the fields of sociology, social psychology, and psychiatry. Furthermore, he was one of the first area specialists outside East Asia. Except for several brief stints at Paris, he served abroad only in Turkey, at his own insistence.[199] In Washington he was chief of the Near Eastern Affairs Division. Combining the social background and noblesse oblige of the older generation with the intellectual qualifications and interests of the new, he was the perfect bridge between them.

Shaw acted from strong faith and conviction. A devout Roman Catholic and passionate humanist, he believed that life centered on a personal ideal built by the individual for himself that governed and directed experience. Intense involvement with human beings, an involvement of seeing, caring, feeling, believing, giving, enriched and extended the fabric of the "intimate self." Success in living depended on the freest possible development of the personality according to its own dictates, not society's judgment in terms of material rewards. In this ideal of individualism, the profession could be a source of satisfaction in life only to the extent that it had social value.[200] Shaw's own ideal directed him down two paths of social action: a lifelong interest in prison reform and treatment of juvenile delinquency and improvement in the personnel management of the Foreign Service.[201]

199. Shaw, "American Foreign Service," p. 327; Heinrichs, *Grew*, p. 160; Interview with Shaw, January 6, 1959; Carr Diary, April 21, 1937, Carr Papers.

200. Shaw, "Success," *Commonweal* XXVI (1937), 510–11.

201. Heinrichs, *Grew*, p. 160; Bertram Hulen, *Inside the Department of State* (New York, 1939), p. 182. Shaw was a member of the board of trustees and board of visitors of the National Training School for Boys,

The fundamental weakness of the Foreign Service was its inherent tendency to mediocrity, Shaw believed. The work as defined was routine, requiring neither superior skill nor intensive mental effort. In the important positions work was ill-defined, and the man made the job. The poorly educated, the insecure person attracted by the status and privileges of diplomacy, the "rigid, unimaginative bureaucrat," the "yes" man, got by easily enough. But the service needed officers who were not likely to fall into a rut, self-contained and self-sustaining individualists with zest for life, imagination, and strong ambition. Shaw believed there was even room for the supreme individualist, forever dissenting, upsetting complacency, and laughing at solemnities, the man who was prepared to take a calculated risk. Of course the Foreign Service officer required basic skills of thought and expression and an effective personality, but he must also possess "insatiable intellectual curiosity," independence of mind, and capacity for constant self-evaluation and criticism. Shaw felt that recruiting this type was not the main difficulty; the post-Rogers Foreign Service officers were of excellent quality. The problem was management. By concentrating on organization and not on the man and his work, the leadership of

---

vice-president and director of the Children's Village, Dobbs Ferry, N.Y., director of the National Conference of Juvenile Agencies, and member of the boards of directors of the Prison Association of New York, the National Probation Association, the Boys' Club of New York, the National Committee for Mental Hygiene, and the executive committee of the National Jail Association. The therapeutic approach to prisoners has the effect of transforming prisons from commonweal organizations concerned with the protection of the public into service organizations, oriented primarily to the needs and interests of the prisoner "clients," and one consequence is a reduced dependence on bureaucratic procedures. See Blau and Scott, *Formal Organizations,* p. 57. The same would apply more strongly to organizations dealing with young offenders. Shaw's connection with this therapeutic movement suggests that he may have conceived of the Foreign Service in the same way and sought to add the dimension of a service organization concerned with the needs of its officer "clients" to a bureaucratic commonweal organization.

the service reinforced the tendency to mediocrity and stultified the capable young officers it already possessed.

The answer was administration that provided an atmosphere conducive to the development of each officer according to his interests and abilities. Shaw deplored the Jack-of-all-trades approach that put diplomats into consular work and vice versa. Consular work required organizing and administrative capacity, whereas diplomatic work called for more "individuality, initiative and imagination." The man who could do anything usually did nothing well. Shaw suggested a service organized by type of work, for example, administrative (mostly consular), economic-financial, research, negotiation, and the area specialties. He also suggested an easier entrance examination followed by ten years of experimentation by the junior officer in various lines of work, during which he would find out what he was best at. Then would come a second, searching examination in financial, economic, legal, and political subjects which would determine advancement to the higher grades.

His idea of specialization combined bureaucratic and professional modes with emphasis on the latter. More sophisticated functional specialization fully accorded with the bureaucratic pattern. However, organizational needs would not necessarily fit individual competencies. Shaw valued the development of the individual according to his own dictates and capacities. Specialization on that principle would require some adjustment of the needs of the organization to those of the individual, contrary to the bureaucratic rationale. Furthermore, advancement was based on further specialization rather than capacity to direct the activities of others. Indeed, if administrative work was "ready-made," as Shaw defined it, competence in that field would tend to defeat advancement. The cream of the service would be those who had developed an esoteric knowledge, an intellectual elite oriented more professionally than bureaucratically.[202]

Shaw would professionalize the service by strengthening its professional organization, the American Foreign Service Association. Established in 1924 for active and retired officers, the association had no formal connection with the government, ran itself on an elective basis, and published a monthly journal. The *Foreign Service Journal* was usually a gossipy house organ only fitfully taking an interest in the larger needs and interests of the service.[203] In 1935 Shaw sought to revive the *Journal* with a letter to the editor in which he said:

> Foreign Service is a profession, the purpose of which is to render certain public services. If this definition is correct then it logically follows that the *Foreign Service Journal* should possess the characteristics of a professional journal and these are the very characteristics which, it seems to me, it does not now possess. Members of a profession, as a rule, do a certain amount of thinking concerning their work and concerning methods by which it can be improved. The results of this thinking they are anxious to discuss with their colleagues, orally and in writing. In the case of the Foreign Service, the members of which are scattered all over the world, this discussion should be carried on in the *Foreign Service Journal.*[204]

At first the response was disappointing, but later issues offered more reviews of books dealing with diplomacy, a re-

202. Shaw, "American Foreign Service"; Editorial by Shaw, "Why Go Into the Foreign Service," *American Foreign Service Journal* VII (1930), 27; Shaw, "The Individualist and the Foreign Service," *ibid.*, IX (1932), 218; Shaw, "The Foreign Service: What Is It and How to Prepare for It," *ibid.*, XV (1938), 40; Shaw, "Foreign Service Personnel," *ibid.*, 172; Grew Diary, August 22, 1930, Grew Papers.

203. See Seldin Chapin's criticism of the *Journal* in "American Foreign Service," *American Foreign Service Journal* XIV (1937), p. 748.

204. Letter to the Editor by Shaw, *ibid.*, XII (1935), 328.

print of an article by Harold Nicolson on the British Foreign Service, and articles from the field, two of them by junior Foreign Service officers, calling for more specialization and in-service professional training. One of these younger officers, Selden Chapin, dealt extensively with recruitment, promotion, and administration and called for freer discussion of professional problems.[205] That same year Shaw entered into a position of direct influence in the association with his election to chairman of the executive committee.

Shaw's second move was to secure control of the administration of the Foreign Service. A "significant step towards a more democratic system of personnel administration," he argued, would be to "give to the Service a measure of real self-government." He publicly attacked its current administration in January, 1936, with a prize essay in a contest sponsored by a retired old-school diplomat, Robert Woods Bliss. The essay, which appeared in *Foreign Affairs,* was a comprehensive statement of what he felt was wrong with the service and what corrective steps should be taken.[206] In November of that year he sought Carr's support for the position of chief of the Division of Foreign Service Personnel, the position in which the incumbent was ineligible for promotion at the time and for three years after. Needless to say, Carr opposed him.[207] Then in 1937, with the world crisis deepening, Roosevelt decided on a major shuffling of the State Department's command. He settled on Welles to replace Phillips as undersecretary, chose Hugh Wilson as a policy assistant secretary, and sent Carr to the field.[208] The old Diplomatic Service was

205. Harold Nicolson, "The British Foreign Service," *ibid.* XIII (1936), 429 ff.; George V. Allen, "The Utility of a Trained and Permanent Foreign Service," *ibid.* 5 ff.; Chapin, "American Foreign Service." pp. 643 ff. and 718 ff.; "Saturn," "Field Notes on Service Needs," *ibid.* XV (1938), 199–200.

206. Shaw, "American Foreign Service," pp. 323–33.

207. Carr Diary, November 14, 15, 1936, April 21, 1937, Carr Papers.

208. Moley, "Shake-up," p. 44.

once again respectable. As Carr's replacement Roosevelt selected George S. Messersmith, a highly regarded Foreign Service officer who had risen from the consular ranks to become minister to Austria and whose reports on the threat of Nazism had been outstanding.[209] The new chief of Foreign Service Personnel under Messersmith was Shaw.

In the four years that remained before World War II, the Foreign Service sought to recruit officers of the highest intellectual caliber. Shaw encouraged a broad liberal arts background with specialization in the social sciences, particularly social psychology and sociology.[210] He argued that the modern diplomat must consider international relations from a broader point of view than classical political science and economics. Behavioral scientists like Harold Lasswell offered valuable insights into nations' tendencies to pathological conduct and ways of resisting such tendencies.[211] At the same time, Messersmith and Shaw strongly discouraged talk of a national academy of foreign affairs on the order of West Point and Annapolis. A service academy would encourage premature vocational education, Shaw warned.[212] Meanwhile, mathematical reasoning and manipulation of symbols replaced arithmetic in the entrance examination; questions demanded more analysis and written exposition.[213] Experts

209. Robert Dallek, "Beyond Tradition: The Diplomatic Careers of William E. Dodd and George S. Messersmith, 1933–1938," *South Atlantic Quarterly* LXVI (1967), 236–37.

210. Shaw, "The Foreign Service: What Is It and How to Prepare for It," pp. 41–42.

211. "The Modern Diplomat," by "H," *Foreign Affairs* XV (April, 1937), 513. Comparison with Shaw's other articles strongly suggests that he wrote it. Shaw, "The Foreign Service: What Is It and How to Prepare For it," p. 42.

212. Memoranda, Shaw to George S. Messersmith, April 18, 1938, and Messersmith to Cordell Hull, April 13, 1938, File 120.313/68–1/2, State Department Archives.

213. Memoranda, Joseph C. Green to Shaw, September 14, 1937, and Green to Messersmith, February 6, 1939, File 120.1121/139,152A, State Department Archives.

scrutinized the oral examination and found wide variations in the judgments of examiners, but were at a loss to discover a more scientific method of evaluation.[214]

Within the service the spirit verged on the utopian. At the Training School, officers just back from their first tour lectured on the position of the Quichua Indian in the social structure of Ecuador, the labor movement in Mexico, minorities and irredentism in Hungary, and Sanskrit as a cultural force in the Near East and Indo-China.[215] Shaw pressed his scheme of matching the functional requirements of posts with data he was accumulating on the capabilities, health, morals, family condition, and preferences of officers, whom he urged to come and talk freely about "all their problems" without the slightest fear that anything they said might be used against them. He in turn would tell them their general standing, especially if their efficiency ratings were beginning to slip. With funds once again available for university instruction, Shaw assigned a dozen or so specialists, mostly in economics, to Harvard, Georgetown, Chicago, Princeton, and New York University. He hoped to extend the program to other fields, and one junior officer urged that up to thirty or forty men a year be permitted to use their leaves of absence for full-time university study without specification as to field; but there were practical limitations even in the Shaw era.[216]

The larger interests of the Foreign Service were prospering as well. With an improving economy and deepening

214. Secretary Hull to Professor Carl C. Brigham, April 28, 1939 and enclosed Memorandum on the Oral Examinations, File 120.1121/158, State Department Archives.

215. David T. Ray, "Activities of the Foreign Service Officers' Training School," *American Foreign Service Journal* XVI (1939), 668.

216. Shaw, "Foreign Service Personnel," 139–40, 172–73; File 120.378/24–33, State Department Archives; James W. Gantenbein, "Study by Foreign Service Officers in American Universities," *American Foreign Service Journal* XVI (1939), 541, 562–63.

world crisis, Congress eased appropriations and officers advanced more rapidly. By the time of Pearl Harbor an average of 45 percent of each of the top four classes had received an appointment within two years and only 20 percent had been in class longer than four years.[217] In 1939 Messersmith won a battle Carr had been fighting for years: under the Reorganization Act of that year the president incorporated the attaché services of the Departments of Commerce and Agriculture into the Foreign Service, which finally became the only foreign service of the United States.[218] Shaw, who was appointed assistant secretary of state for administration in 1941, worked to overcome the public image of the service as a rich man's club by providing figures showing the wide geographical distribution of candidates and the large number of colleges and universities represented. In the new "streamlined" Foreign Service, the argument went, a man was more likely to be of modest means, or even poor, than wealthy, and was as likely to be a graduate of a middle western university as of Harvard. It would have been delusive to suppose that the service had more than a tenuous hold on the affections of the American people, but favorable comment on its more representative and democratic character did appear.[219] As a result of these developments, the Foreign Service on the eve of World War II was stable, confident, and improving. This was perhaps the most favorable position it would ever achieve.

217. Department of State, *Foreign Service List, October 1, 1941* (Washington, 1941).

218. Barnes and Morgan, *Foreign Service*, pp. 222–23; Ilchman, *Professional Diplomacy*, pp. 241–43. On Messersmith's role see File 120.1/304–389, State Department Archives.

219. Joseph H. Baird, "Professionalized Diplomacy" (extracted from *Washington Star*, Aug. 6, 1939), *American Foreign Service Journal* XVI (1939), pp. 542–43; Ellery C. Stowell, "The Appointment of Assistant Secretary of State G. Howland Shaw and Our Foreign Service," (reprinted from *American Journal of International Law*, April, 1941), *American Foreign Service Journal* XVIII (1941), 632–33, 655–66; *Washington Post*, Nov. 24, 1940.

The war disrupted the pattern of orderly growth of an elite career service. Closing of posts in war zones, emergency needs, and proliferation of new functions prevented rational matching of needs and capacities. New demands found the service understrength. It has grown too slowly in the prewar years, only 30 percent since the Rogers Act, as a result of economy measures and highly selective recruitment.[220] With examinations suspended for the duration and officers subject to the draft beginning in 1944, the career service actually declined in strength, from 833 officers in 1939 to 785 in 1945. The Foreign Service Auxiliary, a temporary force, supplied staff for cultural, informational, and economic work in the higher ranks and consular work in the lower ranks.[221] Although the auxiliary officers were temporary, much of their work remained permanent. Clearly, in the postwar world the United States would have vast new responsibilities and interests requiring greatly enlarged overseas representation. The question was whether the Foreign Service should conduct these activities, and if so, how it should expand to undertake them.

Despite wartime difficulties, the Foreign Service emerged in a favorable position to map its future. In 1944 Shaw retired from government and leadership passed to Selden Chapin, a graduate of St. Paul's School and Annapolis, and one of the first to enter the Foreign Service under the Rogers Act. A specialist in Latin American affairs with the naval officer's strong sense of professionalism as well as a long-standing interest in the welfare of the service, Chapin was a fitting successor. Assisting him were Julian Harrington, a consular

220. For example, of 483 who took the written examinations in 1940–41, only 43 were appointed. Stowell, "The Appointment of Assistant Secretary Shaw," p. 633. In that crisis year the Service in all likelihood could have secured funds for as many new officers as it felt it needed. See also Editorial, *American Foreign Service Journal* XXI (1944), 74.

221. "Personnel Inventory of the Foreign Service," *ibid.*, XXII (1945), 13–14, 47; Barnes and Morgan, *Foreign Service*, 242–47.

specialist, and a group of post-Rogers officers that included
Andrew Foster, Alan Steyne, and Edmund Gullion, graduates respectively of Dartmouth, Yale, and Princeton. This
Foreign Service group controlled the Office of the Foreign
Service, a new, high-level administrative unit with its own
planning staff. Assistant Secretary for Administration Julius
C. Holmes was a former Foreign Service officer and a close
friend of Chapin, and his successor, Donald Russell, was
anxious to appease service opinion to facilitate the intensive
postwar negotiations of Secretary of State James F. Byrnes.
Congress, after the Roosevelt years, favored detailed legislative prescriptions for the executive branch, and members of
the relevant subcommittee of the House Foreign Affairs
Committee were favorably disposed toward the administration, Byrnes, or the Foreign Service. The Moses-Linthicum
Act of 1931 required a major overhaul, and Chapin and his
colleagues, after the fashion of Carr, took the initiative in
drafting it.[222]

The basic problem facing the drafters was how to relate
the new foreign relations functions of the United States to
the Foreign Service. At one extreme, the service might remain a closed career with appointment at the bottom and
promotion from within. At the other extreme, it might embrace cultural, information, technical, scientific, fiscal, and
administrative specialists at appropriate rank, and in so doing fundamentally alter its character. A similar challenge
faced the Diplomatic Service after World War I. Shaw, who
undoubtedly remembered the unfortunate consequences of
resistance to change in the twenties, had been leaning to-

222. On the background of the Foreign Service Act of 1946 see: "The
Foreign Service Act of 1946," in Harold Stein, ed., *Public Administration
and Policy Development: A Case Book* (New York, 1951), pp. 661–737;
Arthur G. Jones, *The Evolution of Personnel Systems for U.S. Foreign Af-
fairs: A History of Reform Efforts*, Carnegie Endowment for International
Peace Foreign Affairs Personnel Study No. 1 (1965), chap. 3.

ward the latter solution. An enthusiast for specialization, he welcomed the new functions. Specialists from other agencies could be incorporated on a temporary basis while the Foreign Service developed its own new experts, using several different types of examination.[223] His thinking seems to have been running toward a multibranch career system such as the British installed in their Foreign Service in 1943.[224] In Shaw's conception, officers with academic and area specialties, an aptitude for political work, and what Kennan calls "roundedness of education, judgment and personality" would always gravitate toward the top positions, but alongside, if somewhat lower, would be other career ladders as well.[225] The object must be to retain control of all foreign affairs activities, he insisted. Exclusiveness that forced other agencies to set up their own foreign services would result in a setback from which the Foreign Service would take years to recover.

The position taken by Chapin and his drafting groups was a compromise. While receptive to demands from outside the service for a more flexible and responsive system, they faced strong pressure from within to keep it a closed career. Behind this service conservatism lay the defensive reaction of men who had contracted for one career system, devoted years to it, and now feared a change of terms. Also contributing to resistance was the Carr tradition that any officer should serve in any capacity; "generalists" opposed recruitment for a specific function. Most significant was the exclusiveness of a solidary profession with its distinctive selection

223. Shaw, "The War: The State Department and Its Foreign Service in Wartime," State Department *Bulletin* IX (1943), 291–92; Shaw, "Post-War Problems of the Foreign Service," *American Foreign Service Journal* XXI (1944), 65, 107–8.

224. Strang, *Foreign Office,* pp. 51–70.

225. George Kennan, "The Future of Our Diplomacy," *Foreign Affairs* XXXIII (1955), p. 571.

procedures, prolonged apprenticeship, and shared way of life. Chapin was no less sensitive to such opinion than Grew had been to the concerns of Diplomatic Service officers. The draft bill responded to new demands by creating two auxiliary branches, a Foreign Service Staff corps for administrative, clerical, fiscal, technical, and consular work, and a Foreign Service Reserve for higher-grade specialists such as labor attachés and information officers. At the same time, the bill protected the Foreign Service officer corps by limiting reserve appointments to four years and by restricting admission above the bottom grade to reserve, staff, and department personnel who passed written and oral examinations administered by the Foreign Service. The Chapin group envisaged amalgamation of Department and Foreign Service personnel, but gradually over a period of ten years or so. Essentially the draft bill ensured the Foreign Service officers a protected, privileged, unitary career service.

The draft bill was almost everything several generations of professionals could have wished. It created a class of career ministers, giving the service a regular place among the prized positions of diplomacy. A director general, himself a Foreign Service officer, administered the service and was a member of its policymaking board. Thereby the service finally achieved a permanent role in its own governance. Provision for retirement of those who failed to qualify for promotion would speed the rise of able officers and set stricter performance standards. Inspection, examination, promotion, and training were under the exclusive or preponderant control of the service. Once again, better salaries, allowances, and retirement benefits made the career more attractive.

The Chapin group skillfully maneuvered their bill through the Department of State and other interested departments, side-stepped Budget Bureau objections, and delivered it to their friends in Congress, where it slid easily to passage in

July, 1946, as the Foreign Service Act. On appeal from Secretary Byrnes in Paris, President Truman signed it over objections from advisers who contended it made lateral entry too difficult and unduly limited the administrative discretion of the secretary of state. The Foreign Service secured its interests but left a reserved if not hostile attitude in the executive branch. Professionalism triumphed at the expense of bureaucracy.[226]

Years of the locust followed. The Foreign Service stubbornly clung to its closed career, taking in few officers at the higher grades and shying away from new postwar functions. The United States Information Agency established its own service, and the Department of Agriculture gained authority to reestablish its Foreign Agricultural Service. Congress shifted powers vested in the director general back to the secretary of state. Outside dissatisfaction increased: three successive management studies called for a more open service embracing a variety of skills. In the early fifties, McCarthyism, personnel cuts, and suspension of recruitment brought the service to a state of "administrative ruin," according to Kennan. In 1954 a major bureaucratic reconstruction, the Wriston Program, folded large numbers of departmental, reserve, and staff officers, particularly specialists, into the Foreign Service.[227] A service demoralized and then tripled in size lapsed into passivity for a number of years, but finally found its voice again. In 1963 Deputy Undersecretary William J. Crockett, a Foreign Service officer, began reforms to enhance the status of the service and prod it into greater creativity. Then a "Young Turk" movement of frustrated and

226. Stein, ed., "Foreign Service Act," pp. 664–731. The text of the Foreign Service Act of 1946 is in Childs, *Foreign Service*, Appendix A.

227. Jones, *Evolution of Personnel Systems*, chaps. 4–6; John E. Harr, *The Development of Careers in the Foreign Service*, Carnegie Endowment for International Peace Foreign Affairs Personnel Study No. 3 (1965), chap. 1; Kennan, "Future of Our Diplomacy," p. 568.

disillusioned junior and middle grade officers took control of the Foreign Service Association and demanded redefinition of the role of the diplomat and more dynamic leadership.[228] After the 1968 election a Foreign Service reform group urged the Nixon administration to grant greater autonomy and self-management to the service.[229] These professional stirrings indicate that the dialectic of change in American career diplomacy continues.

228. John Ensor Harr, "The Managerial Crisis," in Smith Simpson, ed., *Resources and Needs of American Diplomacy, Annals of the American Academy of Political and Social Science* CCCLXXX (November, 1968), 34–37; Elizabeth A. Bean, "The Junior Foreign Service Officer," *ibid.,* 77–81.

229. *New York Times,* Dec. 6, 1968; "Nixon and State," *New Republic* CLIX (November 23, 1968), 9–10. See also Simpson, *Resources and Needs of American Diplomacy.*

The United States a World Power, 1900–1917: Myth or Reality?

PAUL A. VARG

IN 1899 John Bassett Moore, then serving as assistant secretary of state, wrote that the United States, during the preceding ten years, had moved "from a position of comparative freedom from entanglements into the position of what is commonly called a world-power." "Where formerly we had only commercial interests," he explained, "we now have territorial and political interests as well."[1] The annexation of the Philippines, Hawaii, and Puerto Rico and the temporary occupation of Cuba appeared to have thrust the United States into the vortex of international politics.

However, no one explanation of the United States' reaction to its new power position is possible. A study of the course pursued in relations with China shows that the administrations in Washington moved with a restraint approaching that of a mere observer. In Cuba the same administrations acted with energy. These two case studies, constituting the body of this essay, argue against any simple

1. Edwin Borchard *et al.*, eds., *The Collected Papers of John Bassett Moore*, 7 vols. (New Haven, Conn., 1944), II, 202.

explanation of American policy in the years after the Spanish-American War.

The differences in response do not alter the fact that measured in economic terms, the United States had achieved great power status. By 1900 there were 193,000 miles of railroad track spanning the continent linking even remote hamlets to great metropolitan centers. The prime result was a national economy based upon the availability of great natural resources and a market of continental dimensions. The value of manufactures by 1899 stood at $13,000,000,000 and surpassed in value the products of agriculture. In 1900 the value of iron and steel products reached $803,968,000. The production of iron and steel almost equaled that of Germany and Great Britain combined. The conditions for mass production had already been achieved. At the turn of the century, it was estimated that the per capita consumption of manufactures in the United States was 50 percent higher than that in Great Britain and twice as great as that in Germany and France.[2]

Unprecedented material success inspired confidence among many Americans that the world at large would inevitably follow in America's wake. The more sober-minded among them pondered the question of the relations of this new economic colossus to the outside world. Some, like the historian John Fiske and the sociologist Franklin Henry Giddings, envisioned an extension of Anglo-Saxon political and economic institutions to more remote parts of the world. Others, like Brooks Adams and Alfred T. Mahan, impressed by contemporary struggles for security, prestige, and markets, concluded that the United States must for reasons of survival build a strong navy, protect the sea lanes of the

2. Harold U. Faulkner, *The Decline of Laissez Faire, 1897–1917* (New York, 1951), pp. 10, 121; Chester W. Wright, *Economic History of the United States* (New York, 1941), p. 707; Fred A. Shannon, *America's Economic Growth* (New York, 1940), p. 626.

world's commerce, and extend its own trade for purposes of counteracting the influence of other powers.

At the same time there emerged the view among many congressmen, journalists, and some business representatives that the capacity to produce goods was outrunning the economic demand of the home market. All were agreed that foreign markets were of increasing importance because of the danger of an industrial surplus. Some set forth a reciprocal trade program as the best answer to this problem. Others adhered to the traditional protective tariff policies and thought the solution to the surplus lay in a policy of opening up foreign markets by aggressive pursuit of colonies, or by strong pressure on governments to open the door to American goods.

The new look outward captured the churches and expressed itself in a rapid growth of interest in the expansion of Christianity. The organization of the Student Volunteers for Foreign Missions at Dwight L. Moody's Northfield in the summer of 1887 marked the beginning of a church crusade calling for "the evangelization of the world in this generation." China soon gained the highest priority and became by 1900, as Sherwood Eddy said, the lodestar of young college students ready to Christianize the world.[3] The crusade never lost its religious orientation, but many of the vigorous young men became passionate crusaders for sheering away anachronisms of superstition, ignorance, and social injustice. In turn they aroused an interest in China among a part of the churchgoing public and encouraged the belief that in the whole realm of foreign relations, China occupied a position of prime importance.

Those charged with the conduct of foreign relations shared the view that the United States was entering upon a

3. Sherwood Eddy, *Pathfinders of the World Missionary Crusade* (New York, 1945), p. 50.

new era. Among these were Theodore Roosevelt, his two
secretaries of state John Hay and Elihu Root, his friend
Henry Cabot Lodge, a leader in the Senate, and other senators including Cushman Davis of Minnesota. Roosevelt's
predecessor in the presidency, William McKinley, although
a man with a reputation for moving cautiously, shared the
vision of a new role for the United States. McKinley, for all
his later protestations of anguish in making up his mind on
the question of annexing the Philippines, had acted decisively on that issue in the summer of 1898, when he dictated
the basis for negotiations with Spain. On no point was he
more firm than on the stipulation that negotiations could
only be entered into if Spain agreed that the islands were
negotiable.[4] Neither, according to the testimony of John
Bassett Moore, was McKinley averse to demanding a sphere
of influence in China when the outbreak of the Boxers in
June, 1900, opened up the prospect of a partition of China.
In spite of his earlier caution in moving toward war with
Spain, McKinley was on the side of those who advocated an
energetic foreign policy.

The transition to a new age of bold engagement in world
affairs, greeted with eagerness by many, evoked the concern
of others. Entangling alliances continued to be anathema,
and not even the most ardent proponents of the "large policy" advocated a departure from the tradition against them.
Usually, moves toward involvement had to be clothed in
terms of duty and national obligation or described as necessary to protect the helpless against the imperialism of others.
Those opposed to the new developments tended to phrase
the argument in terms of anti-imperialism versus imperialism; those in favor more often saw the issue as narrow, self-
centered nationalism versus internationalism.

4. *Collected Papers of John Bassett Moore*, II, 143.

The propensity toward moralistic argument obfuscated the more vital concerns of those who preferred to eschew moralistic arguments or purely intellectual speculation on cosmic tendencies. The public debate set up categories that were often irrelevant to the more immediate questions of what were the vital interests of the nation and how they could be defended or advanced. Those charged with direct responsibility for foreign relations concerned themselves with the more immediate. Although they sometimes contributed to the confusion by resorting to generalizations loaded with value judgments, they reached decisions on the basis of pragmatic and mundane considerations.

What appeared to be a defense of the sovereignty and independence of less-favored nations evoked popular support as long as the defense was limited to moral support. In advising Secretary of State John Hay, John Bassett Moore pointed to the popularity of the Monroe Doctrine. Its popularity, said Moore, was due to the generally held notion that the policy had saved Latin America from European imperialism. No one knew better than Moore the falsity of this popular idea, but he urged Hay to issue the circular note of July 3, 1900, calling for support of China's territorial and administrative integrity and independence, for reasons of national interest, and assured him that the public would interpret the notes in altruistic terms and therefore approve of them.[5]

At the turn of the century, Europeans expressed concern over the future United States role in world affairs. Their concern had its source in the obvious capacity of American industry to flood the markets of Europe and the world with manufactured goods and also in the fears aroused by United States acquisition of an empire as a result of her victory over Spain. A writer for a British magazine, the *Spectator,* wor-

5. Memorandum of Conversation with Secretary of State John Hay, July 1, 1900, John Bassett Moore Papers, Library of Congress.

ried over the towering strength of the United States, but he was even more puzzled and disturbed by the failure of American policy to conform to familiar standards of big-power behavior. He dreaded an American monopoly of world trade and efforts to control the wealth of the world, but he feared equally the American unwillingness to see any but the native powers in control of the richest countries of Asia and America's refusal to take South America or let anyone else take it.

The catapulting of the United States onto the stage of world politics understandably caused concern in the capitals of Europe. Americans appeared to decry alliances, colonization, and imperialism. Among Europe's statesmen, these were not evils but devices for ordering the world's affairs so as to protect the interests of individual nations while at the same time preserving the peace. The behavior of the United States appeared unpredictable to European leaders while at the same time they acknowledged her power.

Americans who welcomed the new role of the United States boldly justified the uniqueness of their policy. The editor of the *Journal of Commerce* replied to the writer in the *Spectator* that Americans did not aim to control all the wealth in the world, but neither were they prepared to deny themselves the gains within their reach. Like all nations not infected with Oriental fatalism, he wrote, Americans were "doing the best we can for ourselves, and our energy and wealth are such that we are quite likely to end by dominating some important industries, and though we shall not own all the wealth of the world, we may be creditors of all nations."

The editor of the *Journal of Commerce* also gave his own explanation of the policy of the United States in Asia and South America. The Chinese and the South Americans were entitled to independent governments. Americans, he wrote, wished exclusive control nowhere, but they likewise were determined not to be excluded. As to South America, Americans had no reason to take it, but neither would they permit their own security to be threatened by permitting European states to establish themselves there. "The South Americans have their own governments," he wrote, and he found them no worse than some European governments. "What they need," he concluded, "is less of Europe; not more of it." [6]

However flamboyant American rhetoric, the American government usually behaved with restraint. When examined closely, specific actions of the United States in world affairs argue against easy generalizations about imperialism or world power status. The variety of approaches reflected the different assessments placed upon the importance of national interests in the many areas of the world. A comparative study of the developments in each major theater, the Far East, Latin America, and Europe, reveals a common tendency toward greater involvement but likewise marked differences.

A series of half-truths have become part of the popular lore concerning relations with China in the years between 1890 and American entry into World War I. It has been too readily assumed that China was considered to be of major importance by the policy-makers, that altruistic considerations advocated by both missionary leaders and church organizations weighed heavily in the councils of statesmen charged with foreign affairs, that the China market was viewed as so important to the American economy that an alliance of business groups and the Department of State assumed a major role in Chinese affairs, and that the Open Door policy provided at least a minor shield for the protec-

6. Editorial, "Europe and the United States," *Journal of Commerce and Commercial Bulletin,* April 29, 1904.

tion of China against European and Japanese imperialism.

The acquisition of the Philippines was both a result of an awakening interest in China and, later, a reason for being concerned about developments on the mainland of Asia. Yet, possession of the islands did not give to the United States the leverage in Chinese affairs that was anticipated. Other powers—Russia, Japan, Great Britain, and, to a somewhat lesser degree, France—were much more effective in making their influence felt in Peking. The weak government of the Manchu dynasty could only effectively resist demands made upon it by any one of these if it could enlist the support of one or more of the others. China did, on occasion, turn to the United States for support; but Washington had little influence because everyone, including the Chinese, recognized that the American government was not ready to resist a determined foe. Other governments, especially Russia and Japan, having much more at stake, were more adamant in demanding or in opposing the demands of others. Their own security, and likewise their important trade and investments, assured firmness in their negotiations.

The United States, on the other hand, had strictly limited interests. Its major concern was the security of the Philippines, and the islands were far removed from the path of the storm brewing in Manchuria at the close of the Boxer Revolt. To be sure, American trade centered in the northern provinces, and the inroads of Russia and Japan raised the specter of Americans being excluded, but this trade was not of sufficient importance to call for a strong policy. Although protests in the defense of equality of commercial opportunity flowed from Washington with regularity, these were conveyed in a spirit of pious hope rather than from a posture of unswerving determination. Moreover, the promise of a future market increasingly faded, especially after 1905, when exports to China failed to increase. Even at the peak of the optimism concerning the China market, the American business community made little effort to expand sales in that part of the world.[7] American investments in China were even less important.

Consequently, the government in Washington treaded water whenever it found itself headed toward a dangerous confrontation. Only when American lives were in danger was there a willingness to proceed boldly. The Boxer Revolt provided such an occasion, and there was no hesitancy in sending a military expedition. On lesser occasions the navy went to the rescue or displayed sufficient force to calm the waters.

The caution of the Department of State before deciding on the Circular Note of 1900 illustrates the point. Pressed to pledge support of China's integrity by Consul-General John Goodnow, who spoke for the leading viceroys in the Yangtze Valley, Hay weighed this proposal and at the same time pondered upon the support of President McKinley and his attorney general for seizing a leasehold and laying claim to a sphere of influence. Hay strongly opposed the latter. In issuing the Circular Note calling for support of China's independence and territorial and administrative integrity, he sought no more than to provide a catalyst whereby the nations would, for a brief time, be enabled to extricate themselves from a race for partition and find security for their interests in a common program of restraint. China could not herself resist their demands, and they could not themselves find security unless there was a mutual commitment to restraint. John Bassett Moore remarked to Hay "that the idea might, by many, be thought to be fanciful, but that after all, it might not be found to be impracticable."

Hay had no need to worry that he was making a hazard-

7. For a detailed factual account, see the author's "The Myth of the China Market," *American Historical Review* LXXIII (1968), 742–58.

ous commitment. He did no more than commit his own government not to violate the principle enunciated; other parties were invited to join in the policy of self-denial, but they were not served notice that the United States would come to China's aid if her independence and administrative and territorial integrity were threatened. Hay did show concern that Russia would probably reject the pledge she was to be invited to make and that France would blindly follow in the steps of the czar's government, but if this should happen, Hay would suffer no more than minor embarrassment.

Moore, in advising Hay, made no reference to the importance of the China market. He advanced only two arguments in favor of the United States' taking a stand. The United States, he said, had an immediate interest "in the fate of China in consequence of holding the Philippines. If Russia, or Russia and powers in alliance with her, held China," Moore argued, "we should be at their mercy in the Philippines." Second, he pointed out "that the idea of supporting the independence and integrity of China would accord with the sentiments of our people; that it was the principle of helping other nations to maintain their independence and integrity that had made the Monroe Doctrine so popular amongst them. . . ."

Moore not only eschewed the argument of the importance of the China market but dismissed as foolish the other consideration that held the attention of missionary-minded interests. According to Moore's memorandum of his conversation with Hay, Moore remarked

> that some of our people, mostly students and men unfamiliar with practical affairs, had conceived that it would be a good thing if the Powers would take China under their tutelage, and reorganize her and transform her; that this seemed to leave out of consideration the 300,000,000 or 400,000,000 people in China, with an ancient and persistent civilization,

and was, in my opinion, on the whole a fantastic conception, based on erroneous principles.[8]

Placing the Circular Note of 1900 in the context out of which it emerged reduces it from a ringing declaration in behalf of China to a cautious pronouncement by a government that did not view China as of vital importance to its own interests.

The estimate of the Department of State of China's importance to American interests did not change, although there were occasions when the vigor of diplomatic notes suggested the contrary. In spite of apparent determination to affect the course of developments, the United States moved with a restraint that accorded with the relatively low estimate the nation at large placed upon its interests in Asia.

There were, however, those in the United States who held those interests to be vital and, therefore, called for a policy of unyielding opposition to the aggressiveness of Russia or Japan. Before the Russo-Japanese War the most ardent advocates of a strong posture were the small group of commercial interests within the business community who spoke through the American Asiatic Association and the *Journal of Commerce and Commercial Bulletin.* The editorials of the New York weekly newspaper affirmed that the nation's economic future hung on access to the China market and that the United States as a Pacific power could not sit idly by while Russia unilaterally absorbed Manchuria and put itself in a position to dominate Peking. "Opinions may be divided as to the source from which the most serious obstacles to an agreement have come," wrote the editor in March, 1901, "but unless western civilization is to confess itself baffled by the Chinese problem, there must be an end to the pursuit

8. Memorandum of Conversation with Secretary of State John Hay, July 1, 1900, Moore Papers.

of individual ambitions at the expense of the common cause." He closed by proclaiming: "The United States is in a position to lend a powerful impulse to greater unity of action, and it is to be hoped that no weak fear of foreign entanglements will allow the opportunity to slip." [9]

Russia's attempts to strengthen its hold over Manchuria after the Boxer Revolt did cause the Department of State to make some moderately vigorous protests. For a brief period the policy seemed to harmonize with the position of the *Journal of Commerce*. Given the lead taken by Japan and Great Britain, the United States could show firmness without facing the danger inherent in being in the forefront of the resistance. The alignment with Tokyo and London reached its peak when Washington turned its negotiations of a new commercial treaty with China into a campaign for opening cities in Manchuria to foreign trade and residence.[10] Russia saw a threat in the requests of the United States to its own program and therefore used its influence in Peking to have the Chinese decline the American request. Throughout the spring and early summer of 1903, Secretary of State John Hay and W. W. Rockhill, his adviser on Far Eastern affairs, doggedly pushed forward. An almost pathological distrust and dislike of Russia increased their firmness.

In July, 1903, they changed course. It was during that month that Japan and Russia entered upon negotiations that clearly portended a showdown. Too close alignment with Japan and Great Britain posed the danger of involvement in possible war. Neither American interests nor public opinion provided support for a dangerous course. By the end of July the United States quietly withdrew from insisting that three

9. Editorial, "The Negotiations at Peking," *Journal of Commerce and Commercial Bulletin,* March 25, 1901.

10. U.S. State Department, *United States Foreign Relations, 1903* (Washington, 1904), p. 53; John Hay to Theodore Roosevelt, April 28, 1903, John Hay Papers, Library of Congress.

cities in Manchuria be opened by a specific date and that they be open to foreign residence. The removal of these two points by the United States enabled Russia to withdraw her opposition to the commercial treaty.[11] Russia's opposition had rested largely on the fear that her own sphere in Manchuria would be inundated by Japanese settlers if the cities were open to foreign settlement.

Manchuria was clearly not worth military involvement. However, after Japan's victory over Russia in 1905, American attention was once again focused on the sprawling plains north of China proper. Americans had looked upon Japan as fighting their war and believed that a victory over Russia was a victory for the principles of the Open Door. War did not solve the problem. Russia and Japan, within their newly defined spheres, sought to improve their positions.

Both countries had important railway interests they were determined to protect. Given the weakness of Chinese administration and the consequent threats of disorder, both St. Petersburg and Tokyo made moves to control the municipalities that were important railway centers. Russia moved first. Harbin, an important terminus on the Chinese Eastern Railway, was the scene of disorder, and unruly elements deprived the more stable citizenry of a feeling of security. Late in 1907 the Russian subjects in Harbin and the officials of the railway proposed a set of municipal regulations that would, in effect, have made the railroad company the real governing authority.

Fred Fisher, the American consul at Harbin, called the proposals to the attention of Willard Straight, consul-general at Mukden, and Henry Fletcher, chargé d'affaires at Peking.[12] Straight promptly endorsed Fisher's protest and ar-

11. Payson J. Treat, *Diplomatic Relations between the United States and Japan, 1895–1905* (Stanford, Calif., 1938), p. 186.

12. Fred Fisher to Assistant Secretary of State, November 25, 1906, State Department Papers, National Archives.

gued that the real importance of the issue would be in its
influence on the Japanese, who would use it as a precedent
for establishing their own governments in the towns along
the South Manchuria Railway. William Phillips, third assistant secretary, after study of these reports, wrote in early
March that acceptance of the Russian regulations would
amount to relinquishing a part of American treaty rights in
China because American residents would be subject to the
Russian municipal authorities and thereby be deprived of
their extraterritorial rights. To accept the Russian view, said
Phillips, would be to acknowledge "that China's sovereignty
had been violated." He concluded with the observation:

> The results of a recognition now by the United States Gov-
> ernment of an absolute Russian administration at Harbin
> would be our formal acquiescence in the principle of the
> erection by Russia and Japan of large and commercial cities
> within Manchuria wholly independent of China, and main-
> tained on the supposition that they are appurtenances to
> Railway property. The integrity of China would then be at
> an end.[13]

This conflict with the principles enunciated earlier by
John Hay rested on legalisms. It had little relationship to
American interests. The Russian minister in Peking told
Henry Fletcher that "there were but 'one and a half' American citizens there and that our interests in Harbin did not
seem to justify the active opposition of our consul." By April
the Department of State learned that the protests against
the proposed municipal regulations for Harbin had set off
much discussion and widespread newspaper editorials in
both Russia and Japan decrying American interference and

13. Memorandum from William Phillips, Third Assistant Secretary,
March 6, 1908, State Department Papers.

speculating on what far-reaching imperialistic design the
United States was about to launch.[14]

A vigorous protest from St. Petersburg early in June
against the actions of the American consul at Harbin compelled Secretary of State Elihu Root to look at the consequences of pursuing the controversy with firmness. The earlier legal interpretation, however correct, did not square
with the realities. Root now called for caution: "We do not
wish to be bumptious or disputatious or unfriendly in the
assertion of our rights, or to become a protagonist in Manchuria," he noted. Our interests, Root observed "are the future interests of the open door and there is no present interest which would justify us in exhibiting undue excitement in
this quiet and firm maintenance of our position." [15]

Root clearly did not consider American interests in China
of sufficient importance to justify boldness. A little more
than a year later, the new secretary of state, Philander C.
Knox, naïvely imagined that he could gain acceptance of a
scheme for neutralizing the railroads of Manchuria by winning the support of Great Britain, Germany, and France to
pressure Russia and Japan into disposing of their valuable
holdings. Knox suffered a severe rebuke, and his action
caused Russia and Japan to join hands in a treaty completed
in July, 1910.[16] Knox clearly underestimated the importance
to Russia and Japan of their holdings in Manchuria, and he
likewise failed to recognize the importance the other powers
attached to their interests.

Woodrow Wilson took a kindly interest in China. He
shared the missionary view of China and sympathized with

14. Montgomery Schuyler to Elihu Root, April 4, 1908, and Thomas
O'Brien to Root, April 16, 1908, State Department Papers.

15. Root to Alvey A. Adee, June 19, 1908, State Department Papers.

16. Edward H. Zabriskie, *American-Russian Rivalry in the Far East: A
Study in Diplomacy and Power Politics, 1895–1914* (Philadelphia, 1946),
p. 169.

the work of the missionaries. When he became president, he refused to support the bankers' consortium on the ground that the conditions of the loan posed a danger to China's sovereignty. He demonstrated genuine sympathy with the Chinese when Japan presented her Twenty-One Demands early in 1915 and again at the close of World War I when Japan insisted on retaining the rights Germany had acquired in Shantung. However friendly to China as he was, he did not find it possible to do more for her than to protest in a cautious manner against Japan's actions in Shantung. He confronted a powerful Japan, and Japan had the support of both Great Britain and France, both of whom had committed themselves on this question in secret treaties in 1917. Wilson, in turning his back on China, responded to the realities of the power situation. Short of endangering relations with Great Britain and France, he could only launch protests, and he needed both British and French support for his plans for Europe. He placed a higher priority on Europe than he did on Asia.

Looking back on the relations between the United States and China in the years 1900 to 1917, it is clear that the United States, although involved in the China question, did not wield the same degree of influence in the Asian area as that exerted by the other world powers. Her restraint was dictated by an awareness that neither her security interests nor her economic interests at the time justified a bold course. China's importance, as American statesmen saw it, lay in the future. Whatever the importance of the China market might become, it was not important at the time. Other nations had heavy investments in railways, mining, and other enterprises. As late as 1914, the United States portion of these investments was only 3 percent.[17] To the degree that there was a public interest in China, it was in large part an

17. C. F. Remer, *Foreign Investments in China* (New York, 1933), p. 76.

intangible, nonmaterial interest associated with dreams of providing tutelage of China in the transition from an ancient to a modern society. Missionaries and their allies in the church leadership at home shared this vision, but their point of view struck almost no response among men of practical affairs, whose concern was bound by considerations of security and the state of the economy.

By almost any standard, the United States record in the Caribbean area differed sharply from the minor role it played in Asia. By World War I, five Caribbean states had been subordinated to protectorate status, and no nation would have openly challenged the dominance of the United States. The differences lay in felt concerns as to security and the presence of economic interests. In contrast to the restraint that characterized the response to developments in Asia, the United States overreacted to both dangers and opportunities in the Caribbean. In part, the difference can be explained by the proximity of the small island republics and by the absence of any power capable of seriously testing American capability.

In fact, the most serious deterrent to Yankee imperialism in the Caribbean came from within the American body politic and not from without. Imperialism had a free rein from the public when American action could be defended as negating Europe's imperialism. It met strong opposition when American behavior came into conflict with democratic values antithetic to domination of another people. Sometimes the opposition was based on no more than the defense of special economic interests. At other times, the opposition came from politicians seeking political gains by putting the ruling party's policies in the worst possible light. Regardless of motives, those who were opposed, by appealing to traditional values, paid tribute to their survival.

Historians have parted ways over the question as to whether strategic considerations or economic interests shaped the policy of intervention. It is probably futile to weigh the comparative importance of these two factors and more profitable to recognize that the new industrial society that had come into being fostered ambitions to achieve those attributes by which greatness among nations was measured. Among these badges of greatness were the capacity to wield an influence abroad and to dominate some one region.

In the aftermath of the Spanish American War, the problem of future relations between the island of Cuba and the republic that had intervened to make it independent of Spain served as a test as to whether the old or the new ideals were to dominate. Whatever private motives existed aiming at the advancement of personal or corporate interests, Congress and the country at large saw the goal as emancipation of the Cubans from Spanish rule. The Teller Amendment promised that Cuba was to be independent, not only of Spain, but likewise of the United States. Some privately questioned the wisdom of the self-denying amendment but did not dare do so publicly.

Senator Teller of Colorado gave expression to the sentiment of the great majority when he introduced his resolution. To be sure, there were those who had never favored independence for Cuba. They probably voted for the amendment simply for the political reason that they did not wish to stand apart from an obviously popular move. Their votes do not explain the general support of the amendment.

The granting of independence to Cuba was something assumed by a majority of Congress in the debates that preceded the war. Senator Teller later explained that he introduced his measure for another reason than that of curbing annexationists moves on the part of the United States. Independence for Cuba was so generally accepted, said Teller, that a resolution was not necessary. The reason for the Teller Amendment, according to its author, was to diminish the danger of European intervention. President McKinley, according to one senator, greatly feared that Europe would intervene in one way or another. He warned two senators who called upon him: "Remember, Senators, if this war breaks out, it may be a world's war." Europe was cynical about the aims of the United States and did not believe that she would go to war against Spain and then set Cuba free. Senator Spooner explained that it had been necessary to dispel this cynicism because it could have led some European governments to intervene.[18] That a nation should make war against another in order to take over a colony of the other would set a most dangerous precedent. It was thought that the Teller Amendment, put before the Senate by the Committee on Foreign Relations and approved by the Senate, would deprive the European powers of a reason for intervening.

Once the fighting started, the pious resolutions lost their sanctity. Raw motives of self-interest and irrational fears cradled in a sense of Anglo-Saxon superiority came to the surface as Americans came face to face with Cuba's insurgents. The army showed its attitude when it restricted its commands to the rebels, our Cuban allies, to orders to carry out the menial tasks of transporting supplies and digging ditches. After the battle of San Juan Hill, General Lawton complained that the Cuban troops sat on a high hill to the rear of the scene of battle and failed to join in the attack. When Santiago was under siege, General Shafter protested that the Cuban troops failed to prevent the entry of Spanish reinforcements.

This was only the beginning of complications. The Cu-

18. *Congressional Record*, 57th Cong., 1st Sess. (1902), 5805–6.

bans, led by General García, were bitter over the Americans ignoring them. And the Americans reciprocated. Upon the close of hostilities, Stephen Crane, correspondent for the *New York World,* reported that the Americans had come to despise the Cubans. The contempt for the Cubans carried over to the political realm, raising questions about their capacity to govern themselves. General Shafter, after his return to the United States in December, 1898, was asked: "How about self-government for the Cubans?" "Self-government!" he replied. "Why, these people are no more fit for self-government than gun-powder is for hell."

The opinions of soldiers and correspondents found their way into the newspapers. The Cubans, so recently the heroic resistors of Spanish tyranny, were soon dismissed as rabble and as wholly unprepared to govern themselves. The revised view was expressed by the Cleveland *Leader:* "While our Government disavowed a purpose of conquest, it may be absolutely necessary for us to keep Cuba and make it a part of the United States." [19]

The distrust that attended the fighting increased in the months ahead. President McKinley reassured the Cubans that they would establish their own government once tranquillity had been achieved, but the Cubans also heard Americans who seemed to favor annexation. In June, 1899, General Leonard Wood, in an interview with the *New York Times,* said that the propertied classes and Spaniards in Cuba favored annexation by the United States. These groups, he reported, wanted a stable government. Wood observed that "the establishment of another Haitian Republic in the West Indies would be a serious mistake." [20]

The Teller Amendment became an object of regret. Gen-

19. David F. Healy, *The United States in Cuba, 1898–1902: Generals, Politicians, and the Search for Policy* (Madison, Wis., 1963), pp. 30–36.
20. *Ibid.,* p. 91.

eral James Harrison Wilson, who was in command of one
part of Cuba, did not propose to alienate the Cubans by
breaking the pledge, but he envisioned arrangements that
would tie Cuba to the United States economically and in
foreign affairs. Senator Joseph B. Foraker of Ohio supported
General Wilson. When Elihu Root became secretary of war
on August 1, 1899, he took over responsibility for governing
Cuba. Root, fearful that Cuban resentment would trap the
United States into the same bitter kind of warfare in which
it was already involved in the Philippines, moved cautiously
and tried to reassure the Cubans that there was no plan for
annexation. Root proposed the establishment of local governments before moving to the problem of drafting a Cuban
constitution. Like many others, Root feared the control of
Cuba falling into the hands of the illiterate and propertyless
classes. Consequently, he prescribed a suffrage based on
literacy, property, or service in the army.[21]

On July 25, 1900, the military government of Cuba called
for the election of a constitutional convention. The convention began its sessions the following November. The Cubans
enjoyed complete freedom in framing their own government, but soon found that the United States notions on the
subject of the relations of the two countries did not conform
to their own. Root wrote to Hay early in January, 1901, out-
lining his ideas on this subject. He wished to have incorporated in the Cuban constitution four provisions. The United
States should have the right to intervene "for the preservation of Cuban independence and the maintenance of a stable government." The Cuban government should not be free
to enter into agreements with foreign powers "which may
tend to impair or interfere with the independence of Cuba,
or to confer upon such foreign power any special right or

21. Philip C. Jessup, *Elihu Root*, 2 vols. (New York, 1938), I, 304–5.

privilege without the consent of the United States." The
United States should have the right to acquire naval stations. Finally, actions taken during the American occupation
and all rights acquired during the course of the occupation
should be maintained and protected.[22]

General Leonard Wood conveyed Root's stipulation to the
Constitutional Convention's Committee on Relations. The
committee resolved

> that some of these stipulations are not acceptable, inasmuch
> as they modify the independence and sovereignty of Cuba.
> Our duty consists in making Cuba independent of all other
> nations, including the great and noble American nation;
> and if we bind ourselves to ask the consent of the United
> States to our international treaties; if we allow them to re-
> tain the right to intervene in our country to support or dis-
> place administrations, and to fulfill rights which only
> concern the Cuban government; and if, lastly, we concede
> to them the right to acquire and maintain any title over any
> lands whereon they may establish naval stations, it is plain
> that we should appear to be independent of the rest of the
> world, but surely we should never be so with relation to the
> United States.[23]

In the United States, men like Elihu Root and Senator Platt
of Connecticut replied that certainly the United States in
intervening to free the Cubans from Spanish misrule, at
great cost in lives and in money, could not be so derelict in
its responsibility as to set Cuba adrift to become the scene
once again of chaos and disorder.

American leaders gave only polite attention to the plain-
tive protests of the Cubans, but they did find it necessary
to reconcile for their own sake the Platt Amendment with

22. *Ibid.*, p. 310
23. Quoted in Albert G. Robinson, *Cuba and the Intervention* (New
York, 1905), p. 238.

the promise of independence given in the earlier Teller Amendment. How those leaders who promoted it reconciled the imposition of these limitations on Cuban sovereignty with the Teller Amendment explains something about difficulties inherent in the peculiar idealism of the American people when it embarked on a crusade to free a foreign people from alleged tyranny and misgovernment.

Congress had in large part voted for the Teller Amendment in good faith, but an independent Cuba soon appeared to present dangers. The editor of the *Journal of Commerce,* in February, 1901, argued that the United States "must have regard to the protection of its own interests no less than to what the Cuban people may think would be best for themselves." In fixing the relation of Cuba to the United States, he wrote, "There may be a higher law to be observed than the Teller resolution, and other considerations to be taken into account than the impatience of the Cuban people to try the experiment of self-government." [24] In February, 1901, Elihu Root, the secretary of war, instructed General Leonard Wood to call on the Cubans to incorporate in their constitution his four earlier proposals plus an additional provision that the Cuban government must not contract debts beyond its ability to pay.[25] The Cubans were strongly opposed, especially to the United States' having the right to intervene. They gave their consent only because they had no real alternative to yielding. Quite clearly, the United States, so recently ready to fight against European imperialism in the Caribbean, had now stepped forth as the imperialist. Both houses of Congress approved the Platt Amendment in February, 1901, but the vote followed strictly party lines.

24. Editorial, "The United States and Cuba," *Journal of Commerce and Commercial Bulletin,* February 28, 1901.
25. Jessup, *Elihu Root,* I, 312.

One historian, after a detailed and careful study of the factors that led to the Platt Amendment, has given his view of what happened.

> The real explanation seems rather to lie in a general recognition that the amendment represented a true compromise. It promised to give the Cubans real internal self-government and at least the semblance of independence, to end the dangers and vexations of United States rule, and at the same time to safeguard American interests in the island as thoroughly as anyone could reasonably desire. Besides, no one could find an alternative that had any reasonable chance of acceptance in both Cuba and the United States. The Platt Amendment seemed to represent at once the least that the McKinley administration was willing to take, and the most that Cuba could be expected to give.[26]

This view accords with the political realities of February, 1901.

The more interesting question to be answered is why Congress and the McKinley Administration found the degree of control retained by the United States necessary. The explanation seems to lie in its disrust of Cuban society even more than in its concern for American economic investments or any concern for the security of the proposed isthmian canal. As concerns the latter, there was almost no mention of the canal. Security considerations did enter the discussion, but it was the security of the coastline from the mouth of the Mississippi to Florida.

In April, 1901, the *North American Review* published Senator Beveridge's justifications of the Platt Amendment. Beveridge, who was privately a supporter of Cuban annexation, defended it as necessary to prevent foreign intervention and instability and revolt. The danger of revolt had its

26. Healy, *The United States in Cuba*, p. 167.

basis in the fact of race. The Latins, argued Beveridge, were an unstable people given to revolution. The instability, he contended, was a racial quality; he made no reference to the economic and social factors that at least explained in part the many revolutions in Latin America he cited as evidence.

The senator found it easy to defend intervention by appealing to traditional liberal ideals ordinarily marshaled to condemn European imperalism. He wrote:

> We are not depriving Cuba of liberty; we are helping her to liberty. Landowners are not to be robbed; they are to be protected. Cities are not to be sacked; they are to be defended. Equal rights are not to be violated; they are to be preserved and enforced. Free speech is not to be suppressed; it is to be fostered. Education is not to be destroyed; it is to be built up. But anarchy is to be kept down, foreign powers kept at bay, and the elements that oppose Cuban progress held in check. All this is not the denial of liberty; it is the bestowal of liberty; for liberty cannot live without law and order.[27]

Beveridge's argument harmonized with the appeals made in 1897 and 1898 in behalf of the Cubans. Then the cry had been that they must be liberated from Spain and permitted to have their independence. By 1901, when it had become clear that the society of Cuba—poor, illiterate, and torn by class divisions—was likely to shape itself after the patterns of other similar societies in Latin America, it was easy to justify intervention in almost identical terms.

The idealism that led to intervention in 1898 was employed in 1902 to justify the Platt Amendment. The reasoning was logical even if it ignored a number of realities. If

27. Albert Beveridge, "Cuba and Congress," *North American Review* CLXXII (1901), 546–48.

concern for human rights was a legitimate concern, the legitimacy would not, in the eyes of its ardent exponents, become illegitimate when it transcended national boundaries. The imperialists condemned such a view as parochial. However, the logical next question would have been the legitimacy of the use of force. Few questioned the rightness of employing force to free the Cubans from Spain. Why should they have questioned provisions for the use of force in Cuba itself as long as the end was to them legitimate? Obviously, Beveridge did not.

The thinking of Senator Beveridge, however interesting and however accurately it reflected one segment of the public, did not accord with the views of Secretary of War Elihu Root. It was he who carried the major share of responsibility for affairs in Cuba and for working out future relationships. He drafted the Platt Amendment, and he it was who pierced the underbrush of argument set forth by self-seeking interests, sentimental and idealistic verbiage, and the views that stemmed from parochial nationalist feelings.

Root faced realistically factors in the situation that were not taken into account by others. He ruled out annexation as unacceptable to the majority of Cubans and as an invitation to a protracted struggle. On the other hand, he accepted as a fact that the United States would never sit idly by if another power intervened in Cuba. It was wiser, he thought, to face this possibility and to provide for the right of the United States to intervene, a right she held under international law only for the duration of the occupation under the terms of the Treaty of Paris.[28] The possibility of intervention, remote in retrospect, did not appear so then. German intentions were viewed with great suspicion. No evidence of such German intentions is to be found in the German ar-

28. Jessup, *Elihu Root,* I, 287–88, 309–15.

chives, and the fear was exaggerated; but given the adventurous policies of the European powers in various parts of
the world, the fear was not wholly unreasonable. Given the
inability of Cuba to defend itself and the very real possibility of ineffective government even in internal affairs,
which would in turn endanger foreign interests, the possibility of a European government being drawn into the situation was not imaginary. Root, a conservative man intent on
seeking to take into account the most remote contingencies,
preferred to risk a degree of Cuban resentment rather than
leave any flank exposed.

Root likewise considered how his fellow American citizens might react to some future crisis in Cuba. There was
much sentiment in favor of annexation. Even anti-imperialists like Josiah Quincy, who strongly opposed the annexation of the Philippines on the ground that the rule of the
Filipinos by the United States would undermine republican principles at home, favored the annexation of Cuba. The
Cubans, Quincy argued, would soon be capable of self-
government. Immigration to Cuba from the United States
would strengthen self-government. Cuba should be annexed
when the Cubans so proposed, and it should be made a
state. It was because Cuba could become a state that Quincy
viewed the annexation with favor.[29] However, Root opposed
annexation and sought to put blocks in the way of its hap-
pening.

Years after the Cuban crisis, Root confided to his biographer, Philip C. Jessup, that it had been necessary "to guard
against the possibility that the United States itself might
try to annex Cuba through some foreclosure procedure." He
wrote: "In all foreign relations it is just as important to
guard against the injustice of one's own country as of any

29. Josiah Quincy, "Political Aspects of Cuba's Economic Distress,"
North American Review CLXXIV (1902), 12–19.

other." "This is true," wrote Root, "although you can't talk much about it in public." [30]

Concern for economic interests and security contributed to the support of the Platt Amendment, but liberal ideology facilitated intervention in the Caribbean.

Some found it necessary to justify every move by idealistic argument. It was wholly irrelevant to the consideration of others. A year after Congress debated the Platt Amendment, the Committee on Ways and Means of the House of Representatives held hearings on commercial reciprocity with Cuba. No more mundane discussion could have taken place. Cuban representatives, spokesmen for New York merchants, agents of the cane growers of Louisiana, and sugar beet interests in California, Colorado, and Michigan argued with the vehemence of bargainers at an Oriental bazaar. Two questions dominated the discussions. Did the price of sugar production in Cuba, given current market prices, make the harvesting of the current crop unprofitable, and would, therefore, the Cuban economy spin into bankruptcy and lead to widespread unemployment and violence? Second, if this were true, did the United States have an obligation to rescue the sugar economy by opening the American market to sugar, or should the obligation be met, as the sugar beet representatives argued, by the American people as a whole and not by the small segment who happened to be domestic producers of sugar? [31]

The backdrop for this sugar extravaganza was the situation of the world market. World sugar production had gradually increased from 1,481,000 tons in 1853–54 to 10,710,000 tons in 1901–2. Germany was by far the greatest producer of sugar. Austria, France, and Russia were next in order.

---

30. Jessup, *Elihu Root,* I, 315.

31. *Reciprocity with Cuba,* Hearings before Committee on Ways and Means, 57th Cong., 1st Sess. (Washington, 1902), pp. 205–34, 258–96.

The world price was determined by Hamburg. To promote exports, Germany and France subsidized exports of sugar so that the price of German beet sugar in London averaged 25 percent of the price in Germany. In 1898 an international cartel had been established whereby both production and prices could be controlled. In brief, the problem facing the sugar planters in Cuba had its source in capitals far removed from both Havana and Washington. Yet, if the United States lowered the duty on sugar imports from Cuba alone by a reciprocal agreement, the Cubans would gain at least temporary relief.[32]

Cuba's distress was also the United States' opportunity. Members of the Ways and Means Committee showed at least as great an interest in capturing the Cuban market for American goods as the Cubans showed in gaining access to the American market. The best informed witness on this phase, Colonel T. H. Bliss, collector of customs at Havana, testified that the United States had a monopoly of the markets in fresh beef, pork, eggs, flour, coal, coal oil, machinery, and railroad iron. This, however, was more than counterbalanced by the imports of a list of ninety articles chiefly from other countries. Others controlled the Cuban markets in cattle, rice, wines, olive oil, salt, preserved fruits, dried beef, cottons, linens, woolens, silk, shoes, hats, and many other commodities.

These articles, said Bliss, could be secured from the United States, and would be if a tariff was arranged that gave the price advantage to the American products. "Thus," he said, "a tariff arrangement that would give the United States the control of the trade tabulated . . . would enable her to control at least 86 percent of the entire inward trade of Cuba." "This," he estimated, "on the basis of last year's

32. See testimony of Dr. Harvey W. Wiley, Chief of Bureau of Chemistry, Department of Agriculture, *ibid.*, pp. 474–519.

figures, would have made their export trade to Cuba amount to $56,904,000 or just double what it actually was."

The casual estimate interested the committee members, but only in the long run would the proposed reciprocal trade program have these results. Bliss informed them of many of the difficulties. Almost all importers in Cuba were Spaniards with long associations with European business houses. New ties would not be established at once. There were other problems, too. Bliss cited the willingness of European cotton manufacturers to meet highly exact weight requirements and to guarantee the exact number of threads in a piece of goods. These determined in part the rate of import duty, and this in turn made the difference between profit and loss. Bliss likewise stressed how the practice of limiting credit to thirty days handicapped American sales.[33]

Cubans pleaded for reciprocity because of the desperate situation of the sugar industry, and they recognized that it would be necessary to offer concessions in return. However, they were not unaware of the danger of Cuba becoming an economic colony of the United States. Their fears were nourished by the British minister, Sir Lionel Carden, who advised them that the principal benefits would go to the Americans and that the Cuban government would suffer sharp losses in revenue. In his report to the Foreign Office, Sir Lionel stated that the very existence of British trade with Cuba was threatened. "These arguments," he wrote "I have not failed to urge on several of the leading Cuban delegates, who are already opposed on political grounds to too intimate a connection with the United States, and it is to be hoped that their efforts may have the effect of neutralizing the action of the planters and their sympathizers."[34]

President McKinley, Secretary of War Root, and General

33. *Ibid.*, pp. 382–83, 386.
34. Quoted in Warren G. Kneer, "Great Britain and the Caribbean, 1901–1913: A Study in Anglo-American Relations," Ph.D. Dissertation (Michigan State University, 1966), p. 179.

Leonard Wood put the argument for a reciprocal trade
treaty in terms of the plight of the Cuban sugar economy
and the moral obligation of the United States, inherent in its
intervention in Cuba, to enable the Cubans to achieve economic recovery. Economic disaster at the close of the United
States military occupation would reflect unfavorably upon
the nation and upon the administration. This was the overriding consideration. Theodore Roosevelt, calling on Congress to approve a reciprocal trade treaty, stressed the obligation of the United States to assist the Cubans. At the
same time these leaders expressed sympathy for the Cubans,
they were mindful of other dimensions of the question than
the immediate crisis. When the final bill was before the
House of Representatives, Roosevelt urged its approval "not
only because it is eminently for our own interests to control
the Cuban market and by every means to foster our supremacy in the lands and waters south of us, but also because
we, of the giant republic of the north, should make all our
sister nations of the American Continent feel that whenever
they will permit it, we desire to show ourselves disinter-
estedly and effectively their friend." [35]

Winning the confidence of the peoples of the Caribbean
by recognizing their problems and responding to their pleas
for assistance guided Roosevelt and Root. The administration saw as its goal constructive leadership and friendly relations based upon mutual interests. The hope of a future
market was almost incidental. However, the frankness of
Roosevelt in stating that the United States aimed at control
of the Cuban market and supremacy "in the lands and waters south of us" supports the Cuban critics who later
charged that the aim was to reduce the island to an economic colony.

The negotiation of a reciprocal trade treaty went forward,

35. Russell H. Fitzgibbon, *Cuba and the United States, 1900–1935*
(New York, 1964), p. 207.

but there was strong opposition from the domestic beet-sugar interests, and Elihu Root for a time had little hope of getting the approval of Congress.[36] In December, 1902, the treaty was completed, and it was approved by Congress the following March. The beet sugar interests won a major concession when a provision was introduced making the 20 percent reduction in duty on Cuban sugar dependent upon the continuation of the high Dingley tariff duties on sugar from all other countries.

Some historians charge that the aim of the United States in negotiating the treaty was economic domination of Cuba. Eventually, Cuba did become an economic colony, but this was not a result of the trade treaty. Shortly after Congress approved of the treaty, Parker Willis, an economist who had long favored reciprocal trade, criticized the treaty as falling far short of the ideals of reciprocity. He maintained that the Cuban reduction of duties on American manufacturers was not sufficient to promise any real increase of exports to Cuba.[37]

The reciprocal trade agreement did not lead to immediate American domination of the Cuban economy. It was Cuba that derived the greater gain. Imports from Cuba rose from $31,371,704 in 1900 to $122,528,037 in 1910. Sugar accounted for $93,543,897 of these imports. The 20 percent reduction of the regular duties on sugar originating in Cuba explained in part the increasing importance of the commercial tie. Almost the entire amount of sugar produced in Cuba was exported to the United States. Imports of tobacco were valued at $17,915,616 in 1910 and likewise benefitted by the 20 percent reduction.[38]

36. Jessup, *Elihu Root*, I, 326–27.

37. H. P. Willis, "Reciprocity with Cuba," *Annals of the American Academy of Political and Social Science* XXII (1903), 129–47.

38. Bureau of Statistics of the Department of Commerce and Labor, *The Foreign Commerce and Navigation of the United States for the Year Ending June 30, 1910* (Washington, 1910), pp. 30, 346, 354–55.

The exports of the United States to Cuba in 1910 fell far short of the optimistic predictions that had been made during the discussion in 1902 of the benefits to be gained by a reciprocal agreement. Exports did increase from $26,513,400 in 1900 to $52,858,758 in 1910, but Cuba continued to buy from Europe in large part rather than from the United States. British cotton goods far outsold American cottons.

American investments in Cuba spiraled upward much more rapidly than exports of goods. In 1898, prior to the war with Spain, they approximated $50 million. By 1911 they had risen to more than $200 million.[39]

The question of whether the United States had attained the status of a world power depends obviously on how the term is defined. By the turn of the century, the United States had by any economic measure moved to the front rank. It was likewise a major power in the Pacific Ocean area, where it possessed a series of important island bases and the Philippines plus a strong navy. Any nation seeking to bring about change in this region would have confronted a determined United States. However, while it exerted a modest influence in Eastern Asia and had established its right to a voice in international affairs in that area, the United States had only minor interests in China, and it did not affect significantly the course of events in the Manchu empire. Only in the Caribbean did the United States take on heavy commitments and dominate political developments. In Europe it was aloof. Except for its lasting impact on Spain in depriving her of the last of her empire and participation in the Algeciras Conference of 1906, the United States played no part in European affairs, although she was important to Europe as an economic competitor and as a supplier of both agricultural and manufactured goods.

The most significant development in American foreign

39. Kneer, "Great Britain and the Caribbean," p. 13.

relations was not an increasing impact on the course of world diplomacy but the emergence of foreign relations as a major problem. Varied responses to the question came to the fore ranging from a clamor for markets, speeches, and editorials on America's mission in the world, to thoughtful probing of the question of national interests. Much of the debate centered on duty and on opportunity and almost none of it on the complexities.

The heritage of a generation determines in large part the conduct of its diplomacy. At the turn of the century the heritage included neither a sense that the nation's welfare was in any way dependent upon developments abroad nor any significant public awareness that the existing world order, so benign in terms of American interests, rested on the complex arrangements of treaties, dominance of underdeveloped areas by the European powers, and control of the seas by Great Britain. Apart from a few leaders, such as Theodore Roosevelt and, to a lesser degree, Woodrow Wilson, there was no recognition of the advantages to the United States of the existing order in Europe. The heritage continued to nourish parochialism and counterbalanced the thrust of new forces. However, the dawn of a new era was at hand. New concerns made themselves felt and new ambitions came to the fore.

The United States and the Failure
of Collective Security in the 1930s

MANFRED JONAS

"IN MY OWN MIND," Senator Arthur Vandenberg of Michigan confided to his diary some time after the event, "my convictions regarding international cooperation and collective security for peace took firm form on the afternoon of the Pearl Harbor attack. That day ended isolationism for any realist." [1] Vandenberg had been slow to reach the conclusion that the development of the United States into a major power and the increasing interdependence of nations brought on by the technological advances of the twentieth century had rendered the traditional American approach to foreign policy obsolete. But when the Japanese forcibly demonstrated that this country was also no longer safe from foreign attack, even the Michigan senator, a longtime congressional isolationist and former member of the Nye Committee, underwent a conversion.

By 1944 Vandenberg had become the champion of an international organization capable, should it prove neces-

1. Arthur H. Vandenberg, Jr., ed. (with Joe Alex Morris), *The Private Papers of Senator Vandenberg* (Boston, 1952), p. 1.

sary, of maintaining peace through cooperative military action, and he promoted this objective as a member of the United States delegation to the San Francisco conference in 1945.[2] There can be little doubt that most Americans underwent a similar conversion during this period. From a nation overwhelmingly committed to the avoidance of any and all "entanglements," the United States moved, certainly by the end of 1941, to the realization that it had an important stake in world peace and world order that it must work actively to preserve.[3]

To describe his new cause, Vandenberg used the phrase "collective security," a term that had gained currency in Europe and in some circles in the United States during the decade. Political scientists generally define collective security as that system of power management in international relations which occupies "the middle zone of the spectrum in which balance of power and world government represent the terminal points."[4] Such a system, of necessity, requires the establishment of an international organization whose members are committed to the settlement of controversies through discussion, arbitration, or the decisions of an international tribunal, and who agree to the use of diplomatic, economic, and perhaps even military force against nations

2. *Congressional Record*, 79th Cong., 1st Sess. (1945), 7957; see also Inis L. Claude, Jr., *Swords into Plowshares*, 2d ed. (New York, 1959), pp. 77 ff.

3. This subject is treated in some detail in Walter Johnson, *The Battle against Isolation* (Chicago, 1944); William L. Langer and S. Everett Gleason, *The Challenge to Isolation, 1937–1940* (New York, 1952); and Donald F. Drummond, *The Passing of American Neutrality, 1937–1941* (Ann Arbor, Mich., 1955). For the conversion of the isolationists during this period, see Manfred Jonas, *Isolationism in America, 1935–1941* (Ithaca, N.Y., 1966).

4. Inis L. Claude, Jr., *Power and International Relations* (New York, 1964), p. 94; see also Willard N. Hogan, *International Conflict and Collective Security: The Principle of Concern in International Organization* (Lexington, Ky., 1955), pp. 179–81.

seeking to make good their claims by warlike acts. The idea
of collective security in this sense was implied by Theodore
Roosevelt, both in his Nobel Peace Prize address in 1910
and in subsequent pronouncements, advanced during World
War I by the Netherlands-based Organisation Centrale
pour une Paix Durable and by its American counterpart,
the League to Enforce Peace, and incorporated in Woodrow
Wilson's proposal for a League of Nations.[5]

It would be difficult to prove, and is indeed unreasonable
to assume, that Vandenberg and most other Americans had
such a precise notion of the course on which they were prepared to embark by 1941. It is far more likely that they regarded collective security as nothing more than a synonym
for international cooperation for peace, "as a large envelope,
into which could be stuffed any and all forms of active participation in world politics."[6] Yet, they were willing to carry
on this cooperation within the framework of an international
body endowed with real, if limited, enforcement powers.
Indeed, the United States was to become the major force
behind the establishment of the United Nations Organization, and thus behind the reestablishment of potentially effective collective security machinery. Considering that this
country never effectively supported the League of Nations
or encouraged efforts to make collective security a reality
in the early thirties, America's championing of collective
security after 1941 represents a fundamental shift in American attitudes and a major turning point in American foreign
relations.

The League of Nations, embodying the collective security

5. Hermann Hagedorn, ed., *The Works of Theodore Roosevelt,* Memorial Edition, 24 vols. (New York, 1923–26), XX, 97, 185; Claude, *Power
and International Relations,* pp. 107–8; Ruhl J. Bartlett, *The League to
Enforce Peace* (Chapel Hill, N.C., 1944), *passim.*

6. Claude, *Power and International Relations,* p. 117.

principle, had been conceived by Woodrow Wilson as an alternative to the balance-of-power system that had failed to prevent a world war, and may, indeed, have been one of its causes. Wilson saw the League as embodying *"an entirely new course of action"* and urged the American people to accept participation in it on that basis.[7] But either for tactical or other reasons he never clearly spelled out just how new that course would be. For collective security in the Wilsonian sense to become operative, all, or at least almost all, nations must be either persuaded or coerced into acceptance of the belief that international peace is their primary national goal and that other national goals in conflict with that must perforce yield precedence. Acceptance of that belief, however, and agreement to act so as to assure its universal acceptance involves a diminution of freedom of action, and thus of national sovereignty, greater than that which any major power had ever been willing to accept.

There is some evidence to indicate that the European powers were ultimately willing to accept the League of Nations not as a new course of action but, simply, as a stronger, stabler, and more sophisticated version of the old alliance system.[8] Wilson could hardly hope to sell the League on this basis in an America nurtured on contempt for this system, but he also, in the final analysis, could not persuade the United States to relinquish the degree of sovereignty that the covenant, taken literally, would have required. Henry Cabot Lodge could, and did, endorse the program of the League to Enforce Peace and argued eloquently that "nations must unite as men unite in order to preserve peace and

7. D. H. Miller, *The Drafting of the Covenant,* 2 vols. (New York, 1928), I, 42.
8. See Edward H. Buehrig, *Woodrow Wilson and the Balance of Power* (Bloomington, Ind., 1955), pp. 273–74; Thomas A. Bailey, *Woodrow Wilson and the Lost Peace* (New York, 1944), p. 315; Miller, *Drafting of the Covenant,* II, 372–73.

order." But what he had in mind was simply a kind of international *posse comitatus,* a vigilante committee in which peace-loving states like the United States would voluntarily get together to stop international lawbreakers.[9] Such an arrangement would not restrict the sovereignty of the participants. But the covenant went far beyond this and correctly appeared to Lodge and the many Americans who shared his view as a clear limitation of American sovereignty and a general alliance more permanent and more entangling than anything Washington might have foreseen.

The case has often been made that most Americans and, indeed, a majority in the Senate favored American adherence to the League of Nations, albeit with some reservations. It would follow from this that Wilson's own intransigeance was a major factor in the defeat of the Versailles treaty. It is equally true, however, that the reservations proposed by Lodge would have emasculated the League Covenant, and thus effectively prevented the establishment of a genuine collective security system.[10] Although it might, for practical purposes, have been better for the United States to join even an emasculated League, there can be little doubt that Wilson was correct in his judgment that neither the irreconcilables nor the reservationists accepted the principle of collective security that he saw as essential to the proper functioning of the League of Nations. Unhappily for him, neither did the American people.

If the rejection of the Treaty of Versailles thus appears as a clearcut rejection of the collective security principle by the Senate and the American people, the efforts made by

9. *Works of Theodore Roosevelt,* XX, 185, 198; Henry Cabot Lodge, *Maintenance of Peace: Address Delivered at Union College Commencement, June 9, 1915* (Washington, 1919); A. Lawrence Lowell, "A League to Enforce Peace," *Atlantic Monthly* CXVI (1915), 400.

10. The reservations are listed in Bartlett, *League to Enforce Peace,* 163.

the United States to reach a *modus vivendi* with the League during the 1920s do nothing to alter this picture. American participation in the nonpolitical work of the League, the sending of judges to serve on international tribunals, and even the eventual sending of observers to the political discussions at Geneva, in no way reflect even a minimal acceptance of the collective security idea. Nor does the work of those organizations friendly to American League membership in the twenties suggest a different conclusion. The founding members of the League of Nations Non-Partisan Association, the forerunner of the League of Nations Association, agreed in 1923 merely to endorse American entry on terms "consistent with our constitution and consonant with the dignity and honor, the moral responsibility and power of our Republic." In its subsequent educational efforts, the organization promoted the League not as an instrument of collective security but merely as a *"method of cooperation* open to those states which wish to use it." The other groups which were formed to promote a greater degree of internationalism in American thinking, such as the Woodrow Wilson Foundation, the Foreign Policy Association, and the Council on Foreign Relations, did no more.[11]

If the concept of collective security was developed, and rejected by most Americans, during the years surrounding World War I, the term itself did not gain currency until the 1930s. It was first given prominence when it became the subject of the seventh and eighth International Studies Conferences held under the auspices of a League of Nations affiliate, the International Institute of Intellectual Co-operation, at Paris in 1934 and London in 1935. It provided the subject for the annual meetings of the Geneva Institute of International Relations in 1935 and 1936, and for the twelfth

---

11. Robert A. Divine, *Second Chance* (New York, 1967), pp. 12, 16, 18–23.

Institute under the Norman Wait Harris Foundation held at the University of Chicago, June 23–July 2, 1936.[12]

Why the term should come into vogue after 1934 is by no means clear, but it would be unwise to reject as flippant C. W. A. Manning's suggestion of August 22, 1935, that "it was invented, quite recently, as a sly means of suggesting to the more 'soft-boiled' Americans that somehow their country, in signing the Kellogg Pact, had inadvertently and against its desires assumed a quasi-membership in the League." [13] If so, the means were not sly enough, however. Certainly American individuals and groups friendly to the League of Nations were involved in the early discussions of the subject. Philip C. Jessup represented the Council on Foreign Relations as a participant in both International Studies Conferences and submitted for consideration of the London conference a lengthy memorandum on the American role in collective action for peace. Allen W. Dulles, William C. Scroggs, Isaiah Bowman, Raymond Leslie Buell, Joseph P. Chamberlain, Tyler Dennett, Edwin F. Gay, Admiral William V. Pratt, DeWitt C. Poole, James T. Shotwell, General George S. Simonds, and Quincy Wright served along with Jessup on the committee responsible for the report, which was seen as the definitive statement of views of what was rather grandiloquently designated as the National Coordinating Center in the United States for organizations engaged in the study of international relations.[14]

12. The published results of these meetings are to be found in Maurice Bourquin, ed., *Collective Security: A Record of the Seventh and Eighth International Studies Conferences* (Paris, 1936); Geneva Institute of International Relations, *Problems of Peace, Tenth Series: Anarchy or World Order* (London, 1936) and *Problems of Peace, Eleventh Series: The League and the Future of the Collective System* (London, 1937); and Quincy Wright, ed., *Neutrality and Collective Security* (Chicago, 1936). The Harris Foundation Lectures had dealt with problems related to collective security in 1924, 1927, and 1930, but the term itself was not used before 1936.

13. Geneva Institute, *Anarchy or World Order*, p. 152.

14. Philip C. Jessup, *International Security: The American Role in Collective Action for Peace* (New York, 1935), p. vii and *passim*.

At the International Studies Conference in London, Jessup was joined by Hamilton Fish Armstrong, the editor of *Foreign Affairs*, Malcolm W. Davis of the European Center of the Carnegie Endowment for International Peace, and Allen W. Dulles. Dulles, who had left the United States Diplomatic Service in 1926 and had subsequently served as legal adviser to the American delegations to the Three-Power Naval Conference in 1927 and to the Geneva Conference for the Reduction and Limitation of Armaments in 1932–33, was chairman of the study meetings of the conference and delivered one of the opening addresses.[15] The 1936 Harris lectures included one on "The United States and Collective Security," by Dean Edwin DeWitt Dickinson of the School of Jurisprudence of the University of California, and the entire series of lectures was published by Quincy Wright under the title *Neutrality and Collective Security*.[16] The lectures on the subject *Anarchy or World Order* delivered under the auspices of the Geneva Institute of International Relations in 1935 included one on "World Organization through Democracy," by Clarence K. Streit, then the Geneva correspondent for the *New York Times*, and another by Professor John B. Whitton of Princeton University that raised the question "Is American neutrality possible?"[17] The 1936 series included not only another lecture by Streit but also contributions by Professor Phillips Bradley of Amherst College, and by Otto Nathan, a New York University economist.[18]

Nevertheless, it was clear even to the American participants in these events—and they represented an infinitesimal

15. Bourquin, *Collective Security*, pp. 40–41, 488, 490–91, 496–97.

16. Wright, *Neutrality and Collective Security*, esp. pp. 157–82.

17. Geneva Institute, *Anarchy or World Order, passim*.

18. Geneva Institute, *The League and the Future of the Collective System, passim.*

minority of the American people—that the United States
was opposed to the notion of collective security that perforce
involved the possibility of sanctions. "The United States,"
Philip Jessup concluded, "will not now enter into any treaty,
pact, covenant, agreement or understanding, which binds it
in advance to use its military, air, or naval forces as a means
of bringing pressure on a state which threatens to resort to
war or actually begins hostilities. There is no realistic advantage from the American standpoint in discussing such
an arrangement at this time." "Further," he continued, "it
may be asserted that the United States is also unwilling to
bind itself in advance to apply economic or financial sanctions." [19]

The failure of the United States to respond affirmatively to
the collective security discussion of the middle 1930s had
roots deep in history. Washington's Farewell Address had
made the case that America's "detached and distant situation" permitted this country to follow a course different
from that of other powers. He had foreseen the time when,
given unity and efficient government, "belligerent nations,
under the impossibility of making acquisitions upon us, will
not lightly hazard the giving us provocation"; and he had
warned against "interweaving our destiny with that of any
part of Europe" and thus entangling our peace and prosperity "in the toils of European Ambition, Rivalship, Interest,
Humour or Caprice." Hamilton had urged avoidance of the
wars engendered by the French Revolution on much the
same grounds. Both men, if we may couch their statements
in more modern terminology, had argued that the security
of the United States could not be threatened unless, indeed,
this country embraced collective arrangements of some sort.
"All the armies of Europe, Asia and Africa combined," the

19. Jessup, *International Security*, p. 126.

youthful Abraham Lincoln had told the Young Men's Lyceum of Springfield, Illinois, in 1838, "with all the treasure of the earth (our own excepted) in their military chest, with a Buonaparte for a commander, could not by force take a drink from the Ohio, or make a track on the Blue Ridge, in the trial of a thousand years." And Carl Schurz had assured the readers of *Harper's Magazine* in 1893 that "in our compact continental stronghold we are substantially unassailable." [20]

Given this long-standing commitment of the United States to an independent foreign policy, it would have required the realization on the part of the American government and people that American security was actually threatened and that the United States was incapable of countering such a threat on its own to make the idea of collective security appealing. There is no evidence to support the assumption that such was indeed the case. Quite the contrary, the traditional view of the relationship of the United States to the rest of the world enjoyed wide acceptance throughout the 1930s. The halls of Congress echoed to the claims of Representatives John B. McClellan of Arkansas, Eugene B. Crowe of Indiana, Henry Ellenbogen of Pennsylvania, Martin Dies of Texas, and others that America was safe because it was separated "by thousands of miles of ocean and natural barriers" from the rest of the world.[21] Most military experts shared these views. Major General Johnson Hagood was certain that we could "build a fence around our property

20. James D. Richardson, ed., *A Compilation of the Messages and Papers of the Presidents, 1789–1897,* 8 vols. (Washington, 1899), I, 221–23; Henry Cabot Lodge, ed., *The Works of Alexander Hamilton,* Constitutional Edition, 12 vols. (New York and London, n.d.), V, 88–89; Roy P. Basler, ed., *The Collected Works of Abraham Lincoln,* 9 vols. (New Brunswick, N.J., 1953–55), I, 109; Frederic Bancroft, ed., *Speeches, Correspondence and Political Papers of Carl Schurz,* 6 vols. (New York and London, 1913), V, 207, 258–59, 264–65.

21. See for example *Congressional Record,* 74th Cong., 2d Sess. (1936), 2247, 2261, and 75th Cong. 1st Sess., (1937), Appendix 748.

and warn everybody to keep out." Major George Fielding
Eliot praised "Providence in its infinite mercy and wisdom"
for having given this country a geographical position far
removed from danger and expressed the opinion that aggressive warfare could not reach American shores. "No military
tidal wave could prevail against our continental and hemi-
spherical impregnability," the *New York Times*'s Hanson
Baldwin assured the readers of the *American Mercury* as
late as 1939.[22] The Senate Foreign Relations Committee
heard the same views expressed by Bernard Baruch, General
Hugh Johnson, and L. D. Stillwell of Dartmouth College.[23]
Even Phillips Bradley, a participant in the Geneva Institute
of International Relations lecture series on collective security in 1936, wrote in *Amerasia* in 1937 that "our geographical position, unique among the nations, makes avoidance of
other people's wars possible. We are insulated against effective attack." He had spoken at Geneva of his hope for a
"coincidence" between American foreign policy and the
principle of collective security.[24]

Such a "coincidence" was not likely to occur, however,
without some concern that American security could not be
maintained by the unaided efforts of this country. In the
absence of a perceived threat, the advice and counsel of the
Founding Fathers, which had been the mainstay of American foreign policy from the outset, was likely to prevail. John
Adams claimed to have told the Continental Congress in

22. Johnson Hagood, "Rational Defense," *Saturday Evening Post* CCIX
(October 24, 1936), 6, 40–43, and *We Can Defend America* (Garden City,
N.Y., 1937), pp. 2–29; George Fielding Eliot, *The Ramparts We Watch*
(New York, 1938), p. 351; Hanson W. Baldwin, "Impregnable America,"
American Mercury XLVII (1939), 267.

23. U.S. Senate, 76th Cong., 1st Sess., *Neutrality, Peace Legislation and
Our Foreign Policy: Hearings before the Committee on Foreign Relations*
(Washington, 1939), pp. 55, 280, 562.

24. Phillips Bradley, "Neutrality and War," *Amerasia* I (1937), 79;
Geneva Institute, *The League and the Future of the Collective System*,
p. 126.

1775 that "our real if not our nominal independence would consist in our Neutrality." Hamilton's abstract of points for possible inclusion in Washington's Farewell Address included the admonition that the "greater rule of our foreign politics" ought to be to have little or no connection with foreign nations and to "cherish the sentiment of *independence*." Washington, of course, had warned of permanent alliances and Jefferson of entangling ones, and Monroe's doctrine envisioned separate spheres of influence for the United States and Europe.[25] All of them ruled out meaningful collective action, and the loud echoes of their sentiments persisted well into the thirties, when they were tested in a number of crises, the first of which arose in connection with the Japanese invasion of Manchuria.

The Manchurian crisis fell into the term of Herbert Hoover, whose opposition to any form of collective security had been unequivocally expressed on numerous occasions. In an Armistice Day address in 1929 he had described the application of force to compel nations to settle their difference as a road the United States had refused to travel, and expressed the hope that aggression could be countered successfully by merely subjecting it "to the searchlight of public opinion." Five months later, Hoover had reaffirmed to the Daughters of the American Revolution his basic belief that America was sufficiently secure without collective arrangements:

> Because of our geographical situation, because of our great resources and of the American genius for organization, we have, in a sense that no other country has it, security from attack and harm by other nations. We are not only more free from attack, but our people are more free from the haunting fear of attack than are any other people in the world.

25. "The Autobiography of John Adams," Adams Papers (microfilm; Boston, 1954–56), Pt. III, No. 180; Felix Gilbert, *To the Farewell Address* (Princeton, N.J., 1961), pp. 138–39, 141; Richardson, *Papers of the Presidents*, I, 222, 323.

This freedom, he argued, did not diminish America's responsibility to work for world peace, but that responsibility could "only be fulfilled to its fullest measure by maintaining the fullest independence," and in particular by "independence from any combination pledged to the use of force" to maintain peace.[26]

In a memorandum the president read to his cabinet shortly after the Mukden Incident had caused China to bring the whole issue before the League of Nations, Hoover applied these views directly to the Far Eastern crisis. Calling the Japanese action immoral and an outrageous affront to the United States, he nevertheless insisted that "the Nine-Power Treaty and the Kellogg Pact are solely moral instruments based upon the hope that peace in the world can be held by the rectitude of nations and enforced solely by the moral reprobation of the world." "We are not parties to the League of Nations, the covenant of which has also been violated," he added with something less than regret. Once again, the conclusion followed logically:

> We should co-operate with the rest of the world; we should do so as long as that co-operation remains in the field of moral pressures. . . . But that is the limit. We will not go along on war or any of the sanctions either economic or military, for those are the roads to war.[27]

Although the United States cooperated with the League of Nations during the Manchurian crisis to a greater degree than ever before, it never deviated from this policy. The most obvious possibility for passing beyond "the field of moral pressures" lay in the application of economic sanctions

26. William Starr Myers, ed., *The State Papers and Other Public Writings of Herbert Hoover*, 2 vols. (Garden City, N.Y., 1934), I, 128, 234–35, 239.

27. *Ibid.*, pp. 156, 158–59; *The Memoirs of Herbert Hoover: The Cabinet and the Presidency, 1920–1933* (New York, 1952), pp. 368–70.

against Japan. The League itself never committed itself to move in that direction, and the United States neither urged it to do so nor seriously contemplated this step on its own. China initially appealed to the League on September 21 to take immediate steps "to prevent the further development of a situation endangering the peace of nations." But it did so under Article XI of the League Covenant, rather than under Articles XV and XVI under which sanctions might have been applied. In response to this, the League considered the idea of sending an investigating commission to Manchuria. Since Japan was opposed to such a commission, and since Secretary of State Henry L. Stimson believed that the Tokyo government did not support its army in Manchuria and could be persuaded to call off the action if it were not pushed too hard, the United States opposed even the sending of a commission.[28]

When Japan continued its advance into Manchuria in early October, the State Department for the first time began even to discuss the question of sanctions,[29] but there is no evidence of any favorable consideration at this time. The League too, speaking through its secretary-general, Sir Eric Drummond, still regarded sanctions to be "entirely out of the question." [30] The United States did agree to send its consul at Geneva, Prentiss Gilbert, to sit with the League Council during its meeting, which began on October 16; but Gilbert's instructions limited him to participation in discussions relating to possible application of the Kellogg-Briand Pact,

28. Henry L. Stimson, *The Far Eastern Crisis: Recollections and Observations* (New York, 1936), pp. 38, 42–43; Prentiss Gilbert to Stimson and Hugh Wilson to Stimson, September 22, 1931, and Stimson to Wilson, September 23, 1931, in U.S. State Department, *Foreign Relations of the United States, 1931*, 3 vols. (Washington, 1946), III, 35–36, 37, 48–49 (hereafter cited as *Foreign Relations*).

29. Stimson, *Far Eastern Crisis*, p. 57.

30. Gilbert to Stimson, October 7, 1931, *Foreign Relations, 1931*, III, 130.

which, as Hoover had repeatedly pointed out, relied entirely on moral pressure for its effectiveness.[31] When the League attempted to draw Gilbert into a more general discussion of the problem, Stimson instructed him to cease to attend meetings and only reluctantly agreed, after a telephone call from British Foreign Secretary Lord Reading, to permit him to go to one more secret and one more open session, but only as an observer at a seat away from the conference table. When it turned out that there were no seats away from the table and when Briand added his plea that Gilbert should nevertheless remain, Stimson reluctantly agreed to "let him go on sitting at the damned table," on condition that he "keep his mouth shut." [32]

On October 24 the League Council, without any further advice or participation by the United States, voted to urge China and Japan to compose their differences and asked Japan to evacuate Manchuria, hopefully prior to the next Council meeting on November 16. No such action was, of course, forthcoming. On November 10 the United States decided to send someone to Paris, where the Council meeting was to be held. Accordingly, Stimson called the ambassador in London, Charles G. Dawes, and asked him to go to Paris, not to attend Council meetings, but merely to be available for discussions with League members in his suite at the Ritz.[33] When the Council reconvened, the subject of eco-

31. Stimson, *Far Eastern Crisis*, pp. 64–65; Stimson to Gilbert, October 16, 1931, *Foreign Relations, 1931*, III, 203. In a telephone conversation on the same day, Stimson urged Gilbert "to keep in the background" and "not give Japan occasion to feel that we are seeking to guide the whole thing" (*ibid.*, 203–7).

32. Robert H. Ferrell, *American Diplomacy in the Great Depression* (New Haven, Conn., 1957), pp. 142–43; Stimson Diary, October 20, 1931, Stimson Papers, Yale University Library; Stimson to Gilbert, October 19, 1931, and telephone call of same date, Reading to Stimson, *Foreign Relations, 1931*, III, 248, 259–60, 248–58.

33. Ferrell, *American Diplomacy*, pp. 142–43; telephone conversation, Stimson to Charles G. Dawes, November 10, 1931, *Foreign Relations, 1931*, III, 407–14.

nomic sanctions received attention for the first time, at least in private conversations. On November 17 the New York *Herald-Tribune* carried, under a Washington dateline, the announcement that it had learned from "high official authority" that the Japanese ambassador in Washington had been officially informed that the United States would not support League sanctions or the withdrawal of diplomatic representatives from Japan. Stimson denied this in a cable intended for Dawes, and Undersecretary of State William R. Castle, Jr., informed the British ambassador in Washington that the denial was correct. Castle did not imply, however, that the United States favored sanctions, but insisted simply that this country had "reserved complete liberty for future action." [34]

On the very same day Dawes informed Stimson that Dr. Alfred Sze, the Chinese counsel at Geneva, had told him that China planned to ask the League within the next day or so to proceed under Articles X, XII, XV, and, if necessary, XVI, and thus to raise officially the question of collective action, probably in the form of sanctions. The American reply was immediate and definite. Stimson called Dawes in Paris and ordered him to stay away from League meetings especially now, "because they are going to take up the question of sanctions." Stimson was certain that the United States would not interfere with an embargo decided on by the League—though he did not wish to say so publicly—but he also expressed doubt "whether it is advisable for the League to go on with an embargo." "We do not ourselves believe in the enforcement of any embargo by our own government." he added.[35]

34. Stimson to G. Howland Shaw, November 17, 1931, and Castle Memorandum, November 18, 1931, *Foreign Relations, 1931,* III, 466–67, 477.

35. Shaw to Stimson, November 18, 1931, and telephone conversation, Stimson to Dawes, November 19, 1931, *ibid.,* pp. 484–85, 488–98, esp. 489, 496.

Outside official circles some sentiments favorable to American imposition of sanctions were expressed. Upton Close and John Dewey advocated such a course in speeches to the New York chapter of the League for Industrial Democracy, and the National Council for the Prevention of War, the Foreign Policy Association, and the League of Nations Association among other groups were sympathetic to such action. On balance, however, it seems clear that opposition to sanctions, and for that matter opposition to any cooperation with the League of Nations, overshadowed these views. Even the sending of Gilbert to attend the meetings at Geneva had been attacked as "a Wilsonian delusion" and a "sample of nitwit diplomacy." [36]

The claim that Secretary Stimson initially favored sanctions and "constantly returned to this idea" was made by Herbert Hoover and seconded by William Starr Myers.[37] But though Stimson may have toyed with the idea of sanctions, at least in the fall of 1931, and indeed discussed the matter with Hoover, the evidence already presented as well as entries he made in his diary suggest that he never really espoused such a course and eventually came to oppose it vigorously. At a meeting in the State Department on December 6, the secretary's principal advisers, Allen T. Klots, James Grafton Rogers, and Stanley K. Hornbeck expressed themselves as inclined to use sanctions, provided that some nation other than the United States took the initiative. Undersecretary Castle was unalterably opposed, and Stimson, though still tempted by the idea, was already considering the safer alternative of "non-recognition" and eventually supported Castle's position. As a result, the others retreated, and no

36. Armin Rappaport, *Henry L. Stimson and Japan* (Chicago, 1963), p. 88; *New York Times,* Nov. 12, Dec. 13, 1931; Stimson Diary, December 6, 1931, Stimson Papers; *Literary Digest* CXI (October 31, 1931), 3–4.

37. Hoover, *Memoirs: The Cabinet and the Presidency,* pp. 366–67; William Starr Myers, *The Foreign Policies of Herbert Hoover, 1929–1933* (New York, 1940), pp. 162–63.

action was taken.[38] When he came to write his own account
of events, both independently in 1936 and with MacGeorge
Bundy in 1947, Stimson never mentioned that he favored
sanctions actively at any time during the Manchurian crisis.[39]

On December 10 the League of Nations finally took action. With the consent of Japan it sent the Lytton Commission to Manchuria to investigate the situation in the hope
that military action in the area would cease while the commission was carrying out its task. The United States had
taken no part in this decision and was not officially represented on the commission. It did, however, agree to the appointment of an "unofficial" American, General Frank Mc-
Coy, to serve on the commission.[40] When the sending of the
commission failed to halt hostilities or stem the advance of
the Japanese, Stimson was incensed and turned his mind
once more to positive action. It was not to sanctions or to
any form of collective action that he turned. Instead, he
resurrected an idea first advanced by Secretary of State
Bryan in 1915 and, with the consent of Hoover, who had
earlier thought along these lines, formulated the well-known
nonrecognition doctrine with which his name is usually associated. When Chinchow fell to the Japanese on January
2, 1932, he began preparing the note that, on January 7,
informed Japan and the world that the United States "does
not intend to recognize any situation, treaty, or agreement
which may be brought about by means contrary to the cov-
enants and obligations of the Pact of Paris." [41] In relation

38. Rappaport, *Stimson and Japan,* pp. 89–90, 92–94; Stimson Diary,
November 7, 14, 1931, Stimson Papers; Ferrell, *American Diplomacy,* pp.
155–56.

39. Stimson, *Far Eastern Crisis, passim.;* and Stimson and McGeorge
Bundy, *On Active Service in Peace and War* (New York, 1947), esp. p. 233.

40. Benjamin B. Wallace, "How the United States 'Led the League' in
1931," *American Political Science Review* XXXIX (1945), 113.

41. Ferrell, *American Diplomacy,* pp. 155–58; Rappaport, *Stimson and
Japan,* pp. 92–94; Stimson Diary, January 3, 4, and 6, 1932, Stimson Papers.
The text of the note is in *Foreign Relations, 1931,* III, 7–8.

to the issue of collective security, it should be noted that his
doctrine was once again an appeal to public opinion and not
to coercion; that it was based on the Kellogg-Briand Pact,
which also was a "moral" document; and that the action
taken was wholly unilateral. Stimson had informed foreign
ambassadors of his plans and hoped that other nations
would follow the American example, but his doctrine was
neither a collective formulation nor a commitment to positive enforcement action. "Non-recognition," Sir John T.
Pratt has pointed out, "was a peculiarly American technique, the fruit of American isolationism." [42]

Isolationist or not, the Stimson Doctrine did not immediately find support in the world community, particularly
not in Great Britain, whose cooperation Stimson regarded
as essential. Certainly it did not inhibit Japan, which, on
January 28, produced the most startling evidence of its aggressive intent by attacking Shanghai. Stimson was outraged
and once more sought more positive action. The United
States sent troops and naval vessels to Shanghai to protect
American interests and persuaded Britain, France, and Italy
to join in asking Japan to stop fighting and to enter into
negotiations with China in the presence of neutral observers.
Japan refused the offer on February 4. [43]

It was at this point that the idea of sanctions came once
again into the realm of public discussion in the United
States, at least within the academic and business communities. [44] Stimson, always at least half-tempted by the idea, was
realistic enough to realize that no massive support for such
a course would be forthcoming either within or without the

42. John T. Pratt, *War and Politics in China* (London, 1943), p. 226;
see also, Ferrell, *American Diplomacy*, pp. 162–69.
43. Stimson, *Far Eastern Crisis*, pp. 147–50; Ferrell, *American Diplomacy*, pp. 178–79.
44. *New York Times*, Feb. 2, 18, 1932; Rappaport, *Stimson and Japan*,
pp. 137–38.

government. Faced by the need for some action, however, he now attempted to unite the signatories to the Nine-Power Treaty in an effort to invoke the provisions of that pact. The Nine-Power Treaty, of course, provided for nothing more than "full and frank communication between the Contracting Powers" in the event of a breach in its provisions; but Stimson regarded its invocation both as a form of "collective protest" and as a step which, in the likely event that it prove ineffective, might push American sentiment in the direction of sterner action, provided, of course, that the League of Nations took the initiative.[45]

By mid-February the idea of an embargo had gained some public support. Organized by Raymond Rich of the World Peace Foundation and led by Newton D. Baker, Wilson's secretary of war, and President A. Lawrence Lowell of Harvard, a movement sprang up in support of sanctions. On February 17 Lowell delivered a nationwide radio address urging the United States to join a League boycott of Japan. A petition was subsequently circulated asking the president and Congress "to signify to the League of Nations that the United States will concur in any economic measures the League may take to restore peace." Twelve thousand signatures were collected, many from the academic community; and a number of other petitions, including one containing the signatures of 5,000 civic leaders from all sections of the country, were submitted to Congress. To coordinate all of these activities, an American Committee on the Far Eastern Crisis was set up, with headquarters in the New York office of the Twentieth Century Fund. The Fund, a private research organization, had itself set up a Committee on Economic Sanctions headed by Columbia University President Nicholas Murray Butler, to consider the possibility of add-

45. Stimson, *Far Eastern Crisis*, pp. 160–61; Ferrell, *American Diplomacy*, p. 180; Hoover, *Memoirs*, II, 375.

ing an economic-sanction protocol to the Kellogg-Briand Pact.[46] "They drove at me," President Hoover complained, "with all the usual propaganda weapons." [47]

The movement for sanctions made little headway, however. Not only did Hoover remain unalterably opposed, but all members of the cabinet and all but two senators shared that opposition. Walter Lippmann and Edwin M. Borchard added their voices to the chorus of protest, and so did the editors of the Chicago *Tribune* and the *New York Herald-Tribune*. The Gannett and Hearst chains firmly opposed sanctions, and so did the *Nation* and the *New Republic*. In May, George Soule contributed an article to *Harper's* entitled "The Fallacy of the Boycott." [48] Under the circumstances, neither Stimson nor anyone else worked actively to commit the United States to the invocation of sanctions, or indeed, to persuade the League to follow such a course. Since the major League powers opposed sanctions as likely to lead to war, no action was forthcoming from that quarter other than the Assembly resolution of March 11, which deplored the existing state of affairs in China, urged the parties to submit the dispute to peaceful settlement, and echoed the Stimson nonrecognition principle of January. The pressure for sanctions, Hoover noted with satisfaction, simply "evaporated," [49] and Stimson proceeded to take his next step. It took the form not of collective action nor of the application of any kind of sanctions. As a last resort, Stimson merely issued a policy statement that, for diplomatic reasons, he

46. Rappaport, *Stimson and Japan*, p. 138; various relevant petitions are reprinted in *Congressional Record*, 72d Cong., 1st Sess. (1932), 4586–4588.

47. Hoover, *Memoirs*, II, 371.

48. Stimson Diary, February 20, 1932, Stimson Papers; *New York Times*, Feb. 14, 21, 24, 1932; *Congressional Record*, 72d Cong., 1st Sess. (1932), 4654 ff.; George Soule, "The Fallacy of the Boycott," *Harper's Magazine* CLXIV (1932), 702–9; Rappaport, *Stimson and Japan*, p. 139.

49. Denna Frank Fleming, *The United States and World Organization, 1920–1933* (New York, 1938), pp. 431–32; Hoover, *Memoirs*, II, 371.

couched in a letter to Senator William E. Borah, in which
he reviewed the entire Open Door policy, reiterated the
Stimson Doctrine, and vaguely threatened Japan that the
United States, in the face of continued Japanese violations
of the Nine-Power Treaty, might no longer feel itself bound
to observe restrictions on naval construction or the fortifica-
tion of Pacific bases that it had accepted under the complex
of agreements coming out of the Washington conference.[50]

It would be difficult to read into this series of events any
serious American commitment to the principle of collective
security, however vaguely defined. In the face of trouble in
the Far East, an area that had been the focus of America's
earliest foreign interests and the arena in which the only
consistent American foreign policy—that of the Open Door
—had been developed, the United States reacted more
strongly than at any time since 1917. Under the administration of a president with some awareness of the interdependence of nations and a secretary of state who had some activist leanings, the United States moved a few cautious steps
closer to some form of international cooperation. But there
is no evidence either that the United States ever seriously
contemplated genuine collective action of any sort or, for
that matter, any course going beyond the stage of moral
suasion. And there is ample evidence that anything else
would have encountered the determined opposition of both
the Congress and the American people. The most that Stimson ever tried to do was to keep the Japanese guessing in
regard to America's real intentions, and it was for that reason that he always objected to American official statements
opposing an embargo. "A word unspoken," he told Walter
Lippmann "is a sword in your scabbard, while a word spoken

50. Ferrell, *American Diplomacy*, pp. 183–88; *Foreign Relations: Japan,
1931–1941*, 2 vols. (Washington, 1943), I, 83–87.

is a sword in the hands of your adversary." He never forgave
Castle for telling the American Conference of International
Justice in May, 1932, that boycotts led to war and that the
United States would not go beyond nonrecognition, nor
Hornbeck for telling essentially the same thing to the American Society of International Law.[51] His quarrel with Hoover
rested on the same grounds. Yet even in Stimson's strongest
anti-Japanese statement—his speech of August 8, 1932, to
the Council on Foreign Relations, which was applauded in
Europe as signifying the end of American neutrality and
roundly condemned for this reason in much of the American
press—he suggested nothing more definite than "branding
the aggressor." Three days later, Hoover restated the official
American position in his acceptance speech to the Republican national convention: "We shall, under the spirit of that
[Kellogg] Pact consult with other nations in times of emergency to promote world peace. We shall enter no agreements committing us to any future course of action or which
shall call for the use of force to preserve peace." [52]

When the League took its final action in the Manchurian
matter on February 24, 1933, by passing a resolution condemning Japanese actions in China, withholding recognition from Manchukuo, and calling for Japanese withdrawal,
Stimson replied within twenty-four hours to the effect that
the United States was in substantial accord with the Assembly's "measured statement of conclusions" and expressed
"general endorsement of the principles thus recommended."
But he reiterated that American support of the League in-

51. *New York Times,* May 5, 7, 1932; *Proceedings of the American Society of International Law, 1930* (Washington, 1930), p. 70; Stimson to
Lippmann, May 19, 1932, quoted in Rappaport, *Stimson and Japan,* p. 160.
52. Stimson Diary, July 14, 18, 23, 25, 26, 27, 28, 1932, Stimson Papers;
New York Times, Aug. 9, 1932; Myers, *State Papers of Herbert Hoover,* II,
260. See also Robert A. Divine, *The Illusion of Neutrality* (Chicago, 1962),
pp. 19–20.

cluded this country's "reserving for itself independence of judgment with regard to method and scope." [53]

In terms of collective security it seems clear that even the words and actions of Henry L. Stimson, the leading international activist in the government, were little more than a bluff designed to intimidate the Japanese, a maneuver not backed by any real expectation that the United States would act decisively when the chips were down. The United States in the early 1930s was neither convinced that its security was actually threatened by events in the Far East nor particularly inclined to see collective action in the crisis as necessarily the best course. At various points, as in initial opposition to sending an investigating mission, in the nonrecognition note, and in the Borah letter, the United States acted quite unilaterally. And the foot-dragging of Great Britain and the other League powers on matters like the invocation of the Nine-Power Treaty, where the United States did believe some form of collective action to be necessary, did nothing to enhance the virtues of collective security arrangements in American eyes.

D. F. Fleming's detailed analysis of press reaction to the final action of the League in February, 1933, disclosed widespread, though by no means unanimous, endorsement of that course. But support for further action, in the form of an economic boycott, was not common. Fleming found at least vaguely positive reactions to this idea in the Newark *Evening News*, the Louisville *Courier-Journal*, the Daily *Oklahoman*, the Galveston *Tribune*, the Albuquerque *Journal*, the Portland *Oregonian*, and the *Rocky Mountain News*. The list of clearcut opponents, led by the Chicago *Tribune* and the Hearst newspapers, was much longer. Although the

53. Fleming, *United States and World Organization*, p. 452; see also W. W. Willoughby, *The Sino-Japanese Controversy and the League of Nations* (Baltimore, 1936), pp. 500–501.

press seemed far more favorably inclined toward the League of Nations than before, there is little evidence of a movement toward American participation in a genuine system of collective security. It is likely that enthusiasm for such a course would have been even less had the crisis arisen in Europe, where the dangers of American involvement in war, as well as of a general entanglement in big power politics, were greater.[54]

An agreement to impose economic sanctions was not, of course, the only way in which the United States might have indicated its willingness to participate in collective security arrangements. Another way might have been through a policy of selectively controlling the trade in arms and ammunition so as to withhold war materials from "aggressors," violators of international agreements, or other nations engaged in activities that endangered world peace. Although the United States had been active throughout the twenties in promoting general disarmament and had participated in all of the international conferences dealing with that subject, it had not seriously considered using the control of American arms export as a device for maintaining world peace. Indeed, the United States had failed to ratify both the Convention of Saint-Germain of September 10, 1919, which provided for the general regulation of arms traffic under the supervision of the League of Nations, and the Geneva Arms Traffic Convention of June 17, 1925, which was specifically designed to remove American objections to the Saint-Germain proposals.[55]

54. Fleming, *United States and World Organization*, pp. 457–94, esp. 465, 471, 472, 475–76. Some reasons for the differing attitudes toward Europe and Asia are suggested in Jonas, *Isolationism in America*, pp. 23–24, 104, 200–201.

55. Elton Atwater, *American Regulation of Arms Exports* (Washington, 1941), pp. 172–76; *Foreign Relations, 1920*, 3 vols. (Washington, 1936), I, 180–96; U.S. State Department, *Press Releases*, XIII (June 29, 1935), 484–85.

Early in 1933, mounting American arms shipments to Latin America, occasioned by the Chaco War between Bolivia
and Paraguay, aroused the concern of both the president and
Congress. Under these circumstances, Stimson was able to
persuade Hoover to send a special message to Congress on
January 10 urging ratification of the Geneva Arms Traffic
Convention or the adoption of legislation that would give
the president authority to forbid, in conjunction with other
arms-manufacturing nations, the shipment of arms and ammunition from the United States. The control of such shipments to areas of international conflict, Hoover explained,
"would greatly aid the earnest and unceasing efforts which
all nations now make to prevent and lessen the dangers of
such conflicts." [56]

Hoover's message was accompanied by a letter dated January 6, which the president had received from the secretary
of state. In it Stimson had gone a great deal further in the
advocacy of a more active role for the United States in collective peace efforts. "There are times," Stimson had written,
"when the hands of the Executive in negotiations for the
orderly settlement of international differences would be
greatly strengthened if he were in a position in cooperation
with other producing nations to control the shipment of
arms." [57] Despite Stimson's words, the implications of the
proposal seem to have been lost on both the Foreign Relations Committee and its chairman, Senator William E.
Borah. The committee, without serious discussion, unanimously reported Senate Joint Resolution 229, which would
have prohibited the export of arms and munitions from the
United States to any country or countries designated by the

56. State Department, *Press Releases*, VIII (January 14, 1933), 18–19;
Divine, *Illusion of Neutrality*, pp. 45–46; Atwater, *American Regulation of
Arms Exports*, p. 182.
57. Stimson to Hoover, January 6, 1933, in State Department, *Press
Releases*, VIII, 22.

president whenever he had found that such exports would "promote or encourage the employment of force in the course of a dispute or conflict between nations" and "after securing the cooperation of such governments as the President may deem necessary." The Senate adopted this resolution by unanimous consent and without debate on January 19, with Borah taking the initiative in urging its immediate adoption.[58] Only on the following day did some senators have second thoughts. At that point the conservative Connecticut Republican Hiram Bingham moved for reconsideration on the grounds that the discretionary powers the resolution gave to the president might involve this country in war.[59] As a result of this maneuver, the resolution did not go to the House. Undersecretary of State Castle, however, persuaded the chairman of the Foreign Affairs Committee, Samuel D. McReynolds, to introduce a separate but identical resolution there. This resolution was amended in committee to apply only to American countries and was reported out in this form on February 15. No action was taken before the Seventy-second Congress adjourned.[60]

The incoming president, Franklin D. Roosevelt, had already expressed his support of a discretionary arms embargo on January 11.[61] At the urging of Secretary of State Cordell Hull and of Norman H. Davis, the American delegate to the Geneva Disarmament Conference, the president agreed, on March 10, to recommend introduction of a new arms embargo resolution to the chairmen of the Foreign Affairs and Foreign Relations committees. In the House the new McReynolds resolution, identical to that of the last Congress,

58. *Congressional Record*, 72d Cong., 2d Sess. (1933), 2096.

59. *Ibid.*, pp. 2134–35.

60. *Foreign Relations, 1933*, 5 vols. (Washington, 1950–52), I, 358–59; *New York Times*, Jan. 31, Feb. 16, 1933; *Congressional Record*, 72d Cong., 2d Sess. (1933), 4209.

61. *New York Times*, Jan. 12, 1933.

was passed after a bitter partisan debate by a roll-call vote of 254 to 109.[62] The majority of the Congressmen still saw the issue simply in terms of interdicting an undesirable form of trade and believed it was intended to apply primarily to situations like the Chaco War, but the administration was exploring the possibility of using its new authority, were it to be granted, for a somewhat wider purpose.

In early March, British Prime Minister Ramsay MacDonald offered a new plan for disarmament that would have provided for consultation among the European powers in case of aggression. At the same time, the chairman of the Geneva Disarmament Convention, Arthur Henderson of Great Britain, approached the American delegates with a scheme to bring the United States at least marginally into the collective security picture. Its essence was that the United States would consult with the major powers and, if it agreed on the identity of the aggressor, halt its trade in arms and thus passively cooperate in the use of sanctions. Norman Davis discussed the matter further with British diplomats in April and urged the United States to agree to the plan.[63] When MacDonald and French Premier Edouard Herriot came to Washington late in April, Roosevelt discussed the issue with them and agreed in principle that this country would "undertake to refrain from any action . . . which would tend to defeat the collective effort which the States in consultation might have decided upon against the aggressor." On May 22 Davis announced this new American policy in a speech at Geneva. "We are willing," he told the delegates,

62. Divine, *Illusion of Neutrality*, pp. 48–51; *Congressional Record*, 73d Cong., 1st Sess. (1933), 581, 1850. The bill was HJR 93.

63. Hugh Gibson to Cordell Hull, March 8, 12, 1933, and Norman H. Davis to Hull, April 16, 1933, in *Foreign Relations, 1933*, I, 26, 32, 89–92, 96–97.

to consult the other states in case of a threat to peace, with a view to averting the conflict. Further than that, in the event that the states, in conference, determine that a state has been guilty of a breach of the peace in violation of its international obligations and take measures against the violator, then, if we concur in the judgment rendered as to the responsible and guilty party, we will refrain from any action tending to defeat such collective effort which these states may thus make to restore peace.[64]

Davis's speech was the closest the United States came to a definite offer of cooperation with collective security measures, and the reaction in Congress was immediate and drastic. The Foreign Relations Committee, which had been considering the arms embargo proposal for some weeks and had been only partially reassured by Hull's statement that the administration planned to apply the embargo to both Paraguay and Bolivia but not to Japan, acted on May 24 to make the arms embargo apply impartially and automatically to all belligerents. In accepting this amendment offered by Hiram Johnson of California, the committee changed the entire sense of the resolution, converting it from a potential collective security measure to a clearly isolationist one, and bringing it, as Hull pointed out, "directly in conflict with our proposal at Geneva as expressed by Norman Davis." [65] Roosevelt, after first accepting this new version of the proposal, quickly recognized the conflict and decided to drop the whole matter. On May 24 Congress passed a bill pro-

64. Franklin D. Roosevelt Papers, President's Special File, Box 30, Franklin D. Roosevelt Library; Sir Robert Vansittart Memorandum, April 23, 1933, and William Phillips Memorandum, April 26, 1933, in *Foreign Relations, 1933,* I, 103–4, 109–10; U.S. State Department, *Peace and War: United States Foreign Policy, 1931–1941* (Washington, 1943), pp. 188–89.

65. *New York Times,* May 25, 26, 30, 1933; Divine, *Illusion of Neutrality,* p. 52; *The Memoirs of Cordell Hull,* 2 vols. (New York, 1948), I, 229–30; *Congressional Record,* 73d Cong., 1st Sess. (1933), 4967.

hibiting the sale of arms to Bolivia and Paraguay, without reference to any action that might be taken by the League or by other powers.[66]

The effort to align the United States, if only passively, with a policy of collective security thus largely failed because of the determined opposition of Congress and the unwillingness of the president to push the matter. Not only did this leave this country farther than ever from a position of meaningful collaboration with other powers in the preservation of peace, it also brought to the fore the idea of an impartial arms embargo against belligerents, an idea that became a key element in the policy designed to preserve at all costs the neutrality of the United States.

Just how far the United States remained from meaningful collaboration with other powers was once again demonstrated in January, 1935, when the administration reintroduced in the Senate the long dormant proposal for American adherence to the World Court. Nine years before, the Senate had voted to join the court by a vote of 76–17, but only with five reservations, including, as the fifth, insistence that the Court have no connection with the League and would not "without the consent of the United States entertain any request for an advisory opinion touching any dispute or question in which the United States has or claims an interest." [67] This last reservation had met with objections from all of the other powers save Cuba, Greece, Liberia, Albania, and Luxembourg, and the counterproposal they made was in turn unacceptable to President Coolidge.[68] Not until 1929,

66. Divine, *Illusion of Neutrality*, pp. 60–62.

67. *Congressional Record*, 69th Cong., 1st Sess. (1926), 2556–57; Manley O. Hudson, *The World Court, 1921–1934*, 4th ed. (Boston, 1934), pp. 8–9, 226–27.

68. Denna Frank Fleming, The United States and the World Court (Garden City, N.Y., 1945), pp. 74–81; *New York Times*, Nov. 12, 1926; Hudson, *The World Court*, pp. 232–39.

and then largely through the efforts of Elihu Root, was a compromise worked out that seemed acceptable both to the United States and to the Tenth Assembly of the League of Nations. The United States signed the compromise proposal on December 9, 1929, and President Hoover forwarded it to the Senate for ratification on the following day.[69] By that time, however, the United States was deeply involved in the deepening domestic economic crisis, and proposals to finalize American accession to the Court were repeatedly put off by the Senate Foreign Relations Committee. In January, 1935, the first quiet Senate session in many years seemed in the offing, and President Roosevelt decided to submit the protocols for the accession of the United States to the Senate in the sanguine expectation that they would meet with little opposition.[70]

Adherence to the World Court by the United States would not have represented a serious or binding commitment to the principles of collective security, since nothing would have compelled this country to join in the enforcement of any decisions the tribunal might reach. Yet the mere fear that adherence to the Court could be the prelude to further commitment led the United States to reject such a step.

Senator Hiram Johnson of California began the attack on the protocols with an impassioned and lengthy speech in which he declared that acceptance of the protocols would simply represent another attempt "to meddle and muddle, under an hysterical internationalism, in those controversies that Europe has and that Europe never will be rid of" and that "going into the Court will ultimately mean going into the League of Nations as surely as that night follows day."

69. Hudson, *The World Court*, pp. 249–51, 261; State Department, *Press Releases*, I, 437 (December 13, 1929); League of Nations, *Official Journal* (1929), p. 1857.

70. *Congressional Record*, 74th Cong., 1st Sess. (1935), 468, 480, 483; Fleming, *United States and World Court*, pp. 117–18.

Of particular concern to Johnson was the possibility of involving the United States in the enforcement of the Court's decisions through sanctions imposed by the League, that is, by genuine collective action. "Sanctions!", he exclaimed. "If there are sanctions behind any decision that this Government may render, then this Government has departed so widely from its traditional policy that every American ought to hang his head in shame." Such views were vehemently supported by a sizable group of senators, including Huey Long of Louisiana, Robert R. Reynolds of North Carolina, and Henrik Shipstead of Minnesota. "To enter the World Court means entering the court of intrigue," Reynolds insisted, " . . . means entering the League of Nation." "I do not believe," Shipstead concluded, "the national policy of the United States is one that should make us enter either the League or its instrument—the League Court." [71]

To make certain that no one would be likely to interpret the acceptance of the protocols by the Senate as a step in the direction of collective security, Senator Vandenberg offered the following amendment to the instrument of ratification:

> That adherence to said protocols and statute hereby approved shall not be so construed as to require the United States to depart from its traditional policy of not intruding upon, interfering with, or entangling itself in the political questions of policy or internal administration of any foreign state; nor shall adherence to the said protocols and statute be construed to imply a relinquishment by the United States of its traditional attitude toward purely American questions.

The Vandenberg amendment, although defeated in the Foreign Relations Committee by a vote of 11–9, was reintro-

71. *Ibid.*, pp. 563–78, 773, 875.

duced in the Senate and there approved by a voice vote on January 24.[72]

Numerous other crippling amendments were introduced, including one by Senator George W. Norris of Nebraska, which would have reconstituted the objectionable "fifth reservation" of 1926 in an even more rigorous form. These amendments were defeated, but, as it turned out, defeated by a process similar to that which marked the debates over the Treaty of Versailles in 1919 and 1920; that is, by a combination of the Court's opponents with its anti-reservationist champions. Accordingly, the protocols themselves went down to defeat in January by a vote of 52–36, seven short of the required two-thirds majority, and almost the identical tally by which the League of Nations Covenant had been rejected in 1920.[73]

America's belated adherence to the World Court, hedged about as it would have been with reservations, would not have been a significant step toward involving this country in collective security arrangements. In rejecting the Court, however, the Senate clearly demonstrated that the mere suggestion of such arrangements was still regarded as contrary to United States policy, and that this country had moved barely, if at all, from the position it had adopted in the immediate postwar years.

By the middle of 1935 it became apparent that the world was rapidly approaching a new crisis in which the threat of a general war once more became a reality. Japan had already flouted world order and the League of Nations, and Italy and Germany were about to embark on similar courses.

72. *Ibid.*, pp. 636, 893; Fleming, *United States and World Court*, pp. 124–25.
73. *Congressional Record*, 74th Cong., 1st Sess. (1935), 893, 977, 1055, 1124–40, 1167.

Mussolini's attack on Ethiopia confronted the League with the first European challenge to its effectiveness as a peace-keeping and crisis-resolving body, and it offered one more chance to test America's stand on the concept of collective security.

The first official information about Italian plans in Ethiopia reached the State Department on September 18, 1934. On that date the War Department forwarded a report from the assistant military attaché in Rome, who had reported on August 29 that "the General Staff of the Italian army have drawn up plans for the military conquest and occupation of Abyssinia" to be undertaken "whenever Abyssinia commits an 'overt act.' " [74] It was with some sense of relief, however, that the State Department received, in answer to its inquiry, a memorandum from Ambassador to Italy Breckinridge Long that failed to confirm this report and concluded that a "very frank and apparently sincere statement" made to him by the Italian Undersecretary of State for Foreign Affairs Fulvio Suvich to the effect that "the Italian Government has no present intention of attacking Abyssinia" should be accepted at face value. At the same time, the American military attaché in Rome, Colonel J. G. Pillow, repudiated the earlier report of his subordinate by placing a rather innocuous interpretation on Italian preparations in Eritrea and Somaliland.[75]

Despite such reassurances, it became clear as autumn wore on that a crisis was developing between Italy and Ethiopia. On November 23 an armed Ethiopian escort for the Anglo-Ethiopian boundary commission encountered an Italian military post at the Wal Wal waterhole in the Oga-

74. Report No. 14028, August 29, 1934, *Foreign Relations, 1934,* 5 vols. (Washington, 1951–52), II, 754.

75. Breckinridge Long Memorandum, September 19, 1934, and Report No. 14057, September 21, 1934, *ibid.,* II, 755–57.

den desert, some sixty miles within Ethiopian territory. The
Italians refused passage, and the Ethiopians dug in at positions facing the Italian post. The long-awaited "overt act"
was now imminent, and the Italo-Ethiopian crisis had moved
from the realm of speculation to that of reality. On December 7 the Italian press carried reports of an attack on Wal
Wal, claimed to be on Italian territory, by six hundred
Ethiopian troops, an attack that had been repulsed by "colonial troops and aeroplanes." [76] Within a week frantic moves
developed in various European capitals to keep the crisis
under control, and by December 17 the chief of the Division of Near Eastern Affairs of the State Department,
Wallace Murray, thought it "not unlikely that sooner or
later there will be a move to invoke the Kellogg Pact in this
dispute." "If so," he told Undersecretary of State William
Phillips, " . . . we ought to leave such invocation to the
League of Nations and make every effort to avoid having
the matter dumped in our lap." [77]

Even more unwelcome than possible invocation of the
Kellogg Pact was the suggestion contained on the following
day in a telegram from W. Perry George, the American
chargé d'affaires in Addis Ababa, that Ethiopian Emperor
Haile Selassie was considering asking for American mediation. Secretary Hull immediately asked for confirmation of
this report, reminding George that the United States had
not acted in 1931 until after the council of the League of
Nations had invoked the Kellogg Pact, and instructing him
to "scrupulously refrain from taking any action which would
encourage the Ethiopian Government to request the mediation of the United States." [78] When the Rumanian minister

76. Alexander Kirk to Hull, December 8, 1934, ibid., II, 767.

77. Wallace Murray to Phillips, December 17, 1934, ibid., II, 767.

78. W. Perry George to Hull, and Hull to George, both December 18,
1934, ibid., II, 769–70.

in Washington reminded Hull that Italy's experience in Ethiopia—i.e., the action or nonaction of other powers in this conflict—would strongly influence Italian attitudes toward the European situation, and offered to inquire of his government whether it believed any American efforts at this time might prove useful, the secretary promptly gave a negative reply and indicated that the United States "preferred to pursue its present policy and attitude of observer." He further asked Chargé George in Addis Ababa to explain to the emperor that "this Government considers that it could not usefully or properly take *any* action," though it, of course, followed "with sympathetic interest" efforts made to settle the dispute.[79] Even more clearly than in the early stages of the Sino-Japanese conflict, the United States thus made plain its intention to avoid both involvement in the dispute and participation in collective schemes to end it.

The Ethiopian crisis, of course, produced the greatest difficulties not for the United States, which simply reasserted its "traditional" policy, but for Great Britain and France, for whom Il Duce's actions appeared as a direct threat to the already precarious European power balance. The real threat to this balance was Hitler's Germany, and both Britain and France, particularly France, looked to Italy as a possible counterweight to German ambitions. Mussolini's action in rushing troops to the Brenner Pass after the murder of Austrian Chancellor Dollfuss in August, 1934, a move widely interpreted as intended to forestall a German annexation of Austria, was taken as evidence that Italian cooperation was vital to any effort to thwart Hitler's designs. When the Wal Wal incident muddied the waters, therefore, French Foreign Minister Pierre Laval journeyed to Rome to resolve outstanding Franco-Italian differences. The Rome

79. Hull Memorandum, December 20, 1934, and Hull to George, December 21, 1934, *ibid.*, II, 771–72, 774. Italics added.

Agreements, which were concluded in January, 1935, contained a secret provision whereby France renounced all interest in Ethiopia save for the Djibouti–Addis Ababa railroad, a renunciation widely interpreted as giving Mussolini carte blanche in that area in return for continued support of the French policy of containing Germany.[80] In the same spirit Great Britain failed to raise the question of Ethiopia at the Stresa Conference that summer and thus could acquiesce in a communiqué stressing agreement with Italy and France on "all international questions which are posed."[81]

Given this attitude, it is not surprising that Britain and France opposed efforts by Ethiopia to bring the matter before the League of Nations. When Ethiopia did appeal to the Council under Article XI of the covenant on January 15, Britain and France persuaded Italy, which also did not want the matter before the League, to agree to seek a settlement of the matter under the terms of the Italo-Abyssinian Treaty of Friendship of 1928. With a sigh of relief, the Council thereupon postponed consideration of the Ethiopian request.[82] Subsequent British and French policy was impaled on the horns of a dilemma: if the credibility of the League as a peace-keeping organization was to be maintained, then it must clearly act; but if Germany was to be checked in Europe, good relations among Britain, France, and Italy had to be maintained. The United States, of course, was not as directly involved with these issues as were the European powers. But it is clear that the British and French dilemma could have been resolved if the United States had in fact

80. D. C. Watt, "The Secret Laval-Mussolini Agreement of 1935 on Ethiopia," *Middle East Journal* XV (1961), 77; Brice Harris, Jr., *The United States and the Italo-Ethiopian Crisis* (Stanford, Calif., 1964), pp. 8–9. But see also Pierre Laval, *The Diary of Pierre Laval* (New York, 1948), p. 20.

81. Harris, *United States and Italo-Ethiopian Crisis*, p. 12.

82. Prentiss Gilbert in Geneva kept the State Department informed of these developments. See Gilbert to Hull, January 11, 15, 16, 17, 19, 1935, *Foreign Relations, 1935*, 4 vols. (Washington, 1953), I, 594–99.

committed itself to cooperate with the efforts to halt both
Italian aggression and the German threat, i.e., if the United
States had committed itself to full participation in some kind
of collective security scheme. But the United States in fact
was moving in the opposite direction.

While the Italo-Ethiopian crisis was coming to a head and
raising the specter of a new European war, the United
States was increasingly concentrating its efforts not on ways
and means to prevent such a war through cooperative actions with other powers but on schemes to avoid involvement in war once it had broken out. The Senate, on April 12,
1934, set up what was to become known as the Nye Committee for the purpose of investigating the munitions industry.
The basic assumption on which the committee acted was
that the greed of munitions-makers and other vested interests was responsible for American involvement in World
War I, and the committee's well-publicized activities thus
fostered widespread acceptance, at least for a time, of what
Charles Beard was to call the devil theory of war.[83] The
logic of the devil theory led to conclusions that made the
concept of collective security seem irrelevant. If America's
wars essentially resulted from the activities of selfish men,
be they bankers, businessmen, munitions-makers, or whatever, then they could be best prevented, not by concerted
international action to stop all wars, but by domestic legislation designed to curb the dangerous proclivities of the
vested interests. Accordingly, the United States turned to
the business of drafting so-called neutrality legislation.

As early as April 17, Hull asked J. Pierrepont Moffat, the
chief of the Division of Western European Affairs, Under-

---

83. *Congressional Record*, 73d Cong., 2d Sess. (1935), 6485; Hull,
Memoirs, I, 399; Jonas, *Isolationism in America*, pp. 144–47; Charles A.
Beard, *The Devil Theory of War* (New York, 1936), *passim*. The best
account of the activities of the Nye Committee is John E. Wiltz, *In Search of
Peace* (Baton Rouge, 1963).

secretary Phillips, Assistant Secretary R. Walton Moore, and
the Department's legal adviser Green H. Hackworth, to begin a study of the question of neutrality legislation "with a
view to keeping us out of further trouble." They immediately turned for advice to Charles Warren, acknowledged
as a leading American authority on international law, who
obliged with a 210-page memorandum entitled "Some Problems in the Maintenance and Enforcement of the Neutrality
of the United States." The Warren memorandum called for
an impartial arms embargo on belligerents and the limitation of arms shipments to neutrals, a ban on American travel
on belligerent vessels, and the restriction of "contraband"
trade with belligerents to prewar levels. In substance Warren's proposals differed only slightly from those being developed by the Nye Committee and virtually assumed the
inevitability of a European war and the consequent useless-
ness of a determined effort to prevent such a war through
collective action.[84] Roosevelt expressed strong interest in
these proposals and asked the State Department to prepare
neutrality legislation for submission to Congress.[85]

While the State Department was still wrestling with this
problem early in 1935, Roosevelt met with the Nye Committee on March 19. Ignoring a memorandum by Hull in
which the secretary had urged the president not to encourage the committee in any way, Roosevelt told the senators
"that he had come around entirely to the ideas of Mr. Bryan"
about prohibiting American ships and American citizens

84. Divine, *Illusion of Neutrality*, p. 70. A copy of the Warren Memorandum is in File 811.04418/28, State Department Papers, National Archives. For Warren's view see also Charles Warren, "What Are the Rights of
Neutrals Now, in Practice?", *Proceedings of the American Society of International Law, 1933* (Washington, 1933), pp. 128–33, and "Troubles of a
Neutral," *Foreign Affairs* XII (1934), 377–94.

85. R. Walton Moore to Franklin D. Roosevelt, August 27, 1934, and
Roosevelt to Hull, September 25, 1934, Files 811.04418/28 and /29, State
Department Papers.

from traveling to belligerent nations in time of war, and asked the committee to consider the entire neutrality question with a view to introducing appropriate legislation.[86] Though Roosevelt requested the committee to show him the draft proposal before submission, he could hardly have been unaware of the isolationist character of the group or have had doubts that a rigid plan for mandatory neutrality legislation would be forthcoming. Yet there is no evidence that he even raised the crucial issue of presidential discretion or made any suggestion that American neutrality policy should be integrated somehow into a general collective security scheme.

The president's meeting with the Nye Committee spurred the introduction of a neutrality bill and brought again to the fore this key issue of 1933. Any neutrality legislation was bound to include an arms embargo. In 1933 feeble attempts by the administration to get congressional approval for a measure that would have empowered the president to prevent arms shipments to any country at his discretion had been scrapped in favor of a proposal for an impartial, mandatory embargo on arms shipments to all belligerents. The Warren memorandum supported the impartial embargo idea, but opinion in the State Department was divided, with Hull, Phillips, and Joseph C. Green of the Division of Western European Affairs favoring discriminatory embargoes. Roosevelt agreed to support a discriminatory arms embargo in a conversation with Phillips on July 21, but made no public statement to that effect.[87] He did not then or at any other time indicate, as Hull repeatedly did, that unless the embargo proposal were of a discriminatory nature, he would

86. Hull to Roosevelt, March 14, 1935, and Joseph C. Green Memorandum, March 21, 1935, *Foreign Relations, 1935,* I, 318–23, 363–64; Divine, *Illusion of Neutrality,* p. 86.

87. Hull, *Memoirs,* I, 410–11.

oppose all neutrality legislation. He did approve a resolution calling for presidential discretion in the application of the law, which the State Department had prepared for submission to Senator Key Pittman of Nevada, the chairman of the Senate Foreign Relations Committee. But the resolution was not sent after Pittman told presidential secretary Stephen Early that "if he wants this done, I will introduce it . . . but he will be licked as sure as hell." In the absence of a firm stand on the part of the president, Congress passed the Neutrality Act on August 23, which, among other things, provided for a mandatory, nondiscriminatory arms embargo for a period of six months.[88]

The Neutrality Act of 1935 was a victory for congressional isolationists and thus a defeat for the collective security principle. Its underlying premise was the belief that this country could preserve its security by insulating itself from the quarrels of others, and that this represented a safer course than the allegedly quixotic effort to keep peace everywhere through concerted international action. Roosevelt and Hull doubted the effectiveness of this scheme for avoiding war and had a more realistic understanding of the complexity of international relations and of America's world role. The president realized, for example, that "the wholly inflexible provisions of Section I of this act might have exactly the opposite effect from that which was intended," [89] and he hoped that after expiration of the six-month measure more flexible provisions might be substituted. Moreover, he noted with some gratification that the Act would not interfere with any future decision by the League of Nations to prohibit the sale of arms to Italy. But neither Roosevelt nor

88. Key Pittman to Stephen Early, August 19, 1935, in Edgar B. Nixon, ed., *Franklin D. Roosevelt and Foreign Affairs,* 3 vols. (Cambridge, Mass., 1969), II, 609; *Congressional Record,* 74th Cong., 1st Sess. (1935), 14370, 14434.

89. State Department, *Peace and War,* p. 272.

Hull envisaged genuine American participation in a collective security scheme at that time, or fully realized that their acquiescence in a restatement of American isolationism might have an adverse affect on the actions of those European powers seeking to preserve peace through the League of Nations. As Italy and Ethiopia moved toward war in the summer of 1935, the United States continued to repel the efforts of Emperor Haile Selassie to secure positive American support for his position.

On July 3 the emperor called the American chargé, George, to the palace in order to ask the American government "to examine means of securing Italy's observance of engagements as signatory of the Kellogg Pact" in view of the unsatisfactory progress of the discussions at Geneva. Hull's reply, sent even before the official text of Haile Selassie's request reached Washington, in effect rejected the emperor's request for American action. Hull expressed gratification with what the League was doing, looked for "a decision satisfactory to both of the Governments directly concerned," and stated that the United States was "loath to believe" that either Ethiopia or Italy would resort to other than pacific means to settle their dispute. Though Hull reaffirmed American support of the Kellogg Pact, his message was sufficiently ambiguous to leave the contrary impression with Haile Selassie and with most of the world press, and to produce a headline in the *New York Times* that read, "President Rejects Ethiopia's Appeal for Peace Effort." [90] This reaction caused Hull to issue a new statement on July 12, in which he clearly indicated the United States' continued support of the pact, without however suggesting that this country might seek to invoke it.[91]

90. Harris, *United States and Italo-Ethiopian Crisis*, pp. 34–35; George to Hull, July 4, 1935, and Hull to George, July 5, 1935, *Foreign Relations, 1935*, I, 723–24, 725.

91. See Phillips to William E. Dodd, July 13, 1935, *Foreign Relations, 1935*, I, 731–32.

There can be little doubt that the American government and the American public sympathized with the plight of Ethiopia,[92] but it is equally apparent that neither was prepared to pay more than lip service to the cause of peace. On July 31 Roosevelt expressed "the hope of the people and the Government of the United States that an amicable solution will be found" but once again laid the responsibility for maintaining peace on the League and gave no indication how the United States might aid that effort.[93] Two weeks later Hull cabled the chargé in London to keep him informed of developments in order to determine "whether any further action . . . within the limits of . . . established policy" would have a beneficial effect. A similiar communication to Paris brought back the suggestion that a direct, but unpublished, message to Mussolini might be in order. After some debate Hull sent a message on behalf of the president, expressing the American hope for a peaceful resolution of the conflict and characterizing the possible failure of such a resolution as a calamity. Mussolini's response was to inform Roosevelt and Hull that it was too late to avoid an armed conflict.[94]

Even after this development, the United States made no attempt to play a stronger role. When Haile Selassie, in a desperate move to involve the United States more directly in the dispute, granted an extensive oil concession to the African Exploration and Development Corporation, a subsidiary of the Standard Vacuum Oil Company, the State Department was aghast. On September 3, senior officers of the company were called to the Department and urged to terminate the concession, which they agreed to do. When the

92. Harris, *United States and Italo-Ethiopian Crisis,* pp. 38–42.

93. Phillips to Robert W. Bingham, July 31, 1935, *Foreign Relations, 1935,* I ,732–33.

94. Hull to Roy Atherton, August 15, 1935; Theodore J. Marriner to Hull, August 17, 1935; Hull to Kirk, August 18, 1935; and Kirk to Hull, August 19, 1935, *ibid.,* I, 732–33, 735, 735–36, 739, 739–42.

American chargé in Addis Ababa suggested that he might try to explain to a disappointed emperor that the American action was intended to be helpful to Ethiopia, he was quickly informed by Hull to change that statement to "helpful in the cause of peace." [95] A final request for American mediation made by Haile Selassie on September 10 produced a lengthy negative reply, which once again referred the matter to the League. The nature of the entire American approach was admirably summed up by Hull on the eve of the actual outbreak of war. "We have given our moral support," he cabled to Cornelius Van H. Engert in Addis Ababa, "to all the efforts that have been made to arrive at a peaceful settlement, and we shall continue this support by any action which we can properly take in the light of our limitations as occasions arise." [96] The nature and extent of "our limitations" was clear. The United States would not, even indirectly, participate in the work of the League, and it would not, in the absence of League action, move to take the lead in efforts to find alternative solutions. On September 20 Hull informed Ray Atherton in London that the United States would not participate in the imposition of sanctions, and could decide its attitude toward collective actions that might be taken by the League only after careful study. A week later he asked Ambassador Bingham in London to discourage British Foreign Secretary Sir Samuel Hoare from calling even a consultative conference of the signers of the Kellogg Pact. Such a move, Hull insisted, would only bypass the League.[97]

95. Cornelius Van H. Engert to Hull, August 30, 1935; Hull to Bingham, September 3, 1935; Engert to Hull, September 4, 1935; and Hull to Engert, September 5, 1935, *ibid.*, I, 778, 781–82, 783, 784.

96. Engert to Hull, September 11, 1935, and Hull to Engert, September 12, 1935, *ibid.*, I, 744, 751–52.

97. Hull to Atherton, September 20, 1935; Hull to Bingham, September 27, 1935; *ibid.*, I, 836, 767–68.

The Italian invasion of Ethiopia began on October 2, and the United States issued its Neutrality Proclamation on October 5, prohibiting the export of arms, ammunition, and implements of war to belligerents and forbidding Americans to travel on belligerent vessels. Roosevelt accompanied this proclamation with a statement that persons engaging in any transactions with belligerents henceforth did so at their own risk. The League Council did not decide that Italy had made war in disregard of the covenant until October 7, and did not impose the first sanctions, those on arms shipments, until October 11. Although Hull had opposed proclaiming American neutrality before the League had decided there was a war,[98] he used the argument of prior action to resist mounting pressures that the United States clarify its intentions with regard to future actions of the League. In telegram after telegram Hull stated the American position. This country had taken independent action to limit arms shipments and had imposed credit restrictions before anyone else had acted. It had made its desire for peace clear on numerous occasions. It would not now serve with, or give advice to, the League committee charged with formulating the policy of sanctions, and it would not commit itself in advance to support any course the League might decide upon. "It must be clear to them by this time," he informed Prentiss Gilbert in Geneva, "that this Government is acting upon its own initiative and proceeding separately and independently of all other Governments or peace organizations." [99] This was hardly a ringing endorsement of the collective security principle. In subsequent communications with the British and Italian ambassadors, Hull made it even clearer that Ameri-

98. Hull to Roosevelt, October 5, 1935, *ibid.*, I, 798–800.
99. Hull to Gilbert, October 17, 1935, *ibid.*, I, 846–48. See also Hull's reply to Dr. Augusto de Vasconcellos, President of the Committee of Coordination of the League, October 26, 1935, *ibid.*, I, 852–54.

can actions with regard to the Italo-Ethiopian War were "developed under our own separate, independent course and initiative and without the slightest relationship to sanctions or any other movements of other nations or peace agencies at Geneva," and were designed primarily to keep the United States out of war.[100]

The League's initial decision to embargo arms to Italy did not test this position. But the subsequent move to extend the embargo to cover strategic materials, particularly oil, did so. The League had to obtain American cooperation if an oil embargo were to be effective, and the world's other oil-producing nations were understandably reluctant to commit themselves to an embargo unless they were assured in advance that the United States would participate.

Roosevelt's initial message of October 5 had attempted to discourage all trade with belligerents by withdrawing government protection from it. When this did not prevent the rapid increase of exports of strategic materials to Italy, Hull and Roosevelt pressed for this so-called moral embargo both in public and in private, most forcefully in a statement by Hull on November 15 that denounced the increasing trade in oil, copper, trucks, tractors, scrap iron, and scrap steel as "contrary to the policy of this Government" and "to the general spirit of the recent neutrality act." Hull's careful explanation that the moral embargo applied essentially to increased exports and not to all trade lent further credence, however, to his oft-repeated assertion that American neutrality policy was designed to avoid entanglements and bore only a passive relation to collective schemes for punishing aggressors.[101] In any event, the value of American exports of

---

100. Hull Memorandum, December 2, 1935, *ibid.*, I, 866–69.

101. Hull Statement, October 10, 1935, *ibid.*, I, 803–4; Hull, *Memoirs*, I, 435; State Department, *Press Releases*, XIII, 338–39 (November 2, 1935). See also Herbert Feis, *Seen from E.A.: Three International Episodes* (New York, 1947), pp. 193 ff.

petroleum products to Italy and her African colonies rose from a monthly average $480,000 in 1932–34 to over a million dollars in October, 1935, and to $2,674,000 in November, while discussion of a possible oil embargo was going on in Geneva.[102]

The situation at Geneva was extraordinarily complex. The British, who in September had set in motion the machinery by which sanctions were initially imposed, had agreed with the French that sanctions were not to be pushed to a point that might force Mussolini to retaliate. They now feared that oil sanctions might have that effect, and found confirmation for their fears in an Italian message to the French that indicated Italy would regard an oil embargo as a military sanction and could not be responsible for any consequences.[103] British Foreign Secretary Sir Samuel Hoare and his French counterpart Pierre Laval therefore sought a means for settling the conflict before the League would have to act on the oil issue. The result of their deliberations, on December 7, was the Hoare-Laval Plan, which would have resolved the conflict by, in effect, handing control of Ethiopia over to Italy. The immediate rejection of this plan by the British government kept the oil issue before the League and left Britain and France with no alternative but to stall for time.

In doing so, they repeatedly referred to the inability of the United States to control its oil shipments to Italy and pointed out the necessity of awaiting the outcome of the neutrality debate then raging in Congress. Only after the United States had reached a decision, Laval told the Chamber of Deputies on December 28, could the League Council decide whether to act on the oil issue. "I cannot," he added, "prejudge the decision which will be taken by Congress, the

102. Feis, *Seen from E.A.*, p. 307.
103. Harris, *United States and Italo-Ethiopian Crisis*, pp. 65–66, 103.

authority which will or will not be given to Roosevelt, the usage which Roosevelt will or will not make of his powers." [104] Although he was clearly using America's ambiguous position as an excuse for his own reluctance to act affirmatively, Laval's statement was given credibility by the American record. Had Congress proceeded to authorize the president to embargo certain raw materials, that credibility would have been diminished and those League members actively supporting sanctions might have found further encouragement. Such was not to be the case, however.

In his annual message to Congress on January 3, 1936, Roosevelt called for a "twofold neutrality" program, and bills incorporating the president's ideas were introduced the next day in both the House and Senate. They called for the continuance of the mandatory, nondiscriminatory arms embargo, but also authorized the president to limit trade in strategic materials to any or all belligerents to prewar levels. [105] In hopes of winning quick congressional approval, Roosevelt thus sacrificed once again the idea of a discriminatory arms embargo. Moreover, he sought no authority to prohibit strategic trade with belligerents, but merely a way to prevent its increase. Had Congress approved this scheme, the United States would have enacted into law the idea, already promulgated by Stimson at the beginning of the decade, that this country would not actively undermine or otherwise interfere with sanctions adopted by the League. But the United States would have continued, as indeed it did continue, to operate under legislation that made active participation in collective security arrangements impossible. Without the possibility of discriminating in its arms sales

104. Quoted in *ibid.*, p. 115.

105. *New York Times*, Jan. 4, 1936; the text of the bill may be found in U.S. House of Representatives, 74th Cong., 2d Sess., *American Neutrality Policy: Hearings before the Committee on Foreign Affairs* (Washington, 1936), pp. 1–6.

or of withholding strategic materials from an aggressor, this country could not throw its full weight into the collective balance. Congress, as it turned out, was not even willing to keep the United States from interfering with the collective efforts of others.

The trade quota proposal almost immediately ran afoul of those members of Congress who opposed presidential discretion in any form and of those who opposed restricting American trade in materials other than arms and ammunition on traditional international law grounds. In the controversy that ensued, the administration bill was lost entirely, and, when time for further discussion ran out, the Act of 1935 was simply extended until May 1, 1937. Roosevelt accepted this resolution of the problem at a cabinet meeting on February 7.[106] He also signed without comment the final bill, despite the fact that it made American neutrality policy even more rigid by adding a ban on loans to belligerents and requiring extension of the arms embargo to any nation that might join a war already in progress. The United States thus refused to cooperate with possible sanctions through a trade embargo, while at the same time threatening the League powers with an arms embargo if they decided to intervene in the Italo-Ethiopian conflict.

If the signing of the new American Neutrality Act on February 29 did nothing to encourage the proponents of oil sanctions at Geneva, the German march into the Rhineland on March 7 effectively ended all possibility of further action. The League turned from further consideration of sanctions to an appeal for conciliation, urging Italy on April 20 "to bring to the settlement of her dispute with Ethiopia that spirit which the League of Nations is entitled to expect from

106. *The Secret Diary of Harold L. Ickes,* 3 vols. (New York, 1953–54), I, 533; see also Jonas, *Isolationism in America,* pp. 175–82, and Divine, *Illusion of Neutrality,* chap. 5.

one of its original Members and a permanent Member of the Council." [107] The result was a foregone conclusion.

During the entire course of the Italo-Ethiopian conflict, the United States had gone to great pains to assure friend and foe, the nations of the world and the American public, that it was pursuing an independent policy wholly removed from any collective security arrangements. Its actions did nothing to call this assurance into question. American policy was undoubtedly popular at home, and the failure of the League in the crisis was used as further evidence of the wisdom of American "independence." It is unlikely that the League would have passed this, its most crucial test in any event, for none of the major powers were prepared to risk war for themselves in order to stop Italy. But there can be little doubt that the refusal of the United States to associate itself clearly with the efforts at collective action made the work at Geneva more difficult and contributed to the failure there.

Though Roosevelt and Hull were certainly more internationalist-minded than the policy they accepted and carried out might indicate, there is no evidence that either of them ever seriously contemplated anything beyond passive cooperation with whatever the League might decide to do. Their extreme caution may have been dictated by domestic political considerations, by the fear of offending both the isolationist majority in Congress and the general public. But the reluctance to exert effective leadership to overcome this opposition suggests strongly that the administration shared to a large degree the general belief that events in Europe did not immediately threaten the security of the United States and could probably best be handled by the European states themselves. The result was that any approach to col-

107. Albert E. Highley, *The First Sanctions Experiment, Geneva Studies,* Vol. IV, No. 4 (July, 1938), p. 118.

lective security remained low on the list of priorities of a
president who believed it necessary to devote most of his
energies to the continuing domestic crisis. That such an attitude further undermined the already precarious collective
security structure within the League and thus gave tacit
encouragement to Germany, Italy, and Japan was too little
understood.

The failure of the League to prevent the Italian conquest
of Ethiopia effectively marked the end of efforts to preserve
world peace through collective international action. Hitler
began to implement his expansionist plans while the Italo-
Ethiopian conflict was still in progress and continued on the
course that led directly to the invasion of Poland in September of 1939. Shortly thereafter, Japan began to resume its
conquest of China, which ultimately led to Pearl Harbor and
American involvement in war. At no point on this road to
war was a concerted international effort made to prevent
disaster, and at no point did the United States attempt to
initiate such an effort. The major League powers, surveying
the wreckage of the sanctions efforts of 1935–36, abandoned
collective schemes for more traditional diplomacy, and even
strong partisans of collective security had second thoughts.
"Perhaps," concluded Albert Highley, "the ideal of collective
security should be abandoned, for it is better not to have it
at all than to have it fail." [108]

For the United States there was nothing to abandon.
Though the ideal was implicit in Woodrow Wilson's proposal
for a League of Nations, it had been steadfastly rejected by
the American people. And during the time when the League
might have developed into an effective collective security
organization, no American administration had given it sufficient encouragement. Even Stimson, Hull, and Roosevelt

108. *Ibid.*, p. 127.

never proposed anything more than an American policy that would not negate the collective efforts of others, and they were unsuccessful in establishing even this limited form of international cooperation as official policy. The actions taken by the United States during the Manchurian crisis were, without exception, taken unilaterally; and in the Italo-Ethiopian conflict, no action was taken at all. In neither case did this country suggest by word or deed that it was willing to join, even indirectly, in a collective effort to preserve world peace by bringing concerted economic and military pressure to bear on potential or actual aggressors.

In his Quarantine Speech of October 5, 1937, Roosevelt called for "positive endeavors to preserve peace." He never explained precisely what he had in mind, and his image of the peace-loving 90 percent of the world's nations who might somehow get together to stop the lawless 10 percent is as vague as the *posse comitatus* idea that Henry Cabot Lodge embraced in 1915. But there is much in the record of his first term of office to suggest that Roosevelt would have shied away from genuinely collective efforts to set up a quarantine much as Lodge had shied away from the obligations of the League Covenant. "We are looking for some way to peace," he told a press conference on October 6, "and by no means is it necessary that that way be contrary to the exercise of neutrality." [109] If the way to peace was not contrary to the exercise of neutrality, collective security surely was.

Not until the United States came to see a clear and present threat to its own security in the actions of Germany, Italy, and Japan did the American attitude undergo a significant change. For a few Americans, including Roosevelt, that

109. State Department, *Press Releases*, XVII, 276–79 (October 9, 1937); Samuel I. Rosenman, ed., *The Public Papers and Addresses of Franklin D. Roosevelt*, 13 vols. (New York, 1938–50), VI, 422–24. See also Dorothy Borg, "Notes on Roosevelt's Quarantine Speech," *Political Science Quarterly* LXXII (1957), 405–33.

moment had come by the time Poland was conquered. For many others it came with the fall of France. For some, like Senator Vandenberg it did not come until the Japanese finally demonstrated at Pearl Harbor that collective action might be required to safeguard not only the peace of the world but the very existence of the United States. Only then did the threat to American sovereignty posed by its enemies come to seem greater than the threat to sovereignty inherent in collective security arrangements. And only then was the United States ready to set out on the course that Woodrow Wilson had proposed.

The United States and the Atlantic Alliance: The First Generation

LAWRENCE S. KAPLAN

NATO HAS BEEN a phenomenon in international relations. Unlike most multinational organizations of the past, it has survived for a generation, thereby fulfilling at least the minimal expectations of its founding fathers. Even more phenomenal for Americans has been the identification of the United States with an idea, a particular group of nations, and an organization that were all repugnant to a tradition that specifically isolated America from Europe. The origins of the North Atlantic Treaty are inextricably linked with the rediscovery of Europe by the United States.

No American tradition had older and more powerful roots than isolationism. The language of American foreign policy in the nineteenth century and in the first half of the twentieth century repeated the words and echoed the emotions and preconceptions of Washington's Farewell Address, Jefferson's First Inaugural Address, and the Monroe Doctrine. Even the verbiage of the Open Door at the turn of the twentieth century and the circumstances of America's entrance in World War I suggested a *Novo Ordo Seclorum*, with the implication in the former of a superiority of American methods and goals over Europe's in the Far East, and in the latter of a refusal to "ally" with the European cobelligerents in the war against the Central Powers.

In the generation preceding World War II the United States had never appeared more resolute in its isolationism. The Western democracies that had betrayed America's faith in the Treaty of Versailles seemingly deserved the fate the Axis powers had in store for them. If most Americans did not look upon the destruction of Europe with satisfaction in the 1930s, they certainly felt that they had no personal stake in the outcome of another European war, despite efforts of President Roosevelt to alert his countrymen to the Nazi peril.

Both the Japanese attack on Pearl Harbor and the United Nations convention at San Francisco appear at least superficially to be suitable landmarks in the changing history of twentieth-century isolationism. Yet, neither the fears of 1941 nor the hopes of 1945 ultimately served as sufficient catalysts to shake the nation from its illusions about American autarchy in a chaotic world. Isolationism had always been more than a description of isolation; it had elements of ideology that involved a state of mind and a course of action.[1] Historians have frequently claimed that the United States had never turned its back on the world, had always been concerned with external affairs, and had often exploited the troubles of the outside world for the advantage of special groups—Wall Street financial interests, missionaries in the Far East, or Franklin D. Roosevelt's political career.[2] But

1. See Selig Adler, *The Isolationist Impulse: Its Twentieth Century Reaction* (New York, 1957); Alexander DeConde, ed., *Isolation and Security* (Durham, N.C., 1957), particularly the editor's Chapter 1, "On Twentieth-Century Isolationism."

2. Charles A. Beard, *American Foreign Policy in the Making, 1932–1940: A Study in Responsibilities* (New Haven, Conn., 1946); William Appleman Williams, *The Tragedy of American Diplomacy* (Cleveland and New York, 1959).

isolationism in the American tradition is specifically identified with Europe, notably with England and France, and is
equated with revulsion from political connections with Europe. Washington's "great rule of conduct" in 1796 had pro-
nounced that America was a new society freed from the Old
World's wars, corruption, and other social evils; and America's later history seemed to have vindicated his judgment
that ties other than commercial would enmesh the United
States in the snares of Europe. This identification was not to
be found in 1945.

On the contrary, the assumptions of Americans about the
world continued to reflect the emotions of the isolationist
tradition. Hence, the idea of war as a permanent institution
in international society remained an un-American idea
blamed on the European balance-of-power system and without validity for the United States. The precipitate mass demobilization of the war economy and military establishment
was done with little more thought about its impact on the
outside world than was the case in 1865 or in 1918. The war
was over, and it followed that all wars would be irrelevant
to the new world order.[3] In this light the United Nations
served as a surrogate foreign office of the United States behind which Americans could withdraw to more important
domestic matters. The Four or Five Policemen of the
Security Council would provide a routine patrol for a world
in which violence would come from smaller irresponsible
powers. Such differences as existed among the Great Powers
would be resolved on the basis of their common goal of maintaining world peace.

America's expectation of involvement without responsibility did not last long. The Soviet Union's refusal to observe

3. Dexter Perkins, *The American Approach to Foreign Policy* (Cambridge, Mass., 1951), particularly Chapter 5, "The American Attitude toward War."

Western requirements for elections in Eastern Europe, its support of communist subversive groups in Greece, and its pressures on Turkey and Iran all pointed to Russian unwillingness to endorse America's image of the postwar world. To cope with the Russian posture required not only a recognition that the Soviet Union was a powerful physical threat to Europe but also that no other power was available to subdue the threat. In understanding this problem, American policymakers also had to face the fact that the balance of power was a reality in 1946 and that American power was the vital element in the maintenance of the balance.

The Truman administration's response to the unexpected pressures of the outside world resulted in an ambivalence toward the Soviet Union that reflected the understandable confusion of an inexperienced leadership. On the one hand, President Truman shared the eagerness of the nation to return to "normalcy" as fast as the soldiers could be returned to civilian life. To justify the hasty demobilization required a reasonably peaceful future for Americans and Russians, and the efforts of Secretary of State James F. Byrnes to reach binding agreements with the Soviet Union bear witness to the importance the administration attached to fulfilling the vision of a world without major conflicts of interests. On the other hand, policymakers if not politicians were forced to recognize within a year after the war's end that the differences with the Soviet Union over elections in Eastern Europe, over the future of atomic weapons, and over the ultimate disposition of the German problem represented more than a breakdown of communications between East and West. They were also a reflection of their respective interpretations of history. To Americans, Russia's harnessing of Eastern Europe to the communist system was a betrayal of treaty promises and a cynical display of Soviet aggression rather than a means of ensuring security against future German resurgence abetted by the capitalist powers. To Russians, American attempts to force elections on Eastern Europe were simply the predictable acts of an imperialist power advancing its capitalist interests rather than an expression of an idealist reordering of Europe in the image of American democracy to avoid future wars.

As early as February, 1946, George F. Kennan, chargé d'affaires in Moscow, sent a cablegram to Washington that contained the seeds of his notable statement on containment in the July, 1947, issue of *Foreign Affairs*. In this message he observed that in the Soviet Union, "we have . . . a political force committed fanatically to the belief that with us there can be no permanent modus vivendi." [4] Out of this kind of thinking emerged a reevaluation of Roosevelt's claim that Yalta "spells the end of the system of unilateral action, the exclusive alliances, the spheres of influence and balances of power and all other expedients which have been tried for centuries—and have always failed." [5] In place of a universal organization like the United Nations, which was consistent with the spirit of isolationism, the United States was forced into a new consideration of the balance of power.

What was needed in 1946 first was the acceptance of the balance of power as a rule of international life and secondly the assertion of leadership in maintaining the balance. Only an American presence in Europe could restrain the Soviet Union's impulse toward expansion, and this presence could better be expressed by diplomacy than by military weapons. In time, Kennan speculated, the United States can "force upon the Kremlin a far greater degree of moderation and

4. Kennan's cablegram of February 22, 1946, from Moscow to Department of State, in Barton J. Bernstein and Allen J. Matusow, eds., *The Truman Administration* (New York, 1966), p. 209.

5. Roosevelt's address to the Congress on Yalta, March 1, 1945, in Samuel I. Rosenman, ed., *The Public Papers and Addresses of Franklin D. Roosevelt*, 13 vols. (New York, 1938–1950), XIII, 586.

circumspection than it has had to observe in recent years, and in this way to promote tendencies which must eventually find their outlet in either the break-up or the gradual mellowing of Soviet power." [6]

When Kennan's message finally became the Truman policy, it was expressed, as Kennan was to point out later, in an unsophisticated and excessively military form.[7] It was Britain's confession of inability to continue its assistance to Greece and Turkey in their struggle against communist pressures that opened to the United States a channel along which American power might be brought to bear in behalf of ailing Europe. The alternative to immediate action appeared to have been the loss of Greece and Turkey, and perhaps even the loss of Europe itself, to communist subversion and ultimate conquest. On this high ground of principle and in the customary Manichean language of American isolationism, President Truman observed that "the free peoples of the world look to us for support in maintaining their freedoms. If we falter in our leadership, we may endanger the peace of the world—and we shall surely endanger the welfare of our own Nation." [8] The $400 million in emergency aid, which was all the British had anticipated in their approaches to the State Department, was dwarfed by the larger challenge implied in the Truman Doctrine, something that the Labour government had not quite anticipated when it laid down its burden in the Mediterranean.[9]

6. George F. Kennan "The Sources of Soviet Conduct," *Foreign Affairs* XXV (July, 1947), 582.

7. George F. Kennan, *Memoirs, 1925–1950* (New York, 1967), pp. 358–59, in which he blames himself for ambiguities in the "X" article that permitted a misinterpretation of "containment."

8. President's message to joint session of the Congress (Truman Doctrine), March 12, 1947, in Department of State *Bulletin* XVI (1947), 537.

9. Elizabeth Lane Furdell, "The United Kingdom, the United States and the Truman Doctrine," Ms., Seminar in American Diplomatic History, Kent State University, 1967.

The presidential speech of March 12, 1947, was only a beginning. The supplies to Greece and Turkey represented an emergency military support. The administration then sought a form of assistance that would deal with the economic chaos left in the wake of war. While the details of the Truman Doctrine were discussed and investigated, the new Policy Planning Staff of the Department of State examined ways of deepening and widening the channel of aid so that massive economic assistance might be provided to Europe as a preventive as much as a curative of the communist infection. The result was the Marshall Plan, organized by Undersecretary of State for Economic Affairs William L. Clayton, tried out in a speech at Cleveland, Mississippi, by Undersecretary of State Dean Acheson, and popularized by Secretary of State George C. Marshall at the Harvard University commencement exercises of June 5, 1947.

The contrast between American behavior after 1918 and after 1945 is instructive, and suggests that nations can learn some lessons, if not always the appropriate ones, from history. The United States joined rather than rejected a league of nations, it abandoned loans to Europe in favor of outright grants of aid, and it considered the consequences of withdrawal from Europe in terms of its effect on the balance of power in the world. True, the European Economic Cooperation Act, which in 1948 gave life to the European Recovery Program, met opposition in the Congress; but the opposing arguments went beyond familiar cries of criminal waste and ungrateful beneficiaries to unfamiliar alarms over the fate of the United Nations and the incompatibility between the military character of the Truman Doctrine and the economic function of the Marshall Plan.[10] The ECA not only passed the scrutiny of the Congress but promised in its execution

10. See Henry A. Wallace, "My Alternative for the Marshall Plan," *New Republic* XXXVIII (January 12, 1948), 13–14; Walter Lippmann, *The Cold War: A Study in U.S. Foreign Policy* (New York, 1947), pp. 52–57.

to promote the building of a new Europe with a continental economy rather than merely national economies. The American image of the future was, of course, a United States of Europe.

The very year in which the nation committed itself to a new view of Europe was also the year in which that continent felt itself to be in greater danger than ever before. The American commitment was to be strengthened by new crises. In February, 1948, Czechoslovakia, a Westernized country whose leaders Eduard Beneš and Jan Masaryk had close ties with the United States, fell prey to a communist coup; and in June the Soviet Union used its presence in East Germany to blockade Berlin, severing all land and water links to the West. Here was the crest of the communist westward wave, whether propelled by the winds of communist doctrine or by a reaction to American measures. What could the United States do to stem the tide?

Europe's own answer was immediate though elliptical. In March, 1948, in the wake of Czechoslovakia's fall, five Western nations—the United Kingdom, France, Belgium, the Netherlands, and Luxembourg—organized in Brussels the Western Union, pledged to mutual defense and to economic cooperation. The significance of this pact was not lost on American planners. On one level, the Brussels treaty emphasized that economic recovery was impossible without military security. On another, it intimated that only the United States could provide that security. By emphasizing the principles of self-help and mutual aid, the Brussels Pact powers appealed to the sentiments that had already made the Organization for European Economic Cooperation successful: namely, that American assistance serve the ends of European unification—political, economic, or military. And the assistance they wanted on this occasion was American participation in the organization.

The closest the United States would come to gratifying

this wish was the Vandenberg Resolution of June 11, 1948, when the Senate endorsed by an overwhelming majority of 64 to 6 the "progressive development of regional and other collective arrangements for individual and collective self-defense," and underlined this endorsement by associating the United States, "by constitutional process, with such regional and other collective arrangements as are based on continuous and effective self-help and mutual aid and as affect its national security." If the Marshall Plan may be likened to enlightened application of World War I loans, then military aid to the Western Union would be an improved version of World War II lend-lease, with the important distinction that weapons and supplies were intended to deter attack rather than to repel invasion after it had begun.

Tailored though the Brussels Pact was to just such a response as the Vandenberg Resolution provided, the member nations were not satisfied. No resolution would be meaningful to them unless "association" was equated with membership in the alliance, and embraced Article 4 of the Treaty: "If any of the High Contracting Parties should be the object of an armed attack on Europe, the other High Contracting Parties will, in accordance with the provisions of Article 51 of the Charter of the United Nations, afford the Party so attacked all the military and other aid and assistance in their power." Could this kind of assurance be granted?

American planners were not at all sure in the spring of 1948 that the nation would give such guarantees. To join a military alliance, particularly a European military alliance with a life span of fifty years, would pit an insecure administration squarely against a tradition that went back to Washington's warnings of 1796 and to the Convention of Mortefontaine of 1800, which terminated the last alliance with a European country. Such a relationship would be of a

different order from direct military assistance to a beleaguered country and even from the carefully programmed
economic support of a group of countries. It would openly
depart from the profession of faith in the United Nations and
professions of distaste for the balance of power made concur-
rently with the unilateral actions that underlay implementation of the containment plan. Senator Vandenberg at the
time of the Senate's hearings on the North Atlantic Treaty
made a point of observing that three of the six paragraphs
in his resolution were designed to make the Charter of the
United Nations more workable.[11]

The problem of reconciling Europe's needs and demands
with America's interests and political limitations had been
the subject of discussion at an important meeting in Blair
House on April 27, 1948, before introduction of the Vandenberg Resolution. Secretary of State Marshall, Undersecretary
Lovett, Senator Vandenberg, and John Foster Dulles gathered to examine the implications of the State Department's
idea of having the Senate approve a resolution in favor of a
North Atlantic regional pact, to be followed by the president's calling for a convention of North Atlantic states "to
frame some sort of regional compact under Article 52 and
collective guarantee under Article 51 of the United Nations
Charter." They all expressed reservations about this maneuver. Vandenberg in particular expressed concern about the
effect of such a regional compact upon the United Nations
and produced a preliminary draft of a resolution that would
avoid a special conference on Charter revision. Dulles wondered if Article 51 of the Charter was not too brittle a base
on which to build a new treaty. Additionally, he speculated
on the dangers to which the United States would be exposed

11. Senator Arthur H. Vandenberg, Hearings, *North Atlantic Treaty,*
U.S. Senate Committee on Foreign Relation, 81st Congress, 1st Session
(1949), Part I, 242. Hereafter cited as *Senate Hearings.*

if one of the allies fell under communist control or if any or all of them would use too firm an American commitment to reduce their own efforts toward economic recovery and military protection. They adjourned without resolving the question of compatibility with the United Nations, the danger of a permanent European dependency on the United States, or their unstated fears of a resurgent isolationism in America.[12] In light of these deliberations the Vandenberg Resolution appears as a cautious compromise.

It was also a compromise that could not last. There was no genuine alternative to alliance in which the United States was fully joined to Western Europe if the purposes of both the Marshall Plan and the Brussels Pact were to be served. And national reception of the Vandenberg Resolution encouraged continuation of negotiations with Europe. Indeed, military collaboration became increasingly important after the Soviet blockade of Berlin forced the United States to grapple with the problems of protecting "West Germany" from Soviet aggression and protecting Western Europe from the specter of a revived Germany. Could these problems be resolved without further American participation in the defense of Europe? America's negative answer was reflected not merely in the Berlin airlift but also in military conversations between the United States and the United Kingdom during the summer of 1948. The special links forged in World War II could be used to bind a larger organization in the Cold War, but no action could be taken until the American presidential campaign had ended. Presumably, a potentially lame-duck president could not carry the nation into the alliance, and so the United States would be better

12. Dulles's Memorandum of Conference at the Blair House—George C. Marshall, Robert A. Lovett, Arthur H. Vandenberg, John Foster Dulles, April 27, 1948, in Dulles Papers, Princeton University. For a different view of the conference, see Arthur H. Vandenberg, Jr., ed., *The Private Papers of Senator Vandenberg* (Boston, 1952), p. 406.

able to handle the issue after the fevers of campaign oratory had subsided.

In his Inaugural Address of 1949, President Truman pointed the way out of the dilemma by stating clearly that the United States was "working out with a number of countries a joint agreement designed to strengthen the security of the North Atlantic area. Such an agreement would take the form of a collective defense arrangement within the terms of the United Nations Charter." The Treaty quickly followed. After a year's debate in European and American councils, it is not surprising that a number of changes had been made in the framing of the document before it was brought to the attention of the public; but it is fair to judge that despite some carefully opaque language in the final form, the original intention of providing a credible deterrent to Soviet attack and a psychological prop to Western morale had been achieved.

A significant difference between the ideas of 1948 and 1949 appeared in the geographical boundaries of the alliance. In the April meeting at Blair House the area under consideration had been widened to include Scandinavia, Iceland, and Canada, the latter being of particular importance in identifying a "North Atlantic" character that could justify American adherence to a new pact. By January, 1949, Italy and Portugal had joined the group, despite misgivings in both cases; Italy was some distance from the Atlantic, and Portugal did not fit the image of a democracy. Sweden ultimately dropped out of the projected treaty, partly because of heavy Soviet pressure, partly because of the historic success of its neutral stance. But notwithstanding political factors that ultimately determined the result, by the winter of 1949 the five nations of Brussels had become the twelve nations of the North Atlantic Pact.

The sensitive issue of the relationship between the Treaty

and the Charter was met obliquely. Under American encouragement the language of the Treaty conformed as best as it could to the letter of the Charter. The founding fathers of the Treaty sprinkled the text liberally with references to the Charter, and specifically to Article 51. By likening the Treaty to the Rio Pact, they claimed by inference a regional status that the framers wished to identify with the North Atlantic system without making a formal commitment to Articles 52 and 53 of the Charter. Had they done so they would have had to subject the deliberations of the new organization to the full scrutiny of the Soviet Union in the Security Council. But by avoiding explicit claims on regional status, the planners invited charges of duplicity for suggesting functions that the new treaty could not possibly have included.[13]

Still another difficulty for the treaty-makers was the issue of a military alliance implied in the Treaty, and with it possible entanglement in a future war as a consequence of obligations to the new allies. The strictures of the Founding Fathers were directed against permanent alliances with the very countries that would be the heart of the Atlantic alliance. Could a twenty-year alliance be fitted in the category of Washington's "temporary alliances for extraordinary emergencies"? Even if the answer was affirmative, the new relationship could run afoul of the constitutional power of the Congress to declare war. Senators Forrest Donnell of Missouri and Arthur Watkins of Utah repeatedly made the point in the hearings on the Treaty that Article 5, in which "the Parties agree that an armed attack against one or more of them in Europe or North America shall be considered an attack against them all," could force the United States into

---

13. "The North Atlantic Treaty," Department of State Publication, No. 3462 (March, 1949); James Reston in *New York Times,* Apr. 22, 1949.

war without the approval of the Congress if Norway were invaded or Paris bombed. Even if the caveat in the wording of this article was truly sufficient to permit escape, would not Article 3 of the Treaty, calling for "continuous and effective self-help and mutual aid," be only a vehicle for unlimited shipments of material to Europe? [14]

Behind these questions lay the habits of isolationist thought. The administration in handling them had to ask itself if the nation would accept the blunt truth that isolationism was obsolete, that the Monroe Doctrine separating the Old from New Worlds was irrelevant, that military alliances were not necessarily evil, and that the balance of power had not only not disappeared but that the nation's survival depended upon its proper functioning. The familiar language of the past had not disappeared from the vocabulary of the administration leaders themselves, as Secretary of Defense Louis Johnson discovered to his embarrassment. Shortly before assuming office and shortly after the signing of the Brussels Pact, he had identified that treaty as the perfect example of a European military alliance that illustrated the differences between the European and American outlooks on the world. Or so it seemed to an appreciative audience of the Daughters of the American Revolution.[15]

Given these circumstances, the administration decided against a direct assault on tradition. The eastern shores of the Atlantic merely became the new boundaries of the New World of the Monroe Doctrine; military alliance became "partnership for peace"; the balance of power became "preponderance of power for peace." In other words, the North Atlantic Treaty was semantically assimilated into the isolationist past with the imagery of Washington's Farewell Ad-

14. See, for example, the exchange between Acheson and Senators Donnell and Watkins, *Senate Hearings*, Part 1, pp. 62–87.

15. *Ibid.*, pp. 146 ff.

dress, Jefferson's First Inaugural Address, and above all the Monroe Doctrine serving to blur distinctions. The Iron Curtain, rather than the Atlantic Ocean, now separated the Old World from the New World.[16]

Despite the impressive display of bipartisanship that united Vandenberg and Connally, and Dulles and Acheson, opponents of the Treaty vigorously rejected the idea of its compatibility either with the United Nations or the Monroe Doctrine, and many of them braved the wrath of an intimidating chairman of the Senate Foreign Relations Committee, Tom Connally, to say so. The voices of the Communist party, the Progressive party of Henry Wallace, pacifist devotees of the United Nations, conservative isolationists, and traditional Anglophobes, all warned the nation against the pact, and failed.

Not even the intervention of Senator Robert A. Taft of Ohio, the most influential of all congressmen, could stir the public, although he stated his willingness to see the Monroe Doctrine extended to Europe provided it remained a unilateral action on the part of the United States.[17]

The administration won its gamble. By a vote of 82 to 13 the Senate approved the North Atlantic Treaty on July 21, 1949, a margin sufficient to suggest that the United States had abandoned its isolationist tradition. Given the apathetic response of public opinion to the arguments of the pact's enemies, it may be argued that the nation no longer needed the comforting language of isolationism to support the break with tradition. Probably it was prepared to accept NATO as it had accepted the Truman Doctrine or the Berlin airlift: namely, as part of the price for power in the postwar world.

16. Ambassador Austin on the "Balance of Power," *ibid.*, p. 97. See also Lawrence S. Kaplan, "NATO and the Language of Isolationism," *South Atlantic Quarterly* LVIII (1958), 204–16.

17. *Congressional Record*, 81st Cong., 1st Sess. (1949), 9206.

The meaning of the North Atlantic Treaty in the year immediately after passage has yet to be fully comprehended or documented, but there are generalizations that may be reasonably made. Whether or not there was a causal connection between the new Atlantic alliance of April and the lifting of the Berlin blockade in May, it is reasonable to assume that the Treaty underscored the failure of the Soviet action in Germany and accelerated the abandonment of the blockade. Important as this victory was, NATO performed an even more important and certainly a more demonstrable function in serving as midwife to the birth of the Federal Republic of Germany on May 8, 1949. Without the protection of the Treaty, it is questionable if even a partially sovereign Germany would have been palatable to its former victims only four years after the end of World War II.

The passage of the Treaty also assured the success of the Mutual Defense Assistance Act of 1949, the beginnings of a massive transfusion of military supplies to the allies under color of Article 3. The Congress's objective, of course, was an integrated military defense system for Europe conforming to economic objectives of the Marshall Plan and underpinning them.[18]

How successful military aid was in the early days of NATO is open to the same kind of question that can be raised about NATO's contribution to the German problem. With respect to Germany, Berlin was saved and the Federal Republic was born, but the relations between the new Germany and NATO were murky even though the allies knew that German manpower and German geography were factors military planners ordinarily would have taken into account. But Europe's visceral fears of a revived Germany made such calculations politically unacceptable. As for the

18. William Adams Brown, Jr., and Redvers Opie, *American Foreign Assistance* (Washington, 1953), pp. 455 ff.

product of military assistance, there was little evidence that anything more than lip service was given to the principle of integration. Indeed, the organization itself was only a paper affair in 1949 and 1950, with no organs to implement a co-ordinated defense system. Perhaps the fact that only a few understaffed divisions confronted a powerful Soviet force of twenty-five divisions in Central Europe made military assistance at best a morale factor to promote a sense of security among the beleaguered allies rather than cogs in a sophisticated military machine.

At any event, the organization that grew out of the Treaty in the summer and fall of 1949 was more shell than substance. Under Article 9 a North Atlantic Council was established that was to "set up such subsidiary bodies as may be necessary; in particular it shall establish a defense committee which shall recommend measures for the implementation of Articles 3 and 5." At its first meeting in September, 1949, the Defense Committee, made up of the defense ministers of each nation, was established along with a chain of command similar to that of the Western Union. Advising the committee would be a Military Committee represented by all the chiefs of staff, which in turn would be guided by the advice of its steering committee, the Standing Group, composed only of representatives of the United States, the United Kingdom, and France. Under this command would be five regional planning groups covering all the geographic areas of NATO. A month later the Council created two parallel groups: a Defense Financial and Economic Committee of finance ministers and a Military Production and Supply Board to support the Defense Committee's efforts to standardize weapons and equipment.[19]

19. North Atlantic Council communiqué, Washington, September 17, 1949, and November 18, 1949, in Lord Ismay, *NATO: The First Five Years, 1951–1954* (Paris, 1954), pp. 173–82.

The flurry of activity in the wake of these acts of establishment appeared more significant than it actually was. When
one considers that most of these groups, including the Council itself, were composed of such dignitaries as the secretary
of state and the secretary of the treasury, the question of
how much time and energy these busy men were able to
devote to their NATO assignments inevitably arises. How
much effect could these groups have had when they met
infrequently at such diverse centers as London, Rome, Paris,
and Washington, and lacked a focus of authority, a direct
line of command, and even the means to bring together the
results of their separate efforts. In partial recognition of this
problem the North Atlantic Council, which was composed of
three cabinet officers from each country, set up a Council
of Deputies at its fourth session in May, 1950, that would
meet in continuous session to formulate issues supervising
the workings of subordinate bodies.[20]

Actually, a year's experience was not necessary to inform
NATO officials that its operation was inefficient. If they
waited that long to make even a superficial change, the
reason lay in the special services of the United States to the
organization. The extraordinary functions of the United
States were never fully articulated, but their outlines are
clear. General Omar D. Bradley, chief of staff in 1949, expressed their spirit when he observed two days after the
Treaty was signed that the military power of the United
States was borne "on the wings of our bombers." The allies
must be confident that this air power would be used in the
event of an enemy attack.[21] His Army Day speech contained
the assumption that the defense of Europe rested not on any
particular military structure the NATO Council might fab-

20. North Atlantic Council communiqué, London, September 15–18,
1950, *ibid.*, pp. 182–83.
21. Cited in *Senate Hearings,* Part 1, p. 182.

ricate, and not on the amount of assistance the United States might offer to the military forces of the alliance individually or collectively. Rather, it rested on the credibility of American air power's promise to provide an immediate response to external aggression. NATO's security, therefore, depended upon the nuclear weapons of the American intercontinental bombers based in Omaha, Nebraska, with striking capabilities that would deter hostilities.

Although NATO's defense preparations were expected to advance beneath the shelter of American air power, the major effects were psychological rather than military. If the various disparate organs of NATO were ever to collate their efforts and implement an integrated defense plan, the time would be in the relatively distant future. Not until January, 1950, did the United States even complete bilateral agreements with eight of the NATO allies, an inevitably slow process that demanded closer inspection of the economies of the recipient countries than the latter had anticipated or had wanted. Although the initial prediction of the secretary of state was that over 50 percent of the military aid program would be finished by the end of the fiscal year 1950, the first shipments were not made until March, 1950. Of the $1.3 billion authorized, only $42 million had been obligated, and $3.5 million spent on Western Europe, according to the first semiannual report of the Mutual Defense Assistance Program covering the period to April 6, 1950.[22]

The leisurely pace of the flow of aid came to a sudden and dramatic end with the Korean crisis of June, 1950. The North Korean invasion of the South and the United Nations response forced the United States either to transform NATO or to abandon it. The latter was a genuine alternative, for

22. *First Semiannual Report to Congress on Mutual Defense Assistance Program, October 6, 1949, to April 6, 1950,* in Brown and Opie, *American Foreign Assistance,* pp. 481–83.

the explosion of war in the Far East called the nation's attention to traditional American interests in Asia, which in turn could have awakened isolationist sentiment. Given the Asian content of so much of Senator Joseph R. McCarthy's jingoistic rhetoric in this period, withdrawal from Europe might have been a logical concomitant. Such was not the case, partly because the fear of communism stimulated by McCarthy and the Soviet success with the atomic bomb inhibited retirement from the world scene despite the pleas of Herbert Hoover or Joseph Kennedy.[23] Instead, NATO was throughly reorganized, with special recognition that the Strategic Air Command was an insufficient deterrent to aggression if unaccompanied by effective ground troops prepared to hold back the initial wave of the enemy's attack. What happened in Korea could happen in Europe, even though the latter, unlike the former, was formally enclosed within the American defense perimeter. So went the reasoning of NATO planners.

Conceivably, NATO's structure might have been revised without the prodding of a Korean conflict. The Russian breaking of the American monopoly on atomic weapons in September, 1949, had serious implications for NATO's security. Still, changes probably would have been milder and more piecemeal than was the case in the last six months of 1950 when the regional planning groups were swept away to be replaced by a Supreme Headquarters in Paris under a Supreme Allied Commander. As an American, he would symbolize American commitment to the defense of Europe and provide a deterrent against communist advance at the

23. Herbert Hoover, "We Should Revise Our Foreign Policies," in *Addresses upon the American Road, 1950–55* (Stanford, 1955), pp. 11–22 (broadcast February 9, 1951); Joseph P. Kennedy's speech before the Law School Forum of the University of Virginia on December 12, 1958, in Manfred Jonas, ed., *American Foreign Relations in the Twentieth Century* (New York, 1967), pp. 140–44.

border and not in Washington or in Omaha. So while Mac-
Arthur's forces were liberating South Korea in September,
1950, the NATO Council in New York was trying to devise
a defense system that would make liberation unnecessary.

A major element in the reorganization of NATO would be
the presence of American troops alongside Europeans under the command of the charismatic figure of General
Dwight D. Eisenhower. Such American soldiers as were already in Europe belonged to occupation forces with functions that could eventually be fitted into the new defense
scheme. Accordingly, the joint chiefs of staff recommended
that six American divisions be assigned to Europe, including
the two already there in occupation service, with the twofold
function of serving as a deterrent against attack and as a
spur to the morale of the allies. The European members
would provide the bulk of the necessary ground forces with
the full knowledge that the American presence in their midst
would guarantee an American participation in the event of
attack.[24]

As attention moved toward practical considerations of
defense problems, the NATO planners reassessed the geographical boundaries of NATO and found them too restrictive. Greece and Turkey, the original beneficiaries of American support, not only remained exposed to communist
threats but in turn exposed the southeastern flank of Europe.
The allies added a protocol to the North Atlantic Treaty that
admitted Greece and Turkey in October, 1951.[25]

Far more serious to both the Americans and Europeans
was the problem of Germany's relations with the alliance.

24. Statement of Secretary of Defense George C. Marshall, *Hearings,
Assignment of Ground Forces of the United States to Do Duty in the
European Area*, Senate Committee on Foreign Relations and Committee on
Armed Services, 82d Cong., 1st Sess., p. 40.

25. The Greece-Turkey Protocol, London, October 22, 1951, in Ismay,
NATO, pp. 20–21.

From the beginning of the movement toward an Atlantic community Germany had been a problem, one that involved not only the defense of allied-occupied Germany from Soviet threats but also the protection of Europeans from a new German menace. The memories of Nazism were still fresh in the minds of its former victims, and the trauma left in its passing was deeper and more disturbing than anything communism might do to Europe. If Americans did not share these memories or sentiments, the Brussels Pact members did; Article 7 of that treaty called for the convocation of the Consultative Council whenever a threat to peace should arise, most specifically "in case of a renewal by Germany of an aggressive policy." No such notice was given of potential Soviet aggression in that document. Though the Atlantic Pact itself was free of such clearly expressed fears, Germany was consciously excluded from the alliance. As Secretary of State Dean Acheson observed, the absence of German sovereignty automatically removed Germans from a position of significance beyond the obvious benefits derived from the fact that an attack on the occupational forces in Germany would call for a NATO response.[26]

The Korean War raised again the German question, and might have provided Americans an occasion to claim that the Federal Republic, created after the signing of the Treaty, possessed attributes of sovereignty sufficient to permit a role in NATO. The imperatives of the time forced a confrontation with the allies that revealed clearly that Americans, no matter how sympathetic to Europe's sufferings under the Nazis, would see in them a barrier to German rearmament or to other forms of German assistance in the defense of Europe. To Americans, Germany was a source of wealth and manpower that should be exploited for the bene-

26. *Senate Hearings,* Part 1, p. 61.

fit of the alliance. Since Germans would benefit from NATO, the least they should do is to offer a contribution toward its effectiveness. "A program for Western Europe which does not include the productive resources of all the countries of Western Europe," asserted Acheson in August, 1950, including "Western Germany, as well as France, will not be effective in the long-range political sense." [27] Given this American attitude, the omission of German collaboration from the communiqué of the NATO Council a month later reflected a schism within the alliance that might have had as serious consequences for the future of NATO as the Korean crisis itself. The most the United States was able to win from its allies was a promise to end the technical state of war between the Federal Republic and the NATO allies of World War II.[28]

But American pressures persisted. And from a military standpoint, Europe recognized that German matériel and troops were of vital importance to the common defense. Politically and economically, the involvement of Germany in its own defense as well as in the support of NATO would be a major step forward in the creation of a united Europe. Countering these benefits was the specter of a revived Germany, militarily strong and willing to take advantage of the Cold War to resume the destructive objectives of Nazism. To blunt American importunities and to exorcise its own fears, France proposed a compromise to solve NATO's problems over Germany. This was the construction of a European Defense Community, a supranational body within NATO in

27. *Hearings, Supplemental Appropriations for 1951*, U.S. Senate Committee on Appropriations, 81st Cong., 2d Sess. (1950), pp. 284–85. See also Lawrence S. Kaplan, "NATO and Adenauer's Germany: Uneasy Partnership," *International Organization* XV (Autumn, 1961), 618–19.

28. North Atlantic Council communiqué, New York, September 16–18, 1950, in Ismay, *NATO*, pp. 185–86; communiqué of the Foreign Ministers of the United Kingdom, France, by the United States, New York, September 19, 1950, Department of State *Bulletin* XXIII (1950), 530–32.

which Germany would abstain from acquiring some customary sovereign powers in return for the privilege of participation in the defense of Europe.

The European Coal and Steel Community was a useful precedent. This functional unit within Western Europe, the work in large measure of two Frenchmen, Robert Schuman and Jean Monnet, joined Germany with France, Italy, and the Benelux countries in a plan to intertwine French and German industries in such a way that neither of the partners would be able to exploit their national economic power to the detriment of their neighbors without inflicting irreparable damage on their own economies. At the same time the Schuman Plan would accelerate the recovery and expansion of all Europe's economies. Here was a long stride toward European unity. A European army within NATO would be another.

On October 24, 1950, Premier René Pleven presented the plan for a European Defense Community to the General Assembly of France. Such details as the size of national and multinational units had yet to be arranged, and the extent of German equality was not at all clear; but at least it provided a response to the American challenge. When the treaty establishing the EDC was finally signed in May, 1952, it stipulated that a council of ministers of the member nations would control a European army composed of national units of 13,000 to 15,000 men. Above this division level would be the multinational corps. What made this form of German militarism palatable to the French and other Europeans were two factors in the treaty designed to limit Germany's freedom of individual action. The first was the specific placement of the European army under the control of the Supreme Allied Commander, General Eisenhower and his American successors. The second was the imposition of specific restrictions upon German membership in the EDC, notably the implicit exclusion from NATO and the explicit prohibition of manufacture of "aircraft, atomic weapons, chemical weapons, biological weapons, heavy ships and other specified items in 'strategically exposed regions' without the unanimous approval of the Council." [29]

Despite the apparent European initiative in the EDC, most of the demands for new and more vigorous means of rearming Europe or of sacrificing traditional practices to the needs of the alliance came from the United States. The response was primarily military. In Korea, General MacArthur led the United Nations forces; in Europe, General Eisenhower symbolized American willingness to do no less than the United States was doing in the Far East. It was American pressure that pushed the alliance by means of a Temporary Council Committee established at the Ottawa conference of September, 1951, to examine the precise extent to which each member might support the common effort. Escalation of the military program was climaxed at the Lisbon Conference in February, 1952, when the Council announced plans to produce fifty NATO divisions by the end of that year, 4,000 aircraft, and a firm recommendation that the German contribution to the alliance be quickly settled. At the same time the office of secretary general was established to assist the Council by absorbing all existing civilian agencies. [30]

The critical American presidential election of 1952 only served to underline the clear identification of Adenauer's Germany with NATO. Indeed, the new president and his

29. Outline of the provisions of the treaty establishing the European Defense Community, signed in Paris on May 27, 1952, in Chatham House Study Group Report, *Atlantic Alliance: NATO's Role in the Free World* (London, 1952), p. 160.

30. Ismay, *NATO*, pp. 41–48; North Atlantic Council communiqué, Lisbon, February 20–25, 1952, *ibid.*, p. 191. Robert S. Jordan, *The NATO International Staff/Secretariat, 1952–1957: A Study in International Administration* (London, 1967), pp. 30–32.

secretary of state, John Foster Dulles, had claimed that they
would wage a more vigorous Cold War than the Democrats
had conducted. Professing disturbance over the negative
image projected by the Truman containment policies, Dulles
attacked the Democrats not for undertaking the responsibilities of world leadership, including the NATO role, but
for their inability or their lack of desire to win the Cold War.
Containment was insufficient. "We should be dynamic; we
should use *ideas* as weapons; and these ideas should conform to *moral* principles. That we do this is right, for it is
the inevitable expression of a faith—and I am confident that
we still do have a faith. But it is also expedient in defending
ourselves against an aggressive, imperialistic despotism. For
even the present lines will not hold unless our purpose goes
beyond confining Soviet Communism within its present
orbit." [31]

A prerequisite to rolling back Soviet forces in central Europe and to liberating the captive peoples was German cooperation, a factor that promoted the mutual good will between Dulles and Adenauer. Equally important in this
deepening German-American relationship was Dulles's respect for Adenauer's commitment to a united Europe in
which German militarism of the past would be forever
buried.[32] And while Germany was being reborn within the
new Europe, NATO and EDC would be instruments in
bringing together the East and West Germany. The Soviet
Union would give partial recognition to the strength of the
revived Europe by giving up its control of its occupied zone.
Such were the hopes of Dulles in the early part of the Eisen-

31. John Foster Dulles, "A Policy of Boldness," *Life* XXXII (May 19, 1952), 154.
32. Louis L. Gerson, *John Foster Dulles,* vol. 17, *The American Secretaries of State and Their Diplomacy,* ed. Robert H. Ferrell and Samuel
Flagg Bemis (New York, 1967), pp. 318–19; Konrad Adenauer, *Memoirs,
1945–1953,* trans. Beate Ruhm von Oppen (Chicago, 1965), pp. 435–37.

hower administration, hopes that if realized would be a reflection of the "virile" liberation policy of Republicans as opposed to the "sterile" containment policy of Democrats.

The shelving of the EDC in 1954 brought an abrupt although not permanent end to these hopes. It is true that Germany ratified the EDC, although only after soul-searching by pacifists concerned with rearmament, by nationalists disturbed about the inferior role in the EDC, and by Germans everywhere fearful of a permanent division of Germany as a result of NATO membership. But the other members of Europe were even more reluctant to ratify the document, and France never did ratify it. Long before the French Assembly effectively killed the EDC by demanding new reservations in August, 1954, it was obvious that France had no intentions of implementing its objectives. France had proposed the treaty and had signed it to deflect American plans from something even less palatable, and had managed to stall the proceedings for almost three years. Unfortunately, American tempers on the subject in Germany were shorter in 1954 than they had been in 1951. By a vote of 88 to 0 on July 31, an angry Senate, anticipating the final evasion of France, had urged the president to grant Germany its sovereignty unilaterally; and the Senate Armed Services Committee was prepared to cut off all aid to France if the EDC Treaty was not ratified by the end of the year. Secretary Dulles accused France of turning her back on "her own historical proposal" when the French Assembly postponed indefinitely debate on the EDC.[33]

The consequence of this schism within the alliance might have been the dissolution of NATO. But before the United States could do more than verbalize its pique, Anthony Eden laid the ground for a satisfactory détente at conferences in

33. *New York Times*, Aug. 1, July 15, Sept. 1, 1954.

London and Paris in September and October, 1954, at which the occupation status of Germany was ended, the Brussels Pact was converted into a Western European Union that would include Germany and Italy, and Germany was to be admitted in 1955 as the fifteenth member of NATO with its military forces directly under the Supreme Allied Commander in Europe. The provisions in the aborted EDC barring Germany from production of biological, chemical, or atomic war materials were retained under the new dispensation.[34]

For France the compromise offered guarantees of both British and American protection within the Western Union and NATO rubrics, respectively; for Germany it offered membership in the Atlantic and European communities on almost equal terms as well as a promise of ultimate reunification of the divided nation. For Russia, German participation was a setback; but at the same time it stiffened the Iron Curtain by bringing into being in 1955 the Warsaw Pact, the Soviet counterpart of NATO. For the United States it offered what most policymakers had wanted from the beginnings of NATO: full exploitation of German resources.

With the temporary solution of the German problem to its credit, the NATO record in the mid-fifties gave reason for Americans to boast of success in their mission. First, the pervasive threat of Soviet military action against the West had failed to materialize. Though Soviet power still remained, the fears that it inspired had diminished since 1948 or 1950. Consequently, as the size of Europe's armies increased and as the internal power of communist minorities

34. Department of State Publication, no. 5659, "London and Paris Agreements, September–October, 1954" (Washington, 1954), pp. 9–20; Anthony Eden, *The Memoirs of Anthony Eden: Full Circle* (Boston, 1960), pp. 168–94.

in Western Europe shrank, the conditions of security that could make American assistance useful to the economies of Europe were now present. The result was the blossoming not only of the European gross national product and the standards of living of their peoples but also of the institutions of unity. The European Economic Community, following the European Coal and Steel Community, represented a functional implementation of the ideal of European unity. Perhaps the most intensive area of change was in the military, often overlooked because new forms of integration were unexpected by-products of military developments.

The fact of supranational leadership within NATO helped erode national sovereignties. When a German general could command the allied land forces of central Europe with troops from countries recently victimized by Nazi brutality, the idea of European unification had gone beyond the rhetorical stage. And even when the alliance was threatened by such serious challenges as the Suez crisis of 1956, which separated France and England from the United States, and the periodic Cyprus crises inflaming Greece and Turkey, the process of military integration continued. While full standardization of weapons, an early dream of NATO fathers, languished, new modes of integration almost surreptitiously made themselves apparent. One of them was "infrastructure," a term borrowed from French railroaders to identify such prerequisites for military operations as fuel storage facilities, pipelines, port installations, and signal communications systems. Within a ten-year span NATO could take credit for the building or improving of 140 airfields, 5,000 miles of fuel pipelines, and 15,000 miles of land telephone and telegraph lines. These facilities ran freely across the territories of NATO nations and were the joint property of all the allies. Out of this growing interdependence a NATO force emerged that meshed the various defense systems of the member nations and unwittingly undermined a major foundation of nationalism.[35]

For Americans operating primarily in another continent, the effects of a common infrastructure were slight. American contingents were a relatively small portion of the NATO armies, and their major military contribution, nuclear weapons, was outside the control of the allies. The principal challenge to American sovereignty came from another source; namely, from the difficulties of reconciling constitutional guarantees to American troops abroad with the very different legal practices of countries in which they were stationed. The question stirred deep emotions in both hosts and guests. It was one thing for American soldiers and civilians to enjoy the privileges of extraterritoriality, notably the protection of American laws, when they were occupation forces in Germany or liberators in France. It was quite another for them to enjoy these privileges when they were in Europe as equals, as guests in a host nation, as allies in a common cause. In the latter circumstances, whose jurisdiction should offenders fall under when the laws of the host country were violated outside the line of duty? If the old occupation status remained in force, the sensibilities of new allies would be ruffled; if Americans abroad were to be subject to a European court, constitutional rights to a trial by jury might be sacrificed.

Risking political dangers, the United States and its allies signed a series of status-of-forces agreements that effectively placed Americans abroad on military and civilian missions under the authority of foreign courts. Such outcries as were made in the Congress were usually too exaggerated in their

35. Lawrence S. Kaplan, "NATO Retrospect," *Review of Politics* XXIII (October, 1961), 452–53.

fears to win conviction.[36] The logic of the situation demanded this concession. So did the host governments, which
subsequently proved to be more lenient with wrongdoers
than American military courts would have been with their
wayward soldiers.

But even as NATO's objectives appeared to meet success
in a number of critical areas, new waves of discontent broke
out in the late 1950s, most of it among European members.
Ironically, much of the malaise concerned the very militari-
zation of the alliance that had seemed so necessary a few
years before. European unhappiness was probably unavoidable under any circumstance. The United States with its
worldwide commitments inevitably pursued policies and
took some actions that did not always satisfy the national
or European aspirations of the allies. Hence the irritation or
concern when the United States revived the economy and
prolonged the life of Fascist Spain by placing missile bases
on Spanish territory; when the United States seemed to join
the Soviet Union in support of neutralist or hostile Arabs at
the expense of England and France in 1956; when American troops left the NATO command to land in Lebanon in
1957; when Dulles's brinkmanship over Formosa in 1958
might have precipitated a world war in which the allies
might have been committed without their approval.

A more direct objection, but one difficult to satisfy, was
the display of the American presence in Europe. Continuous
affronts to European pride were made by the fact that American officers directed the organization—an American general
in Paris, an American admiral in Norfolk, Virginia, an American chief of staff in Washington. Although the civilian
counterparts of the military leaders were well represented

36. Statement of Senator John W. Bricker, *Supplementary Hearing,
Status of Forces of the North Atlantic Treaty,* 83d Cong., 1st Sess. (1953),
pp. 2–8.

by Europeans, few of them carried much authority, and most of them were unknown to the peoples of the Atlantic Community. The secretaries general, Europeans all—Ismay, Spaak, Stikker, and Brosio—lacked the power and the charisma of the American generals—Eisenhower, Ridgway, Gruenther, Norstad, Lemnitzer, and Goodpaster. Given the nature of America's contribution to the alliance, it was unlikely that the trappings of leadership could have been made invisible—or have gone unresented by Europeans. By the end of the decade a confident Europe, its economies flourishing again and moving toward unity as well as toward prosperity, raised questions about the extent of America's power in Europe and about its wisdom in exercising it.

Europe's major charge against the United States was its rigidity in clinging to ideas about the military challenge to NATO at a time when the challenge had changed character, when a new and more apparently moderate regime succeeded Stalin's in the years after 1953. If the Cold War could thereby be ended, the powerful, expensive, and American-dominated military organization would be an obstacle to a détente with the Soviet Union. At Geneva in 1955 the Soviet Union talked about disarmament and the unification of Germany in a "spirit of Locarno" that implied a new relationship with the communist world. And within two years the military response to the Soviet Union seemed obsolescent since the development of new weapons of mass destruction made war too horrible to accept as a means of settling political differences. The Soviet Union not only possessed the hydrogen bomb but in the fall of 1957 had orbited an earth satellite that in perfected form would seem to have upset the balance of power NATO had effected. Therefore, from two somewhat contradictory sources came arguments against the established pattern of NATO defense: first, that the Soviet Union had abandoned the methods if not the intentions of Stalin's regime; second, that the United States and NATO lacked the will and power to protect Europeans in light of the Sputnik Revolution. Such were the fears of many NATO partners.

Some Americans shared these reservations about the course of NATO, with George Kennan as the most articulate critic in 1957. Although retired from government service as a member of the Institute for Advanced Studies at Princeton, he maintained an active interest in public affairs and was particularly concerned about the continuing distortion of his ideas about containment. But unhappy as he was over the way the concept was translated into NATO, he was more disturbed about immediate dangers posed by the confrontation of troops in central Europe. In his widely publicized Reith lectures broadcast from London, he proposed a disengagement of forces that would leave Germany free of foreign troops, thereby reducing the level of tension between East and West. He did not suggest that NATO itself had no mission, but that "if there could be a general withdrawal of American, British, and Russian armed power from the heart of the Continent, there would be at least a chance that Europe's fortunes might be worked out, and the competition between two political philosophies carried forward, in a manner disastrous neither to the respective peoples themselves nor to the cause of world peace." [37]

In conformity with its new image in the West, the Soviet Union of Bulganin and Khrushchev provided a solution calculated to annoy the United States and to cater to Europe's growing fear of impending nuclear destruction and to Germany's growing disillusionment over the prospects of unification. Adam Rapacki, Poland's foreign minister, presented a plan in February, 1958, only a few months after Sputnik's

37. George F. Kennan, *Russia, The Atom and the West* (New York, 1958), p. 61.

success, that would create a denuclearized zone in Central Europe, including both Germanies, where "nuclear weapons will neither be manufactured nor stockpiled." The four major powers would undertake "not to maintain nuclear weapons in the armaments of their forces stationed on the territories included in this zone." [38]

The United States rejected both the Rapacki plan and the Kennan proposals. The official answer to the Polish government was couched in useful diplomatic phrases. Recognizing the good intentions of Rapacki, the Eisenhower administration claimed that the plan was too limited in scope to reduce the danger of nuclear war or to provide a dependable basis for the security of Europe.[39] In appropriately opaque language the United States communiqué complained that the Rapacki plan would implicitly remove the American presence from the Continent, while the Soviet Union would remain on the periphery to resume at will whatever disruptive tactics it might wish to try next.

The reply to Kennan was more blunt, and was most clearly expressed by Dean Acheson, who remained as firm in his support of military power in Europe as he had been during his tenure as secretary of state. Although now retired from public life and in the ranks of his Democratic opponents, Acheson shared Dulles's views on this problem. To both statesmen withdrawal would represent defeatism and timidity that could draw down upon the heads of West the very dangers this new and supposedly more sophisticated appreciation of the Soviet threat was designed to thwart. A neutralized Germany would not only make the defense of Europe almost impossible to maintain but would breed re-

38. Foreign Minister Adam Rapacki to U.S. Ambassador to Poland Jacob Beam, February 14, 1958, Department of State *Bulletin* XXXVIII (1958), 822–23.

39. Beam to Polish Deputy Foreign Minister Josef Winiewicz, May 3, 1958, *ibid.*, pp. 821–22.

sentments in Germany that could revive the ugly passions of the German past.[40]

In his defense of a militant NATO Acheson did not hesitate, however, to criticize the Eisenhower administration's excessive reliance on "massive retaliation" that tended to make the proposed defense seem as fearsome as the potential enemy's threat.[41] Many Germans had never recovered, for example, from Operation Carte Blanche, a war game in 1955 that hypothecated the decimation of much of Germany and the death of 1,700,000 people in atomic destruction before NATO armies would liberate the country. And de Gaulle's France would never be convinced that the United States, now exposed to atomic retaliation, would ever use the weapon in defense of Europe.[42] Something better was needed to deter aggression.

The answer, according to Henry Kissinger in his influential *Nuclear Weapons and Foreign Policy,* was not merely the continuing presence of Americans in Europe but the arming of NATO forces with tactical atomic weapons that could both increase enormously the effectiveness of infantry troops and control the destructiveness of atomic warfare. This strategy had the additional virtue of compensating with increased firepower the lagging military contributions of the NATO partners.[43]

40. Dean Acheson, "The Illusion of Disengagement," *Foreign Affairs* XXXVI (April, 1958), 376–77; Dulles's "Remarks to U.S. Ambassadors to Europe," Paris, May 9, 1958, NATO Ministerial Meeting, Conference Dossiers, Dulles Papers, cited in Walter LaFeber, *America, Russia, and the Cold War, 1945–1966* (New York, 1967), p. 210.

41. Acheson, "The Illusion of Disengagement," p. 381.

42. Speech of Erich Ollenhauer reported in *Das Parliament* (Bonn), July 6, 1955, cited in Gordon Craig, "Germany and NATO: The Rearmament Debate, 1950–1958," in Klaus Knorr, ed., *NATO and American Security,* (Princeton, N.J., 1959), p. 240; see de Gaulle Press Conference on NATO, September 5, 1960, excerpts in *New York Times,* Sept. 6, 1960; Raymond Aron, *Charles de Gaulle* (Paris, 1964), pp. 253–55.

43. Henry Kissinger, *Nuclear Weapons and Foreign Policy* (New York, 1958), pp. 306–15.

Despite the barrage of criticism from a number of directions, NATO survived the decade. It is unlikely that the prospect of the converting of atomic weapons from strategic to tactical instruments, as advocated by Professor Kissinger, accounted for the maintenance of a strong military posture. Nor was it a result of optimism over a German solution that in 1960 seemed farther away than in 1955. Still less was it a product of renewed confidence in American leadership, which since 1958 had been under increasing attack by the most difficult and most articulate of all NATO partners, Charles de Gaulle. Essentially, NATO's firmness was a consequence of the erratic course of Soviet behavior under Khrushchev.

The Berlin crises of 1958 and 1959, which the Russians precipitated, reminded the allies that Stalin's death had not removed the danger of war with the Soviet Union. For many Europeans the abrupt demand for a new status for Berlin nullified the good impression left by apparent Soviet interest expressed at summit conferences in ending the Cold War, and was hard to reconcile with the homely peasant image of the Soviet premier.

In November, 1958, Khrushchev announced that the Soviet Union would end its occupation regime in Berlin and demanded that the allies withdraw their forces from West Berlin, which would then become a "free city." American, British, and French access to the city would be a matter of negotiation with the Soviet-sponsored German Democratic Republic. Should the West fail to respond to this proposal, the Soviet Union would turn over the supply routes to the city to the administration of the East Germans.[44]

By these actions the Soviet Union was not only attempting to consolidate the division of Germany but also to split the

44. U.S.S.R. note to U.S., November 27, 1958, in Department of State *Bulletin* XL (1959), 81–89.

alliance at one of its most vulnerable seams: where the NATO promise of a united Germany coexisted with the NATO fear of a united Germany. Ten years after the signing of the North Atlantic Treaty, the Russians had hopes of exposing NATO's ambivalent feelings about Germany, thus inflaming Germans against their allies, unveiling America's unreliability as a leader, and stampeding fearful members of the alliance into accommodation with the Soviet Union.

Many of the Russian expectations were met. The alliance did indeed creak under the strains of reaction as the British and the Scandinavians pressed for negotiations over Berlin and even for recognition of East Germany, while the Germans and the French remained adamant against any change. Confidence in American leadership was more in question by 1960 than ever before as the rigid certainties of Dulles's militant stance were replaced after his death by hesitant gestures toward bilateral détente with the Soviet Union and by the confused responses to the U-2 spy plane incident of the last year of Eisenhower's presidency. Rejected in his attempt to reconstruct NATO as a triumviral operation, de Gaulle undertook an independent challenge to American hegemony in Europe and to the Anglo-American monopoly on atomic weapons.

Yet, Khrushchev failed in the short run. Despite all his bluster, he retreated in the face of Dulles's firm position that the United States is "solemnly committed to hold West Berlin if need by military force." [45] It was a retreat, screened though it was by grins and scowls, delays and diversions, and finally by a wall around East Berlin. None of the problems relating to Berlin were settled in Geneva in May, 1959, at a conference in which the West attempted to tie the fate of Berlin to peace with a unified Germany. But the deadline

45. News Conference of November 7, 1958, *ibid.* XXIX (1958), 813.

set by Khrushchev passed without further action. Nothing happened on that day beyond the funeral of the cancer-stricken Secretary of State Dulles.[46]

When finally a summit meeting was arranged for the following spring, the Soviet Union used the occasion of the U-2 incident—the capture of an American plane 1,200 miles inside the country—to denounce the United States for its invasion of air space and for espionage, and to cancel peremptorily the Paris summit meeting. Although the president was personally humiliated by the experience, it is worth observing that the Soviet premier, having failed to budge the West on Berlin, had diverted world opinion from his failure. Khrushchev wavered at the brink of war. To this extent, Dulles won vindication for his brinkmanship a year after his death as well as on the day of his funeral.

In 1960, NATO partners and enemies alike awaited the end of the Eisenhower administration, which after November would have a "lame duck" status no matter which party won the presidential election. That the situation in NATO remained perilous was understood in America as well as in Europe. It was equally clear that the major difficulties stemmed from internal rather than external problems; for example, oscillation of American leadership from threat of instant destruction to private agreements with the Russians at the expense of allied interests, and the increasing intransigency among all the allies over America's exclusive control over atomic weapons. Much of the difficulty stemmed from the very success of the alliance in providing the infrastructure for Europe's pride in its power. Europe was not the distraught continent of 1949; it was a strong,

46. C. L. Sulzberger, "The Double Funeral at Arlington," *New York Times,* May 27, 1959.

confident group of countries that as a unit could stand apart from both America and Russia.

It was to this new Europe that President Kennedy addressed himself in 1961 as the new Democratic administration reviewed American foreign policy. Kennedy wanted to infuse the tired alliance with the vigor he had promised America. The New Frontier became the Grand Design of NATO, in which an old military alliance would be transformed by a twofold reconstruction: first, a recognition of NATO as a genuine partnership in which Europe and America would meet as equals rather than one serving as a ward of the other; second, an effort to subordinate the dominant military emphasis of the alliance to political, economic, and cultural purposes, which had been promised in Article 2 of the Treaty and which unobtrusively had been implemented ever since the organization had formed.

The foundation of Kennedy's reconstructed alliance was the idea of a broad community of interests embracing all aspects of Western civilization and resting on two great pillars standing astride the Atlantic, each indispensable to the other. "The future of the West," asserted Kennedy in 1963, "lies in Atlantic partnership—a system of cooperation, interdependence, and harmony whose peoples can jointly meet their burdens and opportunities throughout the world. Some say this is only a dream, but I do not agree." [47]

The excitement engendered by this approach to NATO was reflected in the Atlantic Convention of NATO Nations whose Declaration of Paris endorsed in 1962 the transformation of NATO into an Atlantic Community. This change was expected to lead to the end of the Cold War but not to the

47. President Kennedy's Address at the Paulskirche in Frankfurt, June 25, 1963, in *Public Papers of the Presidents: John F. Kennedy, 1963* (Washington, 1964), p. 517.

end of the American link with Europe.[48] The vision still informed the alliance even after France had expelled all NATO organs from its soil. The first major declaration of NATO in its Brussels headquarters, for example, was to reaffirm the idea of NATO as a political community rather than simply as an alliance.[49]

Yet the Grand Design was always too grandiose to be meaningful and too vague in its language to be translated into specific reforms. The old problems remained to disturb the organization, and not even the soaring rhetoric of Kennedy could banish them. Apathy was one of them. The threat of war had diminished as the old fears of the Soviet Union receded into the background. The Communist parties of Italy and France had lost their vigor. Because of the restiveness among the Warsaw Pact members, the rise of bourgeois habits in the Soviet Union, and the increasing bitterness of the Sino-Soviet dispute, Russia had become a paper tiger for many Europeans no matter how loudly Khrushchev roared.

Counterbalancing the image of a stronger Europe and a weaker Russia was the division of Berlin, and with it the larger question of the future of Germany. The raising of the Berlin Wall, sealing East Berlin from the West in the summer of 1961, was a physical symbol of the continuing Cold War. Although the Soviet Union may have regarded the wall as a defensive measure and may have generally behaved as if this was its primary intention, neither NATO nor the Warsaw bloc could be certain that reactions against the wall on the part of the West Germans or the figurative extension of the wall on the part of the East Germans might not unleash the holocaust everyone feared. Such was the un-

48. Text of the Declaration of Paris in *NATO Letter* XI (June, 1963), 13.
49. *New York Times*, October 17, 1967.

spoken concern of Europeans in the spring of 1965, when the European press altered its accustomed anti-American tone to worry about the Federal Republic's decision, made independently of its allies, to hold a Bundesrat meeting in Berlin, thereby risking retaliation from the East Germans.[50] In this circumstance the existence of NATO with its American contingent was an important source of psychological security even if the military expression of NATO's power was less clear than it had been ten years before.

Yet, coexisting with a continuing dependence upon America's military power was Europe's resentment of the atomic monopoly and its concurrent doubts about America's fitness for Western leadership. The Kennedy administration was sensitive to this sentiment, and felt it could employ a device that served the spirit of the Grand Design: namely, the establishment of a multilateral force (MLF) that would jointly possess atomic weapons.

The idea of providing some allied involvement in nuclear matters had its origins in the Eisenhower administration when American planners tried to reconcile legitimate European demands for a role in their own security with congressional requirements that had placed nuclear weaponry under the exclusive control of American commanders. Part of the conflict was the obvious affront to European sensibilities; but, additionally, there were always the doubts about American leadership of the alliance, leading Europeans to question America as a fit custodian of critical weapons. The periodic Russian-American meetings without allied involvement fed European suspicions of American intentions to arrange a nuclear détente at the expense of the NATO allies. And the United States, for its part, was fearful of sharing its nuclear knowledge with its allies if by doing so it would

50. See, for example, George Penchenier, "L'Irredentisme en Allemagne Occidentale," *Le Monde Diplomatique,* March, 1965, pp. 9–12.

place the awesome power in the hands of fourteen, or at least thirteen, other nations. Would not this increase the risk of war? Would it also reawaken Europe's distrust of Germans if the Federal Republic, despite the treaty provisions, should share the control of nuclear arms?

To resolve this conundrum, General Lauris Norstad, NATO's Supreme Allied Commander in Europe (SACEUR), proposed in 1960 that NATO be given its own nuclear force composed of land-based medium-range ballistic missiles. The North Atlantic Council at its December meeting in 1960 responded to this counsel by approving a revised version of the MLF with a Polaris-armed flotilla of twenty-five ships, each ship armed with eight missiles and each ship manned by contingents of several allied nations.[51] Although the new Kennedy administration that assumed power the following month seized on the MLF as its contribution to the principle of nuclear sharing, the plan failed to win the support of other powers and subsequently died without fanfare. The obituary was buried in the elliptical language of a joint communiqué that followed a meeting of President Johnson and Prime Minister Harold Macmillan of the United Kingdom in December, 1964.[52]

The trouble with the MLF in 1950 or in 1964 is still the trouble with the alliance in 1970. Nuclear sharing merely dramatized one of the many fissures in the alliance that time has only served to widen. On the one hand, there was Europe's reluctance to expend the large amounts of money required to participate in the MLF at a time when Europe had lost its fears of a Soviet invasion. On the other hand, there was the undeniable fact that no matter how much

51. North Atlantic Council communiqué, Paris, December 16–18, 1960, in *NATO Letter* IX (January, 1961), 13.

52. Joint communiqué of President of the United States and Prime Minister of the United Kingdom, December 8, 1964, in Department of State *Bulletin* LI (1964), 903.

money each partner offered, the United States would still have an exclusive voice in the actual decision to use the Polaris missile; decision-making was not a matter of sharing. This knowledge deepened resentments and confirmed France in its intentions to perfect its own nuclear capabilities. Germany, the only ally to display genuine interest in the plan, was angered by an anti-German element in Europe's coldness to the MLF. But many of the smaller members of the alliance, such as Denmark, opposed the plan primarily because it appeared to be an unwitting agent in reviving the Cold War.

The most vociferous and most effective critic of the United States was France's President de Gaulle, and he struck a responsive chord in Europe. Although his pretensions to leadership of a Europe from the Atlantic to the Urals met with derision among most Europeans, and his vendetta against England agitated the European Economic Community in 1963, and again in 1967 evoked strong protests in the Common Market, his anti-American diatribes won understanding if not agreement in the alliance. No other member removed itself from the alliance's organization as France did in 1967; and no other member openly championed the Soviet Union as a counterpoise to American domination of Europe, as France did increasingly throughout the 1960s. But he may be said to have spoken for most of the members when he condemned the war in Vietnam, or when he urged resistance to America's economic presence in Europe in the form of petroleum, automobile, or electronics interests. In the spring of 1967 Harold Wilson, prime minister of the country with the putative "special relationship" with the United States, asserted that Britain was more effective than France in resisting the domination of American industrial power.[53] And in the Federal Republic of Germany all parties

53. Harold Wilson's Address on the Common Market, *Vital Speeches of the Day* XXXII (1967), 482–94.

could warm to that aspect of de Gaulle's complaints which
involved the exclusion of Europe from the industrial benefits that nuclear oligopoly had given the superpowers.

American reactions to Europe's unhappiness were relatively sluggish, perhaps because the nation's attention was
drawn to the Far East rather than to Europe in the middle
and late 1960s. Perhaps, too, there was a recognition among
Americans that the burdens of leadership included a heavy
weight of blame for all the wrongs of the world. If the partners did not want the MLF, or the vague British alternative
offered in 1964, it was not a matter of great moment. Public
opinion supported the administration in leaving the issue of
nuclear sharing alone as long as possible. But the aplomb
with which the nation accepted criticism had certain limits,
and the increasing complexity of the war in Vietnam combined with the increasing stridency of European criticism of
that war invited American retaliation.

Such was an explanation for the pressure in 1966 and 1967
to reduce the size of America's troop commitment to Europe
from sources no less elevated than the level of Senator Mike
Mansfield, majority leader of the Senate.[54] By returning
American troops, the dollar gap caused by American expenditures abroad would be reduced, European nations
would be encouraged to make more impressive contributions to the SHAPE armies, and the needs of other parts of
the world would be recognized. From more conservative
ranks came talk of raising tariff barriers against unfriendly
allies, thereby undermining the painfully constructed foundations of free trade that the United States had laid in the

54. Text of Senator Mansfield's statement on resolution calling for a
reduction of American troops in Western Europe, *Congressional Record,*
89th Cong., 2d Sess. (1966), 20554–55; official Department of State response, N.E.T. interview with Secretary of State Rusk, May 5, 1967, in
Department of State *Bulletin* LVI (1967), 782–83; Mansfield's plans to
revive campaign for troops reduction in Europe, *New York Times,* Jan. 11,
1968.

Kennedy Round of GATT in 1967.[55] Although the administration combatted every specific attack on the nation's commitment to NATO, President Johnson's proposed restrictions
on the American dollar abroad in his New Year's Day news
conference in 1968 was another revelation of the fissures
splitting the Atlantic Alliance.[56]

These problems were accentuated by the disenchantment
of intellectuals on both sides of the Atlantic who looked
upon NATO as an ugly and unnecessary relic of the Cold
War that should be dispatched as soon as possible. Ronald
Steel, speaking for a new generation of foreign policy analysts in the mid-1960s, identified NATO with the blind anti-
communism of the McCarthy era and found it an unwitting
means of expressing an American imperialism: "We acquired an accidental empire, and have maintained—and
ever expanded—it because we have found ourselves in a
global struggle with an ideology." [57] In the Senate the eloquent voice of Senator J. William Fulbright in a series of
addresses, beginning with his influential "Old Myths and
New Realities" in 1964, gave authority to the idea that
NATO and its purposes represented an old myth.[58] If it was
true that Europe's security had progressed to the point
where the alliance was unnecessary or even provocative, the
next step for America might be logically a return to isolationism, or at least to a retirement from the Continent.

Twenty years after the Treaty of Washington, this step

55. Text of GATT Statement on Kennedy Round, May 15, 1967, in *New York Times*, May 16, 1967; Senator Percy's response to Senator Dirksen's support of legislation to restrict tariff, *Congressional Record*, 90th Cong., 1st Sess. (1967), 15378.

56. Transcript of the President's News Conference on Foreign and Do-mestic Affairs, January 1, 1968, in *New York Times*, Jan. 2, 1968.

57. Ronald Steel, "The American Empire," *Commonweal* LXXXVI (1967), 355.

58. "Old Myths and New Realities," *Congressional Record*, 88th Cong., 2d Sess. (1944), 6227–29; "The Fatal Arrogance of Power," *New York Times Magazine*, May 15, 1966, pp. 29 ff.

has not been taken. Too many links have been forged and tightened over this period to have permitted an abrupt fracture of the alliance, or even a purposeful atrophying of the association. Even the most audacious critic of the organization, former French President de Gaulle, did not withdraw from the alliance, and France continues to supply the new headquarters at Brussels with its personnel. And few pundits predict that the Treaty will not continue beyond 1970, or that fewer than the present fifteen members will comprise the alliance of the 1970s.

More than the claims of habit or sentiment account for the survival of NATO. In many ways the problems of 1949 are the problems of 1970. The German question is unsolved, and Europe's trust in the new Germany as a NATO partner is less than complete. An alliance lacking an American military component would leave Germany the most powerful member, a fact of political life that gave a special meaning to America's participation in NATO. But even if the pervasive distrust of Germans should dissolve, Berlin would remain a problem—a city divided, walled, and always vulnerable to Soviet pressure. The Soviet occupation of Czechoslovakia in August, 1968, exposed again the weakness of the Federal Republic's morale, as NATO readdressed itself to the Russian military threat against Western Europe. Talk of cuts in troop strength ended abruptly in the fall of 1968, and George Kennan, erstwhile champion of a disengagement in Germany, now urged the shipment of 100,-000 additional American soldiers to West Germany until Russia evacuated Czechoslovakia.[59]

In the Mediterranean the Russians had made their challenge to NATO clear for over a decade. The Soviet initiative in the Middle East, which stimulated Arab aggressiveness

59. Endre Marton, Interview with George F. Kennan, *New York Times,* Sept. 22, 1968.

toward Israel, bore a major responsibility for the Arab-Israel conflict of June, 1967. Among the lessons for NATO in that war was the extent of Soviet interest in the Eastern Mediterranean and its willingness to take some risks to advance its Middle Eastern objectives. Would those risks be made more freely and more frequently if there were no alliance in the way? Had the Soviet Union normalized its relations with the rest of the world in such a way as to make NATO unnecessary in the late 1960s?

With the exception of France, Europe's response to such questions left few doubts that NATO still had a role to play. Whether that role should be dominated by the military form that had characterized the organization since the Lisbon Conference of 1952 is another matter. NATO must respond to the end of the bipolar world of a generation ago beyond replacing "massive retaliation" with a "flexible response." Some observers were modest in their suggestions, such as former Secretary General Paul-Henri Spaak, who supported "the idea of a non-aggression pact between the NATO Pact Powers and those of the Warsaw Pact." [60] Anthony Eden, writing in October, 1967, urged NATO to move into the diplomatic arena and leave the military behind. NATO, he felt, might assume some of the burdens American diplomacy alone had taken in the leadership of the West.[61] Still another view is that of General André Beaufre, whose idea of reform —a French idea—envisaged NATO as an interim organization whose mission was to give birth to a new all-European organization that would embrace the two Germanies, Spain, Switzerland, and the Soviet satellite nations.[62]

60. Paul-Henri Spaak, "The Alliance Must Go On," *NATO Letter* XV (March, 1967), p. 6. Spaak reflected a hope for a détente with the Soviet Bloc that was fully expressed in the findings of the Harmel Report at the Reykjavik Meeting of the North Atlantic Council in December, 1968. See report of the special study group, *ibid.* XVI (March, 1968), 10–13.

61. *New York Times*, Oct. 14, 1967.

62. André Beaufre, *NATO and Europe* (New York, 1966), pp. 158–59.

Of the three courses suggested above, the broadening of NATO's objectives to include diplomatic and political functions has always been attractive to NATO critics. In fact, NATO has sporadically attempted to realize this objective, which was as old as the Charter itself. Article 2 of the North Atlantic Treaty, emphasizing the "strengthening of free institutions" and the encouragement of "economic collaboration between any and all of them," had been the vehicle for promoting the Atlantic Community, attracting such diverse groups as the federalists of the Atlantic Union Committee in 1949 and the architects of the Grand Design of 1960 as well as the Atlantic diplomatists of 1967. NATO had always dabbled in diplomacy. It ranged from vague intentions to continue efforts at cooperation with Eastern Europe, officially announced in a Council communiqué in December, 1966, to successful mediation between Greece and Turkey on the Cyprus problem in November, 1967, to which Secretary General Manlio Brosio had made a NATO contribution.[63]

Although it is unlikely that the NATO of the 1970s will become a fully integrated political community, still less is it likely that it will keep the military alliance of the 1950s and 1960s intact. Its military function remains, but in many ways the uneasy balance of terror effected between the Soviet Union and the United States has returned the military deterrent to the posture of 1949, with the guarantee of American involvement through the Treaty inhibiting, or at least ameliorating, Soviet adventures in Europe.

Such a guarantee was implicit in President Nixon's dramatic tour of Western Europe, including NATO headquarters, at the beginning of his term of office. Equally implicit

63. North Atlantic Council communiqué, Paris, December 16, 1966, in *NATO Letter* XV (January, 1967), 13; *New York Times*, Nov. 25, 30, 1967.

was a recognition that the alliance of the 1970s will not have as large a military contribution from the United States as it had in the first generation of NATO; the recurrent congressional demands for troop withdrawals are reflections of a sentiment that will be satisfied by the administration. But there is little reason to doubt that its response to these pressures will take a form that will convince the world that disengagement from Vietnam is not setting the stage for disengagement from Europe or for the revival of American isolationism. For America, the maintenance of the alliance remains not only a major factor in its function as a world leader but also a symbol of its continuing rejection of the once powerful and always attractive isolationist tradition.[64]

64. Portions of this chapter have appeared in *Review of Politics* XXXI (October, 1961), 210–22, and in *NATO Letter*, XVIII (June, 1970), 14–18.

Canada in North America

ROBERT CRAIG BROWN

CANADA'S RELATIONS with the United States were in a
state of bad repair in 1900. Two years before, after protracted negotiations between Great Britain and the United
States, a Joint High Commission had been appointed to discuss, and hopefully to settle, a host of outstanding problems
in Canadian-American relations. Many of those problems
were of minor international importance, essentially "housekeeping" issues common to amicable relations between
bordering states, such as agreement on alien labor legislation, the conveyance of prisoners, and laws concerning the
wreckage and salvage of ships. But the commissioners were
also empowered to find solutions to a number of major disputes between Great Britain and the United States that centered upon Canada. All of these were of long standing and
were of such magnitude that they either had caused, or potentially could cause in the future, an open break in Anglo-
American diplomacy. Canadian concern was thus twofold:
the survival of the fledgling Canadian nation was in no small
measure dependent upon Anglo-American friendship, and,

equally, in all of these major disputes it was Canadian interests, commercial interests, that were threatened by the United States.

The North Atlantic fisheries problem evolved out of the admittedly harsh provisions of the Anglo-American agreement of 1818 that forbade the entrance of American fishing vessels into the inshore waters of British North America except, as the agreement put it, "for the purpose of shelter and of repairing damages therein, of purchasing wood, and of obtaining water, and for no other purpose whatever." In short, American fishermen could enter the inshore waters only if survival dictated their doing so; they could not fish in those waters for bait, nor could they enter Canadian harbors to transship their catch, to resupply, or to hire Canadian crews. At various times—under the Reciprocity Treaty of 1854, the Washington Treaty of 1871, and, after 1888, under the licensing provisions of an Anglo-American *modus vivendi*—these restrictions had been waived. But the provisions of the *modus vivendi* were tenuous at best, and the Canadian government could refuse to issue licences and revert back to its exclusive privileges under the Convention of 1818. Then, too, the dispute was incredibly complex because the precise definition of Canadian inshore waters, especially in bays, was unclear and involved complicated questions of international maritime law.

The second major issue faced by the Joint Commission of 1898–99 was the Bering Sea dispute. In the mid-1880s Canadian seal fishermen, shipping from British Columbia, began pelagic sealing in the open waters of Bering Sea, hunting on the high seas seals that had come to give birth to their young on the American-owned Pribilof Islands. In 1886 and in 1887 United States revenue cruisers had seized some of these Canadian vessels on the high seas and brought their masters to trial for violating American municipal law. By so doing, the United States had explicitly, though dubiously, claimed property rights in the seals beyond the recognized three-mile limit around the Pribilofs and implicitly claimed the Bering Sea as a *mare clausum,* or closed sea. Again, complicated questions of international law were at stake as well as Canadian commercial interests. The Canadians claimed that the Americans were violating the doctrine of freedom of the seas and threatening an important new Canadian industry with extinction.

A third major problem concerned the definition of the boundary between Canada and Alaska. Various attempts at a settlement had been made since the United States had purchased Alaska in 1867, and, in fact, by the time the Joint High Commission met, only the panhandle portion of the boundary was in dispute. But it was just in the panhandle— more precisely at two points along the panhandle, the head of Lynn Canal and the southernmost tip at Observatory Inlet —that Canadian and American interests were in conflict. Despite the confusing provisions of the Anglo-Russian Treaty of 1825 that attempted to define the panhandle boundary, or, perhaps, because of them, the United States exercised de facto control of the headwaters of Lynn Canal. This was of critical importance during the Yukon gold rush because the Americans could control the major access routes to the Canadian Yukon Territory and hence control the enormous trade in gold and supplies in the Yukon. The boundary at Observatory Inlet was only an area of potential conflict in 1898–99 but would be the main point of grievance of the Canadians in 1903 when the award of the Boundary Tribunal was announced. But as early as 1886, a Canadian who had been working on the boundary problem observed the source of trouble at Observatory Inlet. "The inlet," Colonel D. R. Cameron reported, "is nearer to Japan and China than the present railway terminus [the Canadian Pacific

Railway's western terminus in Vancouver], and . . . at no distant date one may reasonably expect this remarkable waterway to become the channel of a very large volume of trade." [1]

These substantive problems considered by the Joint High Commission illustrated one side of Canada's role, and problem, in North America. What was of concern to Canada and the United States was the control of the resources of the British North American half of the continent. The rivalry went back to the American Revolution and the formation of the second British Empire. And the rivalry would continue to be the central issue in Canadian-American relations until the present day. For the Canadians, Canadian control of these resources would be the keystone of Canadian nationhood.

The form of the Joint High Commission illustrated the other side of Canada's role and problem in North America. In 1898 Canada was, as Richard Jebb put it, a "colonial nation" within the British Empire, decidedly more than a colony but not possessing all the attributes of nationhood. Technically, of course, Canada's voice in diplomacy was the British Foreign Office. But over the years, and especially since Confederation in 1867, the Canadians had won an increasingly important role of participation in diplomatic exchanges concerning their country. A very brief illustration will make the point. In 1854 the governor-general, Lord Elgin, had negotiated the Reciprocity Treaty. In 1871 Sir John A. Macdonald had served as one of the commissioners who negotiated the Treaty of Washington, and he took his instructions from London. In 1887–88 Sir Charles Tupper was one of the three British commissioners who negotiated the abortive Treaty of 1888, and all three were guided in

1. D. R. Cameron to Colonial Office, October 29, 1886, Vol. 1, Macdonald Papers, Public Archives of Canada (hereafter cited as P.A.C.).

their deliberations by instructions from both London and Ottawa. Finally, in 1898–99, there were four Canadian commissioners, and the British government's representative, Lord Herschell, was to accept the advice of the chief Canadian commissioner, Prime Minister Sir Wilfrid Laurier. The foreign secretary, Lord Salisbury, observed that "several of the questions included in the list furnished by the Canadian Government for discussions are of a purely local character, about which this Department [the Foreign Office] at least, is without information on which any instructions to the British Representatives on the Commission could usefully be framed." "The direct representation of Her Majesty's Government," he added, "should take their instructions from the Dominion Government." [2] The ultimate force of Canadian diplomacy remained, of course, the willingness of the mother country to stand behind the Canadian position with her military might. But within those limits, the participation of Canada in the diplomatic process had become ever greater, and, apparently, her voice was now decisive.

Just how decisive was revealed by the outcome of the deliberations of the Joint High Commission. The Canadians insisted on a "package deal." They were willing to give the Americans a point on the Bering Sea or the North Atlantic fisheries in return for an American tariff concession. But with a growing self-confidence about Canada's ability to "go it alone" in North America and a clear reluctance on the part of Laurier's ministers in Ottawa to accept any agreement that would appear to surrender Canadian interest to American power, Laurier and his colleagues demanded an accord on all issues before the Joint High Commission. And when the Commission could not resolve the Alaska boundary problem, the Canadians went home. There were assurances, in

2. Foreign Office to Colonial Office, December 10, 1897, Colonial Office Papers, C.O. 42/854, P.A.C.

1900, that the Commission was only adjourned and pious pledges on both sides that it would reconvene. But it never did.[3]

There was satisfaction in Ottawa with the abortive results. The Canadians had withstood pressure from both the United States and Great Britain to back down from a firmly held, if legally dubious and inherently weak, position on Alaska. (They demanded a Canadian harbor at the head of Lynn Canal and a Canadian corridor from there to the Yukon Territory.) Sir Wilfrid Laurier told a friend that "there is a question of dignity involved which must make it incumbent upon us to refuse to negotiate on anything else, and this we will unless they [the United States] give way." [4] Laurier's government certainly wanted to settle all outstanding problems with the United States, but the prime minister was also acutely aware that the confident mood of his country would not allow him to do so at the price of a sacrifice of Canadian "dignity." As one newspaper put it:

> Canada is capable of holding her place and her privileges in relation to the United States with dignified consciousness of a desire to maintain international friendliness and in a confident knowledge at the same time that United States friendliness towards us is by no means essential to our well-being, whatever reasons may exist for courting it from an Imperial point of view.[5]

Three years later, in October, 1903, the "Imperial point of view" prevailed, and the logjam of irresolution of Canadian-American disputes was broken with the announcement of

3. Canadian-American relations in the latter part of the nineteenth century are discussed in detail in C. C. Tansill, *Canadian-American Relations, 1875–1911* (New Haven, Conn., 1943), and Robert Craig Brown, *Canada's National Policy, 1883–1900* (Princeton, N.J., 1964).

4. Sir Wilfrid Laurier to A. S. Hardy, February 16, 1899, Box 100, Laurier Papers, P.A.C.

5. *Regina Leader*, Mar. 2, 1899.

the Alaska boundary award. The offense to Canadian dignity was beyond measure. The mother country had taken the diplomatic initiative on Alaska back from Canada; had consciously surrendered to the bluster, the threats, and the deception of President Theodore Roosevelt; had agreed to a "judicial tribunal" of the boundary over Canada's protest; had acquiesced in the appointment of Secretary of War Elihu Root and Senators Henry Cabot Lodge of Massachusetts and George Turner of Washington as America's "eminent jurists"; and had accepted a boundary award that Canadians regarded as both unjust in form and dangerous to their interests in substance. Indeed, it was the *matter* as well as the *manner* of the award that offended Canadians. The American control of the headland at Lynn Canal was confirmed, and correctly so; but when Lord Alverston, the British jurist, agreed with the Americans that the tiny islands of Kannaghunut and Sitklan at the outlet of Observatory Inlet belonged to the United States, the Canadian jurists, Aylesworth and Jette, claimed that he had reversed his decision under intense diplomatic pressure from the United States and the Foreign Office in order to get a final decision the United States would accept. The "judicial" character of the decision was a farce. A diplomatic deal in the anterooms of the Foreign Office, the sacrifice of the Canadian lamb on the altar of Anglo-American friendship, was the only possible interpretation of the award in Ottawa. Moreover, the Canadians believed that the islands so awarded to the United States controlled the shipping lanes to Port Simpson in Observatory Inlet. And in 1903 Colonel Cameron's prediction was coming true: Port Simpson was the projected western terminus of the Canadian government's recently charted second continental railway.[6]

Fearful of further British surrenders to American diplo-

6. See Craig Brown, "The Nationalism of the National Policy," in Peter Russell, ed., *Nationalism in Canada* (Toronto, 1966), p. 161.

macy in the interest of the mother country's strategic neces-
sities and in the name of Anglo-American friendship, and
suspicious of any further dealings with an untrustworthy
American government, the Canadians withdrew within
themselves. When asked in the spring of 1904 about the
possibility of reconvening the Joint High Commission, Laurier replied that "we are always ready to . . . negotiate
with them on fair terms, but we shall not take the initiative
for new negotiations. If new negotiations are to be made,
it must be on their initiative." [7]

The Americans did take the initiative. In 1906 Secretary
of State Elihu Root made tentative overtures to the Canadians about settling outstanding problems, and in January,
1907, he made his first "pilgrimage" to Ottawa. Root came
away from the visit aware of the extreme sensitivity of the
Canadians, even of their hostility to "cleaning the slate."
Moreover, he was convinced that another Joint High Commission was not an appropriate method of settlement; it
was at once too formal and too cumbersome, and issues
became confused in a maze of concessions and countercon-
cessions. Fortunately, Root's desire was heartily seconded
by the governor-general of Canada, Lord Grey, and by the
British ambassador in Washington, James Bryce. This trio,
working hand-in-hand with Laurier over the next few years,
accomplished the remarkable feat of disposing of nearly all
important Canadian-American problems. The new attitude
in Ottawa was reflected in Laurier's statement to the House
of Commons that

> we have come to this position in our relations with the people
> of the United States: we can never conceive of war between
> us, or of war between Great Britain and the United States.

7. Quoted in A. C. Gluek, Jr., "Pilgrimages to Ottawa: Canadian-
American Diplomacy, 1903–13" (Paper presented to the Canadian Historical Association, Calgary, June, 1968), p. 5.

We mean to settle all our difficulties with that nation by peaceful means, by diplomatic action, by negotiations, but never by war.[8]

In part, Laurier was simply stating the cold strategic reality of Canada's place in North America. For some time the British government had based its military and naval planning on the assumption of the improbability if not the impossibility of war with the United States,[9] and it was most unlikely that British military or naval might would be used to buttress any Canadian position in difficulties with the United States. But Laurier was also saying that given an appropriate mood in Washington and appropriate negotiations, a more desirable state of Canadian-American relations was within reach. Quietly and relatively quickly, solutions were found. The North Atlantic fisheries dispute was referred to the Hague Tribunal in 1909, which found the case in Canada's favor. And in 1911 an agreement between the United States, Russia, Japan, and Great Britain (signing for Canada) provided for effective international regulation of the exploitation of fur seals in the North Pacific ocean.

As important as the settlement of problems held over from the nineteenth century was the provision of guidelines for the resolution of the disputes of the new century. Perhaps most notable of all the agreements reached by Root, Bryce, Grey, and Laurier was the signing of the Boundary Waters Treaty in 1909. Four years earlier the Americans had been anxious to reach an agreement with Canada regulating the diversion of water for hydroelectric power from the Niagara River to minimize the danger of this diversion to Niagara

8. J. C. Hopkins, ed., *The Canadian Annual Review of Public Affairs, 1907* (Toronto, 1908), p. 401.

9. Kenneth Bourne, *Britain and the Balance of Power in North America, 1815–1908* (London, 1967), chap. 10, and Samuel F. Wells, Jr., "British Strategic Withdrawal from the Western Hemisphere, 1904–1906," *Canadian Historical Review* XLIX (1968), 335–56.

Falls. Through their respective representatives on the International Waterways Commission, established in 1905, the two governments carried on extensive negotiations, Canada taking the position that it would not "consent to a Treaty for Niagara Falls alone, to the exclusion of all other points of contention of the International Waterways between the two countries." [10] The resultant treaty embodied the Canadian principle of referring all such problems to the International Joint Commission, the successor body to the International Waterways Commission. The treaty was a recognition of the growing urbanization and industrialization along the Great Lakes water boundary, and it anticipated the inevitable conflicts that would arise over shared water resources in the future. It further provided a vehicle, in the I.J.C., for the discussion and resolution of highly technical problems in an atmosphere relatively free from political pressure. Finally, in method it foreshadowed the creation of similar expert commissions to settle complex technical and economic problems during and after World War II. [11]

Laurier's government wished to put a fitting end to "cleaning the slate" by settling the most persistent of all Canadian-American problems, the trade question. In the spring of 1911 the government announced the completion of a comprehensive reciprocity agreement to be implemented by concurrent legislation. Robert Borden's Conservative opposition, aided and abetted by the extremely powerful transcontinental railways, the Canadian Manufacturers' Association, and a

10. George Gibbons to G. Clinton, April 6, 1906, quoted in A. O. Gibbons, "Sir George Gibbons and the Boundary Waters Treaty of 1909," *Canadian Historical Review* XXXIV (1953), 126.

11. A side-effect of this intense and varied period of negotiation was the creation, in 1909, of the Department of External Affairs of the Canadian government, urged especially by Bryce and Grey to bring order and consistency to Canadian negotiations. See James Eayrs, "The Origins of Canada's Department of External Affairs," in Hugh L. Keenleyside et al., *The Growth of Canadian Policies in External Affairs* (Durham, N.C., 1960), pp. 14–32.

number of entrenched Conservative Provincial governments, forced Sir Wilfrid's Liberals into an election and defeat of the government and its reciprocity program. Echoes of mistrust of the United States after the Alaska boundary award punctuated the Conservative campaign. Reciprocity was pictured as the "thin edge of the wedge" of annexation. Borrowing a singularly unfortunate phrase from President Taft's assessment of the reciprocity agreement and wrenching it from its intended context, Borden agreed that Canada was "at the parting of the ways. This compact made in secret and without mandate points, indeed, to a new path. We must decide whether the spirit of Canadianism or of Continentalism shall prevail on the northern half of this continent." Appealing to the traditional arguments of his party, Borden easily equated the Conservatives' protectionist sympathies with "Canadianism" and charged the apparently free-trader Liberals with lack of patriotism and dangerously adopting a "continentalist" or annexationist policy.

Borden's campaign was significantly strengthened by the aid of Canadian manufacturing and railway interests. Their opposition to the reciprocity agreement was summarized in a manifesto of eighteen Toronto businessmen who bolted from Laurier's Liberal party over reciprocity because, *inter alia,*

> the present unexampled prosperity of Canada is the result of the policy which has been pursued in the development of her trade and of her natural resources; because this has involved the expenditure of hundreds of millions of dollars upon railways, canals, steamships, and other means of transportation between East and West and West and East and the obligation to incur further great expenditure for the same purpose; and because further development along the same lines would be seriously checked by the proposed Reciprocity agreement and the benefits of the expenditures referred to would be to

a great extent lost; [and] because as a result of the proposed Agreement the freedom of action possessed by Canada with reference to her tariffs and channels of trade would be greatly curtailed, and she would be hampered in developing her own resources in her own way and by her own people.[12]

Safely in office with what he regarded as a mandate for "Canadianism," Borden quickly reassured Bryce that of the many questions facing his new cabinet,

those which concern the relations of Canada with the United States are among the most important. . . . It is needless to say that we are most desirous of maintaining relations of the most friendly character with the Government and people of the United States, and to dissipate any suspicion of unfriendliness which may have arisen out of the result of the recent elections.[13]

Good direct relations with Washington, the establishment of mutual trust and confidence, were doubtless of great importance to Borden. But of even greater urgency, in view of the increasing danger of war in Europe, was the part that Canada might play in maintaining friendly relations between the United States and Great Britain. Again, just after assuming the prime ministership, in November, 1911, he put Canada's relations with the United States in this larger context before a Halifax audience.

Canada is an autonomous nation within the British Empire and is closely and inseparably united to that Empire by ties of kinship, of sentiment, and of fealty, by historic association

12. Henry Borden, ed., *Robert Laird Borden: His Memoirs*, 2 vols. (Toronto, 1938), I, 327–28; J. C. Hopkins, ed., *The Canadian Annual Review of Public Affairs, 1911* (Toronto, 1912), pp. 48–49.
13. Robert L. Borden to James Bryce, October 14, 1911, no. 4315, OC 104, Borden Papers, P.A.C.

and tradition, by the character of its institutions, and by the free will of its people. By like ties of kinship, by constant social and commercial intercourses, by proximity and mutual respect, and good-will, this country is closely associated with the United States. Canada's voice and influence should always be for harmony and not for discord between our Empire and the great Republic and I believe that she will always be a bond of abiding friendship between them.[14]

This concept of Canadian-American relations successfully met the test of World War I. Unlike the United States, Canada was committed to a full war effort from the beginning; and in several speeches in the United States in the early war years, Borden took special care to explain British and Canadian war aims. There was, of course, much distress in both government and business circles in Canada that so many war orders from Britain were being filled in the United States and so few in Canada in the early years. Canada had entered the war with her government under severe financial stress and with high unemployment throughout the country. The war effort put an even greater burden upon her economy and made the acquisition of substantial orders from Great Britain all the more necessary. In November of 1914 the prime minister advised his high commissioner in London that "a very painful and even bitter feeling is being aroused throughout the Dominion. Men are going without bread in Canada while those across the line are receiving wages for work that could be done as efficiently and as cheaply in this country." [15] Indeed, throughout the war the Canadian government appeared to be in sharper conflict with the mother country than with its neighbor to the south. In the procurement of war materials, the deployment of Canadian troops, and the determination of war policy, at least until 1917, the British

14. Hopkins, *Canadian Annual Review, 1911*, p. 295.
15. Borden to G. Perley, November 27, 1914, Box 2, Perley Papers, P.A.C.

government seemed to regard Canada less as "an autonomous nation within the British Empire" than as a crown colony whose manpower and resources could be used without consulation.[16]

Canadian-American business increased throughout the war and especially after the United States entered the conflict. The "changed relations" that American participation brought about led the Canadian government to cable to Borden in London suggesting the appointment of a "permanent representative at Washington . . . having regard disposition nickel as well as vital commercial materials such as coal, railway cars, boats, such representative . . . necessary at least while war continues."[17] By October, 1917, Borden had decided to make the appointment, noting that "in matters that may concern the whole Empire he will of course consult with the [British] Embassy but in matters solely touching our own affairs he would communicate direct with the United States Government and its various commissions."[18]

The British government countered Borden's decision with the suggestion of an appointment of a Canadian subordinate to the British ambassador. When the prime minister replied that he had in mind the appointment of one of his cabinet ministers as "an important representative to the Government [of the United States] who, in respect of matters directly and solely concerning Canadian interests should have recognized diplomatic status," the colonial secretary informed the governor-general that such a proposal would "raise a grave

16. For one instance of the high-handed British use of Canadian war production facilities, see Gaddis Smith, *Britain's Clandestine Submarines, 1914–1915* (New Haven, Conn., 1964). See also Gaddis Smith, "Canadian External Affairs during World War I," in Keenleyside, *The Growth of Canadian Policies in External Affairs*, pp. 33–58.

17. Arthur Meighen to Borden, April 14, 1917 (telegram), no. 45807, OC 440, Borden Papers.

18. Borden to Perley, October 13, 1917, no. 58137, OC 534, *ibid.*

constitutional issue," and Borden backed down.[19] In January, 1918, the prime minister established a compromise Canadian War Mission in Washington, headed by the Canadian representative on the Imperial Munitions Board there, Lloyd Harris.[20] The Canadian, American, and British governments all finally agreed on the appointment of a Canadian minister in Washington in 1920, and the first appointment, after much delay, was made in 1926.[21]

Routine business between Canada and the United States was handled by the Canadian War Mission for the remainder of the war. More important questions of policy were resolved by frequent visits to Washington by Sir Joseph Pope [22] and Loring Christie of the Department of External Affairs, various cabinet ministers, or Borden himself. In February, 1918, President Wilson suggested to Borden the establishment of direct telegraphic communication between Washington and Ottawa.[23] Later in the same month the prime minister visited the president and requested the placing of American war matériel orders in Canada to help offset Canada's unfavorable balance of trade with the United States. Wilson, Bernard Baruch of the War Industries Board, and Secretary of the Treasury William G. McAdoo were willing to meet the request, McAdoo suggesting that Canada should be singled

19. Governor General to Colonial Secretary, October 18, 1917, no. 58145; Colonial Secretary to Governor General, October 24, 1917, no. 58149; Governor General to Colonial Secretary, November 5, 1917, no. 58155, OC 534; *ibid.*

20. J. W. Flavelle to Borden, November 9, 1917, no. 45853; Borden to Flavelle, November 10, 1917, no. 45854, OC 440; Diary of Sir Robert Laird Borden, January 19, 20, 24, 26, 31, 1918; *ibid.*

21. See John S. Galbraith, *The Establishment of Canadian Diplomatic Status at Washington* (Berkeley, Calif., 1951), *passim;* H. Blair Neatby, *William Lyon Mackenzie King, 1924–1932: The Lonely Heights* (Toronto, 1963), pp. 192–93, and *What's Past Is Prologue: The Memoirs of the Right Honourable Vincent Massey* (Toronto, 1963), pp. 109–70.

22. Cecil Spring-Rice to Borden, January 21, 1918, no. 13078-9, OC 169, Borden Papers.

23. Borden Diary, February 22, 1918, *ibid.*

out "for distinctive assistance" and that "we shd. pool our resources and our endeavours." [24]

The opening of the Imperial War Cabinet to dominion representatives in the latter years of the war gave the dominions a voice in the planning of war policy and later, through the British Empire delegation at Paris, the peace-making policy of the empire. It also provided the Canadians with a forum in which to urge strengthening of Anglo-American cooperation. Two issues were of particular interest to the Canadian prime minister, the disposition of captured German colonies and the future foreign policy of the empire. Both, Borden believed, were potential causes of Anglo-American discord.

During a discussion of the captured colonies problem in December, 1918, Borden said that "one of the most important assets that we could get out of the war would be assured good will and a clear understanding between Great Britain and the United States." Borden quoted from some of Wilson's speeches on the question and added that "so far as Canada was concerned, she did not go into the war in order to add to the territory of the British Empire." He would agree to the territorial ambitions of South Africa, Australia, and New Zealand, but "on one consideration, and one only, and that was that their acquisition was necessary for the future security of the Empire. As regards the remaining conquered territories, he was in favour of entrusting their control and dominion to whichever State was appointed as mandatory for that purpose by the League of Nations. . . ." [25] And Borden was even more blunt about the future foreign policy of the Empire. A few days later he told the Imperial War Cabinet:

24. *Ibid.*, February 27, 28, 1918.
25. *Imperial War Cabinet* 44, Minutes . . . December 20, 1918, Vol. 45, File 79, Foster Papers, P.A.C.

Future good relations between ourselves and the United
States were, as he had said before, the best asset we could
bring home from the war. . . . He wished . . . to make
clear that if the future policy of the British Empire meant
working in co-operation with some European nation as
against the United States, that policy could not reckon on the
approval or the support of Canada. Canada's view was that
as an empire we should keep clear, as far as possible, of
European complications and alliances. This feeling had been
immensely strengthened by the experience of the war, into
which we had been drawn by old-standing pledges and more
recent understandings, of which the dominions had not even
been aware. . . .[26]

Borden deliberately brought the point of view of North
America to the councils of the empire, a point of view that
reflected the growing identity of Canadian and American
interests. He feared that with the conclusion of the war the
United States would withdraw within itself; he hoped that
Canada's neighbor would assume a major responsibility for
world order—at one point he urged American control of the
captured German colonies [27]—and more particularly for "a
league of the two great English-speaking Commonwealths"
as the foundation stone of the postwar peace settlement.[28]
Borden, like so many Americans, and like Prime Minister
Mackenzie King in later years, distrusted "European complications and alliances" and was particularly unsympathetic
to Article X of the League Covenant. His successor, Arthur
Meighen, advised by Loring Christie, carried the Borden
policy of interpreting North America to the empire to its
logical conclusion when he led the fight in the Imperial Conference of 1921 against the renewal of the Anglo-Japanese
alliance and in favor of the resulting Washington Con-

26. *Imperial War Cabinet* 47, Minutes . . . December 30, 1918, *ibid*.
27. *Imperial War Cabinet* 44, Minutes . . . December 20, 1918, *ibid*.
28. *Imperial War Cabinet* 38, Minutes . . . November 26, 1918, *ibid*.

ference. Canada, alone among the Imperial Conference members, opposed renewal of the alliance while, for obvious security reasons, the Australians led the argument for renewal. In one sense, direct Canadian interests were not involved. But the renewal of the alliance was vigorously opposed by the United States: renewal would jeopardize Anglo-American relations, and this could result in greater difficulties for Canada in its relations with the United States. The Canadian argument, skillfully formulated by Christie, eventually won out in London and led to the more general agreement for security in the Pacific adopted in Washington.[29]

The clearly growing emphasis upon the North American character of the country was partly a corollary to Canada's evolving status both in empire-commonwealth and in international affairs. Full membership in the League of Nations, the power to appoint diplomatic missions in foreign capitals, and the ability to sign treaties with foreign governments without an additional signature from the British ambassador —the first instance was the Halibut Treaty with the United States in 1923—all signaled the weakening of the old imperial ties. North Americanism, in this connection, was part of the search for a new identity; more importantly, however, it was a recognition of the importance of Canada's ties with the United States in the development of Canada itself.

Canada's most important trading partner, despite the protective tariffs on both sides of the border, was the United States. As Professor Brebner once noted, "Common sense and real dependence . . . triumphed substantially over the ex-

29. See John Bartlett Brebner, "Canada, the Anglo-Japanese Alliance and the Washington Conference," *Political Science Quarterly* L (1935), 45–57; J. S. Galbraith, "The Imperial Conference of 1921 and the Washington Conference," *Canadian Historical Review* XXIX (1948), 143–52; and M. G. Fry, "The North Atlantic Triangle and the Abrogation of the Anglo-Japanese Alliance," *Journal of Modern History* XXXIX (1967), 46–64.

travagance of economic nationalism when it became apparent that Canadians would have some American products at almost any cost and Americans vice versa."[30] Ever since the adoption of the National Policy tariff of 1879, American investment in Canada had played a major role in the development of Canadian industry, and by 1926 the United States had replaced Great Britain as Canada's principal source of foreign capital.[31] Hundreds of thousands of American farmers had shared in the opening of the "last best West" at the turn of the century. Both before and after World War I they drew inspiration from, and gave inspiration to, their counterparts in the United States in the agrarian protest movements that swept across the Great Plains.

It was not surprising, then, that the similarity of Canadian and American interests was especially evident in the interwar years. Isolationism was a North American rather than an American attitude toward international affairs, as effectively pursued under Mackenzie King's doctrine of "Parliament will decide" as by any government in Washington.[32] The Canadian government even reexamined its own defense policy and declared, through the *Canadian Defence Quarterly* in 1924, that

> the history of the United States and Canada, the common civilization of the two countries, the intimacy of their economic and social ties, and the impossibility of making ade-

30. John Bartlett Brebner, *North Atlantic Triangle,* Carleton Library No. 30 (Toronto, 1966), p. 248.

31. See Hugh G. J. Aitken, "The Changing Structure of the Canadian Economy, with Particular Reference to the Influence of the United States," in Hugh G. J. Aitken *et al., The American Economic Impact on Canada* (Durham, N.C., 1959), pp. 3–35.

32. See James Eayrs, " 'A Low Dishonest Decade': Aspects of Canadian External Policy, 1931–1939," in Keenleyside, *The Growth of Canadian Policies in External Affairs,* pp. 59–80; and K. W. McNaught, "Canadian Foreign Policy and the Whig Interpretation: 1936–1939," in Canadian Historical Association, *Report of the Annual Meeting, 1957* (n.p., n.d.), pp. 43–54.

362   TWENTIETH-CENTURY AMERICAN FOREIGN POLICY

quate preparation for the defence of the border, all make war with the United States too remote a possibility for serious consideration.[33]

Canadian and American scholars pooled their resources to produce the mammoth "Canadian-American Relations" series of volumes, initiated by Canadian scholars in the United States and financed by the Carnegie Endowment for International Peace. A Canadian adviser to the project sounded the typical cliché of the era concerning Canadian-American relations: "Nowhere else in the world does there exist so peculiar a relationship as that between your country and Canada." [34]

But similarity of Canadian and American interests was not to be confused with identity of interests; North Americanism was an expression of Canadian nationalism, not continentalism; of Canada's growing confidence in herself as a separate nation on the North American continent. That was the point made by John W. Dafoe, editor of the Winnipeg *Free Press,* in his lectures at Columbia University in 1933, and later published under the revealing title *Canada an American Nation.*[35] That was also the point of the *Report of the Royal Commission on Broadcasting* (1929)—"Canadian radio listeners want Canadian broadcasting"—and the establishment of the CRBC (forerunner of the CBC) in 1932. Public broadcasting in Canada was essential to counter the influence of American programming. As Prime Minister Richard B. Bennett explained,

33. Quoted in James Eayrs, *In Defence of Canada,* 2 vols. (Toronto, 1964), I, 75.
34. Borden to James C. Shotwell, October 1, 1932, no. 147582–83, Post 1921 Series, Folder 51, Borden Papers. Equally typical of Canadians was Borden's next observation that "in each country, *but especially in the United States,* there is a lack of understanding with respect to the ideals, institutions and outlook of the other." (Italics added.)
35. Ramsay Cook, *The Politics of John W. Dafoe and the Free Press* (Toronto, 1963), pp. 289–90.

this country must be assured of complete Canadian control of broadcasting from Canadian sources, free from foreign interference or influence. Without such control radio broadcasting can never become a great agency for the communication of matters of national concern and for the diffusion of national thought and ideals, and without such control it can never be the agency by which national consciousness may be fostered and sustained and national unity still further strengthened.[36]

The immediate response of both Canada and the United States to the depression decade was to isolate themselves from each other. The Hawley-Smoot tariff in the United States was matched in Canada by Bennett's successful electoral campaign in 1930 with its promise to "blast" Canada's way into world markets with higher protective tariff rates. In 1932, at the Imperial Conference in Ottawa, Imperial Preferential Trade Agreements were signed by Great Britain and the dominions. These agreements, for Canada, placed even further restrictions upon Canadian-American trade (though they also further stimulated United States capital investment in Canada). Even so, the Canadian government refused to enter into fiscal or monetary agreements with its Commonwealth partners because Canada's commercial and credit relations with the United States were "more important" than corresponding ties with the Empire.[37]

By November, 1934, it was clear that protectionism was not working, and the Canadian government dropped, if ever so slightly, its policy of reciprocity of tariffs with the United States and edged toward a policy of reciprocity of trade. "The time has come for definite action," the Canadian minister in Washington wrote to Secretary of State Cordell Hull.

36. Canada, Parliament, *House of Commons Debates,* May 18, 1932, 3035.
37. Memorandums on "Monetary and Financial Questions, Recd for file Sept 20/32," no. 112587–607, Bennett Papers, P.A.C.

"The declared desire of both governments to improve conditions of trade between the two countries should now be carried into effect by the negotiation of a comprehensive trade agreement." [38] Immediately after the 1935 election, the new prime minister, Mackenzie King, traveled to Washington for talks with Hull and President Roosevelt and the signing of the Canadian-American reciprocity agreement.[39] Canada extended most-favored-nation treatment to the United States and reduced the duties on a number of American goods imported into Canada. The United States gave a number of Canadian natural products free entry and reduced the duties on many more, as well as placing Canadian imports on a most-favored-nation basis.

For Mackenzie King the 1935 trade agreement was something more than just the beginnings of lowering tariff barriers between Canada and the United States. It was true that substantial obstacles remained. Canada was still committed to the Imperial Preferential Agreements of 1932, which were of five years duration, and before further progress could be made, tripartite revisions between Canada and Great Britain and the United States would be necessary. But more than freer trade was at stake. For King, like Cordell Hull in Washington, multilateral freer trading relations was the essential condition for maintaining peace in an increasingly warminded world; in Hull's terms, freer trade was "the spear point of the approach to peace." The secretary of state regarded the 1935 agreement as the first chink in the armor of the Ottawa agreements of 1932, and he ceaselessly campaigned to get the British government itself to give up the restrictive and discriminatory agreements. Taking the op-

38. W. D. Herridge to Cordell Hull, November 14, 1934, in W. A. Riddell, ed., *Documents on Canadian Foreign Policy, 1917–1939* (Toronto, 1962), p. 633.

39. See Richard N. Kottman, "The Canadian-American Trade Agreement of 1935," *Journal of American History* LII (1965), 275–96.

portunity of having a like-minded colleague in Ottawa who had influence in London, Hull pressed King, in a conversation in March, 1937, to carry the gospel of freer trade to the forthcoming Imperial Conference. "I wanted action rather than a policy of waiting," he later wrote; "I knew that Mackenzie King would faithfully interpret to the British Government what I said." [40] A long discussion with the president later in the day followed similar if somewhat broader lines, Roosevelt also seeing peace being maintained by alleviating world economic rivalry and proposing a "Permanent Conference on Economic and Social Problems." [41]

The judgment of the Americans was correct; in King they found a ready and sympathetic interpreter. "The bringing together of hostile nations in round table conference," the prime minister wrote to Roosevelt,

> and gaining their acceptance of the principle of investigation before resort to hostilities, would, I believe, mark the dawn of a new era in the history of the world. It would give a fresh impetus to round table conference in industrial as well as international relations.
>
> Only the substitution of an enlightened public opinion as more fruitful of justice than an appeal to force, can save the world today from internal and international strife. [42]

King assured Hull that he was anxious to inform the Imperial Conference of the 1935 agreement and urge an Anglo-American agreement and Anglo-Canadian and further Canadian-American agreements along the same lines.

> I shall be greatly surprised if I do not find, in London, fairly general agreement that the most effective measures that

40. Cordell Hull, *Memoirs,* 2 vols. (New York, 1948), I, 528.
41. W. L. Mackenzie King to Franklin D. Roosevelt, March 8, 1937, King Papers, P.A.C.
42. King to Roosevelt, March 17, 1937, *ibid.*

nations can take for the preservation of peace lie in the field
of economic collaboration. . . .

   . . . I am hopeful, as I explained to Mr. Armour [United
States minister to Canada] in the course of a conversation,
in which he impressed me with the importance that you
and the Government of the United States attach to the attitude of the countries of the British Commonwealth in the
matter, that there will be an opportunity during the forthcoming Conference to explore the possibilities of more active
collaboration in the work for economic and international
peace.[43]

By 1938 the series of agreements between Canada, the
United States, and Great Britain had been signed further
reducing tariff barriers, and Mackenzie King was justifiably
proud of the important part he had played in their completion.

But the effort was both too little and too late. By 1938 it
was becoming clear that Canadian-American cooperation
to wage war would take priority over efforts to preserve
peace. In February the chiefs of staff of the two countries
met in Washington to discuss mutual defense of the Pacific
coast. In August, at Kingston, the president spoke of Canada
as "part of the sisterhood of the British Empire" and pledged
that "the people of the United States will not stand idly by
if domination of Canadian soil is threatened by any other
Empire." And three days later, at Woodbridge, King cited
Canada's "obligations as a good friendly neighbour" that
"should the occasion ever arise, enemy forces would not be
able to pursue their way, either by land, sea or air to the

   43. King to Hull, April 23, 1937, *ibid.* I am grateful to Professor Donald
Forster, executive assistant to the president, University of Toronto, and to
Professor H. Blair Neatby, the biographer of William Lyon Mackenzie King,
for allowing me to read the memorandums prepared by Professor Forster on
the trade agreements, 1937–1938, and for bringing to my attention the material cited in this and the two previous footnotes.

United States, across Canadian territory." In October the
president suggested cooperation in problems of defense
production to the prime minister. And in August, 1939, a
few days before the beginning of hostilities, Canadian officials, including the chairman of the Canadian Defence Production Board, were in Washington to confer about avoiding
as many problems as possible when the president was forced
to invoke the neutrality legislation of the United States.[44]

The cooperation between Canada and the United States
during World War II was unparalleled. From the beginning
of the war the chief concern was the defense of North America, and at Ogdensburg in October, 1940, the prime minister
and the president agreed to establish the Permanent Joint
Board on Defense to achieve that end. The work of the
Board resulted in the plans for American direction of Canadian forces in eastern Canada in the event of the collapse of
Britain and in the building of the Alaska highway by United
States armed forces using Canadian contractors and material. As in World War I, war production again caused a
serious balance-of-payments problem with the United States
for Canada. The Roosevelt-King Hyde Park Agreement of
April, 1941, provided an answer to the problem by establishing greater North American integration of defense production. The agreement was supplemented by numerous joint
committees charged to eliminate wasteful production and
to allocate resource use on a continental basis. Of great significance was the fact that neither agreement was regarded
by either party as a strictly wartime measure. The Joint
Board on Defense was "Permanent," and a directive to one
of the committees established under the 1941 agreement to
plan for "reducing the probable post-war economic disloca-

44. W. R. Riddell to King, August 28, 29, 1939, *ibid.*

tion consequent upon the changes which the economy in each country is presently undergoing" assumed continued economic cooperation after the war.[45]

At the beginning of the war Canada's role of interpreter between the United States and Great Britain was of great importance. As Mackenzie King put it during a visit to Roosevelt at Warm Springs in April, 1940: "Just now, with the world situation as it was, Ottawa was a very important centre even as between Britain and the United States. That much could be done there by conference in different ways that would be helpful in furthering mutual interests."[46] Within a month of the visit Hugh Keenleyside of the Department of External Affairs came to Washington, at Roosevelt's request, to hear of the president's concern over the possible loss of the British fleet to Germany and of his suggestion that, in the event of a British defeat, the fleet be moved to the dominions and the king reside in Bermuda, both pieces of information to be passed through Mackenzie King to Churchill.[47]

But as the role of the Permanent Joint Board on Defense declined after the entry of the United States into the war in favor of direct contact between respective staff officers, so too did King's "lynch-pin" function decline after personal contact between Churchill and Roosevelt was firmly established. Despite the crucial role King portrayed for himself in his diary at the time of the first Quebec Conference, for example, a more accurate picture was probably given in a later letter of recollection: "I was, as you recall, not so much

45. Edgar W. McInnis, *The Unguarded Frontier: A History of American-Canadian Relations* (New York, 1942), p. 363. See also Gerald M. Craig, *The United States and Canada* (Cambridge, Mass., 1968), chap. 15, and Stanley W. Dziuban, *Military Relations between the United States and Canada, 1939–1945* (Washington, 1959).

46. Diary, April 24, 1940, as in J. W. Pickersgill, *The Mackenzie King Record*, Vol. I, *1939–1944* (Toronto, 1960), p. 111.

47. *Ibid.*, pp. 117 ff.

a participant in any of the discussions as a sort of general host, whose task at the Citadel was similar to that of the General Manager of the Chateau Frontenac." [48]

Canada emerged from World War II as the world's fourth-ranking power and committed to a continuing active role in international affairs. She also emerged from the war more intimately linked to the United States than ever before in both military and economic terms. By 1945 American capital invested in Canada had risen to $4.99 billions, and the American capital commitment to postwar development would skyrocket to $20.48 billions by 1963.[49] It was just because of the influence of the United States upon Canada that Canada's own definition of her new role in international affairs as a "middle power" was so important to Canadians, suggesting, as it did, the nation's determination to pursue a course in international relations that would be at once in cooperation with the United States but decidedly independent of American domination. "Middlepowermanship" became elevated to the heady realms of ideology to guide the diplomats from External Affairs and found its most practical focus in unwavering Canadian support for, and commitment to, the United Nations.[50] From it followed the commitment of the third largest national force to the Korean War and what Canadians would come to regard as a role peculiarly suited to themselves, peacekeeping, most notably at the Gaza Strip and in Cyprus. From it also followed a continued and unprecedented Canadian military presence in Europe after the

48. King to Lord Moran, June 9, 1950, quoted in *Churchill: Taken from the Diaries of Lord Moran: The Struggle for Survival, 1940–1965* (Boston, 1966), p. 117 n. 3.

49. By contrast, British investment, expressed in millions of dollars, was 1,750 in 1945 and 3,331 in 1963. That from other countries was 352 in 1945 and 2,384 in 1963. See Craig, *The United States and Canada*, p. 354.

50. See Paul Painchaud, "Middlepowermanship As an Ideology," in J. King Gordon, ed., *Canada's Role As a Middle Power* (Toronto, 1966), pp. 29–35.

war through the multilateral North Atlantic Treaty Organization. "We in Canada," Prime Minister Louis St. Laurent explained to the House of Commons during the debate on the
NATO treaty,

> recognize that there is neither peace nor security for Canada
> if western Europe, quite as much as any part of this hemi-
> sphere, is in danger; but we feel that, by uniting our efforts,
> by making our peaceful intentions clear, by making our
> preparations serious, and by forcing the totalitarian rulers of
> the communist states to realize that we mean business, we
> are not contracting our strength but expanding it. We will
> create a situation which will enable us to speak in the only
> language they recognize, the only language they understand
> —the language that speaks from strength.[51]

Moreover, "middlepowermanship" meant a much more active participation in Commonwealth affairs than had been
the case before the war; it meant Canadian initiative to clear
the path of obstacles to the admission of new Asian and
African states to membership, and it meant the focusing of
Canadian foreign aid on the Colombo Plan. In sum, as historian William Kilbourn has observed, "middlepowermanship" for Canada

> was not so much a matter of her physical strength *vis à vis*
> the great powers—a relatively small quantity can hardly be
> compared to something like the absolute—but rather a mat-
> ter of function. There was a series of jobs to be done that no
> great power, especially one with an imperial past or present,
> could possibly perform.[52]

51. *House of Commons Debates,* March 29, 1949, 2064.
52. William Kilbourn, "The 1950s," in J. M. S. Careless and R. Craig
Brown, eds., *The Canadians, 1867–1967* (Toronto, 1967), p. 331. A less
favorable view of "middlepowermanship," pointing out the problems it
raises for Canadian military policy, has been made by James Eayrs: "I will
contend . . . that the main and overriding motive for the maintainence of
a Canadian military establishment since the Second World War has had little

But in the 1960s "middlepowermanship" appeared to many Canadians to be a decreasingly effective functional counterweight to American influence in Canadian military policy and in Canadian diplomacy. NATO's image became increasingly one of token "multilateralism" and real subservience to the United States. Similarly, the preponderance of American influence in North American defense was more and more apparent. In North America the wartime partnership for common defense, a Canadian general recalled, was continued upon American initiative and "expanded to include exchange of information in the fields of intelligence, weapons, research and development. Joint defence plans were prepared for the approval of the Chiefs of Staffs of both countries. Air defence was to be a joint effort." [53] The joint efforts took the form of the building of the various radar networks in the 1950s, the creation of NORAD in 1958 with a Canadian deputy commander at Colorado Springs, and, after the controversial 1963 election and the victory of Lester B. Pearson's Liberal party, the acceptance of nuclear warheads for Bomarc missiles in Canada and for Canadian army and air force units in Europe.

The placement of two Bomarc bases in eastern Canada and a defense production-sharing agreement with the United States were the main elements of the defense policy that the Diefenbaker government provided after its decision,

---

to do with our national security as such; that it has had everything to do with underpinning our diplomatic and negotiating positions vis a vis various international organizations and other countries. That what is required in the way of military expenditure and military equipment for the performance of this nonmilitary function is, to say the least, difficult to calculate. That, as a consequence, our military policies have been marked by uncertainty and disarray. That we have made grave mistakes in the past, are making grave mistakes right now [1965], and will probably be making grave mistakes ten years from now" (James Eayrs, "Military Policy and Middle Power: The Canadian Experience," Gordon, ed., *Canada's Role As a Middle Power*, p. 70).

53. Quoted in Jon B. McLin, *Canada's Changing Defence Policy, 1957–1963: The Problems of a Middle Power in Alliance* (Baltimore, 1967), p. 9.

in 1959, to scrap the Canadian-built CF 105 Arrow fighter. The Arrow had been the last Canadian attempt to produce wholly Canadian weapons. Henceforth, the government having decided that "the independent development of major military systems by Canada" was simply too expensive, the pretense of an independent role in defense production was given up. The defense industry in Canada thrived on American subcontracts, and the Canadian forces relied increasingly on American production of sophisticated military hardware.[54]

The reaction to the Arrow decision and the resultant further dependence upon the United States for defense of Canada was decidedly hostile. Clearly implied in these decisions was the suggestion that Canada had surrendered her "middle power" status to become a satellite of the United States. As the influential Toronto *Globe and Mail* put it,

> we may drift into a condition uncomfortably like that of certain Middle Eastern and Latin American countries which draw their entire supply of modern weapons from one of the Great Powers, and in consequence find themselves bound to support the policies of their armorer on pain of being suddenly left defenceless. A nation in that position may be independent in name, but it has no real independence in fact.[55]

That, indeed, was the message of the chief correspondent of the CBC in Washington, James Minifie, in his best-selling book *Peacemaker or Powder-Monkey,* in which he advocated Canadian withdrawal from NORAD and NATO. And there is no doubt that withdrawal from NORAD or NATO, or both, were acceptable alternatives to American dominance

---

54. James Eayrs, "Sharing a Continent: *The Hard Issues,*" in John Sloan Dickey, ed., *The United States and Canada* (Englewood Cliffs, N.J., 1964), p. 67, and McLin, *Canada's Changing Defence Policy,* pp. 60–84.

55. Quoted in McLin, *Canada's Changing Defence Policy,* p. 88.

in military and foreign policy for a growing number of Canadians.

There was, of course, another side to the argument over American influence in Canadian foreign policy. James Eayrs has pointed out that "a distinctive, if not the dominant ingredient in Canada's response to its unenviable positioning along the route to holocaust has been an irrational anger," adding that

> though much was done, much more might have been done. There was no invitation to the United States to treat the territory of northern North America as a possible home for whatever bombers or missiles its defence authorities might have wanted to base there; no offer of Canadian airfields as forward bases for United States interceptor aircraft; no *carte blanche* for S.A.C. overflights (the United States command deemed it expedient to route its aerial alert force around Canada rather than over it).[56]

Canadian concern over the preponderant influence of the United States was expressed over the whole compass of Canadian life during the 1950s and 1960s. A measure of the intensity of this concern was the number of Royal Commissions established by the Canadian government to study the problem and recommend policies to protect the Canadian identity. The reports of these bodies were sufficiently and perhaps predictably alarming enough to force at least a modicum of government action. The Royal Commission on the National Development in the Arts and Letters and Science, chaired by the former minister to the United States and later governor general, Vincent Massey, concluded that American culture was stifling Canadian creativity and compared the seriousness of the threat with military defense. In the realm of identity, cultural defense was equally impor-

56. Eayrs, "Sharing a Continent: *The Hard Issues*," pp. 62, 64.

tant; the Commission gravely noted that "the two cannot be separated." [57] The response to the Massey Commission was the establishment by the government of the Canada Council in 1957 to assist financially Canadian cultural endeavors, or to put it in less favorable light, to establish "cultural protectionism." [58] Similar concern was expressed by the Royal Commission on Broadcasting (1957), and the government replied by imposing minimum "Canadian content" regulations for both the Canadian Broadcasting Corporation and privately owned stations. Again, in 1961, the Royal Commission on Publications found that

> the tremendous expansion of communications in the United States has given that nation the world's most penetrating and effective apparatus for the transmission of ideas. Canada, more than any other country, is naked to that force, exposed unceasingly to a vast network of communications which reaches to every corner of our land; American words, images and print—the good, the bad, the indifferent—batter unrelentingly at our eyes and ears. [59]

And again the government answer was tax measures to encourage advertising revenue away from so-called Canadian editions and toward Canadian publications. (*Time* and *Reader's Digest*, the main objects of the Royal Commission's attack, were eventually exempted from these penalties.)

More important for Americans was the Report of the Royal Commission on Canada's Economic Prospects, chaired by Walter Gordon, at the end of the 1950s. It warned of the control the enormous postwar American capital investment

57. Craig, *The United States and Canada*, p. 301.

58. One Canadian author, Mordecai Richler, acidly remarked that the end product of such concern for Canadian culture would be the creation of literary figures "world famous in Canada and deservedly unknown just about everywhere else" (Gerald Clark, *Canada: The Uneasy Neighbor* [New York, 1965], p. 360).

59. Quoted in Eayrs, "Sharing a Continent: *The Hard Issues*," p. 89.

had purchased over Canadian industries and resources, of
the control of Canadian labor by American-based unions,
and of the inevitable loss of Canadian political independence if economic integration continued. In 1961 Mr. Gordon
carried on his campaign with the publication of his book
Troubled Canada. Two years later, as minister of finance, he
brought down his first budget, including proposals (later
withdrawn) to give tax benefits to Canadian companies that
increased the Canadian share of their ownership and to tax
by 30 percent the sale to foreigners of shares of Canadian
companies in excess of $50,000. Mr. Gordon resigned from
the cabinet in 1965 but was reinstated by Mr. Pearson two
years later and was responsible for the report "Foreign
Ownership and the Structure of Canadian Industry," published by the government in 1968. The report recognized the
benefits to Canadian development from foreign investment
but expressed concern "about the implications of foreign
control for Canada's long-run prospects for national independence and economic growth." It concluded with a plea
for "A New National Policy."

> The old National Policy served Canada in its day, as an
> instrument of nation-building and a means of facilitating
> economic growth. The challenges have changed and a new
> National Policy is required. The nation has been built, but
> its sovereignty must be protected and its independence main-
> tained. A diversified economy has been created, but its effi-
> ciency must be improved and its capacity for autonomous
> growth increased.[60]

The economic historian Harold Adams Innis regretfully
observed in 1948 that Canada had "moved from colony to

60. Canada, Privy Council Office, *Foreign Ownership and the Structure
of Canadian Industry: Report of the Task Force on the Structure of Canadian
Industry* (Ottawa, 1968), pp. 1, 415.

nation to colony." [61] That proposition is at the heart of the postwar Canadian debate over Canada's role in North America. Evidence has been, is, and will continue to be marshaled in the press, the universities, and Parliament, from Canadian history and cultural life, from contemporary economic and foreign policy, to prove or disprove the last two words of the proposition. What is undisputed is the recognition by Canadians of the enormous influence of the United States, its life-style and the policies of its government, upon Canada. What is disputed, and long will be, is what can or should be done about it. Perhaps the last word in this brief survey of Canadian-American relations in the twentieth century should go to a Canadian scholar who rejected Innis's judgment and the emotionalism surrounding it and made a plea for realistic assessment of the Canadian-American relationship. If that relationship, James Eayrs told the American Assembly in 1964,

> is to flourish to the mutual benefit of its partners, it will be because statesmen of both countries resist the temptation, to which they have yielded in the past, of believing their politics to be neighbourly rather than international. They must realize that the two nations of North America are of the states-system, not beyond and above it, and shape their policies accordingly. President Johnson, with the best intentions in the world, observed in his first official reference to the Canadian-American relationship that "Canada is such a close neighbor and such a good neighbor that we always have plenty of problems there. They are kind of like problems in the hometown." They are kind of not like that at all. They are the problems not of neighbours but of friendly foreign powers.
>
> What is really required is a certain reserve, a sense of live and let live, even of aloofness on occasion, in the treatment

61. Harold Adams Innis, "Great Britain, the United States and Canada," in *Essays in Canadian Economic History* (Toronto, 1956), p. 405.

of the smaller country by the larger. "Good fences," American leaders are fond of quoting on their Canadian visits, "make good neighbors." They could usefully remember that good neighbours make good fences.[62]

62. Eayrs, "Sharing a Continent: *The Hard Issues,*" pp. 93–94.

Recent United States–Mexican Relations: Problems Old and New

LYLE C. BROWN
JAMES W. WILKIE

DURING the past century and a half, relations between the United States and Mexico have featured periods of harmony and times of conflict.[1] Although the United States welcomed Mexico's independence from Spain and received the first Mexican diplomat in 1822, many Americans coveted Texas and other territories to the south and west. The struggle by English-speaking Texans for independence and the subsequent annexation of Texas by the United States in 1845 resulted in the Mexican War of 1846–48. As a result of Mexico's defeat, the Treaty of Guadalupe Hidalgo conferred upon the victor more than half of Mexico's territory; thus Upper California and New Mexico, along with Texas, were brought within the United States.

Although the United States was prepared to encroach upon the sovereignty of her southern neighbor, similar ac-

1. For detailed accounts of United States–Mexican relations, see J. Lloyd Mecham, *A Survey of United States–Latin American Relations* (Boston, 1965), pp. 342–81; and two works by Howard F. Cline: *The United States and Mexico*, rev. ed. (New York, 1963) and *Mexico, Revolution to Evolution: 1940–1960* (New York, 1963).

tion by another power was not to be allowed. When French forces entered Mexico in 1861, strong protests were made by the Lincoln administration; however, preoccupation with the Civil War prevented effective action against France. With the end of that war, United States pressure was exerted; and in the spring of 1867 the last French troops sailed from Veracruz, leaving Emperor Maximilian to be captured and executed by the regime of President Benito Juárez.

In the years that followed, border incidents involving raids on United States territory by lawless Mexican elements created minor problems that marred relations between the two countries. But during the thirty-five years that General Porfirio Díaz dominated Mexico (1876–1911), outlaws were suppressed and the International Boundary Commission was established to deal with problems caused by the shifting course of the Rio Grande. Under Díaz, Mexico became a magnet for foreign capital; and United States citizens invested millions of dollars in Mexican land, railroads, oil, and mines. By 1910 most of Mexico's land, industry, and commerce was in the hands of foreign investors and a relatively few wealthy Mexicans.

With the outbreak of the Revolution of 1910 and the overthrow of Díaz in the following year, United States–Mexican relations entered a troubled decade that culminated in the United States naval bombardment and occupation of Veracruz and General John J. Pershing's punitive expedition into northern Mexico in pursuit of Pancho Villa. During the 1920s civil strife declined in Mexico, but application of provisions of the Constitution of 1917 adversely affected the interests of American landowners and oil men in that country. Meanwhile, American presidents granted or withheld recognition of Mexican governments as a means of seeking protection for the lives and properties of United States citizens in Mexico. During the Cristero Rebellion (1926–29) many

Americans called for intervention to protect the Catholic church against repressive policies of the Mexican government. Ambassador Dwight W. Morrow played a leading role in terminating that religious conflict and in causing the Mexican government to adopt a more conciliatory attitude toward United States interests, but the election of President Lázaro Cárdenas in 1934 led to new difficulties.

Cárdenas launched a sweeping land reform program that divested many United States citizens of their rural estates, and his support of militant labor unions resulted in strikes that were costly for American business interests. A labor dispute in the petroleum industry finally provoked expropriation of foreign-owned oil properties in March, 1938. This action caused powerful business groups to demand United States intervention, but President Franklin D. Roosevelt was more concerned about promotion of the Good Neighbor policy than protection of his country's oil companies. Subsequently, war clouds gathered in Europe; and in 1940 Mexican voters elected President Manuel Avila Camacho. Under the new president the Mexican government toned down the revolutionary zeal that had inspired policies detrimental to United States interests; also, Mexico entered World War II against the Axis powers and supplied vital raw materials and agricultural laborers to support the United States war effort. During the war American investors became interested in manufacturing opportunities south of the Rio Grande; at the same time the United States government began providing financial assistance for the purpose of speeding Mexico's industrial development.

Because post–World War II problems have been rooted in the international politics of the past, it is against this historical background that United States–Mexican relations since 1945 must be analyzed. In surveying significant developments in the relations of these two nations over the past quarter of a century, attention has been focused on a variety of problems. Some are old, and some are new: disease and insects harmful to livestock, control and protection of alien contract labor, long-standing arbitration controversies, salinity of international rivers, fishing rights in coastal waters, interventionism in the Americas, and means of financing economic development. Some of these problems have been resolved fully; others have been resolved in part; still others remain unresolved and constitute challenges to the presidents and lawmakers, to the businessmen and diplomats, and to the concerned citizens of both countries. In general, it is apparent that a spirit of compromise and cooperation has prevailed in United States–Mexican relations during the post–World War II era. This contrasts sharply with the pattern of crisis and conflict in earlier decades. The objectives of this study are to determine how and why such a transformation has come to pass.

Foot-and-mouth Disease and the Screwworm Fly

Although not as dramatic as international problems involving recognition policy or charges of "imperialism," threats of disease to the livestock herds of the United States and Mexico have prompted cooperation that has become increasingly characteristic of relations between these two nations since World War II. Through joint efforts over a period of seven years, an outbreak of foot-and-mouth disease (or *aftosa*, as it is known in Mexico) was checked and then eradicated; more recently the Mexican government has cooperated to a limited extent with American efforts to free this country of screwworm flies and to make possible the eradication of the harmful insect from Mexican territory as well.

Although mainly a disease of cattle and swine, foot-and-mouth disease affects all cloven-footed animals. Prior to 1930 both the United States and Mexico suffered repeated costly outbreaks of the disease.[2] In that year a convention, signed by representatives of the two countries, became effective. It committed the United States and Mexican governments to take precautions against importation of "domestic ruminants or swine" under conditions involving a risk of introducing animals infected with foot-and-mouth disease or rinderpest.[3] For a period of sixteen years no outbreaks of the former occurred in either country. Then in 1946, despite American protests, Mexico permitted the landing of two shipments of Zebu bulls from Brazil. The United States reaction was to close its borders to importation of all cloven-footed animals from Mexico. Later, when a survey by United States Department of Agriculture personnel revealed no evidence of foot-and-mouth disease in areas where the Brazilian cattle were located, the quarantine was lifted. In December, 1946, an outbreak of the disease was confirmed in the State of Veracruz; consequently, the quarantine was reimposed. The fact that the controversial Zebu bulls had been brought to the area where this outbreak occurred provided strong circumstantial evidence that earlier protests by United State authorities had been fully justified.[4]

Mexican efforts to check the spread of foot-and-mouth

2. See U.S. Department of Agriculture, Agricultural Research Service, Animal Health Division, *Foot-and-Mouth Disease . . . A Menace to North American Livestock*, ARS-91–58 (Hyattsville, Md., 1967), pp. 4–6.

3. U.S. Department of State, *Convention between the United States and Mexico: Safeguarding Livestock Interests through the Prevention of Infectious and Contagious Diseases*, Treaty Series No. 808 (Washington, 1930).

4. See Early B. Shaw, "Mexico's Foot-and-Mouth Disease Problem," *Economic Geography* XXV (1949), 1–3; John A. Hopkins, "The Joint Campaign against Foot-and-Mouth Disease in Mexico," *U.S. Department of State Bulletin* XVI (1947), 711; and Guillermo Quesada Bravo, *La Verdad Sobre el Ganado Cebú Brasileño, y la Cuarentena en la Isla de Sacrificios, Veracruz* (Mexico, D.F., 1946), *passim*.

disease were to no avail; thus United States assistance was requested. Realizing that neither charges against Mexico of convention violation nor quarantine efforts at the border would protect American livestock from the northward-advancing plague, Washington responded positively to the request for aid. Signed by President Truman on February 28, 1947, Public Law 80–8 authorized the Department of Agriculture to cooperate with Mexican authorities for the purpose of eradicating foot-and-mouth disease from that country.[5] This prompt response could be cited as an example of the Good Neighbor policy in action, but it was dictated as much by the interests of the United States as by the needs of Mexico.

Directed by the Mexican–United States Commission for the Eradication of Foot-and-Mouth Disease, an intensive campaign was waged to free Mexico from the disease through slaughter of all infected or exposed cattle, sheep, goats, and swine. Finally, after some incidents involving armed violence by angry owners of condemned livestock, the Commission agreed to discontinue the slaughter method alone and to carry out a program combining quarantine, vaccination, and, "when necessary," slaughter. Subsequently, an effective vaccine was developed; and by December, 1954, authorities of both countries were convinced that Mexico was definitely free from foot-and-mouth disease.[6]

During the 1947–54 period, United States expenditures in combatting this threat to its multibillion-dollar livestock in-

5. See *Congressional Record*, 80th Cong., 1st Sess. (1947), 1070–72, 1305–19, 1345–46; and *U.S. Department of State Bulletin* XVI (1947), 454.
6. For a scholarly account of the Commission's work, see Manuel A. Machado, Jr., *An Industry in Crisis: Mexican–United States Cooperation in the Control of Foot-and-Mouth Disease* (Berkeley and Los Angeles, 1968). For informal descriptions of experiences by United States personnel, see Fred Gipson and Bill Leftwich, *The "Cow Killers": With the Aftosa Commission in Mexico* (Austin, Tex., 1956); and James A. Porter, *Doctor, Spare My Cow* (Ames, Iowa, 1956).

dustry amounted to $136 million. Mexico's direct expenditures were lower, but the Mexican government supplied the indispensable services of large numbers of military and civilian personnel.[7] Since 1954 there has been no recurrence of foot-and-mouth disease in either country; and the Commission for the Eradication of Foot-and-Mouth Disease has been converted into the Commission for the Prevention of Foot-and-Mouth Disease. In addition to its preventive responsibility, the Commission is currently involved in research and planning activities that promise to lead to eradication of yet another threat to livestock herds of both countries: the screwworm fly.

A female screwworm fly lays her eggs at the edges of wounds of warmblooded animals or of people. When the eggs hatch, tiny white worms enter the wound and feed on live flesh. An untreated infestation usually results in death for animals and even for humans. Research by United States Department of Agriculture scientists has resulted in development of a technique whereby man-reared sterile flies are produced from pupae exposed to cobalt-60 radiation; when released, sterile male flies mate with fertile females, which then lay infertile eggs. Since the female screwworm fly mates only once, continued release of large numbers of sterile flies can free an area of this insect within a few months. In this manner United States territory east of the Mississippi River was cleared of the screwworm in 1958–59 at a cost of slightly more than $10 million.[8]

Because the screwworm fly is capable of traveling nearly two hundred miles, and perhaps farther, and since this in-

7. See Edward G. Miller, Jr., "Achievements of Inter-American Cooperation," *U.S. Department of State Bulletin* XXVII (1952), 703; and U.S. Department of Agriculture, *Foot-and-Mouth Disease*, p. 8.

8. See Edward F. Knipling, "The Eradication of the Screw-worm Fly," *Scientific American* CCIII (1960), 54–61.

sect is no respecter of international boundaries, permanent eradication of the pest in the Southwest is dependent on eradication in Mexico also. Beginning in 1962, with the consent of Mexican authorities, sterile flies have been air-dropped by American planes in northern Mexico so as to create a sterile-fly barrier.[9] But recognizing the fact that an extension of the barrier farther southward would be even more advantageous to livestock raisers of both countries, the United States Congress in 1966 amended Public Law 80–8 to authorize the Department of Agriculture to cooperate with the Mexican government in carrying out screwworm eradication measures throughout Mexico. It was expected that such cooperation would be conducted on a cost-sharing basis and that the expense of establishing a barrier at the Isthmus of Tehuantepec or at the Guatemalan border would be much less than the $5 million per year that the United States spends in maintaining the present barrier in northern Mexico.[10] As he signed the measure on July 27, 1966, President Johnson described it as "another example of the spirit of cooperation and warm friendship which exists between the people of Mexico and the United States."[11] To date, however, arrangements have not been made for implementing a jointly financed eradication program. Meanwhile, some Mexican flies succeed in penetrating the existing barrier. As a result, stockmen in the Southwest continue to suffer animal losses from sporadic outbreaks of screwworm infestation; and in 1968 a resident of San Antonio, Texas, died from

9. U.S. Department of Agriculture, Agricultural Research Service, *Facts about the Screwworm Barrier Program*, ARS 91–64 (Hyattsville, Md., 1967), pp. 7–8.

10. For example, see U.S. Congress, Senate, *Eradication of Screwworms in Mexico*, Hearing before a Subcommittee of the Committee on Agriculture and Forestry of the United States Senate on S. 3325 and H.R. 14888, 89th Cong., 2d Sess. (June 23, 1966), *passim*.

11. *U.S. Department of State Bulletin* LV (1966), 232.

this cause.[12] Thus the screwworm fly problem has been resolved only in part; however, one agricultural problem that
once provoked heated controversy was laid to rest at the
end of 1964. This was the contract farm labor problem.

Farm Labor

From the days of World War II until the mid-1960s, millions of Mexican citizens came to the United States to perform farm labor in border states from Texas to California
and, to a lesser extent, in other agricultural areas of the country. Those who crossed the border illegally, sometimes
swimming or wading the Rio Grande, were called "wetbacks"; *braceros* entered the United States legally as contract laborers. Related problems of halting the stream of
wetbacks and of guaranteeing equitable treatment for
braceros figured prominently in United States–Mexican relations for over two decades.

According to the terms of notes exchanged on August 4,
1942, it was agreed that the United States government would
serve as the primary contractor for bracero labor. This meant
that a contract would be signed by the worker and a representative of the Farm Security Administration, with supervision by the Mexican government. American farmers, in turn,
were required to subcontract with the Farm Security Administration for workers to fill their particular labor needs.
Mexican officials were convinced that such an arrangement
would best protect the braceros from unfair treatment.[13] In

12. See "Bleak Outlook for Screwworm Program," *Farm Journal*, Febru-
ary, 1969, p. 42; "Screwworm Situation Described Critical," *Sheep and Goat
Raiser*, September, 1968, pp. 10–11; and Mary K. Mahoney, "Screwworm
Buildup Critical," *Cattleman*, October, 1968, pp. 23, 186.

13. Otey M. Scruggs, "Evolution of the Mexican Farm Labor Agreement
of 1942," *Agricultural History* XXXIV (1960), 147–49.

view of widespread social discrimination against Mexicans in Texas, the Mexican government refused to allow the recruitment of braceros for employment in that state. Nevertheless, desperate wetbacks crossed the Rio Grande in large numbers, and the United States authorities made only limited efforts to deny Texas employers the labor supply that was deemed necessary. At the end of 1947 the United States government ceased to contract for braceros; and although arrangements were made for continuation of the bracero program, contracting was carried out directly between braceros and farmers or farm associations, with contract supervision entirely in the hands of the Mexican authorities.[14]

Unsatisfied with arrangements for bracero contracting and with the failure of United States authorities to curb employment of wetbacks, the Mexican government early in 1951 called for a review of the farm labor problem. In view of the American labor shortage caused by the Korean conflict, Mexico was in a strong bargaining position.[15] During discussions held in Mexico City from January 26 to February 3, Mexican officials insisted that the contracting of braceros should be carried out by a United States government agency, as had been the case between 1942 and 1947. Department of State representatives agreed to this demand;[16] and in June the United States Congress enacted Public Law 78, which authorized the secretary of labor to recruit braceros, operate

14. For a candid account of exploitation of wetback labor in Texas, see John McBride, *Vanishing Bracero: Valley Revolution* (San Antonio, 1963); also see two articles by Otey M. Scruggs: "The United States, Mexico, and the Wetbacks, 1942–1947," *Pacific Historical Review* XXX (1961), 149–64, and "Texas and the Bracero Program, 1942–1947," *ibid.*, XXXII (1963), 251–64.

15. *U.S. Department of State Bulletin* XXIV (1951), 188. For a summary of United States–Mexican farm labor agreements between 1947 and 1951, see George O. Coalson, "Mexican Contract Labor in American Agriculture," *Southwestern Social Science Quarterly* XXXIII (1952), 231–35.

16. *U.S. Department of State Bulletin* XXIV (1951), 300.

reception centers, provide for transportation from the recruitment centers in Mexico to the reception centers, provide subsistence and medical care during transportation and while at reception centers, assist braceros and their employers in negotiating contracts, and guarantee fulfillment of contract terms by employers.[17]

Following enactment of Public Law 78, diplomatic notes were exchanged on August 11, 1951, putting into effect a new Migrant Labor Agreement.[18] Periodically amended and extended, this agreement served as the basis for the bracero program until the expiration of Public Law 78 at the end of 1964. During the intervening thirteen years the Mexican government pressed for higher wages and greater protection for braceros, but within Mexico some employers insisted that they were adversely affected by the labor drain that the bracero program produced. Other protests came from elements whose national pride was wounded by the spectacle of their countrymen traveling long distances to another country in search of better employment opportunities than could be found at home.[19] In view of the unemployment problem prevailing in many areas of rural Mexico, and appreciating the fact that braceros returned with badly needed dollars that could be used to pay for imports from the United States, the Mexican government saw more good than evil in the program.[20] Within the United States, however, labor unions and other social action groups charged that Mexican contract labor had the effect of holding wages for farm la-

17. See *Congressional Record*, 82d Cong., 1st Sess. (1951), 7519-26, 7538-42.

18. *U.S. Department of State Bulletin* XXV (1951), 336.

19. See S. W. Coombs, "Bracero's Journey," *Americas* XV (1963), 7-11.

20. For a study of the impact of the bracero program on a Mexican state that supplied a large number of contract laborers, see Richard H. Hancock, *The Role of the Bracero in the Economic and Cultural Dynamics of Mexico: A Case Study of Chihuahua* (Stanford, Calif., 1959).

borers at low levels and of displacing native workers who could not compete with cheap foreign labor.[21]

When the House of Representatives voted on May 29, 1963, to reject a bill authorizing extension of the bracero agreement due to expire at the end of that year, Ambassador Antonio Carrillo Flores addressed a note to Secretary of State Dean Rusk in which he argued that termination of the bracero program would result in illegal but unavoidable employment of wetbacks. At the same time, he denied that utilization of braceros by some American employers had a harmful effect on employment opportunities for native workers. Perhaps of greatest significance, however, was the ambassador's expressed concern for the impact that termination of the bracero program would have on Mexico's employment situation.[22]

Although the House of Representatives reversed its action and extended Public Law 78 for another year, with the end of 1964 the bracero program was terminated.[23] Thus some United States farmers, who for over twenty years had depended on foreign labor to harvest their crops, were faced with the necessity of offering wages that would attract American citizens to the fields or of investing in new machinery that would replace hand labor. At the same time, thousands of Mexican farm laborers were forced to seek other types of employment.[24] In a sense the bracero program had served as an escape valve for Mexico's rapidly growing

21. For example, see Ruth Graves, "Research Summary on Effects of the Bracero Program," report submitted to the Texas Committee on Migrant Farm Workers, Austin, Texas, January 11, 1961.

22. Dated June 21, 1963, the letter was first made public by Senator J. William Fulbright during the course of debate over extension of Public Law 78. See Congressional Record, 88th Cong., 1st Sess. (1965), 23172–73.

23. Ibid., p. 23223.

24. For statements concerning problems of adjustment resulting from termination of the bracero program, see ibid., 89th Cong., 1st Sess. (1965), 4472–84.

rural population; with the expiration of Public Law 78 this escape valve was closed. By its failure to extend Public Law 78, the United States government unilaterally liquidated the contract farm labor problem. This was a simple solution to a complex problem that involved Mexican national pride as well as economic interests. But if Mexico suffered economically as a result of the loss of dollars previously earned by braceros, in the future the proud nation would be spared the indignity of seeing tens of thousands of her best workers trek northward periodically in search of higher-paying employment on foreign soil.

El Chamizal and the Pious Fund

Also affecting Mexican national pride were two unsettled arbitration cases that had been subjects of widespread concern in Mexico for several decades, although most citizens of the United States were completely unaware of the disputes. Both cases had their origins in events that transpired over one hundred years ago, and both cases involved arbitration awards handed down in the early years of the twentieth century.

Under the terms of the Treaty of Guadalupe Hidalgo (1848) and the Gadsden Treaty (1853), the international boundary was established along the deepest channel of the Rio Grande; but subsequent to the Emory-Salazar survey of the 1852–53, the river moved southward at El Paso until some 600 acres of former Mexican territory known as the Chamizal tract had been added to the north bank. In 1895 the Mexican government placed before the International Boundary Commission the case of a Mexican citizen who claimed ownership of Chamizal land. When the commissioners failed to agree as to whether the river's movement

had involved accretion (slow erosion resulting in loss of title
to the disputed Mexican territory and a change in location
of the international boundary) or avulsion (sudden shift in
the river channel that would affect neither property ownership nor boundary location), they recommended that a neutral commissioner should be appointed to act as an arbiter.[25]
Subsequently, in 1910 an arrangement was made for the
Honorable Eugene Lafleur, a Canadian jurist, to sit with the
commissioners. When the case was heard in 1911, Lafleur
ruled that the disputed Chamizal area should be divided between Mexico and the United States along the boundary
that had been marked by the river's deepest channel in 1864.
Insisting that the 1864 boundary could not be located and
that the Commission must determine whether title to the
whole Chamizal tract was held by the United States or by
Mexico, United States Commissioner Anson Mills refused to
accept the ruling and was supported in this action by the
Department of State.[26]

In the half-century that followed, repeated attempts were
made to achieve a diplomatic settlement of the Chamizal
dispute.[27] Few American citizens were aware of the unresolved problem; but within Mexico the matter was the subject of continued public discussion and was greatly exploited
by anti–United States elements who appealed to Mexican
nationalist sentiment.[28] Then in June, 1962, President John

25. See U.S. Department of State, *Proceedings of the International
(Water) Boundary Commission, United States and Mexico. Treaties of
1884 and 1888. Equitable Distribution of the Waters of the Rio Grande* 2
vols. (Washington, 1903), I, 42–100.

26. For documents concerning the arbitration proceeding, see U.S. State
Department. *Foreign Relations of the United States, 1911* (Washington,
1918), pp. 287–99.

27. For detailed coverage of the Chamizal case from its origin, see Gladys
Gregory, "The Chamizal Settlement: A View from El Paso," *Southwestern
Studies* I (1963), 5–38; and Sheldon Liss, *A Century of Disagreement: The
Chamizal Conflict, 1864–1964* (Washington, 1965).

28. For example, see Mario Gil, *Nuestros Buenos Vecinos* (Mexico, D.F.,
1957), pp. 135–39.

F. Kennedy visited Mexico and conferred with President Adolfo López Mateos on various matters, including the Chamizal controversy. As a result, in a communiqué issued on June 30, they announced that instructions had been given to United States and Mexican officials "to recommend a complete solution to this problem." [29] Over a year later, on August 29, 1963, United States Ambassador Thomas C. Mann and Mexican Foreign Minister Manuel Tello signed in Mexico City a convention providing for relocation of the river channel so as to satisfy, for the most part, Mexico's claim. [30] By a vote of 79 to 1 the convention was approved by the United States Senate on December 17, 1963. [31] Then four years later, on October 28, 1967, Presidents Lyndon B. Johnson and Gustavo Díaz Ordaz traveled to Ciudad Juárez, where they participated in public ceremonies officially recognizing the boundary change and where they jointly declared, "We thus lay to rest a century-old dispute." [32]

For most American citizens, this resolution of an old problem passed almost without notice. The war in Vietnam, the approaching presidential election of 1968, and other more pressing matters held their attention. In Mexico, however, the boundary change was treated as a matter of the greatest national importance. Although probably few Mexicans had a factual understanding of the legal aspects of the arbitration question, there was a conviction that Mexico's cause was just and that a major diplomatic victory had been scored over a more powerful neighbor. [33] From the standpoint of the United States government, the loss of a few acres of territory and the expenditure of a few million dollars required

29. U.S. *Department of State Bulletin* XLVII (1962), 137.

30. See U.S. Department of State, *United States Treaties and Other International Agreements*, XV, Part 1 (1964), 21–36.

31. See *Congressional Record*, 88th Cong., 1st Sess. (1963), 24850–73.

32. U.S. *Department of State Bulletin* LVII (1967), 684.

33. For examples of the extensive press coverage given to the Chamizal settlement, see *Hispano-Americano*, November 6, 1967, pp. 3–34; and *El Día*, October 29, 1967.

for relocation of the boundary constituted a small price to be paid for removal of a source of irritation that for so many years had affected adversely relations with one of Latin America's leading states.

Even before the formal boundary change, announcement of a diplomatic settlement of the Pious Fund claim gave evidence of the beneficial influence of the Chamizal agreement on attempts to resolve another long-standing problem. The Pious Fund had its origin in gifts entrusted to the Society of Jesus for the purpose of spreading Catholicism in Upper and Lower California. With the expulsion of the Jesuits in 1767, the Spanish crown took over administration of the fund; and after the termination of Spanish rule, the Mexican government continued to administer it. In 1842 President Santa Anna directed that Pious Fund properties should be sold and that the money obtained thereby should be placed in the national treasury; an annual interest of 6 percent was to be paid by the government in support of missionary activities in the Californias.

After Upper California became part of the United States under the terms of the Treaty of Guadalupe Hidalgo, the Mexican government refused to give the bishop of Monterey and the archbishop of San Francisco any further share of interest derived from the fund. On behalf of the two California prelates, the United States government sought a settlement before the United States–Mexican Claims Commission. Eventually payment was obtained of annuities due during the 1848–69 period. Then in 1902 a five-member Hague tribunal directed the Mexican government to make payments to cover unpaid annuities from 1869 to 1902; also, that tribunal declared that Mexico was obligated to pay perpetually an annuity of 43,050.99 pesos. Payments ceased with the overthrow of the conservative regime of General Victoriano Huerta in 1914; and during the half-century that followed, American diplomats failed in their attempts to obtain resumption of Pious Fund payments for the benefit of the Catholic church.[34]

In response to a United States note of December 4, 1964, discussions on the Pious Fund problem were renewed; and in April, 1966, a payment of 43,050.99 pesos was made as a token of good will. Then on August 1, 1967, a final settlement was effected through an exchange of notes in Mexico City. Under the terms of this settlement, Mexico agreed to pay the peso equivalent of $662,099 to cover annuities that had accrued since 1914. The exchange rate of Mexico's peso in terms of United States dollars in effect on each annuity date was taken into account in arriving at this total. Also, in order to relieve itself of the obligation to pay future annuities, Mexico agreed to make a lump sum payment, equivalent to $57,447. As explained in the Mexican note, "This amount has been determined by taking into account the fact that, at 6 percent per year, it would produce an annuity equal to the one fixed by the arbitral award of October 14, 1902." [35] Thus another arbitral case was finally disposed of; and, whereas the Chamizal settlement had been more favorable to Mexico, the Pious Fund settlement satisfied an American claim. Without doubt, the latter could not have been obtained had the United States not agreed to the former at an earlier date.

Rio Grande and Colorado River Waters

While negotiations concerning the arbitration cases were being conducted, United States and Mexican diplomats

34. See "The Pious Fund Case between Mexico and the United States" in James Brown Scott, ed., *The Hague Court Reports* (New York, 1916), pp. 1–54; and Francis J. Weber, "The Pious Fund of the Californias," *Hispanic American Historical Review* XLII (1963), 78–94.

35. U.S. Department of State, *Settlement of the Pious Fund Claim*, TIAS 6420 (Washington, 1968), p. 5.

were confronted with two new and related problems: increasing salinity of the Rio Grande and the Colorado River. This development brought heavy financial losses to certain farmers utilizing the waters of these international streams for irrigation purposes; consequently, agricultural interests demanded remedial action, which required new programs involving United States–Mexican cooperation.

With headwaters in the snow-fed streams of Wyoming and Colorado, the Colorado River winds in a southwesterly direction through 1,300 miles of United States territory, then forms the United States–Mexican boundary for eighteen miles, and finally cuts through Mexico for 100 miles before emptying into the Gulf of California. Rising in the state of Colorado, the Rio Grande flows southward, bisecting New Mexico; then for a distance of 1,200 miles, from El Paso to Brownsville, it separates Texas from northern Mexico before reaching the Gulf of Mexico. Both international streams traverse arid regions with millions of acres of fertile lands capable of producing abundant crops if properly irrigated. When the present United States–Mexican boundary was outlined by the treaties of 1848 and 1853, this border area was sparsely populated; but in later years, as population increased on both sides of the boundary and as irrigation projects were developed along the two rivers, disputes arose over division of limited water supplies.

Allocation of Upper Rio Grande water was arranged under the terms of a 1906 treaty, but repeated attempts to reach agreement on division of Lower Rio Grande and Colorado River waters were unsuccessful.[36] Finally, after lengthy formal negotiations begun in 1943, the Mexican Wa-

36. See Charles A. Timm, *The International Boundary Commission, United States and Mexico* (Austin, 1941), pp. 175 ff.; and Norris Hundley, Jr., *Dividing the Waters: A Century of Controversy Between the United States and Mexico* (Berkeley and Los Angeles, 1966), pp. 17–96.

ter Treaty was signed in 1944 and duly proclaimed by the presidents of both countries in November, 1945. Article 10 guarantees annual delivery to Mexico of 1,500,000 acre-feet of Colorado River water "from any and all sources." [37] Quality of irrigation water is as important as quantity; thus it is not surprising that later this provision was to become the subject of troublesome dispute.

Within sixteen years the Mexican government was complaining about the high degree of salinity of the Colorado River water received. In part this was due to decreased precipitation in the Rocky Mountain region and to increased American usage of Colorado River waters; but the principal cause was construction of the Wellton-Mohawk drainage channel to carry highly saline ground water pumped from Arizona farmland along the Gila River. Channeled for a distance of fifty miles to a point near the junction of the Gila and Colorado rivers, the Wellton-Mohawk drainage caused the Colorado River to reach a salt content of 2,700 parts per 1,000,000 parts of water during the last months of 1961. Since such water was unsuitable for irrigation purposes, Mexican farmers in the Mexicali area of Baja California refused to accept delivery; and the Mexican government protested to Washington concerning resulting crop losses. [38]

A Department of State press release dated December 21, 1961, took the legalistic position: "The United States considers that it is fully complying with its obligations under

37. For authoritative analyses of the treaty, see Charles A. Timm, "Water Treaty between the United States and Mexico," *U.S. Department of State Bulletin* X (1944), 282–92; Charles J. Meyers and Richard L. Noble, "The Colorado River: The Treaty with Mexico," *Stanford Law Review* XIX (1967), 367–419; and Roberto Cruz Miramontes, "La Doctrina Harmon, el Tratado de Aguas de 1944 y Algunos Problemas Derivados de su Aplicación," *Foro Internacional* VI (1965–66), 49–120.

38. See Norris Hundley, Jr., "The Colorado Waters Dispute," *Foreign Affairs* XLII (1963–64), 495–500; Hundley, *Dividing the Waters*, pp. 172–75; and Don C. Piper, "A Justiciable Controversy Concerning Water Rights," *American Journal of International Law* LVI (1962), 1019–22.

the treaty, which placed no obligation on the United States to deliver any specified quality of water." Nevertheless, the State Department announced eight days later that "both Governments . . . will enter at once into intensive discussions seeking to resolve all questions at issue and to explore every possibility of removing the basic problem for the future." [39] Later, on March 16, Presidents Kennedy and López Mateos released similar statements concerning the urgent need for a satisfactory solution to the salinity problem. They revealed that United States and Mexican members of the International Boundary and Water Commission had been given forty-five days in which to formulate recommendations concerning remedial measures that should be taken. Qualified soil and water scientists were to be consulted by the commissioners. [40] Then at the end of Kennedy's state visit to Mexico in June, the joint communiqué summing up results of the Mexico City talks reported that the two presidents were determined "to reach a permanent and effective solution at the earliest possible time with the aim of preventing the recurrence of this salinity problem after October, 1963. [41]

Subsequently, American and Mexican scientists engaged in study and discussion; the Mexicali Valley's fall cotton crop was badly damaged by saline irrigation waters; leftist political agitators capitalized on resulting economic problems in Baja California; and some persons speculated on the possibility of taking Mexico's case before the International Court of Justice. [42] Nevertheless, the month of October, 1963, passed, and no solution acceptable to Mexico had been reached. Few American citizens were even aware of the ex-

39. *U.S. Department of State Bulletin* XLVI (1962), 144.
40. *Ibid.*, p. 542.
41. *Ibid.*, XLVII (1962), 135.
42. See *Hispanic American Report* XV (1962), 207–28, 887, 989–90; XVI (1963), 234, 657.

istence of the problem; but for the people of Mexico, especially residents of the Mexicali area, it was a matter of great
importance. Therefore, after conferring with President Johnson at Palm Beach in February, 1964, President López
Mateos told reporters, "The main issue of my talks with
President Johnson was precisely the excess of salt in the waters that Mexico receives from the Colorado River." [43] The
importance of this matter was underscored further in the
presidents' joint communiqué of February 22, which reported: "President López Mateos observed that the government of Mexico and Mexican public opinion consider that
this problem is the only serious one between the two countries and emphasized the importance of finding a permanent
solution as soon as possible." [44]

Another year passed. Finally, on March 22, 1965, President Johnson announced that the United States and Mexico
had reached an agreement on measures to be taken for resolving the Colorado River salinity problem. Formulated by
the International Boundary and Water Commission, the
agreement obligated the United States to construct and
maintain at its expense a bypass channel for the purpose of
carrying Wellton-Mohawk drainage to a point on the Colorado River below Mexico's Morelos Dam diversion facilities,
which direct irrigation water to the Mexicali Valley. At
times when Mexico receives large water deliveries, it will
be possible to discharge above the Morelos Dam if requested
by Mexican authorities. Regardless of whether the drainage
is diluted with better quality water and utilized for irrigation
purposes, or whether it is conveyed to the Colorado River
at a point below the dam and allowed to pass unused into

43. *Ibid.*, XVII (1964), 113.
44. *U.S. Department of State Bulletin* L (1964), 396.

the Gulf of California, the agreement still specifies that drainage is to be charged against Mexico as part of the guaranteed annual delivery of 1,500,000 acre-feet of water "from any and all sources." [45] Built at a cost of $2.5 million, the 13-mile bypass was completed in November, 1965.[46]

In much the same way that the Wellton-Mohawk drainage canal produced a Colorado River salinity problem for the Mexicali Valley of Baja California, Mexico's El Morillo canal was carrying in the summer of 1962 a flow of 11,900 parts of salt drainage to the Rio Grande at a point near Mission, Texas.[47] This drainage had an adverse effect on crops of citrus, vegetables, seedlings, and cotton grown on 780,000 acres of irrigated Texas land and on similar crops produced on a smaller Mexican acreage. When Mexico failed to resolve the salinity problem, the International Boundary and Water Commission recommended construction of a conveyance channel to carry El Morillo drainage to the Gulf of Mexico.[48]

On December 30, 1965, Presidents Johnson and Díaz Ordaz announced their support of the recommendation.[49] Subsequently, the United States Congress enacted Public Law 89–584, which authorized the Department of State to enter into an agreement whereby both countries share equally in construction, maintenance, and operating costs of a diversion channel to be built and managed by Mexico under supervision of the International Boundary and Water Commission. The act imposed ceilings of $690,000 for total United States construction costs and $20,000 for this coun-

45. *Ibid.*, LII (1965), 555–57.

46. Hundley, *Dividing the Waters*, p. 179.

47. *Ibid.*, pp. 219–20.

48. See excerpt from Senate Committee on Foreign Relations Report No. 1485 printed in *Congressional Record*, 89th Cong., 2d Sess. (1966) 20180–81.

49. *U.S. Department of State Bulletin* LIV (1966), 118.

try's share of annual operation and maintenance costs; also, it stipulated:

> Before concluding the agreement or agreements, the Secretary of State shall receive satisfactory assurance from private citizens or a responsible group that they will pay the United States Treasury one-half of the actual United States costs of such construction, including costs of design and right-of-way, and one-half of the actual costs of operation and maintenance.[50]

On September 19, 1966, at the time that he signed the act, President Johnson stated that nearly 90 percent of the required contribution had been raised and placed on deposit in the United States Treasury by Texans benefitting most directly from the drainage diversion project. Then on February 10 he announced that Mexico had begun initial construction work and that the channel would be completed in 1968.[51] Actually, the project, which involved constructing a new channel of 24.6 miles and improving an old drainage facility fifty miles in length, was not completed until June 30, 1969.[52]

From the Gulf of Mexico to the Pacific Ocean, the arid borderlands have serious water supply and utilization problems. Neither American nor Mexican citizens can live and prosper in this area without adequate amounts of fresh water of good quality. As long as water is the key to life and prosperity in the Rio Grande and Colorado River basins, it is probable that international disputes over water rights will

50. *Congressional Record*, 89th Cong., 2d Sess. (1966), 21894–95.

51. *U.S. Department of State Bulletin* LV (1966), 686; LVI (1967), 428–29.

52. See the International Boundary and Water Commission's brochure and map entitled *The Morillo Drain Diversion Canal: A Joint International Project of the United States and Mexico for Improvement of the Quality of Water of the Lower Rio Grande* (July, 1960).

arise; however, both the Water Treaty of 1944 and the recent experiences in dealing with salinity problems suggest that important steps have been taken toward developing a tradition of United States–Mexican cooperation in resolving such issues.

Coastal Fisheries

Not only have Mexico and the United States engaged in disputes involving the waters of international rivers, but they also have differed sharply over the issue of fishing rights in their coastal waters. Thus, an agreement establishing the width of those coastal waters wherein exclusive fishing rights are to be recognized represents another significant achievement in United States–Mexican relations since World War II.

On October 27, 1967, during the course of President Díaz Ordaz's state visit to Washington, Secretary of Foreign Relations Antonio Carrillo Flores and Secretary of State Dean Rusk met in the United States capital and exchanged notes for the purpose of effecting an agreement concerning fishing rights in the coastal waters of their countries. Earlier, at the Geneva Conferences on the Law of the Sea held in 1958 and 1960, Mexico had contributed to the defeat of United States proposals designed to establish for all nations the breadth of the territorial sea and the zone of exclusive fishing rights. Therefore, the 1967 exchange of diplomatic notes represented an attempt to deal on a bilateral basis with a portion of the greater problem that had been left unresolved at Geneva.

Territorial waters are defined as a maritime zone adjacent to a state's territory over which it exercises, or has the right to exercise, jurisdiction. During the eighteenth and nineteenth centuries, the United States and leading European naval powers were in general agreement that the width of this zone was limited to three nautical miles and that a littoral state might reserve fisheries therein for the exclusive use of its citizens.[53] At the Hague Codification Conference of 1930, however, several states insisted on wider belts of territorial waters; and although three miles was recognized as a minimum width, no agreement was reached on the maximum width.[54] On August 29, 1935, President Cárdenas issued a decree proclaiming the breadth of Mexico's territorial waters to be nine nautical miles. Later, in response to United States protests, Secretary of Foreign Relations Eduardo Hay insisted that there was no fixed rule of international law regarding the subject.[55]

Although the United States continued to insist on the three-mile rule in regard to territorial waters and exclusive fishing rights, this position was undermined by an increasing number of more extensive claims advanced by other nations. Several Latin American countries came to share Mexico's disregard for the three-mile rule and advanced claims to territorial seas of six, twelve, and even two hundred miles in breadth.[56] Eventually, the United States was prepared to abandon the three-mile rule also. At the 1960 Geneva Conference, the United States joined Canada in sponsoring a proposal for a six-mile territorial sea plus an additional six-mile zone where a littoral state would enjoy exclusive fish-

53. J. L. Brierly, *The Law of Nations: An Introduction to the International Law of Peace,* ed. Sir Humphrey Waldock, 6th ed. (New York and Oxford, 1963), p. 203.

54. See Jesse S. Reeves, "The Codification of the Law of Territorial Waters," *American Journal of International Law* XXIV (1930), 486–99.

55. See U.S. State Department, *Foreign Relations of the United States, 1936,* 5 vols. (Washington, 1953–54), V, 758–70.

56. See C. Neale Ronning, *Law and Politics in Inter-American Diplomacy* (New York, 1963), pp. 106–25.

ing rights subject only to the limitation that historic fishing rights of other states would be recognized for ten years beginning on October 31, 1961. Strongly opposed by the Soviet Union and Mexico, this United States-Canadian proposal failed by a margin of one vote to obtain the necessary two-thirds majority of states present and voting. Had Mexico voted in favor of the measure, or even abstained from voting, the United States would have won a significant diplomatic victory, and the community of nations would have achieved the long-sought goal of adopting a badly needed rule for delimiting territorial waters and coastal fishing zones. Mexico was interested primarily in excluding American shrimp and tuna fishermen from her coastal waters in the Gulf of Mexico and the Pacific Ocean; and since these areas had been the scene of American fishing operations for many years, the Mexican government was strongly opposed to any arrangement that would recognize historic fishing rights.[57]

In the aftermath of the failure of the 1960 Geneva Conference, several states proceeded through unilateral and multilateral actions to extend their territorial seas and exclusive fishing zones. Consequently, some American officials reached the conclusion that the time had arrived for the United States to enlarge its exclusive fishing zone even though no changes were made in regard to the width of the territorial sea. Complaints by American fishermen that Soviet fishing fleets were taking increasingly large catches

57. For a detailed and authoritative account of the 1960 conference written by the chairman of the U.S. delegation, see Arthur H. Dean, "The Second Geneva Conference on the Law of the Sea: The Fight for Freedom of the Seas," *American Journal of International Law* LIV (1960), 751–89. For criticism of Dean's article and for further explanation of Mexico's position, see Alfonso García Robles, "The Second United Nations Conference on the Law of the Sea—A Reply," *ibid.*, LV (1961), 669–75; Dean's response is printed on pages 675–80.

within the 3- to 12-mile coastal area spurred members of Congress to introduce bills for the purpose of establishing a 12-mile exclusive fishing zone. Significantly, Douglas MacArthur II, the assistant secretary of state for congressional relations, when queried by Senator Warren G. Magnuson, replied that his department was not opposed "to establishing a 12-mile exclusive fisheries zone subject to the continuation of such traditional fishing by foreign states as may be recognized by the U.S. government." Also, he commented that such action "would make it more difficult, from the standpoint of international law, to extend the zone beyond 12 miles in the future."[58] Thereafter, Public Law 89–658 was passed early in October, 1966. It established exclusive United States fishing rights within the 12-mile coastal zone, but authorized recognition of historic fishing rights of foreign states.[59]

Thus the way was paved for negotiations between United States and Mexican governments regarding a problem that had been the source of friction for several years. Frequently, Mexico had complained about American fishermen encroaching upon her waters, and in some instances United States vessels had been seized and fishermen had been fined; but as long as the United States refused to recognize the 9-mile territorial sea limit, American diplomatic officials disregarded such complaints.[60] An end to this controversy,

58. This document is printed in *International Legal Materials* V (1966), 616–17.

59. For congressional debate on the measure, see *Congressional Record,* 89th Cong., 2d Sess. (1966) 13606–12, 24859–69, 25291.

60. Under terms of Public Law 680 (68 Stat. 883), owners of U.S. vessels "seized by a foreign country on the basis of rights or claims in territorial waters or on the high seas which are not recognized by the United States" are to be reimbursed by the secretary of the treasury for fines paid to secure release of a vessel and crew. For an account of the seizure of two U.S. fishing vessels by the Mexican government in February and April, 1962, see "State Responsibility and International Claims," *American Journal of International Law* LVII (1963), 899–902.

and a step toward resolution of differences that had divided
United States and Mexican delegations at the Geneva Conferences, was suggested in a Department of State announcement on May 25, 1967, which stated that "informal and
exploratory conversations . . . on fishery questions of mutual interest" had been concluded in Washington that date.[61]
Further discussions took place in Mexico City from September 11 to 19, and on September 21 a Department of State
press release disclosed that "the delegations agreed on recommendations to their Governments which would regulate
the fisheries of each country operating within the contiguous
fishery zone of the other." [62] Then on October 27, when President Díaz Ordaz was in Washington and at a time when the
Chamizal settlement had brought United States–Mexican
relations to a high point of harmony and good will, Secretary
of State Rusk and Minister of Foreign Relations Carrillo
Flores exchanged notes providing for reciprocal fishing
rights during the 1968–73 period within 9- to 12-mile zones
where Mexican and United States vessels had carried on
fishing operations for shrimp and various species of fish
"during the five years immediately preceding January 1,
1968." The agreement, however, stipulated that fishing in
these zones is to be continued in such a manner that the total
catch by American and Mexican vessels will not exceed the
levels of the five years prior to that date. Concerning the
matter of territorial waters, it is specified that the fisheries
agreement

> does not imply a change of position or an abandonment of
> the positions maintained by each Government regarding the
> breadth of the territorial sea, this matter not being the object
> of this agreement, nor does it limit their freedom to continue

61. *U.S. Department of State Bulletin* LVI (1967), 919.
62. *Ibid.*, LVII (1967), 475.

defending them in the international forum or in any of the
ways recognized by international law.[63]

The United States–Mexican coastal fishery agreement
represents a compromise. Mexico has recognized American
historic fishing rights in the 9- to 12-mile zone of Mexican
coastal waters, although the Mexican delegation at the
Geneva Conferences opposed recognition of any historic
fishing rights. At the same time, while not recognizing
Mexico's claim to a 9-mile territorial sea, the United States
has accepted the Mexican claim to exclusive fishing rights
within that area; and though American fishing vessels are to
be allowed to operate in the 9- to 12-mile zone until the end
of 1973, after that time it is agreed that American fishermen
will be denied access to those waters also. Since relatively
few Mexican vessels have fished in United States coastal
waters as compared with the number of American vessels
that historically have fished off Mexico's coasts, the agreement of 1967 represents an especially good bargain for Mexico. There may be reason to doubt, however, whether Mexico
will be able to develop a fishing industry large enough to
exploit fully the 12-mile coastal zone from which all American fishermen are to be excluded at the beginning of 1974.
But regardless of what Mexico's fishermen may be able to
achieve in the coastal waters that they will monopolize, a
troublesome controversy has been settled.

Interventionism in the Americas

Unfortunately, there are other problems that have not
been resolved. Prominent among the latter is the sharp dis-

63. U.S. Department of State, *Agreement between the United States of
America and the United Mexican States on Traditional Fishing in the Ex-
clusive Fishery Zones Contiguous to the Territorial Seas of Both Countries.*
TIAS 6359 (Washington, 1968).

agreement between the United States and Mexico concerning diplomatic recognition and a related matter—interventionism.

Mexico's post–World War II policy of diplomatic recognition has been influenced by the Estrada Doctrine, which was spelled out by that country's minister of foreign relations on September 27, 1930. Condemning recognition practice "which allows foreign governments to decide on the legitimacy or illegitimacy of another regime," Génaro Estrada asserted that

> the Mexican Government limits itself to maintain or recall its diplomatic agents, as it may deem advisable, and to continue to accept, also as it may deem advisable, similar diplomatic agents which the respective nations have accredited in Mexico, without judging, hastily or *a posteriori*, the right which foreign nations have to accept, maintain or substitute their governments or authorities.[64]

Though the Estrada Doctrine pertained to recognition, in reality it enunciated the principle of nonintervention.[65] This policy reflected Mexico's long-standing opposition to United States intervention in Mexican affairs and seemed to offer a diplomatic way to avoid intervention in any other country's internal affairs.[66]

64. Translated by Edna Monzón de Wilkie from text given in Luis G. Franco, *Glosa del Período de Gobierno del C. Gral. e Ing. Pascual Ortiz Rubio, 1930–1932; Relaciones Exteriores* . . . (Mexico, D.F., 1947), pp. 189–90.

65. Ann Thomas and A. J. Thomas, Jr., *Non-Intervention: The Law and Its Import in the Americas* (Dallas, 1956), p. 50. For comments by three prominent Mexican political figures (Marte R. Gómez, Vicente Lombardo Toledano, Emilio Portes Gil), see James W. Wilkie and Edna Monzón de Wilkie, *México Visto en el Siglo XX: Entrevistas de Historia Oral* (Mexico, D.F., 1969), pp. 137–38, 396–97, 525–26.

66. As early as 1918, for example, President Venustiano Carranza stated in his message to Congress: "No country should intervene in any form or for any reason in the internal affairs of another"; see quotation and discussion in Peggy Fenn, "Mexico, la no Intervención y la Autodeterminación en el Caso de Cuba," *Foro Internacional* IV (1963–64), 1–19.

The Estrada Doctrine has taken on a special importance in the Cold War era. Citing Estrada's principle of nonintervention, Mexico has refused to sanction an international hemispheric police force for the Organization of American States (OAS). Also, at the Tenth Inter-American Conference in Caracas (1954), the doctrine provided a rationale for Mexico's abstention from voting on the United States plan to censure implicitly "Communism in Guatemala." More recently it has been used to justify Mexico's refusal to support collective police action by the OAS against Cuban-sponsored guerrilla activity directed at other Latin American governments. For example, when Fidel Castro sought to export violence to Venezuela by sponsoring insurrection and political assassination, Mexico declined to vote for, or to honor, the OAS resolution to break diplomatic and economic relations with Cuba.[67]

Having experienced United States intervention during the earlier years of this century, Mexico has reacted by formulating a general rule that precludes unilateral or multilateral intervention in any country's internal affairs.[68] Thus it may appear that Mexican foreign policy encourages guerrilla invasions by opposing collective intervention designed to deal with such actions. Actually Mexico is simply caught in a series of contradictions inherited from a traditional fear of American power. As for Mexico's Cuban policy during the past ten years, probably it can be explained best in terms of

67. See Olga Pellicer de Brody, "Mexico en la OEA," *Foro Internacional* VI (1965–66), 288–302; and Javier Rondero, "Mexico at Punta del Este," in Carlos A. Astiz, ed., *Latin American International Politics: Ambitions, Capabilities and the National Interest of Mexico, Brazil and Argentina* (Notre Dame, Ind., 1969), pp. 111–36.

68. See, for example, Foreign Minister Manuel Tello's outline of Mexican history in his speech at the Seventh Meeting of Foreign Ministers, San José, Costa Rica, 1960. Here Tello insists that once a revolution is underway, it must take its course without foreign intervention if a people are to learn from their experience. A summary of this discourse is given in *Política*, September 1, 1960, pp. 32–36.

a Mexican nationalism that is sensitive to all suggestions that Mexico's foreign policy should be subject to United States direction in any way. Because of a desire to see Latin America free of nuclear weapons, however, Mexico backed President Kennedy in the crisis of October, 1962, by asking Castro to remove offensive missiles from Cuban soil.[69] Also, in January of that same year, Mexico abstained and did not vote against Cuba's expulsion from the OAS or against prohibiting the sale of arms to Cuba, because, as her minister of foreign relations noted, "it seems without doubt that there exists a deep-rooted incompatibility between membership in the Organization of American States and a Marxist-Leninist political belief." [70]

United States Investment in Mexico

Closely akin to Mexico's sensitivity concerning United States influence over her foreign policy is Mexico's preoccupation with a fear of "economic imperialism." In other words, Mexico is on guard against economic as well as political controls that might be exercised by her northern neighbor. Thus, in recent years, American private investors have been viewed by many Mexicans as dangerous instruments of imperialism.

Writing in 1952, Howard F. Cline described the period of United States–Mexican relations since 1940 as an "Era of Good Feeling" in which economic matters rather than political affairs had been emphasized; and he commented, "The flow of capital, goods, ideas, and men from the northern republic to the southern has been an important element in

69. See the Mexican Foreign Office declaration reprinted in *Política*, November 1, 1962, p. 3.
70. See *Política*, February 1, 1961, pp. 34–38, especially p. 38.

the economic and industrial revolution taking place in Mexico." [71] Cline's description of United States–Mexican relations extends into the 1970s. At the same time, one must recognize that the heritage of American intervention and influence in Mexico and other Latin American countries has continued to affect United States–Mexican economic relations. Despite denials from American businessmen and diplomats, some Mexicans are convinced that United States interests have conspired to dominate Mexico through economic means.

An example of this thinking is found in a book by José Luis Ceceña, a Mexican Marxist whose anti–United States ideas are rather typical of those frequently expressed in Mexico's intellectual circles. Ceceña charges that a very significant part of Mexico's economy is "controlled by four super groups [i.e., financial groups] that act as one monopolistic bloc making them the most important factor in the decisions of the [Mexican] private sector." He insists that the interlocking directorates of these four financial empires (Morgan Guaranty, First National Bank of New York, Du Pont-Chemical Bank, and the Chase-Rockefeller interests) not only control the economic life of the United States (along with the Mellon interests) but also dominate Mexico's most important economic activities. Ceceña claims that since the early 1960s foreign interests (83 percent United States and 17 percent other countries) have controlled 28 percent of the 2,000 largest companies in Mexico and have greatly influenced another 14 percent. "Control," according to Ceceña, involves ownership of over 50 percent of an enterprise's stock; influence refers to stock ownership ranging between 25 and 50 percent. Thus he insists that "only colonial territories and some countries cultivating a single

71. Cline, *The United States and Mexico,* p. 387.

crop present a situation of greater dependency than Mexico." Regarding this "economic occupation" of Mexico, especially by United States "monopolies," he is particularly concerned that United States capital has controlled or heavily influenced at least 69 percent of the capital in 10 of Mexico's 20 most important economic sectors. Noting that in the early 1960s 26 of the 40 most popular television programs were produced north of the border and sponsored by American firms, he sees evidence of both cultural and economic imperialism. Ceceña believes that Mexico is dependent on foreign capital (which makes Mexican development subservient to the international money market) and is exploited by "decapitalization" (which means that the remittance of profits abroad puts a brake on capital accumulation in Mexico). In order to cure these abuses, Ceceña would make the state the motor of development, nationalize banking and insurance operations, and limit foreign investment.[72]

Although the Mexican government has not seen fit to go to the extremes advocated by Ceceña and others of his persuasion, in this decade it has taken some steps to curb American influence within certain areas of the nation's economy. For example, the government purchased outright the foreign-owned light and power companies in 1960 and, in conjunction with private Mexican interests, obtained control of the Pan American Sulphur Company in 1967. Also, a new mining law of 1961 limits all new mining concessions to a maximum of 34 percent foreign capital; and, in order to encourage "Mexicanization" of concessions already granted, the government has offered a 50 percent tax reduction to mining com-

72. José Luis Ceceña, *El Capital Monopolista y la Económia de México,* (Mexico, D. F., 1963), pp. 108–9, 145–46, 155, 172–74, 177–78, 196–98. For another work that condemns United States foreign investment, see Pablo González Casanova, *La Ideología Norteamericana Sobre Inversiones Extranjeras* (Mexico, D.F., 1955). In contrast, see Manuel Gómez Morín in Wilkie and Wilkie, *México Visto en el Siglo XX,* pp. 208–9.

panies limited to 49 percent foreign capital.[73] In view of
these actions by the Mexican government, American diplomats and investors are quite aware that continuing pressures
and restrictions on foreign capital can be expected in the
future.

Can such actions against foreign capital be attributed to a
dramatic expansion of American investment activity in that
country that has had a detrimental effect on Mexican businessmen? In order to answer this question, comparisons will
be made between American direct investment since World
War II and Mexican public and private investment during
this period. First, however, it seems important to point out
that between 1940 and 1946, United States direct investment decreased from $358 million (1,970 million pesos at
the exchange rate of 5.504) to $316 million (1,534 million
pesos at the exchange rate of 4.855); at the same time, total
Mexican public and private investment increased from 793
million pesos to 3,287 million pesos. After 1946 American
direct investment increased, but at a much lower rate than
Mexican public and private investment; and by 1967 the
former stood at $1,342 million (16,755 million pesos at the
exchange rate of 12.5) while the latter had reached 50,600
million pesos. Thus, the ratio of American direct investment
to Mexican public and private investment reveals the following decline: in 1940, 2.5; in 1946, .5; in 1967, .3. Such a de-
clining ratio suggests that the influence of American investment in Mexico has been reduced significantly since World
War II and that complaints by Mexican nationalists against
alleged domination by United States capital are rooted more
in history than in present-day fact. Though some Mexicans

73. In *El Nacionalismo Mexicano y la Inversión Extranjera* (Mexico,
D.F., 1967), Miguel S. Wionczek discusses nationalization of the electric
power industry (especially pp. 138 ff.); the mining law of 1961 is discussed
cogently on pages 245–48.

claim that American investment is harmful to Mexico because it causes a "decapitalization" by which profits are remitted abroad, this view is contradicted by current official United States policy that seeks to limit American private investment in foreign countries because it in effect "decapitalizes" the United States and produces a negative balance of payments. Without attempting to analyze in detail the controversial matter of repatriation of profits, it can be shown that income from American direct investment in Mexico has been relatively low. (The authors define income as the sum of dividends, interest, and branch profits paid to owners in the United States, after foreign taxes but before payment of any United States taxes.) At no time since 1950 has income as a percentage of book value for American direct investments in Mexico exceeded 9.7 percent; and in 13 of the 18 years between 1950 and 1967, income amounted to 6 percent or less. For example, in 1967 income on American direct investment totaling $1,342 million amounted to $62 million, which represents a 4.6 percent return. By any standards, this is a low return on invested capital.[74]

Though one may argue that American capital may control certain Mexican industries, obviously American investors have not stifled the growth of Mexican national investment, as Ceceña would have us believe, nor has it "displaced, absorbed, or subordinated national investment."[75] Rather,

74. "Direct investment" includes all business enterprises in which U.S. investors have a controlling interest or an important voice in management (usually a 25 percent minimum of voting stock); and this investment excludes miscellaneous holdings of those stocks and bonds issued by foreign corporations or governments, which ordinarily are termed "portfolio investments." See U.S. Department of Commerce, Office of Business Economics, *Direct Private Foreign Investment of the United States: Census of 1950* (Washington, D.C., 1953), pp. 4, 27, 36–42. Data on U.S. investment has been developed from various sources and set forth in detail by the authors in their "United States–Mexican Relations Since 1940," a manuscript currently in preparation.

75. Ceceña, *El Capital Monopolista*, p. 177.

American investment undoubtedly has influenced Mexico's economic growth by encouraging establishment of industries that otherwise might not have been developed. In this process Mexican capital has developed supply and support industries and has organized competing companies.

The rapidly growing influence of American customs and styles on Mexican life cannot be attributed simply to American investment and advertising in Mexico; instead, such changes must be explained in terms of a common desire for peoples of the world, regardless of class or nationality, to be consumers as well as workers. But increased consumption in Mexico must await expansion of production facilities; this development, in turn, depends on a continued flow of capital into the country. Since the supply of Mexican capital is not sufficient, and since private foreign investment is not welcomed on an unrestricted basis, financial assistance must be obtained from other sources.

United States Financial Assistance to Mexico

Mexico's successful economic development since World War II has been predicated to a great extent upon extensive international financial assistance. Out of a total of $1,954.1 million committed to Mexico during the 1946–67 period, 53 percent ($1,033.5 million) took the form of United States grants and loans. The World Bank supplied 32 percent, and the International Development Bank provided about 10 percent. Lesser amounts were obtained from the International Finance Corporation and UN agencies; Alliance for Progress loans to Mexico from the Social Progress Trust Fund amounted to only $35.5 million by 1967. Three-fourths of United States financial assistance for the 1946–47 period ($776.3 million) was made available through the Export-

Import Bank for the purpose of financing United States exports to Mexico. Military assistance totaled a mere $10.3 million, or about 1 percent. Of the $1,033.5 million committed to Mexico by the United States over the 22-year period under discussion, about 87 percent took the form of loans, and the remainder was represented by grants. In only 2 of the 12 years between 1956 and 1967 did loans fall below 86 percent of the United States' net financial commitment. Mexico's position in relation to total international aid ($1,954.1 million from all sources) may be summarized by noting that over 91 percent has consisted of loans that must be repaid at various rates of interest. Indeed, this is a tremendous burden.[76]

As has been pointed out in an earlier study, Mexico appears to have discovered a key to development that involves devoting up to 36 percent of federal expenditures (1961) for amortization of, and interest on, the public debt.[77] Providing that the United States and the rest of the Western world continue to enjoy economic prosperity, Mexico may expect to obtain large loans that can be repaid with new loans. Should circumstances develop under which this financial assistance is no longer forthcoming, Mexico may experience painful financial difficulties. In this regard it must be emphasized that the United States exercises a strong influence over international lending agencies and that this country

76. Financial assistance data is based on information provided in the following U.S. Agency for International Development sources: USAID/Washington, Statistics and Reports Division, "Worksheet," January 10, 1969; *U.S. Overseas Loans and Grants and Assistance from International Organizations: (Special Report Prepared for the House Foreign Affairs Committee), Obligations and Loan Authorizations, July 1, 1945—June 30, 1967,* pp. 47, 163. Mexico's situation is in sharp contrast to that of Bolivia, which until 1963 depended on large grants rather than loans from the U.S. and international agencies. See James W. Wilkie, *The Bolivian Revolution and U.S. Aid Since 1952: Financial Background and Context of Political Decisions* (Los Angeles, 1969).

77. Wilkie, *The Mexican Revolution,* p. 279.

supplied slightly over half of the grants and loans received
by Mexico during the 1946–67 period. In some years the
United States supplied all financial assistance for Mexico,
and in 1967 the United States share amounted to 67.4 percent.[78] Certainly, Mexican government leaders are very much
aware that their nation's financial health depends in a large
measure on the availability of new loans from the World
Bank and the Inter-American Development Bank; and to an
even greater degree is Mexico dependent on the ability and
the willingness of her northern neighbor to supply loans and
grants.

Conclusion

In view of the crises and conflicts that were so prominent
in relations between the United States and Mexico during
the three decades between the outbreak of the Mexican
Revolution of 1910 and the end of the Cárdenas administration in 1940, the achievements of more recent years are
truly impressive. How can one account for this turn of
events? First, it is apparent that Mexican presidents since
Cárdenas have followed policies of moderation that have
provoked fewer conflicts with the northern neighbor. Second, and more important, is the fact that the United States
has displayed greater readiness to make concessions to
Mexican demands. While engaged in the Cold War struggle
with the Soviet Union and Communist China, both the
United States Congress and the White House occupants—
especially under the administrations of Kennedy and
Johnson—have shown great concern for maintaining cordial
relations with nations of the Western Hemisphere. Given a

78. USAID, *U.S. Overseas Loans and Grants* . . . *July 1, 1945—June
30, 1967*, pp. 47, 163.

strong United States desire to minimize friction with Mexico while contending with the Communist powers in Europe and Asia, the Mexican government has been able to protect and advance its national interests through successful negotiations with the more powerful northern neighbor. Operating in the hostile and often violent atmosphere of the mid-twentieth-century world, policy-makers in Washington have found a friendly neighbor and a secure southern border much to be desired, especially if the cost is not excessive.

In regard to problems that have been fully or partially resolved, Mexico has been able to secure agreements on terms that have tested the ability of the United States to be a "good neighbor." Thus, after more than half a century of controversy, Mexico obtained most of the Chamizal territory claimed under the disputed arbitral decision of 1911. Subsequently, the Pious Fund dispute was resolved by an arrangement that allowed Mexico to make a lump sum payment to terminate what had been a perpetual annuity obligation. Negotiations relative to the Colorado River salinity problem resulted in payment by the United States of the entire cost of constructing a canal needed for the purpose of carrying Wellton-Mohawk drainage; on the other hand, when a similar problem developed in the Rio Grande Valley, the United States paid half the cost of constructing a canal needed for diverting El Morillo drainage through Mexican territory to the Gulf of Mexico. In the case of the 1946 foot-and-mouth disease outbreak, which appears to have resulted from Mexico's importation of Zebu cattle in spite of convention restrictions and protests from the United States government, the disease was checked and then eradicated through joint United States–Mexican efforts. Although the United States made a large direct financial contribution to the foot-and-mouth disease eradication program, in later years Mexico has not responded in a similar manner to United States

efforts to protect both countries from screwworm fly infestation. Scientists have developed a technique for eradicating
the screwworm fly, and the United States Congress has
authorized necessary cooperation with the Mexican government; to date, however, Mexico has not seen fit to enter into
a large-scale eradication campaign conducted on the cost-
sharing basis envisioned by American authorities. As for the
coastal fisheries problem, through a 1967 bilateral agreement
Mexico has obtained an arrangement whereby American
fishermen will be excluded from waters within twelve miles
of Mexico's coasts by 1974, despite the fact that American
shrimp and tuna fishermen have fished for many years in a
portion of this coastal zone. Probably the only settlement
with which the Mexican government was not completely
satisfied concerned the matter of contract farm labor. Here,
as a result of political pressures exerted by American labor
and other interests, Congress ended the bracero program
that had been an important source of dollar exchange for
Mexico and had provided employment for large numbers of
Mexican rural laborers.

Major unresolved problems in the field of United States–
Mexican relations concern the issue of interventionism in the
Americas (particularly as related to Cuba and the OAS) and
the means of financing Mexico's economic development. In
regard to the former, the principal difficulty stems from
Mexico's attachment to the antiquated Estrada Doctrine
and a deep-seated fear of United States intervention in her
internal affairs. As for the latter, Mexico has a strong preference for grants and loans from international agencies and
foreign governments. Where direct foreign investment is
allowed, restrictions have been imposed that are designed
to ensure that certain private enterprises will be under Mexican majority control.

In recent years Mexico has come to rely less and less on

direct American investment; however, at the same time Mexico has become heavily dependent on loans from the United States government and from international agencies greatly influenced by the United States. To date, United States and Mexican foreign policy differences regarding Cuba have not affected Mexico's supply of vital financial assistance. There is no guarantee, however, that the future may not bring a change. Certainly there is much irony in the fact that Mexico's increased freedom from the influence of American private capital has been accompanied by greater dependence on United States government loans. Only the future will reveal whether this situation will continue, and if so, whether it will promote cooperation or conflict.

The United States and Cuba: The Uncomfortable "Abrazo," 1898–1968

ALLAN R. MILLETT

REFLECTING on the American influence on Cuban politics, Enrique José Varona in 1906 sadly concluded that his homeland needed to be pushed some thousand miles out into the Atlantic. Nothing less would sever the ties of ideology, economics, sentiment, and security that bound the two nations. Varona despaired for the life of the Cuban republic, for Cuba and the United States seemed linked in an unequal embrace in which intervention was the norm and only the modes changed.[1]

Intervention has so characterized the interplay of Cuban and American politics that it is difficult to escape the term. What is crucial is a discriminating understanding of what intervention has meant to the two nations. For Cuban nationalists, intervention has meant any American commercial or diplomatic act that has influenced Cuban history; this

1. Enrique José Varona to *El Comercio* (Havana), December 3, 1906, in Case 1943/40, Numerical File, 1906–1910, General Records of the Department of State (Record Group 59), National Archives.

definition includes advice to successive Cuban administrations. For the United States, intervention has been military action to protect the physical security of the United States, to safeguard American lives and investments, and to satisfy a desire to foster democratic government abroad. Such intervention has been episodic and marked by the ebb and flow of crisis.[2]

Clearly this description does not exhaust the range of Cuban-American relations. The most obvious alternative theme has been extragovernmental: the continuous role of American business in shaping sugar monoculture and latifundia in Cuba. It has been, moreover, but a step to seeing Cuban-American diplomacy as economic imperialism, with American power either broadly supporting the security of private capital and the class that holds it or narrowly pro-

2. Historical interpretations of Cuban-American relations proliferate like a tropical rain forest. American scholarship follows two broad paths: the security-ideological apologists and the economic-ideological anti-imperialists. Among the first are Charles Chapman, Russell Fitzgibbon, Dana G. Munro, Dexter Perkins, Samuel Flagg Bemis, and David A. Lockmiller, who are sympathetic to American policy-makers because of their security-consciousness and liberal impulses. The economic determinists are not crudely so, emphasizing the psychological motivations behind American global enterprise. The most recent decriers of America's "anti-revolutionary imperialism"—Philip Foner, David Zeitlin, Robert F. Smith, and Walter LaFeber—take their cue from William A. Williams; but this genre begins with the exposés of Albert G. Robinson, Leland Jenks, and Carltón Beals. A common flaw in both groups is a tendency to overemphasize American influence on Cuba's domestic development. Cuban accounts of American diplomacy almost all uniformly deplore American influence, and with decreasing gentility after the 1920s. The best scholars—Rafael Martínez Ortiz, Ramiro Guerra y Sánchez, Fernando Ortiz, Emilio Roig de Leuchsenring, and Herminio Portell Vilá—feel that Cuba never developed the sense of cultural independence and social cohesion it needed because of sugar monoculture and the threat of annexation and occupation, both American imports.

For a recent discussion of Cuban-American relations, see Lester D. Langley, *The Cuban Policy of the United States* (New York, 1968), which argues that American diplomats used nineteenth-century ideals to justify twentieth-century policies. For a review of contemporary issues, see the essays in John Plank, ed., *Cuba and the United States: Long Range Perspectives* (Washington, 1967).

tecting American investments from destruction or expropriation.[3]

There is another thread of consistency that ties the domestic concerns of Americans, the interventions of their presidents, and the unhappy history of the Republic of Cuba: it is
the twentieth-century American abhorrence of violence as a
means of political expression. As much a sentimental vision
as a reality in American history, this abhorrence was more
than a continuing fear of property loss; it was the product of
the Civil War and the class and ethnic conflicts of a complex,
industrializing society. Whatever the causes, American
politics has been a "game" seldom played with submachine
guns, mobs, prisons, guerrillas, and torches. It is the American vision of the happy society that conditioned relations
with Cuba: a unified people, secure, stable, affluent, tolerant,
wanting consensual change if change be necessary. It was
the American willingness to universalize on its own experience, to prefer unstable peace to violent social and political
change, that triggered intervention. This cultural imperialism—the moral stand on political violence and the universal
efficacy of democracy—was as important a factor in Cuban-
American relations as the biggest loan and the most vulnerable sugar *central*.

Violence has been and is an inextricable part of Latin
American politics, and it has been a *norteamericano* dilemma how to deal with the bewildering range of coercion
with which Latins wield power. Political violence has not
been the monopoly of the feudal Latin American countries,
but characterizes the modernizing ones as well. Frustrated

3. See Leland H. Jenks, *Our Cuban Colony: A Study in Sugar* (New
York, 1928); Robert F. Smith, *The United States and Cuba: Business and
Diplomacy, 1917–1960* (New York, 1960); Fernando Ortiz, *Cuban Counter-
point: Tobacco and Sugar* (New York, 1947); Ramiro Guerra y Sánchez,
Sugar and Society in the Caribbean (New Haven, Conn., 1964).

expectation as well as grinding poverty bring violence. Force is not the peasant's tool; it is sanctioned by the middle sectors and technically advanced military officers. Violence may be the product of urbanization and industrialization as well as caudilloism. It may be preferred to free and unpredictable elections. It is a real factor in Latin American political behavior, and democratic political processes, as alternatives to coercion, have not had the legitimacy they enjoy in North America.[4]

Cuba's history as a colony and republic has been rife with political violence. The acceptability of violence was pervasive in Cuban society, a corollary to heroic, manly behavior, the clannishness of family and ethnic group, and the desperate need of high-status public employment of the non-working-class elite.[5] The Cuban acceptance of violence, furthermore, seems directly related to the thirty-year guerrilla war against Spain rather than being only the product of an authoritarian cultural tradition. Violence and politics were by 1898 synonymous in Cuban minds; Antonio Maceo preached that liberty could best be secured by the cutting edge of a machete long before Mao Tse-tung discovered that political power grew out of the barrel of a gun.

Defeating Spain, the Cubans lost their battle with them-

4. Robert F. Smith, "The United States and Latin American Revolutions," *Journal of Inter-American Studies* IV (1962), 89–104; William H. Stokes, "Violence as a Power Factor in Latin American Politics," *Western Political Quarterly* V (1952), 445–68; K. H. Silvert, "Political Change in Latin America," in Herbert L. Matthews, ed., *The United States and Latin America* (New York, 1959), pp. 59–80; Roberto Ortigueira, "La Desintegración Estado Normal de Paises en Desarrollo," *Journal of Inter-American Studies* V (1963), 471–94; Seymor Martin Lipset, "Some Social Requisites of Democracy: Economic Development and Political Legitimacy," *American Political Science Review* LIII (1959), 69–105; Arthur P. Whitaker *et al.*, "The Pathology of Democracy in Latin American," *American Political Science Review* XLIV (1950), 100–49.

5. Wyatt MacGaffey and Clifford R. Barnett, *Cuba* (New Haven, Conn., 1962), pp. 90–103; Lowry Nelson, *Rural Cuba* (Minneapolis, 1950), pp. 139–61, 174–200.

selves for a more secure, democratic, and pacific society.[6]
Instead, the animosities of race, class, national origin, and
economic status that fragmented Cuban society found free
rein in the electoral process, which, however liberal in
theory, was notoriously undemocratic in operation.[7] Political
violence was a sign of patriotic fervor rather than a crime
against the community.[8]

Cuban-American relations after 1898, then, were conditioned by two widely different attitudes about the way man
handles his ambitions and desires in his social environment.
On one side was the fundamental American disapproval of
violence; on the other, the Cuban conviction that coercion
was an equally fundamental attribute of individual liberty
and political action. The result was seventy years of intervention and cultural imperialism by the United States and
seventy years of exploitation of American public opinion by
Cuba's political leaders.

I

From its involvement in the Cuban revolt against Spain
until the rise of the Machado dictatorship, the United States

6. Enrique José Varona, *Mirando en torno* (Havana, 1910) and "Nuestra
indisciplina," *Cuba contemporanea* IV (1914), 12–16; Carlos Marquez
Sterling, *Alrededor de nuestra psicología* (Havana, 1906); Fernando Ortiz,
"La decadencia cubana," *Revista bimestre cubana* XIX (1924), 17–45;
and, in fiction, Carlos Loveira, *Generales y doctores*, ed. Shasta M. Bryant
and J. Riis Owre (New York, 1965), and J. Riis Owre, "*Generales y
doctores*-After Forty-Five Years," *Journal of Inter-American Studies* VIII
(1966), 371–85.

7. Mario Riera Hernández, *Cuba política, 1899–1955* (Havana, 1955);
Russell H. Fitzgibbon, " 'Continuismo' in Central America and the Carrib-
bean," *Inter-American Quarterly* XI (1940), 55–74.

8. Charles E. Chapman, *A History of the Cuban Republic* (New York,
1927), pp. 526–46; Manuel Secades y Japón and Horacio Díaz Pardo, eds.,
La justicia en Cuba: los veteranos y los indultos (Havana, 1908) and *La
justicia en Cuba: patriotas y traidores*, 2 vols. (Havana, 1912, 1914).

government played the role of impartial arbiter in Cuban elections, at the same time attempting to eliminate the causes of political violence with periodic intervention, "interference," and private capital. The Platt Amendment was both the symbol and active force of this self-assumed stewardship. Throughout the period there was, behind the screen of party labels, essential policy continuity in both countries. In the United States the policy-makers were committed to the belief that a nation should concentrate on economic self-improvement in a reformed capitalist system while adjusting controversies non-violently through a democratic political system. In Cuba the political leadership was dominated by the insurgent elite of guerrilla officers, lawyers, doctors, and intellectuals. Rapacious but idealistic, practical oligarchs but rhetorical republicans, masters of coercion and deception whose patriotism was not so strong as to seriously challenge American political supervision or Cuba's colonial economy, these Cuban *políticos* were revolutionaries without a revolution, without national purpose. Although they could claim some American collusion in their inability to attack Cuba's problems, their weaknesses lay within themselves and their society.[9]

When revolt against Spain broke out once more in 1895, Cuban society was already deep in the process of fundamental change. The mechanization of the sugar industry and its rapid growth, the influx of foreign capital, and the end of slavery were altering rural Cuba. Political divisions between Spaniard, Loyalist, Cuban autonomist, and Cuban republi-

9. Cuban-American relations for 1898–1935 are best surveyed in Russell H. Fitzgibbon, *Cuba and the United States, 1900–1935* (Menasha, Wis., 1935) and Dana G. Munro, *Intervention and Dollar Diplomacy in the Caribbean, 1900–1921* (Princeton, N.J., 1964). Valuable Cuban studies covering the same period include Ramiro Guerra y Sánchez, *et al., Historia de la Nación Cubana* 7 vols. (Havana, 1952), Vols. VII and VIII, and Emilio Roig de Leuchsenring, *El intervencionismo, mal de males de Cuba republicana* (San José de Costa Rica, 1931) and *Historia de la Enmienda Platt*, 2 vols. (Havana, 1935).

can were wide. The uncommitted masses, *los pacíficos*, were already wedded to a life of survival. Economic activity was increasingly vulnerable to the seasonal rhythms of sugar growing and the not so predictable influences of the world market for foodstuffs, finance capital, and American tariffs. Guerrilla war, accompanied by vast destruction, death, and population resettlement, further fragmented what might have been a Cuban nation.

In their attempt to end Spanish rule the Cuban insurgents knew their cause would be materially advanced if they could count on the United States as a sanctuary and source of money, men, and supplies. The Cuban Revolutionary party, lead by José Martí and Tomás Estrada Palma, counted on American public sympathy to blunt President Grover Cleveland's official neutrality, though Martí feared that American expansionism might endanger Cuban independence. Consequently, the Cuban junta launched a successful effort to align Americans with their cause. Their most useful tool was to publicize the barbarity of Spanish actions against the rebels. Through the formation of a Cuban League, through mass meetings, doctored press releases, able lobbying, and with the assistance of the American press, the junta had by 1896 created widespread sentiment for the recognition of Cuban belligerency and independence. In the election of that year Republicans, Democrats, and Populists all called for support of the Cubans. American statesmen found rational reasons for such aid in strategic theory, the Monroe Doctrine, and economic gain; but the public was most moved by emotional appeals about liberty, democracy, and the sanctity of person and property. Such sentiments moved Presidence William McKinley to accuse Spain of genocide in his inaugural address, led Senator Shelby Cullom to call Cuba a "charnel house of ruin," and Hearst and Pulitzer to call in their newspapers for a crusade to end the bloodbath in the "new Armenia" within eighty miles of the American coast. That the war involved "uncivilized" methods on both sides generally escaped notice; it was "Butcher" Weyler, not "Butcher" Gómez or Maceo.[10]

Before the wreck of the *Maine* had settled in the mud of Havana harbor, the McKinley administration found itself committed to act as well as talk about Cuba's future. The congressional debate preceding intervention had produced two crucial political decisions: to seek no other permanent relationship other than Cuban independence and to disavow the insurgent generals as leaders of the Cuban people. Instead, McKinley searched for a politically acceptable tutelary relationship and for "responsible" Cubans while the U.S. Army attempted the pacification and reconstruction of the ravaged island.[11]

For the first year of military occupation, weak guidance from Washington and the benign conservatism of General John R. Brooke, the military governor, left American policy unclear and placed the political initiative with two of

10. For American reaction to the revolt, see Ernest R. May, *Imperial Democracy: The Emergence of America as a Great Power* (New York, 1961), and Walter Millis, *The Martial Spirit* (Boston, 1931). On the press and public opinion: Joseph E. Wisan, *The Cuban Crisis as Reflected in the New York Press (1895–1898)* (New York, 1934); M. M. Wilkerson, *Public Opinion and the Spanish-American War* (Baton Rouge, 1932); George W. Auxier, "Propaganda Activities of the Cuban Junta," *Hispanic American Historical Review* XIX (1939), 286–305, and "Middle Western Newspapers and the Spanish-American War," *Mississippi Valley Historical Review* XXVI (1940), 523–34; Raymond A. Detter, "The Cuban Junta and Michigan, 1895–1898," *Michigan History* XLVIII (1964), 35–46; William J. Schellings, "Florida and the Cuban Revolution, 1895–1898," *Florida Historical Quarterly* XXXIX (1960), 175–86. For a scholarly Cuban account that emphasizes annexationism rather than altruism, see Herminio Portell Vilá, *Historia de Cuba en sus relaciones con los Estados Unidos y España*, 4 vols. (Havana, 1938–41). On the conduct of the insurgency: Lawrence R. Nichols, "The Bronze Titan: The Mulatto Hero of Cuban Independence, Antonio Maceo," (Ph.D. dissertation, Duke University, 1954).

11. I have based the discussion of the 1898–1902 occupation on two recent scholarly studies: David F. Healy, *The United States in Cuba, 1898–1902* (Madison, Wis., 1963) and James H. Hitchman, "Leonard Wood and the Cuban Question, 1898–1902," Ph.D. dissertation (University of California, Berkeley, 1965). See also Portell Vilá, *Historia de Cuba*, IV, 13–290.

Brooke's subordinates, James H. Wilson and Leonard Wood. Although Wilson had greater faith in the *políticos* than Wood had and urged a major governmental role in agricultural reform, the two generals were agreed that continued American supervision was necessary. Both hoped for eventual voluntary annexation to the United States, though Wilson favored immediate independence and free trade as the vehicle. Wood, a secular messiah for good citizenship, advocated continued tutelage. Both recognized the fragmented nature of Cuban society and the island's economic vulnerability, views common throughout the military government.[12]

By 1900, however, despite Wood's rise to the governorship, the McKinley administration began to plan for the end of the occupation. McKinley and his able secretary of war, Elihu Root, saw the limits of moral suasion more clearly than Wood and feared the domestic reaction to the shooting "pacification" in the Philippines. The violent reform of colonial peoples was a policy unlikely to win favor with the American electorate, however correct Wood's assessment that immediately transplanting democratic government was impossible.[13]

12. Leonard Wood to William McKinley, April 12, 1900, and to Theodore Roosevelt, July 12, August 18, 1899, Wood Papers, Library of Congress; Leonard Wood, "The Existing Conditions and Needs in Cuba," *North American Review* CLXVIII (1899), 593–601; James H. Wilson to Joseph B. Foraker, June 29, July 24, 1899, and to Elihu Root, November 3, 1899, Wilson Papers, Library of Congress; Col. T. H. Bliss to Col. C. R. Edwards, Chief, Division of Insular Affairs, April 23, 1901, Bliss Papers, Library of Congress; Capt. F. S. Foltz to Inspector General, Division of Cuba, March 19, 1900, File 1670, Letters Received, 1900, Records of the Military Government of Cuba, Record Group 140, National Archives; Hugh L. Scott, *Some Memories of a Soldier* (New York, 1928), 234–35; Maj. J. E. Runcie, "American Misgovernment in Cuba," *North American Review* CLXX (1900), 284–94.

13. Elihu Root, "The Principles of Colonial Policy," extract from the Report of the Secretary of War for 1899, in Robert Bacon and James Brown Scott, eds., *The Military and Colonial Policy of the United States* (Cambridge, Mass., 1916), p. 162; Root to C. W. Eliot, May 4, 1900, Root

Root, however, saw that Cuba's strategic importance and economic potential (to benefit both countries) made some tutelage essential, and Wood's strident condemnation of the *políticos* had its impact. Altruism and self-interest both, the general wrote, cried for continued supervision; to do otherwise was to sanction the violence and instability endemic to the Caribbean.[14] To a large degree this was also the conclusion of the congressional majority: the Cubans should be saved from themselves—but with minimal American responsibility for the *políticos'* behavior after independence.[15]

Root found the Cuban problem perplexing; rebellion and institutional change and collapse had made Cuba a republic unfit to intelligently and pacifically govern itself. Still, he sought some way:

1. To secure a conservative and thoughtful control of Cuba by Cubans during the formative period, and avoid the kind of control which leads to the perpetual revolutions of Central America and the other West India Islands.

2. To make the suffrage respected so there will be acquiescence in its results.

3. To stimulate the people to thrift and education.

I do not believe any people, three-fourths of whom are contented to remain unable to read and write, can for any very long period maintain free government.[16]

Papers, Library of Congress; Root to Roosevelt, December 18, 1901, Wood Papers; Foraker to Wilson, November 20, December 15, 1899, Wilson Papers.

14. Wood to Root, February 16, 1900, Root Papers; Wood to Root, January 19, 1901, Wood Papers; Wood to Root, February 19, 27, 1901, Frank R. McCoy Papers, Library of Congress; "Report of the Military Governor," *Civil Report of Brigadier General Leonard Wood, Military Governor of Cuba, 1902*, 6 vols. (Washington, 1902), I, 12.

15. Orville H. Platt, "The Pacification of Cuba," *Independent* LII (1901), 1464–68, and "Our Relation to the People of Cuba and Puerto Rica," *Annals of the American Academy of Political and Social Science* XVIII (July, 1901), 145–59; Albert J. Beveridge, "Cuba and Congress," *North American Review* CLXXII (1901), 535–50; Foraker to Wilson, February 5, 1900, Wilson Papers.

16. Root to Paul Dana, January 16, 1900, Root Papers.

With the imperialism issue muted by McKinley's reelection in 1900 and Wood's government scoring superficially
impressive gains in Cuba, Root began to work out the details
of American supervision, the political and legal restraints of
the Platt Amendment. As Root mulled over the importance
of a free Cuba to American security, he recognized that
Cuban society would have to become politically pacific to
avoid foreign interference. In the letters that provided the
genesis of the Platt Amendment, he decided that only restraints imposed by the United States could accomplish this
task.[17] As adopted in 1902 by Congress and 1903 (reluctantly
by the *políticos*) by constitution and treaty, the Platt
Amendment provided the United States with future justification for adjudicating Cuban politics. Pressed by a delegation
from Havana, Root emphasized that Article III, the major
provision for intervention, was to guard Cuba from external
assault only. It did not sanction "intermeddling or intervention in any manner" in internal affairs. Root added, however,
that intervention might occur "when there may exist a true
state of anarchy within the Republic." Asked to be more
specific by Domingo Méndez Capote, Root explained "anarchy" as an "absence of government." [18]

For the next thirty years the Platt Amendment conditioned
Cuban-American relations; only the successive sugar tariffs
and trade agreements had equal importance in the diplomatic exchanges. Whatever the wisdom of its provisions for
naval bases and yellow fever control and its admonitions on

17. Root to Wood, January 9, 1901, Wood Papers; Root to John Hay,
January 11, 1901, Root Papers. For a scholarly reconstruction of the drafting of the Platt Amendment and later interpretations, see Lejeune Cum-
mins, "The Formation of the Platt Amendment," *Americas* XXIII (1967),
370–89, and James H. Hitchman, "The Platt Amendment Revisited: A
Bibliography Survey," *ibid.*, 343–69.

18. "Report of the Committee Appointed to Confer with the Government of the United States, Giving an Account of Its Labors," República de
Cuba, Sentado, *Memoria, 1902–1904*, No. 72, Document M, Copy in Cuba
subject file, Root Papers.

the importance of treaty-respecting and fiscal responsibility, it was, nonetheless, an overcommitment. The English political observer James Bryce pointed out that Cuban internal politics could easily distort the amendment. Senator Joseph B. Foraker went further, pointing out that the pledge of intervention was an invitation to internal revolt since the "ins" and "outs" could compete for American support.[19]

It was just such a situation that precipitated armed intervention in 1906, four years after the Roosevelt administration had presided over the election of Tomás Estrada Palma and withdrawn the military government. After 1902 Estrada Palma, a seventy-year-old former exile of great probity, had become increasingly a captive of the *políticos*, finally aligning himself with the immoderate Moderates. They proceeded to dominate the elections of 1905 and 1906 by coercion. In August, 1906, the opposition faction, the Liberals, took to the hills in open revolt.[20]

This civil war found Theodore Roosevelt and Root, now secretary of state, attempting to soften Latin criticism of the seizure of the Canal Zone and intervention in the Dominican Republic. Neither had relinquished, however, his moral opposition to violent politics at home or abroad. Roosevelt, in fact, in a letter read by Root to the Cuban Society of New York, had warned that nonviolence was the sine qua non for avoiding American intervention in the Caribbean, a stand shortly embodied in the Roosevelt Corollary.[21] Roosevelt,

19. James Bryce, "Some Reflections on the State of Cuba," *North American Review* CLXXIV (1902), 449–56; *Congressional Record*, 56th Cong., 2d Sess. (1901), 3151.

20. For Estrada Palma's unhappy tenure: Carlos Manuel Trelles y Govín, *El Progreso (1902–1905) y el retroceso (1906–1922) de República de Cuba* (Havana, 1923); Rafael Martinez Ortiz, *Cuba: los primeros años de independencia*, 2 vols. (Paris, 1921); Carlos Marquez Sterling, *Don Tomás: biografía de una epoca* (Havana, 1953).

21. Roosevelt to Root, May 20, 1904, in Elting E. Morison, ed., *The Letters of Theodore Roosevelt*, 8 vols. (Cambridge, Mass., 1951–54), IV, 801.

responding to Estrada Palma's request for troops and the Liberals' threats to destroy foreign property, offered to mediate; he erroneously assumed that any Cuban patriot would do all he could to avoid another occupation. Such was not the case, for the warring factions explicitly said they preferred an American administration to that of their opponents.[22] This position, coupled with Roosevelt's reluctance to accept a rebel government or to fight a Philippine-style pacification campaign, ended in another period of War Department administration until the spring of 1909.

The second intervention was like the first: peaceful, reformist and temporary in impact. The provisional governor, Charles E. Magoon, and the Army officers of his staff were aware that they were doing little more than liquidating the intervention, not its causes. The officials of the provisional government recognized that violence was endemic to Cuban politics, and that nothing short of a long occupation or true revolution would change this political behavior. Indeed, the Army officers, lead by Colonel Enoch H. Crowder, favored longer direct supervision and the virtual elimination of Cuban party politics and elections.[23] Roosevelt and Root vetoed continuing American control, created the Cuban Army advocated by the *políticos,* and eventually elected away the occupation. None of the observers of the occupation thought that it had changed a thing, except that the *políticos* now had a precedent to further encourage them to manipulate American interests to their own advantage with little fear of annexation.[24]

22. Allan R. Millett, *The Politics of Intervention: The Military Occupation of Cuba, 1906–1909* (Columbus, Ohio, 1968), pp. 59–119.

23. *Ibid.,* pp. 192–270.

24. Lord James Bryce, British Ambassador to the United States, to Sir Edward Grey, January 15, January 22, March 9, 1908, FO 371–446, Public Record Office, London; C. E. Magoon to Theodore Roosevelt, April 16, 1908, Roosevelt Papers, Library of Congress; Frank M. Steinhart to Capt. F. R. McCoy, November 23, 1908, Hugh L. Scott Papers, Library of Con-

II

William Howard Taft, fully aware of the dangers of military occupation after his service as governor of the Philippines and mediator in Cuba in 1906, turned to a more congenial diplomatic policy: reducing the likelihood of violence by encouraging economic progress in Cuba with foreign capital. Unfortunately, the American investments supposed to "replace insecurity and devastation by stability and peaceful self-development" created new hostages for the rebel.[25] Dollar diplomacy, whether loans to underwrite the Cuban government or private investment, exacerbated the conditions that encouraged intervention. However alluring its pacifism, dollar diplomacy did not, in the opinion of American minister John B. Jackson, conform with Cuban realities. Jackson pointed out that no Cuban government could prevent political violence, but a revolt had little chance of success without intervention. There were only two ways a rebel might change the government: assassination or forcing mediation and compromise by burning foreign property. The alternative was to sponsor reform by putting "honorable and capable" Cubans in power and keeping them there. If the United States could not do this, it should rule out intervention absolutely at times of crisis.[26]

---

gress; Maj. H. J. Slocum to Wood, November 25, 1907, and Capt. J. W. Wright to Wood, December 31, 1908, Wood Papers; Dr. Juan Guiteras to Maj. Jefferson R. Kean, March 6, 1908, Kean Papers, University of Virginia Library; Portell Vilá, *Historia de Cuba*, IV, 561.

25. For the purpose of "Dollar Diplomacy," see Philander C. Knox's address to the National Civic Federation, December 11, 1911, quoted in Herbert F. Wright, "Philander C. Knox," in Samuel F. Bemis and Robert H. Ferrell, eds., *The American Secretaries of State and Their Diplomacy*, 16 vols. to date (New York, 1927–), IX, 327–28, and speech by Assistant Secretary of State Huntington Wilson, May 4, 1911, quoted in W. H. Callcott, *The Caribbean Policy of the United States, 1890–1920* (Baltimore, 1942), p. 309.

26. John B. Jackson to Philander C. Knox, August 30, 1910, 837.00/425; memo, "Political Conditions in Cuba," April 27, 1911, 837.00/480, in the

The Taft administration, however, could not resist inter-meddling when threats of revolt and actual violence began again—a reaction predicted in Cuba. When a group of vet-erans pressed President José Miguel Gómez to purge any bureaucrat who had served the Spanish, Secretary of State Philander C. Knox rattled the Platt Amendment to silence the *veteranistas*.[27] No sooner had this crisis passed than an outlawed, all-Negro political party asked Taft to intercede in its behalf and force Gómez to give it jobs and recognition. Rebuffed, the Negroes, in May, 1912, went "to the field" in Oriente province and threatened to destroy foreign property. The State Department pushed Gómez to quash the revolt and guard foreign property, tasks he had neither the troops nor the will to accomplish. The American government then sent ships and marines to Cuba "to protect American lives and property by rendering moral support or assistance to the Cuban government," a move Gómez welcomed privately but condemned publicly. The arrival of marines sparked racial violence outside Oriente and brought more pleas from the rebels. Hounded by the Cuban army and increasingly desperate, the Negro guerrillas actually burned some cane-fields five weeks after their first threats. Only five more months of fighting, marked by massacres and looting, brought the revolt to a close; but "the impression still seems to prevail . . . among the ignorant classes and even among the large part of the more intelligent, that all a discontented party need do is to take to the woods for a brief sojourn, burn

Decimal File, Records of the Department of State, included in Records of the Department of State Relating to Internal Affairs of Cuba, 1910–1933, in the National Archives of the United States (Microfilm Collection No. 488) (hereafter cited by 837 number).

27. Jackson to Knox, November 10, 1911, 837.00/502; Minister A. M. Beaupré to Knox, January 10, 1912, 837.00/539; Knox to Beaupré, January 16, 1912, 837.00/541; Beaupré to Knox, January 18, 1912, 837.00/546.

a few canefields and railroad culverts and bring about American intervention." [28]

The Taft administration, however, denied that its military acts had established a precedent for supporting incumbent governments, and it rejected a congressional attempt to commit American troops by law behind every Cuban regime. Rather, it preferred an interpretation of the Platt Amendment that would allow the president to intervene before violence began, recognizing that a Cuban government might be guilty of acts justifying revolt.[29]

By the time Woodrow Wilson and his associates were confronted with a "Cuban problem," they had already seen how bloody democracy, self-determination, and constitutionalism could get in Haiti, Mexico, and the Dominican Republic. Although the Wilsonians tried to curb economic imperialism, they had not, however, abandoned the belief that those who seized power by force begot further violence and were not fit for American recognition. Even after successive Caribbean occupations, Wilson did not question the righteousness of his decisions:

> So long as the power of recognition rests with me the Government of the United States will refuse to extend the hand of welcome to anyone who obtains power . . . by

28. William H. Taft to José Miguel Gómez, May 27, 1912, 837.00/614; Knox to Beaupré, May 23, 1912, 837.00/598A; Beaupré to Knox, May 24, 1912, 837.00/637; November 7, 1912, 837.00/949.

29. *Congressional Record*, 62d Cong., 2d Sess. (1912), 7891–92. In introducing SB 7075, Senator A. O. Bacon said that the United States could deter revolt by formally supporting the Cuban government. The Taft administration thought this dangerous. Taft to Senator C. S. Page, May 30, 1912, 711.37/41; Knox to Root, August 12, 1912, 711.37/42; Henry L. Stimson to Knox, August 9, 1912, 711.37/42; Brig. Gen. E. H. Crowder, "Memorandum for the Secretary of War," August 6, 1912, 711.37/42, Records of the Department of State Relating to the Political Relations of the United States and Cuba, 1910–1929 (Microfilm Collection No. 509). Hereafter cited by 711.37 number.

treachery and violence. No permanency can be given the affairs of any republic by a title based upon intrigue and
assassination. . . . I am more interested in the fortunes of
oppressed men and pitiful women and children than in any
property rights whatever. Mistakes I have no doubt made in
this perplexing business, but not in purpose or object.[30]

Wilson, Bryan, and Lansing were in essential agreement
that American security and economic growth would be
served best in the Caribbean by applying the ideals of democracy, believing that in so doing they were making a
sharp break with past policy. Their error was in assuming
that "Dollar Diplomacy" had been conceived as economic
imperialism and that Republican interventions had been to
protect American investments.

They themselves consistently reinforced the impression
that the United States government would not tolerate any
acts that violated American preconceptions of how a society
should be governed.[31] And Cuba, for the Wilsonians, seemed
to vindicate the wisdom of condemning violence. The Platt
Amendment was for them a wise tool to restrain illiberal
behavior and protect Cuban self-determination. William E.
Gonzales, their man in Havana, wondered if they understood
that such a position only encouraged Cuban politicians to
appeal for American intervention. He himself could not

30. Speech accepting the Democratic nomination, September 2, 1916,
at Shadow Lawn, N.J., reprinted in *Congressional Record*, 64th Cong., 1st
Sess. (1916), Appendix, 1984–87.

31. Arthur S. Link, *Wilson: The Struggle for Neutrality, 1914–15*
(Princeton, N.J., 1960), pp. 495–550; Ray Stannard Baker, *Woodrow Wilson: Life and Letters,* 8 vols. (Garden City, N.Y., 1927–39), V, 73–75;
Statement to the press by Wilson, March 11, 1913, U.S. State Department,
Foreign Relations of the United States, 1913 (Washington, 1920), p. 7
(hereafter cited as *Foreign Relations*); Robert Lansing, "Present Nature
and Extent of the Monroe Doctrine, and Its Need for Restatement," June 11,
1914, U.S. State Department, *The Lansing Papers, 1914–1920,* 2 vols.
(Washington, 1939), II, 460–65; Selig Adler, "Bryan and Wilsonian Caribbean Penetration," *Hispanic American Historical Review* XX (1940), 198–
226.

make up his mind whether the United States should unequivocally support an incumbent regime to deter revolt
or simply refuse to interfere under any circumstances, however fearful. That violence was an intrinsic part of Cuban
politics and the electoral process he had no doubt.[32]

In 1916 the Cuban president, Mario G. Menocal, reversed
an earlier pledge and began to engineer his own reelection.
His opponents, the Liberals, concluded that the elections
would be stolen and planned a revolt, 1906 style. Anticipating such an act, Gonzales urged the State Department to
back Menocal in order to eliminate Cuban confusion about
what Wilson meant by self-determination; the *políticos*
thought it included the right of rebellion. The elections
were, in fact, stolen, but the State Department hoped that
the Liberals might be appeased without American interference as an example to the world of Cuban democracy.[33]

The plea for constitutionalism was too late, for in February, 1917, the Liberals started a widespread revolt and
army mutiny against Menocal, designed to force American
intervention.[34] The State Department's reaction, however,
was to condemn violent solutions to political grievances;
this position was explicit in an open diplomatic note pub-

32. For an account based on manuscript sources, see George Baker, "The
Wilson Administration and Cuba, 1913–1921," *Mid-America* XLVI (1964),
48–63; William Jennings Bryan to Robert Lansing, June 20, 1915, reprinted
in Paola E. Coletta, ed., "Bryan Briefs Lansing," *Pacific Historical Review*
XXVII (1958), 383–86; W. E. Gonzales to Bryan, November 3, 1914,
837.00/1012; Gonzales to Division of Latin American Affairs, November 9,
1916, 837.00/1045.

33. Gonzales to Lansing, January 21, 1916, 837.00/1021; Alfredo Zayas,
"A Statement on the Elections in Cuba Held November 1, 1916,"
837.00/1253; Lansing to Gonzales, February 10, 1917, 837.00/1059.

34. Orestes Ferrara and Raimundo Cabrera to Lansing, February 10 and
12, 1917, 837.00/1066–69; Diary of John R. Bullard, Jobabo, Cuba, February 12 to March 10, 1917, 837.00/1472; Gonzales to Lansing, February 25,
1917, 837.00/1138; Gaston Schmutz, American consul-general, to Lansing,
February 26, 1917, 837.00/1165; Ferrara to Lansing, March 6, 1917,
837.00/1177; Memo, Lt. Col. Edmund Wittenmyer, military attaché, to
Secretary, War College Division, War Department General Staff, February
28, 1917, 837.00/1196.

lished in Cuba. The Wilson government then committed
ships and marines to Menocal's campaign to defeat the
rebels. Support of a regime whose electoral frauds were
well known was justified in several ways: that with American entry into the World War a rebellion that endangered
the sugar crop or suggested German intrigue could not be
tolerated and that American lives and property were endangered. But the long-term interpretation of Wilson's intervention, decisive to the rebel defeat, was that the United
States had formally outlawed rebellion as a form of political
action, however undemocratic the character of the *de jure*
government.[35]

By 1920 the consensus in the State Department was that
political parties and honest elections (despite the adoption
of a new electoral code drafted by Major General Enoch H.
Crowder in 1919) were beyond Cuba's capacity and that
only American supervision could guarantee a peaceful transfer of government. Some officials thought that more active
tutelage, not armed intervention after violence occurred,
would be a preferable policy. This view was also held by
José Miguel Gómez, the Liberal leader of the 1917 revolt
and his party's presidential candidate in 1920.[36] As it became
increasingly clear that Menocal was going to see that his

35. Leo J. Meyer, "The United States and the Cuban Revolution of
1917," *Hispanic American Historical Review* X (1930), 138–66; Entry,
February 27, 1917, in E. David Cronon, ed., *The Cabinet Diaries of Jo-
sephus Daniels, 1913–1921* (Lincoln, Neb., 1963), p. 106; Robert Lansing,
War Memoirs (Indianapolis, 1938), pp. 311, 313–14; Lansing to Gonzalez,
February 1, 1917, 837.00/1101; Lansing to Newton D. Baker, May 10, 1917,
837.00/1347a; J. M. Walcott, American consul in Santiago, to Lansing,
April 20, 1917, 837.00/1374; Maj. Rigoberto Fernández to Lansing, July 9,
1917, 837.00/1393; Roberto Mendez, Rogerio Zayas Bazán, and Elisée
Figueroa to Woodrow Wilson, January 16, 1918, 837.00/1456.

36. Enoch H. Crowder to Acting Secretary Frank L. Polk, May 8, 1919,
837.00/1549; Gonzales to Lansing, November 7, 1919, 837.00/1549; José
Miguel Gómez to Manuel Márquez Sterling, January 13, 1919, 837.00/1505;
José Miguel Gómez to the Secretary of State, July 15, 1920, 837.00/1700;
Crowder to Secretary of State, August 30, 1919, *Foreign Relations, 1919*,
2 vols. (Washington, 1934), II, 29–77; Quarterly Report No. 1, American
Legation, Havana, May 1, 1919, 837.00/1551.

candidate, the Liberal apostate Alfredo Zayas, would win the presidency, the Wilson administration again had to face the possibility of revolt. The State Department proposed to send American electoral supervisors to Cuba under General Crowder, reinforce the marines in Cuba, and continue its notes to Menocal on the democratic process.[37]

Wilson and his third secretary of state, Bainbridge Colby, however, rejected any American attempt to influence the election. Only armed insurrection justified such an infringement of Cuban sovereignty. Colby made clear that the United States would not supervise the election to ensure its honesty, but was opposed to fraud and intimidation as well as "any attempt to substitute violence and revolution for the processes of government."[38] Though they rejected sanctions as the evidence of Menocal's coercion mounted, Wilson and Colby did allow State Department agents to collect evidence of fraud in Cuba and, as a last attempt to save Cuban democracy, they intended, even before the election, to send a special envoy to Cuba to press the new president "to undertake a definite and thorough going program of reform."[39] But faced with the specter of military occupation, Wilson and Colby acquiesced to another Cuban election dominated by intimidation.[40]

37. "Minutes of a Conference on the Cuban Electoral Situation, Held at the Department of State on July 14, 1920," 837.00/1701 (Among those present: Leo S. Rowe, Crowder, and Sumner Welles); Assistant Secretary of State Norman H. Davis to Woodrow Wilson, August 21, 1920, 837.00/1860a; Memo, Division of Latin American Affairs, to the Under Secretary of State, August 27, 1920, 837.00/1764; Boaz Long, Minister to Cuba, to Colby, September 16, 1920, 837.00/1766.

38. Colby to Francis White, chargé d'affaires, Havana, August 25, 1920, 837.00/1737.

39. Colby to Wilson, July 28, 1920, 837.00/1860a with notation "Approved. Woodrow Wilson." See also Wilson to Davis, October 18, 1920, 837.00/2117; Colby to Long, October 20, 1920, 837.00/1809; Daniel M. Smith, "Bainbridge Colby and the Good Neighbor Policy, 1920–1921," *Mississippi Valley Historical Review* L (1963), pp. 56–78.

40. The election of 1920 provides a case study for political practices in the Cuban republic. See Long to Davis, October 8, November 3, November 5 (2 letters), 1920, 837.00/1819, 1858, 1869 and 1870; for eyewitness ac-

From January, 1921, until January, 1923, the United States, through money and moral suasion, made its last effort to make Cuba a liberal, democratic republic. Two conditions precipitated this exercise in nation-building: a financial crisis and uncertainty about the victor of the 1920 election. The financial crisis was caused by the collapse of the sugar market, which caught the Cuban banks and the Menocal government badly overextended. The usual rapacity of the *políticos* and bankers obstructed reform, and only the intervention of foreign credit and American financial experts restored Cuba's financial system—at the price of another foreign loan and increased foreign banking control. The financial crisis, however, was but a short-range concern and quickly adjusted. The disputed election seemed more fraught with peril, and military intervention was a possibility. To resolve the electoral crisis, the State Department dispatched its one-man crusade to reform Cuba, Major General Enoch H. Crowder.[41]

Using the promise of American financial aid as a lever on the Menocal government, Crowder was instructed to settle the electoral dispute without violence.[42] His arrival alarmed the Menocal-Zayas forces and encouraged the Miguelistas until it became obvious that the United States would not supervise the partial elections of March, 1921, upon which

counts, see Maj. N. W. Campanole, USA., "In Regard to Threatened Uprising in Cuba," October 5, 1920, 837.00/1799, and Dr. H. J. Spinden, "The Evils of the Present Electoral Situation in Cuba," October 22, 1920, 837.00/1835, and "Shall the United States Intervene in Cuba," *World's Work* XLI (1921), 465–83.

41. For scholarly, sympathetic accounts of Crowder's mission: David A. Lockmiller, *Enoch H. Crowder: Soldier, Lawyer, Statesman* (Columbia, Mo., 1955), pp. 217–46; Chapman, *A History of the Cuban Republic*, pp. 413–49.

42. Acting Secretary of State Norman H. Davis to Maj. Gen. E. H. Crowder, December 31, 1920, 837.00/1952b; Davis to Long, December 31, 1920, 837.00/1947a, and January 4, 1921, 837.00/1949; Crowder to Davis, January 17, 1921, 837.00/1967; Entries for January 1 and 4, 1921 in Cronon, ed., *Cabinet Diaries of Josephus Daniels*, pp. 583, 585.

the presidency depended. Instead, fearing an army mutiny and hoping that Menocal would seize this last chance to foster Cuban democracy, Crowder restricted his influence to issuing admonitions; this was all the departing Wilsonians or the new Harding administration would allow. Without American supervision, coercion was again widespread, and to save their honor the Liberals boycotted the polls. They insisted that the American position on political violence gave them no other recourse but symbolic protest.[43]

The resolution of the presidential dispute did not end Crowder's mission, for the general believed that one more attempt should be made to reform Cuban public life and that Alfredo Zayas, the new president, could be pressured to make changes. Despite Zayas's unsavory reputation, Crowder thought his malleability and the financial straits of his regime would make persuasion work. Zayas's desire for a favorable change of the sugar tariff and his need for a large foreign loan could be exploited, while, Crowder thought, pressure from Havana's businessmen and professionals of all nationalities was at last forcing the government to curb corruption and increase its efficiency. With the State Department's approval, Crowder approached Zayas and found him willing to appoint honest ministers, cut the budget, purge the bureaucracy, and check peculation, but only if these reforms were forced on him "more or less in terms of an ultimatum" with the United States clearly bearing the onus for their enactment. The risks seemed worth it, for

43. Long to Davis, January 28, 1921, 837.00/1986; Juan Gualberto Gómez to Crowder, January 7, 1921, and Crowder to Philander C. Knox, February 7, 1921, Crowder Papers, Western Historical Manuscripts Collection, University of Missouri Library; Crowder to Menocal, February 3, 1921, 837.00/1994; Warren G. Harding to Crowder, February 20, 1921, 837.00/2207; Charles E. Hughes to Crowder, March 5, 1921, 837.00/2016a; Faustino Guerra, President, Liberal Party, to Hughes, March 14, 1920, 837.00/2029; Crowder to Hughes, March 12, 1921, 837.00/2080; José Miguel Gómez, "Memorandum on Cuban Elections," March 31, 1921, 837.00/2095.

Crowder feared that without reform another occupation was inevitable.[44]

From February, 1922, until January, 1923, Crowder attempted, through Zayas, to create a Cuban progressive movement. Counting on support from the State Department and a group of Havana business-professional associations, he persuaded Zayas to appoint efficient and honest cabinet officers and presented a legislative program in the famous "Fifteen Memoranda," designed "to foster and promote in every way possible the welfare and prosperity of the Cuban people."[45] From February until July, Crowder periodically presented his reforms, suggesting that compliance would not only encourage the United States to approve another loan and make tariff concessions but that such reform would obviate later American interference by making Cuba a prosperous and peaceful nation.[46] Crowder's "moralization program" urged balanced and limited budgets, legislative control of finances, constitutional reforms to make democratic processes a reality at the polls and in the courts, and the elimination of nepotism, graft, and corruption in the government.

The Crowder reform program was short-lived, for the

44. Crowder to Hughes, March 24, 1921, 837.00/2049; Hughes to Crowder, March 28, 1921, 837.00/2049; Crowder to Hughes, April 28, 1921, 837.00/2093; Crowder to Hughes, May 21, 1921, 837.00/2210; Harding to Hughes, June 8, 1921, 837.00/2211; Crowder to Hughes, August 21, 1921, 837.00/2158.

45. Crowder to Zayas, February 9, 1922, Crowder Papers. On Cuban support: Cord Meyer, "Memorandum," January 24, 1922, 837.00/2196. Crowder later observed: "When I returned from Cuba to Chicago and witnessed the corruption of municipal politics in that city, I felt a sense of shame in recalling the memorandum which I found necessary to send to President Zayas." Quoted in H. F. Guggenheim, *The United States and Cuba* (New York, 1934), p. 157.

46. The Fifteen Memoranda are scattered throughout the 837.00 file of the State Department's Decimal File, but they are easily accessible in the Crowder Papers. They are numbered 1A (February 24, 1922), 1 to 13 (March 6–July 21, 1922), and enclosure 1 to Dispatch 205 (July 14, 1923). They are located in Files 308–314 and File 339 in the Crowder Papers. On the "Honest Cabinet," see Crowder to Hughes, June 19, 1922, 837.002/53.

forces working against it were more than the elderly, right-
eous, self-effacing general could control. Zayas had the
subsidized Havana press charge Crowder with destroying
Cuban national identity. Other *políticos*, a few radical intellectuals, and Zayas's business favorites made the protests a
chorus. The death blow came, however, from the State Department. Crowder found Secretary of State Charles Evans
Hughes's approval of the "moralization program" did not
include charging Cuba with violating the Permanent Treaty
or allowing the memos to "carry any kind of threat of intervention." [47] Moreover, although Hughes understood that
only Zayas's hope for a loan made him a reformer, Crowder
found the secretary increasingly reluctant to use this carrot
to keep Zayas on the path to "large reconstruction and
reform." [48] Instead, Hughes became apprehensive that
Crowder's militancy was being read in Cuba as a threat of
intervention and that the general's zeal was deepening
Zayas's need for State Department support as the reforms
destroyed his political following.[49] The major factor, however, that ended the "moralization program" was the State
Department's approval of a $50 million loan to Zayas. With
the ink hardly dry on the contract, Zayas, despite his assurances that moralization would continue, forced the four
most reformist secretaries from his cabinet. By the summer
of 1923 he had abandoned the Crowder reforms and smaller
budgets as the general helplessly watched. Despite some
spread-eagle rhetoric about the Permanent Treaty in the
loan contract, Crowder knew that even verbal coercion was

47. Crowder to Francis White, Chief of the Latin American Division,
May 4, 1922, Crowder Papers.
48. Crowder to Hughes, August 21, 1922, 837.00/2234, and Crowder to
Hughes, June 23, 1922, Crowder Papers.
49. Hughes to Harding, September 17, 1922, 837.00/2263; Zayas's interview with Mr. Clarence Marine, Superior Bank Liquidating Commission,
July 11, 1922, 837.00/2234.

out of the question. Only a complete breakdown of the Cuban government, Hughes told him, justified American intervention.[50] The general assumed that though he could continue to give advice, Hughes approved of this activity only "for the purpose of passing up to the Zayas administration one hundred percent responsibility for failure." Francis White, chief of the Latin American Division, agreed that this was indeed the secretary's policy.[51]

By the spring of 1923, then, Crowder had lost the leverage of State Department support for reform; but his program did not completely die, for in Cuba "moralization" gained other champions. Disillusioned by the fall of the "Honest Cabinet" and Zayas's rapacity, a group of Havana intellectuals, professionals, and businessmen formed the Cuban Committee of National and Civic Renovation in March, 1923. The moving spirit of the group, Dr. Fernando Ortiz, renowned anthropologist and historian, went so far as to solicit Crowder's thoughts on an American-backed coup. Ortiz proposed that a provisional government be established, corruptionists jailed, the traditional political parties be dissolved, and the constitution rewritten in order to wrest political power from the *políticos* and their illiterate followers.[52] Ortiz warned Crowder, too, that if the United States would not assist the intellectual-economic elite to seize power and purify the government, then it would have to accept politi-

50. Hughes to Crowder, March 31, 1923, 837.002/60a; Hughes to Crowder, April 3, 1923, 837.002/62; Hughes to Crowder, April 4, 1923, 837.002/62 Suppl.

51. Crowder to White, April 4, 1923, and White to Crowder, April 11, 1923, Crowder Papers.

52. Fernando Ortiz, memo, "The Cuban Crisis," March 17, 1923, File 1264, Crowder Papers. For a description of the Committee's leadership, see Ortiz memo, "Cuban Renovation," March (?), 1923, File, 1263, Crowder Papers. The central directorate was Ortiz, Luis Morales, Ramiro Guerra y Sánchez, Martínez Inclán, Felipe Pazos, Gonzalo Freyre de Andrade, Raul de Cárdenas, Oscar Barceló, Luciano R. Martínez, José A. Cosculluela and José Grau San Martín.

cal violence. Ortiz feared that Cuba was heading for increasingly oligarchical government and that the public wanted radical change, now. The political system was bankrupt, financially and morally, and "the North American Government must think seriously of giving us, in the end, a definite and radical solution." [53]

Crowder communicated Ortiz's bleak predictions and his own concern to the State Department, but Hughes was unreceptive. The general emphasized that his "moralization program" had so heartened the "responsible non-political elements of Cuba" that he sensed a growing disapproval of corrupt government, at least among the urban elite. Not coincidentally, he also felt a growing tide of anti-Americanism, stimulated not only by Zayas but also by reformers who saw American interference as the source of Cuba's ills. The general believed that popular frustration was mounting so rapidly that peaceful elections in 1924 were unlikely.[54]

Although aware that Harding and Hughes were no longer interested in Cuban reform or in jeopardizing the hope for Pan-Americanism, Crowder continued to warn the State Department that United States influence was waning in Cuba. Zayas had returned to a bacchanalia of graft in order to solidify his political support and appease his business favorites. Crowder despaired that democratic processes would ever flourish without tutelage and felt the chance to exercise that guidance was decreasing unless the United States acted to check the rising anti-Americanism:

53. Ortiz memos, June 26, 1923, and March 20, 1923, Crowder Papers. Ortiz, a member of the House of Representatives, also provided Crowder with massive documentation of the Cuban government's corruption. Another source of confidential information was Dr. Gonzalo Freyre de Andrade, another congressman, later killed by Machado's gunmen.

54. E. H. Crowder, "Memorandum for the Secretary of State: Recent Cabinet Crisis," April 21, 1923, 837.002/85; Crowder to White, April 26, 1923, 837.00/2610; Crowder to White, June 21, 1923, 837.00/2312; Crowder to Hughes, July 12, 1923, 837.00/2318.

The people argue, with some force, that as no relief against corrupt government can come through corrupt elections, and as the right of armed revolt against such a Government has been denied them by the policy of the United States here and elsewhere in Latin America, the responsibility for the continuance of corrupt government here lies with the United States, and that relief can come only through a much more aggressive attitude of our Government.[55]

The reform movement that Ambassador Crowder predicted became an active force in Cuban politics in August, 1923. Although labeled the Veterans and Patriots Movement, the reformers were an amalgam of groups committed to national reconstruction. The Veterans and Patriots Association, a group of ex-guerrillas led by *políticos* Carlos García Vélez, Tomás Recio, Domingo Méndez Capote, and Carlos Mendieta, lent its prestige, but was the least reformist of the movement's constituent parts; its goals were power for the leaders and pensions for the rank and file. The other groups, however, represented new forces in Cuban politics, an alliance of reform interests that should have warmed the hearts of American progressives: the Committee of One Hundred, the Good Government Association, the Havana Stock Exchange, the Association of Sugar Mill Owners and Planters, the Industrial Association, the National Federation of Economic Corporations, the Women's Club of Cuba, the Rotary Clubs of Cuba, and the Association of University Students. Gathered in congress in Havana, the reformers in a series of manifestoes challenged Zayas to purify the government and parties, but their interests were even

55. Quote from Crowder to Hughes, July 15, 1923, Crowder Papers. On the failure of Cuban government, see Crowder's memos to the Secretary of State, "Cuban Electoral Frauds and Legislation Remedial Thereof" (July 14, 1923) and "The Cuban Congress" (July 17, 1923), *ibid.* On the end of Crowder's reforms, see Harding to Hughes, May 9, 1923, 837.002/93.

broader than administrative reform. The assembly, which included labor leaders, intellectuals, and student radicals, offered a program of sweeping change: the "nationalization" of the working class, the end of corporate privileges, sweeping social reform, women's suffrage, and an end to the Platt Amendment. As one State Department analyst noted: "An interesting element of a socialistic nature was introduced by the demand that the people should participate in the exploitation of agriculture, the industries, and commerce." Moreover, the movement seemed to be reaching people outside the parties by creating committees of propaganda at the provincial and municipal level, thus stimulating an interest of "alarming proportions." Part of the army was thought to be sympathetic.[56]

The reformers, however, could not decide on how to bring about change. They were divided on whether they should curry American intervention; equally divisive was the issue of armed revolt. The latter prospect alarmed the "economic corporations" and seemed hopeless in the face of American intransigence on political violence. Torn with discord, the Veterans and Patriots Movement began to unravel internally by the end of September, assisted by Zayas and the State Department. The Cuban president arrested or scattered the movement's most ambitious leaders, bought off others, and dramatically pledged himself to the assembly's reforms. The State Department remained mute to pleas for support from both Zayas and the assembly. Within six months all that remained of the movement was increased anti-Americanism

56. Latin American Division, Department of State, "The Veterans' Movement in Cuba," September 12, 1923, 837.00/2350; W. S. Howell, chargé d'affaires, to Hughes, August 20, 1923, 837.00/2327; Howell to Hughes, August 27, 1923, 837.00/2337; Howell to Hughes, October 13, 1923, 837.00/2383; Latin American Subsection (M. I. 2-a), Military Intelligence Division, War Department General Staff, "Survey of the Political Situation in Cuba," September 19, 1923, 837.00/2375.

and a brief rural revolt near Cienfuegos, quickly halted by Zayas and an American arms embargo.[57]

With another Cuban presidential election approaching in 1924, the State Department and Crowder continued to insist that political violence was incompatible with reform, however grievous the corruption of the Zayas regime. Hughes believed that a public statement on Cuban politics would only feed anti-Americanism. As the election approached, it also seemed possible that the prospective winner, Liberal *político* and millionaire businessman Gerardo Machado, might be an improvement over Zayas. Crowder, after several conversations with Machado, was convinced that the Liberal candidate sincerely wanted to fulfill that treaty commitment of 1903 "in such a way that no question could arise under the Platt Amendment." Machado might even sponsor a reform administration since he was already wealthy. He was, however, airily unconcerned about the increasing violence of the campaign, which, Crowder warned, might occasion intervention.[58] Machado knew the strength of his position, for he assumed that Crowder could not get Hughes to use any diplomatic tool that might lead to American intervention.[59] Indeed, the only thing Crowder could do as Machado swept to victory (with Zayas's help) was to persuade the loser, Mario G. Menocal, to accept defeat gracefully and not stage a revolt.

57. Howell to Hughes, October 26, 1923, 837.00/2400, and December 4, 1923, 837.00/2453; Crowder to White, January 14, 1924; Maj. W. H. Shutan, attaché, "The Cuban Political Situation," March 24, 1924; Dr. Charles E. Chapman to Crowder, June 25, 1924, all in Crowder Papers.

58. Crowder to Dwight Morrow, August 26, 1926, Crowder Papers; Crowder to Hughes, August 25, August 26, and September 5, 1924, 837.00/2541, 2544, 2547.

59. Crowder to White, September 19, 1924, Crowder Papers; Crowder to Hughes, September 26, 1924, 837.00/2557; Hughes to Crowder, October 8, 1924, 837.00/2555; Hughes to Crowder, November 24, 1924, Crowder Papers.

III

Gerardo Machado entered office a reformer; it was his commitment to overdue economic and political change, not corruption, that eventually turned his government to terrorism and repression. Machado was a positivist, a modernizer. He saw his mission as bringing Cuba into the twentieth century, a task that called for governmental intervention in all phases of Cuban life. "The government of our nation must be the great motor of social life," he said, ensuring equal justice, improved wages and employment, better roads, education, and public works, and an end to crime and immorality. As he told the faculty of the University of Havana, the masses of the world wanted economic improvement, not abstract liberties, parties, parliaments, and theories; since the World War, only centralized authority could cope with the problems of modernization. Machado was determined that if the *políticos* stood in the way of honest and efficient government, then force would be used to subdue them, but it was vital that Cuba rescue itself from its economic distress and corrupt government.[60]

The Machado administration concentrated upon ending Cuba's economic stagnation by raising sugar prices. Beginning with the Verdeja Act of 1927 and culminating with the Chadbourne Plan of 1930, the Cuban government attempted to assist the planters by setting domestic crop quotas, establishing central marketing agencies, and agreeing upon mar-

60. Manifesto by Gerardo Machado, *Diario de la Marina* (Havana), September 10, 1924, 837.00/2549; Speech to the faculty of the National University, reprinted in *El Mundo* (Havana), June 1, 1926; Crowder to Secretary of State Frank B. Kellogg on Machado address to the staff of the National Military Academy, August 25, 1925, 837.00/2597; Machado speech to the Cuban Exhibition, New York City, November 16, 1925, 711.37/80; Crowder to Kellogg on Machado address to Liberal Party officials, November 11, 1926, 837.00/2619.

keting quotas with other international producers. Although Machado's efforts were backed by American business interests in Cuba, the United States government remained adamant that Cuban sugar was already receiving preference in the American market. No new reciprocity treaty was negotiated. Without a change in this policy, sugar prices remained low; Cuban agriculture entered its Great Depression long before 1929.[61]

Machado believed that Cuba's economic plight was so desperate that the government could no longer tolerate party factionalism and administrative corruption. As his sugar policies faltered, he increasingly turned to public works spending to stimulate the economy, a program for which he needed foreign loans and, thus, demonstrated fiscal restraint. Although his public speeches were appropriately anti-*yanqui,* Machado turned to Cuba's nonpolitical business associations for support. At the same time, he begged, bought, and coerced the three traditional parties into a docile pro-Machado front and initiated an effective police attack on crime and political dissent. So sure was Machado of his power and his mission of modernization that he decided to run for reelection in 1928 despite a one-term pledge.[62]

61. Alberto Martínez-Piedra, "Land Reform in Cuba, 1933–1958," (Ph.D. dissertation, Georgetown University, 1962), pp. 37–52; James R. O'Connor, "The Political Economy of Pre-Revolutionary Cuba," (Ph.D. dissertation, Columbia University, 1964); Crowder to Dwight Morrow, March 25, 1925, Crowder Papers; Stokely W. Morgan, Chief, Division of Latin American Affairs, memo of conversation with Cuban ambassador Orestes Ferrara, February 20, 1927, 711.37/101; Crowder to Kellogg, December 6, 1926, 837.00/2623; on reciprocity, see U.S. Tariff Commission, "Operation of the Reciprocity Treaty of 1902 Between the United States and Cuba," June 12, 1926, Crowder Papers.

62. Francis V. Jackman, "America's Cuban Policy during the Period of the Machado Regime," (Ph.D. dissertation, Catholic University, 1964), pp. 7–21; Crowder to Kellogg, October 25, 1926 (837.00/2616) and February 14, 1927 (837.00/2627); Dwight Morrow to Carlos Miguel de Céspedes, March 31, 1926, and Crowder to Dr. Charles E. Chapman, Crowder Papers.

The State Department knew that Machado was creating an opposition to his regime; both Crowder and Noble B. Judah, his replacement as ambassador, reported growing dissatisfaction. The sources of discontent, however, did nothing to persuade Secretary of State Frank B. Kellogg that the United States should express concern, for the most prominent critics were ambitious *políticos* like Menocal, Carlos Mendieta, and Mariano Miguel Gómez, son of José Miguel and former mayor of Havana, or disgruntled American speculators. Kellogg and his ministers agreed that Machado was indeed modernizing Cuba and that he enjoyed the support of Cuba's economic elite, native and foreign. Furthermore, there was no desire to resort to "intermeddling" for to do so risked occupation and increased anti-Americanism in Latin America. Despite its awareness that Cuba's political parties, elections, and constitutional democracy might disappear, the State Department was not convinced that such sacrifices were altogether bad.[63] Still smarting from an electoral intervention in Nicaragua and impressed by Machado's messianic zeal in creating peace, prosperity, and passive *políticos*, the State Department made no effort to keep Machado from another term. Aware that he quite probably had had some critics killed and was drifting into a military-backed dictatorship, the department was satisfied that Machado would remain in control and was not injuring American strategic and commercial interests.[64]

63. Crowder to Kellogg, March 19, 1927, 837.00/2633; Kellogg to Crowder, May 13, 1927, 837.00/2646; memo, "Amendments to the Cuban Constitution," June 17, 1927, synopsis of conference of Kellogg, Crowder, Francis White, and Orestes Ferrara, 837.00/2675; Stokely W. Morgan, "Memorandum of Conversations between the President of Cuba and the Chief of Latin American Affairs," April 25, 1927, 837.00/2655; Noble B. Judah to Kellogg, June 26, 1928, 837.00/2703.

64. C. B. Curtis, chargé d'affaires, to Kellogg, October 29, 1928, 837.00/2714; Curtis to Henry L. Stimson, June 13, 1929, 837.001/M18/42; H. C. Lakin to Machado, January 26, 1929, Crowder Papers; Crowder to Ma-

The State Department knew that Machado was becoming increasingly unpopular, but there seemed to be little connection between the active critics—old-line party politicians, liberal intellectuals, and a handful of student and labor radicals—and what it viewed as Cuba's gravest problem, its economic depression. At least until 1931 the State Department was substantially correct in believing that Machado's most powerful opponents were the same breed as the president himself, that Cuba's poverty and violence were chronic but not at the heart of the opposition, and that the critics were playing for American intervention. Although it may have underestimated the economic insecurity of the elite, the State Department did not think that the Cuban upper class was really revolutionary. Whenever United States officials generalized on the sources of unrest they invariably blamed the collapse of sugar prices.[65] As long as American policy was attuned to Machado's economic policies, the State Department could not justify intervention, however arbitrary the regime. No government had been a model democracy. When the Congress in 1928 investigated charges against Machado, the State Department had no difficulty convincing the Senate Foreign Relations Committee of Cuba's generous treatment of American business;

---

chado, January 26, 1929, Crowder Papers; Manifesto of June 21, 1928, *Declarations of General Gerardo Machado y Morales* (Havana, 1928), Crowder Papers; Bryce Wood, *The Making of the Good Neighbor Policy* (New York, 1961), pp. 48–117.

65. Crowder to Kellogg, May 13, 1927, 837.00/2659; Stokley W. Morgan, memo of conversation with Dr. Fernando Ortiz, "Political Situation in Cuba," May 3, 1927, 837.00/2657; Curtis to Stimson, November 20, 1929, 837.00/2776; Memo, Division of Latin American Affairs, to Assistant Secretary Francis White, September 16, 1929, 837.00/2759 1/2. For economics and the elite, see Henry C. Wallich, *Monetary Problems of an Export Economy: The Cuban Experience, 1914–1947* (Cambridge, Mass., 1950), p. 200. For contemporary economic explanations of Cuban instability, see Philip G. Wright, *The Cuban Situation and Our Treaty Relations* (Washington, 1931), and Fernando Ortiz, "La responsabilidad de los Estados Unidos," *Revista bimestre cubana* XXIV (1929), 484–90.

the violence revealed to the Congress was habitual. Although there was private concern about Machado's desire to perpetuate his regime, State Department officials saw little reason to interfere.[66]

That Machado was by 1929 a dictator is undeniable, but his most vocal opponents until 1931 were *políticos* whose goal was intervention under the Platt Amendment. Both Machado and the State Department were wary; both believed that economic recovery or public works spending would curb mass unrest. Although the American embassy reported growing anti-Machado sentiment among university students, labor leaders, intellectuals, and professional men, these groups were considered pawns of Mendieta's Unión Nacionalista and Menocal's Opposition Conservatives. The State Department, fearing a repeat of past interventions, insisted that threats or acts of violence would not bring American troops running, but that political liberalization might assist economic recovery and the negotiation of another loan.[67]

Secretary of State Henry L. Stimson and Ambassador Harry F. Guggenheim were correct enough in identifying the Opposition's spokesmen as "outs," but they underestimated the depth of feeling in the Cuban intelligentsia that the crux of Cuba's problems was the alien nature of its political system. By 1930 the idea was common among Opposition radicals that Cuba had to be redeemed from American

66. *Congressional Record*, 70th Cong., 1st Sess. (1928), 6591; Judah to Stimson, May 10, 1929, 837.00/2747; Senator William E. Borah to Stimson, September 12, 1929, 711.37/131 1/2; Memo, Undersecretary of State J. Ruben Clark to Stimson, April 26, 1929, 837.00/2749.

67. Stimson to Judah, April 23, 1929, 837.00/2730; H. F. Guggenheim to Stimson, July 15, 1930, *Foreign Relations, 1930*, 3 vols. (Washington, 1945), II, 650–51; Guggenheim to Stimson, October 23 to December 13, 1930, *ibid.*, 667–80; "Memorandum of Conference by the Secretary of State with the Press on October 2, 1930," *ibid.*, 662–65; William E. Walling, "President Machado's Administration of Cuba," *Current History* XXXII (1930), 257–63.

cultural domination. Though the island's economic system was part of the problem, it was secondary to the belief that the constitution of 1901, the Platt Amendment, the Crowder Code of 1919, the traditional political parties, the electoral interventions, and now Machado were all part of a bankrupt political system that could only be broken by fundamental revolution, free of American influence. The United States became the source of every menace to Cuba: poverty, corruption, crime, political oppression, the influx of Haitian and Jamaican workers, illiteracy, disease, the degradation of Hispanic culture, and the materialism of Cuban life. Angry, frustrated, as yet politically impotent, the "Generation of 1930" assaulted Machado not only for what he was but also as a symbol of American domination.[68]

In 1931 the Machado regime and American policy weathered a traditional rural uprising designed to bring United States intervention. Machado by now had had his own term of office and that of the incumbent congress extended by constitutional amendment. He had made it impossible for new political parties to organize and had gotten a favorable supreme court decision on the constitutionality of his regime. He had secured a multimillion dollar loan from the Chase Bank. The army and police remained loyal. Thus far the radical oppositionists were small, fractious gangs severely harried by the Havana police. The major threat was the factions of Mendieta, Menocal, and Mariano Miguel Gómez; but when this coalition staged a revolt, it was quickly broken

68. For the development of Cuban nationalism, see Federico G. Gil, "Antecedents of the Cuban Revolution," *Centennial Review of Arts and Science* VI (1962), 373–93; C. A. M. Hennessy, "The Roots of Cuban Nationalism," *International Affairs* XXXIX (1963), 345–59; Cosme de la Torriente, "The Platt Amendment," *Foreign Affairs* VIII (1930), 364–78; Raymond L. Buell, *Cuba and the Platt Amendment* (New York, 1929); Robert F. Smith, "Twentieth-Century Cuban Historiography," *Hispanic American Historical Review* XLIV (1964), 44–73; Duvon C. Corbitt, "Cuban Revisionist Interpretations of Cuba's Struggle for Independence," *ibid.*, XLIII (1963), 395–404.

up by the Cuban army. Machado began to talk compromise with the *políticos,* at the urging of Guggenheim and Army Chief of Staff Alberto Herrera, and by year's end promises of political liberalization appeared to have ended the crisis.[69]

The Opposition, however, no longer drew its strength from the *políticos.* Resistance to Machado now became urban guerrilla warfare in Havana, waged against the regime by the "ABC," a secret society of professional men and intellectuals, and the young radicals of the Student Directorate. Their campaign of bombings and assassination was a new phenomenon in Cuban political violence. Machado immediately recognized the threat and unleashed his own terrorists, "La Porra," on the Oppositionists. For the next year a tide of murder, torture, mutilation, and execution ebbed and flowed in the capital. Though the rebels were never a coherent single unit nor were they agreed on a post-Machado policy, many were now committed to the new idea that no American interference of any kind could be permitted in the reconstruction of Cuban life. In the meantime, the State Department insisted that the Cubans must determine their own government, hopefully through constitutional means, a position that bolstered the Machado regime and helped keep the army loyal. The killings went on into 1933.[70]

Stimson and Guggenheim found themselves in a most

69. Francis White, "Memorandum by the Assistant Secretary of State," April 10, 1931, *Foreign Relations, 1931,* 3 vols. (Washington, 1946), II, 51–54; Guggenheim to Stimson, August 10–September 9, 1931, *ibid.,* 67–76; Guggenheim to Stimson, December 24, 1931, *ibid.,* 80–82; Jackman, "America's Cuban Policy during the Period of the Machado Regime," pp. 21–29.

70. Guggenheim to Stimson, January 25, 1932, *Foreign Relations, 1932,* 5 vols. (Washington, 1948), V, 533–38; E. L. Reed, chargé d'affaires, to Stimson, May 25, 1932, *ibid.,* 548–50; Guggenheim to Stimson, July 25, 1932, *ibid.,* 552–54; Guggenheim to Stimson, January 5, 1933, *Foreign Relations, 1933,* 5 vols. (Washington, 1950–52), V, 270–74. For detailed descriptions of the Havana terrorism, see Ruby Hart Phillips, *Cuba: Island of Paradox* (New York, 1959), pp. 3–94, and Carleton Beals, *The Crime of Cuba* (Philadelphia, 1933), pp. 239–399.

annoying dilemma. Both adhered to the conservative Root interpretation of the Platt Amendment; both believed that the drift to intermeddling after 1902 had been the basic flaw in Cuban-American relations. In 1932 there was no threat of foreign intervention and, as yet, no loss of American lives and little property damage. Yet the State Department was being urged by Cuban exiles, assorted congressmen, and American liberals to end Machado's inhumanity against Cuba's "best people." Stimson, however, thought that there was little public taste for armed intervention and that sponsoring impartial elections was a policy that moved Americans but had little meaning in the Caribbean. Yet no interference was interpreted as approval of Machado and steadily increased the chance of a revolution of unforeseeable dimensions.[71]

Upon taking office in the gloomy spring of 1933, Franklin D. Roosevelt, Secretary of State Cordell Hull, and Assistant Secretary Sumner Welles thought the Cuban insurgency too important to be ignored. Cuba, as well as the United States, needed a New Deal; and as committed Wilsonians, the administration's policymakers believed that only the tactics of Wilsonian idealism, not its assumptions, needed change. Roosevelt, Hull, and Welles were not against interfering in the cause of democracy, social harmony, and constitutionalism; they only wanted to avoid military occupation. More positively, they wanted to stimulate Latin American progress by lowering tariff barriers and to make Wilsonianism

71. Stimson quoted in *New York Times*, Feb. 7, 1931; Stimson to Guggenheim, March 26, 1932, *Foreign Relations, 1932*, V, 543–47; Wood, *Making of the Good Neighbor Policy*, pp. 52–59; Henry Stimson, "Bases of American Foreign Policy during the Past Four Years," *Foreign Affairs* XI (1933), 383–96. Ambassador Guggenheim, counseled in Havana by Root's biographer, Philip C. Jessup, went further, advocating a new treaty to replace the Platt Amendment. (Guggenheim, *The United States and Cuba*, pp. 231–50). For public and congressional opinion: *Congressional Record*, 72d Cong., 1st Sess. (1932), 7874, and 73d Cong., 1st Sess. (1933), 2891–93; *Literary Digest* CXV (February 25, 1933), 10.

multilateral through Pan-American diplomacy. Such Good
Neighborliness was also clearly in America's interest, too,
because it insured the strategic security of the hemisphere
and promised wider markets for a prostrate economy. Thus
liberal idealism, Pan-Americanism, hemispheric security,
and economic recovery blended in happy harmony in the
New Deal for Cuba.[72]

For the Opposition, Roosevelt's inauguration was a signal
to step up resistance to Machado. United in their assault,
they were, however, organizationally and ideologically fragmented. The Unión Nacionalista, the Marianistas, and the
Menocalistas envisioned a restoration of the pre-Machado
political system by free elections. For the "Generation of
1930" (the core of the ABC, the ABC Radical, the Organi-
zación Celular Radical Revolucionaria (OCRR), and organized labor) restoration was not enough. There must be
sweeping reform: a wholesale purge of the machadistas, a
new constitution, a parliamentary government, limited suffrage, redistribution of wealth by law, and an end of American tutelage. More radical still, the Student Directorate,
with its faculty and intellectual companions, questioned
whether democracy or capitalism was worth saving, especially if the price was the continued American imperialism
of loans, investments, and elections. The differences in the
political prescriptions of the Opposition were basic; adding
the fearful maneuverings of the "cooperating" parties, the

72. Franklin D. Roosevelt, "Our Foreign Policy," *Foreign Affairs* VI
(1928), 573–86; "From Now On, War by Government Shall Be Changed
to Peace by Peoples," Address before the Woodrow Wilson Foundation,
December 28, 1933, in Samuel I. Rosenman, ed., *The Public Papers and
Addresses of Franklin Delano Roosevelt*, 13 vols. (New York, 1938–50), II,
544–49; Cordell Hull, *Memoirs*, 2 vols. (New York, 1948), I, 308–13;
Charles C. Griffin, ed., "Welles to Roosevelt: A Memorandum on Inter-
American Relations, 1933," *Hispanic American Historical Review* XXXIV
(1954), 190–92; Sumner Welles, *The Time for Decision* (New York, 1944),
pp. 191–94; E. David Cronon, "Interpreting the New Good Neighbor
Policy: The Cuban Crisis of 1933," *Hispanic American Historical Review*
XXXIX (1959), 538–67.

army, and the business community, the political climate of Cuba was for the first time truly revolutionary.[73]

To deal with a political elite disillusioned with consensual reform, constitutionalism, and aggregate economic progress, Franklin Roosevelt sent a personal representative who viewed all three as holy writ, Sumner Welles. Career diplomat, Wilsonian reformer of Caribbean nations, Welles was dispatched to Havana to mediate away the Machado regime without a military occupation, without violence, and without antagonizing the rest of Latin America. Welles's instructions, by emphasizing the essentialness of constitutionalism in settling the Cuban insurgency, asked him to restore the order and social harmony that Cuban politics had never had. Feeling it "obligatory" not to let Cuba dissolve in anarchy and ruin, Roosevelt reverted to the "preventive policy," sending Welles to give "friendly advice" on political compromise and to begin negotiations on a new trade agreement and, perhaps, modification of the Treaty of 1903. But Cuba must first return to the path of constitutionalism.[74]

Appalled by Machado's complacent acceptance of the violence in Havana ("he never gave the slightest indication that these acts of barbaric cruelty were anything but justified"), Welles remained convinced that a Cuban solution

73. For the fall of Machado, see Jackman, Wood, and Cronon, previously cited, and K. Duff, "Relations between Cuba and the United States, 1898–1934," in Arnold J. Toynbee, ed., *Survey of International Affairs, 1933* (London, 1934), pp. 361–93; Charles A. Thomson, "The Cuban Revolution: Fall of Machado," *Foreign Policy Reports* XI (1935), 250–60; Hubert C. Herring, "The Downfall of Machado," *Current History* XXXIX (1933), pp. 14–24; Charles W. Hackett, "Guerrilla Warfare in Cuba," *ibid.*, XXXVIII (1933), 469–71.

74. "Statement of Mr. Sumner Welles, Assistant Secretary of State," April 24, 1933, *Foreign Relations, 1933*, V, 278–79; Hull to Welles (Instruction No. 1), May 1, 1933, *ibid.*, pp. 279–86; Welles to Roosevelt, May 18, 1933, quoted in Cronon, "Interpreting the Good Neighbor Policy," p. 540. For a Cuban reaction by a key figure in the Conservative Opposition, see Horacio Ferrer, *Con el rifle al hombro* (Havana, 1950), pp. 297–98, 300, 302, 313, 336. Ferrer, working to replace Machado through the army, thought a coup would mean immediate occupation.

"must" be based on maintaining the "structure of constitutional government" if peace, prosperity, Good Neighborliness, and nonoccupation were to flow from his mediation. His first contacts with the Unión Nacionalista, the Menocalistas, and the Marianistas impressed him that he had found in these Opposition *políticos* equal devotees to the democratic process. They, too, wanted no revolution, preferring to phase out the "Machadato" through a constitutional succession and elections.[75]

Through June and July, 1933, Welles labored to find a peaceful and graceful way to remove Machado; but though he was able to draft a plan, he was unable to find either a provisional president or a Cuban political consensus. Initially he conducted his mediation with Opposition representatives (either "extremely radical" or "decidedly conservative") from among the Unión Nacionalista, Marianistas, Menocalistas, the OCRR, the ABC, the university and institute professors, and the "women of the Opposition." The Student Directorate, author of much of Havana's terrorism and prime target of La Porra, resisted Welles's call to compromise, but curtailed its raids and bombings. Machado, then, in the name of a constitutional settlement, had Welles add representatives from the "cooperating" political parties. The talks went on. By mid-July Welles had his formula: the Opposition and government would agree on basic reforms to purify Cuban politics, the Congress would pass the reforms, a constitutional assembly would be elected and changes made to restore the vice-presidency, elect a vice-president, and have Machado retire. To the Cuban radicals the plan was a betrayal, an impression reinforced by two amnesties

75. Welles, *Time for Decision*, pp. 195–96; Welles to Hull, May 13, 1933, *Foreign Relations, 1933*, V, 287–90; Welles to Hull, *ibid.*, 295–96; Welles to Acting Secretary of State William Phillips, June 2, 1933, *ibid.*, 299–301; Welles to Hull, June 21, 1933, 837.00/3555, quoted in Jackman, "Machado Regime," p. 101.

Machado arranged for the *porristas*. Another warning was Welles's growing ties with the "Generation of '95" and his commitment to their most popular leader, Carlos Mendieta. On July 26, when the first open talks began with Machado's own ministers, the ABC abandoned the mediation.[76]

Cuban politics were beyond constitutional solution. On August 5 the ABC, Student Directorate, and assorted labor leaders turned a transport workers walkout into a city-wide general strike. Panic-stricken, Machado and his coterie sent the police and *porristas* on a rampage, denounced Welles's mediation, and tried to rally support by accusing the United States of planning imminent invasion. The Machadato saw itself on the brink of revolutionary extermination. The threat of occupation, however, persuaded the officers of Havana's garrisons to abandon Machado; though Welles had hinted such action to General Herrera, he was converted by his subordinates, not by Welles. The bloodshed and paralyzation in Havana mounted and spread to a few other towns. On August 11 Machado fled. His police and political apparatus dissolved in mob reprisal. Welles's mediation had fallen, with Machado, to an army coup, but there had been no occupation.[77]

Encouraged by Welles and the army, the constitutionalist Opposition formed a cabinet, named Dr. Carlos Manuel de Céspedes president, and restored successively the constitutions of 1928 and 1901. Although the cabinet included leaders of the ABC, OCRR, and the university professors, the

76. Jackman, "Machado Regime," pp. 104–10; Thomson, "Cuban Revolution," pp. 253, 252–54; Duff, "Cuban-American Relations," p. 377; Welles to Phillips, July 11, 1933, *Foreign Relations, 1933,* V, 317; "Presidential Message to Delegates of Opposing Factions in Cuba, July 1, 1933," *Public Papers and Addresses of Franklin Delano Roosevelt,* II, 263; Welles to Roosevelt, July 17, 1933, *Foreign Relations, 1933,* V, 323–25; La Célula Directriz del ABC, *El ABC en la Mediación* (Havana, 1934).

77. Ferrer, *Cin el rifle al hombro,* pp. 320–37; William Phillips, "Memorandum by the Acting Secretary of State," August 2, 1933, *Foreign Relations, 1933,* V, 331–32; Welles to Phillips, August 2–7, 1933, *ibid.,* 332–37, and Welles to Hull, August 8–11, 1933, *ibid.,* 340–46, 355–56.

rank-and-file radicals, especially the students, saw the Céspedes government as a Welles-sponsored restoration of the *políticos*. Welles himself recognized the increasing pressure for purges, for rapid, extralegal economic and political reforms, and for his own recall, but he and Roosevelt stoutly insisted that the United States could only lend "feasible aid" through "constitutional government." [78] Welles saw "a general process of disintegration going on," and despite his plea for elections and the promise of American economic aid, "none of the real leaders of public opinion" were satisfied with the Céspedes regime. Neither elections nor trade treaties seemed to move the radicals. As Welles recognized, the demoralized Cuban army now held the balance of power. [79]

On the night of September 4, an army mutiny organized by a group of sergeants and student radicals toppled the Céspedes government. Although the mutiny probably began as a reaction to the threat of restricted promotions and reduced pay, it quickly became a political movement that rejected the constitutional nostrums of the American embassy and the conservatism of the Céspedes restoration. The new insurgents proposed, rather, to create a "modern democracy" of "pure national sovereignty" responsive to the masses' needs, but free of the political sins of the old Republic. The insurgents, however, swore that they recognized the sanctity of lives, property, and international obligations. [80] In the

78. Roosevelt's statement of August 13, 1933, *Public Papers and Addresses of Franklin Delano Roosevelt*, II, 322–23; Welles to Hull, August 14, 15, and 30, 1933, *Foreign Relations, 1933*, V, 363–67, and 376–78.

79. Welles to Hull, August 19, 22, and 24, 1933, *Foreign Relations, 1933*, V, 367–73. The matter of foreign loan payments does not appear to have concerned Welles. He and a panel of experts led by A. A. Berle, Jr., warned the State Department that any Cuban government would probably have to call a moratorium on debt payment in order to meet its payroll, a matter of highest importance in quieting Havana. Welles to Hull, August 20, 1933, *ibid.*, 587–80, and "Preliminary Report on Cuban Finances Prepared by American Financial Experts," September 5, 1933, *ibid.*, 583–88.

80. La Agrupación Revolucionaria de Cuba, "Proclama al Pueblo de Cuba," September 4, 1933, reprinted in Ferrer, *Con el rifle al hombro*, pp. 354–55; Welles to Hull, September 5, 1933, *Foreign Relations, 1933*, V

crisis Welles threw his support to the Céspedes regime and its constituents. He argued by phone and cable that supporting a constitutional regime toppled by an army mutiny was the essence of Good Neighborliness. He thought a military demonstration would fell the insurgents, which could be followed by the "elections which the Cuban people unanimously desire." Roosevelt shied away from landing troops, but agreed that the new government should not be recognized.[81]

Acting thereafter on Welles's advice, the Roosevelt administration refused to recognize the insurgent government of Dr. Ramón Grau San Martín. The State Department knew that it ran the risk of an occupation and hemispheric disapproval, but it accepted Welles's *obiter dicta* that not only were the radicals a minority but that the ousted factions spoke for "the enormous majority of the Cuban people." To receive recognition, the new regime must not only end violence but also offer "conclusive evidence" of its own stability and majority support, which for Welles meant appeasing the organized factions, army officers, and business and commercial groups. This he thought was impossible, and without American recognition, his judgment became a self-fulfilling prophecy.[82]

Until Grau left office, the American position was that elections and civil order had to precede reform. Supported by his

381–83; J. M. Puig Casauranc, Mexican minister of foreign affairs, to Hull, September 7, 1933, *ibid.*, 394–95; Jorge Mañach, "Revolution in Cuba," *Foreign Affairs* XII (1933), 46–56.

81. Memoranda of four telephone conversations, September 5 and 6, 1933, between Welles, Hull, and Assistant Secretary of State Jefferson Caffery, *Foreign Relations, 1933*, V, 380, 385–86, 389–90; Welles to Hull, September 7, 1933, *ibid.*, 390–92, 396–98. For events in Havana, see Hubert C. Herring, "Can Cuba Save Herself," *Current History* XXXIX (1933), 151–58, and Charles A. Thomson, "The Cuban Revolution: Reform and Reaction," *Foreign Policy Reports* XI (1936), 262–76.

82. Welles to Hull, September 8–12, 1933, *Foreign Relations, 1933*, V, 405–7, 416–18, 422–26; Welles, *Time for Decision*, p. 198.

conviction that Grau had only academic visionaries, imma-
ture students, and ignorant soldiers with which to govern,
Welles consistently rejected granting recognition. To have
done so, he thought, would have been to sanction a government that did not have "the confidence of all." If the United
States did not continue to support a compromise satisfactory
to the displaced factions and businessmen, large and small,
the alternatives were widespread violence or a more radical
government that "would assume completely dictatorial powers and abandon the program for the reestablishment of constitutional government as the result of national elections." [83]
Conversely, when the Grau government passed popular economic decrees that struck against two foreign companies and
ruthlessly crushed two countercoups, Welles did not equate
its capacity for survival with true stability. He persisted not
only in picturing the insurgent government as a beleagured
clique (which it was) but also in attributing mass support to
its opponents (which they did not have). Recognition of
such a regime, said a public statement written for Roosevelt
by Welles, would be "an obstacle to the free and untram-
meled determination by the Cuban people of their own
destinies." [84]

Spokesmen and sympathizers of the insurgent regime insisted that nonrecognition was the source of Cuban violence
and that Grau's government was embarked on a program of
political and psychological regeneration, not revolution.
They challenged the existence of any Cuban consensus and
pointed out the failures of every preceding regime. Even
the army shared the revolutionary ideal: "not only a change

83. Welles to Hull, September 25, 1933, *Foreign Relations, 1933,* V,
457–58.
84. Quote from Phillips to Roosevelt, November 23, 1933, *ibid.,* 525–26.
See also Welles to Hull, October 16, 1933, *ibid.,* 487–91; Welles to Hull,
November 10, 1933, *ibid.,* 519–20; Welles to Phillips, December 7, 1933,
ibid., 533–36.

of leaders but a change of system." [85] Finally, the State Department conceded that by a tally of arms and raw numbers Grau had supporters, but they were only "the army and ignorant masses who have been misled by utopian promises." [86]

Aware that Roosevelt would not be easily persuaded to land troops (though naval vessels patrolled the coastline), Welles looked among the Cuban factions for a force for order and constitutionalism. As early as September 21, he found his man in Colonel Fulgencio Batista, Grau's parvenu army chief of staff. Welles found Batista sympathetic to the ambassador's views: reform could come only after peace was restored and after it had "the consent of a majority of the Cuban people through the medium of a constituted government." [87] The question was Batista's control of the army, a matter not decided until December. His grip on the army firm, Batista deserted the radicals and ousted Grau San Martín.

With Machado and Grau in exile, the Roosevelt administration quickly acted to please its Cuban and domestic constituents. It recognized the provisional government of Carlos Mendieta and within the year negotiated a new reciprocity treaty and replaced the Treaty of 1903 with a new agreement purged of tutelary responsibility. In a nationally broadcast address in March, 1934, Sumner Welles announced that in a crisis American policy had met the liberal

85. H. F. Matthews, chargé d'affaires, to Phillips, December 14, 1933, on meeting with representatives of the Student Directorate and Colonel Fulgencio Batista, *ibid.*, 541–42; two cables, Josephus Daniels, U.S. ambassador to Mexico, to Hull, September 9, 1933, *ibid.*, 413–15; address of Dr. Angel Giraudy, chairman of the Cuban delegation, December 4, 1933, in Department of State, *Report of the Delegates of the United States of America to the Seventh International Conference of American States* (Washington, 1934), pp. 107–12; Secretary to President Roosevelt (Steve Early) to Phillips, November 22, 1933, *Foreign Relations, 1933*, V, 524.

86. Jefferson Caffery to Phillips, January 10, 1934, *Foreign Relations, 1934*, 5 vols. (Washington, 1951–52), V, 95–96.

87. Welles to Hull, October 1, 1933, *Foreign Relations, 1933*, V, 461–62.

test: it had not been shaped by corporate business and was democratic, resting "solely upon our sincere desire to pursue a policy of justice and fairness to Cuba and to the Cuban people." [88] Moreover, Welles's diplomacy had been a victory for constitutionalism and Good Neighborliness, having removed the odious provisions of the Platt Amendment and freeing Cuba to full comity in the family of nations. [89] Paralyzed equally by its fear of an American military occupation and of an insurgent regime that did not meet its Wilsonian standards of conduct, the Roosevelt administration turned over the task of modernizing Cuba to Fulgencio Batista's army.

To more dispassionate observers, the administration's diplomacy did not appear enlightened. For Josephus Daniels, Russell H. Fitzgibbon, Hubert C. Herring, and a special Commission on Cuban Affairs led by Raymond Leslie Buell, the legacy of Welles's mission was almost immediately discernible. American policy had, they agreed, frustrated the first really democratic political movement in Cuban history. Instead of preserving a sympathy for constitutionalism, peaceful reform, and other American political values, the State Department had instead alienated Cuba's most effective mass political leaders and had given them a cause—the Frustrated Revolution—with potential mass support. [90]

88. Address by Sumner Welles, Assistant Secretary of State, "Relations Between the United States and Cuba," March 21–29, 1934, Department of State, *Latin American Series*, No. 7 (Washington, 1934), 12, 16.

89. Hull to Caffery, March 4, 1935, *Foreign Relations, 1935*, 4 vols., (Washington, 1953), V, 476–77; Hull, *Memoirs*, I, 342–44; "The President Offers a Toast at the State Dinner for the President of Cuba," December 8, 1942, *Public Papers and Addresses of Franklin Delano Roosevelt*, XI, 530–31.

90. Daniels to Hull, July 10, 24, 1934, quoted in Cronon, "Interpreting the Good Neighbor Policy," p. 564; Russell H. Fitzgibbon, "Cuban Elections of 1936," *American Political Science Review* XXX (1936), 724–35; Hubert C. Herring, "Another Chance for Cuba," *Current History* XXXIX (1934), 656–60; Raymond Leslie Buell, *et al.*, *Problems of the New Cuba* (New York, 1935), pp. 492–500.

IV

The fall of Grau San Martín did not restore order or resurrect liberal constitutionalism in Cuba, but the renunciation of the Platt Amendment, the establishment of the sugar quota system, and the continuing competition of Fulgencio Batista and the "Generation of 1930" for control of the "Revolution" shaped Cuban-American relations for the next thirty-eight years. After the Welles Mission, the Roosevelt administration and its successors concentrated on economic issues and hemispheric defense in their diplomacy, having relinquished the role as *poder moderado* to the Cuban Army.

Despite the facade of economic diversification and progress, neither Batista nor Grau San Martín's Cuban Revolutionary Party (Auténtico) was able to transform the growing demands of Cuba's organized interest groups into consensual reform. The economic and professional elite preferred court politics or withdrawal; the radicals remained committed to conspiracy and violence. Both Batista and the Auténticos pledged themselves to Cuban nationalism and to basic institutional change, engineered by the state, but both compromised the social and economic goals set for the state by the Constitution of 1940. Neither was able to stir a stagnant economy, a corrupt national administration, or a demoralized society still marked by insecurity and disorder. As the years went by, their will to make changes also waned. Institutionally, Cuba remained a fragmented, poverty-ridden, and class-conscious nation, despite a veneer of modernization in Havana and the growth of a technical-managerial middle class.[91]

91. Ramiro Guerra y Sánchez, *et al.*, *Historia de la Nación Cubana* (Havana, 1952), VIII, 81–95, 99–176, 340–65; Economic and Technical Mission to Cuba, International Bank for Reconstruction and Development, *Report on Cuba* (Baltimore, 1951), pp. 9–12, 58–60, 358–75, 424–29, 454–55; William S. Stokes, "The Cuban Parliamentary System in Action,

Ironically, by 1952, Cuban elections and party organization had begun to show signs of both free choice and civic awareness when Batista arranged his last barracks revolt. Batista's justification was that political violence and corruption were endangering the government's programs for economic diversification, social welfare, and the evolutionary improvement of rural life; he raised the specter of communism, although the Partido Socialista Popular had been his ally. Only the order provided by his control of the army, Batista contended, could ensure the long-range economic development Cuba needed. To this end, and for his own political and financial renaissance, Batista prevented the probable electoral victory of the reformist Party of the Cuban People (Ortodoxo).[92]

Batista's rule after 1952 did bring increased aggregate prosperity and did satisfy the organized urbanites and businessmen who placed highest priority on economic growth; Batista, too, was supported by those who saw radical reform as a threat to their own religious, racial, economic, and social privileges. Like Nuri al-Said and Ngo Dinh Diem, Batista counted on tacit American approval (especially of his anti-communism) and long-range economic progress to obscure the illegitimate and authoritarian character of his rule. But the army coup and the rigged elections that followed either alienated or demoralized the Auténtico-Ortodoxo constitutionalists and delivered the initiative in the anti-Batista op-

1940–47," *Journal of Politics* XI (1949), 335–64, and "The 'Cuban Revolution' and the Presidential Elections of 1948," *Hispanic American Historical Review* XXXI (1951), 37–79; Hugh Thomas, "The Origins of the Cuban Revolution," *World Today* XIX (1963), 448–60.

92. William S. Stokes, "National and Local Violence in Cuban Politics," *Southwestern Social Science Quarterly* XXXIV (1953), 57–63; Robert F. Smith, "Castro's Revolution: Domestic Sources and Consequences," in John Plank, ed., *Cuba and the United States: Long Range Perspectives* (Washington, 1967), pp. 45–68; William Appleman Williams, *The United States, Cuba, and Castro* (New York, 1962), pp. 55–79; Fulgencio Batista, *The Growth and Decline of the Cuban Republic* (New York, 1964).

position to young "action groups" committed to terrorism and guerrilla warfare. Pitted against armed forces riven with dissension and mentally and professionally ill-equipped for counterinsurgent operations, drawing on the sympathy abroad created by Batista's terrorism, the Opposition, specifically the 26 of July Movement, shot and talked its way to power.[93]

As most students of Cuban history concede, Fidel Castro dominates the Revolution and has, as much as any leader can, decided his country's course since January 1, 1959. To the radicals and previously powerless Cuban rural poor, he is an amalgam of Santa Claus, Christ, and Liborio, the Cuban cartoon Everyman who has struggled against "monopolists" and *políticos* for three generations. Given the Cold War context of the Cuban Revolution, Cuba's military and economic ties with the Soviet Union, and the conversion of the Maximum Leader and his revolutionary elite to Marxism-Leninism, it is understandable why the debate about Castroism has concerned itself with the communist nature of the Revolution and the megalomania and charisma of Castro himself.[94] But there is another conceivable view of the Revolution and Fidel: it and he are the first national "in-power" expression of nineteenth-century anarchism, and the rejection of all Cuba's pre-1959 institutions is rooted in the revo-

93. Harold R. Aaron, "The Seizure of Political Power in Cuba, 1956–1959," (Ph.D. dissertation, Georgetown University, 1964); Loree Wilkerson, *Fidel Castro's Political Programs from Reformism to "Marxism-Leninism,"* (Gainesville, Fla., 1965); Information Department, Royal Institute of International Affairs, *Cuba: A Brief Political and Economic Survey* (Oxford, 1958).

94. Theodore Draper, *Castro's Revolution: Myths and Realities* (New York, 1962), and *Castroism: Theory and Practice* (New York, 1965); Andrés Suárez, *Cuba: Castroism and Communism, 1959–1966* (Cambridge, Mass., 1967); Ward M. Morton, *Castro as Charismatic Hero* (Lawrence, Kans., 1965); Boris Goldenberg, "The Cuban Revolution: An Analysis," *Problems of Communism* XII (September–October, 1963), 1–9; Richard R. Fagen, "Charismatic Authority and the Leadership of Fidel Castro," *Western Political Quarterly* XVIII (1965), 275–84; Ernst Halperin, "The Castro Regime in Cuba," *Current History* LI (1966), 354–59.

lutionaries' view of the interrelationship of Cuban domestic development and Cuban-American relations since 1898.

For the Fidelistas their revolution is to free man from unjust, exploitive institutions, to return him to an Adamic state of nature best achieved through nationalism, rural living, hard work, and selflessness. In essence the Fidelistas want all Cubans to go through the spiritual purification of their own lives in the Sierra Maestra; Cubans all must go through the hell of survival, violence, and moral regeneration that the Fidelistas say they experienced as guerrillas. Only this national social trauma will cleanse Cuba of its past corruptions and sins. The United States, to the Fidelistas a combination of Miami and Mississippi run by the CIA, had been for Cuba the wellspring of poisoning institutions: standing armies, powerful churches, cities, economic and racially-determined classes, banks, corporations, courts, electoral political parties, and bureaucracy. These institutions were *yanqui* inventions, unwittingly accepted in Cuba after 1898, which had for sixty years corrupted individuals and oppressed "the masses." Only a rapid, violent disembowelment of the Cuban republic (indeed, of all non-European nations) could move "the people" to social, political, and economic equality, an equality characterized by minimal institutional restraint and maximal shared hardship.[95]

95. In addition to the above sources, see C. Wright Mills, *Listen, Yankee* (New York, 1960); Ché Guevara, *Guerrilla Warfare*, Vintage Books edition (New York, 1968); Regis Debray, *Revolution in the Revolution*, Grove Press edition (New York, 1967); Luis E. Aguilar, "Regis Debray: Where Logic Failed," *The Reporter* XXXVII (December 28, 1967), 31–32; Philip W. Bonsal, "Cuba, Castro, and the United States," *Foreign Affairs* XLIV (1967), 260–76; Edward B. Glick, "Cuba and the Fifteenth UN General Assembly: A Study of Regional Disassociation," *Journal of Inter-American Studies* VI (1964), 235–48; Irving P. Pflaum, "Castro Cuba in Mid-1960: Fidel of Cuba, By Voice and Violence," American Universities Field Staff, *Reports Service*, Mexico and Caribbean Area Studies (New York, 1960), V, No. 1–13; Dudley Sears, *et al.*, *Cuba: The Economic and Social Revolution* (Chapel Hill, N.C., 1964); Leslie Dewart, *Christianity and Revolution: The Lesson of Cuba* (New York, 1963). Both Draper and Williams see "populist" influences in the Fidelista rhetoric; both, sympathetic to Castro and socialism, shrink from the characterization of the Castro regime as "anarchical."

Castro's uneasy alliance with the Soviet Union for economic and military assistance reflects his determination to break the *abrazo* of the United States and "counterrevolution." The Fidelistas' pathological hatred of America goes deeper, however, than trade embargoes and Playa Giron. Since its first objections to the execution of *batistiano* terrorists to the bombing of North Vietnam, the United States, in the Fidelista view, has continued to impose hypocritical, "reactionary" standards of behavior on the rest of the world. As Fidel himself has said, American imperialism is "its desire to impose outside its frontiers the kind of government system it thinks other states and peoples should have." [96]

Still joined in the uncomfortable *abrazo*, Cuba will perhaps learn that coercion, contempt for liberal institutions, and unchecked personal power are unjust answers to the ills of modern nations, and the United States can ponder whether political change is really ever consensual and nonviolent.

96. Quoted by Lee Lockwood, *Castro's Cuba, Cuba's Fidel* (New York, 1967), p. 188. For the American reaction to Castroite violence and the decision to support the Cuban exiles, see Arthur M. Schlesinger, Jr., *A Thousand Days* (New York, 1965), pp. 215–97; Theodore Sorenson, *Kennedy* (New York, 1965), pp. 291–309; U.S., Congress, Senate, Committee on the Judiciary, Subcommittee to Investigate the Administration of the Internal Security Act and Other Internal Security Laws, *Hearings: Communist Threat to the United States through the Caribbean*, 86th Congress, 1st Session (Washington, 1959), and 90th Congress, 1st Session (Washington, 1967), 18 parts.

The United States and Great Britain:
Uneasy Allies

A. E. CAMPBELL

THE PHRASE "uneasy allies" applied to Britain and the United States is worth a moment's reflection.[1] It states both that the two countries are allies and that their cooperation is not so cordial as that of allies should be. Yet Britain and the United States were not formal allies till 1941, and they have been allies only when each has had many other allies also. Since 1941 it is by no means obvious that their cooperation has been worse or more difficult than that of other allies. Why, then, does a phrase like "uneasy allies" come so readily to mind? It does so because of the belief that Britain and the United States are in some sense natural or preordained allies, and that they "ought" to find it easier to work together effectively than do other states. It rests, in short, on the implicit hypothesis that there is a special Anglo-American rela-

1. It would be pointless to develop an essay from the analysis of a phrase if the phrase were merely the author's invention. The title of this essay was independently suggested by the editors; and I believe that many students of politics naturally think of Anglo-American relations in some such terms. The phrase itself, of course, appears in the title of Leon D. Epstein, *Britain—Uneasy Ally* (Chicago, 1954).

tionship.[2] Anglo-American cooperation is tested by standards unusually severe; only against those standards does the performance appear inadequate.

The nature of the relationship between Britain and America has been a subject of debate since the time of the American Revolution and before. As the quarrel between Britain and the thirteen colonies developed, some Britons argued that the colonies must not be allowed to gain independence. The political tie was essential. If it were broken, Britain would lose at once a large part of her strength; the defection of the mainland colonies would be inevitably followed by that of other parts of the empire; and, worse still, the colonies would move naturally into hostility to Britain and alliance with any European foe.[3] The same blow that reduced British power would enlarge the threat that it had to meet. Others in Britain rejected this whole contention. They insisted that the basis of the connection between Britain and the colonies had been the common interest of both. To this the political tie had contributed nothing. If it were broken —and there was no point in trying to maintain it—the force of self-interest would continue to act as before. There was no reason to expect that an independent United States would be either more hostile or less useful to Britain than the colonies had been—rather, the reverse. Still a third

2. Belief in, and hostility toward, a special relationship between Britain and the United States is, of course, widespread on the continent of Europe. It seems to me beyond dispute that the relationship is in many ways special, and will remain so; but we should not conclude without further inquiry that it is politically effective. It is not surprising that men excluded from a relationship should think it sinister. What is surprising is that they should so readily suppose it effective enough to be dangerous.

3. This is a view that could still find an echo in the twentieth century. "The English-speaking nations have either got to bring themselves under one sovereignty or they will drift into antagonism" (Philip Kerr, later eleventh marquess of Lothian, to Lionel Curtis, September 2, 1927, quoted in Max Beloff, "The Special Relationship: an Anglo-American Myth," in Martin Gilbert, ed., *A Century of Conflict, 1850–1950: Essays for A. J. P. Taylor* [London, 1966], p. 161 n. 2).

school, more influential after it was clear that independence must be granted than before, took a middle course, regretting the breaking of the political tie, which they ascribed to British folly, but hoping that a better substitute might be created, a tie based on common language, traditions, culture, and race, which would ensure the friendship of the two countries.[4]

These three attitudes—modified, of course, to meet the circumstances of American independence—have been the basic British attitudes to the Anglo-American relationship ever since. They are, so to speak, the primary colors of the relationship. They can be blended, they can be used to paint various pictures, and each of them has a complementary color. Through most of the nineteenth century, in the heyday of British power, the second attitude seemed the most plausible. By "interest" was meant essentially private economic interests, which had full play while government activity was minimal and while the economies of the two countries were still largely complementary. As the activity of governments has grown, and as rivalry in trade has overshadowed beneficent exchange, this school of thought may have weakened. But the notion is with us yet that if one can only get the economies of two countries thoroughly entangled, they will not be able to afford hostility. The third attitude is a more mystical one. It readily slips from the hope that ties of language and the like may be helpful into the belief that they must be so, into supposing that a special relationship exists whatever the outward appearances may suggest; and this is natural enough for, by contrast with the first two schools, there is little that either individuals or governments can do to reinforce ties whose origin is in the past.

4. For an excellent analysis of the theme of this paragraph, see Vincent T. Harlow, *The Founding of the Second British Empire, 1763–1793*, 2 vols. (London, 1952–64), I, chap. 5.

Whichever view they took, almost all Britons who looked across the Atlantic at the time of the Revolution underestimated American nationalism, the force of the simple desire to have independence and to be seen to have independence. When, after the War of 1812, Americans were persuaded that their independence was acknowledged, most saw no particular reason to concern themselves with Anglo-American relations. If they had a world view, there was no special place for Britain in it. Not until the end of the nineteenth century, when immigration had already made it much less plausible, did some Americans briefly come to share the British view that there was a racial link between the two countries. It is paradoxical that this sympathy in the field of ideas should have developed at a time when the two countries were engaged in a whole range of diplomatic disputes; and it is paradoxical also that when the disputes were settled the ideas should have been abandoned. Before World War I most Americans had reverted to the traditional posture—a wary suspicion of European states and, among others, of Britain as the great imperial power that clung to territory not her own and to unjustifiable pretensions.

The most obvious thing about all these attitudes, British and American, is how general they are. They all attempt to relate Anglo-American relations to some grand conception of how the world operates. That this should have been so at the time of their origin is not surprising. The British ideas were developed when an empire was breaking up. It was natural to peer into the future, to try to find explanations for the upheaval, and to devise generalizations that would justify either resistance or acquiescence. Equally, the last decade of the nineteenth century was a period in which Americans were concerned to reconsider the course that the world was taking and the place of their country in it. But not all periods are so portentous as the 1770s, or seem so portentous as the 1890s, yet the Anglo-American relationship retains the sweeping character given to it first in George III's reign. None of the attitudes sketched above gives much weight to specific, temporary events. They do not emphasize that relations between two countries, and so between the United States and Britain, may be now good, now bad; may be good over one issue, bad over another; may be good in one part of the world while bad elsewhere. They do not allow that often it does not matter much whether relations are good or bad—they may be merely indifferent—and that they may sometimes be bad without posing any serious threat of war.

Almost equally remarkable is that these attitudes, British and American alike, require judgments about the domestic politics of the other country. At the time of the Revolution, much British discussion turned on different analyses of how many Loyalists there were in the colonies and how they might be strengthened. In later years the question was how many Americans there were who felt some affection for Britain, or at least sympathy for British purposes, and how they might be encouraged. Conversely, it was thought important not to give color to the malicious fictions of Britain's enemies, Irish-American, German-American, or whatever they might be. Perhaps most striking is that British analyses of American domestic politics tended to cast Britain's opponents into two groups—those opposed to Britain by reason of their racial origin, and those opposed to Britain from ignorance or parochialism. Little was made of the possibility that men who disliked Britain's domestic politics might deduce that her international purposes were equally offensive, as, for example, many Populists did. Yet this was the more important stream in American thinking. Most Americans who were ready in the 1890s to suppose some community of purpose between the two countries did so for ideological rather than for merely racial reasons.[5]

Here a difficulty developed almost at once. In the early years, when Americans were acutely conscious of the gulf between their republican institutions and the monarchical institutions of Europe, the sympathy of most Americans was with British radicals, men in the nature of things almost always in opposition. There was little scope for governmental cooperation. As time passed and Britain became more democratic, this difficulty disappeared. The sympathy of the 1890s probably owed more to a similarity of social outlook among important groups in the two countries than to any other factor.[6] But the difficulty was soon to be replaced by another. The natural community of social outlook was between Americans and British Conservatives, both upholders of the capitalist system. But Conservatives were also the most ardent defenders of the British empire, to most Americans a dangerous anachronism. The British Labour party, which seemed more ready to move toward self-determination and the abandonment of empire, became more and more committed to dogmatic socialism. Most Britons were either right on domestic matters but wrong in foreign affairs, or right in foreign affairs and wrong on domestic matters.

5. One characteristic quality of the thought of the 1890s was the supposition that race and ideology were in some way connected, and especially that some peoples were politically more talented than others. This theme is one that is almost always mentioned in writing on the period, but one that still lacks, to the best of my knowledge, a full analysis, though Bradford Perkins, *The Great Rapprochement: England and the United States, 1895–1914* (New York, 1968), has much of interest to say on the subject. Even today this belief contributes to one school of thought on the special relationship.

6. D. C. Watt, "America and the British Foreign-Policy-Making Elite, from Joseph Chamberlain to Anthony Eden, 1895–1956," *Review of Politics* XXV (1963), reprinted in *Personalities and Policies* (London, 1965); Cushing Strout, *The American Image of the Old World* (New York, 1963), chap. 8.

Where were Americans of good will to find their natural allies? [7]

For observers in Britain there were thus good, or at least right-thinking, Americans, and those that were ill-disposed or foolish; American observers similarly divided Britons into categories. The bad were to be frustrated and the good encouraged. There is nothing unusual in this. It is almost certain that within any country, some groups will advocate a policy more favorable to another country than will others. But it is noticeable in Anglo-American relations how little these attitudes had to do with policy. They were not short-term and specific attitudes, as those determined by policy are. They were persistent and long-term. They survived specific policy issues because they were detached from them. One supported friends and discouraged opponents in the other country, less by policy than by adding credibility to a general picture of one's own country and its place in the world. [8]

The reason for this may be suggested by an analogy with domestic politics. In domestic politics active men attach themselves to a party or a cause, which they then abandon with great reluctance if at all. They may often be grieved or outraged by the folly of their own side, or by its capture by the wrong elements; but they show great resilience and ingenuity in clinging to it nevertheless. They regard these lapses as temporary. To move over to the other party is a

7. In 1945 Representative Celler (Democrat, New York) felt both horns of the dilemma. See his opinion that the loan to Britain "would promote too much damned Socialism at home and too much damned Imperialism abroad" (quoted in Richard W. Gardner, *Sterling-Dollar Diplomacy* [Oxford, 1956], p. 237; and D. G. Watt, "American Aid to Britain and the Problem of Socialism, 1945–51," *American Review* II (1963), reprinted in *Personalities and Policies*, p. 61).

8. A specific policy of one country may often be damaging to another without making relations much worse. What is important is that the policy should not be judged inevitable, part of some larger hostile plan.

last resort, usually undertaken in some much more fundamental disillusionment. This attachment to a chosen group
is not blind loyalty, mere stubbornness or obscurantism. It
follows naturally from the fact that the group was chosen
in the first place because it seemed to embody some vision
of the large, long-term political good, a fundamental prediction about the course of future progress. Such commitments
cannot be, and should not be, lightly abandoned. In particular they should not be abandoned by reason of some dispute
about policy. A policy, after all, may usually be changed. It
seldom determines the foreseeable future.

Similarly, very few specific issues that arise between two
countries can be regarded as having fundamental importance. Since men are quarrelsome animals, they probably
give too much importance to most issues; and, of course,
those most important capture the attention of historians as
of contemporaries. But most are hard-fought at the time
and forgotten when settled or overtaken by some new concern. Issues that imperatively require a recasting of one's
world view are fortunately few. They have been few in
Anglo-American relations. A whole range of specific issues
has arisen between the two countries from independence to
the present. In settling these the United States has, inevitably, been generally successful. What is important is that at
no time have most Britons been driven to the conclusion
that this or that American success threatened any fundamental British vision of the future. One of the established attitudes toward the United States could always be modified to
take account of American progress.[9] On the other side,
progress was for most Americans in the nineteenth century
an article of faith. It could be relied on to solve most prob-

___

9. I have tried myself to explore this theme for one short but important
period in *Great Britain and the United States, 1895–1903* (London, 1960),
especially chap. 7.

lems, including those of Anglo-American relations. After independence had been won, any later threat must seem trivial by comparison. If Britain were foolish enough to oppose the legitimate aspirations of the United States—and to Americans they were all legitimate—these should be firmly defended, but American progress would ensure that any issue could be reopened later if that should be necessary, with better hope of success. No settlement need be regarded as final.[10]

In terms of national power, American progress was a fact. According to some theories of international relations at least, the very great change in the relative power of the two countries ought to dominate the relationship. In the first years of American independence, Britain was unquestionably the major power. It is true that one British attitude derived from a sense of weakness, from the belief that Britain, shorn of the thirteen colonies, would not long be a match for France. But twenty years served to renew British confidence, and for much of the nineteenth century she was, both in British estimation and in fact, the greatest of the powers. During those years the speed of American advance served to give the United States a confidence that greater British power did not daunt and that even the Civil War hardly called into question. It is not difficult to suppose that a sense of rough equality between the two countries may have developed shortly after 1814 and survived perhaps till World War I. Thereafter, of course, the picture is entirely different. The United States has advanced till she is, by any test, the greatest of the powers; Britain has settled

10. For much of the nineteenth century there was little occasion for Americans to determine their attitude to other states. Their confidence that their expansion could be limited only by themselves is, however, a quality that no historian has been able to overlook. Manifest destiny was more often assumed than debated. It has received its most consistent and persuasive exposition in R. W. Van Alstyne's admirable study, *The Rising American Empire* (Oxford, 1960).

into a group of secondary powers. If power plays a dominant part in the formation of national attitudes, it seems unlikely that ideas appropriate to the earlier period would be appropriate to the later. In a sense, they are not; and it is the thesis of this essay that they are beginning to give way. But they have been remarkably durable and have begun to give way much later than one might have expected from calculations of mere power.

For this there have been a number of explanations. Those who believe in the force of the special relationship insist that the ideas survive because they are valid and true. They were never based on calculations of relative power, and they are not, therefore, invalidated when power relationships change.[11] Those who discount the force of the special relationship argue rather that it is a cozy British myth, whose purpose is simply that of shoring up British self-esteem and sparing Britons the necessity of coming to terms with the world. As it once enabled Britons to accept the loss of the American colonies, so it now enables them to accept their loss of world power. Meanwhile, Americans have long lost any interest they had in the relationship. They do not discuss it, and if, from time to time, one catches an echo of old phrases and modes of thought in American public discourse, it is no more than an echo. Old clichés will do because the subject is not important enough to require new thought.[12]

11. The leading exponent of this view is H. C. Allen. See *The Anglo-American Relationship since 1783* (London, 1959), and *The Anglo-American Predicament: The British Commonwealth, the United States and European Unity* (London, 1960).

12. "In the last fifteen years . . . practically all the debate has been in Britain. This is not surprising: since the war America has in the nature of things loomed enormously larger on the British horizon than Britain has on the American horizon" (Coral Bell, *The Debatable Alliance: An Essay in Anglo-American Relations* [London, 1964], p. 1). Max Beloff, "The Special Relationship," gives most of his space to the analysis of British attitudes. It is worth emphasizing that the terms of the British debate have often been quite unrealistic.

Both lines of explanation lead to the same dilemma. If the Anglo-American special relationship is permanently valid, why should it be now breaking down? If the Anglo-American special relationship had long lost all practical relevance, why should we now recognize the fact, when it was not necessary to recognize it earlier? [13]

The difficulty arises because neither account of the Anglo-American relationship refers to the real world at the level at which political attitudes are formed. One is too general, the other too specific. The fault of the first school—dubbed "sentimental" by its opponents—is not sentimentality but simply that its doctrine is one that no event or chain of events could confirm or disprove. The fault of the rival doctrine is that it seeks disproof or confirmation at the wrong level of political activity—a level too limited and too parochial. Though politicians may try to make what use of the relationship they can, for analysts it is the course of events that must determine the nature of the relationship, and not the other way about. It follows therefore that the relationship must be fitted into place among the other concerns of both British and Americans. It is not merely the direct relationship between the two powers that has changed. The world preoccupations of both have also changed. To say so is a truism. It is almost equally a truism to suggest that this change must have affected their view of each other. It is perhaps less of a truism to emphasize how recently these changes have become of dominant importance.

Both the attitudes set out above are unhistorical. The first —that Britain and the United States are connected by a whole network of cultural ties *that are politically significant*

13. See Lord Chalfont's television address of October 9, 1967, as reported in the *Times,* October 10, 1967, under the headline, "Britain Drops Special Link with U.S." Among other things he said that "everyone should remember that unless Britain could help to strengthen Europe 'we are going to be taken over by America.'"

—is indeed historical in origin; but once formed, it is not open to modification by other historical events. The second —that cultural ties do not have any important effect on international relations—is not even historical in origin. It is an a priori belief, which cannot be affected by historical evidence. Yet Anglo-American relations are a historical phenomenon, and they have not been equally good at all times. In the effort to take account of that fact, two further lines of inquiry have been developed. One is to consider the groups actually responsible for the conduct of the relations, in the attempt to discover how far sympathy or lack of sympathy between them can be correlated with good or bad relations.[14] Such an inquiry is a natural extension of traditional diplomatic history. A more elaborate approach has applied techniques of modern political science to the analysis of a whole complex of links between the two countries in the effort to discover how changes in these have affected intergovernmental relations.[15] This attempt rests on more precisely stated conceptual foundations than the other, but it is much less satisfactory. For it must inevitably neglect changes in the relationship that it is designed to elucidate—changes in the interests, purposes, and international standing of the two states.

To say this is to imply that states have interests—it is hardly too much to say, personalities—that are more than the mechanical resultants of the interests of their citizens. For convenience historians, of course, constantly write as if they accepted the implication, writing of "Britain" or "the United States," "London" or "Washington," as if a single entity were in question. This convention would not be useful unless, more often than not, it was largely true. Patriotism

14. Watt, "America and the British Foreign-Policy-Making Elite."
15. Bruce M. Russett, *Community and Contention: Britain and America in the Twentieth Century* (Cambridge, Mass., 1963).

is an autonomous force. Men often support their country not to further their private interests but in spite of them. On many occasions their commitments to their country dominate or override their other commitments to other groups. Naturally, it is these occasions that are of most concern to the student of international relations. When they arise, men's attitudes are no doubt affected by beliefs formed in other circumstances and for other reasons. There will usually be some scope for domestic debate as to just what the national interest requires.[16] But attitudes are not determined by such prior beliefs. Equally important—or rather, more important —is some more or less formed view of the national purpose and the national interest. It will hardly be disputed that men of different nations, whose outlook, background, and private interests are in every respect very similar, and who take the same view of public issues in which their countries are neutral, may differ very sharply when their countries and their countries' interests seem to differ.[17]

If this is conceded, it follows that we ought to try to discover what function one country serves for another, what use it is to the other. Hence we must discover what common purpose, if any, a nation has. Since a nation is immortal, its fundamental purposes must be distant and, because distant, imprecise. (There may be critical periods in its history, when immediate interests are dominant, but these are important just because, if they are safely passed, the nation has an indefinite future.) To determine what the fundamental purpose of a nation is, is difficult; and the attempt invites attack from several directions. Statements cannot be precisely documented: they are therefore suspect to the diplomatic

16. The American domestic debate on the Vietnam war has become unusually violent. But then, the war has been unusually unsuccessful.

17. For some discussion of this, see K. E. Boulding, "National Images and International Systems," *Journal of Conflict Resolution* III (1959).

historian. They cannot be buttressed by statistical or quantitative evidence: they are therefore virtually meaningless to one school at least of political scientists. We are entering "the marshy fields of intellectual and social history" [18] where that venture has traditionally been most disapproved. Any statement made can at best be persuasive. Yet enthusiasts for the special relationship, to whom such a general approach might be appealing, are likely to be alienated because the presumptions from which it starts are not theirs.

It will be the contention of this paper that the special relationship rested on a common interest in the maintenance of peace. That is, Britain valued American prosperity and power chiefly as making the maintenance of peace more likely; and the United States valued British prosperity and power for the same reason. This common interest in turn derived from the fact that Britain and the United States were the chief beneficiaries of the international system established in 1815 and shored up, or patched up, till 1945. In international affairs the governments of both countries were highly conservative, and because conservative, peaceable. (To say that a shared interest in peace rested on shared conservatism is not to deny that it had a moral element also; nor, on the other hand, need we deny that the two nations had interests that were sometimes opposed.) As a basis for cooperation this was inadequate, for conservative states find it easiest to cooperate when their cooperation is least needed; yet it explains the underlying stability of Anglo-American relations, stability that superficial difficulties barely disturbed.

Anglo-American relations can best be studied in the two areas in which they have been of importance—Europe and the Far East. Until very recently the Middle East was not an area in which the United States took an interest. Even to

18. The phrase is Herbert Butterfield's; see *Man on His Past* (Cambridge, 1955), p. xvi.

Britain, in spite of the British love affair with the desert, it was of interest chiefly as one route to the Far East. The British interest in the Middle East was quite simply strategic; and the Middle East was strategically important because Britain lay on one side and her Far Eastern interests on the other. In a manner equally simple, geography determined that the United States had no interest in the Middle East. Oil might have made a difference—ought to have made a difference, one might say. But though oil gave the Middle East an independent value for both countries, it had remarkably little impact on their relations. The rivalries of oil companies in the area affected neither governmental relations to any significant extent nor the attitudes of the two peoples. The chief explanation for this was that the politics of the area were reasonably stable till World War II. After the war, of course, many more significant changes were also at work.[19] Europe and the Far East remain, then, the areas in which Anglo-American relations were formed, were potentially significant, and can be tested.

It is the essence of the special relationship that it is unique. That is, the links between Britain and America are of a kind that neither state can have with any third power. Good relations between Britain and other powers, between America and other powers, will be of a different and, it is implied, a less significant kind. For Britain such a relationship was for long plausible enough. As a powerful, Western, non-European state, the United States stood alone. There could be no similar relationship with any other power, for there was no similar power. The relationship—if it existed—did not conflict with any other British commitment or with any

19. For a revealing account of the Anglo-American rivalry over the oil of the Middle East that developed in the later years of the war, and of its part in the general relations of the two countries, see Gabriel Kolko, *The Politics of War: Allied Diplomacy and the World Crisis of 1943–1945* (London, 1969), chap. 12, especially pp. 294–313.

British prejudice. At worst it sometimes jarred awkwardly against certain concepts of empire, though never against those most generally held. Above all, it had no particular consequences for the conduct of British relations with European states. Nothing in the special relationship dictated one set of European alignments rather than another. On the question of how Britain should order her relations with Europe, the Anglo-American relationship gave no guidance. Had the United States been in Europe—*per impossibile*—it is hard to envisage any special relationship developing.

For Americans the problem was more difficult. Britain was in Europe, one major power among others. Why should one develop, how should one justify, a special relationship with one of those powers as against the others? More and more Americans had their roots in continental Europe, and to take sides in European controversies was, besides, to abandon a political tradition that went back to the origin of the country. The dilemma is a familiar one. On the level of policy it was not resolved, nor could it be resolved. But on the level of political ideology it gave almost as little trouble as did British relations with America. Americans were looking to the distant future, and saw Britain as the example of an ideology. Whatever defects Britain might have in American eyes—and they were many—other European states had in equal or greater measure; and, still more important, Britain was usually thought the country most likely to improve. This did not call for positive support of Britain; rather, the reverse. Keeping out of the struggles of Europe would usually be the most educative as well as the most inexpensive policy. The advance of Britain in terms of power was not necessary or desirable. But neither was the decline of Britain if that decline implied also a decline in the values for which America was thought to stand. Insofar as calculations of power determined the American attitude, they were calculations not so much of British power relative to the United States as of British power relative to other European nations.

This suggests the purpose of the special relationship for Americans, a purpose that determines its proper limits. Britain is seen not as the stock from which America sprang but rather as a country on the same side, valued as sharing the same values. This identification is not always equally strong. When Britain is secure and confident, points of controversy between Britain and America come to the fore, and common interests can be left to take care of themselves. It once again becomes apparent to Americans that, though the two countries may be engaged in some common enterprise, Americans must form their own judgments of what that enterprise is. They cannot merely follow a British lead. Familiar American doubts revive as to whether Britain really is committed to virtue. Yet when Britain is weak or in danger, another dilemma presents itself. Not Britain per se but Britain as an ally in the cause is what is valuable. How much effort should be put into saving an ally; how many risks can properly be run for him? Might not the cause be better served by independent action? Does not British weakness itself indicate internal flaws that cast doubt on Britain's value to the cause?[20] For Americans the special relationship places Britain not in a special category that no other nation can enter but rather in a class. Britain is top of the class, but that is a position that can be lost; and it can be lost, let us note, by a failure in performance no less than by a change in purpose.

20. Gabriel Kolko, discussing Anglo-American relations during World War II, has an admirable phrase that might be given wider application. The American object, he says, was to ensure that Britain would be "neither too strong nor too weak to cooperate" (*The Politics of War*, p. 290). Though American opportunity to further it was greater in wartime, the object was not a new one. It may well be the only sensible object of any nation dealing with another, at any time.

When American attention—or for that matter, British attention—was concentrated on the Far East, it was Britain active and imperial that Americans saw. In the late nineteenth century Britain was anxious for her position there, which seemed threatened, immediately in China and more remotely in India, by Russian expansion. Her efforts, however, to develop cooperation with the United States were unavailing. Their basis was the supposition that Russian activities, if they limited trade in China or hastened the break-up of that empire, were as offensive to the United States as to Britain. So indeed they were; but because the interests of both Britain and America in China were comparatively slight, and because the two countries were themselves rivals, mutual distrust prevented cooperation. What both countries expected and were willing to accept was that the independent activity of each would benefit the other also. When, after the Russo-Japanese War and World War I the Russian threat in the Far East was removed, cooperation between the two countries was still more difficult. The ambitions of Japan seemed to threaten the interests of both, yet they could not agree on any policy either to check or to come to terms with Japan. The reason is straightforward enough—American dislike of Britain's Far Eastern empire. In the Far East Americans feared that any action of theirs would benefit Britain more than themselves; their devices were designed to limit Britain hardly less than Japan. Britain, increasingly preoccupied in Europe, could not act effectively in the Far East. Americans were reluctant to undergo expense for the advantage of Britain, even if they had been able to devise a policy. Yet had Britain been stronger and more active, it is hardly likely that her policy would have been pleasing to the United States or have solved any American dilemma. While any sort of equality between the two countries survived, they were bound to be, in the Far East, either ineffective or rivals, and most usually both.[21]

In Europe, by contrast, Britain was for most Americans the exemplar of virtue, the country that came closest to sharing their ideals.[22] Britain was not an equal, of course, and suffered from a whole range of political vices. Nevertheless, Britain had attained the only position necessary and possible. There was no reason to prefer any other European state to Britain, and some reason to prefer Britain to other states. It is notable that those very Americans who were outraged by almost any British activity in the Western Hemisphere, and mistrustful of British activity in the wider world, were entirely content to see Britain powerful and active in Europe. Britain-in-Europe and Britain-elsewhere were almost two separate entities.

Part of the explanation of this is a shared interest in the balance of power in Europe. From that balance (including Britain-in-Europe) the United States was the chief beneficiary, as Britain was of the continental balance. It was desirable that the balance should be as fine as possible, for any spare energy of the powers would be given to activity in the wider world that would be disadvantageous to the United States. This explanation will hardly suffice, though there is something in it. It is very doubtful whether most Americans thought of the balance of power in this way. Their thinking, then as later, was much more inclined to the idea of a Euro-

21. For Anglo-American relations in the Far East in two different periods, see Campbell, *Great Britain and the United States*, chap. 6, and H. G. Nicholas, *Britain and the United States* (London, 1963), chap. 6. It is arguable that the defense of a common interest is never an adequate basis for an alliance.

22. The exceptions to this generalization were the German-Americans and the Irish-Americans. It was because they so obviously had special reasons for being out of line that the idea of "hyphenated Americans" had some plausibility.

pean concert.[23] Second, no theory of the balance of power will explain why it was desirable that *Britain* should retain her position. Why should a small shift, bringing Germany, for example, into the position previously held by Britain, be a matter of any concern to the United States? What the United States wanted in Europe was not a balance of power but peace and quiet; and, in Europe, the continuing strength of Britain was a guarantee of peace and quiet, for Britain was the chief satiated power. It is hardly too much to say that in American eyes the role of Britain was to keep Europe quiet. Since in American eyes Britain was fully the equal in virtue of other European states, and the superior of most, quiet did not mean merely uneasy peace under effective tyranny. It was satisfactory in the present, and offered hope for the future.

In such circumstances the future becomes the distant future. Change is, in principle, acceptable; but the weight of conservatism is thrown against it. When force is then invoked to bring about change, the attempt to use force identifies a wrongdoer. In practice, the demand that change must be brought about peacefully usually conceals the determination that it shall not be brought about at all. For Europe this determination was shared by Britain and the United States; or, rather, while it was a British determination, and while Britain could make it good, the United States was relieved of the need to take an interest in European politics. The shared interest, however, survived only in peacetime. When World War I broke out, it was a widespread American belief that among the powers Britain at least had been forced into war. So far the belief in British virtue was reinforced. But British treatment of Amer-

23. In this matter, to take only one example, Woodrow Wilson's critics and his supporters had much in common. Only peace in Europe enables Americans to avoid taking sides.

ican shipping quickly called it into question.[24] Indeed, British participation in the war revealed the limits of the shared interest. Both powers had hoped to continue business as usual, standing aside from the quarrels of Europe. Once Britain, rightly or wrongly, was drawn in, the community of interest disappeared. It is not an accident that American entry into the war did not restore cordiality between the two countries. The suspicion that developed at the peace conference was not merely the result of temperamental differences between Wilson and Lloyd George. It reflected differences of interest that were bound to arise whenever activity by either power was in question.[25] They could agree only in preferring inactivity.

The interwar years demonstrated that World War I had settled very little. Germany's bid for a larger share in the affairs of Europe had been frustrated only by American intervention. That intervention had not been determined by any clear conception of its purposes, and was withdrawn at the war's end. As the European powers began to recover, the imbalance that had been the underlying cause of World War I was seen to have survived it. After a period of uncertainty, the problem for Britain was again identified as that of checking the ambitions of Germany, now, under Hitler, more aggressive than ever. It might be supposed that American aid in accomplishing this would be welcome and would be offered. Here, if ever, a common interest in stability should

24. The best discussion of this problem is in Arthur S. Link, *Wilson: The Struggle for Neutrality, 1914–1915* (Princeton, N.J., 1960), especially chaps. 4, 6, and 10; and *Wilson: Confusions and Crises, 1915–1916* (Princeton, N.J., 1964), *passim.*

25. Seth P. Tillman, *Anglo-American Relations at the Paris Peace Conference of 1919* (Princeton, N.J., 1961). See also Arthur S. Link, *President Wilson and his English Critics* (Oxford, 1959), and Harold I. Nelson, *Land and Power: British and Allied Policy on Germany's Frontiers, 1916–19* (London, 1963). Arno J. Mayer, *Politics and Diplomacy of Peacemaking: Containment and Counterrevolution at Versailles, 1918–1919* (London, 1968), massive in learning, is disappointing in that the theme suggested by the subtitle is lost in detail.

be discernible. But cooperation between Britain and the
United States proved impossible to arrange. The final and
best-known episode is the rejection of President Roosevelt's
offer to call an international conference in Washington
early in 1938.[26] For this historians have tended to blame
Chamberlain. Roosevelt in those years gets a better verdict.
So far as he failed, it was due to preoccupation with domestic matters and to the force of isolationist sentiment.[27] Probably the general verdict calls for modification. If we inquire just what Britain and the United States were to cooperate to do, we get no precise answer. Chamberlain, who
overestimated his powers of negotiation, had decided on a
policy of appeasement. Was he to be induced to turn to a
policy of resistance by a promise of American support? If so,
what form could that American support take? It is highly unlikely that Roosevelt could have given any undertaking of
military support, or that he would have tried. Failing that,
what had he to offer? If his idea was that Hitler might be
induced to give way by the prospect of gaining American
good will as well as British, it was hardly a realistic one.
American inactivity was all that Hitler desired; he already
had it. It is hard not to think that Roosevelt, like Chamberlain, exaggerated the part that his personality could play.

This fault, however, was not simply one of personality. It
was one forced on both Chamberlain and Roosevelt by the
circumstances in which they found themselves. Both wanted
stability in Europe, and stability without fighting for it.

26. U.S. State Department, *Foreign Relations of the United States,
1938*, 5 vols. (Washington, 1954–56), I, 115–32. For discussions see William
L. Langer and S. Everett Gleason, *The Challenge to Isolation, 1937–1940*
(London, 1952), pp. 24–32, and Nicholas, *Britain and the United States,*
pp. 24–28.

27. We should remember that there is another school of historians that
has accused Roosevelt of paying too little heed to public opinion and of
dragging the United States toward war. See, for example, Charles Callan
Tansill, *Back Door to War: The Roosevelt Foreign Policy, 1933–1941*
(Chicago, 1952).

There is nothing discreditable in that. Inevitably, however, it placed them at the mercy of the restraint, or lack of it, of other statesmen. Faced with a man who wanted to overturn the old order and who had no objection to war, they were helpless. They ceased to be so only when they took the decision to resist, but it was precisely over the nature, the timing, the method, and the conditions of that decision that they were bound to disagree, for each hoped that the other would do the main work. Americans hoped that if Britain took a firm line, Hitler would recognize the limits of German expansion, and stability without cost would be again attained. The British were of two minds. They wanted to limit Hitler, but they saw well the risks they ran. Too intransigent a policy would not only bring on a war but would lose them American sympathy as well. Too feeble a policy would lose the objective and again would lose American sympathy. Yet any middle course also held dangers. They might have American support, but the brunt would fall on Britain; and while American forces were not committed, as they might well not be, there was danger of American withdrawal at some awkward moment. The experience of World War I suggested to Europeans no less than to Americans that Europe should settle its own affairs.

It is thus hardly too much to say that the function of Britain, in American eyes, was to maintain the peace and stability of Europe. When she was seen as doing that, she was good; when some other British activity came to the forefront of American attention, she was bad. The function was one that Britain became less and less able to fulfill. Americans therefore had to reconsider their position. It was as well for Anglo-American relations that the Nazi regime in Germany was so degraded that accommodation with it was offensive to most Americans. Hitler destroyed the case of those who were disposed to seek agreement with him. The course of World War II had two main effects. It gave many Americans an emotional sympathy for Britain—an emotional devotion to Sir Winston Churchill—that survived the war; and it gave many Americans an exaggerated impression of British power. The United States was the stronger partner in the alliance, of course; but the British performance was more than respectable, and it largely concealed the cost in national exhaustion at which it had been made. At the war's end, when the alliance with the Soviet Union began to break up, there remained a relationship between Britain and the United States that was genuinely "special"—that of the two Western world powers that had fought the war together. It was symbolized by the continuance, or revival, of cooperation in atomic matters.

Gar Alperovitz has recently expounded the thesis that the United States early identified the Soviet Union as her postwar opponent, and valued the atomic bomb chiefly as a diplomatic weapon against her.[28] He concentrates his analysis on the period immediately before and immediately after the Potsdam conference, and especially on the period— which came to an end at Hiroshima—when a handful of officials had knowledge that no one else had. Much of his argument is persuasive, but the importance of that short period can be exaggerated. It was thought vital to achieve the "right" settlement with the Soviet Union just because it was hoped that the settlement, once achieved, would be largely self-sustaining. There is evidence to suggest that Americans hoped, and to some extent expected, that Britain would once again take up her old and "proper" task as the guardian of European stability. This hope was based on the failure to realize just how hard-hit Britain had been by the war. The loan to Britain, for example, was justified

28. Gar Alperovitz, *Atomic Diplomacy: Hiroshima and Potsdam* (London, 1966).

largely by Britain's special place in world trade, a place she was expected to resume. To help Britain would be the best, indeed the only, way of restoring world trade quickly. It would not be followed by demands for similar loans to other countries—or, if it was, the demands could be rejected as lacking similar justification—but was rather the best way of ensuring that other loans would not be needed.[29] Again, the history of the settlement in Poland and southeastern Europe is now being revised. But there is no reason as yet to abandon the belief that the object of American policy was a settlement in Europe that would largely sustain itself and that, for the rest, would be sustained by Britain. American efforts to push Britain forward in Europe, and a certain wary British resistance, have been continuing elements in Anglo-American relations almost from that day to this. Nothing else was to be expected.

Had Britain been equal to the task allotted to her, Anglo-American relations in the postwar years might have taken a different course. Since the Soviet regime had no attraction for Americans, their sympathies, if not their support, would presumably have been with Britain. Russia could have exerted no pull such as Germany from time to time exerted in earlier years. Yet a divided Germany would have been able to appeal powerfully to American prejudices. We need spend no time on the might-have-beens. It quickly became clear that Britain could not oppose an equal force to Russia in Europe, and almost as quickly the United States decided to supply the force herself. Here was the end of the old Anglo-American relationship, for, permanently involved in Europe, the United States was bound to develop a European

29. At the time of the negotiation of the British loan, the State Department kept a close watch both on press comment and on expressions of congressional opinion. I am indebted to Mr. H. Schuyler Foster, director of the Public Opinion Studies Staff, for access to some of the material then collected, and for his hospitality.

policy of her own and to form links with other European states, most obviously France and Germany. Nothing in that precluded good relations with Britain also; what it did preclude was the idea of a special, unique relationship. Such elements as served to preserve the relationship—memories of the wartime alliance, or Britain's possession of atomic power—became less and less important as time passed, and remained important for Britons rather than for Americans. American eagerness for Britain to join the Common Market is indicative of this. For America, Britain had ceased to fulfill her proper function. New arrangements therefore had to be made.

Britain proved reluctant to recognize the change. For this there were various reasons, straightforward enough. One was simple insular complacency, which survived the war and was as strong in the Labour party as among Conservatives. More than anything else this underlay the various detailed objections that were raised to British adherence to the Treaty of Rome. Another was the belief that Britain, like the United States and the Soviet Union, was a world power, and that no other Western European state was. It was this assumption that General de Gaulle was most furiously to challenge. But coupled with these, intimately interwoven with them, was the belief in the special relationship with the United States. It nourished both the sense of Britain's superiority to Europe and the belief in Britain's world responsibilities; they were essential to it. For, if Americans had observed that Britain could no longer take the part they had assigned her, and if they were gradually to accept the consequences of that, it was by no means true that the United States was unable to play the part assigned her by Britain. Stronger than ever, her economy stimulated rather than damaged by the war, she was now exercising the world power that the special relationship made, so to say, an extension of British power.

The chief British charges against the United States had been isolationism and complacency. Now that these were being abandoned, the special relationship might well be more fruitful for Britain than ever before. There were, of course, those who saw that a special relationship was appropriate only between equals or near-equals; but Britain suffered from a belief in her capacity to recover that has only begun to crack in the last decade.

Events in Europe thus began to erode the special relationship by weakening American interest or belief in it. Events in the Far East appeared for a time to be strengthening it. In the Far East, as we have seen, American distrust of British imperialism was the chief bar to cooperation, which common fear of Russian expansion was never great enough to overcome. Still less was this so after the Japanese victory in the Russo-Japanese War, when the renewal and extension of the Anglo-Japanese alliance seemed to most Americans a mischievous step. World War I reduced Russian power in the Far East still further, but it also set in train the slow British withdrawal from the area. The Anglo-Japanese alliance was ended, partly, indeed, in response to the knowledge that the United States disliked it; but we should note how little resistance there was in Britain to its ending. The threat it had been designed to meet, and had met with surprising effectiveness, no longer existed. In consequence the alliance lost its value. The interwar years were years in which the chief threat to the existing order in the Far East was clearly Japan, and in which British opposition was as clearly feeble. American opposition was hardly more effective. What is worth emphasizing for our purpose is that in the Far East a more vigorous British policy would have earned American censure.

After World War II the process of dismantling the colonial empires began. Here the British record was a good one.

Britain was not blamed for the upheavals that followed her withdrawal from India, but rather was given credit for the good grace with which the decision to withdraw had been taken. It contrasted, in particular, with the French efforts to hang on to their possessions, and the churlish manner in which the Dutch abandoned theirs. The old American picture of Britain as a grasping colonial power began to fade. It did not follow that cooperation was easy. When Indonesia and Malaya came into conflict, the American tendency, till late, was to suppose that Indonesia was right and Britain wrong. Moreover, the situation was dominated, from an early stage, by American identification of Communist China as the Far Eastern enemy. Largely as a legacy of World War II, the United States was now more active than Britain in the Far East. There was room for dispute about the best way to respond to communism in China; but more important, there was room also for dispute about how to treat the independent states of the Far East so as to render them useful in the anticommunist struggle. The British thought Americans needlessly inflexible in their anticommunism. The Americans suspected the British of hankering after the empire they had lost. As so often in the past each country welcomed in principle the activity of the other, but in practice supposed that activity ill-judged.

Yet there was nothing in this Far Eastern situation to disturb the special relationship. Americans distrusted British activity in the Far East, and did so the more because it distracted British attention from Europe. British insistence that Britain still had a world role seemed to Americans both unrealistic and damaging to the recovery and advance of Europe. Nevertheless, they supposed that British withdrawal would inevitably continue in spite of British nostalgia for an irrecoverable past. From time to time—as, for example, over the question of aid to India during the Chinese attack of

1962—they found it possible to work conveniently with Britain; at other times they found no difficulty in being reasonably tactful. The basic proposition—that the Far East was an area that the United States could handle, and in which British activity was less desirable than British inactivity—did not conflict with the notion of a special relationship. Nor did the British find any more difficulty. They might consider that many specific American actions were ill-judged. They could maintain their hope that with more experience and a little gentle British prodding Americans would learn subtlety and tact. These qualities were all that was needed. There was no objection in principle to having the United States control an area in which Britain felt she had responsibilities rather than valuable interests. What both powers wanted, as ever, was inexpensive stability. While that seemed attainable, there was no cause for either to rethink its position.

What has altered the position, and may have altered it permanently, is the war in Vietnam. Just as Britain's manifest inability to maintain *peaceful* stability in Europe disillusioned Americans with the idea of a special relationship, so America's failure to hold the line *peacefully* in the Far East has disillusioned many Britons. It has not stimulated anti-Americanism except among those who were anti-American already. It has made people reconsider their views who would otherwise have left them complacently unexamined. The problem is not simply that the United States seems to have been drawn into a struggle in which victory is unlikely and which, so critics on both sides of the Atlantic contend, is immoral as well. That would be no more than a temporary setback to Anglo-American relations: it is safe to say that Vietnam will not engage our attention forever. What has been called in question is the assumption that the wealth, power, and influence of the United States

ordinarily serve British purposes as well as American. This
does not suggest an immediate change of policy or, still less,
hostility to the United States. Rather, it suggests a sort of
British Gaullism.[30] There seems no point in being the lesser
part of an Anglo-American partnership. It has inhibited British independence, it has not influenced the United States,
and, most important, it has not kept the peace. The proper
British course is one of more determined independence.

It was argued above that Americans finally lost interest in
the special relationship when Britain became too weak to
maintain European stability and when, in consequence, the
United States intervened directly in European politics. The
present situation in the Far East seems to offer no parallel.
There is no decline in American power, absolute or relative;
and it would be wholly unrealistic to suppose that British
action, whether independent or in support of the United
States, could achieve a result that United States action cannot. Yet there are points of similarity. First, what is under
consideration is not some absolute standard of power but
effective power, power that, given Anglo-American assumptions, is properly measured, and can only be measured, by
the capacity to maintain peace. It is just this capacity, of
course, that the Vietnam war has called into question. Second, since the subject of this analysis is the Anglo-American
relationship, not the alternative policies open to either
nation, the great and obvious difference between British
and American power may be a distraction. Before World
War I, and again before World War II, when the balance in
Europe was clearly unstable, recognition of that fact
strengthened American determination to remain aloof if
possible, determination that any sense of a special relation-

30. It is often remarked that the British were Gaullists before de Gaulle.
The comment refers to British aloofness from other European states and
insistence on a world role, not to British independence of the United States.

ship could do little to counteract. Similarly, if a political struggle is now to develop in Asia, with the United States and China as protagonists, the British disposition will be to stand aside, maintaining so far as possible connections with both.

Britain and the United States have long differed in their attitude to Communist China. While peace in Asia, however fragile, could be maintained, the differences were of secondary importance. In war, or under the immediate threat of war, they are central. Both countries are forced to make calculations, and predictions of the future, that emphasize how different their circumstances are. It is not easy to envisage a future in which it will again be possible to neglect those different circumstances. Anglo-American relations at the moment are not bad. Whatever the outcome in Vietnam, they will often, one may hope, be good in the future. But if good, they will be good as relations between other states are good, and not by reason of any special relationship. The long-range predictions not about Britain or America but about the future of the world and the forces shaping it, which were the basis of the special relationship, have ceased to be plausible.

From Contempt to Containment:
Cycles in American Attitudes
toward China

WARREN I. COHEN

UNDER FIRE in 1967 because of an unpopular war in Southeast Asia, the American secretary of state explained the administration's policy in terms of the need to contain an aggressive China. In 1968, as the season for elections neared in the United States, William Buckley, a leading spokesman for American conservatism, urged upon the Republican party a foreign policy platform that included provision for making Japan into a nuclear power, as a counter to China. The knowledge that Dean Rusk and American conservatives saw China as a threat to the interests of the United States could hardly have come as a surprise to anyone familiar with American attitudes toward China since 1950—when the outbreak of war in Korea led the Truman administration to apply the policy of containment to Asia. Much had changed since the beginning of the century when American attitudes toward China were such as to lead a later student, Harold Isaacs, to categorize the period 1840–1905 as the "Age of Contempt."

Fear now reigned where once contempt had spat—and in

the years between, China had struggled to become a modern nation-state. As China awakened, how did the United States respond? What was the American reaction to the process of modernization in China, to the development of nationalism? To what extent was the United States willing to interpose its power between China and Japan's pretensions to hegemony in East Asia? These are the questions with which I am concerned in this essay, another approach to the study of Sino-American relations in the twentieth century.

I

When Theodore Roosevelt became president of the United States, his inherited secretary of state, John Hay, had already placed the world's major powers on notice of American interest in China. Long involved in Chinese affairs, enmeshed in the treaty system shaped largely by other imperial powers, the United States had chosen not to follow when the Japanese and European powers sought to divide China into spheres of influence. But the interest in China that antedated American independence, the involvement that began in 1784 with the arrival of the first American merchantman at Canton, was not to be abandoned. Indeed, the acquisition of an insular empire in the Pacific in the closing years of the nineteenth century had heightened American concern over the course of events in the Far East, and in 1899 and 1900 in his Open Door notes, John Hay both expressed this concern and requested assurance that the position of the United States in China would not be undermined by the course upon which the powers had embarked.

Over the years there has been much debate over the meaning and wisdom of Hay's message to the powers. There have been suggestions that he benignly and/or foolishly claimed for the United States a role that it had neither the will nor the power to play—that of protector of China. Whatever the merits of the various arguments, it should be patently clear that no matter what else was involved, Hay's policy was intended to serve the interests of the United States. If his notes proved to be of value to China also, that was incidental. But to assert the truism that American policy was designed to serve American ends is not to suggest that this policy was antithetical to the interests of China. At times there may well have been conflicts of interest, but there is no iron law of interests such as classical economists postulated for wages. A nation in the course of serving its own interests may as easily serve as infringe upon the interests of others. In short, to demonstrate that American statesmen, in formulating and executing policy toward China, consistently sought to further the interests of their own country does not prove a priori that they consistently sought to or did exploit China.

Hay, as he wrote his notes, served in a government that held China in contempt. China was less a part of the international order with which he dealt than it was an inert mass to be acted upon. If the other imperial powers expressed their contempt by carving China into spheres, the American government, in defending its interests, did not consult with the Chinese government, nor did Hay at any time seek an expression of Chinese needs. In fact, during the period in which the Open Door notes were formulated and delivered, Hay was involved in a heated debate with the Chinese minister to the United States over the issue of American discrimination against Chinese in Hawaii and the Philippines. September, 1899, the month in which the first notes were sent to the powers was the same month in which the Chinese minister, Wu T'ing-fang, protested against the "utter disregard" of the United States for "the friendly relations which should exist between the two governments." [1]

The American minister to China, E. H. Conger, expressed another facet of the American attitude toward China, explaining the merits of gunboat diplomacy to Hay: "The Chinese Government really care little for anything but power, and an earnest exhibition of it always promptly moves them." As Conger mustered gunboats to protect the rights of Americans in China, Wu T'ing-fang could arm himself only with indignation in his efforts to protect the rights of Chinese in the United States. "Mr. Secretary," he wrote to Hay, "the archives of your Department will show how futile have been the representations of the Chinese Government." He charged officials of the American government with treating the Chinese "not as subjects of a friendly power lawfully seeking the benefit of treaty privileges, but as suspected criminals." Why, he asked, could not the Chinese in the United States receive the same treatment afforded other foreigners—and "demanded and secured" by the Chinese Government "for American citizens in China—an open door and a fair field." [2]

And the answer was that China was weak and held in contempt by the United States no less than by the other powers. And before Wu left for home, Roosevelt, whose contempt for China was rarely concealed, took over the reins of the American government.

Roosevelt's Far Eastern policies have received considerable scholarly treatment, but the major focus, including two recent volumes, has been, justly, on his handling of Japanese-

1. U.S. State Department, *Foreign Relations of the United States, 1899* (Washington, 1901), pp. 202–15 (hereafter cited as *Foreign Relations*).

2. *Foreign Relations, 1900* (Washington, 1902), p. 94; *Foreign Relations, 1901* (Washington, 1902), pp. 76–97.

American relations. The most extensive analysis of Roosevelt's attitudes and policy toward China is probably the
long chapter in Howard K. Beale's *Theodore Roosevelt and
America's Rise to World Power.* In a book that clearly demonstrated Roosevelt's fascination with power politics and his
commitment to imperialism, Beale was particularly critical
of his failure to come to terms with Chinese nationalism, of
his "failure to formulate a foreign policy that would have
helped solve China's basic problems and would have been
in line with China's future role in world affairs." Indeed,
Beale carried the argument one step further and declared
that the rise of nationalism in China "was precisely what
Americans like Roosevelt feared." Moreover, he implied that
in the failure of the United States to befriend Chinese nationalism, to guide it, the United States lost China and
"missed perhaps the greatest opportunity of its twentieth
century career." [3]

Whether greater wisdom or decency in Roosevelt's policy
would have spared the Chinese Communists the necessity
of organizing and averted the unpleasantness that followed
World War II is a question probably best left to some able
Chinese geomancer, but Roosevelt's attitudes toward China
and Chinese nationalism merit examination. And examination immediately indicates a contempt for China so strong
that "Chinese" became in Roosevelt's vocabulary a derisive
adjective. Thus the Russians in June, 1905, by refusing to
come to terms with the Japanese, were accused of behaving
with "Chinese folly." Over the years, his frequent dissatisfaction with the unwillingness of his fellow Americans to

3. For Roosevelt and Japan, see Raymond A. Esthus, *Theodore Roosevelt
and Japan* (Seattle, 1966) and Charles E. Neu, *An Uncertain Friendship:
Theodore Roosevelt and Japan, 1906–1909* (Cambridge, Mass., 1967);
Howard K. Beale, *Theodore Roosevelt and the Rise of America to World
Power* (Baltimore, 1956), pp. 248, 252.

endorse his programs for military preparedness brought
clumsy attempts at analogies with presumed Chinese pacifism, the most picturesque example coming after Wilson's
statement about being "too proud to fight." Roosevelt wrote:
"If I thought the mood was permanent, I would feel that
Uncle Sam would do well to wear a pigtail at once." Herein
lay the source of his attitude toward China and the
Chinese.[4]

For all Roosevelt's inane prattle about Anglo-Saxon superiority, for all his peculiar racial classifications, it was not
race as normally understood that determined his view. No
one could deny his most obvious respect for the Japanese.
He himself expressed this most characteristically to John
Hay: "What nonsense it is to speak of the Chinese and
Japanese as of the same race! They are of the same race only
in the sense that a Levantine Greek is of the same race with
Lord Milner." The Japanese had built a nation—they had
modernized their society. In time, he believed, they would
build a great civilization. For most of his life, however,
Roosevelt did not believe the Chinese could become civilized
—did not believe the Chinese could create a modern
society. Perhaps when the moon was blue: "If China became civilized like Japan," and a number of other wondrous
things occurred, "then," he wrote to Henry White, "an
international disarmament agreement would be possible."
He was repelled by the apparent lack of patriotism in
China, explaining its semicolonial status in terms of the
inability and unwillingness of the Chinese to fight, and he
made frequent invidious comparisons with Japan. In short,

    4. Theodore Roosevelt to Henry Cabot Lodge, June 16, 1905; to Arthur
Hamilton Lee, June 7, 1916, in Elting E. Morison et al., eds., The Letters of
Theodore Roosevelt, 8 vols. (Cambridge, Mass., 1951–54), IV, 1232; VIII,
1055 (hereafter cited as Letters).

Roosevelt's disgust with China was markedly similar to that
of Sun Yat-sen: the Chinese people were as loose sands that
could not be held together to create a modern nation state.[5]

Obviously, Roosevelt's concern for China was not quite
equal to Sun's, but neither was his attitude toward Chinese
nationalism antithetical to Sun's, as Beale's analysis would
suggest. If, to Roosevelt, Chinese rights and aspirations were
never of equal importance to American rights and aspirations, he could still recognize that they existed and fault
those who trod on them—even Americans. For Roosevelt,
the imperialist had obligations as well as privileges, and the
greatest obligation was to behave in a manner that clearly
demonstrated superiority. To Finley Peter Dunne he once
admitted that "your delicious phrase about 'take up the
white man's burden and put it on the coon,' exactly hit the
weak spot in my own theory." So long as this weak spot
existed, so long as this uneasiness existed, the "civilized"
nations had to perform in exemplary manner in the presence
of their victims. Thus Roosevelt was infuriated by the
brutality of European troops in the relief expedition that
liberated Peking during the Boxer Rebellion. He wrote to
Mahan, noting that the American officers in the expedition
felt that the "awful outrages committed by many of the
European troops . . . the wanton so-called punitive ex-
peditions of the German troops, and indeed the original
misconduct of some of the foreigners, notably the Germans
and the Russians, have left the count against us rather than
against the Chinese." Though proud of the role played by
American forces, especially General A. R. Chafee's efforts to
secure justice for the Chinese, he readily called Mahan's attention to reports of misconduct on the part of American

5. Roosevelt to John Hay, September 2, 1904; to Henry White, August
14, 1906, *Letters,* IV, 917; V, 359.

missionaries. Nothing could be lower than an imperial power
that sank to such levels; and in 1905, in the midst of a crisis
in Sino-American relations, Roosevelt, expressing dissatisfaction with China to his minister, W. W. Rockhill, insisted
that "bad as the Chinese are, no human beings, black, yellow
or white, can be quite as untruthful, as insincere, as arrogant
—in short as untrustworthy in every way—as the Russians
under their present system." [6]

Now, in the latter part of the twentieth century, few
Americans would be pleased with the patterns of Roosevelt's
thought, with his overt imperialism and racial condescension.
But his attitudes must be kept in perspective. Russians were
contemptible "under their present system." He was appalled
by the massive inefficient bureaucracy that obstructed
modernization. China was contemptible, not because Chinese were yellow, not because they were Asians, but because
they had no national spirit and made no effort to modernize.
Implicit in his thought was not hostility toward, or fear of,
Chinese nationalism, but rather the assumption that China
would never develop a national spirit—that it would remain
forever a weak clumsy empire with even less capacity to
mobilize its energies than the bureaucratic Russian empire.
Rather than condemn the Chinese to an eternal role as
victim of international politics, he constantly pointed to the
Japanese example as one that the Chinese might well em-
ulate.

In 1905, however, the Chinese surprised Roosevelt with a
nationalist movement that took the form of an anti-American
boycott. Here indeed was a trying test of his attitudes and
policy, and Beale has contended that he "offered the young
Chinese nationalists not sympathy but a show of force," that

6. Roosevelt to Finley Peter Dunne, January 16, 1900; to Alfred Thayer
Mahan, March 18, 1901; to William W. Rockhill, August 29, 1905, *Letters,*
II, 1134; III, 23; IV, 1326–27.

he even "prepared to invade China."[7] Although evidence does exist to support Beale's contentions, this same evidence, *in context,* permits a very different interpretation.

The anti-American movement of 1905 came in response to the immigration policy of the United States and to the discrimination against Oriental immigrants in California. The movement took the form of a boycott against American trade and was undertaken by the Chinese people rather than by their government—although some representatives of the Chinese government, like Wu T'ing-fang, supported it. With regard to immigration policy, Roosevelt's attitude was clear, consistent, and creditable. He accepted the exclusion of Chinese labor that he was powerless to prevent and made every effort to obtain fair treatment for Chinese businessmen and students. This did not satisfy the Chinese, nor should it have. The Chinese exclusion acts were unquestionably a disgrace, a mockery of American ideals—but they were the will of the majority of Americans and not the work of Roosevelt.

Roosevelt dealt with the boycott by attempting to alleviate its causes in the United States and to limit its application in China. On both fronts he had limited success because he had but limited power. Within the United States he could dictate neither to Congress nor to the particular states, which, like California, legalized discrimination against Orientals. Over events in China, he had still less control. To American businessmen, political figures, and friends, he contended that the Chinese had just cause for complaint, that "undoubtedly one of the chief causes of the boycott has been the shortcomings of the United States Government and people in the matter of the treatment of Chinese here." He demanded support, particularly from Pacific Coast sufferers from the

7. Beale, *Theodore Roosevelt,* pp. 242, 247.

boycott, for his efforts "to do justice as well as to exact justice." Of Senator George Perkins of California, Roosevelt asked for help "to secure rational action by Congress in legislation and treaties affecting Chinese merchants, professional men, students, travelers, and the like, so as to secure to them exactly the same treatment in the United States as would be given to similar people of other nationalities." He insisted he was doing what he could and demanded that Pacific Coast representatives aid "in undoing the injustice in our treaties and legislation as regards the Chinese, which has probably been the whole, and certainly the main, cause of the present boycott." [8]

On the administrative level Roosevelt could act alone, and he did. Victor Metcalf, the secretary of commerce and labor, received orders to send "specific and rigid" instructions to immigration authorities "that we will no more tolerate discourtesy or harsh treatment in connection with the Chinese merchant, traveler or student than in connection with . . . [those] who visit us from other nations." He informed the acting secretary of state, Herbert Peirce, that immigration authorities had been put on notice that harshness in the administration of the laws would not be tolerated and that "any discourtesy shown to Chinese persons by any official of the Government will be cause for immediate dismissal from the service." [9]

In his efforts to have the Chinese government stop the boycott, Roosevelt's methods, contrary to Beale's allegations, were unexceptional. The American minister in Peking made frequent protests and warned that the Chinese government would be held accountable for losses sustained by American

8. Roosevelt to George C. Perkins, August 31, 1905; to T. C. Friedlander, November 23, 1905, *Letters*, IV, 1327–28; V, 90–91.
9. Roosevelt to Victor Metcalf, June 16, 1905; to Herbert Peirce, June 24, 1905, *Letters*, IV, 1235, 1251.

businessmen. He demanded the punishment of the man alleged to be the leader of the boycott movement. In short, given the fact that the boycott violated American treaty rights and was, to say the least, an unfriendly gesture, Rockhill's actions were routine. There was no threat of force—even after the Chinese government denied responsibility for the boycott and refused to take further action. And in the fall, after the movement had been sustained for about five months and *Chinese* businessmen began to suffer, the boycott lost its vitality.[10]

Beale's charges of Roosevelt meeting this expression of Chinese nationalism with a show of force and preparations for invasion are misleading. At the close of 1905 the American Asiatic Fleet *was* increased by two cruisers and three gunboats, and Roosevelt *did* ask the War Department to prepare plans for possible operations against China; but neither move was taken with any intention of crushing the boycott in particular or Chinese nationalism in general. In October a number of American missionaries were murdered in China, and as the boycott faded, physical attacks on Americans increased. With the memory of the Boxer uprising only five years old, it would have been irresponsible for Roosevelt not to have considered the possibility of a new relief expedition. And so the secretary of the navy was notified that "the Chinese are not showing a good spirit" and that the United States "ought to be prepared for any contingencies there." Fortunately, no expedition to China proved necessary, "but," Roosevelt wrote to General Leonard Wood, "I wanted to be sure that if it was needed we would not be unprepared." [11]

10. *Foreign Relations, 1905* (Washington, 1906), 204–34.

11. Roosevelt to Charles J. Bonaparte, November 15, 1905; to William H. Taft, January 11, 1906; to Leonard Wood, April 2, 1906, *Letters,* V, 77, 132–133, 205. See also *Foreign Relations, 1933,* 5 vols. (Washington, 1950),

In December, 1905, with the situation in China relatively quiet, Roosevelt chose the occasion of his annual message to Congress to express his essential sympathy with the Chinese cause. Although he condoned the policy of excluding coolies, he insisted that in practice "grave injustice and wrong have been done by this nation to the people of China, and therefore ultimately to this nation itself." He reminded his audience of American insistence upon justice being shown Americans by the Chinese, but warned that "we cannot receive equity unless we are willing to do equity." "We cannot," he maintained, "ask the Chinese to do to us what we are unwilling to do to them." In direct reference to the boycott, he attributed it to the resentment felt by all the Chinese leaders against the harshness of American immigration policy.[12]

Roosevelt's most characteristic expression of sympathy for Chinese nationalism came almost two years later when the Chinese government announced that it intended to reappoint Wu T'ing-fang as minister to the United States. In his previous tour Wu, a master of the English language, had persistently bested the Department of State in exchanges over the treatment of Chinese in America and in the new American empire in the Pacific. A strident nationalist, he had been active in the boycott movement of 1905 and subsequently allied himself with Sun Yat-sen, remaining Sun's principal adviser on foreign affairs until his death in 1922. In 1907 the question was raised as to whether the United States should accept as minister a man who had consistently harassed the American government during his earlier tenure

III, 31–39, for a Department of State review of the events of 1905. This document contains evidence that negates Beale's charge but, by illustrating the *routine* practices of the Asiatic Fleet, precludes any sanguine view of American imperialism in China.

12. Theodore Roosevelt, *State Papers as Governor and President, 1899–1909* (New York, 1925), pp. 376–77 (hereafter cited as *State Papers*).

in office and who had been deeply involved in anti-American activities ever since. And Roosevelt replied:

> My feeling would be strongly that we ought not to object to Wu. He is a bad old Chink and if he had his way he would put us all to the heavy death or do something equally unpleasant with us; but we cannot expect to get a Minister like the one that has just gone, and the loss is far more China's than ours; while I do not object to any Chinaman showing a feeling that he would like to retaliate now and then for our insolence to the Chinese.[13]

During his last two years in office, Roosevelt indicated an awareness of the changes that were occurring in China, of the modernizing (he would have said "civilizing") process struggling to break through the shell of Chinese conservatism—and he did not deny American sympathy or assistance. In his annual message of 1907 he asked for authority to refund the punitive part of the Boxer Indemnity, declaring that the United States "should help in every practicable way in the education of the Chinese people, so that the vast and populous empire of China may gradually adapt itself to modern conditions." Although Beale contended that Roosevelt did not realize that it was nationalism that was emerging in China and that he viewed an exhibition of nationalist aspirations as misbehavior, *before* he left the White House, Roosevelt published an article, "The Awakening of China," which read like a paean to the new spirt there. He called upon his countrymen to note the awakening of China: the increased contact with foreigners, increased trade, modernization of communications, evolution of industry, and a change in attitudes toward Western education. With his usual enthusiasm Roosevelt visualized a new China freed

13. Roosevelt to Elihu Root, September 26, 1907, *Letters,* V, 809.

from the shackles of ancient superstitions. At last there had
come a movement that meant "the growth of a real and intelligent spirit of patriotism in all parts of China."

Having learned much of what he knew of events in China
from missionaries, Roosevelt exaggerated the influence of
Christian education on Chinese nationalism; but that devia-
tion hardly detracted from his message: China had awakened and was preparing to join the modern world, "one of
the great events of our age." And there would be no reason
to fear a modern China provided that Chinese discontent
was met not with repression but with justice and education:
"The best way to avoid possible peril, commercial or military, from the great Chinese people, is by behaving right-
eously toward them and by striving to inspire a religious
life in them." After this expression of regard for religious
works, he concluded by insisting that the object of the missions should not be limited to the saving of souls but should
also work toward the creation of the kingdom of God on earth
—which, after all, was the modest goal of the New Nationalism.[14]

Almost as if to demonstrate that these ideas were not
merely the result of some Sunday morning uplift but rather
an integral part of his view of world politics, Roosevelt expressed them quite differently when addressing T'ang
Shao-i, a prominent nationalist reformer, a few days after
publication of the article. He declared that the United States
hoped, "so far as the opportunity and the power permit, to
aid those Chinese citizens who in working for the betterment
of conditions in China, in working to bring China abreast
of the general movement of civilized mankind, are showing
themselves to be the truest friends and supporters of the
ancient Chinese Empire." Roosevelt's reasons for desiring a

14. Roosevelt, *State Papers*, p. 571; Beale, *Theodore Roosevelt*, p. 251;
Roosevelt, "The Awakening of China," *Outlook* XC (1908), 665-67.

strong China came from his conception of the world's need for a stable balance of power. A weak China invited foreign aggression and a competition for power in East Asia—a competition that provided a much more certain danger of instability than did the emergence of a strong Chinese nation. To T'ang, he declared:

> I believe that the world now realizes more than ever before that normally it is to the advantage of other nations when any nation becomes stable and prosperous, able to keep the peace within its own borders, and strong enough not to invite aggression from without. We heartily hope for the progress of China, and so far as by peaceful and legitimate means we are able we will do our part toward furthering that progress.[15]

Nothing that Roosevelt said or did generally or specifically with regard to Chinese nationalism proves that Roosevelt was any less an imperialist or superpatriot than he appears in others' portraits of him. Even at his most benign, he was condescending to the Chinese, and he never willingly sacrificed any American interests in China, as Beale and others have shown clearly in their studies of the Canton-Hankow railroad dispute. Scholars are agreed that he was willing to acquiesce in Japanese infringements on Chinese sovereignty in Manchuria, rather than risk involving the United States in war with Japan. But if his principal concern was always his country's national interest, the desire for a strong China was not incompatible with American interests. If the United States benefited from a stable international order, a strong China was ultimately a surer guarantee of such an order than a weak China over which other powers vied.

Roosevelt was contemptuous of weak countries that in-

15. Roosevelt to the Department of State, December 2, 1908, *Letters*, VI, 1405–7.

sisted upon retaining their ancient customs and traditional societies. Such countries are currently referred to as "under-developed"—he called them uncivilized. For the Chinese he seemed to have particular contempt, perhaps because a once great civilization seemed unable to revitalize itself, because the Chinese, lacking a spirit of nationalism, were unwilling to create a modern nation-state. When, in 1905, he perceived the new spirit in China, he met it with respect and even admiration. He did not fight for Chinese nationalism because it was not in America's interest to fight China's battles. "Alliance with China," he wrote in 1910, "in view of China's absolute military helplessness, means not an additional strength to us, but an additional obligation which we assume." [16] A strong China might well be in the interest of the entire world; but in Roosevelt's time it did not exist, and he guided his nation through the shoals of world politics with a surer sense of the limits of its power than is apparent in some historians with benefit of fifty or more years of hindsight.

II

In the decade following Roosevelt's brief retirement from American politics, the men who concerned themselves with Far Eastern policy proved to be still more sympathetic to the national aspirations of the Chinese people. But there were differences of tremendous significance. Roosevelt had compartmentalized his thoughts. His sympathy for Chinese nationalism was genuine, but he never let it interfere with his perception of the realities of power. He did not believe that the interests of the United States could be served by

16. Roosevelt to Taft, December 22, 1910, *Letters*, VII, 190.

aligning the country with China in such a way as to antagonize Japan—in his time and for long after the dominant
force in East Asia. With all his rhetoric about America's
mission, he suffered no illusions of a Pax Americana; no
messianic impulse drove him to risk the security and interests of the United States on behalf of China.

His successors, especially Taft and his secretary of state
Philander C. Knox, and Wilson, had a more immediate sense
of the identity of American and Chinese interests—and a
lesser understanding of the role of power in world affairs.
They sympathized with Chinese aspirations, considered
them just, and considered diplomatic and financial support
of these aspirations consistent with the interests of the
United States. That such policy antagonized Japan concerned them far less than it had Roosevelt. For Taft and
Knox, perhaps, it was the power of the dollar, for Wilson, the
power of right; but both administrations dared Japanese
military power without fear of conflict.

Roosevelt's disagreement with Taft and Knox over dollar
diplomacy in Manchuria illustrates the difference between
mere sympathy for China and a policy that, partly on the
basis of sympathy, would have the United States act to assist
China in attaining its goals. Charles Vevier and Raymond
Esthus have shown Willard Straight's role in the schemes
to force Russia and especially Japan out of Manchuria.[17]
Despite differences in their interpretations of Straight's
motives, both men agreed that the neutralization scheme,
whereby an American-sponsored international loan was to
enable the Chinese government to buy up foreign railroad

---

17. Charles Vevier, "The Open Door: An Idea in Action, 1906–1913," *Pa-
cific Historical Review* XXIV (1955), 49–62; Raymond Esthus, "The
Changing Concept of the Open Door, 1899–1910," *Mississippi Valley
Historical Review* XLVI (1959), 435–54.

concessions, would have given China an opportunity to regain sovereignty over Manchuria. Great advantages would also have accrued to American railroad and banking interests, but this was the bait necessary to raise the capital, for neither banks nor railroads are designed to be eleemosynary institutions. And yet, if for the moment dollars were intended to serve the ends of diplomacy, it should not be forgotten that the ultimate purpose of Knox's diplomacy was the furtherance of American trade and investments abroad. Here, in the Far East, this led to an assumption of the congruity of Chinese and American interests. Every step taken to relieve the Chinese from the pressures of European and Japanese imperialism provided a new hope for American profit. To paraphrase Samuel Flagg Bemis, the liberation of China was to provide America's opportunity.

The assumption of the congruence of American and Chinese interests disturbed Roosevelt. In a letter to his son he bemoaned the inability of "poor Taft" to understand that a successful policy toward Japan necessitated a "coherent plan for treating affairs in Manchuria, affairs in China, affairs about immigration." Finally, he went to Taft and told him that Japan could be a serious menace to the security of the United States and its possessions. He noted that the Japanese were very sensitive to threats to their interests on the continent of Asia, especially in Manchuria, "where American interests are really unimportant, and not such that the American people would be content to run the slightest risk of collision about them." With both Taft and Knox he argued that the United States should do nothing that might be construed as challenging Japanese interests in Manchuria. To identify the interests of the United States with those of China was utter madness. Roosevelt contended that to challenge Japan in Manchuria required tremendous military power—a fleet equivalent to England's and an army comparable to Germany's.[18]

Indeed, Roosevelt went further and contended that the Open Door policy of the United States was worthless when a powerful nation chose to disregard it and was prepared to use force if necessary to pursue its ends. To this, Knox took exception, preferring the higher moral ground implicit in his draft for Taft's reply to Roosevelt. He asked "why the Japanese need Manchuria any more than does China who owns it now." And he posed what was to become the crucial problem for those who would determine American policy in the Far East for years to come. Charging that Roosevelt saw no alternative "between silently renouncing our historic policy in China whenever it may cross the interest of another power and being prepared to go to war in defense of that policy," Knox began the quest for that alternative.[19]

To Taft and Knox, as to Willard Straight and perhaps to men of good will everywhere, China had the right to control its own territory and its own resources, as its people sought to create a modern nation. But Japan posed obstacles to the modernization of China, which threatened Japanese hegemony in East Asia. Where Taft, Knox, and Straight differed from others who shared their sentiments was in their conviction that opposition to Japan in support of Chinese aspirations was consistent not only with the ideals but also with the interests of the American people. And they made the effort to provide China with the capital needed to return to the Chinese people control over their internal communications and over the exploitation of their resources.

18. Roosevelt to Lodge, May 24, 1910; to Theodore Roosevelt, Jr., December 5, 1910; to Taft, December 8, and December 22, 1910, *Letters*, VII, 86, 178, 180, 189–90.

19. Henry F. Pringle, *The Life and Times of William Howard Taft*, 2 vols. (New York and Toronto, 1939), II, 685–86.

Knox's plans for Manchuria foundered when Japan and
Russia unexpectedly chose to manuever together and the
complexities of European politics required England and
France to chart courses other than those hoped for by the
United States. But the Chinese themselves, discarding the
jetsam of the Manchu dynasty, sailed forward, hoping to
find in a republican form of government a shorter and calmer
channel to modernization.

III

Of the efforts of Taft and Knox to force American capital
into China, it may be said that the interests of neither China
nor the United States were served thereby. Ultimately, to
Woodrow Wilson was left the future of American participation in the Six Power Banking Consortium, organized to
provide loans to the Chinese government.

In its initial handling of American policy toward China,
the administration of Woodrow Wilson provided a marvel-
ous example of the all too common blend of arrogance and
ignorance. First came the consortium question: the American participants asked if the new administration desired
continued American participation. Perhaps the most striking glimpse of the decision-making process is afforded by
the diary entries of Josephus Daniels. At no time were the
members of the Far Eastern Division of the Department of
State consulted—or the inherited assistant secretaries—or
even the Chinese themselves. Mistrustful of the militarism
and dollar diplomacy of the administrations that preceded
theirs, Wilson and Secretary of State William Jennings Bryan
had no use for the bureaucratic remnants of darker days.
Progress, the new world toward which the new diplomacy

of Wilson and Bryan led, could only be obstructed by the advice of "experts" deeply rooted in the immoral milieu of old style, Old World, power politics.

Bryan needed no one's advice to know that bankers involved in monopolistic practices boded ill for China. Two decades of tilting against the "interests" had taught him at least that. The secretary of the interior, "who had made a long study of Chinese affairs," argued that "old time favoritism" should be dropped now that China "had declared for new ways." He opposed assistance to China that was conditional upon China being "beholden to a group of financiers in the largest nations." The secretary of commerce suggested that withdrawal from the consortium might jeopardize American trade and sought some "proper way" to help China. No one else seemed concerned with economic considerations, and no one at all raised questions about how withdrawal would effect American relations with other nations or the position of the United States in East Asia. Daniels found Wilson "clear in his conviction that we could not request the trust group of bankers to effect the loan, and that we ought to help China in some better way." And so Wilson informed the press that American participation in the consortium would no longer have the support of the government.

At a cabinet meeting shortly thereafter, Wilson explained his decision: "I feel so keenly the desire to help China that I prefer to err in the line of helping that country than otherwise." If the United States had moved on with the consortium, "we would have gotten nothing but mere influence in China and lost the proud position which America secured when Secretary Hay stood for the Open Door in China after the Boxer Uprising." But now, having demonstrated American disinterestedness, having purged itself from association with international bankers, the United States would be in an excellent position to call the imperialists to account. For China, at least, the new order had begun.[20]

Neither the anger of "reactionary" elements in the Department of State nor the outrage of the Japanese imperialists gave Wilson cause to doubt the wisdom or righteousness of his course. More likely these responses confirmed his judgment. And Yuan Shih-k'ai, president of the unrecognized Republic of China, gave further testimony that Wilson had found a "better way." Through the Chinese minister to the United States, he sent word of his appreciation, and to the American chargé d'affaires he announced that Wilson's action would be "of great assistance to us." [21]

If Yuan expected loans on a more generous basis to be forthcoming, he did not live to see them. If his praise of Wilson could be repaid by American recognition of his regime, he was not to be disappointed. Within a week Wilson informed the cabinet that he had decided to recognize the Republic of China. The attorney general wondered if it might not be best to cooperate with the other powers, but Wilson would have none of this. Their ambassadors would be informed confidentially, and they could join with the United States if they wished; but the United States would not be bound by the decision of the other nations. The high moral purpose of the president exhilarated Daniels, but there were complications. The Japanese government called attention to the fact that Sun Yat-sen and his party disputed Yuan's right to the presidency and that recognition at this time "would practically amount to interference in favor of Mr. Yuan." Into cabinet discussions also crept the fact that a "prominent Chinaman" (the Kuomintang leader, Sung Chiao-jen) had been assassinated and that President Yuan

20. E. David Cronon, ed., *The Cabinet Diaries of Josephus Daniels, 1913–1921* (Lincoln, Neb., 1963), pp. 7–8, 17.

21. *Foreign Relations, 1913* (Washington, 1920), 173–75.

might have been involved. But these objections do not seem to have been given serious consideration. The parliament of the new republic was to meet for the first time, and the great democratic republic, the United States of America, extended its blessing in the form of recognition.[22]

But somehow, despite this policy of obvious friendship and good will toward China, little progress was made toward the modernization of China. Little indeed was the evidence that traditional Chinese society had changed, that a sense of nationalism had come with the creation of a republic. Little indeed was the evidence that the Chinese people sought change or that there existed an indigenous leadership prepared to coax or coerce China into the modern era. Developments in industry or internal communications were minimal. To go forward—or perhaps more accurately, to survive—China needed capital and aggressive leaders. As a result of Wilson's decision on American participation in the consortium, China's principal source of economic assistance was Japan, a country that, unlike the United States, did not believe that its interests would be served by a strong, modern China. With the withdrawal of the United States from the consortium and the coming of the war in Europe, Japan established a virtually unchecked hegemony over China's finances. Given the absence of competitors, the Japanese were able to dictate the terms of the loans, exacting concession after concession, gnawing away at Chinese sovereignty. In short, as Tien-yi Li, Arthur Link, and Roy Curry have shown, Wilson's well-intentioned policy toward China, motivated by anti-imperialism, worked to the detriment of China.[23]

22. Cronon, *Cabinet Diaries*, pp. 20–23; *Foreign Relations, 1913*, p. 109.
23. Tien-yi Li, *Woodrow Wilson's China Policy, 1913–1917* (New York, 1952); Arthur S. Link, *Wilson: The New Freedom* (Princeton, N.J., 1956), especially pp. 283–88; Roy W. Curry, *Woodrow Wilson and Far Eastern Policy, 1913–1921* (New York, 1959).

The Japanese entered the war shortly after it began and seized the German concessions in Shantung. Helplessly, the Chinese turned to the United States for assistance. In Washington, Robert Lansing, then counselor of the Department of State, insisted that it would be "quixotic in the extreme to allow the question of China's territorial integrity to entangle the United States in international difficulties." A few months later, he suggested a Rooseveltian bargain by means of which the United States would acquiesce in Japanese policies in Shantung and southern Manchuria in return for an end to Japanese complaints about land tenure legislation in the United States and the directing of Japanese emigrants to Manchuria rather than the United States. Of Bryan he asked: "Can there be any harm in attempting to reach a reciprocal understanding?" For Lansing, American interests in China were limited to commerce, and a Japanese promise not to create monopolies for Japanese trade, not to permit discriminatory railroad rates, and a general agreement to permit equal opportunity for American trade satisfied the requirements of the Open Door. In his analysis and recommendations, there was none of the ebullient idealism that had permeated cabinet discussions of China in 1913, but rather an old-fashioned attempt to assess national interest and to serve this end without particular regard for China. This proved to be too narrow a vision for Woodrow Wilson.[24]

Another view of America's interests in the Far East, one that joined more smoothly with Wilson's attitude toward China, was presented by E. T. Williams, chief of the Division of Far Eastern Affairs. Arthur S. Link refers to Williams as a member of a small but influential group in the Foreign Service who believed that the development of China would

24. *Foreign Relations, 1914, Supplement* (Washington, 1928), pp. 189–90; U.S. State Department, *The Lansing Papers, 1914–1920*, 2 vols. (Washington, 1936), II, 407–8.

provide "America's great economic opportunity in the future." Williams recognized that existing commercial interests were greater in Japan than in China, but believed that the myth of the China market would be the morrow's reality, and "the look ahead shows *our interest* to be *a strong and independent China* rather than one held in subjection by Japan." Williams urged that the United States press Japan to soften its approach to China, then insist that the Chinese do what was necessary to bring order to the country and to be able to defend their country themselves: to create a modern nation-state. "We *can* and *ought* to assist her in this," wrote Williams to Bryan, "and in so doing we shall be building up *a strong defense for ourselves.*" Here, as an alternative to Lansing's proposal, was offered the argument that America's interests as well as the ideals of its people, could best be served by an Asian policy that was aggressively pro-Chinese. And it was in this direction that Wilson ultimately tended.

In the crisis over Japan's notorious Twenty-one Demands, Wilson chose for the United States the role of China's defender—a role Lansing called quixotic and Roosevelt considered mad. Though he carried the torch perilously close to where Roosevelt believed could be found the fuse of Japanese military power, Wilson entertained no thought of war. Indeed, Link contends that neither Bryan nor Wilson seriously considered policies that might provoke war, believing that "American interests in China did not justify taking any such chances." [25]

Japan's pressures on China forced Wilson to recognize China's need for an alternative to Japanese financial assistance, and he realized that only the United States could

25. Arthur S. Link, *Wilson: The Struggle for Neutrality, 1914–1915* (Princeton, N.J., 1960), pp. 276–77. Italics in Williams quote added by Link.

provide that alternative. Significantly, he was forced to reconsider the question of American participation in the consortium, to reexamine his attitude toward monopoly capital.
A man confident of the benefits of the free market, certain
of the salutary effects of competition, committed to the concepts of laissez-faire liberalism, had to find a way to provide
economic aid to an underdeveloped country. Wilson and
Bryan had come to power determined to put an end to monopoly; to clear away the obstructions to competition; to
provide equality of opportunity for all. And just as these
ideas were to prove inadequate domestically, they provided
an inadequate foundation for a policy whose object was to
aid China.

Roy Curry has written that Wilson failed to understand
that American bankers would not be willing to take the risks
of advancing credits or aiding in China's development because banditry and conditions approaching anarchy made
investments unsafe. China could not attract capital on the
free market. To aid China, the American government had to
play a positive role, an active role, such as it was philosophi-
cally unprepared to play even in the domestic economy.
Richard Hofstadter has suggested that it was not until the
coming of the New Deal that the American people and their
elected representatives came to realize that equality of opportunity was not enough; that those who failed in a fair
race still deserved to live. And yet, interestingly enough, in
his policy toward China, Wilson began to move in this direction in 1917: in the creation of the New Consortium, Wilson
demonstrated his understanding that China could not survive in a free market situation and that the desire to aid
China required government intervention in the economy.
Wilson swallowed his pride and asked the bankers to help,
agreeing to their condition that he publicly announce that
the New Consortium would be created, the new loan made,

at the suggestion of the administration. He further agreed
that the government would help the bankers to collect in the
event China defaulted. Good or evil, as in the eyes of the
beholder, it was dollar diplomacy—the use of American capital to serve the ends of American diplomacy in East Asia.
And American ends were stated most succinctly by Breckinridge Long: "to drive Japan out of China." [26]

Ironically, it was the most obvious failure of Wilson's Far
Eastern policy, the defeat at Versailles of his effort to regain
Shantung for China, that provided the occasion for the first
great demonstration of Chinese readiness for change, of
Chinese willingness to enter the modern world: the May
Fourth Movement. After word of the decision to permit
Japan to retain the German concessions in Shantung reached
China, hundreds of thousands of Chinese students took to
the streets in protest, first in Peking, then in cities throughout China. A boycott of Japanese goods was organized, and
allegedly pro-Japanese members of the Chinese government
were attacked. For months the movement steamrollered,
and in September, 1919, the American minister reported:
"A storm of popular indignation swept over the country
which is without parallel since the days of foreign intercourse with China. . . . The mobilization of an active public opinion, definite in its aims, was a new development in
Chinese political life." China's students had become the
necessary ingredient for the jelling of China's "loose sands"
into a powerful nationalist force, and reports of new evi-
dences of Chinese patriotism became commonplace. Businessmen, naval officers, and the visiting philosopher John
Dewey commented enthusiastically on the awakening, the
"real" awakening, of China. As Ch'ou Ts'e-tsung, the leading

26. Curry, *Wilson and Far Eastern Policy*, pp. 26, 191–94; Richard
Hofstadter, *The Age of Reform: From Bryan to F.D.R.* (New York, 1955);
Foreign Relations, 1918 (Washington, 1930), pp. 171–74.

student of the movement has shown now, for the first time, Chinese intellectuals felt a need for the *complete* transformation of Chinese civilization. They had come to realize that the destruction of traditional society was the essential prerequisite to the modernization of China.[27]

Generally, Americans in China responded favorably to the May Fourth Movement in all its manifestations. The social and intellectual changes demanded by the Chinese students led in the direction of civilizing, Westernizing, modernizing China. Politically, the most apparent activity was the anti-Japanese boycott, confirming the American assumption that Chinese nationalism, should it develop, would be directed against Japan and the European imperialists—but never against the United States. In addition, the students were working for an end to the civil strife that had dominated China since the collapse of Yuan Shih-k'ai's regime. If all went well, the movement might reasonably be expected to result in a unified, modern China, friendly to the United States and able to protect its own territorial and administrative integrity. In sum, there was no apparent reason for Americans to respond with anything short of enthusiasm.

Looking back over the decade that followed, the historian obviously has a perspective denied the men who lived through the events of those troubled years. Perhaps the pattern that now seems apparent, the inevitable triumph of anti-imperialism, of Chinese nationalism, is a trick the historian plays on himself. But a process does seem clear now—

27. Paul S. Reinsch to Robert Lansing, July 25, 1919, State Department Numerical File 893.00/3235; T. J. N. Gatrell to F. M. Dearing, June 5, 1919. Copy to Breckinridge Long, 893.00/3184; Annual Report of Commander-in-Chief, Asiatic Fleet. Copy to State Department dated February 1, 1920, item 2 (x), 893.00/3314; ONI to J. V. A. MacMurray, January 24, 1920, 893.00/3456, State Department Papers (National Archives); Evelyn Dewey, ed., *Letters from Japan and China, by John Dewey . . . and Alice Chipman Dewey* (New York, 1920), pp. 237, 246–47; Ch'ou Ts'e-tsung, *The May Fourth Movement: Intellectual Revolution in Modern China* (Cambridge, Mass., 1960).

a process that gives meaning to a decade of nearly constant chaos: the brushing aside of the old order of warlords, warlord armies, inert masses; the power, the energy of the ideas generated by the May Fourth Movement waning, waxing, reaching politicians, soldiers; the attempts to reach the masses, in the cities and even in the countryside, culminating in the successful Northern Expedition of the Kuomintang armies in 1926, in significant mobilization of the masses, and ultimately in a national government that exercised essential control over China proper and could exact at least nominal allegiance from Manchuria. As the decade closed, China was no longer a mere geographic expression: a nation-state had been formed, and its leadership, China's first modern political elite, had notified all the powers that a unified people would no longer tolerate a semicolonial status.

The first substantive American response to this striving for modernization came in the agreements reached at the Washington Conference of 1921–22. At Washington the powers, at the insistence of the United States, made a commitment to allow the Chinese to determine their own destiny, to work out their own problems, free of foreign interference. In addition, they agreed to begin the process of abolishing the "unequal treaties" that provided the legal basis for the privileges of the imperialists in China. Unfortunately, plans for restoring to the Chinese control over their tariff and jurisdiction over foreigners were contingent, in fact, upon the prior restoration of order in China. When the years following the conference brought chaos instead, neither the United States nor the other Washington signatories would take any further initiative.

Some scholars, like William Appleman Williams and Akira Iriye, have been critical of American policy in the 1920s, contending that the United States lost an opportunity to shape the subsequent course of Chinese history. Iriye apparently believes that the United States might have been able to avert the conditions that led to Japanese aggression in the 1930s, and Williams claims that more aggressive support of Chinese nationalism might have prevented the coming of Mao. Both are particularly critical of American coolness or opposition to Sun Yat-sen, which they interpret as hostility to Chinese nationalism.[28]

There can be no denying that Sun was held in low esteem by most American officials. During the Wilson administration Paul Reinsch, the ardently Sinophile American minister to China, had questioned his wisdom, and Lansing had questioned the genuineness of his professed principles. Charles R. Crane, Reinsch's successor, reported that Sun's own associates were embarrassed by his "impractical and grandiose schemes." In 1922 Harding's appointee, Jacob Gould Schurman, confirmed these reports, writing that thoughtful Chinese and foreigners no longer sympathized with Sun. Schurman himself thought Sun "would be impossible as a responsible statesman" and estimated that Sun's influence was ebbing.[29]

It would be a mistake, however, to view this criticism of Sun, offered between 1918 and 1922, as evidence of American opposition to Chinese nationalism. In these years, Sun was not yet the personification of Chinese nationalism, not even to the Chinese. On the contrary, he was merely China's

28. William A. Williams, "China and Japan: A Challenge and a Choice of the Nineteen Twenties," *Pacific Historical Review* XXVI (1957), 259–79; Akira Iriye, *After Imperialism: The Search for a New Order in the Far East, 1921–1931* (Cambridge, Mass., 1965).

29. *Foreign Relations, 1918* (Washington, 1930), p. 94; Curry, *Wilson and Far Eastern Policy*, p. 205; *Foreign Relations, 1921*, 2 vols. (Washington, 1936), I, 325; *Foreign Relations, 1922*, 2 vols. (Washington, 1938), I, 707. See also Charles Evan Hughes to Warren G. Harding, May 24, 1922, Harding Papers, Ohio Historical Society.

best-known politician, consorting with a variety of warlords
in a desperate effort to capture the reins of power. To many
Chinese intellectuals, Sun's ambition seemed the primary
obstacle to internal peace and the unification of China. It
was not, therefore, inconsistent of Schurman to report enthusiastically on China's new sense of nationalism and patriotism and endorse the demands of Chinese nationalists
while simultaneously criticizing Sun.

Against this setting the Harding administration refused
to take Sun's pretensions seriously and scrupulously avoided
any contact with him that could be construed as interference
in China's internal affairs. When the vice-consul at Canton,
Ernest Price, forwarded a letter from Sun to Harding, he
was rebuked for "permitting the Consulate General to make
itself a vehicle of official communication for an organization
in revolt against a Government with which the United States
is in friendly relations." Sun's letter was returned to Canton.
Williams sees in this rebuff evidence of an anti-Kuomintang
policy, which he contends had Hughes's "unqualified approval" despite his awareness "of Sun's new strength and the
Kuomintang's political potential." In fact, Sun's strength
was rapidly approaching its nadir, and it might have been
difficult to find a Chinese who would have wagered any
cash on the Kuomintang's potential. In June, 1922, Sun's
protégé, General Ch'en Chiung-ming, turned on him and
drove him out of Canton, and China's intellectuals demanded that he resign the presidency of the rebel government to clear the way for unification. His "new strength"
had evaporated, and he was fortunate to escape to Shanghai.
Interestingly enough, Akira Iriye is critical of American
policy at this juncture. Such was American coolness to Sun
that he "was refused use of an American naval vessel to
transport him, after his defeat by General Ch'en, to Shanghai." Iriye does not explain why the United States should

have provided an American warship for the use of a man in rebellion against the recognized government of China after his defeat by his own supporters.[30]

By the spring of 1924, with the help of the Soviet Union, Sun's movement had been revitalized. To be sure, Sun had offered the Russians greater concessions against Chinese sovereignty than the warlord regime at Peking had dared offer, but this fact meant little in face of the dogma that the Soviet Union could not be imperialistic nor could great leaders of nationalist movements be their running dogs. Schurman's view of Sun did not change for the better, but he was increasingly impressed by Sun's power. Iriye suggests that if Sun's brand of nationalism disturbed Americans, they could have supported Tuan Chi-jui's Peking government at the close of 1924, to "encourage mild, as opposed to radical, nationalism in China"; but this idea, of course, assumes that nationalist movements can be controlled from outside. How does one nation encourage "mild" nationalism in another nation—how do you ride the tiger? [31]

Without denying the desirability of a better relationship between the United States and Sun, it remains difficult to see how this would have been possible. Had the United States intervened in Sun's behalf, who could divine how the nationalist spirit would have responded to this foreign interference? Who would dare predict the reaction of the other signatories of the Washington agreements? Moreover, the consequences of the American failure to come to terms with Sun were hardly apocalyptic: neither China's destiny nor the future of Japanese-American relations were thereby re-

30. Hughes to George Christian, April 12, 1921, Harding Papers; *Foreign Relations, 1921*, I, 324, 334–35, 339–40; Iriye, *After Imperialism*, p. 47.

31. Jacob Gould Schurman to Calvin Coolidge, April 8, 1924, Schurman Papers, Collection of Regional History, Cornell University; Iriye, *After Imperialism*, p. 45.

vealed. For Sun's successor and for a generation of Japanese and American statesmen, there still existed ample opportunity for constructive action.

But whatever the virtues of observing the traditional principle of nonintervention, the American response to Chinese nationalism in the years between the Washington Conference and the Northern Expedition was unsatisfactory. Chinese patriots demanded the abolition of the "unequal treaties," and, insensitively, the United States clung to its privileges under the treaty system. And the reason for American policy in this instance was not hostility to Chinese nationalism, not the desire to impede China's economic modernization, but the same sterile legalism that critics like George Kennan have seen in other areas of American policy. To the Chinese extraterritoriality was a hated symbol of imperialism—an explosive issue. To the American government it was a matter of law and order to be dealt with dispassionately. The Chinese had certain obligations to protect the lives and property of foreigners, and until they restored order and proved both willing and able to carry out these obligations, the United States could not abandon the extraterritorial system.

In 1925 J. V. A. MacMurray, the leading exponent of this legalistic approach to the demands of the Chinese nationalists, was designated minister to China. He reached his post shortly after the May 30 Incident, in which police of the International Settlement at Shanghai had fired into a crowd of Chinese demonstrators. Nationalism, particularly in its anti-imperialist manifestations, burned with a white heat; but MacMurray still opposed concessions, insisting that treaty revision could not be considered before China met its treaty obligations. To yield, he advised his superiors, would "encourage a spirit of irresponsibility with which even the soberest Chinese have recently been infected through various Bolshevik and juvenile nationalistic influences." [32]

In sum, the failure of the United States to surrender the privileges its citizens enjoyed under the unequal treaties derived first from a failure to appreciate the intensity with which Chinese nationalists, radical or "mild," abhorred these symbolic fetters. Second, the American government attempted at first to deal with these highly emotional issues within the same rational and legal framework that characterized its relations with nations traditionally treated as equals and enjoying the luxury of civil order: it insisted on observance of treaty obligations. Accepting the need for modernization and encouraging the process, the United States nonetheless demanded order, seemingly unaware that the ancient scales of Chinese society could hardly be scraped away without the sword. One thoughtful scholar, C. F. Remer, in a letter congratulating MacMurray on his appointment as minister to China, searched for a parallel, recalling that Carlyle was said to have remarked that "the American civil war was the burning out of a foul chimney." [33]

But as the Northern Expedition gathered force, the United States was confronted with a clearly defined problem. With virtually all Chinese demanding treaty revision and the Kuomintang-Communist coalition indicating its intention to abrogate the treaties unilaterally if necessary, would the United States yield or not? And if not, what action was the American government prepared to take to prevent China from unilaterally abandoning its treaty obligations?

MacMurray's position was clear: firmness and the use of

32. Foreign Relations, 1921, I, 508; transcript of lecture given at the Foreign Service School, J. V. A. MacMurray Papers, Princeton University; MacMurray to Kellogg, quoted in Dorothy Borg, American Policy and the Chinese Revolution, 1925–1928 (New York, 1947), p. 63.

33. C. F. Remer to MacMurray, April 24, 1925, MacMurray Papers.

force, if necessary, would alone contain Chinese foolishness. Aware of Soviet influence in China, he inclined to blame Bolshevism for the unruliness of the Chinese nationalists. In Washington, however, Secretary of State Frank Kellogg and his principal adviser on Chinese affairs, Nelson Johnson, were forced by domestic conditions to try a different tack. As Dorothy Borg has shown, public opinion in the United States would no longer tolerate gunboat diplomacy. The American milieu of the 1920s was increasingly anti-imperialist, increasingly sensitive to the use of force against underdeveloped countries, whether in Latin America or in Asia. Indeed, one legacy of intervention in World War I had been the greatly increased vigor of movements opposed to the use of force in world affairs. At a time when domestic pressures were driving Kellogg toward signing a pact outlawing war, he could not but be hesitant about preserving American privileges in China with military action. Similarly, at a time when increasing numbers of Americans believed that they had been involved in World War I to serve the selfish ends of a privileged few, the American government could not easily respond to the demand for gunboats voiced by the American Chamber of Commerce in Shanghai.

With American opinion virtually united in the view that peaceful solutions to all problems were necessary and possible, the only course was to yield as gracefully as possible to the Chinese demand for treaty revision, brushing aside MacMurray's protests and the legal considerations upon which they were based. Once having determined to yield, the rest should have been relatively easy, but to whom should the United States yield? From October, 1925, to the close of 1928, China was torn by civil strife more violent than that which had plagued that benighted country since 1920. In 1926 the Kuomintang-Communist coalition, though mobilizing the masses behind demands for abolition of the unequal treaties, was in fact opposed to any treaty revision for the simple reason that such revision would aid their enemies by increasing their revenues and their prestige. On the other hand, failure to implement the promises of the Washington Conference was alleged to be unneutral by the enemies of the Kuomintang. Considerations of this kind, rather than hostility to the aspirations of Chinese nationalists, dictated American policy in the years before Chiang Kai-shek achieved at least nominal control over all of China.

Dorothy Borg and Russell Buhite have shown that Kellogg and Johnson, the two men who directed the course of American policy from 1925 to 1928, were driven principally by the desire to retain what they believed to be American primacy in friendship to China. Despite occasional fits of nervousness caused by evidence of Soviet influence in China, Kellogg accepted the basic premise that Remer had offered to MacMurray: that the revolution and its concomitant violence and disorder were necessary to enable the Chinese to slough off the ancient civilization that thwarted their development. Similarly, as he watched China struggle to modernize, he recognized instinctively that the rationale for the old imperialistic perquisites was disappearing: that the United States and all the powers had to prepare to give China complete independence as soon as possible. And if public opposition to the use of force in China made the Kellogg-Johnson policy a necessity, their instincts and assumptions about China converted necessity into virtue. Concerned about Soviet imperialism, they concluded that the success of the Chinese nationalists would be the best defense against that threat. Even before the split between the Kuomintang and the Communists, it was relatively easy from the vantage point of Washington to brush aside MacMurray's fear of Bolshevism with the fragile conviction that communism was too alien a concept, too removed from Chinese realities, to succeed in China. Thus fortified, Americans in Washington could view the Chinese revolution as a worthy imitator of the American revolution—a thoroughly praiseworthy quest for the freedom to determine their own future—a freedom promised to the people of China at the Washington Conference. And if the United States remained in the van, foremost of China's friends, proponent of self-determination, Chinese nationalism could only reciprocate this friendship. In short, the necessary policy of yielding to Chinese demands for treaty revision and the abrogation of the treaty system, of accepting rather than attempting to obstruct the modernization process, was ultimately discovered to be congruent not only with American ideals but with the interests of the United States as well.[34]

Looking back over the decade of the 1920s, whether one admires American adherence to the principle of nonintervention or castigates those responsible for determining policy for failing to give active assistance to Chinese nationalism, it is worth noting that at the close of the decade Americans had cause for satisfaction with their government's policy. The Soviet Union, the nation that had taken the greatest initiative—aiding the Kuomintang, manipulating the Chinese Communist party, giving welcome focus to the nationalist movement—had been rewarded with the almost total expulsion of Soviet influence in China. Japanese meddling won few friends in Nanking. As Iriye is forced to conclude, the other powers—and particularly the United States —"sat by and by their very caution were laying the ground for understanding with Nationalist China." [35]

34. Borg, *American Policy and the Chinese Revolution,* especially pp. 116–23; Russell Buhite, "Nelson Johnson and American Policy toward China, 1925–1928," *Pacific Historical Review* XXXV (1966), 451–65.

35. Iriye, *After Imperialism,* p. 214.

IV

One of the peculiarities of writings on Sino-American relations has been the general assumption that in the years 1931 to 1945 America was most sympathetic to, and most ready to come to the aid of, China. Dorothy Borg's recent work has done much to dispel the illusion for the period 1933–38 —and yet the larger era needs examination.[36]

Probably the most important point to be made about the men who shaped American policy in this period, especially Henry L. Stimson and Franklin D. Roosevelt, is that they were generally uninterested in China or her problems—except insofar as they viewed the difficulties besetting China as part of a threat to the peace machinery of the world. Stimson and Roosevelt viewed events in Europe as of far greater significance to the United States than anything that might occur in East Asia. Neither man considered the preservation of the Open Door essential to the security of the United States or had any illusions about the importance of China to the United States.

The recent scholarship of Iriye and James Crowley has answered many questions about Japanese policy and presented several interesting arguments in mitigation of Japan's crimes, but their work confirms the fact that Japan's aggressive continental policy was her response to the creation of a modern nation-state in China.[37] The question facing the United States from 1931 to 1941 was, given American support for the modernization of China, how to respond to Japanese determination to deny Chinese aspirations.

36. Dorothy Borg, *The United States and the Far Eastern Crisis of 1933–1938* (Cambridge, Mass., 1964).

37. Iriye, *After Imperialism;* James B. Crowley, *Japan's Quest for Autonomy: National Security and Foreign Policy* (Princeton, N.J., 1966).

In 1931 and 1941 the United States led the opposition to Japanese aggression in China. However, it must be recognized that in the first instance, the limited action taken by the United States was motivated far less by any desire to come to the aid of China than to uphold the existing peace machinery and the sanctity of treaty obligations. In the second instance, the Roosevelt administration's appeasement of Japan ended only when Roosevelt became convinced that Japan's ties with Nazi Germany augmented the German threat to American security.

A few months before the Mukden Incident, Nelson Johnson, then minister to China, exchanged ideas on American Far Eastern policy with William Castle, undersecretary of state. Johnson was unquestionably sympathetic to China, and Castle, previously ambassador to Japan, was generally considered friendly to Japan. Nonetheless, Johnson declared that he had no quarrel with Castle's ideas on American policy toward Japan and thought it best to leave Japan alone in the Far East. On the other hand, he expressed the belief that the United States "should follow a policy in regard to the Far East which would encourage the establishment and development of a strong government and nation here in China. I have believed this necessary to the peace of the Pacific." Recognizing that the policies he advocated for Japan and China might be deemed in conflict, he informed Castle that he had "never believed that Japan could or would take charge in China." He reported that Manchuria was daily becoming more Chinese, "but if Manchuria is destined to become part of Japan, I do not see why that should necessarily embroil us." Here was essentially a return to the position of Theodore Roosevelt: sympathy for China and the belief that a strong China fending for itself could best preserve the peace of East Asia—combined with a disinclination to interfere with Japan, the principal power in the area, particularly with regard to Manchuria.[38]

But in one important respect, the world had changed since the day of Theodore Roosevelt. There now existed an international organization, a multilateral promise to leave the Chinese free to work out their own future, and a nearly universal agreement among nations not to resort to war as an instrument of national policy—machinery for the peaceful settlement of disputes and treaty obligations barring military solutions. The United States had rejected membership in the League of Nations, but had been instrumental in working out the Pacific settlement of 1921–22 and in the creation of the Paris Peace Pact, first signed in 1928. The latter treaty had aroused great hopes for perpetual peace among Americans, and it was within the peace movement that Japanese aggression created the gravest concern.

In the Department of State, Stanley Hornbeck, chief of the Division of Far Eastern Affairs, a man long reputed to be pro-Chinese and anti-Japanese, approached the problem not from the standpoint of Japan's threat to China or to specific American interests in the Far East but as a threat to the peace of the world. To Stimson he argued that the Japanese had violated the Paris Peace Pact and "that any American protest should not appear as part of traditional American Far Eastern policy but as cooperation with the international movement for world peace." [39] As Hornbeck apparently realized immediately, the events in Manchuria had a sig-

38. Nelson T. Johnson to William Castle, March 25, 1931, Johnson Papers, Library of Congress. As instructed by Johnson, Castle passed the letter on to Stanley Hornbeck, who endorsed it on May 20, 1931, and filed as 893.00/11642, State Department Papers.

39. Robert H. Ferrell, *American Diplomacy in the Great Depression: Hoover-Stimson Foreign Policy, 1929–1933* (New Haven, Conn., 1957), p. 131. In a letter to Norman H. Davis, May 1, 1925, MacMurray wrote that Hornbeck, under consideration for a position at Columbia University, "has rather too distinctly the attitude of being pro-Chinese and incidently somewhat anti-Japanese," MacMurray Papers.

nificance far greater than the territory involved or the concrete and limited interests of the United States in China.

Herbert Hoover, president of the United States, deeply immersed in the problems of the Great Depression, was almost totally uninterested in the Asian crisis. Stimson, no less concerned with the effort to end economic stagnation, allowed some of his energies to be diverted toward Manchuria —not out of friendship for China, but as Robert Ferrell, Elting Morison, and Richard Current have shown, because of his conception of the importance of treaty obligations to international peace. Nelson Johnson, his representative in China, concurred, remaining indifferent to the fate of Manchuria, but apprehensive of a second world war if the Kellogg Peace Pact and the League were brushed aside. For all Americans who put their hope in international cooperation and regretted the failure of the United States to join the League, the decision by Stimson and Hoover to work with the League provided a new, albeit short-lived, hope.[40]

All of these men—Hoover and Stimson, Johnson and Hornbeck, and even Castle with his great sympathy for Japan—were in complete agreement on two points: first, that American policy had to serve American interests; and second, that American interests in Manchuria in particular and China in general were insignificant. William Neumann has

40. Ferrell, *American Diplomacy in the Great Depression;* Elting E. Morison, *Turmoil and Tradition: A Study of the Life and Times of Henry L. Stimson* (Boston, 1960); Richard N. Current, *Secretary Stimson: A Study in Statecraft* (New Brunswick, N.J., 1954); Russell Buhite, "Nelson T. Johnson and American Policy Toward China, 1925–1941" (Ph.D. dissertation, Michigan State University, 1965); Raymond B. Fosdick to William A. White, October 31, 1931, White Papers, Library of Congress; Fosdick to Herbert Hoover and Henry L. Stimson, November 10, 1931, 793.94/2779; Irene Johnson, League of Nations Association, to Stimson, October 5, 1931, 793.94/1990; Richard R. Wood, Friends Peace Committee, to Stimson, October 9, 1931, 793.94/2085; Memorandum of Conversation between J. G. Rogers, Assistant Secretary, and Frederick J. Libby, National Council for the Prevention of War, December 4, 1931, with enclosure, 500.A 15 A 4/637, State Department Papers.

noted that none of these men, nor any other American statesman of the interwar period, ever offered "a public and explicit statement of the priorities of American interests in
Asia" or indicated which of these interests, if any, would
justify war. Indeed, in departmental memorandums, reports,
and personal correspondence, Hornbeck, Johnson, and Castle made clear their conviction that no American interests
in China justified war—that nothing short of a Japanese attack on the Philippines or on American commerce in the
Pacific would justify war with Japan. Certainly these men
had moved away from the conception of congruent Chinese
and American interests that had led to the anti-Japanese
policies of the Taft and Wilson administrations. But Stimson
in particular had a larger view than that of his aides—though
Hornbeck and Johnson were rarely far behind. In place of
the earlier conception of congruent Sino-American relations,
Stimson had a vision of a worldwide unity of interest in
peace. Only in the sense that Japanese aggression, as it violated Japan's treaty obligations and ignored the League of
Nations, threatened the peace of the world, did it threaten
the interests of the United States. But for Herbert Hoover,
so indirect a threat could not compete with the very concrete
problems he faced within the United States—and not even
Stimson was prepared for the United States to take the
principal role in East Asia when the League members appeared to abdicate their responsibilities.[41]

The failure of words to stop the Japanese shattered one of
the primary assumptions of American policy: that moral
sanctions, appeals to world public opinion, could keep the
peace. And when Japanese actions demonstrated that words

41. William Neumann, "Ambiguity and Ambivalence in Ideas of National
Interest in Asia," in Alexander DeConde, ed., Isolation and Security
(Durham, N.C., 1957); Buhite, "Johnson and American Policy toward
China, 1925–1941"; Castle to Johnson, December 21, 1932, Johnson Papers;
Ferrell, American Diplomacy in the Great Depression.

and empty threats would not suffice, there was no responsible American prepared to take the next step of resort to force. If Stimson doubted that the particular interests of the United States in Manchuria warranted significant protest and doubted that the interests of world peace warranted any more than protests, the administration of Franklin Roosevelt was composed almost entirely of men who were determined not to antagonize Japan on behalf of China or abstract conceptions of the indivisibility of world peace.

The early years of Roosevelt's power found idealism reserved for domestic affairs, a narrow construction of national interest prevailing and a general retreat from the Open Door underway. American interests in Asia were once again measurable, limited to tangibles like commerce, investments, and occasionally missionary activities. Available evidence suggests that all thought of mutuality of interest between the United States and China had vanished for the moment, and even those most sympathetic to China in the past had given up on the Chinese government and had concluded that Chinese modernization under Chinese leadership was probably impossible. Some were even forced to the conclusion that Japanese domination of China would be in the best interests of the United States—and China, too! Not only Grew, but Hornbeck as well, fought vehemently against measures that might give offense to Japan.[42]

In May, 1933, Hornbeck announced that settlement of the Sino-Japanese dispute in North China might be *detrimental* to American interests—that it might be best to keep the Japanese involved in an indecisive struggle in an area where the United States had no vital interests. And the price, al-

    42. Entries for December 31, 1934 and January 7, 1935, Diary of William Phillips, Houghton Library, Harvard University. Hornbeck was particularly upset by the U.S. Navy's announcement of spring naval maneuvers on the same day that Japan denounced the Washington Naval Treaty.

lowing the "principles of our FE policy and our ideals with regard to world peace" to be "further scratched and dented," seemed slight enough. Johnson wrote that none of these Japanese transgressions concerned the United States directly. Not only did they cost the United States nothing, but "the development of this area under Japanese enterprise may mean an increased opportunity for American industrial plants to sell the kind of machinery and other manufactured goods that will be needed where so much energy is being displayed." At a meeting of military and naval intelligence representatives with Undersecretary of State William Phillips and his Far Eastern staff, Admiral Wainright, returning from duty on the Yangtze, informed those assembled that he thought the Chinese "hopelessly miserable" and that Japanese domination would probably be to their advantage.[43]

From all corners came support for what Phillips called our policy of "hands off." He called in MacMurray, for whom he had great respect, and MacMurray recommended the utmost caution in any approaches to Japan—and then before returning to his post at Riga, he prepared a 105-page memo that provided a brilliant rationalization for doing nothing. Wilfred Fleisher, Japan-based journalist, stopped by and advised "a policy of caution, avoidance of pin-pricks, in other words, a reversal of the Stimson policy, in fact the policy we were now pursuing." Even a man like Thomas Lamont, deeply involved in world affairs, an advocate of collective security, and prominent in China famine relief work, could not countenance any other role for the United States in the mid-1930s. To Johnson he wrote that he regretted seeing China under Japanese control, "but if she lacks the

43. Hornbeck memorandum in Franklin D. Roosevelt Papers, quoted in Borg, *United States and the Far Eastern Crisis*, p. 569 n. 101; Johnson to Stanley Hornbeck, June 1, 1933, Johnson Papers; Entry for November 11, 1935, Phillips Diary.

strength to protect herself from aggression and exploitation, she cannot reasonably expect the other nations to do the job for her." He might well have summed up the attitude of the Roosevelt administration when he concluded: "Certainly America is not going to court trouble by any quixotic attempt to checkmate Japan in Asia." [44]

Perhaps the best indication of American indifference to the fate of China can be found in Dorothy Borg's account of United States silver policy and its disastrous effects upon China. The Chinese begged the United States to stop purchasing Chinese silver, and Phillips went to Morgenthau and Roosevelt. The president insisted that the problem was "China's business and not ours; that they could stop the outflow of silver if they so desired and that it was not up to us to alter our policy merely because the Chinese were unable to protect themselves." [45]

Johnson, in China, reported growing dissatisfaction with the United States, but for the most part, it seemed to irritate him. He and Hornbeck often felt it necessary to remind the Chinese that American policy was supposed to serve American ends first. They were quick to counter what they viewed as Chinese suggestions that the United States fight China's battles, quick to tell Chiang Kai-shek and other members of his regime that the United States had done its share and more for China. Hornbeck, approving such a reply by Johnson to Chiang's complaints, added the thought that in relations with China, "we are fortunately situated in that our interests and those of China usually run along parallel lines; at least they do not conflict." As the Japanese began the full-scale invasion of China, Hornbeck made sub-

44. Entries for June 14, 24, 1935, Phillips Diary; Thomas Lamont to Johnson, May 19, 1936, Johnson Papers.

45. Borg, *United States and the Far Eastern Crisis,* pp. 121–37; Entry for December 12, 1934, Phillips Diary.

stantially the same points in a conversation with H. H. Kung, China's minister of finance, and C. T. Wang, Chinese ambassador to the United States. He declared that the United States had always favored "a strong, unified China" but that American policy in the Far East was designed to do more than merely help China. He claimed for the United States the privilege of acting on its own conception of national interest—a privilege which the Chinese sometimes seemed to think was exclusively their own.[46]

In the weeks that followed, Chiang became extremely bitter about the role the United States played, particularly over what he viewed as the American failure to cooperate with Great Britain's efforts on China's behalf. Though Chiang took his case to Roosevelt, he received naught but sympathy at that level and not even that much from Nelson Johnson, who wrote: "Certainly nothing makes me lose patience with my Chinese friends so quickly as when I hear them talk about the responsibility of America for aiding to preserve the independence and integrity of China. . . ." [47]

But if the summer of 1937 provided the nadir of American concern for China, the Japanese attack, coming as hopes for peace in Europe dimmed, forced Roosevelt and men of good will all over the world to think anew of the dangers to the peace and security of their own countries. The interests of the United States in Manchuria, then North China, then Ethiopia, and now the rest of China might not warrant the use of force or the risk of war. The interests of the United States in the Versailles settlement, which it did not sign, in the Pacific settlement, which it had sponsored, and in the Kellogg-Briand Pact might not warrant the use of force or the risk of war. But as violence spread abroad and treaties

46. Hornbeck to Johnson, March 13, 1937, 711.93/350; Memorandum of Conversation, July 10, 1937, 893.0146/549, State Department Papers.
47. Borg, *United States and the Far Eastern Crisis*, pp. 309, 315.

were violated, men troubled by the nationalism of the mid-
1930s spoke again of the need for international cooperation,
of collective security. A man like Norman Davis would readily concede "that our interests in the Far East are not worth
risking a fight" and then go on to shock those with narrower
conceptions of national interest by arguing that "the maintenance of collective action or the defeat of an aggressor like
Japan might be principles that would be well worth waging
war for." [48]

In his famed "Quarantine Speech," Roosevelt groped for
a way to take some action on behalf of world peace but characteristically allowed fine-sounding phrases to outstrip his
thoughts. At the Brussels Conference of the Nine Power
Treaty signatories, nothing was accomplished as Roosevelt
retreated from the implications of his speech. But Davis,
heading the American delegation, indicated clearly to Anthony Eden that the concern of the United States was *not*
primarily China, "that we did not view the problem as
merely a Far Eastern one but as a world problem where the
forces of order had a direct interest in preventing lawlessness
and aggression." Davis failed to win his point at the conference, but his idea was taking hold at home. By Christmas,
1937, J. Pierpont Moffat, a brilliant young career diplomat
who was unsympathetic to Davis's conception of the problem, concluded that the collective security idea was gaining
momentum in the United States "at the very moment when
most countries in Europe have reached the conclusion that
collective action is unworkable and are trying to divest themselves of their responsibilities under the [League] Covenant." Moffat was outraged to find that Clark Eichelberger
of the League of Nations Association had drafted a speech
for the chairman of the House Foreign Affairs Committee

48. Entry for September 29, 1937, Diary of J. Pierrepont Moffat, Houghton Library, Harvard University.

in which he "kept repeating that the violation of the Nine Power Treaty by Japan was more important to us than the sinking of our ships or the danger to the lives of our citizens." [49]

Moffat was, however, overly pessimistic. For the time, the tide of public and congressional opinion still ran with *his* conception of national interest, and the man in the White House, whatever his personal convictions, was taking no chances. Throughout 1938 and well into 1939, the Japanese pushed on, bombing civilians, brutalizing those who did not flee before them; and the United States held its peace. American property was destroyed, American commerce disrupted, American citizens injured, even killed—but the "lessons" of World War I prevailed. Not for the advantage of a few investors, a few merchants, a few Americans who risked their lives in war zones would the United States again be drawn into war.

In the spring of 1939 Moffat's fears approached realization. As the European situation grew more ominous, Roosevelt sought to have the neutrality legislation revised. The very nature of the proposed revision, the extension of the cash-and-carry concept to arms and munitions, indicated relative indifference to the war in Asia. "Cash and carry" meant, simply, that any nation that had the money and the means to transport the goods could purchase anything it needed from the United States. The advantages to Great Britain in the event of a European war were obvious, and presumably Hitler would be forewarned of Britain's ability to secure aid and would have second thoughts about provoking war. But if, as proposed in the bill before the Senate, the new law were applied to the Far Eastern war, the disadvantages to China were equally obvious. China had not

49. Entries for November 2, 1937, December 23–26, 27, 1937, *ibid.*

the cash or any means of transporting purchases from the United States. Japan controlled the western Pacific—at least every conceivable port of entry into China. And the Chinese ambassador protested to Senator Key Pittman, chairman of the Senate Foreign Relations Committee, contending that the proposed legislation had the "unintended effect of helping aggression in the Pacific." [50] Even the program preferred by the Department of State provided nothing for China, no end to the sale of war materials to Japan. Moreover, bills proposing economic sanctions against Japan were opposed by the administration.

And finally, primarily to head off legislation that might antagonize Japan, the administration chose to support a proposal by Senator Arthur Vandenberg, an *opponent* of sanctions, to give Japan the required six-months notice of termination of the 1911 Treaty of Friendship and Commerce. As Herbert Feis has indicated, the administration had no plan for sanctions against Japan. Making a virtue of necessity, Hull decided that this step, without indication of what would follow, might have a salutary effect on the Japanese. Perhaps then it would not be necessary to plan the next step.[51]

Soon after war came in Europe, Roosevelt met with success in his efforts to revise the neutrality legislation. "Cash and carry" became the law, with the attendent benefits to Great Britain—and to Japan. The efforts of pro-Chinese groups like the American Committee for Non-Participation in Japanese Aggression brought little in the way of tangible results. With the coming of the European war, its chairman, Roger S. Greene, and many of its supporters shifted their

50. Hu Shih to Key Pittman, April 10, 1939, SEN 76A-F9 CFR Neutrality China-Japan, Senate Foreign Relations Committee Papers, National Archives.

51. Herbert Feis, *The Road to Pearl Harbor* (Princeton, N.J., 1950), 41.

energies toward what they considered a more vital cause: aid to Great Britain.[52]

Through the winter of 1939–40 and on into the spring, Hull thwarted the efforts of those who sought economic sanctions against Japan. Not until summer, when Japan had made gestures against the British and French positions in Southeast Asia and appeared to be flirting anew with Nazi Germany, did the United States take significant action to retard the Japanese war effort. Even then, Roosevelt was persuaded not to prevent the sale of all scrap iron and oil. In fact, the year following brought a tremendous increase in the sale of petroleum products to Japan.

Clearly, American policy toward Japan was being determined without particular regard for China. Nonetheless, it was also apparent that the American conception of national interest was more broadly conceived in 1940, after the Nazi blitzkrieg, than it had been in the mid-1930s. To the administration and to a growing number of Americans, the survival of the Western democracies was vital to the security of the United States. The administration had embarked on a policy of all aid short of war to support Great Britain's battle, and significant public support was being mustered by the Committee to Defend America by Aiding the Allies—an organization with close ties to the government. To this organization, as to most of the men in Washington, "allies" meant France and England. In May, 1940, Nelson Johnson wrote to William Allen White, chairman of the committee, expressing his concern over the course the world had taken

52. For a contrary view of the accomplishments of the American Committee for Non-Participation in Japanese Aggression, see Donald J. Friedman, *The Road from Isolation: The Campaign of the American Committee for Non-Participation in Japanese Aggression, 1938–1941* (Cambridge, Mass., 1968). For Greene's own estimate, see Roger S. Greene to Admiral Harry Yarnell, February 27, 1941, and Yarnell to Greene, March 3, 1941, Committee to Defend America by Aiding the Allies Papers, Princeton University.

since Mukden, his fear for democracy if the democracies would not fight. Interestingly enough, Johnson, though ambassador to China, focused his attention on the war in Europe; and White, in reply, told of the work of his committee, its efforts on behalf of France and England, making no mention whatever of the Far East.[53]

Stated most simply, few Americans in the summer of 1940 conceived of China as an ally. Few Americans considered the defense of China essential to the security of the United States. Few Americans related the struggle in China to the events in Europe, where their attention was focused. Then, in one of history's greatest diplomatic blunders, the Japanese changed all this. On September 27, 1940, the Japanese concluded the Tripartite Pact with Germany and Italy and with one stroke tied together two wars and elevated China to the status of "ally" in the battle against Axis aggression. Ironically, her use of the pen rather than of the sword proved to be Japan's undoing.

Several scholars, especially Paul Schroeder, have explained the impact of the Tripartite Pact on Japanese-American relations. This is obviously the appropriate focus, but the impact on Sino-American relations must also be kept in mind. Within the administration and within pro-administration organizations like the Committee to Defend America by Aiding the Allies, announcement of the Tripartite Pact raised the isue of regarding China as one of the Allies and prompted even those principally concerned with the war in Europe to agree to aid to China and to adopt the program of anti-Japanese sanctions pressed by the China-oriented lobbies. Without sacrificing stress on the idea of Great Britain's survival as the key to America's future, Clark Eichelberger, national director of the Committee to Defend

53. Johnson to White, May 16, 1940, White to Johnson, May 31, 1940, White Papers.

America, advised chapter heads that the wars in the Atlantic
and Pacific were now one war; "Britain and China in the
Pacific, with Britain in the Atlantic, now constitute our first
lines of defense." And as Schroeder has indicated, Japan now
had to face stepped-up American aid to China and, of even
greater significance, the impossibility of negotiating a new
Pacific settlement without reference to China. Without
doubt, the American response made China the principal
beneficiary of the new Axis alliance.[54]

Even after the Tripartite Pact became expendable—or
very nearly so—to Japan, in the summer of 1941, China's
status as an ally prevented a *modus vivendi* between the
United States and Japan. Until the fall of 1940, appeasement
of Japan had been an easy policy to pursue. Afterward, it
meant the dashing of hopes raised in China and among
China's friends in the United States. It meant betrayal of a
nation so recently labeled a democracy and one of the allies
in the war against aggressors. It meant renouncing all the
"educational" efforts of the previous year. It meant risking
the charge that Roosevelt was concerned only with Great
Britain's chestnuts. Fear of a "Far Eastern Munich" gnawed
at China's friends, and they redoubled their efforts in the
summer of 1941—but they need not have feared.[55] The
United States, having once ceased to supply Japan with "the
sinews of war," could not again accept the role of merchant
of death. Having once proclaimed solidarity with China,
there could be no return to the uncomfortable role of passive observer of China's sorrows. And the war came.

54. Paul Schroeder, *The Axis Alliance and Japanese-American Relations,
1941* (Ithaca, N.Y., 1958); Clark Eichelberger to chapter chairmen, October 15, 1940; to Mrs. Lewis Mumford, October 22, 1940, enclosure,
Committee to Defend America Papers.

55. Greene to Yarnell, June 12, 1941; to T. L. Power, August 20, 1941,
September 19, 1941; Geraldine T. Fitch to Livingston Hartley, August 12,
1941, Committee to Defend America Papers; Geraldine Fitch to White,
August 5, 1941 (mimeographed), White Papers.

V

The war came—and China was an honored ally. But Roosevelt and his advisers continued their focus on the war in Europe. To be sure, there were cries of discontent in high places: Hornbeck, for one, urged more attention and aid for China. Still, those who determined American policy continued in their belief that Germany was the gravest danger to the United States and Great Britain its most important ally. China's task was merely to keep Japan busy until her allies had completed the major task. In the interim, they would provide her with whatever supplies were not needed elsewhere—assuming a way could be found to transport these items over Japanese-held territory, or the Himalayas.

Having viewed the bombing of Pearl Harbor as a heaven-sent reprieve, the Chinese government was bitterly disappointed by the American response. Exhausted by years of civil strife, Japanese pressures, and four years of war, the Chinese could not, would not, muster the men, energies, or morale necessary to meet American demands for action. Herbert Feis has told the story of the ensuing frustrations and frictions; and the problems of supply, command, and strategy are carefully and thoroughly analyzed by Romanus and Sunderland in three outstanding volumes of the history of the army in World War II.[56] The point that remains to be made is that China never had more than symbolic importance to Roosevelt and his advisers. Throughout the 1930s they had been largely indifferent to China's fate, deeming American interests in China as slight, unwilling to concede that Japanese hegemony over China would threaten the

56. Herbert Feis, *The China Tangle: The American Effort in China from Pearl Harbor to the Marshall Mission* (Princeton, N.J., 1953); Charles F. Romanus and Riley Sunderland, *Stilwell's Mission to China; Stilwell's Command Problems;* and *Time Runs Out in CBI* (Washington, 1953, 1956, 1960).

United States. If the morass of China had been a good place to bemire the Japanese in 1935, it was as useful in 1942. China as a victim of aggression concerned men who were advocates of collective security, but they too turned away when Hitler provided them with more important victims.

For the first three years of the Sino-Japanese war, the United States had allowed itself to be the most important supplier of the Japanese war machine. For the last eighteen months before the Japanese attack on Pearl Harbor, the United States gradually tightened the screws on Japan—not out of sudden concern for China but because of the threat posed by Japan's southward thrusts and ultimately by her adherence to the Rome-Berlin Axis. Thus, China was transformed into an "ally"—not a real ally, but a symbolic ally, as she was transformed into one of the "democracies," but not a real one. China received all of the praise and some of the loyalty due an ally, but little of the substance. During the war nothing changed. On their part the Chinese did little to change American estimates of their fighting will or potential. In return the United States renounced the last of its privileges under the "unequal treaties"—at least in theory—and talked much of China as a great power after the war. China was given "face."

Roosevelt's conception of China as a great power was ultimately incorporated into the United Nations Organization—in part compensation for neglect during the war. But Roosevelt also acted upon the assumption of a mutuality of interest between the United States and China; of a China grateful to the United States, *dependent* upon the United States—as Churchill suspected, "a faggot vote" on the side of the United States. Had Roosevelt read Chiang's *China's Destiny* or understood the Chinese Communist movement, he would have known better, would have understood that neither major force in China excepted the United States from the hostility directed against the imperialists. And no matter what the Chinese might themselves have offered the Soviet Union at Yalta, the fact that Roosevelt took it upon himself to dispose of Chinese territory without prior consultation with China was not likely to make him the recipient of Chinese gratitude.

VI

For half a century after the first of Hay's Open Door notes, Chinese aspirations to create a modern nation-state were viewed with favor by the United States. Contrary to the allegations of writers like Beale and Williams, the United States did not at any time evidence hostility toward Chinese nationalism, in part because few Americans could conceive of China becoming a threat to the United States. Except for a few brief moments after the Revolution of 1911 and after the establishment of the Kuomintang regime in the late 1920s, few men anywhere in the Western world could imagine a China able to defend her own borders, and fewer still feared an aggressive China. In addition, Americans assumed that they were assured of China's friendship, as their due. What was salient about the involvement of the United States in the imperialism of the treaty system was *not* that Americans were imperialists but rather that because they denied to themselves the fact of American imperialism, they were confident that a nationalist China would be friendly to them—and thus favored the emergence of a strong, modern China.

Throughout these fifty years, however, sympathy for China was tested by threats to China, especially from Japan. Theodore Roosevelt may not have renounced American interests in face of Japanese power, but he did refrain from supporting China against Japan. In this decision he was guided not by hostility to Chinese nationalism but by the realization of the limits of American power. Unprepared to fight Japan, Roosevelt chose not to dare her. But his successors, both Taft and Wilson, sought ways to offer China positive support, perceiving no danger from Japan. Unconcerned with Japanese power, they asserted American interests and Chinese rights with impunity—if not with success.

The decade following World War I brought a new situation. China was threatened less from outside than by internal chaos—and she required assistance less than patience. In patience some American officials were lacking, but their government was not. And when the Kuomintang established a semblance of order, it did not want for support from the United States. But in 1931 the Japanese, by their actions in Manchuria, posed a new threat to Chinese nationalism, and Stimson led the offensive against Japan. Like Taft and Wilson, however, he did not contemplate the use of force against Japan. In this sense he responded to Japanese pressures on China by seeking the alternative Knox had hypothesized between abandoning China and preparing for war. Where Knox employed dollar diplomacy, Stimson chose moral diplomacy; condemnation rather than investments served as his weapon.

Stimson, however, was moved by an idea far greater than any Knox had ever had, far broader than concern for China. He feared for far more than China: he feared for the peace of the world, if nations could violate their treaty obligations, resort to force, to aggression, whenever it served their purposes. The policy he and Hoover pursued was not so much pro-Chinese as it was anti-Japanese—and it was anti-Japanese because Japan, violating the sanctity of treaties and committing aggression, had acted immorally, had become an outlaw. In all this, China became an abstraction: the victim in a test case of the interwar peace system. The system failed the test; the powers lost the system—and China lost Manchuria.

Franklin Delano Roosevelt returned to the position taken years before by his cousin Theodore. Unprepared to fight Japan, he was unwilling to oppose her, to appear in any way as China's champion. In the mid-1930s the appeasement of Japan was central to his East Asian policy. Informed Americans were increasingly less optimistic about the prospects for the Kuomintang, and informed or uninformed, Americans were at that time less willing to risk involvement in overseas quarrels than at any time in their history. But even as the public view of the role of the United States in world affairs changed when confronted with the events of 1939 and 1940, the Roosevelt administration remained unwilling to oppose—or even stop aiding—Japan. Not until 1940 or 1941 was the United States willing to fight—not for China but for democracy, the Four Freedoms, and world peace, against Japan as a fascist, totalitarian outlaw. In other words, in the years following Hay's notes, not until the fall of 1940 was the government of the United States prepared to use force against Japan—and at that time, for reasons that involved China only incidentally. And when, after the Japanese attack on Pear Harbor, the United States went to war, ultimately defeating Japan, the liberation of China was merely a by-product of Japan's defeat rather than an important American priority.

VII

All this changed after 1949. Although the Chinese Communists had launched a virulent anti-American campaign in July 1946, the American people did not really take cognizance of Chinese hostility until three years later, when the establishment of the Peoples Republic was proclaimed. To this shock of a China neither grateful nor friendly to the United States was added a more severe shock, little more than a year later, when China's "Red Hordes" marched across the Yalu and smashed MacArthur's forces. Suddenly the contempt for Chinese power that World War II experience had only heightened gave way to fear and a new concept of the Yellow Peril. A new cycle of American attitudes toward China had begun.

After 1950 it was clear that for the first time, China's leaders showed signs of successfully mobilizing the peasant masses and of overcoming the corruption inherent in traditional Chinese society. But because they were also Marxist-Leninists, hostile to the West in general and the United States in particular, Americans lost all sympathy for China's aspirations. Regrettably, just when the prospects for the modernization of China seemed most promising, the United States for the *first* time determined to oppose that modernization. There was no longer any question of whether the United States would interpose itself between China and her enemies, for the United States had become China's principal enemy. Beginning in 1950, the United States embarked upon a course designed to isolate, weaken, and ultimately to bring about the collapse of order in China.

NOTES ON THE
CONTRIBUTORS

JOHN BRAEMAN teaches history at the University of Nebraska and is the author of *Albert J. Beveridge: American Nationalist.*

ROBERT H. BREMNER, professor of history at Ohio State University, has written *From the Depths: The Discovery of Poverty in the United States* and *American Philanthropy.*

DAVID BRODY is professor of history at the University of California, Davis, and author of *Steelworkers in America: The Nonunion Era* and *Labor in Crisis: The Steel Strike of 1919.*

LYLE C. BROWN, who has written numerous articles and reviews on Mexican affairs, is professor of political science at Baylor University.

ROBERT CRAIG BROWN teaches history at the University of Toronto and is the author of *Canada's National Policy, 1883–1900: A Study in Canadian-American Relations.*

ALEXANDER ELMSLIE CAMPBELL, a fellow of Keble College, Oxford University, has written *Great Britain and the United States, 1895–1903,* and is the editor of *Expansion and Imperialism.*

WARREN I. COHEN, author of *The American Revisionists: The Lessons of Intervention in World War I,* teaches at Michigan State University.

WALDO H. HEINRICHS, JR., teaches history at the University of Illinois, Urbana-Champaign, and has written *American Ambassador: Joseph C. Grew and the Development of the United States Diplomatic Tradition.*

MANFRED JONAS, professor of history and director of the graduate program in American studies at Union College, has written *Isolationism in America, 1935–1941.*

LAWRENCE S. KAPLAN, author of *Jefferson and France: An Essay on Politics and Political Ideas,* is professor of history at Kent State University and chairman of the graduate program in history there.

ALLAN R. MILLETT, who is associate professor of history at Ohio State University, has written *The Politics of Intervention: The Military Occupation of Cuba, 1906–1909.*

CHARLES E. NEU teaches history at Brown University and is the author of *An Uncertain Friendship: Theodore Roosevelt and Japan, 1906–1909.*

DAVID F. TRASK, professor of history and chairman of the department at the State University of New York, Stony Brook, has written *The United States in the Supreme War*

Council: American War Aims and Inter-Allied Strategy, 1917–1918.

PAUL A. VARG is professor of history at Michigan State University and author of four books, including *Missionaries, Chinese, and Diplomats* and *The Making of a Myth: The United States and China, 1897–1912.*

JAMES W. WILKIE, who is associate professor of history at the University of California, Los Angeles, received the Herbert E. Bolton Memorial Prize for *The Mexican Revolution: Federal Expenditure and Social Change since 1910.*

INDEX